Renaissance Eloquence

Renaissance Eloquence

Studies in the Theory and Practice of Renaissance Rhetoric

EDITED BY JAMES J. MURPHY

University
of California
Press
Berkeley
Los Angeles
London

University of California Press
Berkeley and Los Angeles, California

University of California Press, Ltd.
London, England

© 1983 by
The Regents of the University of California

Library of Congress Cataloging in Publication Data

Main entry under title:
Renaissance eloquence.

Bibliography: p.
Includes index.
1. Rhetoric — 1500 – 1800 — Congresses.   I. Murphy,
James Jerome.
PN171.6.R4 1982   808'.009'03   81-13128
ISBN 0-520-04543-2   AACR2

Printed in the United States of America

1   2   3   4   5   6   7   8   9

Contents

CONTENTS

Part Two

Rhetorical Trends in Renaissance Europe

Part Three

Ethics, Politics, and Theology

CONTENTS

Preface

Modern scholars have long recognized the staggering complexity of Renaissance rhetoric and its manifold applications in a wide variety of contemporary disciplines, from diplomatics to religion. Nevertheless, as Professor Paul Oskar Kristeller points out in one of the essays in this volume, we still lack a comprehensive history of rhetorical theory and practice in the Renaissance. It is indeed a field without even the basic apparatus for historiography — without a canon of authors, without a bibliography, and without many of the other scholarly tools that have been used so often with profit to study other phenomena in our cultural heritage. There is, to take a drastic instance, no institute or research center devoted to this subject.

With this in mind the Newberry Library devoted its Twenty-Sixth annual Renaissance Conference in April 1979 to the topic "Rhetoric in the Renaissance." A generous grant from the National Endowment for the Humanities enabled the Library to bring to Chicago thirty scholars from eleven countries for a three-day meeting. The essays in this volume are selected from papers delivered before the more than two hundred persons attending; each essay has been revised and enlarged by virtue of personal exchanges at the Newberry Library, through later correspondence, and by reflection since that time.

The pervasiveness of rhetoric in the Renaissance is well illustrated by the range of essays in this volume. The first section indicates the progress made and the problems discovered in attempting to define the field. The next section includes four essays that provide insight into major rhetorical trends of that period in Europe. The seven essays in Part Three discuss the role of rhetoric in Renaissance ethics, politics, and theology. Part Four focuses on rhetoric in its dynamic relations to other literary arts such as letter-writing, poetry, fiction, and drama. All in all, the twenty-three studies gathered here can provide both a proof of the complexity of Renaissance rhetoric and a means to understand it.

Special gratitude is owed to Marianne Briscoe of the Newberry Library for her unflagging energy in helping to bring these scholars together. The continued encouragement of John Tedeschi and Lawrence W. Towner of the Library was greatly appreciated. And from the earliest stages of this project, the gentlemanly support of Philip Lilienthal and later of William McClung of the University of California Press was a constant prop to the editor.

It is our hope that this volume will accelerate the study of Renaissance rhetoric. The need for that study is proven time and time again by the writers of the essays within these covers. It is hoped, too, that the essays also point to some fruitful avenues of exploration that can someday result in that "comprehensive history" so earnestly desired by Professor Kristeller.

James J. Murphy
Department of Rhetoric
University of California, Davis

PART ONE

The Scope of Renaissance Rhetoric

Rhetoric in Medieval
and Renaissance Culture

PAUL OSKAR KRISTELLER

The term *rhetoric*, long despised, has become once more respectable
in recent years, but its precise meaning, whether applied to antiquity
or the Middle Ages, to the Renaissance or modern times, seems far
from clear. Rhetoric has been defined or understood as the art of
persuasion, of the probable argument, of prose style and composition, or of literary criticism; and each of these different, though
related, definitions has come to the fore in a different period or
context. The art of composition has at times emphasized the speech,
orally delivered and heard by an audience, and at other times the
letter or the essay, silently written and read. Apart from its own intrinsic meaning, rhetoric has had changing associations with other
subjects and disciplines that have significantly affected the way rhetoric itself has been understood: rhetoric has been associated with
grammar and logic, with poetics, with ethics and politics, to mention
only some of its more significant connections. The place of rhetoric
in the classifications of the arts and sciences and in the curriculum of
schools and universities has also undergone many changes over the
centuries. I cannot hope to do justice to all these aspects in a brief
essay but shall concentrate on Renaissance rhetoric, its medieval antecedents and its place in Renaissance culture. I shall also attempt to
indicate some of the many problems that in my opinion need further
investigation.[1]

1. For supplementary information and bibliography, see Paul Oskar Kristeller,
Renaissance Thought and Its Sources (New York, 1979), esp. the section titled "Philosophy
and Rhetoric from Antiquity to the Renaissance" (pp. 211–59, 312–27). Also see

It has been stated more than once in recent years that rhetoric holds the key to Renaissance humanism and to Renaissance thought and civilization in general.[2] Because of an article I published well over thirty years ago, I am often counted among the supporters of that view.[3] I may be forgiven if I use this occasion to clarify my position on this important subject. I do believe that Renaissance rhetoric is much more important, in need of much more study and attention, than most scholars of the past few generations were willing to admit. However, I never meant to say and I still do not believe that Renaissance humanism, let alone Renaissance thought and learning in general, is reducible to rhetoric alone. Rhetoric was only one of the five *studia humanitatis* cultivated by the humanists, whose work as grammarians (and classical scholars), historians, poets, and moralists cannot be derived from their rhetoric, although this work may often seem inseparable from it. Moreover, as I have kept insisting (although many historians have refused to listen to me), humanism constitutes only one aspect, though an important one, of Renaissance thought and learning; furthermore, the history of theology and jurisprudence, of the sciences and of philosophy, in the Renaissance is not limited to Renaissance humanism, let alone to humanist rhetoric, though this history was in many ways affected by rhetoric.[4] I should like to keep these distinctions firmly in mind when I try to discuss, without exaggerated claims, some aspects of Renaissance rhetoric and its impact on the other areas of humanist and nonhumanist learning in the Renaissance. As usual, I shall focus my attention on Italy since I am acquainted with the history of that country and since in the history of rhetoric, during the Renaissance as well as

George A. Kennedy, *Classical Rhetoric and Its Christian and Secular Tradition from Ancient to Modern Times* (Chapel Hill, N.C., 1980), and Ernesto Grassi, *Rhetoric as Philosophy: The Humanist Tradition* (University Park, Pa., 1980).

2. Hannah H. Gray, "Renaissance Humanism: The Pursuit of Eloquence," *Journal of the History of Ideas* 24 (1963), 497 – 514; Jerrold E. Seigel, *Rhetoric and Philosophy in Renaissance Humanism* (Princeton, N.J., 1968); Hannah H. Gray, "History and Rhetoric in Quattrocento Humanism" (Ph.D. diss., Harvard University, 1956); and Nancy Struever, *The Language of History in the Renaissance* (Princeton, N.J., 1970).

3. Paul Oskar Kristeller, "Humanism and Scholasticism in the Renaissance," *Byzantion* 17 (1944 – 1945), 346 – 74, rpt. in his *Studies in Renaissance Thought and Letters* (Rome, 1956), pp. 553 – 83, and in his *Renaissance Thought* (New York, 1961), pp. 92 – 119, 153 – 66.

4. Paul Oskar Kristeller, "The Impact of Early Italian Humanism on Thought and Learning," in *Developments in the Early Renaissance*, ed. Bernard S. Levy (Albany, N.Y., 1972), pp. 120-57.

during the Middle Ages, the leading role of the Italians is generally recognized.

For a proper understanding of Renaissance rhetoric, as of many other Renaissance developments, we must begin with the ancient sources. For general rhetorical theory, Cicero's *De inventione* and the pseudo-Ciceronian *Rhetorica ad Herennium* were the basic sources throughout the Middle Ages. As standard textbooks, they generated numerous commentaries, especially during the twelfth and fourteenth centuries, and these commentaries have received much attention in recent years.[5] The fifteenth century added the more mature rhetorical works of Cicero, especially the *Orator* and the *De oratore*. They exercised a very great influence on Renaissance literature and thought, an influence that has been noticed in many instances but should be explored in a more comprehensive way. Quintilian, whose work had been known to the Middle Ages only in a truncated version, was also rediscovered in his complete text and widely studied in the fifteenth century. His influence has not yet been fully explored, but it is significant that Lorenzo Valla attributed to him a greater authority than even to Cicero himself.[6] Cicero's orations, some of them long known and others newly discovered, were widely admired and imitated; in fact, the newly found introductions of Asconius to some of Cicero's orations inspired Antonio Loschi and Sicco Polenton to try doing the same for some of Cicero's other speeches. For the composition of letters, those of Seneca and Pliny and, above all, the newly found letters of Cicero provided the chief sources and models.

The expansion of ancient source material during the Renaissance, in rhetoric as in other areas, becomes much more apparent when we pass from the Latin to the Greek sources. The Greek rhetorical sources known to the later Middle Ages were very few indeed: Aristotle's *Rhetoric* and the pseudo-Aristotelian *Rhetorica ad Alexandrum*, the treatise *De elocutione* attributed to Demetrius of Phaleron, and the speech *Ad Demonicum* attributed to Isocrates. The last three texts had a very limited circulation;[7] and since Aristotle's *Rhetoric*, though widely known, was studied by the scholastic philosophers as a

5. John O. Ward, *"Artificiosa Eloquentia in the Middle Ages"* (Ph.D. diss., University of Toronto, 1972); Ward, "From Antiquity to the Renaissance: Glosses and Commentaries on Cicero's *Rhetorica*," in *Medieval Eloquence*, ed. James J. Murphy (Berkeley and Los Angeles, 1978), pp. 25–67.

6. Lorenzo Valla, *Dialecticae Disputationes* 2.20–23; 3.15 (*Opera omnia*, Basel, 1540, rpt. Turin, 1962), pp. 719–31 and 752–56.

7. Paul Oskar Kristeller, *Renaissance Thought and Its Sources*, p. 322, notes 50–53.

part of moral philosophy,[8] but not by the professional rhetoricians, we may safely assert that medieval rhetoric was not affected by any Greek theories or writings except through the intermediary of the ancient Roman rhetorical writers.

During the Renaissance, the entire body of Greek rhetorical literature became accessible to the West, both through the original texts and through Latin and vernacular translations. The humanists came to know not only Hermogenes and Aphthonius, who had dominated the rhetorical tradition among the Greeks in late antiquity and during the Byzantine period, but also pseudo-Longinus, Dionysius of Halicarnassus, Menander, and other minor Greek writers on rhetoric.[9] The *Rhetorica ad Alexandrum* and pseudo-Demetrius became more widely known,[10] and, most important, Aristotle's *Rhetoric* was recognized and widely studied as a work on rhetoric rather than on moral philosophy. When Aldus Manutius published the first Greek edition of Aristotle's collected writings (1495–1498), he significantly omitted the *Rhetoric* (and the newly acquired *Poetics*) and included it instead in the corpus of Greek rhetorical writings he published a few years later (1508).[11] In the sixteenth century, Aristotle's *Rhetoric* had many commentators, all of them humanists and rhetoricians rather than moral philosophers.[12] This whole body of commentaries on the *Rhetoric* should be examined for its contributions to rhetorical and literary theory with the same careful attention that the commentaries on the *Poetics,* some of them by the same authors, have recently received.[13] To the theoretical treatises on rhetoric we must add the actual products of ancient Greek oratory. The Attic orators, especially Lysias, Isocrates, and Demosthenes, were all trans-

8. The medieval commentators of Aristotle's *Rhetoric* include Giles of Rome, Guido Vernani, John Buridan, and John of Jandun.

9. For Hermogenes, see Annabel M. Patterson, *Hermogenes in the Renaissance* (Princeton, N.J., 1970); and John Monfasani, *George of Trebizond* (Leyden, 1976).

10. For Demetrius, see Bernard B. Weinberg in *Catalogus Translationum et Commentariorum,* vol. 2, eds. Paul Oskar Kristeller and F. Edward Cranz (Washington, 1971), pp. 27–41. A Latin translation of the *Rhetorica ad Alexandrum* by Francesco Filelfo was widely diffused.

11. Lorenzo Minio-Paluello, "Attività filosofico-editoriale dell' umanesimo," in his *Opuscula* (Amsterdam, 1972), pp. 483–500.

12. The sixteenth-century commentators on the *Rhetoric* include Daniel Barbarus, Petrus Victorius, M. A. Maioragius, Franciscus Portus, and Antonius Riccobonus. See F. Edward Cranz, *A Bibliography of Aristotle Editions 1501–1600* (Baden-Baden, 1971), pp. 162–63.

13. Bernard B. Weinberg, *A History of Literary Criticism in the Italian Renaissance,* 2 vols. (Chicago, 1961).

lated, read, and imitated; so were some of the later Greek orators, such as Dio of Prusa, Aristides, and Libanius. We may add the speeches found in the works of Thucydides, Dio Cassius, and other historians, speeches sometimes translated and studied as separate pieces.[14] The vast body of Greek letters, most of them late and apocryphal, and hence neglected by modern classical scholars, were enormously popular among Renaissance humanists. The letters attributed to Phalaris, Diogenes the Cynic, Brutus, and others were among the most widely read works of ancient literature, to judge from the number of extant translations, manuscripts, and editions; the letters of Libanius, moreover, were nearly doubled in the fifteenth century by the Latin forgeries of Francesco Zambeccari.[15] Much of this material is still awaiting further bibliographical scrutiny, textual study, and exploration of its influence. The somewhat rough and hasty outline I have been trying to draw will eventually have to be corrected and completed accordingly.

Independent treatises on general rhetorical theory were produced rather rarely, if at all, during the later Middle Ages, and their number was still quite limited during the fifteenth century. This fact may be due to the authority of the ancient textbooks, which humanist teachers were more inclined to gloss than to rival. The early examples known to me include several popular treatises by Gasparino Barzizza and Agostino Dati, a systematic and very influential treatise by George of Trebisond,[16] a work by Guillaume Fichet that attempts to introduce an interesting new terminology,[17] treatises by Giorgio Valla[18] and Philippus Callimachus,[19] and probably a few more. In the sixteenth century, the literature of rhetorical textbooks was quite extensive, but even the bibliographical description of this literature is far from complete.[20] To my knowledge there are no detailed studies

14. For manuscripts containing them, see Paul Oskar Kristeller, *Iter Italicum*, 2 vols. (Leiden, 1963 – 1967), and other catalogues.

15. R. Foerster, *Francesco Zambeccari und die Briefe des Libanios* (Stuttgart, 1878).

16. Monfasani, *George of Trebizond.*

17. Paul Oskar Kristeller, "An Unknown Humanist Sermon on St. Stephen by Guillaume Fichet," in *Mélanges Eugène Tisserant*, Studi e Testi 236 (Vatican City, 1964), pp. 459 – 97.

18. Gray, "History and Rhetoric."

19. Philippus Callimachus, *Rhetorica*, ed. K. F. Kumaniecki (Warsaw, 1950).

20. Donald L. Clark, *Rhetoric and Poetry in the Renaissance* (New York, 1922, rpt. 1963); Charles S. Baldwin, *Renaissance Literary Theory and Practice* (New York, 1939, rpt. 1959); O. B. Hardison, *The Enduring Monument* (Chapel Hill, N.C., 1962); W. S. Howell, *Logic and Rhetoric in England, 1500 – 1700* (Princeton, 1956); F. Buisson, *Répertoire des*

of Renaissance rhetoric comparable to those dealing with the treatises on grammar, logic, or poetics of the same period.[21] I may be imperfectly informed, but I should not know where to turn for precise information on the individual doctrines of specific authors and on their differences from the doctrines of other ancient or contemporary writers. The same is true for the history of individual concepts, topics, or theories, with the possible exception of the figures of speech, which have interested the historians of poetics and of literary criticism. Peter Ramus's reform of logic also involved rhetoric, since he changed the traditional division between the two disciplines, and thus his rhetoric, or rather that of his friend Talaeus, has received attention from recent historians of Ramism.[22]

One specific problem that was important to theorists and writers in the Renaissance, as it had been in late antiquity, was the imitation of ancient models. The humanists all agreed that some kind of imitation was necessary, but there was a lively discussion between the Ciceronians, who recognized only Cicero as their model in prose style and vocabulary, and their opponents, who advocated a more eclectic and in a way a more original prose style. The debate, which found Barzizza, Paolo Cortesi, and Bembo, among the Ciceronians, and Lorenzo Valla, Poliziano, Gianfrancesco Pico, Erasmus, and Lipsius, among their opponents, has been the subject of some scholarly discussion.[23] But it deserves further detailed and comprehensive investigation, as do many other specific concepts and doctrines of rhetorical theory. We may add that the extensive medieval and Renaissance literature on memory, which has recently received some scholarly attention,[24] may be considered to some extent a part of rhetoric. For

ouvrages pédagogiques du XVIe siècle (Paris, 1886, rpt. Nieuwkoop, 1962); and Susan Gallick, "The Continuity of the Rhetorical Tradition: Manuscript to Incunabulum," *Manuscripta* 23 (1979), 31 – 47.

21. G. Arthur Padley, *Grammatical Theory in Western Europe 1500–1700* (Cambridge, 1976); W. Risse, *Bibliographia Logica* (Hildesheim, 1965); and Weinberg, *A History of Literary Criticism*.

22. Walter J. Ong, *Ramus: Method and the Decay of Dialogue* (Cambridge, Mass., 1958) and *Ramus and Talon Inventory* (Cambridge, Mass., 1958); Neal W. Gilbert, *Renaissance Concepts of Method* (New York, 1960).

23. R. Sabbadini, *Storia del Ciceronianismo* (Turin, 1885); Izora Scott, *Controversies Over the Imitation of Cicero as a Model for Style* (New York, 1910); *Le Epistole "De imitatione" di Giovanfrancesco Pico della Mirandola e di Pietro Bembo*, ed. G. Santangelo (Florence, 1954); Erasmus, *Il Ciceroniano*, ed. A. Gambaro (Brescia, 1965); Erasmus, *Dialogus Ciceronianus*, ed. P. Mesnard, in *Opera omnia*, ordo 1, tomus 2 (Amsterdam, 1971), pp. 581 – 710.

24. Helga Hajdu, *Das Mnemotechnische Schrifttum des Mittelalters* (Vienna, 1936); and Frances Yates, *The Art of Memory* (London and Chicago, 1966).

according to ancient theory, memory was one of the five parts of rhetoric, and some of the earliest treatises on memory are actually commentaries on the section of the *Rhetorica ad Herennium* that deals with memory.[25] New fields of investigation have often originated as monographic treatments of what used to be one chapter in a broader traditional discipline.

Much more extensive than the literature on rhetoric in general or on specific topics such as imitation seems to be the literature on the various genres of prose literature, and especially that on the letter, the speech, and the sermon; this fact may be considered a medieval inheritance. The treatise, the dialogue, and the essay, though much cultivated by Renaissance humanists and other writers, did not receive much theoretical attention, though there were a few sixteenth-century treatises on the dialogue.[26]

The theory of the letter as a main genre of prose literature appears rather late and seldom in classical rhetoric, whereas it came to acquire a central place in the Middle Ages.[27] The composition of documents and letters was a legal and administrative necessity throughout the early Middle Ages. In an age of widespread illiteracy, the popes and other church officials, the princes, and later the cities depended on the services of notaries, chancellors, and secretaries properly trained for their tasks. This training was based on formularies and collections of models and probably also on oral instruction. The earliest extant treatise that deals specifically with the art of writing letters, or *ars dictandi,* was composed by Alberic of Montecassino in the late eleventh century. It appears from his work and from the introductions of later works that the *ars dictandi* originated as a part of the larger field of rhetoric and eventually received special treat-

---

25. *Ad Herennium* III. 16, 24 – 28, 40.

26. Rudolf Hirzel, *Der Dialog,* 2 vols. (Leipzig, 1895, rpt. Hildesheim, 1963).

27. James J. Murphy, *Rhetoric in the Middle Ages* (Berkeley and Los Angeles, 1974); Murphy, *Medieval Rhetoric: A Select Bibliography* (Toronto, 1971); Giles Constable, *Letters and Letter-Collections* (Turnhout, 1976); Kristeller, *Renaissance Thought and Its Sources,* pp. 317 – 19; Kennedy, *Classical Rhetoric,* pp. 173 – 94; H. M. Schaller, "Dichtungs lehren und Briefsteller," in *Die Renaissance der Wissenschaften im 12 Jahrhundert,* ed. P. Weimar (Zurich and Munich, 1981), pp. 249 – 71; id., "Ars dictaminis, ars dictandi," in *Lexikon des Mittelalters* (Zurich and Munich, 1980), coll. 1034 – 39. It appears that the ancient Egyptians treated the letter as a literary genre. There are formal letters from the third millennium B.C. and manuals of letter-writing and collections of form letters from the second millennium. See G. Posener, "Les malheurs d'un prêtre égyptien," *Journal des Savants* (1979), pp. 199 – 205, esp. pp. 199 – 201.

ment because of the great practical and professional importance of its subject. The twelfth century produced a very large number of works on *dictamen* that included both theoretical treatises and collections of form letters, many of them anonymous. Most of the authors who have been identified for the early twelfth century were active at Bologna, whereas later in the same century Orléans and other French centers became important and developed a style of their own. During the thirteenth century, the school of Bologna retained its importance and produced some of its most famous masters, such as Boncompagno. Guido Faba, Giovanni di Bonandrea, and Lawrence of Aquileia. Their influence, as we may see from the diffusion of their manuscripts, extended throughout Europe; during the fourteenth century, if not earlier, we find a number of *dictatores* active outside Italy, not only in France but also in England, Spain, Germany, and Bohemia. In Italy, we also find treatises on *dictamen* from the fourteenth and even from the fifteenth century, but characteristically their authors are known as prehumanists and humanists.[28] This fact would seem to confirm my theory, first presented in 1945, that there is a direct link between the medieval *ars dictaminis* and humanist epistolography (I never meant to suggest that humanism as a whole was derived from the *ars dictaminis*).

In their formal aspects, not in their style or specific content, or even in their titles, the humanist treatises on letter-writing and their collections of form letters are the direct continuation of the medieval *artes dictandi;* moreover, in their activity as chancellors and secretaries, with attendant administrative and political functions, the humanists were the direct successors of the medieval *dictatores,* who included such figures as Petrus de Vineis and Rolandino Passeggeri. Many humanists, including Salutati, had notarial training or even the rudiments of legal training. The humanist *ars epistolandi,* which took the place of the medieval *ars dictandi,* inherited certain features from it, such as the emphasis on and the separate treatment of the address *(salutatio)* and the introduction *(exordium),* the theory of punctuation and that of the parts of the letter. The humanists rejected the medieval doctrine of the *cursus* and returned in theory and practice to the ancient theory of the metrical *clausula* known from Cicero. Above all,

28. Paul Oskar Kristeller, "Un 'ars dictaminis' di Giovanni del Virgilio," *Italia Medioevale e Umanistica* 4, 1961, 181–200. Dictamen treatises by Francesco da Buti and Dominicus Bandinus appear in several manuscripts. Also see Paul F. Gehl, "Vat. Ottobonianus Lat. 1854: Apropos of Catalogue Notices and the History of Grammatical Pedagogy," *Revue d'Histoire des Textes* 8 (1978), 303–7 (on Alberic of Montecassino).

they cultivated a different style and followed different models, especially Cicero and their own humanist predecessors. Erasmus's and Vives's treatises on letter-writing have attracted some recent attention, but Mario Filelfo's large collection of form letters has been largely ignored. For the other treatises and model collections of the fifteenth and sixteenth centuries, even the bibliographical spadework remains to be done.[29]

Much more numerous than the treatises and collections of form letters are the extant collections of actual letters, public or private, original or edited. The vast body of extant material has thus far defied any attempt to achieve bibliographical control or a comprehensive study and interpretation based on the actual sources. Some of the state letters of Salutati were published in the eighteenth century,[30] but the state letters of Bruni and other prominent humanist chancellors are awaiting scholarly attention in the archives not only of Florence but also of other Italian and northern centers.[31] Historians, mainly interested in political events, have often been satisfied with calendars and regests. The humanist influence on the chanceries affected the style of handwriting, which has received some recent attention, but above all it influenced the style of composition and the terminology used in addressing popes and princes and in rendering their titles and prerogatives in a humanist Latin that sometimes offended traditional legal or court practice. I once came across a curious episode involving Bartolomeo Scala, whose wording

29. Giles Constable, *Letters and Letter-Collections;* Cecil H. Clough, "The Cult of Antiquity: Letters and Letter Collections," in *Cultural Aspects of the Italian Renaissance,* ed. Cecil H. Clough (Manchester and New York, 1976), pp. 33 – 67; Alois Gerlo, "The *Opus de conscribendis epistolis* of Erasmus and the Tradition of Ars Epistolica," in *Classical Influences on European Culture A.D. 500 – 1500,* ed. R. R. Bolgar (Cambridge, 1971), pp. 103 – 14; Erasmus, *De conscribendis epistolis,* ed. J. C. Margolin, *Opera omnia,* ordo 1, tomus 2 (Amsterdam, 1971), pp. 153 – 579. For the numerous incunabula containing Johannes Marius Philelphus, *Novum Epistolarium,* see Hain 12968-80 and Copinger 4744 – 45. The first edition (Hain 12968) was printed in Paris, 1481, according to Reichling.

30. Coluccio Salutati, *Epistolae,* ed. Josephus Rigaccius, 2 vols. (Florence, 1741 – 1742). See Ronald G. Witt, *Coluccio Salutati and His Public Letters* (Geneva, 1976); Paul M. Kendall and V. Ilardi, *Dispatches with Selected Documents of Milanese Ambassadors in France and Burgundy,* vol. 1 (1450 – 1460) (Athens, Ohio, 1970); and Lorenzo de' Medici, *Lettere,* ed. N. Rubinstein and R. Fubini, vols. 1 – 3 (Florence, 1977).

31. Peter Herde, "Die Schrift der Florentiner Behoerden in der Fruehrenaissance," *Archiv für Diplomatik* 17 (1971), 301 – 35; Thomas Frenz, "Das Eindringen humanistischer Schriftformen in die Urkunden und Akten der paepstlichen Kurie im 15. Jahrhundert," *Archiv für Diplomatik* 19 (1973), 287 – 418, and 20 (1974), 384 – 506.

of the credentials for some Florentine ambassadors was challenged by no less a person than Pope Paul II.[32] Now that the text of the credentials has been found, the controversy can be understood and interpreted in greater detail.[33] We actually need a listing of humanist state letters as they are found in archives and libraries, and a study of their style and terminology, especially where it departs from previous practice. A complete edition of these letters is hardly possible and perhaps not even worthwhile, but certainly some well-selected specimens should be edited as a starting point for further study. To illustrate the medieval connection also in this area, I may mention that we have a small group of manuscripts that contain together the state letters of both Petrus de Vineis and Coluccio Salutati, preceded by a letter from a fifteenth-century father to his student son, who was evidently supposed to study and imitate these medieval and humanist letters combined in this single volume.[34]

The private letters of the Renaissance humanists constitute another vast body of uncharted material. They are much more numerous than the comparable letters from the Middle Ages and hardly less extensive than the extant body of state letters from the fifteenth and sixteenth centuries. These private letters, however, have received greater scholarly attention, with a somewhat larger part printed, both in early and modern editions. In the case of Petrarch, Ficino, and other authors, it has been rightly observed that these letters were usually collected and edited by their authors. This fact can be checked and confirmed when the original letters or copies deriving from the recipient rather than from the sender have been preserved.[35] These private letters are of great interest, not only for their style but also for their content. They are an invaluable record of the life, thought, and scholarship of their authors, and of the literary and political history of their time. We now have good critical editions of

32. Paul Oskar Kristeller, "An Unknown Correspondence of Alessandro Braccesi . . . ," in *Classical Mediaeval and Renaissance Studies in Honor of Berthold Louis Ullman*, ed. Charles Henderson, vol. 2 (Rome, 1964), pp. 311 – 64, esp. 334 – 41; Alison Brown, *Bartolomeo Scala* (Princeton, N.J., 1979), pp. 135 – 92.

33. I have recently found the text of these credentials in Florence, Biblioteca Nazionale, ms. Pal. 1133, f. 19^v – 20^v.

34. Kristeller, *Studies in Renaissance Thought and Letters*, p. 565, note 28. For one of the mss., Naples V F 37, see Kristeller, *Iter Italicum* 1.420.

35. Francesco Petrarca, *Le familiari*, ed. V. Rossi and U. Bosco, 4 vols. (Florence, 1933 – 1942). For the problem, see the studies by Constable and Clough, cited above (note 29), and my article on Braccesi (above, note 32). For Marsilio Ficino, see Kristeller, *Supplementum Ficinianum*, 2 vols. (Florence, 1937, rpt. 1973).

some of the letters of Petrarch and Bruni, of the correspondence of Salutati and Guarino, Ermolao Barbaro, Erasmus. Similar editions for Poggio, Filelfo, Ficino, Pico, Poliziano, and others are now being prepared or should be undertaken.[36] When a critical edition is not necessary or feasible, at least critical lists with regests and selected texts should be published. Special attention should also be paid to certain genres of letters of which medieval and humanist theorists were aware, genres that correspond to the permanent needs of human life and society and that are still with us in the twentieth century: letters of sympathy and of congratulation, letters of recommendation, love letters and invectives, and several more.

The second important genre of Renaissance prose literature we have to discuss is the speech or oration. In classical antiquity, the oration was the very center of rhetorical theory and practice, though among the three types of speech — deliberative, judiciary, and epideictic — the last was to become the most important in the later centuries of antiquity. During the Middle Ages, the secular public speech and the political and social institutions supporting it disappeared more or less completely. The statement, often repeated by historians, that medieval rhetoric was exclusively concerned with the letter and with the sermon, since public oratory was unknown during those centuries, is correct up to a certain point. It is, however, not entirely correct. In Italy, the rise of the city-states and their new institutions brought about a revival of secular, public oratory; and the practice was followed by instruction and theory, and by the composition of treatises and form speeches.[37] The earliest testimonies of the practice of secular oratory date from the twelfth century. From the thirteenth century, well within the accepted area of the medieval period,

36. Petrarca, *Le familiari.* Leonardo Bruni Aretino, *Humanistisch-Philosophische Schriften,* ed. H. Baron (Leipzig and Berlin, 1928). The study of F. P. Luiso on Bruni's letters, printed many decades ago but never published, has now been edited by Lucia Gualdo Rosa (*Studi su l'episìolario di Leonardo Bruni* [Rome, 1980]). Coluccio Salutati, *Epistolario,* ed. F. Novati, 4 vols. in 5 (Rome, 1891 – 1911). Guarino, *Epistolario,* ed. R. Sabbadini, 3 vols. (Venice, 1915 – 1919). Ermolao Barbaro, *Epistolae, Orationes et Carmina,* ed. V. Branca, 2 vols. (Florence, 1943). Erasmus, *Opus Epistolarum,* ed. P. S. Allen, 12 vols. (Oxford, 1906 – 1958). Erasmus, *Correspondence,* tr. R. A. B. Mynors and D. F. S. Thomson, vols. 1 – 5 (Toronto, 1974 – 1979). Thomas More, *The Correspondence,* ed. Elizabeth F. Rogers (Princeton, N. J., 1947, rpt. Freeport, N.Y., 1970). An edition of Poggio is being prepared by Helene Harth, of Francesco Filelfo by Vito Giustiniani, and of Ficino by Alessandro Perosa and Sebastiano Gentile.

37. Alfredo Galletti, *L'eloquenza dalle origini al XVI secolo* (Milan, 1904 – 1938). Kristeller, *Renaissance Thought and Its Sources,* pp. 320 – 21.

we have not only testimonies but speeches actually delivered, form speeches, and theoretical treatises. The *ars arengandi*, as it was called, became an accepted counterpart of the *ars dictandi*, and it was taught and treated by the same authors.

As early as the thirteenth century, the secular speech was frequently composed, delivered, and recorded in the vernacular; and the same also is true for the public and private letter, although later. Secular speeches are mentioned by the historians of the thirteenth century, and a few such speeches have actually been preserved. The handbooks written for the podestà, the city official called in from the outside, contain form speeches for funerals and other occasions.[38] Boncompagno's *Rhetorica novissima* is not a handbook of *dictamen*, as widely believed, but a handbook for lawyers that includes models of judiciary speeches.[39] We have collections of vernacular speeches of all kinds from the same century.[40] The epideictic genre tends to prevail, and we encounter some of the same types of speeches that were to dominate the oratory of the humanist period: funeral and wedding speeches, ambassador's speeches, welcoming speeches for entering officials or distinguished visitors, university speeches delivered at the beginning of the academic year or upon the graduation of successful candidates, and several more. As in the case of the *ars dictaminis*, we have before us again a fully developed medieval pattern, and again I am prompted to repeat what I stated many years ago, namely, that there is an express link between the Italian *ars arengandi* of the late Middle Ages and the oratory of the humanists (again, I never meant to claim that humanism as a whole was derived from the *ars arengandi*). This link consists in the formal and institutional pattern of the speeches, not in their specific literary style or content.

The extant literature of humanist speeches is very large indeed, although perhaps less so than the letters from the same period. It consists not only of individual speeches but also of collections of speeches by one or more authors, and also of collections of speech models, many of them anonymous. The speeches of the humanists

38. Fritz Hertter, *Die Podestaliteratur Italiens im 12. und 13. Jahrhundert* (Leipzig and Berlin, 1910).

39. Boncompagnus, *Rhetorica novissima*, ed. A. Gaudenzi in *Bibliotheca Juridica Medii Aevi*, vol. 2 (Bologna, 1892), pp. 249–97.

40. Guido Faba, *Parlamenti ed epistole*, in A. Gaudenzi, *I suoni, le forme e le parole dell'odierno dialetto della città di Bologna* (Turin, 1889). Matteo dei Libri, *Arringhe*, ed. Eleonora Vincenti (Milan and Naples, 1974).

have been less studied and edited than their letters and treatises,[41] and they need much more research and investigation. We should have a bibliography of humanist orations, manuscript and printed, by known and anonymous authors, in Latin and in the vernacular, with incipits to permit identification — all arranged by genres as well as by authors and dates. The use of a computer might be considered, and this might attract the necessary funds and manpower. In addition to the genres we have mentioned, which are found in medieval specimens as well, we also have orations to congratulate a new pope, bishop, prince, or other official upon his accession; orations delivered at the opening of church councils or synods, of chapters of a religious order, of public disputations (a genre to which Pico's famous oration belongs); orations by a professor given at the beginning of his course, usually in praise of his subject; orations in praise of Saint Jerome, Saint Augustine, Saint Thomas Aquinas, or others, apparently delivered on specific occasions; orations addressed to newly elected public officials or judges, usually in praise of justice (a practice that seems worth reviving).[42] These speeches follow certain patterns that should be examined. They are not as empty as is usually asserted, for they are often written in good Latin (which can be appreciated by those who know Latin), and they are full of interesting details, biographical and historical as well as literary or scholarly and even philosophical and theological. The speeches of the humanists deserve much further study, not only as a distinct literary genre but also in conjunction with the other writings and activities of their authors.

The third genre of rhetorical prose we must briefly consider, besides the letter and the speech, is the sermon. Like the letter, and much more so than the oration, the sermon of the Renaissance was heavily dependent on a strong and prolific medieval tradition. The enormous literature of medieval sermons has but recently become

41. K. Muellner, *Reden und Briefe italienischer Humanisten* (Vienna, 1899).

42. Charles Trinkaus, "A Humanist's Image of Humanism: The Inaugural Orations of Bartolommeo della Fonte," *Studies in the Renaissance* 7 (1960), 90 – 147. For orations on Saint Jerome, see the forthcoming book by Eugene F. Rice, *St. Jerome in the Renaissance.* For orations on Thomas Aquinas, see Kristeller, *Medieval Aspects of Renaissance Learning,* ed. and tr. Edward P. Mahoney (Durham, N.C., 1974), pp. 60 – 62. John W. O'Malley, "Some Renaissance Panegyrics of Aquinas," *Renaissance Quarterly* 27 (1974), 174 – 93. For public speeches in fifteenth-century Florence, see E. Santini, *Firenze e i suoi "Oratori" nel Quattrocento* (Milan, 1922), and Santini, "La *Protestatio de iustitia* nella Firenze medicea del sec. XV," *Rinascimento* 10 (1959), 33 – 106.

the subject of a critical bibliography.[43] Apparently it was customary during the Carolingian era and beyond to recite in church the homilies of the Church Fathers. The composition of new sermons received a fresh impulse with the Cistercians in the twelfth century and with the mendicant orders in the thirteenth. These sermons were composed in a new pattern that involved a verse from Scripture as a theme, a division of this verse into several parts, and a development of these parts through logical arguments and illustrative stories, or *exempla*. The practice of preaching was accompanied in the twelfth and thirteenth centuries by voluminous treatises on the *ars praedicandi*. They have been carefully listed and studied by modern historians.[44]

Preaching in the fourteenth and fifteenth centuries, in Italy as elsewhere, seems to have followed in many ways the practice and theory of the preceding centuries; some curious examples show that even the newly developing art of secular eloquence followed for a while certain patterns of the sermon.[45] But as we go further along in time, the reverse influence of secular eloquence upon its sacred counterpart becomes more and more apparent. Preachers such as Remigio de'Girolami began to deliver sermons not only on holidays and on saint's days, as had been the prevailing custom, but also on the same occasions that were favored by secular orators, such as funerals, weddings, or public events.[46] The famous preachers of fifteenth-century Italy, from Saint Bernardino of Siena to Roberto da Lecce and Girolamo Savonarola, followed to some extent the medieval pattern, but the wide emotional appeal of their sermons must have been due to other factors that to my knowledge have not yet been sufficiently clarified. Alberto da Sarteano, often associated as a preacher with Saint Bernardino, exchanged at the same time elegant letters with contemporary humanists,[47] and we may wonder how these different

43. J. P. Schneyer, *Repertorium der lateinischen Sermones des Mittelalters für die Zeit von 1150 – 1350*, Beiträge zur Geschichte der Philosophie des Mittelalters 43, 7 vols. (Münster, 1969 – 1976).

44. Harry Caplan, *Mediaeval Artes Praedicandi*, 2 vols. (Ithaca, N.Y., 1934 – 1936); Thomas M. Charland, *Artes Praedicandi* (Ottawa, 1936).

45. Petrus de Vineis gave a speech in Padua, taking for his theme a verse from Ovid (Rolandinus Patavinus, *Cronica*, book 4, chap. 10, ed. A. Bernardi, Città di Castello, 1905 – 1908, p. 64). Petrarch took for the speech given at his coronation as a poet in 1341 a theme from Vergil (Attilio Hortis, *Scritti inediti di Francesco Petrarca*, Trieste, 1874, p. 311).

46. For Remigio Girolami as a public orator, see Galletti, pp. 166 – 68, 503 – 6.

47. S. Albertus a Sarthiano, *Vita et opera*, ed. F. Haroldus (Rome, 1688).

interests were reflected in his preaching.

The practice of lay preaching, which may be traced back to the early thirteenth century (Albertano da Brescia is the earliest example that comes to mind), and the increasing influence of humanist scholarship and rhetoric, also among the members of the clergy and of the religious orders, may explain the fact that after the middle of the fifteenth century, especially in Italy, sacred eloquence was influenced increasingly by secular, that is, by humanist oratory. The theme from Scripture is supplemented or even replaced by a regular introduction, and the logical argument makes room for a freer flow of religious considerations and admonitions in a style that conforms to the rhetorical taste of the period. Luther and Erasmus felt offended by this style. Modern historians have echoed these feelings and have often dismissed with contempt the entire area of humanist preaching. They do not seem to notice that they are in fact condemning in literature the same phenomenon that they profess to admire in the art of the same period, namely, a combination of religious content and classical form. More recently, at least some aspects of this literature, such as the sermons delivered before the popes on certain holidays, the funeral sermons for some popes of the period, and the sermons in praise of Saint Thomas Aquinas, have received a fair and competent treatment.[48] It is to be hoped that the same kind of study will be applied to other types of humanist sermons delivered in various cities and on diverse occasions. An especially interesting group, mostly in the vernacular, consists of the sermons delivered by young laymen, many of them later humanists, before the religious guilds of fifteenth-century Florence.[49]

After this very brief survey of Renaissance rhetoric, its major genres and their medieval antecedents, I should like to mention even more briefly the impact of Renaissance rhetoric on the other areas of

48. John W. O'Malley, "Preaching for the Popes," in *The Pursuit of Holiness in Late Medieval and Renaissance Religion*, ed. Charles Trinkaus and Heiko A. Oberman (Leiden, 1974), pp. 408 – 40; John M. McManamon, "The Ideal Renaissance Pope: Funerary Oratory from the Papal Court," *Archivum Historiae Pontificiae* 14 (1976), 9 – 70; and "Renaissance Preaching: Theory and Practice, A Holy Thursday Sermon of Aurelio Brandolini," *Viator* 10 (1979), 355 – 73. And now see also O'Malley, *Praise and Blame in Renaissance Rome* (Durham, N.C., 1979).

49. Collections of such sermons are found in Florence, Biblioteca Nazionale, ms. Magl. XXXV 211, and in Biblioteca Riccardiana, ms. 2204. Kristeller, *Studies in Renaissance Thought and Letters*, p. 105, note 17; Kristeller, *Iter Italicum* 1.141 – 42, 216 – 17. A third manuscript, formerly owned by the Principe Ginori Conti (*Iter* 1.228) is now in the Stanford University Library.

Renaissance civilization. The other *studia humanitatis* were of direct concern to the humanists and were cultivated by them along with rhetoric. Grammar, the first of these *studia,* was considered more elementary than rhetoric, but the borderline between grammar and rhetoric was not always clearly marked. Grammar included not only orthography and metrics but also phraseology, which we may consider a part of composition or stylistics and hence of rhetoric. Valla's *Elegantiae* was by the standards of its time a work of advanced grammar, but it also served for many centuries as a handbook of style and good writing. Rhetoric and poetics were considered sisters by the humanists, for they were thought to provide the rules for writing well in prose and in verse, respectively. This view omitted several important dimensions of both rhetoric and poetics that were well understood in classical Greece, but it accorded with ideas that had been widespread in late antiquity and during the Middle Ages. Long before the term *humanista* had been coined, the humanists called themselves poets and orators, as did their contemporaries. Thus there was in the Renaissance, as for some time before, a close parallelism between rhetorical and poetical theory, and a good deal of mutual influence between the two areas. The historians of rhetoric will do well to study and emphasize these influences, especially since the historians of poetics, under the spell of romantic preconceptions, have ignored or deplored them and have not attempted to understand them.

The relation between rhetoric and history is of a different type. As a chief genre of prose literature, historiography ever since classical antiquity was thought to be subject to the rules of rhetorical theory. The Greek and Roman historians were among the chief prose authors read and interpreted in humanist courses. The introduction to a course that dealt with an ancient historian often included a discussion of the goals and merits of historiography.[50] When the theory of the art of history became the subject of separate treatises in the late sixteenth century, it was considered a counterpart of rhetoric and poetics and was in many ways influenced by the older traditions of rhetorical (and poetical) literature.[51] In a more specific way, the impact of rhetoric on historiography is apparent in the speeches, fictitious at least in their wording, that formed an integral part of

50. Beatrice Reynolds, "Shifting Currents in Historical Criticism," *Journal of the History of Ideas* 14 (1953), 471–92, rpt. in *Renaissance Essays,* ed. Paul Oskar Kristeller and P. P. Wiener (New York, 1968), pp. 115–36.

51. G. Cotroneo, *I trattati dell' "Ars historica"* (Naples, 1971).

historical literature in the Renaissance as well as in antiquity and the Middle Ages. These speeches were composed according to the rhetorical taste of the time. This practice of following the taste of the times is not necessarily bad merely because it has been abandoned in this century, and there is no good reason for blaming the humanists any more than their ancient and medieval predecessors. Conversely, the charge often made that the rhetorical, that is, the literary style of the humanists diminishes their trustworthiness as critical historians, does not stand scrutiny any better. We may dislike the style of the humanists, but their literary ambitions do not stand in the way of their critical judgment or their use of historical evidence any more than is the case with ancient or modern historians. They vary among each other in the quality of both their style and their reliability, and each of them has to be examined and judged according to his own merits or demerits. We surely do not wish to imply that a historian must write badly to deserve our confidence.

The last area of humanist learning and literature that we must consider is that of moral philosophy, which according to the humanists' view included ethics and politics as well as several other subjects. The moral literature of the humanists is influenced by their rhetoric and grammar in more than one way. They revive the classical genres of the treatise and the dialogue in accordance with such favorite ancient models as Plato, Cicero, and Plutarch. They like to restate the doctrines found in the works of ancient writers and to cite these writers as authorities in support of their own opinions. *Auctoritas* is in fact an ancient rhetorical category, one by no means peculiar to medieval theology or jurisprudence, as many historians seem to believe. The humanists cultivate in their treatises and dialogues an elegant, classicizing, and often Ciceronian style, avoiding the tight arguments of the scholastic philosophers and also their precise terminology. Thus they often lose in conceptual clarity what they gain in literary elegance. As professional rhetoricians, they attribute the highest value to eloquence and claim that they achieve in their moral treatises a combination of eloquence and wisdom that had escaped their scholastic predecessors. A leading humanist such as Lorenzo Valla even places rhetoric above or in the place of philosophy.[52] The com-

52. Hanna-Barbara Gerl, *Rhetorik als Philosophie: Lorenzo Valla* (Munich, 1974). See also J. Lindhardt, *Rhetor, Poeta, Historicus: Studien über rhetorische Erkenntniss und Lebensanschauung im italienischen Renaissancehumanismus* (Leiden, 1979) (deals with Salutati).

bination of wisdom and eloquence sounds like a very appealing program, but we cannot help feeling that wisdom is often sacrificed to eloquence or understood in a rather trivial sense. Our feeling is confirmed by a Renaissance thinker like Pico, certainly not unaffected by humanist rhetoric, who defends the scholastic philosophers against Ermolao Barbaro because they subordinate form to content, as befits a philosopher concerned with the discovery of truth.[53]

If we pass from the *studia humanitatis* to the other learned disciplines that were taught at the Renaissance universities and rooted in the late medieval tradition, we must note that Renaissance rhetoric had a special and strong, though perhaps only temporary, influence on logic. A number of humanists, from Lorenzo Valla to Ramus and Nizolius, tried to reform logic by subordinating it to rhetoric, and this development, which affected not only Italy and France but also many other countries including early America, has received a good deal of recent scholarly attention.[54] The humanist influence in the other learned disciplines, such as theology and jurisprudence, natural philosophy and metaphysics, mathematics and medicine, is pervasive but less specific. It appears in the use of literary genres such as the dialogue or the monographic treatise as against the commentary and the question, in the use and imitation of classical sources and authorities, and above all in the elegant literary style that avoids the tight argument and often also the precise terminology developed by the scholastics, often from Greek sources, but alien to the ancient Roman authors.[55] In recent studies, interesting attempts have also been made to link the theory and practice of the visual arts and music with classical and humanist rhetoric, but I do not feel competent to pursue this subject further.[56]

Although I have dealt with a broad and complex problem in a rather summary and superficial manner, I hope it has become apparent that Renaissance rhetoric, though indebted in many ways to ancient and medieval antecedents, had a physiognomy of its own. It

53. Quirinus Breen, "Giovanni Pico della Mirandola on the Conflict of Philosophy and Rhetoric," *Journal of the History of Ideas* 13 (1952), 384 – 426, rpt. in his *Christianity and Humanism*, ed. Nelson Peter Ross (Grand Rapids, Mich., 1968), pp. 1 – 68.

54. See above, note 22. Juan Luis Vives, *Against the Pseudodialecticians*, ed. and tr. Rita Guerlac (Dordrecht and Boston, 1979).

55. For humanism and jurisprudence, D. Maffei, *Gli inizi dell'umanesimo giuridico* (Milan, 1956); G. Kisch, *Humanismus und Jurisprudenz* (Basel, 1955); and Donald R. Kelley, *Foundations of Modern Historical Scholarship* (New York, 1970).

56. Warren Kirkendale, "Ciceronians versus Aristotelians on the Ricercar as Exordium, from Bembo to Bach." *Journal of the American Musicological Society* 32 (1979), 1 – 44.

occupied an important place in the civilization of its period, thanks to its own role in theory and practice, in education and literature, but also because of its impact on other areas of humanist learning and on other sectors of learning and civilization that were outside the proper domain of the humanists. Renaissance rhetoric is a large area that is still insufficiently explored by modern scholarship and badly in need of much further investigation. We need a correct and complete listing of the manuscript and printed sources, as far as that is possible, an analysis of their content, and critical editions of the more important texts. We need monographs on the more important writers who should also help us understand the links between their contributions to rhetoric and their other works and activities. We should try to understand, in this area as in others, the differences that distinguish the various stages within the Renaissance and the various countries, regions, and cities that played a role in the general development. Special attention should also be paid to the differences between Latin and vernacular rhetoric in both theory and practice, and to their mutual influence where pertinent. What we ultimately need, but cannot hope to achieve at this time, is a comprehensive history of Renaissance rhetoric that will be based on a detailed study of the sources and that will describe not only the internal history of rhetorical theory and practice but also its impact on all other areas of Renaissance civilization.

One Thousand Neglected Authors: The Scope and Importance of Renaissance Rhetoric

JAMES J. MURPHY

There is a marvelously profound line in one of Aristotle's works (*Metaphysics* I.i): "Man by nature desires to know."

It seems clear to me that we need to know much more about two important phenomena in our culture: Rhetoric and Renaissance. We need to know about rhetoric — the art or science of men and women communicating with other human beings — in a critically important period in Western civilization that we call the Renaissance.

The general history of rhetoric is gradually being written. There is a verifiably ancient and medieval history of *ars rhetorica*; the names of Aristotle, Cicero, and Quintilian are well enough known to any student of the Renaissance, and recent studies have begun to make familiar such post-classical personages as Geoffrey of Vinsauf, Ranulph Higden, and Guido Faba.[1] The very term *rhetoric* is being clarified in this process, so that we can take it to mean the attempt to explain the process of human communication. A rhetorician, then, is someone who provides his fellows with useful precepts or directions for organizing and presenting his ideas or feelings to them. Martin Luther, for instance, was exceptionally skilled at arguing his point of view but did not attempt to show others how to be so skillful; his

1. See George A. Kennedy, *The Art of Persuasion in Greece* (Princeton, N.J., 1963); Kennedy, *The Art of Rhetoric in the Roman World* (Princeton, N.J., 1972); Kennedy, *Classical Rhetoric and Its Christian and Secular Tradition from Ancient to Modern Times* (Chapel Hill, N.C., 1980); Martin L. Clarke, *Rhetoric at Rome: A Historical Survey* (London, 1953); James J. Murphy, *Rhetoric in the Middle Ages: A History of Rhetorical Theory from Saint Augustine to the Renaissance* (Berkeley and Los Angeles, 1974); Murphy, *Medieval Rhetoric: A Select Bibliography* (Toronto, 1971).

disciple Johann Sturm, by contrast, was so anxious to teach that skill that he wrote more than a dozen rhetorical works specifically designed to lay out the necessary precepts.[2]

Yet how much do we really know today about rhetoric in the Renaissance? It is certainly true that Renaissance scholars customarily acknowledge its importance or influence.[3] It is also true that for one major country (England) we do have a useful survey of the whole period by Wilbur S. Howell[4] and that Spain and Germany have drawn some attention.[5] In addition there are some significant studies of key individuals,[6] and students of literature have explored some specific aspects of the influence of rhetoric.[7]

Nevertheless, the scope of Renaissance rhetoric is barely appreciated. It is a field of human activity that stretched over centuries of

2. For example, *De ratione inveniendi oratoria libri IIII* (Strassburg, 1570); *Scholia ad rhetorica Aristotelis* (Strassburg, 1570). See Pierre Mesnard, "The Pedagogy of Johann Sturm (1507–1589) and Its Evangelical Inspiration," *Studies in the Renaissance* 13 (1966), 200–19.

3. It is interesting that, although medievalists have long had major bibliographic guides (for instance, Louis J. Paetow, *A Guide to the Study of Medieval History*, first published in 1917 and lately revised, New York, 1973), it is only recently that we have seen for the Renaissance such analogues as Jozef IJsewijn, *Companion to Neo-Latin Studies* (Amsterdam, New York, and Oxford, 1977).

4. Wilbur S. Howell, *Logic and Rhetoric in England, 1500–1700* (Princeton, N.J., 1956, rpt. New York, 1960). See also Donald Lemen Clark, *Rhetoric and Poetry in the Renaissance* (1922, rpt. New York, 1963); Walter J. Ong, S.J., "Tudor Writings on Rhetoric, Poetic, and Literary Theory," in his *Rhetoric, Romance, and Technology* (Ithaca, N.Y., 1971), pp. 48–103; and William G. Crane, "English Rhetorics of the Sixteenth Century," in *The Province of Rhetoric*, eds. J. Schwartz and J. A. Rycenga (New York, 1965).

5. Antonio Marti, *La preceptiva retórica española en el Siglo de Oro*, Biblioteca románica hispánica, 1: Trados y monografias, 12 (Madrid, 1972); and José Rico Verdu, *La retórica española de los siglos XVI y XVII* (Madrid, 1973). Helmut Schanze, *Rhetorik: Beiträge zur ihrer Geschichte in Deutschland vom 16.–20. Jahrhundert* (Frankfurt, 1974).

6. For instance, Karl R. Wallace, *Francis Bacon on Communication and Rhetoric, or the Art of Applying Reason to the Imagination for the Better Moving of the Will* (Chapel Hill, N.C., 1943); and Lisa Jardine, *Francis Bacon: Discovery and the Art of Discourse* (Cambridge, 1974). A number of useful monographs have appeared in various periodicals — such as Lawrence Flynn, S.J., "The *De arte rhetorica* of Cyprian Soarez S.J.," *Quarterly Journal of Speech* 42 (1956), 367–74, and 43 (1957), 257–65; Christine W. Sizemore, "The Authorship of *The Mystery of Rhetoric Unveiled* [attributed to John Smith]," *Papers of the Bibliographic Society of America* 69 (1975), 79–81; Jacqueline Ijsewin-Jacobs, "*Magistri Anthonii Haneron* (ca. 1400–1490) *opera gramm. et rhet. I*," *Humanistica Louvaniensia* 24 (1975), 29–69. A systematic survey of such individual studies is hampered by the lack of a critical bibliography of Renaissance rhetoric.

7. Within one year (1970), four such books appeared: Alex Gordon, *Ronsard et la Rhétorique*, Travaux d'Humanisme et Renaissance III (Geneva, 1970); Annabel M. Pat-

time, over scores of national boundaries, and over half a score of languages. It is now clear that books of rhetoric were written in Latin, in Italian, in French, in Spanish, in Greek, in English, in German, in Polish, in Bohemian, in Dutch, in Danish, in Swedish, in Welsh — in virtually every Western language of early modern times. They span over two and a half centuries, from the earliest days of printing to about the year 1700.

One can understand the bewilderment of anyone approaching the study of Renaissance rhetoric. Consider the remarkably diverse events of this period: the rise of empirical science, the new philosophy, the emergence of the New World. Consider some of the great names of the period: John Locke, René Descartes, Christopher Columbus, Martin Luther, William Shakespeare, Johann Gutenberg. Yet the explorer Vasco da Gama is a spiritual brother of the rhetorician Francisco Robertelli; Francis Bacon is a spiritual brother of Giovanni Baptista Bernardi, both trying to harness human knowledge into some kind of understandable whole. That it is an extremely complex period in Western culture is a conclusion surely needing no further proof.

It is manifest therefore that any serious student of the Renaissance must be conversant with philosophy, logic, Latin literature, half a dozen vernacular literatures, mercantilism, the birth of linguistics, the revival of both the Greek and Latin classics, the Reformation, revolutions in education, the role of universities, revolts against scholasticism, the impact of the printing press, the genius of writers like François Rabelais and John Milton, and a dozen other subjects — each of which even by itself would seem to require a lifetime of study. Only a Renaissance man, apparently, could possibly be a modern Renaissance scholar. But how many Kristellers can there be?

What seems to have happened, in the face of this problem of enormous Renaissance diversity and proliferation of human activity, is that many modern scholars have apparently settled, perhaps defensively, for a solution in respect to rhetoric that is both misleading and dangerous. This solution has been to concentrate on a comparatively few rhetorical authors and their works, implicitly declaring,

---

terson, *Hermogenes and the Renaissance: Seven Ideas of Style* (Princeton, N.J., 1970); A. Kibédi Varga, *Rhétorique et littérature* (Paris, 1970); Brian Vickers, *Classical Rhetoric in English Poetry* (London, 1970). A more recent volume, exploring nine Renaissance writers of Italy, England, and France, is that of William J. Kennedy, *Rhetorical Norms in Renaissance Literature* (New Haven, Conn., 1978).

almost by default, that these are the only rhetorical productions worth considering.

Let me pose a challenge to readers at this point. Listed below are the most frequently cited names of Renaissance rhetoricians, the names most often seen in footnotes or heard in learned papers at meetings. Then allow me to ask the test question: Is it possible to name ten more? Is this list of names that dominate our footnotes really the canon of accepted Renaissance rhetoricians? A visitor from Mars might well conclude that these are the most important or critical figures in the history of Renaissance rhetoric, because these are the names that recur time and time again in our publications:

Rudolf Agricola	Marius Nizolius
Francis Bacon	Henry Peacham
Leonard Cox	George Puttenham
Desiderius Erasmus	Richard Rainolde
Pierre Fabri	Peter Ramus
Thomas Farnaby	Johann Sturm
Abraham Fraunce	Joannes Susenbrotus
Luis de Granada	George Trapezuntius
Justus Lipsius	Juan Luis Vives
Philip Melanchthon	Thomas Wilson

This is a list that has launched a thousand footnotes. Every name on it is an important personage, studied and restudied; indeed, almost every one has been the subject of a book. But while this is certainly a list of important figures in any serious history of Renaissance thought about human communication, the question remains: Is it possible to name ten more rhetoricians of the Renaissance who are equally important? I would suggest that most modern scholars could not do so, precisely because these twenty are indeed the core of a generally accepted "canon" of rhetoricians quoted by everyone, analyzed by everyone, assumed by almost everyone to be the only ones worth the effort to study. However, it is a canon by default; the result is a scholarly sin, a sin of synecdoche — of taking the part for the whole. The sin consists in assuming that adroit quotations from only Erasmus or only Vives or only Ramus will ipso facto represent Renaissance thinking about rhetoric.

This sin of synecdoche is indeed dangerous and misleading. It is dangerous because accepting this canon of authors at face value makes it seem to us today that Renaissance rhetoric is only an historical curiosity like the Investiture Controversy or the Battle of Agincourt — in other words, only a matter of antiquarian interest with no relation to today's world. This erroneous assumption excludes rhetoric as a subject deserving serious thought. It is also misleading because it distorts our understanding of a crucial period in our human history; and whatever distorts history, I hope we can agree, performs a disservice to an understanding of our own world. The crucial issue, then, is whether this list of twenty authors is a reasonable canon for the study of Renaissance rhetoric, and this question can be emphatically denied.

At this point, the subtitle of this paper— "The Scope and Importance of Renaissance Rhetoric" — must begin to break apart. How can we possibly determine the *importance* of a subject when we do not yet know its *scope*—its size, its dimension, its geographical spread, its practitioners? For example, G. Arthur Padley has now presented us with a survey of Latin grammar for the Renaissance;[8] thirty-two of the grammarians he treats also wrote treatises on rhetoric. This is but one further evidence of the broad sweep of rhetoric in the period. How can we hope to begin to understand the *importance* of relations between rhetoric and grammar in the Renaissance if we do not first grasp the *scope* of rhetoric itself?

One might have assumed that by now there would be a standard bibliography; that there would be a standard list of authors and their works; that there would be an equivalent of Howell's history for Italy, for Spain, for Germany, for France, and so forth. But in fact the basic apparatus for serious study of this field is still lacking. There is no basic bibliography, there is no internationally recognized canon of authors, there is no Latin Howell, or French Howell, or German Howell. In short, there appears to be no comprehensive mechanism available for the systematic study of Renaissance rhetoric.

This impression is reinforced if we check the bibliographies for current work. For example, there is a bibliography of periodicals in the field of rhetoric — standard at least for Americans — that is, the index of articles in American speech journals from 1917 to 1979.[9] Those include *The Quarterly Journal of Speech, Speech Monographs* (now

8. G. Arthur Padley, *Grammatical Theory in Western Europe, 1500 – 1700: The Latin Tradition* (Cambridge, 1976). See also the general remarks in Aldo D. Scaglione, *Ars grammatica* (The Hague and Paris, 1970).

9. *Index to Journals in Communication Studies Through 1979*, Ronald J. Matlon (Speech Communication Association, 1980).

Communication Monographs), *Western Speech, Central States Speech Journal, Southern Speech Journal,* and *Speech Education* (now *Communication Education*). For the sixty-two-year period of the index, there are just 136 items listed on Renaissance rhetoric out of a total of more than 8,000 articles cited — an average of just one out of every sixty articles published in that period. Other bibliographies reveal similar patterns.[10] If one next checks the important *Renaissance Quarterly,* one finds that major surveys like that of Charles Trinkaus in 1976[11] (discussing Kristeller, Hans Baron, and others) do indeed note the importance of rhetorical influences — "a new sophistication" in modern studies — but stop short of definitive explanations or comprehensive analyses.

Meanwhile, however, Charles H. Lohr has begun publishing his admirable lists of authors of Renaissance Latin Aristotle Commentaries, first in *Studies in the Renaissance* (1974) and thereafter in *Renaissance Quarterly.* In 1972 John O. Ward completed a massive Toronto thesis on the commentators on Cicero's rhetorical works up to the year 1600, though even that study lists only thirty-one printed commentaries on Cicero's *De inventione* and the *Rhetorica ad Herennium.*[12] These two projects, each a model of methodology, when viewed together with Paul Oskar Kristeller's massive *Catalogus* project, make it seem possible to attack head-on the problem of Renaissance rhetoric with its multitude of authors and works. The evident success of these ventures gives added emphasis to a fundamental concept that Kristeller pointed out eighteen years ago in his *Eight Philosophers of the Italian Renaissance:*

10. See, for example, *Bibliographie de l'Humanisme belge, précedée d'une bibliographie générale concernant l'Humanisme européen,* Alois Gerlo avec la collaboration d'Emile Lauf, Institut pour l'étude de la Renaissance et de l'humanisme, Travaux, Instrumenta humanistica I (Presses Universitaires de Bruxelles, 1965); and *Bibliographie internationale de l'Humanisme et de la Renaissance,* Féderation internationale de Sociétés et Instituts pour l'étude de la Renaissance (Geneva, 1966 – [published in 1965]).

11. Charles Trinkaus, "Humanism, Religion, Society: Concepts and Motivations of Some Recent Studies," *Renaissance Quarterly* 29 (1976), 676 – 713; part 2, section B (pp. 694 – 99) is entitled "Rhetoric and Renaissance Historical Consciousness."

12. John O. Ward, "*Artificiosa eloquentia* in the Middle Ages," 2 vols. (Ph.D. diss., University of Toronto, 1972). Ward's list of printed commentaries appears in 2.570 – 81. However, the Bodleian Library alone holds the works of sixty-one authors of commentaries on Cicero's rhetorical works. See also Ward's chapter "From Antiquity to the Renaissance: Glosses and Commentaries on Cicero's *Rhetorica*" in *Medieval Eloquence: Studies in the Theory and Practice of Medieval Rhetoric,* ed. James J. Murphy (Berkeley and Los Angeles, 1978), pp. 25 – 67.

The study of any historical area cannot be placed on a solid foundation until the relevant primary sources are more or less fully inventoried and thus made available for further study.[13]

This obviously sensible injunction ought to weigh heavily on the shoulders of anyone beginning a study of rhetoric in the Renaissance. No single volume can be understood well until there is some way to see how that volume fits into the overall Renaissance scheme of things. Without this knowledge, we cannot hope to comprehend how, say, Francesco Patrizi relates to other authors like Gabriele Zinano or Johannes Spangenberg or Sebastian Fox Morzillo.

Nevertheless, there is mounting evidence that we do not yet fully comprehend the scope of this subject. There seem to be at least a thousand authors of Renaissance rhetorical works, not twenty or thirty (there are more than one hundred *incunabula* alone): a vast and unexplored treasure trove of information about human communication.

We have long had clues to indicate that there are many more Renaissance rhetoricians than our footnotes normally include. When Johan-Henricus Alstedius published his *Rhetorica* at Herborn in 1616, he listed in his frontispiece the titles of the 30 works on style that he used as sources.[14] When Diego Valades, O.F.M., newly returned from the missionary fields in 1579, wrote in his *Rhetorica christiana* about applying European rhetoric to Indian audiences in Mexico, he included an alphabetized index of 157 authors consulted, including 26 rhetoricians ranging from Cicero and Quintilian to Pedro de Guevara and Benito Ario Montano.[15]

One of the most interesting sets of clues of this kind, however, is to be found in the *Thesaurus rhetoricae* of Giovanni Baptista Bernardi, published at Venice in 1599.[16] Bernardi lists in his frontispiece the

13. Paul Oskar Kristeller, *Eight Philosophers of the Italian Renaissance* (Stanford, Calif., 1964). The problem remains even today.

14. *Rhetorica, quatuor libris proponens universam ornate dicendi modum* (Herborn, 1616). Book 1 deals with tropes, 2 with figures, 3 with delivery, and 4 with *rhetorica specialis*. Alstedius is also the author of *Orator, sex libris informatus*, which achieved its third edition in the same year, 1616, as well as *Clavis artis Lullianae* (1609) and *Systema mnemonicum duplex* (1610).

15. Didaco Valades, *Rhetorica christiana ad concionandi, utriusque facultatis exemplis suo loco insertis; quae quidem, ex Indorum maxime deprompta sunt historiis. Unde praeter doctrinam, summa quoque delectatio comparabitur* (Perugia, 1579).

16. *Ioan, Baptista Bernardi, Patricii Veneti. Thesaurus rhetoricae, in quo insunt omnes praeceptiones, quae ad perfectum oratorem, instituendum, ex antiquis, & recentioribus Rhetorum monumentis, accurate desumptae sunt, ordineque admirabili, ac facillimo in unum velut locum*

titles (and editions) of the thirty-nine works he uses as sources for his encyclopedia of about five thousand rhetorical terms. His method is to list the terms in alphabetical order and then to cull from his authors either directly quoted definitions or his own paraphrases of their statements. Hence, a term like *argumentum* merits two columns of separate, short paragraphs giving various authors' views; at the end of each paragraph Bernardi cites his source in some detail: author, title, book, and section or page. Not surprisingly, he gives heavy weight to the *La Retorica* of his fellow Italian, Bartolomeo Cavalcanti (1503 – 1572); this vernacular work, first published at Venice in 1555, had at least six editions by 1585. The bulk of Bernardi's sources, however, are Latin works. It is illuminating to note which "ancient and more recent works of the rhetoricians" are chosen by a knowledgeable encyclopedist at the end of the sixteenth century. The contemporary authors chosen include Germans, Frenchmen, and Spaniards as well as Italians; while Peter Ramus is not listed, his disciple Omer Talon is. Following is the list as Bernardi presents it:

AVTHORES
A QVIBVS OPVS HOC
EXCERPSIMVS,
ET CVIVS IMPRESSIONIS SINT.

Aristoteles impressus in 16. Venetijs 1572.
Aphtonius impressus Basileæ, vnacum Hermogene.
Hermogenes impressus Basileæ.
Theon Sophista Basileæ 1541.
Dionysius Longinus, Venetijs 1555.
Demetrius Phalereus, Florentiæ 1562.
    Vns cum comm. Petri Victorij.
Marc. Tull. Cicero, Lugduni 1562.
Quintilianus impressus Lugduni 1555.
Auerroes Venetijs 1550.
Consult. Chrius Venetijs 1523.
Boethius Basileæ 1546.
Macrobius.
Aquila Rom. Venetijs 1523.
Egid. in Rhet. Arist. Venetijs 1515.

---

digestae, ita ut uno intvitu omnia, quae ad artem pertinent inveniri possint. Opus utilissimum non modo oratoribus & concionatoribus, sed etiam omnibus, qui Rhetoricae operam dant, per necessarium (Venice, 1599). Bernardi is also the author of a work he titled *Seminarium totius philosophiae Aristotelicae et Platonicae* (Geneva, 1599, altera editio). Despite its title it also includes a book on Stoic philosophy.

Pub. Rutilius Lupus Venetijs 1523.
August. Sues. in Rhet. Arist. Venetijs 1521.
Petrus Victorius in Rhet. Arist. Florentiæ 1548.
   In Demetrium Phalereum Flor. 1562.
Georgius Trapezuntius impressus Parisijs 1538.
Daniel Barbarus in Rhet. Arist. Venetijs 1544.
August. Valerius Cardin. Venetijs 1578.
Ludouicus Granata Venetijs 1578.
Marc. Ant. Maioragius in Rhet. Arist. Venetijs 1572.
Sulpicius Victor.
Iulius Camillus Venetijs 1584.
Aud. Thaleus Parisijs 1577.
Hieronymus Regius Venetijs 1568.
Cyprianus Soarius Brixiæ 1581.
Bartholomæus Caualcanti Pisauri 1559.
August. Curius Venetijs 1563.
Rodolphus Agricola Venetijs 1558.
Ioachimus Fortius Lugduni 1531.
Iacobus Ludouicus Strebeus Coloniæ 1582.
Petrus Mosellanus Lugduni 1533.
Iouita Rapitius Venetijs 1554.
Franciscus Robortelius Bononiae 1567.
Emp. Rhetor.
Iulius Rufinianus Lugduni 1533.
Beda Presbyter Lugduni 1533.

For at least one author at the end of the century, then, it is clear that Europe as a whole, rather than his native country alone, is the ground for collecting ideas about rhetoric. It is also noteworthy that Bernardi presents his book not only for orators and preachers but for all who wish to use rhetoric. His book seems worthy of further study beyond its value for the list of sources he provides.

In more recent times there have appeared some useful lists of authors and their works, usually published as appendices to studies of various kinds. An early one of these lists was published by the late Karl Wallace in 1943 as an appendix to his book, *Francis Bacon on Communication and Rhetoric;* Professor Wallace began with the remarkable collection assembled at the University of Illinois Library over many years by T. W. Baldwin and Marvin T. Herrick, and then added to the list a number of items from the admittedly incomplete catalogue under the subject-heading "Rhetoric" at the Library of Congress. Three other useful lists may be found in Lee Sonnino's *Handbook to Sixteenth Century Rhetoric,* in the late Joan Lechner's *Ren-*

aissance Commonplaces, and in Father Walter Ong's *Ramus and Talon Inventory,* which of course deals mainly with pro- or anti-Ramus works. Altogether these modern lists point to two or three hundred authors.[17] The eight separate lists of preaching manuals compiled by Harry Caplan and Henry H. King have never been collated to identify the Renaissance titles.[18]

Nevertheless, Renaissance rhetoric must surely be one of the most-mentioned and least-studied subjects in modern scholarship. The apparatus for study — what economists call the "infrastructure," or basic equipment — is simply not yet fully available to us.

Surely the real scope of this subject will only begin to dawn on us when some systematic survey is undertaken. The study of individual ideas or individual authors may be one way to begin.[19] A preliminary short-title catalogue of authors of rhetorical works published from the beginning of printing to the year 1700, to which has been added a select secondary bibliography, is now available.[20]

Investigation of particular ideas very quickly reveals the staggering complexity of Renaissance rhetoric. One notes, for instance, the widespread interest in the distinction between "general rhetoric" and "special rhetoric," as made by Renaissance rhetoricians like

17. For Wallace see above, note 6. Lee Ann Sonnino, *A Handbook to Sixteenth Century Rhetoric* (London, 1968); Sister Joan Marie Lechner, O.S.U., *Renaissance Concepts of the Commonplaces* (New York, 1962); Walter J. Ong, S.J., *Ramus and Talon Inventory* (Cambridge, Mass., 1968); there is a fair amount of duplication among these lists, and in the case of Wallace there are occasional unannounced translations (into English) of Latin or French titles. There are some regional or national lists, as in P. Kuentz, "Esquisse d'un inventaire des ouvrages de langue française traitant de la rhétorique entre 1610 & 1715," *XVIIᵉ Siècle* 80–81 (1968), 2. 133–42; as Kuentz points out, ". . . il est impossible de tracer une frontière rigoureuse entre ce qui est théorie de la rhétorique et théorie de la littérature. . . . Le choix paraîtra souvent contestable" (p. 133).

18. For Latin treatises, *Harvard Theological Review* 42 (1949), 185–206; for Italian, *Speech Monographs* 16 (1949), 243–52; for Dutch, *Speech Monographs* 21 (1954), 235–47; for French, *Quarterly Journal of Speech* 36 (1950), 296–302; for English, *Speech Monographs* 22 (1955), 1–106; for Scandinavian, *Speech Monographs* 21 (1954), 1–9; for Spanish, *Speech Monographs* 17 (1950), 161–70; and for German, *Speech Monographs* 23 (1956), no. 5, 1–106.

19. An excellent recent example is Hannah-Barbara Gerl, *Rhetorik als Philosophie: Lorenzo Valla* (Munich, 1974).

20. See James J. Murphy, *Renaissance Rhetoric: A Short-Title Catalogue of Works on Rhetorical Theory from the Beginning of Printing to A.D. 1700, with Special Attention to the Holdings of the Bodleian Library, Oxford. With a Select Basic Bibliography of Secondary Works on Renaissance Rhetoric* (New York, 1981). Also see Charles Stanford, "The Renaissance," in Winifred P. Horner (ed.), *Historical Rhetoric: An Annotated Bibliography of Sources in English* (New York, 1980), pp. 111–184.

Bartholomew Keckermann and Clemens Timpler.[21] Franciscans, Dominicans, and Jesuits were forced into what we would call cross-cultural rhetorical studies because of their missionary efforts.[22] A number of continental books on rhetoric also had English editions not otherwise noted in our standard rhetorical studies.[23] It would of course be expected that classical rhetorical works would be widely printed in Renaissance Europe, but some readers may be surprised at the evident and long-lasting popularity of Aphthonius, not only in Greek and in Latin, and in the well-known English version of Richard Rainolde, but in Italian, French, and Spanish as well.[24] Annabel Patterson has now studied Hermogenes for us.[25] Another interesting phenomenon is the resurgence of interest in the so-called rhetoric of the medieval figure Ramon Lulle, long associated with cabbalistic theory and magic; both the Frenchman Sieur Jacob and the German Joannes Alstedius wrote explanations of Lulle's theories.[26]

Naturally, rhetoricians in the Renaissance — as indeed in our own times — could be expected to publish either in opposition to or in support of another rhetorician's views. The Ramists and anti-Ramists are an example. Sometimes these clashes follow predictable religious lines, as with Johann Sturm or Philip Melanchthon, or with Johann Cochleus, who in 1531 wrote a book teaching the rhetoric needed to persuade those whom he regarded as damnable Lutheran

21. Bartholomew Keckermann, *Systema rhetorica, generalis et specialis* (Danzig, 1606). Keckermann notes (p. 538) that "ars quidem potissimum in rhetorica generali, prudentia vero in rhetorica speciali dominatur." And Clemens Timpler, *Rhetoricae systema methodicum per praeceptiones et questiones* (Hanover, 1613). See also note 14, above, on Alstedius.

22. Symptomatic of this concern is the effort to provide teaching tools for the new languages required: the Jesuit Gaspar de Villela on Japanese, the Franciscan Luiz Rodriguez on Nahuatl, the Augustinian Martin de Rada on Chinese; the Dominican Francisco Diaz wrote a book in Chinese dealing with the four cardinal virtues. See note 15, above, on Diego Valades.

23. For instance, *Methodus de conscribendi epistolis a G. Macropedia traditia. Accessit G. Hegendorphini Epistolas conscribendi methodus* (London, 1580). Caplan and King (Latin) report a London 1570 edition of Hepinus, *Formula compendoria de formandis sacris concionibus*, first published in Basle in 1540.

24. One particular Latin version with the commentary of Lorichius, for instance, had a wide use: *Apthonii sophistae progymnasmata, partim a Rodolpho Agricola, partim a Joanne Maria Cataneo latinae donata . . . cum scholiis Reinhardi Lorichii Hadamarii* (Frankfurt, 1553). This version had at least eleven editions by 1600, including three in London, and a further twenty-nine within the next century.

25. See above, note 7.

26. A useful survey of this development may be found in Joseph M. Victor, "The Revival of Lullism at Paris, 1499–1516," *Renaissance Quarterly* 28 (1975), 504–34.

heretics: his title is *Rhetorica divina, sive Ars vincendi haereticos Lutheranos ex sacris scripturis.* But sometimes there is a burst of continuing written controversy, in book and broadside, even among fellows of one religious persuasion; for instance, there was the controversy in seventeenth-century England over the question of "private preaching"—that is, need a preacher be ordained; and if ordained, need he be learned or even educated? In the fifteen years between 1642 and 1657, a rash of seventeen publications flew back and forth, notable more for their passion than their precision of logic. For instance, John Taylor, the Water Poet, joined in the fray with these lines:

> A preacher's work is not to geld a sowe,
> Unseemely 'tis a judge should milk a cow,
> A Cobbler to a pulpit should not mount,
> Nor can Asse cast up a true account.[27]

The reply to this by Henry Walker—no relation to either Obadiah Walker or William Walker—was both crude and violent. Suffice it to say that it involved a suggestion about certain arrangements of the human anatomy that a reasonable person might well consider physically impossible.

The proliferation of texts is a further evidence of the scope of this subject. One visit to the Zentralbibliothek, Zurich, Switzerland, produced the records of twenty-two German and Swiss authors for whom there is no record in either the British Library or the Bodleian Library; only three of the twenty-two were represented in the holdings of the Bibliothèque Nationale in Paris. A Xerox copy of the handwritten subject catalogue—*De arte rhetorica* and *Oratores*—of the Herzog August Bibliothek in Wolfenbüttel, West Germany, loaned by Brian Vickers, indicates the existence of forty-two Renaissance rhetorical works for which there is no other evidence in Oxford, Paris, London, or the Library of Congress. The two-volume bibliographic survey of Spanish language arts by Marcelino Menéndez y Pelayo lists scores of Spanish rhetorical works for which there are no easily discoverable examplars either here or in Europe.[28] Have they

27. John Taylor, *A Swarme of Sectaries and Schismatiques: Wherein is discovered the strange preaching (or prating) of such as are by their trades cobblers, tinkers, pedlars, weavers, sowgelders, and chimney-sweepers.* London, 1641 (Wing T514), p. 2. For a reply see Henry Walker, *An Answer to a Foolish Pamphlet entitled A Swarme of Sectaries and Schismaticks put forth by John Taylor the water-poet,* London, 1641 (Wing W368).

28. Marcelino Menéndez y Pelayo, *Historia de las ideas estéticas en España,* 2 vols. (Madrid, 1974). Also, see above, note 5.

all perished in wars and revolutions? If it is not possible to locate extant copies, can we ever be sure that we understand the real course of Spanish rhetoric?

There is one recurring experience: every visit to a library — whether it is UCLA, the Folger, the Staatsbibliothek München, the Newberry, or Trinity College, Dublin — produces a further list of new book titles. This raises a further, nightmarish question: How many more hundreds (or thousands) of Renaissance rhetorical treatises still remain to be found?

The important caution to be derived from all this is that it is not yet possible to generalize about Renaissance rhetoric. We do not yet have the data to make inductive reasoning possible and we need more studies of individual writers.

One potentially fruitful line of inquiry, therefore, given our present state of knowledge about Renaissance rhetoric in general, would be to undertake detailed studies of individual authors and their works, making each of them in a sense a kind of bench mark against which to assess the field as a whole. The study of one man's works may well identify his peers, enemies as well as friends. The study of the Venetian Giovanni Baptista Bernardi, for instance, has already been mentioned as one way of assessing the influence of the thirty-nine authors he uses as sources. Peter Ramus is of course an obvious example of an author already studied as a bench mark, just as Cyprian Soarez is an instance for a different segment of the field. But we lack such individuated studies even for other well-known writers like Philip Melanchthon, Johann Sturm, Luis de Granada, and a host of others. If we lack rhetorical analyses of even the giants, how much more so do we need exploration of men we are just coming to know!

The Pedro Simon Abril (or Aprileus) who is credited by Menéndez y Pelayo with a Spanish *Progymnasma de Aftonio* also wrote an *Introductiones ad libros logicorum Aristotelis libri duo* (Toledo, 1572) now in the Bodleian Library. That he also composed *La Gramatica Griega, escrita en lengua Castellana* (Madrid, 1587) would seem to indicate an interest in the *trivium* as a whole. He also translated some orations of Demosthenes as well as sermons of Saint Basil and Chrysostom, besides the *Ethics* of Aristotle.

Johan Henricus Alstedius (1588– 1638), professor of philosophy and theology at Weissemburg and sometime opponent of Robert Bellarmine, wrote in addition to his well-known *Encyclopedia* (1630) a

Compendium grammaticae Latinae (1613), a *Clavis artis Lulliande* (1609), and a *Systema mnemonicum duplex* (1610), the first book of which was sometimes printed separately as *Artium liberalium . . . systema.* He is the author of *Orator, sex libris informatus* (Herborn, editio tertia, 1612), which includes *Rhetorica ecclesiastica* as book six. The nearly one thousand pages of his *Theologica prophetica* (Hanover, 1622) includes a vast collection of *conciones* (pp. 88 – 904) in addition to rhetorical theory. His *Methodus SS. Theologis in sex libris tributa* (Herborn, 1612) includes a section on the responsibilities of the listening church congregation *(De officio auditorum).*[29]

Sometimes a single passage will give a striking insight into the whole rhetorical stance of an author like Benito Arias Montanus:

> Damnat perversa quorendam studia, qui nullo in Dialectica iactio fundamento, Rhetoricis incumbunt, vanum quandam verborum & figurarum congeriem affectantes, eamque solam Rhetoricam esse putantes.[30]

Sometimes a title will reveal much about an author, as in the case of Jakob Andrea (1528 – 1590), Lutheran theologian of Tübingen and author of a rather sober *Methodus concionandi* (Frankfurt? 1595). Perhaps more revealing than this book, however, is the title of one of his numerous theological works: *Asinus avis; hoc est metamorphosis nova qua novitius quidam sacramentarius, Marcus Beumlerius, dum tenere in avem falconem transire voluit, ridiculo errore in asinum commutatus est* (Tübingen, 1587).[31] For another example, the brief *Isagoge rhetorices* (Louvain, 1516) of Hadrianus Barlandus (1488 – 1522) shows another side of a certain kind of humanistic ego: for each *exemplum Ciceronis* in his section on figures, he includes an *exemplum Barlandi.*[32]

Sometimes the other interests of an author may provide illumi-

29. For an older but still interesting study of Alstedius, see Percival R. Cole, *A Neglected Educator: Johann Heinrich Alstedius: Translations from the Latin of His Encyclopedia,* Records of the Teachers Association, no. 5, New South Wales, The Teachers College (Sydney, 1910).

30. *Rhetoricorum libri IIII Benedicti Ariae Montani Theologi, ac poetae laureati, ex disciplina militari divi Iacobi Ensigeri* (Antwerp, 1569), p. 7.

31. Marcus Beumlerus (1555 – 1611), an ardent defender of Calvin, was professor of theology in Zurich from 1594 to his death of the plague seventeen years later. His *Elocutionis rhetoricae libri duo* (Zurich, 1598) is a treatise on tropes and figures that includes Hebrew examples from the Old Testament. He also wrote several treatises analyzing the letters of Cicero in the Ramist manner *(an methodum Petri Rami accomodata).*

32. It is interesting that, after studies at Gand and at Louvain, he taught Latin at

nation about him. Caspar Bartholin (1585– 1630) taught medicine at Padua, Wittenberg, and Copenhagen, where he also taught theology in addition to composing a *Rhetorica maior* (Copenhagen? 1616).[33] René Bary, author of *La rhétorique françoise* (Paris, 1653), was not only historiographer to the king but the author of books on morals, logic, and one on *Physique*. The Thomas Blebel who wrote *Rhetorica artis progymnasmata . . . ad puerilem accomodata* (Leipzig, 1584) also published a book on astronomy, *De sphaera* (Leipzig, 1590). Nor was every author tamely quiescent in the usual academic tradition—schoolmasters then, as today, often wrote books. The much-condemned sixteenth-century figure Jacobus Brocardus (who finally found refuge in Nuremburg after condemnations by at least three synods) had mystic visions of applying scriptural passages to contemporary events, but these lofty aspirations did not prevent him from writing two Latin versions of Aristotle's *Rhetoric*.[34]

Surely the study of individual authors—and these examples have been selected merely from the letters A– B in a list of authors—can provide us significant bench marks for understanding rhetoric in the whole period we call the Renaissance.

Another approach might be to take a certain limited time span and assess all the rhetorical works appearing in that period. For instance, from the beginning of printing to the year 1500—the period of the so-called *incunabula*—we now know that at least 117 rhetorical works were printed, mainly on the Continent.[35] The list includes all the ancient authors and many of the medieval authors like William of

Busleiden. After a visit to England, however, he returned to teach rhetoric instead. The British Library has a copy of his *Compendiosa institutiones artis oratoriae, omnia nunc emendatius excusa* (Cologne, 1537). See E. Daxhelet, *Adrien Barlandus, humaniste belge* (Louvain, 1938).

33. For another example, Geraldus Bucoldianus (Gerhardt Bucholtz), author of *De inventione et amplificatione oratoria seu usu locorum libri tres* (Lyons, 1551) and editor of Quintilian (Cologne, 1527), was physician to Ferdinand, King of Rome.

34. Jacobus Brocardus, *In tres libros Aristotelis de arte rhetorica paraphrasis* (Paris, 1549 and 1558); and *Partitiones oratoriae, quibus omnia Aristotelis praecepta breviter et dilucide explicantur* (Venice, 1558).

35. For one incunable produced in England, see James J. Murphy, "Caxton's two choices: 'Modern' and 'Medieval' Rhetoric in Traversagni's *Nova rhetorica* and the Anonymous *Court of Sapience*," *Medievalia et humanistica* n.s. 3 (1972), 241 –55. Conversely, the fairly numerous studies of fifteenth-century English figures like Stephen Hawes seldom penetrate beyond the superficial level in assessing rhetorical influences of that period.

Auvergne, Albertanus Brixiensis, Guidotta da Bologna, Brunetto Latini, Aegidius Romanus, and Ramon Lull. Some of the late fifteenth-century writers are shadowy figures like Salguis *decanus parisiensis*, author of *Ars inveniendi themata* (1482), or simply anonymous like the author of the *Liber novus rhetorice* (Cologne, 1484), now in the Staatsbibliothek, Munich. Some are not recorded in standard works like Hain. Indeed, some seem to be merely printed versions of medieval dictaminal manuscripts, like the *Ars scribendi* (1494?) of Jacobus Barynus (Hain 2661). Others, like the *De fine oratoris pro Ciceronis et Quintiliani assertione* (Brixen, 1492) of Christopher Barzizza, are much more sophisticated in their treatment of current humanistic concerns. It would be useful to have at least a preliminary survey of the rhetorical developments in these works over the comparatively short time span involved.

The incunabular period is after all the period of significant works by people like Ermolao Barbaro, Christopher and Gasparino Barzizza, Benedictus Benedictus, Aurelius Brandolinus, Joannes Caesarius, Lodovico Carbo, Conrad Celtis, Symphorien Champier, Augustino Dathi, Joannes Despauterius, Hieronymus Dungersheim, Desiderius Erasmus, Gulielmus Fichetus, George of Trebizond, Heinrich Gessler, Antonio de Gouvea, Antonio Haneron, Pierre de la Hazardiere, Nicholas Herborn, Jacobus Izelgrimus, Jacobus Publius, Laurentius de Saona, Joannes Lentzberger, the young George Macropedius, Antonio Mancinelli, Claudio Mino, Francesco Nigro, William Obendorffer, Jacobus Paulus Niavis, Antonio de Nebrija, Francisco Filelfo, Aneae Silvia Piccolomini, Raphael and Hieronymus Regius, Johann Reuchlin, Friedrich Riederer, Salguis, Guillaume Tardif, Lorenzo Valla, Johannes Sulpitius Verulanus, Albrecht von Eyb, and Christopher Weidlings. Even the most skeletal survey of these writers could tell us a great deal about rhetoric in the latter half of the fifteenth century. This in turn might well explicate more clearly the rhetorical events of the sixteenth century.[36]

There must surely be a variety of other approaches to begin a

---

36. To give one example, it would be useful to have a competent rhetorical study of the *Margarita poetica* of Albertus de Eyb (Albrecht von Eyb), printed by Georg Husner at Strassburg not later than 1472. This lengthy work includes not only excerpts from Gasparino Barzizza and Stephanus Fliscus as well as Cicero and Quintilian but incorporates the *Praecepta artis rhetoricae* attributed to Aneae Silvio Piccolomini. The title of the work is explained as a dedication to de Eyb's mother: "Tu a genetrice mea dignissima divina Margarita de Wolmerhausen: femina quidem clarissima" (f. 1).

more systematic study of Renaissance rhetoric. Some are small in scope and could be undertaken immediately. The numerous *Tabulae* of the period might also provide some useful indices of contemporary thinking about rhetoric. For example, study of the *Tabulae rhetoricae* (Venice, 1571) of R. C. Angeli, which draws upon both Aristotle and Demetrius Phalereus, would indicate at least Angeli's understanding of these works, just as translations and commentaries so often do.

Other approaches, perhaps more fruitful in the long run, would require carefully planned study over a long period. Despite the work of scholars like Birgit Stolt,[37] we still do not have a definitive study of the rhetoric of Lutheran Protestantism. Despite the efforts of Marshall McLuhan, Walter Ong, and Elizabeth Eisenstein, we probably do not yet have a complete picture of the rhetorical impact of the printing press.[38] Do we yet appreciate fully the effect of rhetoric upon even so obvious a field as education? Diplomatics? Preaching? Science?[39] These are cosmic questions whose answers may require concerted, persistent efforts over time. Yet how can we profess to understand the Renaissance as a whole when we do not yet sufficiently comprehend an element — rhetoric — that so many modern scholars acknowledge to be important?

Obviously rhetoric is but one of many important facets of Renaissance culture — see the cautions of Professor Kristeller elsewhere in this volume — but it is indeed an important one.

37. Birgit Stolt, *Studien zu Luthers Freiheitstraktat mit besonderer Rücksicht auf das Verhältnis der lateinischen und deutschen Fassung zueinander und die Stilmittel der Rhetorik* (Stockholm, 1969).

38. Marshall McLuhan, *The Gutenberg Galaxy: The Making of Typographic Man* (Toronto, 1962); Walter J. Ong, S. J., *Rhetoric, Romance and Technology* (Ithaca, N. Y., 1971). Now also see Elizabeth L. Eisenstein, *The Printing Press as an Agent of Change: Communications and Cultural Transformations in Early-modern Europe,* 2 vols. (Cambridge, 1979).

39. For instance, note the comparative bibliographic paucity of a study like James P. Zappen, "Science and Rhetoric from Bacon to Hobbes: Responses to the Problem of Eloquence," in *Rhetoric 78: Proceedings of Theory of Rhetoric, An Interdisciplinary Conference,* eds. Robert L. Brown, Jr. and Martin Steinman, Jr., Center for Advanced Studies in Language, Style, and Literary Theory (Minneapolis, Minn., 1979), pp. 399–419.

Rhetoric in
the Italian Renaissance

DOMINIC A. LaRUSSO

Most persons embarking upon a study of the Italian Renaissance are immediately impressed with the apparent overwhelming complexity attending the effort. The sheer volume of scholarly studies in a variety of fields from a host of researchers would test the will of the strongest devotee. The phenomenon (as some would title it) of the Italian Renaissance is a kaleidoscope of individual metamorphoses, social interactions, and creative revolutions quite unlike those of any other historical moment. Initial investigation into each of these arenas has uncovered a series of labyrinths not yet totally delimited. The inspired work of Fernand Braudel, *The Mediterranean*,[1] represents this protean condition even better than the classical effort of Jacob Burckhardt.[2] After some four centuries of attention, the problem of definition (period, phenomenon, focus, achievements) remains strong and thriving.[3] And foremost among the subdivisions of this problem is the "abundance of interpretations" attending the dominant current labeled "humanism," which was evident sometime between 1300 and 1600 and a consideration of which proves to be "a

1. S. Reynolds, trans., 2 vols. (New York, 1972). I wish to acknowledge the priceless guidance of the late Joseph G. Fucilla during my work on this essay.

2. *The Civilisation of the Renaissance in Italy*, trans. S. G. C. Middlemore (London, 1890).

3. Of the many, the following serve as good examples of the continuing efforts toward reinterpretations: L. Gundersheimer, "Toward a Reinterpretation of the Renaissance in Ferrara," *Bibliothèque D'Humanisme et Renaissance* 30 (1968), 267 – 81; E. Cochrane, "The End of the Renaissance in Florence," *Bibliothèque D'Humanisme et Renaissance* 27 (1965), 7 – 29.

convenient way to deal with the inner development of Renaissance culture."[4] As noted by Gioacchino Paparelli in his work *Feritas, Humanitas, Divinitas*—extended by Paul Oskar Kristeller in "Studies on Renaissance Humanism during the Last Twenty Years," and detailed more specifically by Donald Weinstein in his careful review, "In Whose Image and Likeness: Interpretations of Renaissance Humanism"—schools of interpretation range from those championing humanism as a philosophical controversy over human values to those viewing it as a *modus operandi* for the life of an active citizen.[5]

A shadow of the first school is that group embracing the notion of *studia divinitas* or humanism as piously motivated and directed. Closer to the second group are those scholars who build upon the image of humanism as *studia humanitatis*, the core of which is the rhetorical tradition. The posture of each group, of course, dictates its method of investigation, focus of study, and resultant conclusions. A reader seeking a view of Renaissance scholarship through the eyes of Giuseppe Toffanin, diligent champion of the first school, would glean a knowledge strong with a tone of religious endowments; rhetorical implications, if noted at all, would be recorded as incidental at best. Turning to the position of Kristeller, that same reader would find rhetorical accomplishments identified more positively, analyzed

4. W. J. Bouwsma, "Changing Assumptions in Later Renaissance Culture," *Viator* 7 (1976), 421. Without pretense at exhausting the possibilities, I suggest that the following efforts ought to be consulted for an appreciation of the spectrum of thought involved: R. Weiss, "Per una storia del primo Umanesimo," *Rivista storica italiana* 60 (1948), 349–66; B. L. Ullman, "Renaissance—The Word and the Underlying Concept," *Studies in Philology* 49 (1952), 105–18; Paul Oskar Kristeller, *Studies in Renaissance Thought and Letters* (Rome, 1956), pp. 553–83; H. Baron, "Burckhardt's *Civilization of the Renaissance* a Century after its Publication," *Renaissance News* 13 (1960), 207–22; F. B. Artz, *Renaissance Humanism 1300–1500* (Kent, Ohio, 1966), pp. 1–49; R. Spongano, "L'Umanesimo e le sue origini," *Giornale storico della Letteratura Italiana* 130 (1953), 238–310.

5. (Messina, 1960); Kristeller, *Studies in the Renaissance* 9 (1962), 7–30; Weinstein, *Journal of the History of Ideas* 33 (1972), 165–76. At this point, mention must be made of the seminal nature of the Kristeller article to the student of Renaissance scholarship—whatever its facet. From the critical appraisals of selected scholars and their works to the bibliographic citations, the article is alive with thoughts indispensable to any serious consideration of humanism or humanists. The interested reader might profit most from a sequential study of Kristeller, "The Place of Classical Humanism in Renaissance Thought," *Journal of the History of Ideas* 4 (1943), 59–63; G. Paparelli, *Feritas* . . . ; Hannah H. Gray, "Renaissance Humanism: The Pursuit of Eloquence," *Journal of the History of Ideas* 24 (1963), 497–514; N. J. Perella, "Humanism and the Spirit of the Renaissance," *Italica* 40 (1963): 132–44; D. Weinstein, "In Whose Image and Likeness?"; W. Bouwsma, "Changing Assumptions"; G. M. Logan, "Substance and Form in

more completely, and implicated more definitely in the vital affairs of the periods under consideration.[6]

Significant in all this controversy is the fact that, while the degree of emphasis may vary between schools and among investigators, all recognize the presence of the rhetorical tradition in matters of law, religion, education, art, philosophy, and civil affairs. Some dismiss this presence as incidental or fatuous; others stress its pivotal nature in Renaissance developments; all find it impossible to ignore.

Of most interest to students of rhetoric is the dialectic within the midst of those already convinced of the impact made by the rhetorical tradition, but divided over the nature and scope of that impact. The exchange between Jerrold Seigel and Hans Baron best typifies the apparent polar positions involved.[7] Essentially a political historian, Baron presents an energetic and unique notion of a mass of humanistic literature untouched by his predecessors that may well have led to a stronger focus upon the role of rhetoric in the lives of prominent civic leaders, although his own perspective of the *Quattrocento* led him to minimize its significance. Seigel and others were moved to embrace the position of Kristeller that the rhetorical tradition served to initiate, develop, and sustain the intellectual and political maturation of Renaissance citizens.[8]

Hidden in all this controversy is a secondary level of definitional problems concerning rhetoric itself. Relating to a similar condition faced by those sifting through the efforts of the ancients, George Kennedy observes that

> Rhetoric, like other faculties, can be viewed in two general ways: as a historical phenomenon or as a systematic discipline. From the former point of view what is most interesting are the differences in different rhetorics and how these differences can be related to art, literature, political and legal institutions, and the philosophical and

Renaissance Humanism," *Journal of Medieval and Renaissance Studies* 7 (1977), 1–34; B. Corrigan and B. Mitchell, "Italian Literature," in *The Present State of Scholarship in Sixteenth-Century Literature,* ed. W. M. Jones (Columbia, Mo., 1978), esp. pp. 8–12.

6. Especial attention should be given to the Corrigan and Mitchell article noted above, in the pages cited as well as the choice bibliography.

7. J. Seigel, "'Civic Humanism,' or Ciceronian Rhetoric?" *Past and Present* 34 (1966), 3–48; H. Baron, "Leonardo Bruni: 'Professional Rhetorician' or 'Civic Humanist'?" *Past and Present* 36 (1967), 21–37. The conclusions of Delio Cantimori are relevant here, "Rhetoric and Politics in Italian Humanism," *Journal of the Warburg Institute* 1 (1937–1938), 83–102, as are those of P. Albert Duhamel, "The Function of Rhetoric as Effective Expression," *Journal of the History of Ideas* 10 (1949), 344–57.

8. Bouwsma, p. 422.

intellectual currents of various periods and cultures. From the systematic point of view, the major focus is on what rhetorics have in common and whether universal, positive statements can be made about what "rhetoric" is, about its parts, its forms.[9]

At the very least, it can be said that the problems of perspective delineated by Kennedy persist in the study of Renaissance rhetoric, with the quantitative advantage on the side of historians whose prime interests center in the words and deeds of *Quattrocento* citizens. Rhetoric is advanced as the core of man's ability to construct cities, influence political development and guide personal achievement.[10] Due largely to the Protagorean credo reinforced by Isocrates and implemented by Cicero, the Italian humanist is shown as believing that

> rhetoric was a coherent body of knowledge of human behavior with a special focus on the relation of discourse to action. For them rhetoric functioned as a psychology which stressed the sophisticated analysis of problems of will and choice, motivation and compulsion; which developed a concrete self-consciousness in the author of the relation of meaning to intention; and which placed a high value on a sense of *opportunità (kairos)*, a grasp of the relation of choice to circumstance.[11]

Stimulated by the thought that rhetoric conduced to freedom in all realms by providing "techniques for either a theory of literature or a statesman's handbook,"[12] some scholars turned to a more systematic perspective in the attempt to know more.

Of those shadows touching the perimeters of this school of systematic analysis, Bernard Weinberg's is among the more obvious. Albeit within a matrix of literary criticism, his prodigious and protracted investigation of major and minor works of *Cinquecento letterati* enriched the rhetorical repository both quantitatively and qualita-

9. "The Present State of the Study of Ancient Rhetoric." *Classical Philology* 70 (1975), 278.

10. Nancy Struever writes convincingly of the historiographic facet of rhetoric using Salutati, Bruni, and Bracciolini as witnesses; *The Language of History in the Renaissance* (Princeton, N. J., 1970). In an earlier discussion, Richard McKeon, *Thought Action and Passion* (Chicago, 1954), presents his stimulating interpretation of the dynamic relationship between history and rhetoric.

11. Struever, *Language of History,* p. 116.

12. McKeon, *Thought Action and Passion,* p. 187.

tively.[13] His insistence upon working from primary sources to expand the real base of critical appraisal led to a reappraisal of scores of manuscripts and printed works available during the 1500s. Moreover, the diligence of scrutiny and general method of investigation, revealing common trends and idiosyncratic notions, resulted in a legacy of enticing research topics for both poetry and rhetoric. In pursuit of the theme of *imitation,* important to both poetry and rhetoric, Weinberg became aware of four principal images of rhetoric, which directed the activities of humanists interested in this "most complicated of all literary sciences of the epoch . . . ,"[14] images that carved out niches of intellectual and practical involvement. First, there is a view of rhetoric as concern for figures and tropes, an inchoate approach to style that divorced *verba* from *res.* A second, more mature notion of rhetoric combines *verba* and *res* to produce various theories of style. In this vein, attention is directed toward developing the various kinds of style delineated by Cicero and others. A third conceptualization of rhetoric stresses it as the theory of literary composition. The canons of *inventio, dispositio,* and *elocutio* were applied by these *letterati* to rhetorical discourse or poetic activity. The fourth prominent posture reemphasized rhetoric as persuasion.

It is fair to state at this point that the scholar interested in the history of rhetoric during the Italian Renaissance has an available base from which to operate. Still, it should be noted that much of this base has been provided by those whose primary goal has been something other than the history of rhetoric; while crucial to any understanding in this area, many of the contributions alluded to thus far touch only indirectly on any attempt to chart the course of rhetorical ideas. What is needed is a concerted effort to survey the field of Ital-

13. When I first began my own labors in earnest during the 1950s, Weinberg was well along in his monumental *History of Literary Criticism in the Italian Renaissance,* 2 vols. (Chicago, 1961), and his *Trattati di Poetica e Retorica del Cinquecento,* 4 vols. (Bari, 1970 – 1974) was in a wispy design. His kind, timely encouragement helped direct my own endeavors toward the vernacular statements of rhetorical concepts.

14. *Trattati,* 1.546 ff. The full comment is "La retorica è forse la più complicata di tutte le scienze letterarie dell' epoca, non soltanto perchè il termine gode di sensi ancora più numerosi di quelli attribuiti all'imitazione, ma anche perchè, al punto storico a cui siamo arrivati, *essa rappresenta una fusione e confusione di arti e scienze in principio diverse ma ridotte ora ad una sola disciplina pressoché universale*" (italics mine). The effect of this research, in spirit and method, is no less significant than that associated with Baron's and Kristeller's. Note the more specialized view of W. J. Kennedy in *Rhetorical Norms in Renaissance Literature* (New Haven, Conn., 1978), pp. 1 – 5.

ian Renaissance rhetoric in a manner much like those requested by the Committee on Renaissance Studies of the American Council of Learned Societies.[15]

While this is not an attempt to present either a survey or a history of the field, it is an effort to highlight certain of the more promising avenues open to exploration and development. Virtually all surveys of intellectual disciplines begin with a call for more bibliographies — general and specialized.[16] Despite the fact that the standard bibliographies such as McKerrow's and the Cambridge series are available to all researchers, including those interested in Italian rhetoric, special additional aid is not easily had. Aside from the specifics extractable from the *MLA International Bibliography of Books and Articles on the Modern Languages and Literatures,* the quarterly list published on Italian Studies in *Italica, The Year's Work in Modern Languages,* the report of recent studies in the Renaissance in *Studies in Philology,* short-title catalogues, special library catalogues, and the works of Kristeller, Cosenza, Galletti, Fontanini, Garin, Santini, Tiraboschi, Weinberg, and a few more, researchers have recourse to no workable book-lists or annotated bibliographies of either major rhetorical treatises or

15. The 1979 Newberry Library Conference on Rhetoric in the Renaissance was obviously designed to provide the framework for such a probe. Among the more helpful models for such a survey one might find: R. Tuve, "A Critical Survey of Scholarship in the Field of English Literature of the Renaissance," *Studies in Philology* 40 (1943), 204 – 55; W. Ferguson, "Recent Trends in the Economic Historiography of the Renaissance," *Studies in the Renaissance* 7 (1960), 7 – 26; Paul Oskar Kristeller, "Studies on Renaissance Humanism during the Last Twenty Years," *Studies in the Renaissance* 9 (1962), 7 – 30; Paul Oskar Kristeller and J. H. Randall, Jr., "The Study of the Philosophies of the Renaissance," *Journal of the History of Ideas* 2 (1941), 449 – 96; L. B. Wright, "Introduction to a Survey of Renaissance Studies," *Modern Language Quarterly* 2 (1941), 355 – 61; F. R. Johnson and S. V. Larkey, "Science," ibid., pp. 363 – 401; R. H. Bainton, "Changing Ideas and Ideals in the Sixteenth Century," *The Journal of Modern History* 8 (1936), 417 – 43 and the very helpful bibliography. A most recent offering in this regard containing a good discussion of the historical-political roots supporting general Renaissance scholarship, is Jones, ed., *The Present State of Scholarship in Sixteenth-Century Literature* (see above, note 5).

16. After viewing the work of two decades on Renaissance humanism, Kristeller still felt the need for more "bibliographies, editions, monographs, and really comprehensive works of reference," in "Studies in Renaissance Humanism," p. 22. The need is greater for the field of Italian Renaissance rhetoric, especially for the *Cinquecento.* Of the work already in hand, including bibliographies, commentaries, and critical appraisals, the bulk pertains to the 1400s and before. Comparatively little has been done with vulgate texts written, published, or utilized during the 1500s. The most complete effort thus far remains that of Weinberg.

special authors.[17] Some efforts have been made visible. As early as 1920, a list of "Italian Critical Treatises of the Sixteenth Century" was published by R. C. Williams as one person's consignment to fill a bibliographic void.[18] Six years later, the same journal published another list, this by W. L. Bullock; for roughly the same period, this list included many new items clearly identified as rhetorically oriented and with many more geographic notations appended.[19] Very noticeable is the absence of special bibliographies and critical surveys of Italian Renaissance rhetorics and related areas on the order of J. W. Holme's "Italian Courtesy-Books of the Sixteenth Century" or the Caplan and King contribution, "Italian Treatises on Preaching: A Booklist,"[20] and the aforementioned studies of Weinberg.

Although mildly reflective of the problems detailed by Kristeller in the preface of *Iter Italicum,* construction of functional bibliographies for the study of rhetorical phenomena in the Italian Renaissance (whether check-lists or in-depth efforts) has problems that are

17. In the course of compiling such bibliographies, one should also refer to the publications issuing forth from the various centers for Renaissance studies such as those at Harvard, the universities of North Carolina, Michigan, London, California at Los Angeles, Toronto, Ohio State, Pittsburg, and so on; the libraries, including Newberry, Huntington, Folger, John Rylands, and others; and the constituent society seminars, many of which are listed in *Renaissance News* 31 (1978), 459 – 62. For aid in contributions of individual authors, see at least: Paul Oskar Kristeller, *Iter Italicum,* 2 vols. (Leiden, 1963 and 1967); M. Cosenza, *Bibliographical and Bibliographical Dictionary of the Italian Humanists of the World of Classical Scholarship in Italy, 1300 – 1800,* 2nd ed., 6 vols. (Boston, 1962 – 1967); A. Galletti, *L'Eloquenza (Dalle Origini al XVI Secolo)* (Milan, 1938); G. Fontanini, *Biblioteca dell' Eloquenza Italiana,* 2 vols. (Venice, 1753); F. Tateo, *"Rhetorica" e "Poetica" fra Medioevo e Rinascimento* (Bari, 1960); E. Garin, et al., *Testi Umanistici su la Retorica* (Rome, 1953); E. Santini, *L'Eloquenza Italiana dal Concilio Tridentino ai nostri giorni,* 2 vols. (Milan, 1923; Palermo, 1928); G. Tiraboschi, *Storia della Letteratura Italiana* (Florence, 1805 – 1813), i – ix; G. Toffanin, *Storia letteraria d' Italia. Il Cinquecento,* 7th ed. (Milan, 1973); E. Bonora, *Retorica e invenzione: studi sulla letteratura italiana del Rinascimento* (Milan, 1970); *Storia della letteratura italiana* (Milan, 1966), vol. 4: *Il Cinquecento.* Additional help can be secured from the particular focus of dictionaries typified by G. Gerini, *Gli scrittori pedagogici italiani del secolo decimoquinto* (Turin, 1896); C. Frati, *Dizionario bio-bibliografico dei bibliotecari e bibliofili italiani del sec. XIV al XIX* (Florence, 1933); *Dizionario letterario Bompiani delle opere e dei personnagi di tutti i tempi e di tutte le letterature,* 9 vols. (Milan, 1946 – 1950); and series 38 on "Pedagogisti ed Educatori" of the *Enciclopedia Biografica e Bibliografica "Italiana"* (Milan, 1939).

18. *Modern Language Notes* 35 (1920), 506 – 7.

19. "Italian Sixteenth-Century Criticism," *Modern Language Notes* 41 (1926), 254 – 63.

20. J. W. Holme, *Modern Language Review* 5 (1910), 145 – 60; H. Caplan and H. King, *Speech Monographs* 16 (1949), 243 – 52.

rarely solved by one scholar. Such work is more properly the result of the coordinated efforts of many, and the recent contributions of participants at the 1979 Newberry Library Conference on Rhetoric in the Italian Renaissance is a move in this direction; a decision to revive the ill-fated project entitled *Biographical Dictionary of Renaissance Rhetoricians* would be another.

Perhaps more in the area of rhetorical scholarship than in related fields, in addition to the bibliographies and special lists sketched above, the need continues for more critical appraisal of the nature, structure, and machinations of the vast number of informal and formal organizations of learning that pressed upon the cultural life of the period. Such explorations are potentially rewarding not only because of the distinctive intrusion of rhetorical concepts in the intellectual ventures of the day but also because most humanists-rhetoricians were directly or indirectly affiliated with such assemblies. Moreover, the 1500s witnessed a veritable explosion in the number of *accademie* established throughout the peninsula. Again, the work of Kristeller on the Platonic Academy serves as general mode, as does Brunetti's "L'Accademia Aldina," and Gilbert's "Bernardo Rucellai and the *Orti Oricellari* . . . ," and De Gaetano's "The Florentine Academy and the Advancement of Learning. . . ."[21] But what of the others located throughout the peninsula?[22] What of their members? What discussions were held? What polemics encouraged? What was the impact of such discussions and polemics on cultural and political matters? An analysis of the early concept and practices of the *studio* as an informal institution of learning should also bear fruit, as Woodward's investigation of various Renaissance peda-

21. Paul Oskar Kristeller, "The Platonic Academy of Florence," *Renaissance News* 14 (1961), 147 – 59; M. Brunetti, *Rivista di Venezia* 8 (1929), 417 – 31; F. Gilbert, *Journal of the Warburg and Courtauld Institutes* 12 (1949), 101 – 31; A. DeGaetano, "The Florentine Academy and the Advancement of Learning through the Vernacular: the *Orti Oricellari* and the Sacra Accademia," *Bibliothèque D'Humanisme et Renaissance* 30 (1968), 19 – 52. This scrutiny of records reveals the names of many who were dedicated to the rhetorical experience, some as rhetors, some as rhetoricians, and some as both (passim). Weinberg once again offers a model in his "Argomenti di Discussione Letteraria nell' Accademia degli Alterati (1570 – 1600)," *Giornale storico della Letteratura Italiana* 131 (1954), 175 – 94.

22. Without pretending to exhaust the possibilities, mention must be made here of L'Accademie: *Fiorentina* (earlier called *degli Umidi*); *della Crusca; degli Alterati; degli Scossi; degli Insensati; degli Intronati; degli Infiammati; degli Elevati; degli Uranici; degli Assorditi* as samples. The index of the 1824 edition of Tiraboschi offers valuable information on this subject, as does the particular analysis of M. Maylender, *Storia delle accademie d'Italia*, 5 vols. (Bologna, 1926 – 1930).

gogues attests.[23] What do we know of the role of rhetoric in these companies of scholars? Aside from studying them to discover who taught what to whom, in what mode, through what exercises, and with what texts, there is value in studying the rhetorical philosophies and practices of the various religious societies and movements as well. While we know more about the rationale and methods of the *ratio studiorum* than about many of the contemporary systems, there remain many shadowy areas regarding rhetoric's role in the cultural and intellectual development of those involved.[24] And what of the

23. W. H. Woodward, *Vittorino da Feltre and Other Humanist Educators* (Cambridge, 1905). Obviously, the early work of R. Sabbadini on da Feltre, da Verona, and Barzizza is indespensable: *La Biblioteca delle scuole italiane* 7 (1897), 33 – 37; *Rivista di filologia e d'istruzione classica* 14 (1885 – 1886), 425 – 34; *Giornale Linguistico* 18 (1891), 3 – 40; *Archivio storico lombardo* 13 (1886), 363 – 78, 563 – 83, 825 – 36; *Revista pedagogica* 21 (1928), 629 – 33. See also E. Garin, ed., *L'Educazione in Europa (1400 – 1600)* (Bari, 1957), particularly chaps. 3 and 4; G. Gerini, *Gli Scrittori . . .* , pp. 42 – 73, 228 – 59, 269 – 81. Of special concern are Paul Oskar Kristeller, "Un' 'Ars Dictaminis' di Giovanni Del Virgilio," *Italia Medioevale e Umanistica* 4 (1961), 181 – 221; G. Billanovich, "Giovanni Del Virgilio, Pietro Da Moglio, Francesco Da Fiano," *Italia Medioevale e Umanistica* 6 (1963), pts. 1 – 3, 203 – 34, and pt. 4, 7 (1964), 279 – 324; G. Cremaschi, "Bartolino da Lodi professore di Grammatica e di Retorica nello Studio di Bologna agli inizi del Quattrocento," *Aevum* 26 (1952), 309 – 48; note also, although attention is to an earlier period, H. Wieruszowski, "Rhetoric and the Classics in Italian Education of the Thirteenth Century," *Studia Gratiana* 11 (1967), 169 – 207; and "Arezzo as a Center of Learning and Letters in the Thirteenth Century," *Traditio* 9 (1953), 321 – 91.

24. An exceptional repository of early documents relevant to the *ratio* is E. A. Fitzpatrick, *St. Ignatius and the Ratio Studiorum* (New York, 1933). Well known is the fact that, at the intermediate level of the Jesuit system, "Rhetorica" is the dominant force directing methods and materials. To my knowledge, a systematic scrutiny of the *De Controversiis* (1586 – 1596) of Cardinal Roberto Bellarmine (1542 – 1621) for its rhetorical concepts and implications has not been done. Yet as student of those involved in forming the *ratio* and as teacher of many who followed, Bellarmine was a factor in the education of the young. Gerard Smith, S. J., ed., *Jesuit Thinkers of the Renaissance* (Milwaukee, Wisc., 1939), presents an interesting and rewarding collection of essays that could prove of aid to further research in this arena. While I have not seen the work, my attention has been called to E. J. Lynch's "The Origin and Development of Rhetoric in the Plan of Studies of 1599 of the Society of Jesus" (Ph. D. diss., Northwestern University, 1968). Applicable as model here is the effort of R. A. Lang, "Rhetoric at the University of Paris, 1550 – 1789," *Speech Monographs* 23 (1956), 216 – 28, as well as "Rhetoric in *Les Petites-Ecoles of Port Royal*," *Speech Monographs* 25 (1958), 208 – 14. See also J. M. Connors, S. V.D., "Saint Charles Borromeo in Homiletic Tradition," *American Ecclesiastical Review* 138 (1958), 9 – 23; and Paul Oskar Kristeller, "The Contribution of Religious Order to Renaissance Thought and Learning," *American Benedictine Review* 21 (1970), 1 – 55, with careful note of the bibliography. See also E. M. Jung, "On the Nature of Evangelism in Sixteenth-Century Italy," *Journal of the History of Ideas* 14 (1953), 511 – 27.

more formal and well-established centers of learning? What of a comparative study of rhetorical curricula, textbooks, and exercises employed at the universities of Florence, Bologna, Ferrara, Padua, Perugia, Siena, and the like?[25] In short, much remains to be done at this basic and indispensable level of search, accumulation, and compilation.

Upon this groundwork, activity designed to service another substantial need—translations, commentaries, and interpretations—could mature more rapidly. Once again we find ourselves recipients of the scholarly expertise of historians of education, science, philosophy, art, and literary criticism. Consider, for example, the necessity for more studies similar to those of Ong's work on Ramus, Breen's splendid exegesis of Giovanni Pico della Mirandola's position on philosophy and rhetoric and his more extended treatise of Mario Nizolio (Marius Nizolius), and those of Garin, Rossi and Vasoli collected in *Testi Umanistici su la Retorica*.[26] Much remains for close scrutiny and appraisal, particularly if one considers *Cinquecento* treatises by persons whose lives render ample proof of the possible balance between *la vita activa* and *la vita contemplativa*, who represent the *civis* of Seigel, Kristeller, and others. [27]

25. J. R. Banker's article, "*The* Ars Dictaminis *and Rhetorical Textbooks at the Bolognese University in the Fourteenth Century*," *Medievalia et Humanistica* n.s. 5 (1974), 153–68, is the clearest example of such a study. Hints are also contained in A. Gherardi, *Statuti della universita e studio fiorentino* (Florence, 1881), who records salary and duties of such persons as Tommaso Corsini (p. 116), F. Bruni, M. Di Loro, and others who affected the course of rhetoric (pp. 297, 445–46, 467). Struever, *The Language of History* (p. 105), notes a passage in the *statuti* emphasizing the use of rhetorical studies. Also useful in this vein are L. Thorndike, *University Records and Life in the Middle Ages* (New York, 1944), and W. Hammer, "Balthazar Rasinus and his Praise of Studies at the University of Pavia," *Studies in Philology* 37 (1940), 133–48.

26. The importance and quality of Father Walter J. Ong's work are well known. At the very least, one should consult *Ramus, Method, and the Decay of Dialogue* (Cambridge, Mass., 1958), with its extraordinary bibliography; Q. Breen, "Giovanni Pico della Mirandola on the Conflict of Philosophy and Rhetoric," *Journal of the History of Ideas* 13 (1952), 384–412; "Melanchthon's Reply to G. Pico della Mirandola," 13 (1952), 413–26; "The *Observationes in M. T. Ciceronem* of Marius Nizolius," *Studies in the Renaissance* 1 (1954), 49–58; "John Calvin and the Rhetorical Tradition," *Church History* 26 (1957), 3–21. Also of note here are L. J. Flynn, S. J., "The *De Arte Rhetorica* of Cyprian Soarez, S. J.," *Quarterly Journal of Speech* 42 (1956), 367–74; D. Aguzzi Barbagli, ed., *Francesco Patrizi, Della Poetica*, 3 vols. (Florence, 1969–1971); L. M. Brisca, "La Retorica di Francesco Patrizio o del Platonico Anti-Aristotelismo," *Aevum* 26 (1952), 434–61; A. Baca, "The *Art of Rhetoric* of Aeneas Silvius Piccolomini," *Western Speech* 34 (1970), 9–16.

27. Suggestive of possibilities in this regard, the following *Cinquenceto* figures remain relatively untouched in terms of their respective roles in affecting the direc-

There is something to be said for the view that a scrutiny of the thoughts and opinions of those who live at the confluence of theory and practice furnish the true voice of *humanitas*. Representative of this group, Bartolomeo Cavalcanti (1503– 1562), an unusual man in a society of uncommon men, deserves such attention.[28]

Cavalcanti's *La Retorica* (1559) merits consideration, at least, as a force in stirring and continuing the rhetorical tradition in an exceptional way. Quite apart from its popularity (ten editions in twenty-six years) and its significance as "the revival of the full classical tradi-

---

tion, substance, and practice of rhetoric: Amaseo, Romolo (1481 – 1552); Barbaro, Daniello (1513 – 1570); Battista, Ignazio (1478 – 1553); Brucioli, Antonio (ca. 1490 – 1566); Camillo, Giulio (1479 – 1550); Della Casa, Giovanni (1503 – 1556); Doni, Antonio (b. 1513); Maioragio, Marcantonio (1514 – 1555); Nifo, Agostino (1473 – 1538?); Patrizi, Francesco (1529 – 1597); Piccolomini, Alessandro (1508 – 1579); Ricci, Bartolomeo (1489 – 1569); Sansovino, Francesco (1521 – 1583); Segni, Bernardo (1504 – 1558); Speroni, Sperone (1500 – 1588); Sigonio, Carlo (ca. 1520 – 1584); Vetori, Pietro (1499 – 1585). Here, also, the shadow of Cicero emerges strongly in the various debates, discussions, contests, courses, and treatises arising from the movement called Ciceronianism. I. Scott's early effort remains the major touchstone in this area, *Controversies over the Imitation of Cicero* (New York, 1910). As they moved through the available Ciceroniana, certain Renaissance figures probed to uncover the underpinnings of faith and philosophy that were the very strength of the Ciceronian eloquence they championed; others, incapacitated by eagerness and dedication, heard only the prosodic features and attended only to the subtle linguistic nuances and proceeded to dismember the total art to highlight the linguistic arm. The debate between these schools persisted well into the following two centuries, though with less heat than that generated during the latter 1500s. A worthy example of work in this circle is that of D. Gagliardi, "Il Ciceronianesimo nel Cinquecento e Ortensio Lando," *Le Parole e Le Idee* 3 (1961), 15 – 21.

28. J. Monfasani, *George of Trebizond* (Leiden, 1976), recognizes the influence of the Italian "politico-oratorical conception of rhetoric in the Ciceronian tradition"; especially in that "from Trebizond to Calvalcanti [*sic*] and Alessandro Piccolomini, the Italian Renaissance witnessed attempts to re-establish the full classical art of rhetoric as vital to civil life" (p. 331). Cavalcanti himself recognizes the affiliation between rhetoric and civil affairs on pp. 9 – 10 in *La Retorica di M. Bartolomeo Cavalcanti, Gentilhuomo Fiorentino. Divisa in Sette Libri Dove Si Contiene Tutto Quello, Che Appartiene All'Arte Oratoria* (Venice, 1569). For a lesser-known witness to this image of rhetoric, see Iason Denores (Giason DeNores), *Breve Trattato Dell'Oratore* . . . (Padua, 1574), 2^r – 5^v. Aside from my own intermittent efforts since 1954, no other systematic investigation of Cavalcanti came to my attention until Christina Roaf's publication, *Bartolomeo Cavalcanti: Lettere Edite e Inedite* (Bologna, 1967). In 1975 personal correspondence with Professor Roaf revealed the existence of her "Bartolomeo Cavalcanti, 1503 – 1562: A Critical and Biographical Study" (Ph. D. diss., Somerville College, University of Oxford, 1959). It offers an outstanding exegesis and critical evaluation of *La Retorica* in addition to other works of Cavalcanti.

tion,"[29] the treatise is notable for reflecting Ciceronian spirit and thought while being designed to do homage to Aristotle and his concept of rhetoric.

The work is from the pen of a man who experienced the intimate communication between private reflection and civil action: author, ambassador, administrator, rebel, rhetor, and rhetorician. Early on, Cavalcanti showed a singular appreciation for political justice, democratic procedures, and discursive interaction—all refined by formal and informal schooling. Thus, when the young Florentine spoke from the steps of the church of Santo Spirito to crystallize the feelings of his fellow citizens against tyranny, it was his sense of public duty that motivated him and helped decide the style of his efforts—symbolic and real. He was mostly lauded as one who could see beyond the distressing particulars of his personal life to capture, describe, and put into practice the important universals necessary to a healthy commonweal.[30]

A prodigious effort divided into seven books, it is the result of a request by Cardinal of Ferrara (Ippolito II d'Este) for a vulgate work on rhetoric designed to reach the unsophisticated person who knew little of the art and less Latin, Greek, or dialectic.[31] Overcoming his original intention to follow strictly the doctrine and design of Aristotle, Cavalcanti adjusts, amends, revises, reinterprets, refines, and extends the precepts of many ancient sources because "it was not possible to . . . follow a single author nor easy to bring into accord [the many] . . . diverse opinions."[32] That he did this well is recorded by the publisher of the 1569 edition, who conjectures that if all the works of

29. Charles S. Baldwin (and D. L. Clark), *Renaissance Literary Theory and Practice* (New York, 1939), p. 63. The 1555 edition cited by Baldwin appears to be an error. Printed copies of *La Retorica* are available in a minimum of twenty-nine libraries in the U. S. At least one copy of every edition but one (1584) can be seen, including the 1564 edition (Pesaro, Heredi di B. Cesano) unavailable to Roaf.

30. B. Robini, Letter, *La Retorica*, pp. ii – iii. Unless otherwise specified, all further references to *La Retorica* are to the 1569 edition. For easily accessible biographical information, see: Lisio, *Orazioni*, pp. 3 – 6; Roaf, *Lettere*, pp. xv – xvii, lxix – lxxi; Tiraboschi, *Storia*, 7, pt. 3, 17, 1525 – 27. Despite the drain of his varied activities and constant movement, Cavalcanti managed to produce a literary record reminiscent of Tully. In addition to both private and professional letters, his thoughts have been preserved in essays on literary criticism, government, and orations and in *La Retorica*; Roaf, "Bartolomeo Cavalcanti," is of the same opinion, pp. 438 – 39.

31. Roaf, *Lettere*, letter 106, p. 135, and the dedicatory letter to Cardinal Ferrara, unnumbered (1569 edition), p. 4.

32. *La Retorica*, dedicatory letter, unnumbered, p. 2.

ancient rhetoricians should be lost, *La Retorica* would serve as a true repository of rhetorical theory.[33]

What is important here is that, in the process of conception and construction, the *magnum opus* appears to have taken on more of a Ciceronian flavor. While the overall design remained — largely Aristotelian (even to the omission of *memoria* as a canon) — the examples and tone are remarkably Tullian. Examples, illustrations, and citations (in the 1569 edition) are drawn from Ciceronian treatises in over half the cases. Whenever models are employed for subject matter, disposition, or style, they speak with the voice of Cicero.[34] Unlike some of his contemporaries who are inclined to blur the distinctions between poetry and rhetoric, Cavalcanti uses speeches to illustrate the principles of speaking well, and, in this vein, the speeches of Cicero dominate. When matters of importance to the community are emphasized, Cicero's spirit and words guide the discussion. Since people follow people rather than ideas *in vacuo*, the good man speaking well was considered a communal treasure by many of the politically active people of the time.[35]

Nowhere is this thought more evident than in Cavalcanti's treatment of *ethos*, which he feels the need to translate as *costume*.[36] Confessing his disappointment with Aristotle's generally obscure discussion of this key concept, the Florentine ambassador-rhetorician reveals his dependence upon Cicero for thoughts that more closely define the fact of rhetorical reciprocity.[37] There is evident here the

33. *La Retorica*, Robini's letter, p. iii.

34. Monfasani, *George of Trebizond*, traces the influence through Trebizond noting "... the great Italian rhetorician Bartolomeo Calvalcanti [*sic*] borrowed from Trebizond's work ..." (p. 321, text and note 14). Interesting parallels are also revealed by a comparison of Cavalcanti's oration "Alla Militia Fiorentina" and Cicero's "Pro Milo." For Cavalcanti's comments on Trebizond, see letter 109 to P. Vettori, 27 Nov. 1545, in Roaf, *Lettere*, pp. 141–43.

35. An interesting point here is that the young Cavalcanti appears to have been influenced by his senior contemporary Noccolò Machiavelli with whom he exchanged, at least, several letters. Some of that influence may be reflected by his use of examples drawn from Machiavelli's *History of Florence*, as noted by Roaf, *Lettere*, pp. xvii, xlv. One immediately notices the differences in tone between the inquiries and comments of Cavalcanti and the didacticisms of Machiavelli. See A. J. Pansini, *Niccolò Machiavelli and the United States of America* (New York, 1969), pp. 1221–23.

36. *La Retorica*, pp. 77–78, 214–41, 349–58, 528, 541, 549; Roaf, *Lettere*, letters 106, 110, 111, 112, 114 reveal Cavalcanti's dilemma.

37. *La Retorica*, pp. 77–78. When Cavalcanti's contemporary Giulio Del Bene (ca. 1574), in an oration delivered in 1574 before L'Accadema degli Alterati, spoke of *costumi* as "impossible to imitate without actions" and "known only in the operation,"

thought that the art's chief impulse is from the dynamic interaction of speaker and listener, both of whom carry contrails of social mores. In the crucible of interaction, individual values are mixed with group mores to produce a probative force necessary to effective persuasion, and, in consequence, the perennial quality of *humanus* is revealed. Thus, the power of the art, reflecting a refined Ciceronian view, rests in the action of discourse, not in the beauty of words; in the viable activity rather than in the finished product.[38]

In very few periods of history were citizens treated to a greater opportunity to play earwitness to divers creations of formal public discourse. Exposed as they were to such a large body of oral dissertations, many learned that a speaking mind capable of sharing intricate thought and personal feeling was the highest goal and the greatest treasure of which a community could boast. In keeping with the classical sentiment, Renaissance *letterati* believed that orations served as an expression of society's *humanitas* (*ratio et verba* fuse into *oratio?*); the values of the many are reflected in the spoken words of one. Yet the study of Renaissance oratory (sacred, ambassadorial, legal, legislative, and ceremonial) has been left virtually untouched, and another window that could provide additional perspectives of an exciting culture remains closed.[39]

he was handling essentially the same thought. See "Due Discorsi," in Weinberg, *Trattati*, 3.202. Important insights might well come from a scrutiny of terms that seem to cluster in humanistic discussions: *eleganza, energeia, costume, urbanità* among the more prominent.

38. McKeon, *Thought Passion and Action*, p. 19, calls attention to the thought that *freedom*, in communal living, is developed by the technique of *rhetoric*, "but the rhetoric is that of speeches used in a *history* to reconstruct the condition and intentions that moved men to action."

39. Among those sources harboring information of this sort, see Fontanini, *Biblioteca;* Galletti, *L'Eloquenza;* G. Lisio, *Orazioni Scelte del Secolo XVI* (Florence, 1897); E. Santini, *Firenze e i suoi 'Oratori' nel Quattrocento* (Milan, 1922); *L'Eloquenza Italiana dal Concilio Tridentino ai nostri giorni* (Milan, 1923), vol. 1: "Gli Oratori Sacri"; and vol. 2: "Gli Oratori Civili" (Palermo, 1928); M. Fancelli, ed., *Orazioni Politiche del Cinquecento* (Bologna, 1941); P. Dazzi, ed., *Orazioni Politiche del Secolo XVI* (Florence, 1866); A. Segarizzi, ed., *Relazioni degli ambasciatori veneti al Senato,* 3 vols. (Bari, 1912 – 1916). A model for analytic consideration of orations is available in Charles Trinkaus, "A Humanist's Image of Humanism: the Inaugural Orations of Bartolommeo Della Fonte," *Studies in the Renaissance* 7 (1960), 90 – 147; Neal W. Gilbert, "The Early Italian Humanists and Disputation," in *Renaissance Studies in Honor of Hans Baron*, eds. A. Molho and J. A. Tedeschi (Dekalb, Ill., 1971), pp. 203 – 26, is relevant here for its light shed upon logical facets of humanist disputation. G. Bertoni, "Orazioni perdute di Ludovico Carbone," *Giornale storico della Letteratura Italiana* 118 (1941), 198–200; E. Allodoli, "L'Orazione

Inasmuch as orations were a part of histories, dialogues, and various dramatic works written by the humanists, another concerted effort seems warranted in a rhetorical analysis of the "nonrhetorical" works of major Renaissance figures. That writers, of whatever age, do influence the conduct, attitudes, and appreciations of multitudes is commonplace. What, then, might be uncovered by researchers wearing rhetorical spectacles? Asking rhetorical questions? Approached this way, even the classic *Divina Commedia* yields new fruit.[40] And even if this masterpiece were exhausted as terrain rich for rhetorical harvest (which it is not), what of the lessons to be learned from *De vulgari eloquentia, De monarchia, Convivio,* and the like?[41] And what of the works of other figures with the stature and influence of Dante? Most recently, there has been a stirring in the Machiavelli camp, but little of Giucciardini or Lorenzo or Michelangelo or Leonardo or Cellini or

di Francesco Robertello per la morte del Guidiccioni," *La Rinascita* 5 (1942), 372 – 406. A small idea of the wealth available in this realm is furnished by even a most rudimentary check list restricted to the 1500s as: Adriani, Giovan Battista (1513 – 1579); Ammirato, Scipione (1531 – 1601); Badoaro, Pietro (ca. 1590); Bellarmino, Roberto (1542 – 1621); Benivieni, Lorenzo (ca. 1530); Borghini, Vincenzio (1515 – 1580); Borromeo, Carlo (1538 – 1584); Carbone, Ludovico (16th cent.); Castiglionchio, Lapo da (16th cent.); Catena, Girolamo Giovanni (16th cent.); Cavalcanti, Bartolomeo (1503 – 1562); Crispo, Giovan Battista (16th cent.); Della Casa, Giovanni (1503 – 1556); Della Fonte, Bartolommeo (1446 – 1513); Del Bene, Giulio (ca. 1574); Doni, Gian Battista (1594 – 1647); Ferrini, Bartolommeo (16th cent.); Fiamma, Gabriele (d. 1565); Frangipane, Cornelio (1508 – 1588); Gaudioso, Sebastiano (d. 1600); Giustianiani, Sebastiano (ca. 1529); Guidiccioni, Giovanni (1500 – 1541); Lollio, Alberto (ca. 1508 – 1568/9); Medici, Lorenzino de' (1514 – 1548); Musso, Cornelio (1511 – 1574); Nardi, Jacopo (1476 – 1563); Neri, Filippo (1515 – 1595); Palestrina, Pier Luigi da (1524 – 1594); Panigarola, Francesco (1548 – 1594); Paruta, Paolo (1540 – 1598); Pesaro, Piero da (ca. 1528); Robertello, Francesco (ca. 1558); Rotta, Isidoro (ca. 1587); Salviati, Leonardo (ca. 1562); Sansovino, Francesco (1521 – 1583); Speroni, Sperone (1500 – 1588); Strozzi, Federico (1547 – 1634); Silva, Ferdinando di (ca. 1537); Tolomei, Claudio (1492 – 1556); Tommasini, Bernadino di Domenico (1487 – 1564); Torelli, Lelio (1489 – 1576); Taverna, Gianfrancesco (ca. 1529); Varchi, Benedetto (1503 – 1565); Visdomini, Franceschino (d. 1573); Vettori, Piero (1499 – 1575). Special studies to determine the degree to which, in one man, the orator heeds the rhetorician (as in the cases of Cavalcanti and Speroni, for example) might prove interesting and rewarding.

40. W. S. Howell's work, "The Method of Dialogue in Dante's *Inferno*" (Ph.D. diss., Cornell University, 1931), has not been pursued very diligently. In the same circle of action is D. Sheehan, "The Control of Feeling: A Rhetorical Analysis of *Inferno* XIII," *Italica* 51 (1974), 193 – 206.

41. F. Capua, *Insegnamenti retorici medievali e dottrine estetiche moderni nel 'De Vulgari Eloquentia,' di Dante* (Naples, 1945); A. Buck, "Gli Studi sulla Poetica e sulla Retorica di Dante e del suo tempo," *Cultura e Scuola* 4 (1965), 143 – 66; H. Wieruszowski, "*Ars dictaminis* in the time of Dante," *Medievalia et Humanistica* no. 1 (1943), 95 – 108.

dozens of others.[42] What has been published by those toiling in the garden of "courtesy books" has not exhausted the possibilities regarding the discovery of rhetorical bases, implications, and influences.[43] The same observation might also be made of investigations into Renaissance epistolography. As revealed by the *epistolari* published in the 1500s, Renaissance citizens had a keen interest in the written mode of expression that, inevitably, bore the imprint of rhetorical tradition. Be they political, reportorial, or familiar, letters from the pens of Italian Renaissance figures provide fertile ground for the rhetorical scholar, especially since "no anthology of Renaissance letters in the English language or in any other translation is today available."[44]

No less significant as a realm of Renaissance activity that might well yield unusual rewards for the rhetorical scholar is that of the *emblemata*. In the course of pursuing his interests, in "Tudor Writing on Rhetoric," Ong notes that

> The emblematists' concern with iconography and all sorts of symbolism is intimately related to rhetorical and dialectical word play and to rhetorical "ornament."[45]

But, in addition to the obvious connections with the exterior aspects of rhetoric, the spate of Renaissance emblem books might well reflect threads of concern and appreciation for the subtle strengths of *inventio, dispositio,* and the traditional purposes of instructing, persuading, and pleasing.[46] From the first impact of Alciati's *Emblematum*

42. E. Raimondi, "Machiavelli and the Rhetoric of the Warrior," *Modern Language Notes* 92 (1977), 1 – 16; W. Wiethoff. "Machiavelli's *The Prince;* Rhetorical Influence in Civil Philosophy," *Western Speech* 38 (1974); "The Martial 'Virtue' of Rhetoric in Machiavelli's *Art of War,*" *Quarterly Journal of Speech* 64 (1978), 304 – 12.

43. Gerald Mohrmann supplies a model with "*The Civile Conversation:* Communication in the Renaissance," *Speech Monographs* 39 (1972), 193 – 204. It is well known that contributions of Baldassare Castiglione, *Il Cortegiano* (1528), and Matteo Palmieri, *Della Vita Civile* (1529), render important ties to the rhetorical legacy. See L. Valmaggi, "Per le fonti del Cortegiano," *Giornale storico della Letteratura Italiana* 14 (1889), 72 – 93; E. Garin, *Storia della Filosofia Italiana* (Turin, 1966), 1.335 – 37; 355 – 56; H. Baron, "Cicero and the Roman Civic Spirit in the Middle Ages and Early Renaissance," *Bulletin of the John Rylands Library* 22 (1938), 93.

44. R. J. Clements, ed., *Renaissance Letters* (New York, 1976), p. xiv. One should read Clements's introduction in its entirety for a good sense of substance and spirit attached to this research quarter.

45. In *Studies in the Renaissance* 15 (1968), 61.

46. One could hardly begin an investigation into this facet without consulting M. Praz, *Studies in Seventeenth Century Imagery* (London, 1939– 1947), vols. 1, 2, and the

liber (1531), a wave of renewed interest for possible ties among *ars pictura, ars poesis,* and *ars rhetorica* was felt among Renaissance intellectuals mindful of communicative necessities.

Those aware of the rhetorical influence on the various cultural and intellectual aspects of Italian life during the Renaissance could hardly ignore the possibility that the laws of rhetoric and the principles of magic may well be intertwined. The evident power of oracy in directing thought, passion, and action toward good or evil—suggested by Plato, recognized by Scripture, and deliberated by medieval philosophers—was earnestly explored by Italian humanists and their contemporaries.[47] Many realized that the rhetorical act was the magical matrix; meaning was extracted from oral symbols and converted into energy that initiated action and reaction and left a residual feeling of spiritual fusion. Could rhetoric work its magic through an expectancy heightened in the audient by virtue of aural and visual images stirred up in the immediacy of the communicative experience? Earlier studies of Lazarelli, Ficino, Bruno, Agrippa, Pom-

---

considerably increased edition (Rome, 1964). Also of enormous help here is the work of R. J. Clements, especially *The Peregrine Muse* (Chapel Hill, N. C., 1959); "Princes and Literature: A Theme of Renaissance Emblem Books, *Modern Language Quarterly* 16 (1955), 114.23; "Pen and Sword in Renaissance Emblem Literature," *Modern Language Quarterly* 5 (1944), 131–41; *Picta Poesis: Literary and Humanistic Theory in Renaissance Emblem Books* (Rome, 1960). Frances Yates supplies some interesting interpretations of what has been termed the "Petrarcan emblem," in "The Emblematic Conceit in Giordano Bruno's *De gli eroici furori* and in the Elizabethan sonnet sequences," *Journal of the Warburg and Courtauld Institutes* 6 (1943), 101–21; and H. Miedema advances new views in "The Term *Emblemata* in Alciati," *Journal of the Warburg and Courtauld Institutes* 31 (1968), 234–50. I would include here a note of personal interest regarding the need for further inquiry into the symbolism of *Lady* Rhetoric. In my collection of over twenty-five professional photographs of sepulchres, *campanili,* pulpit supports, and various church façades designed, constructed, or restored on the peninsula during the Renaissance, all but one show rhetoric as a lady. Quite apart from the ancient tie to the various muses, little thought appears to have been given to determining the extent of any conscious development of this feminine emphasis in both language (rhetorica) and visual design. G. B. Ladner, "Medieval and Modern Understanding of Symbolism: A Comparison," *Speculum* 54 (1979), 223–56, serves as a good source for basic ideas in this direction.

47. D. P. Walker gives a good account of this thread in *Spiritual and Demonic Magic From Ficino to Campanella* (London, 1958); Yates also furnishes much insight into the nature and scope of Renaissance thought on matters of magic, linguistic development, and oracy; see *Giordano Bruno and the Hermetic Tradition* (Chicago, 1964). Garin offers a thorough discussion of one treatise on magic in addition to matters of astrology and science in *L'Età Nuova* (Naples, 1969).

ponazzi, and others provide some answers and even more enticing suggestions for further effort in this regard.[48]

Finally, more remains to be done in the way of comparative analysis of rhetorical concepts and Utopian designs,[49] of the rhetorical positions evident in the famous *lotta della lingua,* which occupied the minds of deeply learned and uncommonly imaginative persons,[50] of rhetorical roots and fragrances manifested in the Conciliar movement, the Inquisition, and secular legal developments.[51]

In the course of this discussion, it has been suggested that even the most cursory view of the work in hand on Italian Renaissance rhetoric would reveal the overwhelming stamp of philosophers, philologists, linguists, and historians. If they appear at all, contributions by rhetorical scholars — qua rhetorical scholars — bear the unmistakable stain of toasts offered by arriving relatives come late to the banquet. A topic that has filled centuries with its rhetorical convulsions

48. See preceding footnote and also the notions of G. Guglielminetti as they are manifested in "Magia e technica nella poetica di Tommaso Campanella," *Rivista di Estetica* 9 (1964), 361 – 400.

49. An obvious point of entry into this realm is the thought of Francesco Patrizi (1529 – 1597) in *Della Retorica Dieci Dialoghi* (Venice, 1562) and in his Utopian treatise, *La Città Felice* (Venice, 1553). Sources that might facilitate studies of this sort include: P. F. Grendler, "Utopia in Renaissance Italy: Doni's 'New World'," *Journal of the History of Ideas* 26 (1965), 479 – 94; J. H. Hexter, "The Loom of Language and the Fabric of Imperatives: The Case of *Il Principe* and *Utopia,*" *American Historical Review* 69 (1964), 945 – 68, and G. Masso, *Education in Utopias* (New York, 1927).

50. Originally an argument between Latin and the vernacular, the *questione della lingua* soon became a debate over a choice between older and newer versions of Florentine speech whose side issues included the matter of imitation. M. Vitale offers *Cinquecento* samples of conflicting arguments in his *La Questione Della Lingua* (Palermo, 1960), pp. 280 – 313. Attention should be given also to *Le Epistole 'De Imitatione' di Giovanfrancesco Pico Della Mirandola e di Pietro Bembo,* ed. G. Santangelo (Florence, 1954) as a repository of both spirit and substance for this debate.

51. The prime target of any investigation into theoretical or practical aspects of conciliar rhetoric is, of course, the Council of Trent (1545 – 1563). E. Santini's *L'Eloquenza Italiana dal Concilio Tridentino ai nostri giorni* (Milan, 1923) is a beginning source for prospective focuses. Despite the fact that even the most cursory review of the disciplines of law and rhetoric seems to argue for a symbiotic relationship throughout their long histories, not a great deal has been done to explicate the nature of this implication for the Italian Renaissance. We need something on the order of Richard J. Schoeck's "Rhetoric and Law in Sixteenth Century England," *Studies in Philology* 50 (1953), 110 – 27; "Early Anglo-Saxon Studies and Legal Scholarship in the Renaissance," *Studies in the Renaissance* 5 (1958), 102 – 10; D. S. Bland, "Rhetoric and the Law Student in Sixteenth Century England," *Studies in Philology* 54 (1957), 506 – 8; and L. Stevens, "The Contribution of French Jurists to the Humanism of the Renaissance," *Studies in the Renaissance* 1 (1954), 92 – 105.

and practical manifestations, which has challenged the minds and affected the lives of multitudes, appears nevertheless as a tangential subject of study in a period marked by its concern for *humanitas,* that unique blend of conception, passion, and expression. What efforts are available need to be augmented by more critical analyses written by scholars whose prime focus is upon rhetoric as an organic art capable of creating the important fusion between the rational and sentimental within individuals and between the personal and social dimensions of communal living.

Oratorical Delivery
and Other Problems
in Current Scholarship on
English Renaissance Rhetoric

GERALD P. MOHRMANN

Our grasp is considerable when it comes to the colors and textures of rhetoric in England during the Renaissance. We can begin with the general trends and the authors and treatises exemplifying them, for, over the years, many important surveys and analyses have appeared. Some of the earliest still offer useful points of entry: Clark's *Rhetoric and Poetry in the Renaissance*[1] and Crane's *Wit and Rhetoric in the Renaissance*[2] come to mind immediately, and for a more recent illustration there is Vickers's *Classical Rhetoric in English Poetry*.[3]

From the perspective of rhetoric as a general approach to the arts of discourse, the fullest account unquestionably is found in Howell's *Logic and Rhetoric in England, 1500–1700*.[4] Many other examples could be cited, of course, and however one may value any of these contributions, the interpretations invariably are interesting, even if the interest stems primarily from a disagreement; almost all these efforts include useful bibliographies.

In these secondary accounts we find the Ciceronian inheritance flowering in all of its manifestations. As Howell rightly observes, the true rhetoric for Cicero is a single entity, one art composed of "the five great arts"[5] of *inventio, dispositio, elocutio, memoria,* and *actio.* Al-

1. Donald L. Clark, *Rhetoric and Poetry in the Renaissance* (New York, 1922).

2. William G. Crane, *Wit and Rhetoric in the Renaissance* (New York, 1937).

3. Brian Vickers, *Classical Rhetoric in English Poetry* (London, 1970), p. 42.

4. Wilbur S. Howell, *Logic and Rhetoric in England, 1500–1700* (Princeton, N. J., 1956).

5. Howell, p. 67.

though *memoria* does not have the urgency in Renaissance England that it had in antiquity, it is fair to say that a full Ciceronian rhetoric controls in Wilson's *Arte of Rhetorique*[6] and in *The Arte or Crafte of Rhetoryke* by Cox.[7] But if a full and unsegmented presentation of the rhetoric found in *De oratore* and *Institutio oratoria* is evident in vernacular accounts, so is the seemingly inevitable drift toward a nearly exclusive concentration on one of the subsidiary arts. This drift always has been most apparent in relation to style as style, and that emphasis operates in Sherry's *Treatise of Schemes and Tropes*[8] and Peacham's *The Garden of Eloquence.*[9] Yet both Sherry and Wilson include model discourses and they point to another dimension of the Ciceronian inheritance — the use of models for imitation. The "formulary rhetoric" is Howell's label for this phenomenon, which is constituted "of compositions drawn to illustrate rhetorical principles and presented as models for students to imitate."[10] Using models for imitation is, of course, vintage practice; in perhaps the best-known English version, *A Booke Called the Foundacion of Rhetorike,*[11] Rainolde bases his vernacular presentation on a Latin translation of the *Progymnasmata* of Aphthonius.

So we know that Ciceronian rhetoric flourished in whole or in part in vernacular presentations in the England of the Renaissance; we know, too, that it continued to flourish in the original, with both Cicero and Quintilian exerting an influence through the Latin texts.[12] The classical inheritance also received support in versions offered by commentators from the Continent, writers such as Melanchthon and Sturm. The impact from that quarter is yet to be systematically assessed, but one suspects that the Continentals were used as best suited the English purposes. For example, in 1570 a small handbook was abstracted from Sturm as *A Ritch Storehouse of Treasurie for Nobilitye and Gentlemen,* and the translator provides a brief guide to education that is founded in Ciceronian rhetoric and guided by conventional religion, the goal being a happy and healthy

6. Thomas Wilson, *The Arte of Rhetorique* (London, 1553).

7. Leonard Cox, *The Arte or Crafte of Rhetoryke* (London, 1532).

8. Richard Sherry, *A Treatise of Schemes and Tropes* (London, 1550).

9. Henry Peacham, *The Garden of Eloquence* (London, 1577).

10. Howell, p. 67.

11. Richard Rainolde, *A Booke Called the Foundacion of Rhetorike* (London, 1563).

12. See John O. Ward, "From Antiquity to the Renaissance: Glosses and Commentaries on Cicero's *Rhetorica,*" in *Medieval Eloquence: Studies in the Theory and Practice of Medieval Rhetoric,* ed. James J. Murphy (Berkeley and Los Angeles, 1978), pp. 25 – 67.

social structure.[13] There is one influence from the Continent, however, that is not purely a reinforcement of Cicero, and it has been investigated quite vigorously. The reference, of course, is to the impact of Peter Ramus.

An anti-Aristotelian, Ramus was not concerned principally with discourse, but when the logic of his intellectual reform was pursued, invention and arrangement were stripped away from rhetoric. Ramus attached his name to no treatise on rhetoric, but his disciple Talon did, and it is in that work that we find the concrete formulation of "the dictate that style and delivery are the whole of rhetoric."[14] Both Ong and Howell have explored Ramism in detail;[15] in fact, in the latter's book, Ramism and responses to it comprise nearly half the discussion of logic and rhetoric in England from 1500 to 1700. It has been questioned whether the subject merits that emphasis,[16] but it cannot be doubted that Ramistic rhetoric became extremely popular in the original of Talon and in the Latin version produced in England by Butler[17] and Dugard,[18] the latter following Talon by nearly a hundred years and presenting a simplified account on Butler's interpretation. Fenner[19] and Fraunce[20] wrote English versions, and most of these Ramistic approaches are recommended in treatises on education of the era.[21] Alongside the Ciceronian inheritance, then, the impress of Ramism is felt, at times most markedly, in England during the Renaissance.

In any event, the surveys and interpretations of general trends available always have reference to specific instances, and so we know much of the original treatises. In addition, many have been reprinted, often with useful introductory analysis, examples including Mair's to *Wilson's Arte of Rhetorique*[22] and Seaton's to the *Arcadian Rhet-*

13. Joannes Sturmius, *A Ritch Storehouse or Treasurie for Nobilitye and Gentlemen,* trans. T. B. Gent (London, 1570).

14. Howell, p. 165.

15. See Wilbur S. Howell and Walter J. Ong, *Ramus: Method, and the Decay of Dialogue* (Cambridge, Mass., 1958). Also now see Peter Sharratt, "The Present State of Studies on Ramus," *Studi Francesci* nos. 47–48 (1972), 201–13.

16. Vickers, p. 42.

17. Charles Butler, *Rhetoricae libri duo* (London, 1629).

18. William Dugard, *Rhetorices Elementa* (Middleburg, 1584).

19. Dudley Fenner, *The Artes of Logike and Rhetorike* (London, 1648).

20. Abraham Fraunce, *The Arcadian Rhetorike* (London, 1588).

21. See Charles Hoole, *A New Discovery of the Old Art of Teaching Schoole* (London, 1660).

22. G. H. Mair, ed., *Wilson's Arte of Rhetorique, 1560* (Oxford, 1909).

oric.[23] Since the writers of the original treatises almost invariably represent the academic establishment and since their efforts sometimes are at one with education as education, it follows that our knowledge of rhetoric in Renaissance England penetrates the educational establishment at several levels. At the broadest level, general theory drew regularly and directly from Quintilian and his *Institutio oratoria,* the general purpose of education being little removed from that of the Italian humanists and their "pursuit of eloquence."[24] Many of the studies already cited could be listed again in this context because a concatenation is unavoidable, but there are those examinations that focus directly on education. Here there are surveys, such as Woodward's *Studies in Education During the Age of the Renaissance, 1400–1600,*[25] and investigations of individuals, such as Watson on Vives;[26] nevertheless, it must be remarked that rhetoric remains incidental to other purposes in most of the modern studies, although it is quite unlikely that Yates would have made basic changes in her study of memory had she come at it from a purely rhetorical perspective.[27] Yet rhetoric ordinarily becomes central only in shorter monographs. For example, the full impress of the tradition is slighted in favor of limited analyses in most of the works on preaching, another topic related to both education and rhetorical theory.[28]

An offshoot of our understanding of the educational system, indeed a rather direct projection of it, is the awareness that rhetorical studies figure importantly in the creation of English literature. Insofar as the Renaissance in England is concerned, it is safe to say that this is the field most tilled in the province of rhetoric, a place that, by itself, would furnish a bibliography sufficient to exhaust the space available here. In addition to works cited earlier, others include those by C. S. Baldwin, T. W. Baldwin, Atkins, Tuve, and Joseph, as well as a host of shorter and more specialized analyses.[29] The most important

23. Ethel Seaton, ed., *The Arcadian Rhetorike* (Oxford, 1950).

24. The usage, of course, is from Hannah H. Gray, "Renaissance Humanism: The Pursuit of Eloquence," *Journal of the History of Ideas,* 24 (1963).

25. W. H. Woodward, *Studies in Education During the Age of the Renaissance 1400–1600* (Cambridge, 1906).

26. Foster Watson, *Vives: On Education* (Cambridge, 1906). Watson's general contributions to the history of education rank with those of Woodward.

27. Frances Yates, *Art of Memory* (Chicago, 1966).

28. See, for example, J. W. Blench, *Preaching in England in the Late Fifteenth and Sixteenth Centuries* (Oxford, 1964); and W. Fraser Mitchell, *English Pulpit Oratory from Andrewes to Tillotson* (London, 1932).

29. Charles S. Baldwin, *Renaissance Literary Theory and Practice* (New York, 1939);

studies range from a close explication of a given text or texts, to examinations of a particular author or genre, to sweeping general surveys. One encounters explorations of the problematic relationship between rhetoric and poetic, attempts to trace rhetorical theory from textbook and classroom through author to text; above all else, we find efforts to ferret out connections between the tropes and figures of rhetorical theory and the finished work of literary art, and if some of the connections occasionally appear rather tenuous, it is clear that the rhetoric of the English Renaissance encouraged the pursuit of eloquence at its most extensive.[30]

Indeed, we do know a great deal about the nature and function of rhetoric during the Renaissance in England and about its relationship to general education, to preaching, to the world of letters; but, sadly, we know less than we should, truly even know less than would appear on the surface. As invariably happens, we all become prisoners of what is known or thought to be known, and that is a causal element limiting our knowledge and meriting our attention.

For example, the impact of humanism on English rhetoric is not yet fully explored. Consider Kristeller's observation that "Renaissance humanism must be understood as a characteristic phase in what may be called the rhetorical tradition in Western culture."[31] In some respects this comment is most applicable to the Italian humanists of the fifteenth and sixteenth centuries, but it also applies to the English humanists — cultural lag and cultural differences notwithstanding. That being so, we should be able to assume that there is considerable understanding abroad of the way in which rhetorical study functioned in Renaissance England. We ought to be able to recount the role of rhetorical theory and practice in the social order of the era, in shaping the concentration of the individual gentleman, and in producing the articulate citizen. I allude, of course, to the earlier studies by Caspari, Kelso, and Ferguson.[32] All have places in

---

T. W. Baldwin, *William Shakespeare's Small Latine & Lesse Greeke*, 2 vols. (Urbana, Ill., 1944); J. W. H. Atkins, *English Literary Criticism: The Renascence* (London, 1947); Rosemond Tuve, *Elizabethan and Metaphysical Imagery* (Chicago, 1947).

30. Sister Miriam Joseph, *Shakespeare's Use of the Arts of Language* (New York, 1947). For a bibliography relating rhetoric to literature in this period, see Charles Stanford, "The Renaissance," in *A Selected Annotated Bibliography of Rhetoric for the English Scholar*, ed. Winifred B. Horner (New York, 1980).

31. Paul Oskar Kristeller, *Renaissance Thought* (New York, 1961), p. 11.

32. Fritz Caspari, *Humanism and the Social Order in Tudor England* (Chicago, 1954); Arthur B. Ferguson, *The Articulate Citizen and the English Renaissance* (Durham, N.C.,

appropriate bibliographies and deservedly so, but in them and in other studies of comparable merit, the direct and explicit influence exerted by the rhetorical tradition is notable primarily for its omission. Such omission is particularly glaring when the writer considers humanist training as it "is brought to bear on the practical issues of public life,"[33] then ignores every significant rhetorical treatise of the period and all that rhetoric contributed to the classroom. Even Rice's very important and fundamental exploration suffers in this regard, for almost all the primary sources to which he turns have basic associations in the study of rhetoric.[34]

This is not to denigrate any of the foregoing studies nor to carp futilely about what might have been; it is merely to point up that a complete vision of the individual in the social structure and the very fabric of that structure must wait upon interpretations in which the part played by rhetoric is sharp and clear, not blurred and indistinct. Baron remarks that Cicero "taught the Renaissance these two things: the primary task of man is action and service for the community; and the contact of the spirit with active life does not distract his powers but stimulates his highest energy."[35] As he, Kristeller, and others stress, this aspect of the rhetorical inheritance enabled humanists to resolve the apparent conflict between the life of contemplation and that of active citizenship. The conflict and its resolution have essential rhetorical dimensions because Cicero's conception must operate when interpersonal and other social relationships have an important place in analyses. The fact too often is ignored in studies of society in Renaissance England.

Vickers helps clarify what we did not know, but he also raises questions about what we thought we knew and underlines the danger of being trapped by what we think we know.[36] This is not to call for revisionism at every turn, especially in so vast and complicated an arena of study, but surely we must learn to use properly what has

---

1965); Ruth Kelso, *The Doctrine of the English Gentlemen in the Sixteenth Century* (Gloucester, Mass., 1964).

33. Ferguson, p. xv.

34. Eugene F. Rice, *The Renaissance Idea of Wisdom* (Cambridge, Mass., 1958).

35. Hans Baron, "Cicero and the Roman Civic Spirit in the Middle Ages and Early Renaissance," *Bulletin of the John Rylands Library,* 22 (1938), 91. We do not yet have for English rhetorical history the kind of study presented for Italian humanism by Jerrold E. Seigel, *Rhetoric and Philosophy in Renaissance Humanism: The Union of Eloquence and Wisdom, Petrarch to Valla* (Princeton, N. J., 1968).

36. Vickers, pp. 40 ff.

been accomplished and not merely become prisoners of the conventional wisdom. For example, Vickers is troubled by the received opinion concerning Ramism, and although that influence upon English rhetoric in the Renaissance was permitted to dominate for too long, a reading of accepted accounts would suggest that theorists in England and on the Continent were so caught up in Ramism that it swept all else away. As noted above, this topic and its ramifications account for half the space of Howell's discussion, and although it has to be admitted that Ramism exerted a dominant force in rhetorical theory, it was far from being preemptive. A single example will be a sufficient test here.

The example is provided by Charles Hoole in his *Art of Teaching Schoole,* for he has been identified as being typical of the influence Ramus exerted upon the teaching of rhetoric throughout the educational system in Renaissance England.[37] Hoole does recommend that the student be familiar with the Ramistic rhetorics of Butler and Dugard, but he remarks that they should then move on to Farnaby, Susenbrotus, "or the like, till they be better able to peruse other authors, that more fully treat the art."[38] Those authors who more fully treat the art include Vossius, Caussin, and Sturm, and though Cicero's theoretical treatises are not mentioned, Cicero as writer and speaker never is far from the student's attention. In truth, Hoole is most notable for a catholicity of sources recommended, and while he demonstrates the impact of Ramism, he demonstrates at the same time that one could patiently pursue the goal of effective communication without elevating the enterprise to the level of philosophical principles. Hoole and others like him who labored at the most elementary levels of education may seem terribly fundamental, even mundane at times, but theirs, too, was the pursuit of eloquence. Perhaps there seems little of grandeur in their ultimate vision, but they expected that the students would achieve some mastery in the arts of discourse and would go out into the world better able to use writing and speech for the betterment of self and society. Given the purposes and given the level of instruction, we have to be very careful about abstracting philosophic positions and pointing to intellectual currents in elementary textbooks and even in many textbooks at a more advanced level.

The hazards of intentional thinking, of determining *a priori* that

37. For instance, Howell, pp. 270–71.
38. Hoole, p. 133.

a certain influence will be manifested, is illustrated by a product of Renaissance education in England, George Herbert. He was University Orator and a lecturer in rhetoric at Cambridge when the school was the hotbed of Ramistic logic in England, but during his tenure the statutes required that his lectures on rhetoric cover Hermagoras, Quintilian, and Cicero. Then, after time in Parliament and a period of indecision, he was ordained and spent his last years as a country parson. During those last years he composed *A Priest to the Temple,* a work demonstrating Herbert knew that "what constitutes gravity, elevation, transparence, and conciseness in a speech depends not so much on the niceties of invention, arrangement, and language as taught by sixteenth- and seventeenth-century logic and rhetoric as it does upon an understanding of the nature and beliefs of an audience."[39] Given the tensions that had to exist in the rhetorical theory and practice to which he was exposed and in which he was an important participant, one wonders how truly illuminating are the explications of Herbert's poems based in some bit of rhetorical theory, wonders whether it is not the invention and style of the explicator that holds our attention, rather than the conviction that we are learning habits of mind inculcated by rhetorical systems. Indeed, it seems more than possible that the converse is true, that our systems of rhetoric, in spite of any differences in particular emphases and dimensions, demonstrate habits of mind typical in Western thought, so typical that they appear regularly when writers treat the arts of discourse.

Certainly, cause and effect relationships must not be asserted casually, and it is imperative that interpretations of the real world that is academia be juxtaposed to and penetrated by influences from the other real worlds surrounding it. For example, Quintilian issues an injunction about the use of the left hand for gesturing; his status supreme in educational theory, the restriction was imposed consistently and mechanically during the Renaissance and on into the eighteenth century. It was not until the nineteenth century that Austin noted that this was merely a sartorial injunction — that the Roman speaker gestured with the left hand at risk of losing his toga.[40] Yet did the centuries of repetition have any effect? I am aware of no single critique in which there is any comment to the point, and even if

39. H. E. Knepprath, "George Herbert: University Orator and Country Parson," *Southern Speech Journal,* 32 (winter 1966), 112.

40. Gilbert Austin, *Chironomia* (London, 1806), p. 402.

one can be found, the doctrine is so simple and direct that one would expect to find critical application with a marked degree of regularity. No doubt the apparent inconsistency is not difficult to resolve, but no resolution can seriously challenge the basis of argument here, the contention that we must proceed with extreme caution when interpreting the influence of activities in the classroom, particularly at the elementary level.

And at the elementary level a further caution needs to be appended regarding the interpretation of textbooks because the authors so often offer a vision not of what "is" but of what they think "ought to be." Schoolmasters, ministers, lawyers — frequently playing more than one role at the same time — want education to produce better citizens and a better-ordered society. All is not uniformity, certainly, but there is a pronounced tendency to adapt the teleological perspective, as Cicero does, and to see speech as the line of demarcation between man and beast, the gift of God that has brought humans into social relationships and that will lead to the triumph of right reason over base passion. This account is not overdrawn; a similar version could be abstracted from most of the elementary works on rhetoric and education in English of the Renaissance. Twentieth-century cynicism may make the writers seem naive and overly optimistic, but we do them a dreadful disservice when we let that cynicism distort the efforts of these men who struggled as best they could to make a better life here and in the hereafter, no matter how vain those efforts may appear today. Perhaps they were guilty of blinking reality when they wrote, but perhaps they very well knew it.

But enough of cautions about what we think we know and what we might know. The coin has its other side: the need for far bolder and sweeping application of what we do know and think we know or might know. Thus, although quite aware that Tristram Shandy freely accepts hobby-horses only so long as the riders do not ask that we also mount the steed, I adduce a personal hobby-horse — oratorical delivery — because it will illustrate the need for greater boldness on the part of those interested in the rhetorical tradition.

That the theory of oratorical delivery and its implications in Western thought have been neglected is hardly surprising. After all, oral presentation is ephemeral, and even for those figures in which delivery is a most patent element (e.g., figures such as *prosopopoeia* and *exclamatio*), no written description can hope to offer the appropriate specificity coupled with an equally appropriate flexibility. Consequently, it is most understandable that the permanent remains have been examined from the points of view available in matters relating to invention, arrangement, and style. Furthermore, when delivery became a focal point and the elocutionary movement eventually produced mechanical excesses, the stage was set for subsequent neglect and misinterpretation in the scholarship. The early elocutionists had a sound rationale, but it long was ignored and the movement was treated as if some accidental aberration of the tradition rather than as a thoroughly inevitable circumstance, a most natural development of Renaissance thought.[41]

The ephemeral nature of delivery aside, the excesses of the elocutionists aside, and the state of scholarship aside, a bold approach to the theory of oratorical delivery can tell us much about the function of the rhetorical tradition in Western thought. For example, it seems impossible to talk with real accuracy about decorum in the English Renaissance until that topic has been interpreted in the light of oral presentation. Explicit in many classical treatises on rhetoric, the oral dimension may only be implicit in analyses of poetic, but it may be so for the very reason that it was all too self-evident. When Horace appropriated the character types from Aristotle's *Rhetoric* and made them the bases for appropriate presentation in poetic, delivery was an essential constituent, and it remained essential throughout the Renaissance in commentaries on poetic. Abstracted from the life by Aristotle, decorum becomes a key feature in discussions of poetry and drama, and art as life turns back upon itself to become life as art when grace and the decorous become central in the living of a life. In the *Ritch Storehouse,* translated from Sturm and cited above, we read that the notion of decorum includes not only an image of "forme, as it were of the outward skinne, but also that of the bloud, veines, sinowes, and the verye brawnes, or force of the muscules may appeere forth and be seene."[42]

The relationships between rhetoric and poetic being the most intimate, those relationships may seem to deserve closest attention with regard to the role played by the theory of oratorical delivery in the conception of decorum, but the theory has other and quite obvious ramifications that connect directly with the conception. Most obvious is the manifestation in the books on courtesy, works such as

41. For comment on the rationale, see Gerald P. Mohrmann, "The Language of Nature and Elocutionary Theory," *Quarterly Journal of Speech* 52 (1966), 116–24. For a typical assessment, see Wilbur S. Howell, *Eighteenth-Century British Logic and Rhetoric* (Princeton, N. J., 1971).

42. Sturmius, pp. 45^r–45^v.

Castiglione's *Courtier* and Guazzo's *Civile Conversatione,* works in which the presentation of the self cannot be separated from the tones, looks, and gestures that constitute delivery. Furthermore, appropriate physical deportment extends beyond the courtesy books, as such, to a wide variety of Renaissance treatises, to those by Palmieri, Charron, Primaudaye, de Vienne, and others, all of which were known in England in the original and via translations. The extension eventually finds its way to the most elementary level of education, and one finds Hoole observing that "the sweet and orderly behavior of Children" is of the utmost significance because "this speaketh to every one that the Childe is well taught, though (perhaps) he learn but little; and good manners indeed are a main part of good education."[43] Precise emphases vary as the works vary, but in all these discussions of the individual functioning as a social animal, the physical element is basic. There are extensions and amplifications of traditional dicta about oratorical delivery, but that does not alter the fact that grace in the living of a life is to be exemplified in graceful physical behavior in the speech act. And it is worth noting, if only in passing, that delivery is a topic wherein tensions between Ramistic rhetoric and the Ciceronian can be at least partially resolved, though in the present context Ramism may ultimately be most significant historically for having nurtured the elocutionary emphasis in the tradition.

In a seemingly quite different sphere, the theory of oratorical delivery makes another fundamental appearance, for it is ubiquitous in Renaissance discussions of painting theory. Lee's interpretation represents the received opinion,[44] and undoubtedly he is correct in stressing the comparison between poetry and painting; nevertheless, he is guilty of the Platonic fallacy when discarding rather too easily the contribution of rhetoric to Renaissance painting theory. (The Platonic fallacy consists of accepting that rhetoric can never have any influence that is anything but malign.) That this is a fallacy in relation to painting theory in the Renaissance is revealed if one undertakes no more than the most cursory examination of Alberti's *Della Pittura,* and any comparison between poetry and painting notwithstanding, his theory of emotional expression in painting assuredly has its proximate sources in the rhetorical tradition, in *actio.*[45] With the advent of mannerism after the High Renaissance, a less

43. Hoole, p. 33.
44. Rensselaer W. Lee, "Ut Pictura Poesis: The Humanistic Theory of Painting," *Art Bulletin* 22 (December 1940), 197 – 269.
45. C. Grayson, *Leon Battista Alberti on Painting and Sculpture* (London, 1972).

happy application appears, for Lomazzo in his *Trattate* evolves prescriptive and stultifying descriptions,[46] but if the two writers reveal the inheritance in quite different fashion, they equally demonstrate that the influence need not be of any particular type, will be what the writer and the time make of it. Whatever shape this influence may take, it functions in English painting theory during the Renaissance and after, and, broad or narrow, oratorical delivery or some other topic, the rhetorical inheritance must be investigated with more vigor and audacity if we are to understand the Renaissance in Great Britain.

That hobby-horse aside — and there are a few more lanes through which it could be ridden — there unquestionably are other points of entry into humanism and into rhetoric of the English Renaissance that would prove as productive or more productive, but whatever the route taken, a measure of audaciousness seems almost obligatory. Some of the audacity may demand perspectives; some ask only that we look closely again at what we thought was within our grasp. Both tacks are suggested in the bibliography that follows this essay, taken from *Renaissance Rhetoric: A Short-Title Catalogue*.[47] Included here is a list of rhetorical works published in Great Britain prior to 1700, with approximately two hundred authors and two hundred fifty titles in all.

When commenting on the short-title catalogue in his essay, Murphy notes the interesting topics that emerge immediately, and even a casual inspection of these British publications brings additional matters to the surface. For example, Cicero has but 7 English entries here; yet his larger total is 399.[48] That fact raises questions about the nature of scholarly intercourse between Great Britain and the Continent; so also do the entries for Melanchthon, Sturm, Susenbrotus, and Vossius. What prompted the comparative frequency of publication for the last two? Was it scarcity? The nature of their works? The earlier impact of Ramism? Personal influence? Perhaps there is no great significance at all, but such questions do arise, and a closer examination of the following bibliography and the larger one from

46. G. P. Lomazzo, *Trattato dell'arte della pittura; Scultura et architettura* (Milan, 1584).

47. James J. Murphy, *Renaissance Rhetoric: A Short-Title Catalogue of Works on Rhetorical Theory from the Beginning of Printing to A.D. 1700, with Special Attention to the Holdings of the Bodleian Library, Oxford. With a Select Basic Bibliography of Secondary Works on Renaissance Rhetoric* (New York, 1981).

48. Ibid., pp. 96 – 131.

which it has been abstracted surely should prompt a variety of useful inquiries.

And whether the focus be on the relationships between English and continental rhetoric or on a more restricted concern such as the debate over private preaching, the exploration of such questions surely can enhance our grasp and increase our reach when approaching English rhetoric in the Renaissance.

First Editions of Rhetorical
Works Printed in Britain to A.D. 1700

The following list includes only
the first appearance of the works cited.
Many were published on the Continent prior to an edition
from Oxford or London; for these continental issues,
and for subsequent English or Scottish issues, see
Renaissance Rhetoric: A Short-Title Catalogue
(note 47 above).

Students of English rhetoric should also note
that, in addition to numerous continental editions
available for purchase in Britain in this period,
some English authors (e.g., Dudley Fenner,
The Artes of Logike and Rhetorike, 1584)
published their own works on the Continent.

Alcuin, Albinus Flaccus (735 – 804). *Compendium Alcuini.* London, 1638.

Allacci, Leone (1586 – 1669). *Epistola de Figura eccl. Graec., etc. ad J. Morinum.* . . . London, 1682.

Ames, D. D., William (1576 – 1633). *Technometria omnium et singularium Artium.* London, 1633.

———. "Of Making Sermons," in *Conscience with the Power and Cases Thereof,* translated out of Latine into English. London, 1639.

———. "Of Ordinary Ministers and Their Office," in *The Marrow of Sacred Divinity,* trans. out of the Latin. London, 1642.

Anaximenes of Lampsacos? [*Rhetorica ad Alexandrum*] in *Aristotle's Rhetoric; or the True Grounds and Principles of Oratory.* . . . *Made English by the Translators of the Art of Thinking. In four books.* London, 1686.

Aphthonius sophista (fourth century A.D.). *Progymnasmata.* Ed. G. Hervet. London, 1520?

———. *De utraque copia, verborum et rerum praecepta, una cum exemplis dilucido brevique carmine comprehensa, ut facilius et iucundus edisci, ac memoriae quoque firmius inhaerere possint.* London, 1583.

_____. *Aphthonii sophistae progymnasmata, partim a Rodolpho Agricola, partim a Joanne Maria Cataneo latinitate donata. . . . Cum scholiis Reinhardi Lorichii Hadamarii.* London, 1572.

_____. *Progymnasmata Latinitate donata. Novissima editio.* [London], 1623.

Arderne, James (1636 – 1691). *Directions Concerning the Matter and Stile of Sermons.* London, 1671.

Aristotle (384 – 322 B.C.). *Rhetorica* (Greek). Cambridge, 1696.

_____. *Aristotelis De rhetorica . . . libri tres, graecolat. Contextu graeco, ad exemplaria selectora emendato; latino paraphrasi, ubi opus, intertexto.* (Greek) Ed. T. Goulston. London, 1619.

_____. *A Brief of the Art of Rhetorique. Containing in substance all that Aristotle hath written in his three bookes of that subject, except onely what is not applicable to the English tongue.* By Thomas Hobbes. London, 1635?

_____. *The Art of Rhetoric, with a discourse of the laws of England.* By Thomas Hobbes. London, 1681.

_____. *Aristotelis artis rhetoricae compendium.* London, 1683.

_____. *Rhetorices artis compendium.* London, 1683.

_____. *Aristotle's Rhetoric, or the True Grounds and Principles of Oratory: Showing the Right Art of Pleading and Speaking in Full Assemblies and Courts of Judicature. Made English by the Translators of the Art of Thinking. In four books* (i.e., with *ad Alexandrum*). London, 1686.

Arnauld, Antoine (1612 – 1694). *Logique, ou l'art de penser.* London, 1664.

_____. *Logica, sive ars cogitandi.* London, 1674.

_____. *The Art of Speaking.* London, 1676.

Arrowsmith, Joseph (fl. 1685). *The Art of Preaching.* N.p., 1685.

The Art of Preaching. N.p., 1685. Anon.

Bacon, Francis (1561 – 1626). "Touching a preaching ministry," in *Certain Considerations touching the better pacification and edification of the church of England.* London, 1604 (complete printed).

_____. *The Two Books of Francis Bacon. Of the Proficience and Advancement of Learning, Divine and Humane.* London, 1605.

_____. *De dignitate et argumentis scientiarum libros IX.* Ed. W. Rawley. London, 1623.

_____. *Opera Francisci Baronis de Verulamio. . . . Iomus primus: qui continet De dignitate et argumentis scientiarum libros IX.* Ed. William Rawley. London, 1623.

Barton, John (fl. 1634). *The Art of Rhetorick, Consisely and Compleatly Handled, Exemplified Out of Holy Writ, and with a Compendous and Conspicuous comment.* London, 1634.

Baxter, D. D., Richard D., of Kidderminster (1615 – 1691). *Gildas Silvanus: The Reformed Pastor: Shewing the Nature of Pastoral Work.* London, 1656.

_____. *An apology for the nonconformists' ministry.* London, 1681.

Bernard, Richard (1557? – 1641). *The faithful shepheard: or the shepheard's faithfulnesse.* London, 1607.

———. *The Shepheard's practice.* London, 1607.

———. *The faithful shepheard: wholy in a manner transposed . . . With the shepheard's practice or his manner of feeding his Flocke in the end.* London, 1621.

Bilson, Thomas (1546/7 – 1616). *The effect of certain sermons touching the full Redemption of Mankind . . . preached at Paules Crosse and elsewhere in London.* London, 1599.

Blount, Thomas (1618 – 1679). *The Academie of Eloquence, containing a Compleate English Rhetorique. Exemplified with Common-Places, and formes. . . .* London, 1654.

———. *The academy of eloquence: containing a compleat English rhetorique, exemplified; common-places, and formula's digested into an easie and methodical way to speak and write fluently, according to the mode of the present times: with letters both amorous and morall, upon emergent occasions. . . .* London, 1656.

Boys, John (1571 – 1625). "The end of preaching"; "Preachers are prophets"; "Plaine preaching" in *The works of John Boys.* London, 1620.

Brandolinus, Aurelius (ca. 1440 – 1497 or 1498). *De ratione scribendi libri tres.* London, 1573.

Brinsley, John (fl. 1633). *Ludus Literarius: or The Grammar Schoole.* London, 1612.

———. *The Preacher's charge, and people's duty about preaching and hearing the word.* London, 1631.

Brown, Robert (fl. 1666). *Rudimentorum rhetoricorum.* Aberdeen, 1666.

The Brownists' Conventicle: or, An assemble of Brownists, Separatists, and Non-Conformists, as they met together at a private house to heare a sermon of a brother of theirs neere Algate, being a learned felt-maker, contayning the whole discourse of his exposition, with the manner and form of his preaching. London, 1641. Anon.

Bulwer, John (fl. 1654). *Chirologia: or the Naturall Language of the Hand. . . . Whereunto is Added Chironomia, or the Art of Manual Rhetoricke, by J. B.* 2 vols. London, 1644.

Burnet, Gilbert (1643 – 1715). *A modest survey of the most considerable things in a discourse . . . entituled, Naked Truth.* London, 1676.

———. *A discourse of the Pastoral Care.* London, 1692.

Butler, Charles (1560 – 1647). *Ramae rhetoricae libri duo in usum scholarum.* Oxford, 1597.

———. *Oratoriae libri duo.* London, 1629.

Byfield, Nicholas (1579 – 1622). *The Paterne of wholesome words.* London, 1618.

———. *The principles or the patterne of wholesome words.* London, n.d. (2nd ed.).

Cartwright, Thomas (1535 – 1603). "An Answer to the admonition," in Tractate II: "What kind of preaching is most effective?" In *The Works of John Whitgift*, ed. John Ayre. London, 1851 – 53 (3, 1 – 13).

Casaubon, Méric (1599 – 1671). *De verborum usu et accuratae eorum cognitionis utilitate, diatriba.* London, 1647.

_____. *A treatise concerning enthusiasms.* London, 1655 (ad ed.).

_____. *The question, To whom it belonged anciently to preach, and whether all priests might or did: discussed out of antiquity: as also, what preaching is, properly.* London, 1663.

Cawdrey, Robert (fl. 1600). *A Treasurie or Storehouse of Similes: both Pleasaunt, delightfull, and profitable.* London, 1600.

Chappell, William (1582 – 1649). *Methodus concionandi* [anon.?] London, 1648.

_____. *The Use of Holy Scripture* (sermon notes on 2 Tim. 3. 16). London, 1653.

_____. *The preacher, or the art and method of preaching, tr. from Latin.* London, 1656.

Charles I (of England) (1600 – 1649). *Directions Concerning Preachers.* Croydon, 1622.

Charles II (of England) (1630 – 1685). *Directions Concerning Preachers.* Croydon, 1662.

Cicero, Marcus Tullius. *Opera omnia.* London, 1585.

_____. *[De oratione, Orator]. Cum . . . Philippi Melanchthonis castigationibus et scholiis.* London, 1573.

_____. *M. I. Ciceronis ad Quintum Fratrem in libros de oratore praefatio incipit.* Cambridge, 1589.

_____. *Rhetoricorum ad C. Herennium libri quattuor. M. I. Ciceronis De inventione libri duo, Ioannis Michaelis Bruti animadversionibus illustrati.* London, 1579.

Clarke, B. D., John (d. 1658). *Transitionum rhetoricarum formulae.* London, 1628.

_____. *Formulae oratoriae in usum scholarum concinnatae, una cum orationibus, declamationibus, etc., deque collocatione oratoria et artificio demum poetico, praeceptiunculis. Quarta editio longe et auctior et emendatior. (Manuductio ad artem carminificam, seu Dux poeticus.)* London, 1632.

_____. *Dux grammaticus tyronem scholasticum ad rectam orthographiam, syntaxin, et prosodiam dirigens. Cui suas etiam auxiliares succenturiavit copias dux oratorius, etc.* London, 1633.

Collier, Thomas (fl. 1691). *The Pulpit-guard routed in its twenty strongholds; or a brief answer to the large and lawless discourse written by one Tho. Hall . . . intituled, The Pulpit guarded with twenty arguments, pretending to prove the unlawfulness . . . of private men's preaching.* London, 1651.

_____. *Pulpit-guard and font-guard routed.* London, 1652.

Collinges, John (1623 – 1690). *Vindiciae ministerii evangelici: a vindication of the great ordinance of God, viz: a Gospel ministry.* London, 1651.

_____. *Responsoria ad erratica pastoris, sive vindicae vindicarum; id est, the shepherds wandrings* [sic] *discovered in a vindication of the great ordinance of God, gospel-preachers and preaching.* London, 1652.

_____. *Vindiciae ministerii evangelici revindicatae; or the Preacher (pretendedly) sent, sent back again, to bring better account of who sent him . . . by way of a reply to a late book* [by John Martin et al.]. London, 1658.

Comenius, John Amos (1592 – 1671). *Ars ornatoriae, sive grammatica elegans, et eruditiones scholasticae atrium; rerum et linguarum ornamenta exhibens.* London, 1664.

Copeland, Robert (fl. 1508 – 1547). *The Art of Memorye, that is otherwise called, The Phoenix: a Boke Uery Behouefell and Profytable to all Professors of Seyences, Grammaryens, Rethoryciens, Legystes. . . . Translated out of French into English by R. C.* London, n.d.

Cox, Leonard (fl. 1524 – 1572). *The Arte or Crafte of Rhetoryke.* London, 1524.

Croft, Herbert (1603 – 1691). *The naked truth; or, the true state of the primitive church, by an humble moderator.* London, 1675.

d'Assigny, S.S.Th.B., Marius (1643 – 1717). *The Art of Memory. A Treatise useful for all, especially such as are to speak in Publick.* London, 1697.

————. *Rhetorica anglorum, vel exercitationes oratoriae in rhetoricam sacram et communem. Quibus adiiciuntur quaedam regulae ad imbecilles memorias corroborandas.* London, 1699.

Dathus, Augustinus (1420 – 1478). *Augustini Dacti scribe sup. Tullianis eloganciis* [sic] *et verbis.* St. Albans, 1479.

Day, Angel (fl. 1586). *The English Secretorie; or Plaine and Direct Method of Enditing of All Manner of Epistles or Letters. . . . Corrected, refined, and amended . . . also tropes, figures, as usually or for ornaments sake are in this method required.* London, 1586.

Demetrius Phalereus (ca. 350 – ca. 280 B.C.). *De elocutione.* Oxford, 1676.

De sacris concionibus. Anon. [Reuchlin] *De arte praedicandi.* [Melancthon] *De officiis concionatoris.* [Hepinus] *De formandis sacris concionibus.* London, 1570?

Doddridge, Sir John (1555 – 1628). *The English Lawyer; describing a method for the managing of the lawes of this land.* London, 1631.

Doelsch, John (fl. 1539). *In D. Erasmus libros de duplici copia verborum ac rerum commentariis M. Veltkirchii* [not exact title]. London, 1569.

Ducci, Lorenzo (fl. 1550). *Ars aulica, or, The Courtiers Arte.* Tr. E. Blount. London, 1607.

Dugard, William (1606 – 1662). *Rhetorices elementa, quaestionibus et responsionibus explicata.* London, 1604.

————. *Rhetorices elementa.* London, 1648.

Eachard, D. D., John (1636 – 1679). *A free and impartial inquiry into the causes of that very great esteem and honour that the non-conforming preachers are generally in with their followers, in a letter to H. M. by a lover of the Church of England and unfeigned piety.* London, 1673.

Erasmus Roterodamus, Desiderius (1465 – 1536). *Dialogus cui titulus Ciceronianus sive de optimo genere dicendi.* Oxford, 1693.

————. *De conscribendis epistolis.* Cambridge, 1521.

————. *De duplici copia rerum ac verborum, commentarii duo.* London, 1556 (Veltkirchii).

Farnaby, Thomas (1575? – 1647). *Index rhetoricus scholis et institutioni tenerioris aetatis accomodatus.* London, 1625.

_____. *Phrases oratoriae et poeticae.* London, 1631.

Fenner, Dudley (1558? – 1587). *The Artes of Logike and Rhetorike, plainlie set foorth in the English Tounge, easie to be learned and practised . . .* (trans. of Ramus's *Dialecticae partitiones* and Talaeus's *Institutiones oratoriae*). Middleburg, 1584.

_____. *The Artes of Logike and Rhetorike, plainlie set foorth in the English Tongue, togither with examples for the practise of the same.* Middleburg, 1584.

Ferriby, John. *The lawfull preacher; or a short discourse shewing that they ought to preach who are ordained ministers, occasionally delivered in some lectures at Epping . . . as also, the Pulpit-Guard-relieved, in answer to a late book called The Pulpit-guard routed, written by Tho. Collier.* London, 1652.

Fleming, Abraham (ca. 1552 – 1607). *A Panoplie of Epistles contayning a Perfect Plaitforme of Inditing Letters of All Sorts . . . Used of the Best and Eloquentest Rhetoricians that Have Lived in All Ages . . . Gathered and Translated out of Latine into English by Abraham Flemming.* London, 1576.

Fraunce, Abraham (fl. 1587 – 1633). *The Arcadian Rhetorike; or, the Praecepts of Rhetorike Made Plaine by examples.* London, 1588.

_____. *The Lawiers Logike.* London, 1588.

Fuller, Thomas (1608 – 1661). "The faithful Minister"; "The controversial Divine"; "Of memory"; "The good bishop"; "The life of Mr. [Wm] Perkins," in *The Holy State and the Profane State.* Cambridge, 1642.

Fulwood, William (fl. 1562). *The Castle of Memorie: wherein is conteyned the Restoring, Augmentyng, and Conserving of the Memorye, and Remembraunce.* English'd by W. Fulwood. London, 1563.

_____. *The Enemie of Idleness, teaching the maner and stile how to endite, compose, and write all sorts of epistles.* London, 1568.

_____. *The Enemie of Idleness . . . newly publ. and augmented by W.E.* London, 1582.

Gérard, Pierre (fl. 1598). *A Preparation to the most holie ministerie.* Tr. by N[icholas] B[ecket]. London, 1598.

Gerardus Hyperius, Andreas (1511 – 1564). *The Practis of Preaching, otherwise called the Pathway to the Pulpet: Conteyning an excellent Method how to frame divine sermons, & to interpret the Holy Scriptures according to the capacity of the vulgar people. First written in Latin by the learned pastor of Christes Church, Andreas Hyperius: and now lately (to the profit of the same Church) Englished by Iohn Ludham, vicar of Wetherffeld.* London, 1577.

Gerbier, Baron d'Ouvilly, Sir Balthazar (1591 – 1667). *The Art of Well Speaking, being a Lecture Read Publiquely at Sir B. Gerbier's Academy.* London, 1650.

_____. *A publique Lecture on all the languages, arts, sciences, and noble exercises, which are taught in Sir B. Gerbiers academy.* London, 1650.

Gil, Alexander (1564/5 – 1635). *Logonomia Anglica qua gentis sermo facilius addiscitur.* London, 1619.

Glanvill, Joseph (1636 – 1680). *An essay concerning preaching . . . written for the direction of a young divine.* London, 1678.

———. *A Seasonable defense of preaching and the plain way of it.* London, 1678 (with *An essay*).

Gother, John (d. 1704). *Good advice to the pulpits; delivered in a few cautions for the keeping up of the reputation of those chairs, and preserving the nation in peace.* London, 1687.

———. *Pulpit-sayings, or the character of the pulpit-papist examined.* London, 1688.

Granger, Thomas (fl. 1616). *Syntagma grammaticum, or an easie explanation of Lillies grammar.* London, 1616.

———. *The application of Scripture; or, the manner how to use the Word to most edifying.* London, 1616.

———. *Syntagma logicum or the Divine Logicke, serving especially for the use of divines in the practice of preaching, and for the further helpe of judicious hearers and generally for all.* London, 1620.

Greenwood, John (d. 1593). *Mr. Some laid open in his couleurs: wherein the indifferent reader may easily see howe wretchedly and loosely he hath handeled the cause against M. Penri.* London? 1588.

Guazzo, Stefano (1530 – 1593). *The Civile Conversation of M. Steeven Guazzo Written First in Italian and Nowe translated out of the French by George Pettie.* Books 1 – 3; Book 4 trans. Bartholomew Young. London, 1581.

Haddon, Walter (1516 – 1572). *De laudibus eloquentiae oratorio.* In *G. Haddoni legum doctoris . . . lucubrationes passim collectae et editae studio et labore T. Hatcheri.* London, 1567.

Hall, Thomas (1610 – 1665). *The pulpit guarded with XVII arguments, proving the unlawfulness, sinfulness, and danger of suffering private persons to take upon them publike preaching . . . occasioned by a dispute at Henley in Arden, August 20 1650, against L[awrence] Williams and 4 other craftsmen-preachers.* London, 1651.

———. *The font guarded with xx arguments.* London, 1651.

Hart, S. J., John (d. 1586). *The summe of the conference betweene Iohn Rainolds and Iohn Hart.* London, 1584.

———. *Summa colloquii J. Rainoldi cum J. Harto de capite et fide ecclessiae.* Trans. from the English by Bishop Henry Parry. Oxford, 1610.

Harvey, Gabriel (ca. 1550 – 1630). *Ciceronianus, vel oratio post reditum habita Cantabrigiae ad suos auditores.* London, 1577.

———. *G. Harveii Rhetor, sive duorum dierum oratio, de natura, arte et excercitatione rhetorica.* London, 1577.

Hawes, Stephen (d. 1523?). *The Passetyme of Pleasure, or the History of Graunde Amoure and la Bel Pucel, conteining the knowledge of the Seven Sciences and the Course of Man's Life in this World.* London, 1509.

Hegendorff, Christopher (1500 – 1540). *Methodus de conscribendi epistolis, a G.*

Macropedio tradita. Accessit G. Hegendorphini Epistolas conscribendi Methodus. London, 1580.

Hemmingsen, Niels (1513 – 1600). *The Preacher, or Methode of Preaching; written in Latine by N. Hemminge, and translated in Englishe by J[ohn] H[orsfall].* London, 1574.

Hepinus, Johannes (1499 – 1553). *Formula compendiaria de formandis sacris concionibus.* London, 1570.

Herbert, George (1593 – 1633). *A priest to the temple, or The Country Parson.* (Ch. 7: "The parson preaching.") London, 1652.

Hieron, Samuel (1576? – 1617). *The preacher's plea.* London, 1604.

_____. *The dignitie of preaching.* London, 1615.

Hobbes, Thomás (1588 – 1679). *A Briefe of the Arte of Rhetorique, containing in substance all that Aristotle hath written in His Three Books of that subject, Except onely what is not applicable to the English Tongue.* London, 1637.

_____. *A compendium of the art of logick and rhetorick in the English tongue, containing all that Peter Ramus, Aristotle, and others have writ thereon* [tr. R. Fage and T. Hobbes]: *with plain directions for the more easie understanding and practice of the same.* [Separately entitled]: *The art of rhetorick plainly set forth, by a concealed author* [by Hobbes?]. London, 1651.

_____. *The Art of Rhetoric, with a Discourse of the Laws of england.* Pt. 2: *The Whole Art of Rhetoric* [i.e., *A Briefe of the Art of Rhetorique*]; *The Art of Rhetorick plainly set forth; with Pertinent Examples* [by Hobbes?]. London, 1681.

Holyday, Barten (1593 – 1661). *Oratio habita cum Aristotelis rhetoricorum librum secundum auspicare.* In *Philosophiae polito-barbarae specimen.* Oxford, 1633.

An Homelye of Basilius Howe Younge Mene Oughte to Reade Poets and Oratours. London, 1557. Anon.

An honest answer to the late published Apologie for private preaching, by T. J. London, 1642. Anon.

Hooker, Richard (1553/4 – 1600). *Of the Laws of Eccelesiastical Polity* (Book 5, chaps. 18 – 22). London, 1597.

Hoole, Charles (1610 – 1666/7). *A New Discovery of the Art of Teaching Schoole, in four small treatises; 1. A petty-schoole; 2. The Ushers duty; 3. The masters method; 4. Scholatic discipline; written about twenty three years ago for the benefit of Rotherham School.* London, 1660.

Horne, Thomas (1610 – 1654). *Rhetoricae compendium, Latino-Anglice.* London, 1651.

_____. *Manuductio in aedem Palladis: qua utilissima methodus authores bonos legendi indigitatur* (Greek). London, 1687.

Hoskins, John (1566 – 1638). *Direccions for Speech and Style.* London, 1599 [MS only].

Hughes, William (fl. 1694). *A practical discourse of silence.* London, 1694.

Isocrates (436 – 338 B.C.). *A perfite looking glasse for all estates. Contained in three orations of morall instructions.* Tr. into Latin by Hier. Wolfius. Englished [by J. Forrest]. London, 1580.

──────. *Isocratis orationes et epistolae. Editio postrema* (Greek). London, 1591.

James I (of England) (1566 – 1625). "Directions concerning preachers. A.D. 1622." [In *Documents Illustrative of English Church History,* ed. Henry Gee and W. J. Hardy.] London, 1896 [pp. 516 – 518].

Jewel, John (1522 – 1571). *Oratio contra rhetoricam. . . . A sermon made in Latine in Oxenford, in the reign of King Edward the Sixt* (but before 1554, when Jewel fled England) *. . . and translated into English by R. V.* In *The Works of John Jewel.* London, 1609.

Jones, Bassett (fl. 1634 – 1659). *Hermaeologium: or, An Essay at the Rationality of the Art of speaking. As a Supplement to Lillie's Grammar.* London, 1659.

Kerhuel, John (fl. 1673). *Idea eloquentiae sive ut vulgo vocant rhetoricae. De periodis, tropis, figuris verborum, figuris sententiarum et integrae orationis partibus methodice differens. . . .* London, 1673.

Kirk, P. (fl. 1690). *Logomachia, or The Conquest of Eloquence.* London, 1690.

Kirkwood, James (1650 – 1708). *Rhetoricae compendium.* Edinburgh, 1696 [2nd ed.].

Knollys, Hanserd (1598 – 1691). *Grammaticae Latinae, Graecae, et Hebraicae. Compendium. Rhetoricae adumbratio. Item Radices Graecae et Hebraicae omnes quae in Sacra Scriptura Veteris et Novis Testamenti occurrunt.* London, 1665.

Lamy, Cong. Orat., Bernard (1640 – 1715). *The Art of Speaking: Written in French by Messieurs du Port Royal: In Pursuance of a Former Treatise Intituled, The Art of Thinking. Rendered into English.* London, 1676.

Le Faucheur, Michel (d. 1657). *An essay upon the action of an orator.* London, [1680?].

Legate, O.S.B., John (fl. 1500). *Prophetica, sive de sacra et unica ratione concionandi tractatus.* Cambridge, 1592 [2nd ed.].

Lever, Ralphe (d. 1584/85). *The Arte of Reason Rightly Termed Witcraft, Teaching a Perfect Way to Argue and Dispute.* London, 1573.

Lex Talionis: or, The Author of the Naked Truth stript naked. London, 1676. Anon.

Liber placitandi. A book of special pleadings. London, 1674. Anon.

Libellus sophistarum ad usum Oxoniensis. [London, R. Pynson], 1499 – 1500. Anon.

Libellus sophistarum ad usum Cantibrigiensis. N.p. [W. de Worde]. 1510. Anon.

Longinus, Dionysius (fl. third century A.D.). *Dionysii Longini . . . liber de grandi loquentia sive sublimi dicendi genere.* Ed. by G. Langbaine. Oxford, 1636.

──────. *Peri Uphous, or D. Longinus of the height of eloquence, rendered out of the originall by J. H.* [John Hall]. London, 1652.

──────. *A treatise of the loftiness or elegance of speech.* London, 1680.

──────. *An essay upon sublime style.* Oxford, 1698.

Lucy, William (1591 – 1677). *A treatise of the nature of a minister in all its offices.* [Section 15 on preaching.] London, 1670.

Lupton, Donald (d. 1676). *The freedom of preaching, or Spiritual gifts defended:*

proving that all men endowed with gifts and abilities may teach and preach the word of God. London, 1652.

Lydgate, John (1370 – 1451). *De curia sapiencie or Court of Sapience.* N.p. [W. Caxton], 1480.

Mackenzie, Sir George (1636 – 1691). *Idea eloquentiae forensis hoderniae: una cum actione forensi ex unaquaque juris parte.* Edinburgh, 1681.

Macropedius, Georgius (fl. 1543). *Methodus de conscribendis epistolis.* London, 1580.

_____. *Methodus de conscribendis epistolis, et epitome praeceptionum de paranda copia verborum et rerum, item ix. speciebus argumentationum rhetoricarum.* London, 1580.

Martin, John (1619 – 1693). *The Preacher sent; or a vindication of the liberty of publick preaching by some men not ordained; in answer to two books . . . 1. Jus Divinum ministerii Evangelici, by the Provincial Assembly of London. 2. Vindiciae ministrii Evangelici. By Mr. John Collinges, Norwich.* London, 1658.

Mason, John (fl. 1610). *Princeps rhetoricus or pilogachia, ye combat of caps.* London, 1648.

Melanchthon, Philip (1497 – 1560). *De officio concionatoris brevis commonefactio.* London, 1570.

_____. *De officiis concionatoris;* in lib. inscript. "De arte concionandi formulae" per Jo. Reuchlinum aliosque. London, 1570.

_____. *Formulae de arte concionandi; et discendi theologiae ratio.* London, 1570.

Milton, John (1608 – 1674). *Joannis Miltoni Angli Artis logicae plenior institutio, ad P. Rami methodum concinata.* London, 1672.

Mosellanus, Petrus (1493? – 1524). *Paedologia Petri Mosellani Protegensis in puerorum usum conscripta et aucta. Dialogi 37.* London? 1532.

Newton, John (1622 – 1678). *An Introduction to the Art of Rhetorick.* London, 1671.

_____. *The English Academy: or A Brief Introduction to the Seven Liberal Arts.* London, 1677.

Nicole, Pierre (1625 – 1695). *Moral Essays, by Messieurs de Port Royal* (i.e., P. Nicole) *rendered into Eng. by a person of quality.* Vol. I. London, 1677.

Officium concionatoris: in quo praecepta utilissima de invenienda habendaque concione iam ante aliquot anno sex optimis auctoribus collecta et quam methodice disposita. Cambridge, 1567. Anon.

Olivier, S.J., Peter (fl. 1672). *Dissertationes academicae, de oratoria, historia, et poetica.* Cambridge, 1674.

Patrick, Symon (1626 – 1707). *A discourse of profiting by sermons and of going to hear, where men think they can profit the most.* London, 1683.

Peacham the Elder, Henry (1576 – 1643). *The Garden of Eloquence, conteyning the figures of grammar and rhetorick.* London, 1577.

Pemble, William (ca. 1592 – 1623). *Enchiridion ortorium a Guliemo Pembelo . . . concinnatum. . . .* Oxford, 1633.

―――. *The works of William Pemble.* London, 1635 [3rd ed.].

Penry, John (1559/63 – 1593). *A Treatise containing the aequity of an humble supplication which is to be exhibited unto hir gracious maiesty and this high court of parliament, in the behalfe of the countrey of Wales, that some order may be taken for the preaching of the gospell among those people.* Oxford, 1587.

―――. *A defense of that which hath bin written in the questions of the ignorant ministerie, and the communicating with them.* London, 1588. Mouldsey, 1588.

―――. *An exhortation unto the governors and people of Wales, to Labour earnestly to have the preaching of the Gospell planted among them; with additions.* [Mouldsey], 1588.

Perkins, William (1558 – 1602). *Prophetica, sive de unica ratione concionandi.* Cambridge, 1592.

―――. *The Art of Prophecying, or A Treatise Concerning the Sacred and Onely True Manner, and Method of Preaching. First Written in Latin by Mr. William Perkins. And now faithfully Translated into English (for that it Containeth Many Worthy Things fit for the Knowledge of Men of All Degrees).* London, 1607.

Perry, Henry (1560? – 1617). *Egluryn phraethineb. Sebh. Dosparth ar retoreq, vn o'r saith gelbhydhyd, yn dyscullhuniaith ymadrodh, a'i pherthynassau.* London, 1595.

―――. *Rhetoreq neurheitheq, a ddechreuwyd gan William Salisbury, a anghwanegwyd ac a orphenwyd gan Henry Perri. 2 argraf. [of] Egluryn fraethineb, seu Dosparth ar retoraq.* Ed. by O. Jones and W. O. Pughe. Issued in parts, as a suppl. to several nos. of *Y Greal.* London, 1807.

Phillips, Edward (1630 – 1696?). *The Mysteries of Love and Eloquence, or, the Arts of Wooing and Complementing* [signed E. P.]. 2 pts. London, 1658.

―――. *The Beau's Academy.* London, 1699.

Pomey, S. J., François Antoine (1619 – 1673). *Novus candidatus rhetoricae, altro se candidior, comptiorque, non Aphthonii solum progymnasmata ornatius concinnata, sed Tullianae etiam rhetoricae praecepta clarius explicare repraesentans. . . . Accessit . . . dissertatio de panegyrico.* London, 1692.

Preston, John (1587 – 1628). *Patterne of Wholesome Words.* In *Riches of Mercy to Men in Misery.* London, 1658.

Prideaux, John (1578 – 1650). *Hypomnemata logica, Rhetorica, physica, metaphysica, pneumatica, ethica, politica, Oeconomica. Per Jo. P[rideaux] coll: Exon.* Oxford, n.d.

―――. *Sacred eloquence, or the art of rhetoric as it is laid down in the scripture.* London, 1657.

Prince, J. *A letter to a Young Divine containing some brief directions for composing and delivering sermons.* London, [1692?].

Puttenham, George (d. 1590). *The Arte of English Poesie.* London, 1589.

Quintilianus, Marcus Fabius (35? – 95?). *Institutio oratoria.* Oxford, 1693.

―――. *Institutio. . . . Nova huic editioni adiecit Fabianarum notarum spicilegium subcisivum D. Paraeus. Accesserunt etiam Quintianorum declamationes.* London, 1641.

_____. *Declamationes quindecim.* London, 1641.

_____. *The Declamations of Quintilian, being an exercitation or praxis upon his XII books, Concerning the institution of an orator. Translated (from the Oxford Theatre edition) into English, by a learned and ingenious hand* (i.e., John Warr). London, 1686.

R. W. (fl. 1680). *The English Orator; or Rhetorical Descants upon Some Valuable Themes Both Historical and Philosophical.* 2 pts. London, 1680.

Radau, S. J., Michaele (fl. 1657). *Orator Extemporaneus seu artis oratoriae breviarum bipartitum.* London, 1657.

Rainolde, Richard (d. 1606). *A Booke Called the Foundacion of Rhetorike.* London, 1563.

Rainolds, John (1549 – 1607). *The summe of the conference betweene Iohn Rainolds and Iohn Hart.* London, 1584.

_____. *Summa colloquii J. Rainoldi cum J. Harto de capite et fide ecclessiae.* Tr. from the English by Bishop Henry Parry. Oxford, 1610.

Ramus, Peter (1515 – 1572). *Audomari Talaei Rhetorica (Audomari Talaei Rhetoricae libri duo Petri Rami praelectionibus illustrati) (Audomari Talaei Rhetorica e Petri Rami praelectionibus observata) (Ramae rhetoricae libri duo).* London, 1584.

_____. *Dialectica libri duo.* London, 1574.

_____. *The logike of the most excellant philosopher P. Ramus.* Newly trans. by Rolland Makylmenaeum Scotum. London, 1574.

_____. *The Art of logick. Gathered out of Aristotle, and set in due form . . . by Peter Ramus . . . Pub. . . . by Anthony Wotton.* London, 1626.

_____. *P. Ramus . . . his Dialectica in two bookes. Not onely translated into English, but also digested into questions and answers. . . .* By R. F(age). London, 1632.

Rapin, S. J., René (1621 – 1687). *Réflexions sur l'usage de l'eloquence de ce temps en général.* Oxford, 1672.

_____. *Reflections upon the eloquence of these times; particularly of the barr and pulpit* [by R. Rapin, trans. by N. N.]. London, 1672.

_____. *A Comparison between the Eloquence of Demosthenes and Cicero.* Translated out of the French [of René Rapin]. Oxford, 1672.

_____. *Reflections upon the Use of the Eloquence of these Times.* Translated out of the French [of René Rapin]. Oxford, 1672.

Reuchlin, Johann (1455 – 1522). *Liber congestorum de arte praedicandi.* London, 1570.

Reyner, Edward (1600 – 1668). *Rules for the government of the tongue: together, with directions in six particular cases.* London, 1656.

_____. *A treatise of the necessity of humane learning for a Gospel-preacher.* London, 1663.

Rhetores selecti. Ed. Thomas Gale *Rhetores selecti* [Greek and Latin] *Demetrius Phalaerus* [*de Elocutione*], *Tiberius Rhetor* [*de Schematibus Demosthenes*], *anonymous sophista [de rhetorica], Severi Alexandrini [ethopoeiae]. Demetrius emendavit, reliquous e Mss. edidit et Latin vertit, omnes notis illustravit Tho. Gale.* Oxford, 1676.

Rhetorices artis compendium (of Aristotle). London, 1683. Anon.

Richardson, Alexander (fl. 1629). *The Logician's School-Master ... Whereunto Are added His Prelections on Ramus His Grammar; Talaeus His Rhetoric.* London, 1629.

Robinson, Hugh (ca. 1584 – 1655). *I. Preces. II. Grammaticalia quaedam.* Oxford, 1616.

Robinson, Robert (fl. 1617). *The Art of Pronuntiation digested into two parts.* London, 1617.

Ross, Alexander (fl. 1650). *Enchiridion duplex, oratorium nempe, et poetrium, ab Alex. Ross, illud a Theod. Morello concinnatum.* London, 1650.

Rutherford, John (d. 1577). *Commentariorum de arte disserendi libri quatuor.* London, 1577.

Seppens, Robert (fl. 1664). *Rex theologicus: The preacher's guard and guide in the didactical part of his duty; or, A vindicating shewing that the king's Majesty's letter to the late L. (Laud) Archbishop of Canterbury is most conformable to the judgement and practice of antiquity.* London, 1664.

Seton, John (1498 – 1567). *Dialectica.* London, 1545.

————. *Dialectica brevem in contextum constricta, eadem in scholiis, per exempla latius explicata.* London, 1560.

Shappell, William (fl. 1656). *The Art and Method of Preaching.* London, 1656.

Shaw, Samuel (1635 – 1696). *Words Made Visible.* London, 1679.

Sherry, Richard (1506 – 1555). *A treatise of the Schemes and Tropes gathered out of the best grammarians and oratours: whereunto is added a declamacion that chyldren Strayt from their infancie should be well and gently broughte up in learnyng; written first in Latin by Erasmus.* London, 1550.

————. *A Treatise of the figures of Grammar and Rhetorike profitable for all that be studious of Eloquence, and in especiall for such as in Grammar Scholes doe reede most eloquent Poets and Orators. . . .* London, 1555.

Smith, John (fl. 1657). *The Mysterie of Rhetorique Unvail'd wherein above 130 of the Tropes and Figures are Severally Divided from the Greek into English together with Lively Definitions and Variety of Latine, English Scriptural Examples.* London, 1657.

Some, D. D., Robert (1542 – 1609). *A goodly treatise containing and deciding certaine questions mooved of late in London . . . a defence of such points as M. Penry hath dealt against; and a confutation of many grosse errours broached in M. Penries last treatise.* London, 1588.

South, D. D., Robert (1634 – 1716). *Sacred Eloquence, or the Art of Rhetoric as it is Layed Down in the Scriptures.* London, 1659.

Spencer, Thomas (fl. 1628). *The Art of Logick, Delivered in the Precepts of Aristotle and Ramus.* London, 1628.

Sprat, Thomas (1635 – 1713). *The error of extempore prayer and preaching.* N.p., ca. 1670.

Stapleton, Thomas (1535 – 1598). *Promptuarium catholicum ad instructionem concionatorum contra haereticos nostri temporis.* Cologne, 1557.

———. *Opera omnia.* Paris, 1620.

Stephens, Thomas (fl. 1648). *Troposchematologia: maximam partem ex indice rhetorica Farnabii deprompta: additis insuper anglicanis exemplis.* London, 1648.

Stockwood, John (d. 1610). *Progymnasma scholasticum.* London, 1597.

———. *The Treatise of Figures at the End of the Rules of Construction in the Latin Grammar* (Lyly's). *Construed . . . by John Stockwood.* London, 1672.

Strada, S. J., Famianus (1572 – 1649). *Eloquentia bipartita; pars prior prolusiones academicas, sive prolixiores exhibet orationes, ad facultatem oratoriam, etc. spectantes; altera, paradigmata eloquentiae breviores proponit.* Oxford, 1662.

Sturm, Johann (1507 – 1589). *A Ritch Storehouse or Treasure Called Nobilitas literata.* Tr. by T. Browne. London, 1570.

———. *Aeschinis contra Ctesiphontem, et Demosthenis pro corona orationes a Joanne Sturmio illustratae.* London, 1624.

Susenbrotus, Joannes (fl. 1535?). *Epitome troporum ac schematum et grammaticorum et rhetoricorum.* London, 1562.

Sutcliffe, Matthew (fl. 1590). *A Treatise of Ecclesiastical Discipline.* London, 1590.

———. *De concionum ad populum formulis.* In *De recta studii theologici ratione liber I.* London, 1602.

Taverner, Richard (1505 – 1575). *The flowres of sencies gathered out of sundry wryters by Erasmus in Latine and Englished by Richard Taverner.* London, 1540.

Taylor, John (1580 – 1653). *A swarme of sectaries and schismatiques: wherein is discovered preaching (or prating) of such as are by their trades cobblers, tinkers, pedlars, weavers, sow gelders, and chymney-sweepers.* London, 1641.

———. *An apology for private preaching.* London, [1642].

Tesmarus, John (fl. 1621). *Exercitationum rhetoricam libri iii.* London, 1621.

Thorne, William (1568? – 1630). *Ducente deo. Willelmi Thorni Tullius, Seu Rhetor* [Greek trans.] *in tria stromata divisus.* Oxford, 1592.

Thurman, Henry (fl. 1660). *A defence of humane learning in the ministry: or, a treatise proving that it is necessary a minister (or preacher) should be skilled in humane learning.* Oxford, 1660.

Tommae, Petrus (ca. 1448 – 1508). *Foenix Domini Petri Ravenatis memoriae magistri.* London, [1548?].

———. *The Art of Memory.* Tr. R. Coplande. London, 1548.

Travers, Walter (1548? – 1635). *Ecclesiasticae disciplinae, et Anglicanae ecclesiae ab illa aberrationis, e verbo dei . . . explicatio.* La Rochelle, 1574.

———. *A full and plaine declaration of ecclesiasticale discipline out off the word off God, and off the declining off the churche off England from the same.* [Middleburg?], 1574.

Traversanus, Laurentius Guglielmus (1422 – 1503). *Nova rhetorica*. N.p. [William Caxton], 1479.

Turner, Francis (1638 – 1700). *Affectuum decidua, or due expressions*. Oxford, 1656.

―――. *Animadversions on a late pamphlet entituled The Naked Truth etc*. London, 1676.

Tuvill, Daniel (d. 1660). *The Dove and the Serpent. In which is contained a large description of all such points and principles, as tend either to conversation, or negotiation. . . .* London, 1609.

Twells, John (fl. 1686). *Tentamina elegantarium bina; or two essays of elegancies*. London, 1686.

―――. *Cicero redivivus; or the art of oratory*. London, 1688.

Valerius, Cornelius (1512 – 1578). *In universam bene dicendi rationem tabula, summam artis rhetoricae complectens*. London, 1580.

Vaughan, William (1577 – 1648). *The Golden-Grove, Moralized in Three Bookes: A Worke Very Necessary for All Such as Would know How to Governe Themselves, Their Houses, or Their Countrey*. London, 1600.

Verepaeus, Simon (ca. 1522 – 1598). *De epistolis Latine conscribendis*. 5 books. London, 1592.

Vicars, Thomas (b. 1591?). *Cheiragogia, Manuductio ad artem rhetoricam Ante paucos annos in privatum quorundam Scholarium usum concinnata*. London, 1619.

Vossius, Gerardus (1577 – 1649). *Elementa rhetorica, oratoriis ejusdem partitionibus accomodata: inque usum scholarum Hollandiae et West-Frisiae edita*. Aberdeen, 1631.

―――. *Rhetorices contractae, sive partitionum oratoriarum libri quinque, editio altera*. Oxford, 1631.

Walker, Henry (fl. 1641). *An answer to a foolish pamphlet entitled A swarme of sectaries schismaticks, put forth by John Taylor the water-poet*. London, 1641.

Walker, Obadiah (1616 – 1698). *Some Instructions concerning the Art of Oratory Collected for the use of a friend a Young Student*. London, 1659.

―――. *The guide in controversies*. London, 1673.

―――. *Of education especially of young gentlemen*. Oxford, 1673.

Walker, William (1623 – 1684). *Troposchematologiae. Rhetoricae libri duo*. London, 1668.

―――. *De argumentorum inventione libri duo*. London, 1672.

Wilkins, John (1614 – 1672). *Ecclesiastes, or a Discourse concerning the gift of preaching as it fals under the rules of art*. London, 1646.

Williams, John (1636? – 1709). *An apology for the pulpits, being in answer to a . . . book intituled Good advice to the pulpits etc*. [i.e., by John Gother]. London. 1688.

Willis, John (d. 1627/28). *Mnemonica, sive reminiscendi ars*. London, 1617.

―――. *The Art of Memory*. London, 1621.

———. *Mnemonica, or The Art of Memory.* London, 1661.

Wilson, Thomas (1525? – 1581). *The Rule of Reason, conteyning the Arte of Logique.* London, 1551.

———. *The Art of Rhetorique, for the Use of All such as are studious of Eloquence, Set forth in English, by T. W.* London, 1553.

Woodall, Frederick (fl. 1658). *The Preacher sent, or a vindication of the liberty of publick preaching, by some men not ordained:* by John Martin, Sam. Petto, and F. Woodall. London, 1658.

———. [Woodall and Petto] *A vindication of "the Preacher Sent"; or a warrant for publick preaching without ordination.* London, [1659].

Wright, Leonard (fl. 1596). *For pastors.* N.p. [London?], 1589 (rpt.).

Younge, Richard (fl. 1661). *The Proof of a Good Preacher.* London, 1661.

Rhetoric, a Story or a System?
A Challenge to Historians
of Renaissance Rhetoric

A. KIBÉDI VARGA

Along the Belgian highways one can see signboards saying "Traffic kills 500 children each year" (Het verkeer doodt elk jaar 500 kinderen). It is obvious that this is a statement-sentence, probably taken from some statistical report; but it is no less obvious that this statement has not been put by chance along the highways, that it is not intended only to convey abstract information to those who happen to read it.

One sentence containing a single message can have different functions, and as far as these functions are persuasive, it is usually very difficult to relate the given function to the grammatical form of the sentence. Conversely, the same piece of information can be expressed by different sentences, and all these sentences are meant to figure in different contexts and fulfill their different functions. Authors of treatises on rhetoric and poetics often display much virtuosity in establishing long lists of synonymous sentences, as for instance Christian Weise, who in his *Curiöse Gedancken von deutschen Versen*, published in 1692, presents twelve sentences as variations of "Ich will in Garten gehen" and twelve others for "Die Türcken sind geschlagen."[1] The author neglects, however, to say that these variants need different contexts and are in reality intended to serve different aims.

I chose my two examples to show (1) that every verbal utterance should be analyzed from more than one point of view, (2) that treatises, old and new, try often to amuse the reader by presenting a large

---

1. Quoted from Marian Szyrocki, ed., *Poetik des Barock* (Hamburg 1968), pp. 240–41.

variety of heterogeneous examples instead of tracing back each example to its context. This lack of context makes them amusing and makes the author seem very eloquent.

Rhetoric is the discipline that should give to every utterance the most general, the largest possible, context by permitting its analysis from every scientifically admissible point of view, that is, on every formally and functionally distinguishable level. Thus rhetoric appears to be a *system based on a strict hierarchy*.

Though the whole framework of rhetoric gives us intuitively the impression of being systematic, the treatises do not really try to present this discipline as a hierarchical system.[2] Each part in a typical book constitutes a different chapter, and the hierarchical relation between these chapters is not pointed out. This seeming disparity can be explained by the traditional view of rhetoric as a pedagogical method for teaching and learning eloquence, and not (as is the case nowadays, especially in Europe) as a semiotic-pragmatic method for analyzing discourse. For use as a teaching method it is useful to adopt a chronological order; rhetoric becomes then the story of a learning process, almost a kind of ideal *Bildungsroman* in which the pupil has to overcome more and more difficult obstacles: first he has to master the grammar, then rhetoric, and if he is gifted enough to go on — and to become, not an orator, but a poet — there is even something called "second rhetoric," that is, prosody.[3] The same thing happens inside the rhetoric itself: even though the handbooks on rhetoric present first the invention, then the disposition, and so on, and consequently follow the hierarchical order, the numerous practical and didactic suggestions and comments hide this hierarchy and tend to present the whole rather as an itinerary in which the point of arrival is more important than the point of departure. Crevier, one of the least quoted but finest French rhetoricians, is profoundly right when he writes that between the various parts of rhetoric, and especially between invention and elocution, "il n'y a nulle égalité," invention being most important.[4] However, most treatises seem to forget this qualita-

2. The most systematic presentation of classical rhetoric is a modern one, Heinrich Lausberg's *Handbuch der literarischen Rhetorik* (Munich, 1960); his rhetoric is a complicated network of cross-references — which corresponds undoubtedly to one part of the reality — but the hierarchy is less visible.

3. In sixteenth-century France, the study of versification was considered a stage coming *after* the study of rhetoric and was called therefore "seconde rhétorique":"on distingue à l'époque deux rhétoriques: la *première* qui est celle de la prose, et la *seconde*, qui est l'art des vers" (Alex L. Gordon, *Ronsard et la rhétorique,* Geneva, 1970, p. 15).

4. *Rhétorique française* (Paris, 1765), p. 2.

tive matter and adopt the point of view of quantity: what takes more space (disposition) is more important.

My point is that, since we use rhetoric no longer as a creative-didactic but as a critical-analytic method, the relations between its parts and proportions have been modified; and our main task should be, and in fact has been for several centuries, to "translate" this *story* into a *system,* to translate this chronology of consecutive activities into a hierarchy of levels. This means that to every phenomenon that appears on a level, however small it may be, something must correspond on another level. In other words, there can be no general remark on *ethos* or on *topics* in the chapter on invention without something equivalent to it (e.g., a *figure*) on the level of the chapter on disposition. Every phenomenon should be defined at its own level but it should also be comprehended at each higher level. Every *figure* should be defined as part of elocution, but at the same time it should be mentioned in relation to the topic within which it usually appears and functions, in the chapter on invention.

It goes without saying that these levels include not only the rhetoric *stricto sensu* but also its traditional allies, or auxiliary disciplines: linguistics, logic, and psychology. On the highest level, which corresponds in my opinion to the *genera dicendi,* one might even wonder whether one should not add psychoanalysis, sociology, and anthropology — disciplines that are not completely foreign to Aristotelian rhetorical philosophy.

In a rather rough and schematic way, I would say that the lowest level is that of *grammar,* the second *elocution* or *style,* the third *invention.* There are, however, two problems in this schema:

1. We see — and the treatises corroborate this — that it is quite natural to pass from *elocution* to *invention* and vice versa, but the place of *disposition,* which fits quite naturally between the two in the didactic itinerary, seems much more problematic in a systematic hierarchy.

2. It is not easy to know what exactly belongs to *invention* and what kind of inner hierarchy one should establish for it. I'd like to suggest as a third level the *topics,* as fourth level the three *appeals* and their three specific kinds of argumentation, as fifth level the *staseis,* or issues, and as the highest the *genera dicendi.*

It is difficult to distinguish these levels, but perhaps a description of the interrelation between them could help us distinguish between them better. We need an exhaustive inventory of possible relations; in the typical books we mostly find some loose remarks only. The eighteenth-century writer Papon says, for instance, that when using a *hypotyposis* one should put all the verbs in the *present tense* — establishing thus a link between *grammar* and *elocution* (my first and second levels). But he does not give a complete description either of the possible grammatical forms of *hypotyposis* or of the way it functions on levels higher than that of elocution.[5] Crevier — to quote another example — notes, without insisting and without any concrete detail, the relation between the *staseis* and certain topics (my third and fifth levels): "il est aisé de voir quels lieux de rhétorique conviennent à chacun des trois états de cause" (p. 145). The least neglected is of course, as we shall see further on, the relation between the second and the third levels, between figures and topics, but even there one finds mostly scattered remarks at best.[6] Considerable difficulties seem to arise especially when one tries to find out the relationships between phenomena on the same level: what is the mutual relation between the three *appeals*? and what between the three *genera dicendi*? It is strange that the relation between *logos, ethos,* and *pathos* has never been seriously studied, though it is a fundamental issue that should influence the structure of the rhetorical system.[7]

As to the three *genera dicendi,* they have always been very well distinguished by comparisons, analogies, and contrasts — but there is probably more to say about the basic human interaction they represent. Some recent work seems to show that, if we are willing to postulate a larger social context for the treatises, admitting hidden presuppositions of the speaker, and so forth, we could reduce the number of the *genera dicendi:* for instance, the epideictic discourse appears then to be persuasive as well but, of course, indirectly so;

5. J. P. Papon, *L'art du Poète et de l'Orateur* (Lyon, 1766) p. 361. Hypotyposis being a "figure of thought," it is probably difficult to assign a fixed grammatical form to it, but it should be possible to study its frequency, its uses, and thus to determine to which topics of invention it should be related.

6. See, for instance, George Campbell: "There is one trope, *irony,* in which the relation is contrariety." *The Philosophy of Rhetoric,* ed. L. F. Bitzer, Carbondale, Ill., 1963, p. 294.

7. Crevier expresses a preference for ethos above pathos (p. 303). On the whole problem some interesting suggestions are to be found in Klaus Dockhorn, *Macht und Wirkung der Rhetorik* (Bad Homburg, 1968). According to Grimaldi, the relation between the three kinds of appeal is secured, in Aristotelian rhetoric, by the concept of the enthymeme (W. M. A. Grimaldi, *Studies in the Philosophy of Aristotle's Rhetoric,* Hermes-Schriften 25 [Wiesbaden, 1972]).

praise or blame is subordinated to some general consideration or to a tacitly admitted ideology.[8]

Some work has been done, of course, to show the interrelation of the various levels, to demonstrate thereby the systematic unity of rhetoric. I do not think of the numerous attempts, ancient and modern, to show the impact of rhetoric on some fields outside it but more or less related to eloquence, though even here some very precise parallels have been elaborated — as for instance, when Gérard de Benat tries to correlate the terminology of rhetoric and poetics by saying: "Les Peintures et les Images sont cette figure que les Rhéteurs appellent *hipotipose*" and "Le portrait est cette figure que les Rhéteurs appellent *Ethopée*."[9] Many similar attempts have been made to establish links between rhetoric and the theory of painting, as is shown for instance in the (tediously and not quite convincingly) elaborate *Parallèle de l'Eloquence et de la Peinture* by Charies Coypel, "peintre ordinaire du Roi" (1732).

The relationship between the various subdivisions of rhetoric has been studied especially in regard to *topics, figures,* and *pathos* (the emotional appeal). In the Renaissance, the classification of figures undertaken by Peacham and by Melanchthon reveals a consciousness of this problem of relation, as Sister Miriam Joseph has pointed out in her well-known study.[10] She is especially interested in the links between topics and figures·and deals with this question in some detail (eleven figures reflect the topics of division, p. 315; "eighteen figures are derived from the relation of subject and adjuncts," p. 319), providing, at the same time, an interesting contribution to the modern problem of determining the relationship between logic and linguistic discourse. More recently, Heinrich Plett and Brian Vickers have worked on describing links between figures and *pathos,* that is, their emotional effect. Plett examines the English Renaissance rhetoric treatises in order to show that the establishing of such links was

8. See Louis Marin, *Le récit est un piège* (Paris, 1979).

9. *L'art oratoire réduit en exemples, ou choix de morceaux d'éloquences tirés des plus célèbres Orateurs, Du siècle de Louis XIV & du siècle de Louis XV* (Amsterdam, 1760), 2.1, 205. It is piquant to note that what are really compared to rhetoric in these quotations are not terms of poetic, strictly speaking, but pictorial metaphors applied to poetics *(peinture, image, portrait).*

10. *Shakespeare's Use of the Arts of Language,* 2nd ed. (New York, 1966), pp. 38 – 39; see also J. Donald Ragsdale, "Invention in English 'stylistic' rhetoric," *Quarterly Journal of Speech* 51 (1965), 164 – 67.

one of their main concerns,[11] and Vickers is consequently right when he protests against the misconception that the elaborate inventory of technical devices presented in Renaissance rhetorics is only a matter of form, that Renaissance rhetorics are only concerned with form. The rhetoricians' interest in *pathos* goes back to antiquity; among other examples, Vickers quotes the emotion of *anger,* which according to Aristotle demands the figure of *hyperbole* and which according to Quintilian "cannot be credibly expressed in neat *antitheses.*"[12] In spite of these interesting and promising attempts, formidable problems remain if we want to give a full description of the hierarchical system of rhetoric. For the time being, I'd like to examine only the two relationships already mentioned.

As to the relation between *topics* and *figure,* much confusion should first of all be clarified. The famous French ecclesiastical orator Bourdaloue deplores that topics are interchangeable:

> Il n'en est guère qui ne puisse être remplacé par un équivalent. La *Définition,* par exemple, qui tire une preuve d'un objet par l'explication qu'elle en donne, n'est pas sans rapport avec l'*Enumération des Parties,* qui analyse les principales circonstances d'un fait, ou qui expose les diverses faces d'une idée.[13]

The problem is even greater when we discover that the distinction between the category of the topics belonging to invention, on the one hand, and the category of the figures belonging to elocution, on the other, is not always sharp. Gérard de Benat notes that "La figure appelée Parallèle a quelque rapport avec la similitude, un des lieux oratoires" (vol. 2, 377). Like similies, *examples* also have an ambiguous position. Thomas Wilson deals with them in his chapter on elocution, but this does not prevent him from giving an interpretation of *exempla* that derives them from the topics.[14] The status of certain schemes

---

11. *Rhetorik der Affekte — Englische Wirkungsästhetik im Zeitalter der Renaissance* (Tübingen, 1975).

12. *Classical Rhetoric in English Poetry* (London, 1970), pp. 91, 94, 101.

13. *La Rhétorique de Bourdaloue,* traduite pour la première fois, conformément au texte latin manuscrit de la bibliothèque d'Alençon, par. A. Profillet (Paris, 1864), p. 53.

14. "We read of *Danae* the faire damosell, whom *Jupiter* tempted full oft, and could never have his pleasure, till at length he made it raigne golde, and so as she sat in her Chimney, a great deale fell upon her lappe, the which she took gladly and kept it there, within the which golde, *Iupiter* himself was comprehended, whereby is none other thing els signified, but that woman have bene, and will be overcome by money." *The Arte of Rhetorique* (1560), as quoted by O. B. Hardison, Jr., ed., *English Literary Criticism, The Renaissance* (New York, 1963), p. 52.

of grammar, sometimes admitted as topics and sometimes considered figures, is at least as problematic as that of comparisons and examples (see Crevier, p. 40). Sister Miriam Joseph is particularly aware of this problem: "some of the figures are identical with logical forms, for example the *dilemma,* which was regarded as both a figure and a form of reasoning" (p. 36).

The second relationship might be defined by asking: How do *figures* and *topics* work in relation to *pathos;* in other words, what is the hierarchical relation of *topics* to *pathos* and of *figures,* through *topics,* to *pathos?* In spite of valuable work in this field, two corollary questions remain unanswered.

First, if we admit that rhetoric is a hierarchical system, we should also attempt to consider where to begin examining the interrelation between its levels. I think that, after having made full inventories of every phenomenon belonging to one level, we should start studying relationships by starting always at the higher level. Every phenomenon on a higher level implies the existence and determines the use of one or more phenomena on each successively lower level. By doing otherwise, we just continue to make tedious inventories and state, for instance, that a given figure "can be used for a great range of effects" (Vickers, p. 120, á propos of *chiasmus*).

Second, the relation among pathos, argumentation, and style cannot be clear as long as we neglect to study the comparatively highest level, that is, *pathos.* We will never be able to reconstruct the system of the traditional psychology. Some modern scholars seem to forget the strict structuring of emotions as they were classified since Aristotle, who devoted the larger part of the second book of his *Rhetoric* to this matter: Pity and Fear, the two composing parts of tragic catharsis, have their fixed place in this classification and should therefore always be studied in this context. The number of emotions can vary: Chrysippus distinguishes four: "*pleasure* from present good, *pain* from present evil, *desire* from future good, and *fear* from future evil."[15] Similar classifications can be found until the seventeenth century, for Bourdaloue gives a subtle elaboration of Chrysippus in his rhetoric and Descartes devotes to this question his famous *Traité des Passions.* Figures and topics of Renaissance rhetoric treatises should be related not just to some kind of general emotional state, but to the rather well-defined contemporaneous categories of emotions.

15. Quoted from A. Levi, S.J., *French Moralists, the Theory of the Passions 1585 to 1649* (Oxford, 1964), p. 12.

I am aware, of course, that we touch here upon a fundamental problem of rhetorical hierarchy: the lower the level, the more precisely we can describe it. We can describe grammar fairly well, but we do not have any exhaustive inventory of behavioral categories at our disposal; yet these categories constitute what is called *pathos,* and as such they determine what happens on lower levels. The highest levels are the most powerful and the least precise; that is the problem and that is why we should try to be as strict as possible, especially with regard to these higher levels.

If we are willing to retranslate the rhetorical curriculum into a hierarchical rhetorical system, we can maintain that the relationship between the lower levels has been studied, even if not enough, by stylistics (grammar-elocution) or by rhetoric (elocution-invention); the relationship spanning the highest to the lower levels, on the contrary, has been traditionally neglected by rhetoric — these problems being examined in the last few years by what we call *Textlinguistik* or *discourse analysis.*[16] If students of classical and Renaissance rhetoric try seriously to reconstruct the complete framework of rhetoric, they could thus offer a very valuable contribution to a modern theory of discourse.

16. Works devoted to these fields are so numerous in recent years that no attempt can be made to mention even a few. I think, on the one hand, of studies on conversation analysis trying to relate syntactic peculiarities to rhetorical devices and emotional states (levels 2, 3, and 4 of this essay) and, on the other hand, of works interested in the question of how logical argumentation appears in natural language, in plain, common-sense texts.

PART TWO

Rhetorical Trends in Renaissance Europe

La Retórica y el Renacimiento:
An Overview of Spanish Theory

DON ABBOTT

The nineteenth-century British critic George Saintsbury, writing of his Spanish counterpart Marcelino Menéndez y Pelayo, observed that the Renaissance had "supplied Señor Menéndez with a tolerably fair herd of humanist rhetoricians to fill the ninety pages of his ninth chapter."[1] Because of the abundance of rhetorical treatises written by Renaissance Spaniards, a complete overview of the subject would indeed require an essay of at least ninety pages. Such comprehensiveness exceeds the mission of the present volume. I have, therefore, chosen to discuss only one aspect of Spanish Renaissance rhetoric, which I shall call, somewhat arbitrarily, the attempt to restructure rhetoric. While the particulars of this restructuring vary considerably among the writers, the broad features are rather consistent. Writers of this orientation express dissatisfaction with traditional rhetoric and seek to redirect its functions and forms. More specifically, invention as an argumentative concept is dismissed; *inventio* as a term disappears almost entirely while its duties are delegated to the imagination. The pivotal terms in this restructuring are, therefore, invention and imagination.

Theorists who strive to alter the inventive and imaginative aspects of rhetoric are many. I have selected three figures to examine in

1. George Saintsbury, *A History of Criticism and Literary Taste in Europe* (New York, 1902) 2.335 – 36. See also Marcelino Menéndez y Pelayo, *Historia de las ideas estéticas en España* in *Edicion nacional de las obras completas de Menéndez Pelayo* (Madrid, 1947), 2.145 – 203. This treatment by Menéndez y Pelayo remains one of the best accounts of Spanish Renaissance rhetoric.

detail: Juan Luis Vives (1492 – 1540), Juan Huarte de San Juan (1529? – 1588?), and Baltasar Gracián (1601 – 1658). Vives appears at the beginning of the Golden Age, Huarte at the middle, and Gracián at its end. Hence an examination of these three figures provides a view of this restructuring at its inception, its midpoint, and its completion.

The Spanish attempt to restructure begins with and receives its most impassioned expression in the writings of Juan Luis Vives. In 1520 Vives denounced scholasticism as a "gangrene" and a "pestilence" that had "infested the minds of men for five hundred years and more."[2] What was needed to combat this infection was a new approach to learning in all arts and sciences. Rhetoric, like other disciplines, was in desperate need of remedial measures. When the ancient democracies declined, "the careful exercise of speech was neglected entirely and the rhetorical art passed, without exception, first into oblivion, and then it was enveloped in darkness and ignorance."[3] Vives vows to correct these intolerable conditions: "Now we, after so long an interval, shall undertake to recall that art out of darkness into the light. We shall not repeat the ancients, but in fact we shall teach something entirely new."[4]

To "teach something entirely new," Vives must first survey the positions of his predecessors and thus insure that the errors of the past would be avoided in the education of the present. This is precisely the approach of "On the Corruption of Rhetoric," in *De disciplinis,* where Vives finds little in classical doctrine that is agreeable. The exaggerated claims of the Roman rhetoricians for the inextricability of wisdom, virtue, and rhetoric are insupportable. Consequently, Vives rejects as overly expansive the definition of the orator as a good man skilled in speaking.

Just as Vives rejects the existence of a necessary link between a good man and a great speaker, so too he denies the inclusiveness of the classical genres of forensic, deliberative, and epideictic oratory. These three are no more than the result of Aristotle's observations on the customs of his times and as such are not exhaustive. From

2. Juan Luis Vives, *Adversus Pseudodialeticos* in *Juan Luis Vives: Obras completas,* trans. and ed. Lorenzo Riber (Madrid, 1948), 2.310. Translations from this Spanish edition of Vives' works are mine.

3. Juan Luis Vives, *De ratione dicendi.* I have used the English translation of this work by Mary Jean Thomas, "The Rhetoric of Juan Luis Vives" (Ph.D. diss., Pennsylvania State University, 1967), p. 136.

4. Ibid.

these genres developed the systems of invention, disposition, and ornamentation, which necessarily remain reflections of these original forms. "Who does not believe," asks Vives, "that thanksgivings, felicitations, consolations, history, and teaching necessitate a very different invention and elocution than for judicial, consultative, and demonstrative discourse?"[5]

But what Vives perhaps finds most objectionable about classical theory is the five-part division of rhetoric into invention, disposition, elocution, memory, and delivery. Memory is simply a part of nature and not the exclusive property of rhetoric. Indeed, memory is a necessity for all arts: grammar, dialectic, arithmetic, and jurisprudence. Nor is delivery a part of rhetoric, for "an orator, by writing, can accomplish his specific function, and be an excellent orator, without gesture."[6] Invention is not peculiar to rhetoric but is, like memory, necessary to all arts. The invention of arguments, however, is reserved by Vives for dialectic. Finally, Vives rejects disposition because of the impossibility of establishing precise rules for the various parts of an oration. Vives's major criticisms of the fivefold division stem from his belief that the classical conception is imprecise and redundant. Simply because one art assists another does not mean that one is a component of the other. Says Vives: "It is better if the architect is also a philosopher. But does this make philosophy a part of architecture?"[7]

The appropriate part of rhetoric is, of course, elocution. But not traditional elocution, which the "infinite subtlety" of the Greeks had made all "schemes and lights."[8] Thus in *De disciplinis* Vives presents an art of rhetoric in need of reform; the reforms themselves are presented in *De ratione dicendi* (1532). In this latter work Vives claims that his "method of teaching the art is absolutely new and quite different from the traditional and commonly known method."[9] Yet he begins with a rather familiar set of definitions: the subject matter of rhetoric is speech; the end is speaking well; the mission of the rhetor is to explain, or to persuade, or to move the soul. Speech consists of words and ideas — words are the body and ideas the soul of discourse. Then, in most characteristic statement, Vives tells what he is about: "Words are public property. They are by no means the property of an art, nor are they private property. What belongs in the

5. Juan Luis Vives, *De disciplinis,* in *Obras completas,* 2.458.
6. Ibid., p. 459.   7. Ibid., p. 456.   8. Ibid., p. 461.
9. "The Rhetoric of Juan Luis Vives," p. 133.

domain of this treatise is the application of words and thoughts and how they may be adapted to the end which is proposed."[10]

Consistent with this view Vives begins his work with an examination of the nature of words. The entirety of book one is devoted to the intrinsic and extrinsic qualities of words considered individually and in composition. Book two considers the qualities of the oration and how the instruments of speech may be adapted to the various ends of the speaker. Finally, book three investigates teaching and the various genres of discourse appropriate to it.

A pervasive theme of *De ratione dicendi* is that of decorum — adaptation, propriety. Vives claims that "every action has an agent from whom it originates and a receiver into which it passes. To these all instruments of this art must be adapted."[11] Later he adds that "the primary duty of adaptation belongs to the speaker, so that the listener will not shun his duty, which happens when he averts his attention from the speaker."[12] Thus for Vives adaptation secures attention, which in turn ensures the attainment of the speaker's desired end.

Vives is reasonably effective in attaining his own end: a new approach to rhetoric. "On the Corruption of Rhetoric" made it unnecessary for him to discuss in *De ratione dicendi* the "good man," the three genres of discourse, or the five-part division of rhetoric. Vives is thus free to present his alternative to the ancients. This alternative is "stylistic" insofar as all other concerns are excluded, but it is not a rhetoric of schemes and tropes. *De ratione dicendi* is indeed the art of expression — the appropriate expression of ideas. Rhetoric is, to paraphrase Donald Bryant, the art of adjusting ideas to words and words to people.[13] As such, Vives's rhetoric may not be entirely new, but neither is it entirely traditional.

A second attempt to restructure rhetoric is contained in Juan Huarte's *Examen de ingenios para las ciencias* (1575). Huarte's point of departure is "an opinion very common and ordinarie amongst the antient Philosophers, to say, That Nature is she who makes a man of habilitie to learne, and that art with her precepts and rules guies a facilitie hereunto, but then vse and experience, which he reapes of particular things, makes him mightie in working. Yet none of them ever shewed in particular, what thing this nature was, nor in what

---

10. Ibid., p. 137.   11. Ibid., p. 263.   12. Ibid., p. 284.

13. Donald Bryant, "Rhetoric: Its Function and Scope," in *The Province of Rhetoric*, eds. Joseph Schwartz and John A. Rycenga (New York, 1965), p. 19.

ranke of causes it ought to be placed: only they affirmed, that this, wanting in him who learned, art, experience, teachers, bookes, and trauaile are of none auaile."[14]

The purpose, therefore, of *The Examination of Men's Wits* is to overcome ancient deficiencies and demonstrate the causes of natural ability. The explanation of the variety of human abilities Huarte provides is a physiological one borrowed from Galen. The brain is controlled by certain qualities, or "humours." Huarte distinguishes three such qualities: hot, moist, and dry. The temperature and moisture of the brain determine the three faculties of the mind: understanding, imagination, and memory. Cold and dry yield understanding, heat insures imagination, and moisture makes memory.

Each faculty, in turn, governs particular arts and sciences. The faculty of memory insures ability in "*Latine Grammer,* or whatsoeuer other language, the *Theoricke* of the lawes, Divinitie positive, *Cosmography,* and *Arithmeticke.*" Within the province of the understanding, Huarte includes "the *Theoricke of phisicke, logicke, natural, and morall Philosophy.*"[15] And finally, "From a good imagination, spring all the Arts and Sciences, which consist in figure, correspondence, harmonie, and proportion: such are Poetrie, Eloquence, Musicke, and the skill of preaching: the practice of Phisicke, the Mathematicals, Astrologie, and the gouerning of a Commonwealth, the art of Warfare, Paynting, drawing, writing, reading."[16]

Huarte devotes two chapters to demonstrating that eloquence derives from the imagination. He does, however, modify this doctrine somewhat, noting that the art of persuasion "springeth from a vnion, which the memorie maketh with the imagination."[17] Accordingly, "wisdoem appertaineth to the imagination, copiousnesse of words and sentences to the memorie" and "ornament and polishment to the imagination."[18]

Much of the subsequent discussion is devoted to proving that the traditional "properties" of rhetoric are indeed derived primarily from the imagination and secondarily from the memory. Invention, therefore, becomes one of several "graces" needed by the preacher. "A perfect orator," says Huarte, must "possesse much invention, or much reading, for if he rest bound to dilate and confirms any matter

14. Juan Huarte, *Examen de Ingenios: The Examination of Men's Wits* (1594). Translated out of the Spanish by M. Camillo Camilli. Englished out of his Italian by Richard Carew. Ed. Carmen Rodgers (Gainesville, Fla., 1959), p. 13.

15. Ibid., p. 103.   16. Ibid.   17. Ibid., p. 120.   18. Ibid., p. 132.

whatsoeuer, with many speeches and sentences applied to the purpose, it behooueth that he have a very swift imagination."[19] Lacking imagination, the orator may resort to reading, but "whatsoeuer books teach, is bounded and limited; and the proper invention is a good fountain which alwaie yeeldeth forth new and fresh water."[20]

Not only does the imagination govern the ability to be eloquent, but eloquence and understanding are indeed inimicable. Huarte says quite simply that "eloquence and finesse of speech cannot find place in men of great understanding."[21] This too has a physiological explanation, for it is because of a "defect of the toung" that "men of great understanding cannot be good orators or preachers."[22] Moreover, those qualities that make for good oratory do not make for good morality. Men of considerable imagination "are of a complexion very hote, and from this quality spring three principal vices in a man; Pride, Gluttonie, and Lecherie."[23] Imaginative men are also "chloricke, subtle, malignant, and cavillers, and alwaies enclined to evill, which they can compass with much readiness & craft."[24]

This rather scurrilous nature of the preacher presents certain theological problems for Huarte, who is, for the most part, content to separate divinity, a product of understanding, from preaching, a product of the imagination. Huarte does hint, however, that this separation may be overcome by divine intervention.[25] The orator or preacher, therefore, need not be a good man skilled in speaking, but simply someone endowed with the great heat necessary to yield a "forcible imagination."

The extreme physiological determinism of Juan Huarte de San Juan produced the *Siglo de Oro*'s most emphatic statement of the subjugation of rhetoric to the imagination and the most explicit declaration of the division between eloquence and understanding.

The final attempt to restructure rhetoric appears appropriately enough in the works of the last great prose writer of the Golden Age, Baltasar Gracián. Gracián's *Agudeza y arte de ingenio* (1649) is a rather unusual rhetorical treatise. And there are those, including Gracián himself, who would deny that it is rhetoric at all. Determining the rhetorical import of the work is made difficult by Gracián's disinterest in precise definitions. Because the key terms *"agudeza"* and *"ingenio"* are never defined, their meanings can only be suggested by corresponding words. *Agudeza* is variously rendered into English as wit,

19. Ibid., p. 131.   20. Ibid., p. 132.   21. Ibid., p. 120.
22. Ibid., p. 139.   23. Ibid., p. 140.   24. Ibid.   25. Ibid., p. 123.

acuteness, subtlety, quickness, grace, and profundity. *Ingenio* is mind, talent, ingenuity, imagination, invention. The title is generally translated into English as *The Mind's Wit and Art*. This book is, most simply put, Gracián's search for wit in all forms of human expression.

This search for wit requires Gracián to cite a truly overwhelming multitude of examples. He justifies the variety of his sources in this way:

> The clergyman will admire the nourishing conceits of St. Ambrose; the humanist the peppery ones of Martial. Here the philosopher will find Seneca's prudent sayings, the historian the rancorous ones of Tacitus, the orator, Pliny's keenness, and the poet, the brilliance of Ausonius. For whoever teaches is indebted everywhere. I took my examples from the languages in which I found them, for if Latin vaunts the eminent Florus, so too Italian has the bold Tasso, Spanish the cultivated Góngora, and Portuguese the tender Camoens. If I frequent the Spanish it is because wit is prevalent with them, just as erudition is with the French, eloquence with the Italian and originality with the Greeks.[26]

Gracián is a man of his word—he discovers excellences of wit in prose and poetry, ancient and modern—for *agudeza* is an eternal and universal concept.

Because wit is eternal and universal, Gracián believes that it extends, indeed replaces, rhetorical principles of previous ages. "The ancients," he says, "found a method for the syllogism and an art of the trope; but wit, either for fear of it or to deprive it of hope, they confined and remitted to the mere swagger of the imagination. . . . But they never came to observe wit carefully, and so never found a system for it, much less perfection."[27] Unlike the ancients, who did not fully appreciate the imagination, Gracián dedicates his work "to the Imagination—to wit in art, a resplendant conception—for even though some of its artifices glimmer in Rhetoric's discipline, still they hardly approach a sparkle: orphan children adopted by Eloquence, since they don't know their true mother. Wit makes use of rhetorical figures and tropes as devices for elegantly expressing its concepts; but they contain within their own limits the material foundations of the nicety and, at best, the ornaments of thought."[28]

26. I have used the translation of the *Agudeza y arte de ingenio* by Leland H. Chambers, "Baltasar Gracián's *The Mind's Wit and Art*" (Ph.D. diss., University of Michigan, 1962), pp. 80–81.

27. Ibid., p. 85.   28. Ibid., p. 80.

The schemes and tropes of classical rhetoric, then, offer only meager insights into the workings of the imagination. But the shortcomings of rhetoric may be rectified by employing its own method. Says Gracián: "Conscious craft cannot be denied where so much complexity reigns. A syllogism is made with rules; with rules, then let conceits be hammered out. Let all skill beg for instruction, all the more when it is a matter of the subtleness of the imagination."[29] Gracián is, therefore, proposing to instruct the imagination in a manner somewhat analogous to the way in which syllogising instructs the understanding. And despite Gracián's disavowal of his dependence on rhetoric, the rules he formulates are very rhetorical indeed. For what Gracián actually proposes is a system of *topoi*.[30] He makes this clear early in the treatise when he writes that "it is the privilege of science to reduce its teachings to general principles; doctrinal maxims are, as the name implies, at the head and source even of good discourse, are the fundamentals of teaching; by royal principle, then, let the queen art commence."[31] This statement can be little else but a definition of *topoi*. The topical nature of Gracián's system becomes more apparent as he explains and enumerates these "general principles": "the subject about which someone reflects and muses ... whether eulogizing or vituperating—is like the center from which the discourse distributes lines of deliberation and cunning to the entities that surround it; that is, to what is adjacent and perfects the subject, as do its causes, its effects, attributes, qualities, contingencies. Circumstances of time, place, manner, etc., and any other conditions belonging to it."[32] These various topics are essential to Gracián's analysis of wit. For his procedure, in the bulk of the book, is to describe a particular conceit, identify the topic from which it is derived, and then exemplify this process from as many sources as possible.

Gracián's sources are primarily poets and preachers, and appropriately so, for the attempt is to subsume poetic and rhetoric into a universal theory of expression. But this effort is not entirely successful, for the conceptual framework remains rhetorical. What Gracián does do is reclaim invention and reassign it to the imagination and transform the topics from the seats of argument to the sources of wit.

29. Ibid., p. 86.
30. For a complete discussion of *topoi* in Gracián, see M. J. Woods, "Gracián, Peregrini, and the Theory of Topics," *Modern Language Review* 63 (1968), 854–63. I have followed Woods's interpretation.
31. "Baltasar Gracián's *The Mind's Wit and Art*," p. 116.
32. Ibid.

The resultant *Agudeza y arte de ingenio* is truly a rhetoric of the baroque.

Juan Luis Vives, Juan Huarte de San Juan, and Baltasar Gracián all sought to restructure rhetoric. Whereas Vives began this movement by rejecting invention, Huarte extended it by reclaiming invention and assigning it to the imagination. Gracián completed the restructuring by continuing the dominance of the imagination over invention while restoring the "rules" that had been so repugnant to Vives and Huarte. So while invention ceased to serve as the primary part of rhetoric and the term *inventio* fell into disuse, its *function,* somewhat altered, continued unabated. Such a result was probably inevitable. As Walter Ong has observed in a different context: "the divorce of rhetoric from dialectic implies at the same time a union of invention and striking expression in any given text."[33] For it is inevitable that rhetoric must seek to answer inventional questions.

This rhetorical restructuring with the resultant "union of invention and striking expression" by no means explains the totality of Spanish Renaissance rhetoric. Contemporaries of Vives, Huarte, and Gracián continued to advocate more traditional conceptions of rhetoric. These more classically inclined rhetoricians include Benito Arias Montano, Bartolomé Bravo, Alfonso García Matamoros, Luis de Granada, and Antonio de Nebrija. Because this list includes the names of many of Spain's greatest humanists, there is an understandable tendency to view the rhetoric of the Golden Age as largely a preservation of classical precepts. Yet it is likely that the restructuring described above is the more representative rhetorical feature of the age. Such questions of interpretation are regrettably difficult to answer because of the paucity of relevant studies.

The greatest weakness of scholarship in Spanish Renaissance rhetoric is that there is so little of it.[34] Studies of Vives and Gracián are voluminous, but consideration of their contributions to rhetoric remain scarce. And most other Spanish rhetoricians have received even less attention. Detailed studies of individual theorists and treatises are clearly needed. Beyond this obvious need I would suggest two areas I believe require exploration.

The first area would be studies of a comparative nature — inves-

33. Walter J. Ong, S.J., *Ramus, Method, and the Decay of Dialogue* (Cambridge, Mass., 1958), p. 102. Ong's comment is in reference to Agricola.

34. This situation has improved considerably with the recent publication of two books: Antonio Martí, *La preceptiva retórica española en el Siglo de Oro* (Madrid, 1972); and José Rico Verdu, *La retórica española de los siglos XVI y XVII* (Madrid, 1973).

tigations of the relation between Spanish and other European rhetorics. Most particularly, I have in mind Spanish Ramism. Ong identifies Francisco Sánchez de las Brozas as the earliest disciple of Peter Ramus beyond the borders of France.[35] Other *Ramistas* include Pedro Juan Núñez and Fadrique Furió Ceriol. Furió Ceriol suggests the difficulties of generalizing about Ramism in Spain. He does indeed divide rhetoric into two parts, elocution and disposition, and not, as one would expect, elocution and delivery. The entire course of Spanish Ramism has been little studied and is imperfectly understood.

The second area I would suggest involves studies of the historical consequence of Spanish Renaissance rhetoric. I believe it impossible to understand eighteenth-century Spanish rhetoric without an appreciation of sixteenth- and seventeenth-century theory. The influence of Renaissance theorists proved to be very persistent. Sánchez's *Organum, dialecticum et rhetoricum* (1579) was designated as the text in rhetoric at the University of Salamanca as late as 1771.[36] This dependence on Renaissance theory, I believe, helps explain how a nation that produced neither a Bacon nor a Descartes was nonetheless able to create an "enlightened" theory of rhetoric largely consistent with the theories of England and France. The contributions of Renaissance theorists continued long after the *Siglo de Oro* was over.

Spaniards of the sixteenth and seventeenth centuries produced a prodigious number of rhetorical treatises. Platonists, Aristotelians, Ramists, and eclectics of all kinds yielded a body of theory of great variety and complexity that has remained largely overlooked by the twentieth century. It is perhaps no exaggeration to say that the Spanish Renaissance was indeed a golden age of rhetoric. In 1553 Alfonso García de Matamoros, himself a rhetorician, wrote a defense of Spanish learning — *Pro adserenda hispanorum eruditione*. I would make his conclusion my own: "In view of the foregoing exposition, let the railers cease to speak ill of our most learned Spaniards. In respect to the antiquity of the arts among us, to the abundance of erudite men in our midst, to mental power, or to their application to the interests of mind and soul, the men of our nation have as ancient a record as any, nor have any surpassed us in quality since the days of the Greeks and Romans."[37]

35. *Ramus, Method and the Decay of Dialogue*, p. 305.

36. See "The 1771 Plan of Studies," in George M. Addy, *The Enlightenment in the University of Salamanca* (Durham, N.C., 1966), appendix 1, esp. p. 249.

37. Cited in Otis H. Green, *Spain and the Western Tradition* (Madison, Wisc., 1968), 3.138.

Problems and Trends
in the History of
German Rhetoric to 1500

HELMUT SCHANZE

While scholars of literary history have been talking about a "renaissance of rhetoric" for almost a decade,[1] it might be queried whether the terms *renaissance* and *rhetoric* should not also be associated with one another in an historical sense. In fact, within the context of this renaissance of rhetoric, the phenomenon of rhetoric (if one can speak at all of rhetoric in specific terms) and the problems associated with it are questions that have been raised almost as a matter of course. Nevertheless, it is strange that, judging simply by the number of publications, these questions are almost completely overshadowed by the dominant question of *Barockrhetorik,* and it is just as odd that it is the seventeenth century that is considered rhetorical in literary scholarship, and not the fifteenth or the sixteenth, not even the eighteenth, and least of all the nineteenth.[2] Thus when we speak of a Renaissance rhetoric in Germany, we are always confronted with two problems. The first is concerned with the history of reception, which we find expressed in the phrase *renaissance of rhetoric,* the recollec-

Translated from the German by Winder McConnell.

1. Compare Heinrich F. Plett, *Rhetorik: Kristische Positionen zum Stand der Forschung* (Munich, 1977), p. 9. Also, Helmut Schanze, ed., *Rhetorik: Beiträge zu ihrer Geschichte in Deutschland vom 16. bis 20. Jh.* (Frankfurt, 1974), p. 8.

2. Concerning the problem of *Barock* rhetoric, compare Renate Hildebrandt-Günther, *Rhetorik und deutsche literarische Tradition im 17. Jh.* (Marburg, 1966); Ludwig Fischer, *Gebundene Rede. Dichtung und Rhetorik in der literarischen Theorie des Barock in Deutschland* (Tübingen, 1968); Wilfried Barner, *Barockrhetorik. Untersuchungen zu ihren geschichtlichen Grundlagen* (Tübingen, 1970).

tion of that old art of speech, now forgotten and considered of little importance. Walter Jens, among others, has repeatedly emphasized that the latter has much to do with public freedom and democracy, with the co-determination of an individual within a social structure. The second problem has to do with the obvious lack of abundant research on this historical subject.[3]

I

It cannot be the intention of the present essay to alter completely the current state of research from one moment to the next. Rather, I can only hope here to draw initial attention to the problems associated with the writing of a history of rhetoric in Germany. In short, the scholar who is interested in a renaissance of rhetoric, in an historical sense that does not neglect its significance for our own time, would also have to be interested in rhetoric in the Renaissance. He would have to be concerned with its specific transformations that, from an historical perspective, introduced the "New Age" of public speech with a "Discovery of the World and of Man" (Jacob Burckhardt). A comparison with the history of rhetoric in other West European countries demonstrates, in itself, that the so-called rhetorical century is definitely connected with those developments in the area of rhetoric that occurred around and before the year 1500. Nevertheless, it is a fact that the concept of the literary *Barock*, as well as the historical terms *Reformation* and *Counter-Reformation*, and not the term *Renaissance*, provided the designations employed to describe the Age of Rhetoric in German literary history.

Apart from this, there is the insistence of German Renaissance scholars that we must speak of a "separate [independent] Renaissance" or even a "Germanic Renaissance,"[4] a view that received considerable ideological support in the 1920s and 1930s. This attempt to bring the term *Renaissance* into line with ideology does not make it any easier to arrive at an objective judgment of the concept as it pertains to Germany; the same is true of the term *Rhetoric*, which has been diversely interpreted, as well as misinterpreted and distorted.

3. Cf. Walter Jens, "Rhetorik," in *Reallexikon der deutschen Literaturgeschichte*, 2nd ed. (Berlin, 1971), pp. 432–56.
4. Heinz Otto Burger, *Renaissance, Humanismus, Reformation. Deutsche Literatur im Europäischen Kontext* (Bad Homburg, 1969), p. 45.

As if to underscore what I just stated, rhetoric is treated only marginally (and then, only with regard to the development of rhetoric in France) in the collection of essays edited by August Buck.[5] To be sure, in the same year Heinz Otto Burger published his influential work *Renaissance, Humanismus, Reformation*. In it, Burger postulated a very different theory: the Renaissance in Germany is to be regarded as a renaissance of rhetoric.[6] While his hypothesis is, of course, somewhat exaggerated, it is, in view of the complete neglect of this question particularly in German scholarship, quite justified. Burger's theory makes us acutely aware that neither cultural history nor the history of ideas, nor literary history, can be written without intensive and extensive study in the area of rhetorical theory and practice. The point first made — and often repeated — by Klaus Dockhorn concerning the "ubiquity of rhetoric" proved, in the light of Burger's work, to be extremely fruitful for research conducted in the areas of the Renaissance, humanism, and Reformation.[7] This problem, the neglect of rhetoric in Germany, which has been so loudly deplored in the so-called rhetoric renaissance, is exemplified here in a subject that seems both far removed and also difficult to deal with.

II

Given the vagueness of the term *Renaissance,* a more precise definition of *epoch* must be offered if we are to come to terms with the problem that surrounds the historicity of rhetoric. We must ask ourselves the following question: Can we determine, in the complex of historical processes in the fifteenth century, the events that for the first time (or specifically) in the German-speaking countries allow us to ascertain instances of public speaking and, consequently, define the theory of speech in a new way? Two events must be mentioned in this regard, events that created new dimensions in the history of

5. *Zu Begriff und Problem der Renaissance,* ed. A. Buck, Wege der Forschung (Darmstadt, 1969). The standard literature is given in James E. Engel, *Renaissance, Humanismus, Reformation,* Handbuch der Literaturgeschichte II, 4 (Bern and Munich, 1969).

6. Burger; and Samuel Jaffé: "Rhetoric and Ideology in a New History of German Literature," *The Journal of Modern Philology* 71, no. 3 (1974), 304 – 24.

7. Klaus Dockhorn, *Macht und Wirkung der Rhetorik. Vier Aufsätze zur Ideengeschichte der Vormoderne* (Bad Homburg, 1968).

rhetoric. They are associated with the names of two cities: Mainz and Wittenberg. In 1453 Gutenberg's Latin Bible, the first large printing with movable type, is completed in Mainz, and with it begins the Gutenberg Age of rhetoric. We should note here that, with the invention of printing, public speaking and its written fixation (exemplary, poetical, and practical) undergo an increasing transformation from pure oral delivery (previously the only medium that had been able to reach a wide public) and basically private manuscripts to this new mass medium. Rhetoric thus becomes in a completely new sense literary rhetoric. The printing press expands literary communication in a manner one had hitherto been unable to observe. If the new printings imitate medieval writing practices, one difference should, nevertheless, be noted: the private skills of medieval writers now become public. Both quantitatively and geographically, no "secret" has probably ever been disseminated more quickly than that of printing. In the space of a few years, German printers are to be found throughout Europe. The printing capital of Venice, with its large number of German printers, offers only one, if highly significant, example in the history of rhetoric. Thousands of copies of manuscripts hitherto jealously guarded are now made available to an ever-increasing number of scholars, thanks to the invention of printer's ink. Mainz, Cologne, Strassburg, Basel, and a considerable number of small German towns, particularly in the south, attract scholars and humanists in the German-speaking areas of Europe. The latter wish to participate in the publication of the sources, as well as their own humanistic treatises, speeches in prose and verse — all with the aid of this new medium.[8]

The second great event of the era occurs two generations later. It is inseparably bound up with the first event: in 1517, Luther nails his ninety-five theses to the door of the Schlosskirche in Wittenberg. These theses are immediately circulated in printed form, and thus begins the period of the Reformation in the history of rhetoric. The new Protestant theory and practice of the sermon, the emphasis on rhetoric in Protestant humanism and in its new system of education, have continued to influence education in Europe to the present day. Luther, together with Melanchthon, turns Wittenberg into the center of book-learning, based on a new concept of rhetoric.

8. Cf. Elizabeth L. Eisenstein, *The Printing Press as an Agent of Change,* 2 vols. (Cambridge, 1979).

I cannot deal definitively here with the influence of the printing press or the Reformation on the theory and practice of oration. However, if it is a matter of arriving at a structure for the history of rhetoric in the Renaissance, we can indeed speak of events that created new conditions during that time, conditions that extended beyond the era. For instance, versions of the classical system of rhetoric, as described by Cicero and Quintilian, now became widely available. But the conditions alluded to above hardly allowed the preservation of an uninterrupted tradition of that system. We can delineate the methodological problem with which we shall have to deal now and later as follows: the description of a qualitative jump in the direction of a new rhetoric, complementing the renaissance of the old. Wherever the classical tradition occurs, it is changed as a whole by the new conditions the media have brought about and by the change in the concept of tradition itself, which is indicated by the term *Reformation* and the problems surrounding it. Once again we have a paradox: precisely that time which advocated a return to the authentic sources basically altered the latter in practice and, consequently, also in theory. Adhering to the idea *ad fontes,* the humanist comes out in support not of the old rhetoric but rather of a new rhetoric. At present we can discern three basic trends in this problematic situation. These three trends are intimately bound up with three men who are prominent in the intellectual development of the period about 1500: Desiderius Erasmus of Rotterdam, Martin Luther, and Philipp Melanchthon. Erasmus may be considered a representative of humanism in general, and, at the same time, he is a prime example of the very close relationship that existed between printer and scholar. He is also largely responsible for the development of a literary rhetoric. Luther is a representative of the Reformation associated with his name, of the new Protestant theology, and, simultaneously, of a new, Lutheran rhetoric. And finally Melanchthon, the *Praeceptor Germaniae,* represents a new system of education, the new humanistic school rhetoric. Melanchthon's middle-of-the-road scholarly theology assured the rhetorical tradition a place in the educational system, and it was not challenged until the advent of Romanticism and neo-humanism in Germany about 1800, when the new idealistic philosophy and esthetic began to take its place.

However, the motives for this disdain of rhetoric appear to be rooted in the period before 1500. On more than one occasion, a structural parallel has been drawn between Renaissance and Romanticism, but it is a comparison not well taken because of its lack of a solid foundation.[9] In particular, the notion of the national, intrinsic value of culture, in comparison to foreign forms, was projected back into the period of the Renaissance.

III

> Revixit etiam eloquentia et nostro quidem seculo apud Italos maxime floret. Spero idem in Theutonia futurum, si tu tuique similes continuare et amplecti totis conatibus oratoriam decreveritis.[10]

This excerpt from Enea Silvio's letter to the Teutonic humanist Gregor Heimburg, written in Vienna on January 31, 1449, appears to me a significant early example of what we might term the theory of the *translatio* of the idea of a renaissance of rhetoric from its origins in Italy to the *nationes* in the north and the west. Enea has been called with justification the great initiator of the German Renaissance, and not just because of this letter. His contribution to humanism and to the Renaissance north of the Alps was immense. Nevertheless, Gregor Heimburg, a famous lawyer and representative of the German nobility in many controversies with Rome, and his humanistic circle in Nürnberg, probably had good reason to be skeptical about this theory of the torch, which, lit in Italy, was then passed on to the other nations. They considered themselves and their humanistic endeavors the equal of those in Italy. In his *Germania* (1457), Enea himself appeared to confirm this national self-esteem and the idea that the German Renaissance was parallel to and concurrent with the Italian endeavors:

> Littere quoque et omnium bonarum artium studia apud vos florent, scholas quoque, in quibus et jura et medicina et liberales tradunter artes, in Germania plures urbes habent, ut Colonia Agrippina, Lovanium, Heidelberga, Praga, Erfordia, Vienna, Rostochium, in quibus viri doctissimi claruerunt et nostra quoque etate non inferiores clarent.[11]

Rhetoric and historical truth become identical. Are we dealing here simply with the inflated rhetoric of the great humanist, appealing in

9. Cf. Hermann August Korff, *Humanismus und Romantik* (Leipzig, [1924]).

10. Quoted from the edition by Berthe Widmer, *Enea Silvio Piccolomini. Papst Pius II. Ausgewählte Werke* (Basel, 1960), p. 296.

11. Ibid., p. 374.

flattering terms to the northern money bags in order to make them more inclined to look favorably upon the desperate appeal of the Holy See for financial support? Or is this a document of modern nationalism, replete with considerable historical material? In any case, the argument taken up remained ambiguous, open to interpretation from both sides, inasmuch as it had been invented. Together with the inspiring *Gravamina der deutschen Nation,* drawn up by Martin Mair, a pupil of Gregor Heimburg, in which the German case, that is, the complaints made by the German nobles against the avarice of the clergy, was set down in effective rhetoric, there evolves a genuinely rhetorical controversy which, as the argument continued, eventually led to the Reformation and to Protestantism. The unity of dialectic and rhetorical invention, emphasized in *De inventione dialectica* (1479) by Rudolf Agricola (a *huomo universale,* equally at home in the north and in the south), theoretically transforms the question of a separation of case and rhetoric into a purely rhetorical question. This is a basic reason for the mistrust in Roman rhetoric that prevailed from the outset of the controversy, a controversy that we may describe as entirely intrinsically rhetorical. In the meantime, however, the theory of the light that emanated from Italy, the hypothesis concerning the translation of Renaissance thought from Italy to the north, remained an argument open to dispute. The Germans did appear to be correct in their refutation of the south-north theory, that is, in their assertion of the equality of the German Renaissance. Insofar as this controversy became historically far-reaching, the problem with the new rhetoric from the very beginning lay in the fact that it was drawn into the controversy in the sense of an insincere, flattering speech. It could be defamed as not national, even if the nationalists themselves made use of it. Rhetoric in Germany became an unpopular art — one normally sees this as a development of the eighteenth and nineteenth century — because the opponents of a specific rhetoric disputed its universal validity, even though they themselves assumed this validity in their deliberations. While a clear differentiation must be made between the concept of nation in the sixteenth century and nation in the nineteenth (a false topicality of the Renaissance movement in the nineteenth century has led to myriad false interpretations), we can detect in the discrepancy mentioned above the common ground between the early and later mistrust of a specific rhetoric and early and later nationalism. The idea of a vernacular rhetoric contains within itself this basic contradiction: there is a tendency to break with the old rhetoric; in a strict sense it is (now only) historically understandable. In the same way, the historical sense of the nineteenth century and its alleged hostility towards rhetoric are deducible. The twosidedness of the Renaissance—on the one hand, a return to the classical prototype, on the other, however, the discovery of individual esteem, the conflict between norm and individuality, which, historically, leads to the concept of national—provokes, in the area of literature, an initial *querelle des Anciens et des Modernes*. In the history of rhetoric, that means that the discovery of the old rhetoric has the paradoxical consequence of bringing forth not one, but rather a considerable number of nationally diversified modern rhetorics in the various national languages. That this first *querelle* simultaneously contains political dimensions may be attributed to the specific association of the Holy Roman Empire of the German Nation with Italy, the land in which the Renaissance originated. In principle, however, this development is true for all of Europe in general. Its historical framework is not just the Renaissance of the fifteenth century, for it is a development that can also be traced in the history of rhetoric in the modern age.

IV

Apart from Burger's extensive depiction of the epoch, the history of humanistic rhetoric still lacks, for the most part, a collection of materials assembled on the basis of this criterion. Incunabula research has proved to be of invaluable assistance in this regard. To be sure, there is a problem in organizing incunabula according to a modern system of knowledge. Despite accurate descriptions in excellent bibliographies, it is extremely difficult to gain an overview of material that can be classified primarily as "rhetorical." We must take into account, furthermore, that the standard bibliographies by Hain, Copinger, Panzer, Reichling, and finally the *Gesamtkatalog der Wiegendrucke* (GW), which has now appeared up to the letter F,[12] all evince different stages of research. There is also the problem of those books

12. We can expect to find a considerable amount of material under "Formularien" in vol. 8, soon to appear. With regard to incunabula research see, in particular, Ferdinand Geldner, *Inkunabelkunde. Eine Einführung in die Welt des frühen Buchdrucks,* Elemente des Buch- und Bibliothekswesens 5 (Wiesbaden, 1978). Approximately 43 percent of the incunabula are from German-speaking areas (p. 43). As an individual printing capital, Venice ranked foremost (p. 37). Further, Geldner, *Die deutschen Inkunabeldrucker des XV. Jahrhunderts nach Druckorten,* 1: *Das deutsche Sprachgebiet* (Stuttgart, 1968).

in German libraries destroyed during World War II. Changes of ownership present further problems still: the libraries of earlier scholars and school libraries have been integrated into larger libraries according to modern criteria, and this integration has destroyed their original cohesion. But even a cursory glance through the larger catalogs, as well as the individual catalogs of larger collections, can be extremely helpful, for they provide us with an idea of the lasting influence of a specific rhetoric on early printings. At the same time, we can note the lack of rhetorical information in the last decades of the fifteenth century, and even in the sixteenth, which is much more difficult to catalog.

One of the first printed books on rhetoric (in Latin) is the *Liber novus rhetoricae* by the Cologne printer Johann Koelhoff of Lübeck.[13] It is quite clear that he was not only the printer of the book but also its compiler or author. He asserts that he has not only done the printing but that the work is also *studiose elaborata*. By no means does the printer wish to be considered inferior to the scholar.

From the perspective of quantity alone, the type *rhetorica et formularium teutsch* (easily identifiable as "rhetoric") has a prominent spot in the incunabula catalogs. These early printings were obviously compiled to fulfill the needs of the town clerks: as such, they are in the tradition of the medieval *artes dictandi*. Nevertheless, they completely conform to the humanistic ideals of style and clearly demonstrate the influence of a rediscovered classical rhetoric. This relationship to tradition is emphasized in the *rhetorica* that precedes each section. The format of a question posed by the pupil and the answer proffered by the teacher makes clear the close theoretical relationship between letter-writing and rhetoric (oratory). Basically, however, models for letters are provided that the pupil is encouraged to imitate. In the process, we can differentiate between a group of printers or compilers from Augsburg and a second group from Strassburg. From 1483 alone we know of four different printings. The printers in Augsburg are Anton Sorg and Johann Schönsperger, in Strassburg, Heinrich Knoblochtzer and Johann Prüss.[14] There followed a

13. ARS DICENDI. SIUVE PERORANDI LUCULETISSIME NOTIFICATA PER ME JOHANE KOELHOFF DE LUBECK COLONIE CIVEM STUDIOSE ELABORATA DIE XVI. APRIL. QUI FUIT VIGILIA PASCHE ANNO GRATIE. M. CCCC LXXXIIII FINIT.

14. Cf. Johannes Müller, *Quellenschriften und Geschichte des deutschsprachigen Unterrichts* (Gotha, 1882, rpt. Darmstadt, 1969). Paul Joachimsen (Joachimsohn), "Aus der Vorgeschichte des Formulare und deutsch Rhetorica," *ZfdA* 37 (1893), 24–121. Joachimsen, "Frühhumanismus in Schwaben," *Württ. Vierteljahrshefte für Landesgeschichte* n.s. 5 (1896), 63–126. Ludwig von Rockinger, *Über Formelbücher vom 13. bis zum 16. Jh. als*

large number of new printings and reprints. A *formularium* from the year 1493 may demonstrate the cooperation between town clerk and printer. In it we find the name of the author or compiler specifically mentioned: the town clerk Heinrich Gessler of Freiburg. The printer is Johann Prüss. The title indicates that we are dealing with a vernacular rhetoric: "New practicirt rhetoric und brieff formulary des adels, stetten und lendern des hochtutschen yetzt louffenden stylums und gebruchs."[15].

According to scholars, the first vernacular rhetoric in Germany is the *Spiegel der wahren Rhetorik* of Friedrich Riederer, the city printer in Freiburg. The title indicates its theoretical basis, almost *Barock* in its characteristics: "Uss M. Tulio C. und andern getutscht."[16] Basically, Riederer translates the rhetoric of Herennius, which, at that time, was associated with the name of Cicero. However, this work, too, contains, in the final analysis, a *formularium*. The standardization of letter-writing according to the rules of classical rhetoric (in contemporary, humanistic reception) that had now been achieved contributed more than any other tradition to the subsequent prevalence enjoyed by the humanistic ideal of style. Moreover, the south German cities are centers for the *studia humanitatis*. The historical reconstruction of this network (bond) among the humanists, the town clerks and the printers may well constitute one of the most fruitful topics of research in the area of historical rhetoric.[17] In particular, the name of

rechtsgeschichtliche Quellen (Munich, 1855). Von Rockinger, *Briefsteller und Formelbücher des 11. bis 14. Jh.* Quellen und Erörterungen zur bayerischen und deutschen Geschichte 9.1.2. (Munich, 1863–64). Recently, Hans Joachim Koppitz, "Einige Beobachtungen zum Stil der Prosaversionen mittelhochdeutscher Ritteromane und anderer mittelhochdeutscher Erzählwerke," in *Studien zur deutschen Literatur des Mittelalters*, ed. R. Schützeichel (Bonn, 1979), pp. 561 f. In the catalogue of the Stuttgart Exhibition "Der Frühdruck im deutschen Südwesten 1473–1500," Peter Amelung has proved a nondated print by Johannes Zaimer of Ulm (around 1482) the first printed *Formulare und deutsch Rhetorica*. Peter Amelung, comp. *Der Frühdruck im deutschen Südwesten. Eine Ausstellung der Württembergischen Landesbibliothek Stuttgart. Katalog* (Stuttgart, 1979), 1.116.

15. Title given by Hans Joachim Lange, *Aemulatio Veterum sive de optimo genere discendi* (Bern and Frankfurt, 1974), p. 243. (Copy in the University Library, Freiburg.)

16. Concerning Riederer, see Jaffé; Geldner, *Inkunabeldrucker*, pp. 281 f. The extremely elaborate title page (both artistically and linguistically) is said to have been produced with the assistance of Albrecht Dürer. In 1494 Riederer published the *Rhetorica minor* of Jacob Mennel (Hain 13914).

17. See Gerhart Burger, *Die südwestdeutschen Stadtschreiber im Mittelater* (Böblingen, 1960), particularly p. 242.

Niclas von Wyle, a humanist and town clerk in Esslingen, must be mentioned here. The influence of his *formularia* extends, via his pupil Burkhard Hirschfelder, not only to the printed *formularia* that appeared about 1480 but also to the first German rhetoric published by Riederer. Thus, the south German town clerks became the "vanguard of the Age of the Renaissance"[18] and, at the same time, the vanguard of a new rhetoric. Riederer himself is further extolled by the humanist Jacob Locher Philomusus in his concluding treatise to *Epitoma rhetorices* of 1496. Riederer himself was the printer. The humanist Locher, in his turn, would now complement Riederer's rhetoric in the vernacular *(lingua vernacula)* with a Latin and pure rhetoric *(latina et pura rhetorica)*.[19]

In this manner, a new, vernacular rhetoric came into being with a practical application and completely in accordance with traditional models. It conformed less to traditional theory, which declined in contrast to the *formularia* part (and not just vis-à-vis quantity). Special rhetorics, such as that of epistolers, tend to dominate in contrast to general rhetoric. Oratory, for its part, is confined to sermons and to the court. In practice, specialized models are needed, models of good writing. The art of speaking (oration) becomes an art of writing.

V

There is another development that occurs completely parallel to the aforementioned: the *termini* of rhetorical theory are transformed into those of humanistic poetics. Locher's *Epitoma,* printed by Riederer, is followed immediately (in a volume of collected essays and such held by the Frankfurt Municipal Library) by his *Oratio de studio humanarum disciplinarum et laude poetarum,* which also appeared in 1496. This treatise undoubtedly conforms to the traditional sequence of theory and practice *(Exempel).* It is not simply coincidence, however, that the example finds the praise of the poets. Whether the poetics of the Renaissance are rhetorical, as is generally assumed, or whether poetics does not rather increasingly take over the role of general rhetoric is a question I can only allude to here. There is early

18. Gerhart Burger, *Stadtschreiber,* p. 244.
19. Copy in the Municipal and University Library, Frankfurt. See Kurt Ohly and Vera Sack, *Inkunabelkatalog der Stadt- und Universitätsbibliothek und anderer öffentlicher Sammlungen in Frankfurt am Main* no. 1817 (Frankfurt, 1967).

evidence for the latter theory in the works of Albrecht von Eyb and Peter Luder. Eyb's principal work, *Margarita poetica*, is, in truth, a *summa oratorum omnium*, for all of the poets, historians, and philosophers are included.[20] The folio volume with over three hundred leaves is not only a document of untiring scholarly diligence; it has also been organized in an extremely rational way for easy use. The arrangement of the work and its register make all of the material contained therein readily accessible for use in rhetoric, including poetry. That it was reprinted several times demonstrates how useful it was in practice. The documentation of all accessible "authorities" makes the work valuable as a catalog of the reception not only of classical sources but also of contemporary rhetorical literary practice.

An early partial printing of the *Margarita*, the *Praecepta artis rhetoricae* (written from 1457 to 1459), is attributed by the printers to Enea Silvio, proof of just how much weight "authority" actually carried.[21]

Peter Luder's inaugural lecture in Heidelberg, a *genus poeticum* within the framework of the *ars oratoria*, has a theoretical foundation. Luder sketches a step-by-step development *(gradus)* from the *genus historiale* through the *genus oratorium* to the *genus poeticum*. Some other important authors whose works appeared early in print include Konrad Celtis, the *poeta laureatus*, Jacob Locher, already mentioned above in connection with the Freiburg Circle and Riederer, Heinrich Bebel, and the great Erfurt humanist, Eobanus Hessus. The totality of their publications demonstrates an elaborate concept of rhetorical poetics that may also be designated as general rhetoric. Konrad Celtis's *Ars versificandi et carminum* of 1486 clearly follows the old rhetorical scheme of *partes*, but in the end it emphasizes the emotional power of poetry in much the same way Luder had done. Jacob Locher and Heinrich Bebel regard themselves both as poets and scholars of poetics, as rhetors as well as rhetoricians. Theory and practice are intertwined. Thus, we cannot view Locher's speech in praise of the poets or Bebel's *Ars versificandi* only from the perspective of traditional poetics. Even a work such as Eobanus Hessus's *Scribendorum versuum maxime compendiosa ratio* is aimed at rhetorical practice.[22] At this point the optics of modern literary history, which is only

20. GW 9529–9537, particularly GW 9530.
21. GW 9542–9543 (1488 ff.). From Albrecht and Enea Silvio Piccolomini to a "literary relationship," see Burger, *Renaissance, Humanismus, Reformation*, pp. 121 f.
22. For titles, see Lange, *Aemulatio Veterum*, pp. 249 ff.

concerned with identifying poetic examples, dissolves the basic unity of poetry and rhetoric in the Renaissance. In a general rhetoric, for which Luder's concept may serve as an example, prose and verse have their assigned place. The high regard for poetry in contrast to oratory does not, then, signify an abandoning of the rhetorical, theoretical framework. Within the *gradus*, the relationship to the rhetorical theory of styles remains recognizable. If one understands the entire theoretical effort of the humanists to develop well-formed, effective figures of speech as an attempt to arrive at a general rhetoric, which, in the same sense, can be regarded as rhetorical poetics, then trends can be discerned here that, if judged by the classical canon of rules, will lead to the dissolution of this system.

Most apparent of all is a tendency to reduce the rhetorical system to individual *partes*. This trend towards dissolution has recently been demonstrated quite convincingly by Hans Joachim Lange in his dissertation *Aemulatio veterum sive de optimo genere dicendi*.[23] Within the rhetorical-poetical system of the sixteenth and seventeenth century, Lange detects an inclination to increasingly neglect *inventio* in contrast to *elocutio*. Whether he has been successful in his attempt to identify this trend as early *Barock* or manneristic remains to be seen. Since we can just as easily detect a neglect of *actio* and *memoria*, while, on the other hand, precisely *memoria* and *inventio* find expression in highly specialized manuals (for example, in philosophical works), it is only *actio* that has been basically phased out. As a result of Lange's findings we can ascertain that before the time of Peter Ramus rhetoric had, in fact, already been reduced to the rhetoric of elocution. *Memoria* and *inventio* are discussed under other headings. The trend towards elocutionary rhetoric and the disappearance of *actio* can be explained by the change in medial paradigma already alluded to above. The spoken word (oration) is confined to sermons or, in humanistic circles, to lectures. In a broad sense, public speaking before a large but varied public becomes possible in a revolutionary new way through the assistance of printing. There now begins an extensive process of reflection on the efficacy of linguistic media as they have been traditionally gathered together in the *elocutio*. The nonverbal media — gestures, mimicry — remain pertinent, to be sure, for the sermon, lecture, and theater. They are to be disregarded in the transformation of oral rhetoric into literary rhetoric, that is, the rhetoric of the printed word. We may, therefore, propose the theory that the

23. Ibid., particularly pp. 35 – 55.

trend towards elocutionary rhetoric in the early sixteenth century can be explained as an expression of the "Gutenberg Age" of rhetoric. The negative confirmation of this theory may be sought in our own times and in the new mass media: it is not simply coincidence that, in an age of visual and auditive media, of film and television, the nonverbal means of communication have again been accorded considerable attention, even in a theoretical sense. We note that there is, simultaneously, a crisis in literary rhetoric — in printed poetics.

VI

The amalgamation of poetics and rhetoric, and the specialization and the reduction of rhetoric, are undertaken by the humanists of the fifteenth and sixteenth centuries, not least of all because of the fascination of a diverse public that could now be reached by the printed book. It is not only because he was the undisputed leader of the humanists that we can sum up this new development under the name of Erasmus of Rotterdam, but also because, through his publications and activities, he serves as a paradigm for this development. Erasmus is not a rhetorical systematizer, and his most theoretical work, *De ratione studii,* is not a rhetoric, although it has a clear basis in rhetoric. With his widely known manual, *De duplici copia rerum et verborum,* Erasmus established the model for a specialized rhetoric, and his formula *res et verba* made a basic systematization of the classical system fruitful for the educational system and the schools in the modern age. *De duplici copia* was reprinted over two hundred times and is one of the most widely circulated books of the Renaissance.

Rhetoric also forms the basis of his masterpiece, the edition of the New Testament (*Novum Testamentum Graece* of 1516). Here, as well, we are not dealing specifically with rhetoric, but rather with practical scholarship inspired by eloquence and the theory of eloquence. A significant example may serve to clarify this point. Erasmus suggests for 1 John 1: "In principio erat sermo."[24] What he means by this is the spoken ("living") word, not just the "word" alone, but also the "thing," in the double unity of *res* and *verba* of rhetoric. The influence of rhetorical theory thus reaches into the very heart of Erasmus's theology; it is a theology that would be inconceivable without rhetoric. It

24. See C. L. A. Jarrot, "Erasmus. In principio erat sermo. A controversial translation," *Studies in Philology* 61 (1964), 35 ff.

represents furthermore a milestone in the reevaluation of rhetoric about the year 1800.

We can say that the guild of *oratores et poetae,* from time to time quite justifiably regarded as disreputable and boastful, gains in the person of Erasmus a representative of European stature. His literary rhetoric (in the broad sense of the word *literary*) encompasses the entire spectrum of education, including theology. That the very basis of Erasmus's thought is to be found in a specifically humanistic reception of rhetoric that, as printed literature and not as public oratory, has retained its effectiveness to the present also signifies a clear shift in the importance of the classical system, if not the subsequent development of a new rhetoric.

VII

We shall now turn our attention to a new, completely different rhetoric that is inspired by a radically theological trend and that, while it may be quite inconceivable without literary rhetoric, is, nonetheless, its counter-model. Among the most dramatic aspects of recent research are the views that with the year 1517 a new chapter begins in the history of rhetoric and that the Reformation could have anything at all to do with rhetoric. At the same time, we have here the key to the problem connected with the writing of a history of rhetoric in Germany. Klaus Dockhorn, Birgit Stolt, and Heinz Otto Burger have demonstrated the uniqueness of Luther's rhetoric. First of all, they have clearly shown that at the core of Lutheran theology, in the concept of faith *(fides),* the corresponding concept of rhetoric has been assimilated and productively transformed. Second, Klaus Dockhorn and Birgit Stolt in particular have proved that Luther's concept of the Holy Ghost corresponds to the idea of a universal orator. Third, they have demonstrated that the Lutheran apothegm "verbum facit fides" is genuinely rhetorical in nature. Finally, Heinz Otto Burger, in particular, has pointed to the rhetorical character of the theory and practice of Luther's translation of the Bible.[25] Never-

25. Birgit Stolt, *Studien zu Luthers Freiheitstraktat mit besonderer Berücksichtigung der lateinischen und deutschen Fassung zueinander und der Stilmittel der Rhetorik* (Stockholm, 1969). And her "Docere, delectare und movere bei Luther. Analysiert anhand der Predigt, 'dass man Kinder zur Schulen halten solle,'" *Deutsche Vierteljahrsschrift* 44 (1970), 433–75. Klaus Dockhorn, "Rhetorica movet. Protestantischer Humanismus

theless, the fundamental difference, when compared as well to the rhetorical theology of Erasmus, remains clear: Luther's rhetoric is aimed at a divine orator, not a human or humanistic one. Seen from this perspective, a *rhetorica contra rhetores* can be discerned in Luther's rhetoric. Erasmus formulated a theory of human understanding. Luther's basis is the *credo*, with regard to the divine word. In his essay "Protestantischer Humanismus und karolingische Renaissance," Klaus Dockhorn expresses quite pointedly that Protestantism under Luther and Melanchthon chose rhetoric as anthropology and that it was precisely in this point that Protestantism differed from Catholicism, which continued to employ arguments in conformity with scholastic dialectic.[26] There is substantial evidence to support this theory in the extensive collection of sources known as the *Corpus Reformatorum*. Rhetoric occupies a major place in the theory and practice of the sermon as well as in the Protestant concept of the school. Until the Jesuits (who also employ identical rhetorical arguments, something I cannot pursue in detail here) appear in the second half of the sixteenth century, rhetoric is clearly prominent. Thus, Lutheran rhetoric (discernible even among his opponents) can be regarded as the second, decisive trend in the history of Renaissance rhetoric. This trend also does not leave the classical system untouched but rather tends to transform it often to the point where it is no longer recognizable. Here I have in mind the work of Reinhard Breymayer on the topic of "pietistic rhetoric." In this instance, the rhetorical principle of the *dissimulatio artis* may have led to an apparent hostility towards rhetoric.

VIII

If the great spiritual leaders of the period around and after 1500 are Erasmus and Luther, we would not be doing justice to the person of Philipp Melanchthon, especially in a history of rhetoric, if we were to describe his work as merely ancillary or as mediating. We are not only obliged to him for the basic theoretical formulation of the new rhetoric, in three different versions,[27] the influence of which extends

und karolingische Renaissance," in *Rhetorik*, ed. Helmut Schanze, pp. 17–42. Heinz Otto Burger, "Luther als Ereignis der Literaturgeschichte," in his *Dasein heisst eine Rolle spielen* (Munich, 1963), pp. 56–74.

26. Dockhorn, "Rhetorica movet," p. 42.

27. *De rhetorica*, 1.3 (1519), *Institutiones rhet.* (1521), *Elementorum rhetor.* 1.2 (1531).

far beyond the "occasionalism" of poets and rhetoricians, but also for his formulation and organization of the extensive Protestant system of education, within the framework of which the new rhetoric was accorded a decisive role.

Nor should we underestimate his ability to integrate the various trends prevalent about 1500. Humanistic scholarship, Luther's concept of faith and, last but not least, even the attempt to differentiate between (and, simultaneously, reintegrate) dialectic and rhetoric, all of these have a place within the program of education proposed by the *Praeceptor Germaniae* in his reformation of the university and higher education. The schools of "old" humanism, following Melanchthon, accord the most importance to a linguistic-literary education based on the principles of rhetoric. It is not until the advent of neo-humanism in Germany in the nineteenth century that we have a break with tradition. The oral side of this educational process, Melanchthon's own idea of the scholar endowed with considerable magnetism, who is highly effective among the public, would also play a notable role. The university in Wittenberg has become exemplary through the person of the great *praeceptor* and the manner of developing personal relationships between teachers and students. The great number of teachers (in the broadest sense of the word) who, on the basis of personal acquaintanceship, chose Melanchthon as a model for their own professional training is in itself astounding and sets up an oral tradition beside the written one.[28]

Such a revolutionary effect can hardly be detected at first glance in the writings of the reformer himself. His works, vis-à-vis rhetoric, appear to be almost traditional, scholastic. But the concept of an integration of philosophical dialectic with rhetorical *inventio*, which Melanchthon advocates through his entire work, is, in fact, revolutionary. *Inventio* is consciously subordinated to the philosophical claim of "searching for truth" in the three versions of the *Rhetorica*. One may question whether this concept was successful for rhetoric specifically, for as *inventio* became more and more a philosophical discipline in school tradition, the core of rhetoric instruction became centered in *elocutio*. In this manner, the humanistic trend toward elocutionary rhetoric was promoted, albeit counter to Melanchthon's intention to integrate.

Almost the same can be said of Melanchthon's introduction of a

28. See Friedrich Paulsen, *Geschichte des gelehrten Unterrichts,* 2nd. ed. (Leipzig, 1896), pp. 257 ff.

separate homiletic genre into the rhetorical system (*genus didascalicon*). What began as an attempt at integration also ended here in specialization, a separate theory of homiletics. The parallel drawn by the great Jesuit Caussin between holy and human rhetoric, based on an even-numbered *genera* model, has likewise remained an exception in the separate development of homiletics.[29]

IX

Erasmus, Luther, Melanchthon: the principal developments in the history of rhetoric in the sixteenth century can be linked to their names. The most important authors refer to the works of these three or are in direct, and even personal, contact with them. The large number of rhetorics for use in schools and the abundance of homiletics and *formularia* are hard to imagine without the educational reform brought about by humanism and the Reformation. In Burger's work, Renaissance, humanism, and Reformation not only represent a specific expanse of time; they also tend to be interlocked with each other, and this makes it problematical to speak of a German Renaissance. The end of this trend towards integration occurs during the Thirty Years War (1618 – 1648) and is perceived as a break with tradition. However, the educational system established by the Counter-Reformation clearly marks the beginning of a new era in the middle of the sixteenth century. I cannot deal here with the manner in which this system differed from the "Wittenbergian" or with the analogies it displayed to the latter, although, from the perspective of the history of rhetoric, they are of considerable interest. In the first half of the sixteenth century, there come into being standard school rhetorics that were still known far into the seventeenth and, to some degree, even in the eighteenth century. Above all, the basic works were constantly supplied with commentary and held ready for use in the schools. I should mention here Murmelius (1510), Christoph Bucoldianus (1535), Hegendorff (1534), David Chytraeus (1558),[30] as well as Kaspar Goldtwurm and his great German rhetoric of 1545, and, finally, the great pedagogue Johannes Sturm from

29. See Franz Günther Sieveke, "Eloquentia sacra: Zur Predigttheorie des Nicolaus Caussinus S. J.," in *Rhetorik*, ed. Schanze, pp. 43 – 68.

30. Titles in Lange as well as in Dieter Breuer and Günther Kopsch, "Rhetoriklehrbücher des 16. bis 20. Jh.," in *Rhetorik*, ed. Schanze, pp. 222 ff.

Schleiden in the Eifel region,[31] who founded in Strassburg his new model of a grammar school based on the principles of rhetoric. The so-called school rhetoric still needs to be investigated in more detail. Thousands of schoolbooks, often with what appeared to be the same titles and frequently distributed under the name of an "authority," abbreviated collections or anthologies, would have to be examined. We can count on the system appearing very much in line with tradition and completely stable. It would, therefore, be necessary to pay close attention to the slightest difference. What an individual author selects from the works of Aristotle and Cicero, the "auctor ad Herennium," for use in the schools and also the way in which he judges certain texts could be of importance here. Lange has undertaken just such a pedantic task and has achieved considerable success utilizing a large body of material, even if it has been collected more or less at random.[32] The reader is directed to this work for individual examples.

One aspect of research that might be pursued would deal with the consequences of an integration of the homiletic genre into the Quintilian system. We might also take a look at the relationship of epistolography to rhetoric. The connection between poetics and rhetoric — a favorite topic of scholars — could, in many respects, be redefined.

All in all we may speak of a new rhetoric in the period beginning about 1500, despite the presence of school rhetoric, which continued to adhere to traditional formulae. We must dispute the view (which the humanists themselves tended to support through their faith in the classical system) that the innovators, in contrast to the old masters, were not capable of achieving any new development vis-à-vis the rhetorical system. This is a theory that has been in vogue for some time and has contributed to the defamation of the rhetorical system by its suggestion that the system was incapable of integrating new linguistic developments. The rather pretentious work *Allgemeine Theorie der schönen Künste,* by the Swiss Johann Georg Sulzer, depicts the dissolution of a now old-fashioned school rhetoric. In the article entitled "Rhetoric," we find a statement to the effect that the innovators had left the theory of this art "at approximately that point where the old masters had left off." The volume in question appeared in

31. On Sturm, see Paulsen, *Geschichte des gelehrten Unterrichts,* pp. 284 ff.
32. Lange, *Aemulatio Veterum,* particularly the bibliography, pp. 217 ff.

1794 — at a time when the theory of Romanticism began to constitute itself as a new rhetoric.[33]

We have now arrived at the starting-point of our deliberations. When we associate the three main developments in rhetoric in the fifteenth century with Erasmus, Luther, and Melanchthon, we intend to show a vital link with tradition, not a stagnant system of Renaissance rhetoric. It must be remembered that the invention of the printing press could not remain without consequence for the system of rhetoric. We believe we have demonstrated a development to literary rhetoric. It must also be noted that the Lutheran Reformation had to contribute to a new rhetoric. Finally, let us not forget that the educational system based on new and old rhetoric inaugurated by Melanchthon was used consistently for a number of centuries in both German and non-German schools.

Nevertheless, we should not underestimate, in this regard, those counterforces that show an (apparently) hostile tendency towards rhetoric. In the rhetoric of Erasmus, this hostility can be witnessed in the trend towards specialization, the tendency to develop a pure literary rhetoric, an isolated elocutionary rhetoric. Lutheran rhetoric employs the classical system in a radically unhumanistic way, as an *ancilla theologiae*. Homiletics alone is left as residue. Finally, Melanchthon's school rhetoric leads to petrification, which makes rhetoric at the end of the eighteenth century in Germany almost obsolete.

Furthermore, the three basic developments that occurred around 1500 in the history of rhetoric cannot be regarded as isolated from one another. Melanchthon was not alone in his efforts to achieve an integration; in the process he created a tradition of his own. In the mid-sixteenth century, similar efforts were undertaken by the school of Johannes Sturm and, apparently in a countereffort, by the educational system established by the Jesuits.

The aims of Sturm's school were threefold: wisdom, eloquence, faith — "Sapiens ac aloquens pietas," or, as Friedrich Paulsen puts it, "Expertise and the gift for presentation in the service of the new evangelical faith."[34] Eloquence, as the standard aim of the school, is pursued in the three formal disciplines: grammar, dialectics, and rhetoric. Sturm thus developed a curriculum whose elements were

33. See Helmut Schanze, "Romantik und Rhetorik. Rhetorische Komponenten der Literaturprogrammatik um 1800," in *Rhetorik*, ed. Schanze, pp. 126–44.

34. See Paulsen, *Geschichte des gelehrten Unterrichts*, p. 284.

by no means arbitrary but which rather culminate in practical rhetoric, in the effective lecture.

I have attempted to demonstrate that Renaissance rhetoric represents a complicated subject but also one that is worth devoting further research to. Despite the four generations of scholarship that have transpired since Jacob Burckhardt made his inspiring statement concerning the discovery of the world and of man, there is still a considerable gap in the history of rhetoric itself. From the perspective of research, this subject ought to be defined, to begin with, as a separate entity, not merely as a part of the history of education or religion. In the study of literary history, the dominant role played by so-called *Barock* scholarship has been chiefly responsible for making us aware of the phenomenon of Renaissance rhetoric. In the final analysis, however, it has treated the latter only as a precursor of *Barock* poetics. Once again, the difficulty that is traditionally associated with the concept of a Renaissance in Germany becomes apparent in the historical details I have provided. Not least of all we find mirrored here the historical experience of a cleavage in faith and a devastating war that, fought on the territory of the old Reich ("Empire"), left as its legacy a distorted consciousness of tradition. This historical experience occurred during a change in era — something unusual for international research — in the stark contrast between Renaissance and *Barock,* which constituted the great dividing line about the year 1600.

Renaissance Commentators on Ciceronian Rhetoric

JOHN O. WARD

In this essay I want to give some idea of the nature and scope of Renaissance commentaries on the *Rhetorica*[1] of Cicero, and to make a few remarks about the significance of the genre in the wider perspective of the Western rhetorical tradition.

The identifying characteristic of Renaissance humanism — itself the keynote of Renaissance culture — is currently defined as the pursuit of eloquence.[2] The sustaining didactic curriculum behind this pursuit of eloquence was classical rhetorical theory, primarily as outlined in the anonymous classical treatise the *Rhetorica ad Herennium*. The centrality, in Renaissance culture, therefore, of the commentaries and glosses on Cicero's *Rhetorica* — and until the sixteenth cen-

---

1. By the term *Rhetorica* here I mean not only the entire Ciceronian rhetorical canon of seven works and the speeches but also the pseudo-Ciceronian *Rhetorica ad Herennium* and the *Institutio oratoria* of Quintilian, which are in the same tradition.

2. W. J. Bouwsma, *The Culture of Renaissance Humanism* (American Historical Association Pamphlet, 1973), p. 9; Bouwsma, "Changing Assumptions in Later Renaissance Culture," *Viator* 7 (1976), 421 – 40; Bouwsma, "The Renaissance and the Drama of Western History," *American Historical Review* 84 (1979), 1 – 15; Hannah H. Gray, "Renaissance Humanism: the Pursuit of Eloquence," in *Renaissance Essays from the Journal of the History of Ideas,* eds. Paul Oskar Kristeller and P. P. Wiener (New York, 1968), pp. 199 – 216; Kristeller, *Renaissance Thought* (New York, 1961, rpt. 1965), esp. p. 11; Nancy Struever, *The Language of History in the Renaissance: Rhetoric and Historical Consciousness in Florentine Humanism* (Princeton, N.J., 1970); Jerrold E. Seigel, *Rhetoric and Philosophy in Renaissance Humanism: the union of eloquence and wisdom, Petrarch to Valla* (Princeton, 1968) but see especially Struever's review of Seigel in *History and Theory* 11 (1972), 64 – 74; and Charles Trinkaus, "Humanism, Religion, Society: concepts and motivations of some recent studies," *Renaissance Quarterly* 29 (1976), 676 – 713.

tury it was still perfectly permissible to regard the *Ad Herennium* as a work of Cicero—hangs on the centrality of rhetoric in that culture. This latter is tied, in turn, to the growth of urban patterns of life and of cultural forms and attitudes appropriate to those patterns. Among such forms and attitudes one might mention the *ars notaria, dictamen,* law, the study of classical Latin literature, and a closer appreciation of some features of the classical ethos and past than had prevailed in the presumably less urban culture of the prior, medieval period.

Under the current reading of Medieval-Renaissance cultural change, therefore, we might expect to find the principal theses on which that reading is based supported by the evidence of the commentaries on the *De inventione* and *Ad Herennium,* the two central texts in both medieval and Renaissance rhetorical study, and, arguably, the most widely used classical Latin writings of all time. We might expect to find, from the time of *pre-umanesimo* onwards, a greater attention paid to the strict understanding of the classical doctrine of rhetoric and a broader concern with its application in contemporary society.[3] Commentaries on the two texts can be expected to have provided the main academic fuel and impetus for the broader study of classical culture and more comprehensive statements of dictaminal and notarial usage.[4] We might expect some shift of attention from the two texts mentioned, particularly the incomplete and inventionally oriented *De inventione,* in favor of the subtler treatment of the *ars rhetorica* found in such writings as Cicero's *De oratore* or Quintilian's *Institutio oratoria,* or in favor of intensified study of Cicero's

---

3. Gray, p. 202.

4. Helene Wieruszowski, *Politics and Culture in Medieval Spain* (Rome, 1971), p. 462, speaking of the Bolognese professor Jacques de Dinant. Note also the close connection between lecturing on the *Ad Her.* and *dictamen* in the teaching careers of Giovanni di Bonandrea and Bartolinus de Benincasa: see J. R. Banker, "Giovanni di Bonandrea and Civic Values in the Context of the Italian Rhetorical Tradition," *Manuscripta* 18 (1974), 3–20, and "The *ars dictaminis* and Rhetorical Textbooks at the Bolognese University in the Fourteenth Century," *Medievalia et Humanistica* n.s. 5 (1974), 153–68; S. M. J. Karaus, "Selections from the commentary of Bartolinus de Benincasa de Canulo on the *Rhetorica ad Herennium*" (Ph.D. diss., Columbia University, 1970). I discuss the links between *dictamen* and classical rhetoric in John O. Ward, "*Artificiosa eloquentia* in the Middle Ages" (Ph.D. diss., University of Toronto, 1972), 1.380 ff. Note also the remarks by Brunetto Latini, *Tresor,* ed. Francesco Maggini (Florence, 1968), p. 5: "the *rector* is he who teaches the science according to the rules and commandments of the art; the orator is he who, having learned the art, uses it in speaking and writing (*dire, dittare*) on questions posed *si come sono li buoni parlatori e dittatori, si come fue maestro Piero dalle Vigne.*" Manuscripts containing the *Ad Herennium* with dictaminal materials

speeches themselves,[5] or even in favor of newly composed humanist rhetorical treatises; equally, however, we might expect the *Ad Herennium* and its commentaries to have remained the main didactic text during the Renaissance, partly because academic concerns are always conservative and partly because no more suitable basic manual of the art of rhetoric, it might be argued, has been written than the anonymous classical treatise itself.

These expectations, which seem to me to arise from any reasonably wide reading of contemporary scholarship on the nature of Renaissance culture, require some preliminary examination of the evidence, and it may be convenient to provide this examination under the following heads:

I. The quantitative survival of Renaissance commentaries and glosses on the *De inventione* and the *Ad Herennium*.

II. The above considered in relation to the survival of commentaries and glosses on other Ciceronian rhetorical works and his speeches.

III. The survival of *De inventione* and *Ad Herennium* glosses and commentaries in relation to the currency of the *rhetores latini minores*, Quintilian's *Institutes*, and classical or late classical Greek rhetorical treatises.

IV. The survival of the "Ciceronian" basic manuals considered in relation to the currency of original Renaissance rhetorical manuals, for example, the *Rhetoricorum libri quinque* of George of Trebizond.[6]

I conclude this survey with some initial considerations of the implications of the commentary evidence.

I

The following broad stages in the development of commentation can already be discerned from the rather large number of commentaries that have so far come to light:

---

are common. Bologna Univ. Bibl. 2461 and Wolfenbüttel Herzog-August-Bibl. 4.15 Auf. 4to, for example, both contain glossed texts of the *Ad Herennium* and dictaminal treatises by Giovanni di Bonandrea.

5. Gray, for example (p. 205), notes humanist emphasis on the *Pro Archia*.

6. On which, see John Monfasani, *George of Trebizond: A Biography and a Study of His Rhetoric and Logic* (Leiden, 1976).

The "pre-Bartolinus" or "Alanus" stage, so-called from the currency of an *Ad Herennium* gloss ascribed in some manuscripts to "Alanus" (of Lille?), written perhaps around the turn of the twelfth and thirteenth centuries and remaining in vogue until the commentary of Bartolinus de Benincasa de Canulo, who taught rhetoric at the *studium* of Bologna in the first half of the fourteenth century.

The "Bartolinus" stage, extending from the commentary of Bartolinus, which has come down to use in three versions, to the commentary of Guarino da Verona, compiled from the latter's lectures in the second quarter of the fifteenth century.

The "Guarino" stage, extending from the currency of *reportationes* of Guarino's lectures until the replacement of the unacknowledged printed version of his commentary by the commentaries of Jerome Capiduro, Francesco Maturanzio, and Antonio Mancinelli in the last decade of the fifteenth century.

The period of currency of commentaries by the last three scholars, which lasted until the mid-sixteenth century, when further sets of *scholiae*, commentaries, and illustrative notes of a more recognizably modern academic flavor began to dominate in the printed texts of Cicero's rhetorical works.

Some remarks and amplification of this schema follow. Bartolinus de Benincasa de Canulo, whose rhetorical teaching has been subjected to careful study by Mrs. Sandra Wertis,[7] was the *repetitor* and *discipulus* of his master, Giovanni di Bonandrea, who seems to have begun teaching *dictamen* and lecturing on the *Ad Herennium* in the Bologna studium in 1303.[8] Upon the latter's death in 1321, Bartolinus was appointed to the chair of rhetoric, where he lectured on the *Ad Herennium* and the *Brief Introduction to Dictamen* of Giovanni, his erstwhile master. There are fifteen fifteenth-century manuscripts of Bartolinus's lectures on the *Ad Herennium*, three of the early version, eight of the later (longer) version, three of a version made up from both the early and late versions, and one containing what seems to be a very early version of the lectures. Surprisingly, perhaps, only three

---

7. See Karaus, "Selections."

8. Banker, Wertis and references cited therein. Giovanni's *Ad Her.* lectures have not yet been identified. See Remigio Sabbadini, *Le Scoperte dei codici latini e greci ne' secoli XIV e XV,* 2 vols. (Florence, 1905–1914), 2.150–51 on early Bolognese rhetorical teaching.

manuscripts have come to light that could date from the fourteenth century: one of the early version, one of the late version, and one of the very early version.[9] Mrs. Wertis and Professor Monfasani cite a 1403 letter of Antonio da Romagna to Pietro Marcello recommending the study of Victorinus or Bartolinus or any other "plain and useful" interpreter of the *Rhetorics* of Cicero.[10] Clearly, by that stage, both the *Ad Herennium* and the *De inventione* were being recommended for rhetorical study, and the most convenient glosses were those of Victorinus and Bartolinus. We may suppose that the dominance of the Bartolinus gloss continued at least until the 1430s, for both Wertis and Monfasani cite George of Trebizond as saying, in his *Five Books of Rhetoric,* which appeared in 1433 – 1434, that in his day

> almost no one of the good arts is held in such abject contempt as oratory: despite the plentiful and elegant books on the subject left behind by our ancestors, Greek as well as Latin, few or none are discovered by our own abandoned times. . . . I think that if posterity was not forced by those who teach rhetoric to transcribe the books of Bartolinus, Alanus and others of this kind — and I know not what their utility is — then the works of good authors would be discovered in place of these triflers, or at least, the hearers, not imbued by these idiocies, might apply more readily their untutored minds to the doctrines of humanity, than which nothing more useful or worthy of man has been assigned by the father of men and the Gods.[11]

This is a curious statement, though by no means the first attempt at self-promotion by denigration of Ciceronian rhetoric.[12] George of Trebizond was a notoriously difficult though formidable intellec-

9. These details will appear in Wertis, with, where relevant, my own additions to the manuscript survival of Bartolinus. Two manuscripts of Bartolinus have subsequently come to light, independently identified by myself and Professor Kristeller: Kremsmünster 147 s.XV and Sankt Paul im Lavanttal Stifsbibl. Codd. Hospit. 137 s.XV. In the case of my own identification, I would like to acknowledge here the help and hospitality of Donald Yates and Julius Plante of the Hill Monastic Microfilm Library, St. Johns University, Collegeville, Minnesota, on the occasion of my visit there in May 1979 and thereafter by letter.

10. Monfasani, pp. 263 – 64.

11. Ibid., p. 71.

12. The example of Buoncompagno comes to mind: *Rhetorica Novissima*, ed. A. Gaudenzi (Bologna, 1892), p. 252. Correspondingly, it is to be noted that Guarino's interest in Greek may well have been sufficiently casual as to encourage Trebizond to stress Hellenistic rhetoric as a way of making his name. On Guarino's Greek interests see Ian Thomson, "Some notes on the contents of Guarino's library," *Renaissance Quarterly* 29 (1976), 169 – 77.

tual, and his *Five Books of Rhetoric* did introduce an important strain of Greek rhetoric into the humanist curriculum — in particular, the works of Hermogenes of Tarsus. They also developed particular sections of the curriculum, for example argumentation.[13] However, underneath the bravura, it is clear that the texts on which Bartolinus and Alanus lectured play no small role in George's rhetoric.[14] In fact, the *constitutio negotialis,* which more sophisticated Latin scholarship, following the lead of the author of the *Ad Herennium,* had succeeded in abolishing from the lecture curriculum, is resurrected by George from Hermogenes and the *De inventione.*[15]

That George refers to Alanus and Bartolinus in the same breath is no surprise. Alanus continued to be consulted after Bartolinus's commentary became current, but his primacy was definitely supplanted. That George does not refer to the lectures of Guarino is evidence — according to Monfasani — that Guarino's lectures were not yet available in circulated form. This is probably the case, although George's antipathy towards Guarino was notorious.[16] Guarino's formal presentation of a course of rhetoric dates, it would seem, only from 1419 (Verona). This phase of his life ended in 1429 with his remove to Ferrara, where, from 1436 to 1460, he held a municipal chair of rhetoric. It is from his teaching in this period, apparently, that our *recollectae* of his *Ad Herennium* lectures derive, although all are the work of his students or his son Battista, who was professor of rhetoric at Bologna 1455 – 1457 and thereafter followed his father's footsteps at Ferrara, where, upon the latter's death in 1460, he succeeded to the chair of rhetoric.[17] According to LaRusso, "the pu-

13. Monfasani, pp. 271 ff.

14. Ibid., pp. 272 ff., 279 – 80, 284, 288 – 89.

15. Ibid., pp. 274, 289. The *De inventione,* according to Professor Monfasani, George "incorporates almost totally."

16. Ibid., pp. 29 ff.

17. See Union Académique Internationale, *Catalogus Translationum et Commentariorum: Medieval and Renaissance Latin Translations and Commentaries,* eds. F. E. Cranz and Paul Oskar Kristeller, 1 (Washington, 1960), 2 (Washington, 1971), 3 (Washington, 1976) (hereafter cited as *CTC*), 1.207 and 257; Monfasani, pp. 7 ff. and index under "Guarino." Sabbadini, *La scuola e gli Studi di Guarino Guarini Veronese* (Catania, 1896), writes: "la commentò *(Ad Her.)* e la prese a tema di quattro corsi almeno, uno a Verona e tre a Ferrara, de quali ci sono rimaste le prolusioni" (p. 62). The earliest (?) recension of Guarino's commentary was compiled in 1445 by a student and approved by the master (Sabbadini, p. 93). See also M. E. Cosenza, *Biographical and Bibliographical Dictionary of the Italian Humanists and of the world of classical scholarship in Italy 1300 – 1800,* 2nd rev. ed., 6 vols. (Boston, 1962 – 1967), 5.870.

pils of Guarino rapidly learned that the *Ad Herennium* was the supreme authority in Rhetoric."[18]

Guarino's celebrity was neither immediate nor universal, although it was considerable. Copies of Bartolinus's gloss were being made as late as the 1450s,[19] and there is considerable evidence of his popularity in the citations of his name in surviving glosses and glossed texts of the *Ad Herennium.*[20] Guarino's gloss has come down to us in some eighteen manuscripts, comprising at least three main versions,[21] and certain other manuscripts conflate his gloss with older material.[22] In addition, one of the versions was stripped of signs of authorship and included in early printed editions of the *Ad Herennium* as the marginal gloss.

Before providing some indication of the printed glosses on the *De inventione* and *Ad Herennium,* we should give an idea of the survival of manuscript commentaries and glosses within the above tradition. The earliest major Renaissance *Ad Herennium* gloss, it would seem, is known by its incipit as *Plena et perfecta.* It is decidedly in the Alanus tradition and is known from a manuscript written in 1342, two others of the fourteenth century, and one owned by Gasparino Barzizza.[23] The commentary shows close links with the Perugia and Cremona versions of the "Alanus" gloss. However, in our manuscripts of the third version of Bartolinus's commentary,[24] which were apparently

18. Dominic A. LaRusso, "Rhetorical Education: Italy 1300–1450," *Western Speech* 4 (1960), 217.

19. 1436, 1456, 1467 are some representative dates found in the manuscripts. MS Vat. Ottob. lat, 1438 contains an *oratio panegyrica ad Alphonsum regem* dated 1443 on fols. 1–5ᵛ and then a copy of Bartolinus's gloss. It was written by Peter de Damiano, a student in rhetoric under Master "Gasparinus de Pergamo" and in the same manuscript is another version of a portion of Bartolinus's commentary copied in 1433 "per me Lucam Melegnyanum de Fogia."

20. The following manuscripts at least contain reference to or uses of Bartolinus: Oxford Bod. Canon. Misc. 7, Perugia Bibl. Com. 584 (H.70), Seville Bibl. Cap.y Col. 83–8–16, Vat. lat. 1696, 2900, Vat. Ross. 975.

21. *Marciana:* Venice Marc. lat. XIII, 84 (3997), Oxf. Bod. Canon. Misc. 165, Basle Öffentl. Bibl. der Univ. F.V. 32, Munich Bay, Staatsb. lat. 28, 137 and lat. 378, St. Gall Stifsbibl. 851, Vat. lat. 5129, Ghent Bibl. der Rijksuniv. 10. *Ambrosiana:* Donau eschingen Fürstlich-Fürst. Hofbibl. 12, Florence Ricc. 681, Milan Ambros. A.36 inf., Schägl Stiftsb. 124 (454 b.51), Vat. lat. 5338. Other variant manuscripts: Flor. Bibl. Naz. Centr. II.1.67, Oxf. Lincoln Coll. 84, Perugia Bibl. Com. 730 (I, 124), Palermo Bibl. Com. 2 Qq D 140, Vat. lat. 11, 441.

22. E.g., Stockholm Kungl. Bibl. Va 10

23. Oxf. Bod. lat. class. d.36, San Gimignano Bibl. Com. 24, Naples Bibl. Naz. V.D. 18, Sotheby Sale 27/3/1950 lot. 30.

24. See text above, between notes 8 and 9. The early books of MS Naples V.D.19

compiled according to marginal annotations, from "Alanus" and "Magister Bartolinus," the portions ascribed to the former are, in fact, from the present commentary. If, as seems likely, this third version of Bartolinus's commentary is the earliest, then it is possible that in his early lecturing days Bartolinus made considerable use of an older commentary, *plena et perfecta,* which is thus possibly to be identified as the gloss of his master, Giovanni di Bonandrea. Its ascription to "Alanus" may rest on a misconception, deriving either from the similarities between the Alanus quotations in Bartolinus's gloss and *plena* or from other similarities between *plena* and "Alanus." The author of the *plena* gloss may even have rested content with "improving" "Alanus" and thereby have contributed to his own anonymity in the face of the greater fame of the older scholar. If the commentary by "Alanus" is certainly French, and late twelfth century in origin, and if that known as *Plena et perfecta* is certainly Italian, and early fourteenth century in origin, then early Renaissance *Ad Herennium* commentation is heavily dependent upon the renaissance of the twelfth century.[25] However, there is only one thirteenth-century manuscript of "Alanus" (the rest being fourteenth and fifteenth century),[26] and the Italian provenance of most of them seems assured. Since rhetorical scholarship in twelfth-century Italy seems to have produced a number of glosses on the *Ad Herennium* or *De inventione,*[27] it is not

(one of the manuscripts of the earliest (?) version of Bartolinus's commentary) seem similar in places to *Plena et perfecta,* and not the same as later (?) Bartolinus versions. Book 3 of MS Naples V.D.19 begins differently from *Plena* but at *Ad Her.* 3.4.7 (V.D.19 f.59ᵛ, V.D.18 [*Plena*] f.53ᵛ) they seem virtually identical again, down to the gloss on *similitudo* (*Ad Her.* IV.45.59). At exactly the point of change-over there is a marginal note (partly trimmed) in V.D.19 f.59ᵛ: "usque huc secundum magistrum Bertolinum et abhinc in antea secundum (commentato) rem Alanum." This is exactly comparable with MS San Michele f.163ᵛ. V.D.19 ends with a gloss similar to the longer, later Bartolinus version but *similitudo* (f.88ʳ) is, in fact, glossed twice: what seems to have happened is that the scribe has had to finish his commentary with the later Bartolinus version, exactly as, according to the researches of Wertis, three manuscripts of the later version of Bartolinus finish book 4 (after *Ad Her.* IV.25 – 26) with a different version.

25. See Paul Oskar Kristeller, *Renaissance Thought* (New York, 1961, rpt. 1965), pp. 107 – 8; and F. Simone's discussion of Renucci in *The French Renaissance,* trans. H. Gaston Hall (London, 1969), pp. 269 ff. Harry Caplan, *Of Eloquence: Studies in Ancient and Medieval Rhetoric* (Ithaca, N.Y., 1970), pp. 269 – 70, is certain of the French origin of Alanus's commentary and (p. 267) supposes a later twelfth-century date.

26. Florence Bibl. Med. Laur. Pl.90.87 *sup.* Other manuscripts: London BL Harley 6324, Florence BML Pl.71, 4, Perugia Bibl. Com. 237 (D 55), Oxford Magdalene Coll. 82, Paris BN lat. 7757, Cremona Bibl. Gov. 125, Breslau Bibl. Uniw. R71.

27. See Ward, "The date of the commentary on Cicero's *De inventione* by Thierry

unlikely that the circulation of the commentary by "Alanus" owes more to Italian rhetorical interests, in the later thirteenth and fourteenth centuries, than to northern French scholarship in the time of Alan of Lille or his immediate successors.

In 1444 a beautiful manuscript of an elaborate marginal *lectura, Elucidarium* or *Viridarium* on the *Ad Herennium*, was compiled at Cagliari, Sardinia. The gloss was written by Philippus de Vicecomitibus de Pisto(r)ia, a *magister* who had studied for seven years at Bologna and then, for twenty years, had taught in many cities and served many of the better-known lords and states of the day. The gloss shows clear signs of dependence on Bartolinus but is independent in many places. It has an elaborate preface, doubtless to rival that found in the later version of Bartolinus's own commentary.[28] Another Seville manuscript preserves a commentary on the *Ad Herennium* in the Bartolinus tradition,[29] while MS Vatican Pal. Lat. 1461 contains a version, sometimes rephrased, especially early in book one, of the Bartolinus short or *felix qui* (early) version, with a new long preface, and the insertion of the text of the *Ad Herennium* in the body of the commentary, on an alternating basis.[30] Another manuscript has the same gloss on the early folios of the *Ad Herennium*, attributed to a "Martinus Rhetorinus glosator."[31]

Among the more independent, and at the same time more problematical, *Ad Herennium* glosses is that contained in MS Milan Ambrosiana I 142 *inf.* This manuscript, given in Kristeller's *Iter Italicum* 1.295 as "misc. XIV" has been very kindly described for me by Professor Giuseppe Billanovich as "a miscellany, prepared for grammat-

---

of Chartres (ca. 1095–1160?) and the Cornifician attack on the Liberal Arts," *Viator* 3 (1972), 219–73. Note the Italian (?) provenance of MS Venice Marc. lat. XI.23 (4686); *De inv.* commentary by Lawrence of Amalfi (?) ca. 1045–1063, in MS Venice Marc. lat. Z.L.497; Florence BML Pl.50, 1; Lucca Bibl. Feliniana 614 (rhetorical *summa* by Bishop Guillielmo de Lucca [d. before 1194], see F. Gastaldelli in *Salesianum* 39, 1977, 693 ff., a reference I owe to Mrs. Fredborg); Oxf. Bod. Barlow 40, S.C. 6480. I hope to have more to say on these and comparable manuscripts elsewhere.

28. MS Seville Bibl. Cap. y Col. 83-8-16, Munich Bay. Staatsb. lat. 23, 716 (1368 a.d.).

29. MS 5-4-13 s.XV.

30. On the habit of using the preface to a gloss course as a display of stylistic erudition see Seigel, "The Teaching of Argyropoulos and the Rhetoric of the First Humanists," in *Action and Conviction in Early Modern Europe*, ed. T. K. Rabb (Princeton, N.J., 1969), pp. 237–60, esp. 250–51. Note Guarino da Verona's *prefatio in incohanda rhetorica Ciceronis* (BL Harl. 2580, 2500 etc.) and Barzizza on the *De officiis, Mediaeval Studies* 33 (1977), 303.

31. Milan Ambros. L 83 sup.

ical and rhetorical studies . . . written very likely at Padua in the first quarter of the fifteenth century and there . . . used by a German student."[32] The *Ad Herennium* portion of the manuscript is extremely ambitious, consisting of an elaborate preface, texts of the *Ad Herennium* and parts of the *De inventione,* facing commentary, and marginal notes. The whole is tied together in an elaborate, and, for the rhetorical glosses, unique cross-referencing apparatus. The preface eschews the elaborate finery of Bartolinus but gives a form of the *accessus* now attributed to the generation of Thierry of Chartres[33] and that known as the four Aristotelian causes. Only the latter appears in the Bartolinus preface. Milan I 142 quotes Aristotle's *Rhetoric,* the *De inventione,* Quintilian, and Alanus on the nature of rhetoric, together with Victorinus and Boethius's *De differentiis topicis.* Bartolinus in his own preface refers to passages from the preface to the *De inventione,* and similarly the present author refers to specific numbered *lectiones* from the same portions of the *De inventione* but includes the passages in his text of the *Ad Herennium.* The author refers repeatedly to his *Ordinarius,* his *Speculum,* Giles of Rome, and Walter Burley's *De vita et moribus Philosophorum* (the latter rather obliquely "in libro que dicitur de vita . . ." and so on). Most interestingly, when he comes to the *causa formalis,* he deals with the "forma tractatus, que consistit in divisione librorum, capitulorum et huiusmodi." He refers under this head to the division of the work into "prohemium et tractatum" but informs his readers that this is a "divisio superficialis et rudis"; there is, he continues, a "divisio fertilior et utilior que procedit per lectiones qua usus fuit, ut fertur, B(eatus) Augustinus cum hanc rethoricam Rome legit." The *Ad Herennium* is divided into four books, of which the first contains sixteen *lectiones naturales;* of these the first is the *prohemium* (the *lemma* is given), and the chapter headings of the *Ad Herennium* follow.

Now, the language used by this author when describing the *forma tractatus* is strikingly similar to that found in such northern scholastic works of the thirteenth century as Jordan (of Saxony?)'s commentary on Priscian, Michael Scot's commentary on the *Sphere* of Sacrobosco, and commentaries on logic by Nicholas of Paris and Robert Kilwardby. Egidius Romanus, we are told by modern scholars, was one of the first to distinguish between the *forma tractandi* and the

32. I quote from a letter to me by Professor Billanovich, March 27, 1976.

33. Ward, "The Date"; Karin Margareta Fredborg, "The Commentary of Thierry of Chartres on Cicero's *De inventione,*" *Cahiers de l'Institut du Moyen-Age Grec et Latin* (Université de Copenhague) 7 (1971), 1–36 (225–60).

forma tractatus in scriptural exegesis.[34] The division (sometimes using the word *forma,* sometimes the word *modus*) was common in many disciplines by the early fourteenth century and appears in Bartolinus's preface.[35] However, I have nowhere found any rejection of the traditional distinction of the *forma tractatus* into *prohemium et tractatus* in place of a division into *lectiones,* except in the manuscript under consideration, and have no further information on what would seem to have been an interesting scholastic controversy concerning the proper initial preparation of the text for lecturing. The term *lectiones,* as is well known, appears in university statutes in reference to convenient divisions of a text for lecturing purposes. In the present author's arrangement of the text, there are 111 *lectiones,* each given with a paragraph mark in red or blue, an arabic numeral, and an initial *lemma.* The full commentary, which occupies the right-hand column of each page, or whole pages, or alternate paragraphs with the text, quotes from Cicero's *De oratore,* the *Orator,* and the *Paradoxa.*

The author of this commentary, then, who seems thus to have been at pains to elaborate the system of lecturing on the *Ad Herennium,* was engaged in giving ordinary lectures on other subjects; he wrote or compiled a *Speculum* and reflects some of the scholastic terminology of the late thirteenth and early fourteenth centuries; he seems unaware of Guarino's lectures, and, as far as I am at present able to determine, is uninfluenced by Bartolinus. Yet certain features of the commentary suggest that it dates from the Bartolinus period or a little later: certainly the author's language seems directed at the treatment of the *forma tractatus* to be found in Bartolinus and Philippus de Vicecomitibus de Pisto(r)ia, the latter of whom he seems almost to be quoting on the division into *prohemium et tractatum.* The manuscript watermarks and other details agree with the date given

34. See A. J. Minnis, "Discussions of Authorial Role and Literary Form in Late-Medieval Scriptural Exegesis," *Beiträge zur Geschichte der deutschen Sprache* 99 (1977), 37–65; M. B. Parkes, "The influence of the concepts of *ordinatio* and *compilatio* on the development of the Book," in *Medieval Learning and Literature, essays presented to R. W. Hunt,* eds. J. J. G. Alexander and M. T. Gibson (Oxford, 1976), pp. 115–41; S. H. Thomson, "Robert Kilwardby's commentaries *in Priscianum* and *in Barbarismum Donati,*" *New Scholasticism* 12 (1938), 52–65; B. Nardi, "Osservazioni sul medievale *accessus ad auctores* in rapporto all' epistola a Cangrande," *Studi e Problemi di critica testuale,* Convegno di studi di Filologia Italiana nel Centenario della Commissione per i testi di lingua (Bologna, 1961), pp. 273–305; and pp. 268–305 of his *Saggi e Note di Critica Dantesca* (Milan and Naples, 1966).

35. See notes 7 and 9, above.

by Billanovich, but I would not be surprised if the commentary were a generation or two earlier than this.

In the third quarter of the fourteenth century, Luigius de Gianfilliaciis, a Florentine orator, diplomat, and lawyer of the time, wrote a *summa dictaminum retorice ex arte veteri et nova collecta,* which proceeds according to the parts of rhetoric rather than the book divisions of the *Ad Herennium* and is accompanied in our manuscript written in 1417, by a text of Victorinus, the rhetorical extract from Cassidorus's *Institutes,* which is commonly found, usually without title, printed as a separate work in the manuscripts, and a note about Victorinus and Remigius of Auxerre.[36] Examination suggests that this work can be usefully grouped with the commentary literature as an interesting example of private rhetorical scholarship, and, as such, it is similar to the *lectiones* on the *De inventione,* written probably in the late fourteenth century by Lorenzo di Antonio Ridolfi (1360 – 1442) in his days as a student of the *trivium* and canon law. Ridolfi subsequently became an eminent statesman and lawyer under Cosimo de' Medici.[37] Both works are clearly to be distinguished from academic glosses by university scholars and suggest the extent to which Florentines of a practical bent in the fourteenth century carried their studies in classical rhetorical theory.

MS Naples Bibl. Naz. V.D.38 carries an anonymous commentary on the *Ad Herennium* apparently pre-Guarino but not obviously dependent upon Bartolinus. Watermarks suggest the manuscript is to be dated towards the very end of the fourteenth century, and the gloss was perhaps compiled in the second half of that century.[38] MS Paris B.N. lat. 14,716 carries a fragment of an anonymous gloss on the *Ad Herennium* (incipit *Benivolos auditores*) possibly composed in Italy in the fourteenth century but copied into a northern manuscript, or

36. MS Vat. Chigi I.VIII.291. On Luigi Gianfigliazzi, see F. Novati "Luigi Gianfigliazzi, giureconsulto ed orator fiorentino del secolo XIV" *Archivio Storico Italiano* ser. 5, 3 (1889), 440 – 47; and L. Martines *The Social World of the Florentine Humanists 1390 – 1460* (Princeton, N.J., 1963), pp. 77, 81, 212, 216, 236 – 37; La Russo, "Rhetoric and the Social Order in Italy 1450 – 1600" (Ph.D. diss., Northwestern University, 1956), p. 122; A. Galletti, *L'Eloquenza* (Milan, 1938), pp. 508, 527 – 28. On the Cassiodorus extract, see V. M. Lagorio, "A text of Cassiodorus's *De Rhetorica* in codex Pal. Lat. 1588," *Scriptorium* 30 (1976), 43 – 45.

37. MS Florence Bibl. Naz. Centr. Fondo Pal. Panciatichiani 147 (60). On Ridolfi, see Martines's index under "Ridolfi Family"; and Vespasiano da Bisticci, *Vite di Uomini illustri del secolo XV,* eds. P. D'Ancona and E. Aeschlimann (Milan, 1951), pp. 380 – 83.

38. Incipit "In principio huius libri tria sunt principaliter inquirenda. . . ."

at least a manuscript with a pronounced nondictaminal, northern flavor to it.[39] A manuscript from the Escorial monastic library contains grammatical definitions, a *De inventione,* a glossed *Ad Herennium,* Giovanni di Bonandrea's *Brief introduction to Dictamen,* and a portion of an *Ad Herennium* commentary (incipit *Ad honorem domini*) that adopts some of the terminology found in Bartolinus's gloss but goes back to the Alanus tradition.[40] The manuscript is from the fifteenth century but the gloss may well be earlier and in view of its conjunction with the *Brevis introductio* of Giovanni di Bonandrea and its "Alanus" features might be examined for early fourteenth-century authorship. In 1415 a *lectura super Tullium de memoria artificiali secundum magistrum Grecum* (incipit *Ad artem memorie*) was delivered at the Council of Constance. After an apparently original introduction, it takes the form of a wide-ranging commentary/treatise based on that portion of the *Ad Herennium* that deals with memory. It is preserved, as far as I know, in only one manuscript.[41]

These are the major full commentaries (or surviving fragments thereof) that fall in the Bartolinus phase of commentation — some clearly dependent on Bartolinus, some independent and suggestive of a variety of teaching schools.

The next group of eight works reveals an obvious dependence upon Guarino's gloss. It includes the following commentaries: *quoniam in hoc opere,* an *Ad Herennium* gloss found with Gasparino Barzizza's *de compositione* and a tractate on artificial memory based on the *Ad Herennium* by Antonius de Malespinis, canon of the church of Verona;[42] *etsi hic posset,* another *Ad Herennium* gloss in a manuscript with work by Gasparino Barzizza and written before 1471;[43] *etsi re-*

---

39. The manuscript contains Buridan's *Quaestiones super Metaphysicam Aristotilis, Tabula Genealogiarum Deorum secundum Jo. Boccaccium, Tabula librorum Alberti de Animalibus, Glose in Platonis Timaeum* etc. According to Fredborg, in MS München Bay. Staats. lat. 14460 "where rhetoric is dealt with according to the theory of Boethius' *De differentiis topicis* bk. IV, ... the section on rhetoric is immediately followed by a section on Plato's *Timaeus* and Boethius' *De consolatione Philosophiae*" (Fredborg, "Buridan's *quaestiones super Rhetoricam Aristotelis,*" in *The Logic of John Buridan, Acts of the 3rd European Symposium on Medieval Logic and Semantics, Copenhagen 16 – 21 November, 1975,* ed. J. Pinborg, Copenhagen, 1976, p. 49).

40. V. III. 11 s. XV.

41. Giessen Univ. bibl. 792. I have to thank Professor Kristeller for this reference and information regarding the manuscript. On memory, see Caplan; Monfasani (pp. 244 – 48); Frances Yates, *The Art of Memory* (London, 1966); and G. A. Zinn, Jr., "Hugh of St. Victor and the Art of Memory," *Viator* 5 (1974), 211 – 34.

42. MS Bay. Staatsb. lat. 6721.

43. Venice Marc. lat. XI, 34 (4354).

thorica, an *Ad Herennium* gloss written before 1454 and mentioning Michael Scot, Guarino, and Bartolinus;[44] and *Ad Herennium* commentary by Philippus de Regio written before 1458 and beginning *Etsi negotiis. Antequam veniamus;*[45] *intuenti et inspectanti,* an *Ad Herennium* gloss written in Italy around the middle of the fifteenth century;[46] *etsi id est,* a fragment of a commentary on the *Ad Herennium* citing Guarino in the Ambrosiana version and apparently using or referring to a series of extracts from Quintilian's *Institutes (extracta Quintiliana);*[47] *solet queri,* part of a commentary on the *Ad Herennium* surviving in a manuscript from the British Library;[48] and *satis ut arbitror,* a fragment of another *Ad Herennium* commentary.[49]

Much the most interesting of the post-Guarino manuscript commentaries is the relatively well-known MS Stockholm Va 10, compiled by the Parisian *magister in artibus* Jean Poulain.[50] Poulain, who held an Orleans license in civil and canon law, completed copying Victorinus at Laon in 1465, together with other commentary material ascribed incorrectly to Grillius. This material is arranged as a massive marginal gloss to a text of the *De inventione.* Three years later, also at Laon, the text of the *Ad Herennium* in the same manuscript was completed; then, seventeen years after that, at the Parisian college of Saint Martin a gloss was completed around the *Ad Herennium,* entitled *apparatus Grillii et aliorum expositorum supra secundam rethoricam Tullii.* The gloss is, in fact, an amalgam of versions of Guarino (who had appeared for the first time in print three or four years previously), "Alanus" and in some parts an immediately "pre-Alanus" gloss of the twelfth century. Poulain was thus availing himself of the most accessible traditions of commentation on his texts. He was also the scribe of a Quintilian manuscript: Paris BN lat. 7721.[51] A careful study of this complicated manuscript has yet to be made; presumably much light can be cast by it on the development of humanism in the north.

In addition to the above, from the fourteenth and fifteenth cen-

44. Oxf. Bod. Canon. Misc. 7, S.C. 19483.

45. Vienna Öst. Nationalb. 3206.

46. Cambridge, Gonville and Gaius Coll. 488.

47. Florence Ricc. 973 (N.I.5).

48. London BM. Add. 11,391.

49. Munich Bay. Staatsb. lat. 28,643.

50. See M. Wisén, *De scholiis Rhetorices ad Herennium codice Holmiense Traditis* (Stockholm, 1905); and Ward (diss.), 2.511 ff.

51. Cf. Ch. Fierville's 1890 edition of Quintilian's *Institutes* I, pp. lxxiv – lxxvii.

turies we have manuscripts of six commentaries on *Ad Herennium* IV, two further fragments of *Ad Herennium* commentaries, a *De inventione* commentary, eight *accessus* or collections of notes on the *Ad Herennium,* one on the *De inventione* and one on both texts (fourteenth century, with canon law texts, philosophical works of Cicero, and some Aristotelian works).[52] Some of these latter occur in rich contexts for the student of Renaissance rhetoric: for example, Vatican MS Reg. Lat. 1568, which contains the *Synonyma* of Cicero, Gasparino's *de compositione,* certain dictaminal exercises, Hugh of St. Victor's soliloquy *de arca animae,* a table of *exempla* from the *Golden Legend* of Jacob of Voragine, names of the books of the Bible, material on preaching and canon law, the *Ad Herennium,* rhetorical tables and notes, figures of rhetoric, and letters of Aeneas Sylvius.[53]

The manuscripts I have examined also contain 11 massive glossed texts of the *Ad Herennium,* one by Johannes Heynlin aus Stein or de Lapide, the celebrated northern humanist and publisher who ended life as a Carthusian monk at Basel,[54] and another by Octavianus Martinus de Suessa, ca. 1401.[55] There are 2 massive glossed *De inventione* texts, 12 minor glossed texts of the *Ad Herennium,* 2 of the *De inventione,*[56] 15 minor to slight glossed *Ad Herennium* texts (including glosses apparently ascribable to Francesco da Fiano), 2 of the *De inventione,* and I have counted a further 118 texts of the *Ad Herennium* that bear some, but not significant, glosses from the fourteenth and fifteenth centuries, and 45 such texts of the *De inventione.*[57] This latter class of texts contains indications of the rhetorical teaching of Georgius de Peurbach, 1423–1469, a celebrated astronomer of Vienna, of William Coste of Merton College, Oxford, and of Pietro da Moglio, in the hand of his disciple Francesco Piendibeni.[58] After approximately

52. Details of these manuscripts will appear shortly elsewhere.
53. I have used the description of this manuscript by Paola Scarcia Piacentini in the files of the IRHT, Paris.
54. Basle Öff. Bibl. der Univ. Inc. 705 (formerly F. IV.36). See Max Burckhardt, *Die Inkunabeln aus der Bibliothek des Johannes de Lapide* (Basle, 1973).
55. Rome, Bibl. Stat. Angelica 1310 (T. 3. 1) s.XV (1450).
56. See note 52, above.
57. These figures are continually expanding as manuscript research continues.
58. Francesco Piendibeni, da Montepulciano: notaio delle riformagioni, *then* di cancelliere del Comune di Perugia, *then* di scrittore nella curia pontificale, *then* di arciprete di Montepulciano, *then* (1414–33) di vescovo di Arezzo (Billanovich, *Italia Medioevale e Umanistica* 6 [1963], 212). MSS Milan Bibl. Naz. Braid. A. G. IX 9, Munich Bay. Staats. lat. 18802. See also Sabbadini, *Le Scoperte,* 2.151. Willelmus Coste de Mertona: MS Uppsala Univbibl. C928.

the year 1500, but still in manuscript, may be found 6 *Ad Herennium* commentaries (including one by Ulricius Zasius, one by Alexander Guarinus, and one written ca. 1580–1582 by Master Hieronimus of Prague), 2 sets of notes on the Ad Herennium, one introduction to the *De inventione,* and 6 glossed texts of the *Ad Herennium.*[59]

It is clear from this detail that the *De inventione* was not abandoned as a curriculum text in the Renaissance. Twenty-eight fourteenth and fifteenth century manuscripts of Victorinus survive to confirm this conclusion. One, Ghent Bibl. der Rijksuniversiteit 10, is a superb large (40 cm. high) volume, beautifully written, ornamented and illustrated, containing addresses and letters to the Holy Roman Emperor Frederick and Maximilian King of the Romans by the Venetian Ambassador Hermolaos Barbaro, by Jean de Carondelet, Chancellor of the King of the Romans, by the Lord Abbot Anthony of Admont, as well as the *De inventione* with Victorinus as a marginal gloss, the *Ad Herennium* with the commentary of Guarino as gloss, Cicero *differentiae sermonum,* Lorenzo Valla *de ratione dicendi, precepta ad orationem ornate componenda,* and Cicero *Synonyma.* The manuscript, of finest vellum, was executed on the order of Raphaël de Marcatelle (ca. 1437–1508) towards the end of the fifteenth century. Raphaël, one of the bastard sons of Duke Philip the Good of Burgundy, Bishop of Roses (Syria) and abbot of the monastery of Saint Bavon, was a renowned bibliophile.[60]

In addition to the *originalia* (i.e., the texts of the *Ad Herennium* and the *De inventione* themselves, and Victorinus's commentary), medieval commentaries on the two classical works were clearly used in the Renaissance. We have, for example, 17 manuscripts of twelfth-century commentaries on the *Ad Herennium* and *De inventione* that

59. See n. 52, above. There are also manuscript notes in various printed editions of the *Ad Herennium* and *De inventione.*

60. On Barbaro, see V. Branca, "Ermolao Barbaro and Late Quattrocento Humanism," in *Renaissance Venice,* ed. J. R. Hale (London, 1973), pp. 218 ff.; U. Tucci, "Il patrizio Veneziano Mercante e Umanistica," in H. G. Beck et al., *Venezia, centro di mediazione fra oriente e occidente (secoli xv – xvi), aspetti e problemi* (Florence, 1977), pp. 335 – 57; and J. B. Ross, "Venetian Schools and Teachers 14th to early 16th centuries: a survey and a study of Giovanni Battista Egnazio," *Renaissance Quarterly* 29 (1976), 521 ff. There is a further Victorinus manuscript from the Bibl. Vallicelliana (Rome) but I do not at present have any indication of its date. There are numerous s. XV manuscripts of the text (full or partial). That the text continued during the Renaissance to have the impact it had in the twelfth century is suggested by Trinkaus ("A humanist's image of Humanism: the inaugural orations of Bartolommeo della Fonte," *Studies in the Renaissance* 7 [1960], 113 – 14); for twelfth-century parallels, see Ward (diss.), chap. 4.

date from the fourteenth and fifteenth centuries. One Renaissance manuscript of the *De inventione* commentary by Petrus Helias, a contemporary of Thierry of Chartres, contains Jerome's *Contra Iovinianum*, Boethius's *De differentiis topicis,* Fortunatianus's *Artis rhetoricae libri tres,* the pseudo-Augustine *De rhetorica liber,* Martianus Capella's *De Nuptiis* V (on rhetoric) with glosses, a *Practica perbrevis in arte dicendi* by Br. Antonius Raudensis Theologus, and the Petrus Helias gloss titled *commentum super rhetorica veteri secundum divum Augustinum se referentem ad opinionem Victorini.* Petrus Helias refers to Victorinus in the first lines of his commentary, and it was known that Augustine praised Victorinus. One is reminded of the Milan I.142 commentator's reference to the Blessed Augustine's lectures at Rome on the *Ad Herennium.*[61] In addition, a number of the twelfth-century manuscripts of twelfth-century commentaries carry Renaissance marginalia and corrections, indicating some later currency.

I have commented elsewhere on the proliferation of commentaries on the *Ad Herennium* and *De inventione* during the era of printing. The first gloss to appear in print was Victorinus, in 1474, with the *De inventione,* from the Milanese printer Antonius Zarotus. The first *Ad Herennium* gloss to appear was the Marciana recension of Guarino's gloss, which Sabbadini thinks is more extended and complete than the Ambrosiana recension that was apparently compiled in 1445 and approved by Guarino himself.[62] The printed commentary, as has been mentioned, was stripped of all indication of

61. Brescia Bibl. Civ. Querin. A. V. 4. Raudensis's *Practica* cites Cicero *Partit. Or., Pro Deiot., Ad Her.,* Quintilian, and so on. Margareta Fredborg reminds me also at this point of the contents of the Thierry of Chartres MS Munich Bay. Staatsb. lat. 3565 s.XV, which includes Egidius Romanus *super Rhetoricam Aristotelis* and our principal fragment of Grillius's *De inventione* commentary.

62. Sabbadini (above, note 17), esp. pp. 93 – 95. My previous discussion of the printed commentaries is contained in Ward, "From Antiquity to the Renaissance: Glosses and Commentaries on Cicero's *Rhetorica,*" in *Medieval Eloquence: Studies in the Theory and Practice of Medieval Rhetoric,* ed. James J. Murphy (Berkeley and Los Angeles, 1978), pp. 26 – 67, esp. pp. 39 – 41. The present discussion supplements those pages and provides more up-to-date statistics. It is noteworthy that the first Renaissance Priscian gloss was, in fact, an eleventh-century text: see M. Gibson, "The Collected Works of Priscian: The Printed Editions 1470 – 1859," *Studi Medievali* 18 (1977), 249 – 60. Percival (in this volume) states that medieval grammatical texts were often used in the Renaissance, although Renaissance scholars discontinued the practice of *commenting* grammatical texts. Yet Juan Vives gives elaborate rules on the composition of commentaries. There are some 163 *incunabula* editions of Alexander of Villedieu's *Doctrinale* and more than 100 sixteenth-century editions (Percival, this volume). Why was grammar so amply served in the Renaissance by medieval texts and not rhetoric? It

Guarino's authorship. According to Sabbadini it derives from a "more correct" manuscript of the Marciana recension, but my own observations suggest that it contains a number of corruptions not found in some of the manuscripts. Guarino's gloss saw seven editions between 1481 – 1482 and 1493. As early as 1490 another gloss on the *Ad Herennium* appeared in print, that of Georgio Valla's student Jerome Capiduro; this gloss, announced as a faculty-approved version of George's own gloss on the *Ad Herennium,* was not printed again until 1541, after which time it saw nine further editions before 1571 and was occasionally reprinted thereafter. By 1599 Victorinus's commentary had been printed some forty-seven times and was to continue in vogue for much longer than that. By 1494 the extremely popular commentary on the first book of the *Ad Herennium* by Antonio Mancinelli (1452 – 1505) had been added to the stable, and within two years the full commentary by Francesco Maturanzio, by that stage in his fifties, had become available. Both were last printed in 1542, after twenty-six or twenty-seven and seventeen editions, respectively.[63] Between 1508 and 1513 three more commentators had added their observations to the text of the *Ad Herennium:* Josse Badius of Aasche, Claudius de Gurgite, who contributed *epitomata* to each chapter, and Marinus Becichemus Scodrensis, who contributed *castigationes* to the *De inventione,* the *Ad Herennium,* and the text of Victorinus. These contributions were printed thirteen or fourteen times each before 1571 in the case of the first and the last, but the

---

might also be pointed out that there were some 150 editions of commentaires by Thomas Aquinas on Aristotle during the fifteenth and sixteenth centuries. It is significant, therefore, that the first printed rhetorical gloss was a *modernus* rather than a time-honored medieval author.

63. Some bibliographers (e.g., Panzer, Maittaire, Graesse) list a 1486 edition of Maturanzio and Mancinelli on the *Ad Herennium,* which, if genuine, would bring their total editions to twenty-seven and eighteen, respectively, and antedate my statement of their first appearance by eight and ten years, respectively. Rafaello Regio wrote a *praefatio* to the *Ad Her.* in 1500. On the history of Ciceronian textual scholarship see the 1823 ed. of Cicero's *Opera* by Christ. Godofr. Schütz (Augusta Taurinorum) l.xxi ff.; pp. 13 ff. give Ernestus's preface to the rhetorical works, including some critical history. The notes at the foot of the page for the rhetorical vols. (1 – 3) are only rarely ascribed, but frequently mention previous glossators. See also I. C. Orellius and Io. G. Baiterius, eds., *M. T. Ciceronis Opera quae supersunt,* vol. 5 (Turin, 1833), pts. 1 and 2 and vol. 6, 242 ff; and J. W. Moss, *A Manual of Classical Bibliography comprising a copious detail of the various editions of the Greek and Latin classics, and of the critical and philological works published in illustration of them with an account of the principal translations,* 2 vols. (London, 1837), 1.285 ff.

epitomata were far less popular (apparently only four printings: 1513, 1517, 1526, 1531). In 1526 and 1531 the editions of the *Ad Herennium* and *De inventione* announced contributions drawn from George of Trebizond (and there is an occasional reference to his *adnotationes* after 1600), but I have so far not been able to identify any notes on these texts by George, or even any extracts made from his *Rhetoricorum libri quinque*. Some of the standard *Ad Herennium* glossators quote Trebizond — Capiduro is an example.

Between 1535 and 1541 three further contributors appeared in print: Gilbert de Longueil, from Utrecht, physician to the archbishop of Cologne, whose annotations saw fourteen editions by 1568; Claudius Pontanus, whose *scholiae* were printed eight times by 1564; and Pietro Vettori, a noted classicist from Florence who devoted much time to the editing of Cicero's works. His *castigationes* on the *Ad Herennium* saw nine printings by 1564. Michael Toxita or Schütz, born 1515 in the Tyrol and later to become a humanist, alchemist, and poet, had a commentary on the *Ad Herennium* printed in 1556 and 1558, allegedly from the *scholia* of Johannis Sturm, the noted Strassbourg classical scholar (1507-1589), who published a corrected Cicero *Rhetorica* in 1548. In the 1560s and 1570s the names of Denis Lambin and the Venetian Giammichele Bruto were added to the list of annotators of both the *De inventione* and the *Ad Herennium*, and by the turn of the century, when the first generations of commentators had outrun their vogue, new scholars were entering print: Fulvio Orsini, Denis Godefroy, and Aldo Manuzio the Younger.[64] In addition, there are several commentators whose works seem to have been printed only once: Juan Luis Vives, the Valencian scholar (b. 1493) who studied and taught in Paris, Bruges, Louvain and Oxford, wrote a *praelectio* on the *Ad Herennium* IV (1538) to introduce a course of lectures on the *pigmenta exornationesve orationis*

64. Denis Lambin 1565, 1566, 1569, 1572, 1585; Bruto 1570, 1579, and his edition of Cicero, *Op. Omn.* (1540) contains notes (Moss, p. 291); Orsini 1581; Denis Godefroy 1588, 1596. For the most part, biographical information about the figures mentioned in this essay can be obtained from the standard reference works: e.g., W. Pökel, *Philologisches Schriftsteller-Lexikon* (Leipzig, 1882, rpt. Darmstadt, 1966), and Sandys, Toffanin, Tiraboschi, Hoefer, Brunet, Michaud, Ist. della Encic. Ital. *Dizionario Biografico degli Italiani* (Rome, 1965– , useful, for example, on Marino Becichemo), *Allgemeine Deutsche Biographie* or *CTC* indices. Moreover, the "Renaissance Latin Aristotle Commentaries" compiled by Charles Lohr contain some information regarding Cicero's commentators: e.g., *Studies in the Renaissance* 21 (1974), 244 on Vitus Amerbach; *Renaissance Quarterly* 28 (1975), 696 on Camerarius; and *Renaissance Quarterly* 29 (1976), 705–6 on Antonius de Gouveia and p. 715 on Christoph Hegendorf.

("quartum Rhetoricorum ad Herennium celeri lectione interpretabimur, quem ubi primum finierimus . . ."); Georgius Acanthius Kelhaimannus published in 1549 at Basle a *partitiones in Ciceronis de rhetorica libros quattuor ad Herennium universam fere huius rei artem complectentes;* and Antonio Riccoboni wrote, according to Pökel (p. 225) a *Commentar. librorum de inventione, partitit. [sic] Topicor. Orat. de oratore* (published at Venice, 1567); his *Commentarius in universam doctrinam oratoriam Ciceronis* was published at Frankfurt in 1596. In 1564 there appeared at Venice the first full-scale printed *De inventione* commentary since the publication of the commentary of Victorinus, by Nascimbaenus Nascimbaenius of Ferrara. Hitherto, apart from a few *castigationes* and the repeated printing of Victorinus's gloss, the *Ad Herennium* had received the lion's share of scholarly attention. After the appearance of the 1564 commentary by Nascimbaenus, which was not popular at all, many of the later commentators provided notes on both the *De inventione* and the *Ad Herennium*.[65]

The above details no doubt establish the continued currency of the two elementary classical Roman rhetorical treatises throughout the Renaissance. However, despite the considerable survival of manuscripts and the evidence of continued interest during the era of printing, it is still surprising how many known teachers of grammar and rhetoric between ca. 1300 and 1600 do not appear to have published glosses on the elementary texts. A list of names here would serve only to underline the problem,[66] and time may still identify various anonymous manuscripts with known teachers of rhetoric. The exact status of commentation on the *Ad Herennium* and the *De inventione* is thus hard to assess. Certainly until the second half of the fifteenth century the *Ad Herennium* seems to have been the standard

65. Nascimbaenius's commentary was printed once, with extracts appearing here and there in editions after 1600 (e.g., Amsterdam, 1724; Paris, 1740). Vives's *Praelectio in quartum Rhetoricorum ad Herennium* is printed, e.g., *Opera omnia* (Valentiae Edetanorum, 1782, rpt. Gregg, 1964), 2.87 – 89. Among the "ghosts" are a Victorinus for 1499, a Venice 1482 commentary of Omnibonus Leonicenus on the *Ad Her., De inv.,* or both (Hain 5086, Goff C-644; cf. Moss 1.310, Venice 1470, *De inventione,* ed. Omnibonus) and a commentary on the *Ad Herennium* by Giorgio Valla (Murphy, *Medieval Eloquence,* p. 40, note 41, the reference to "Lorenzo" Valla being an error).

66. Dominic LaRusso, "Rhetoric and the Social Order in Italy, 1450 – 1600" (Ph.D. diss., Northwestern University, 1956), pp. 122 ff., provides a fuller conspectus of names than in his useful article, "Rhetorical Education: Italy, 1300 – 1450," *Western Speech* 14 (1960), 213 – 19. Some thirty-three professors of rhetoric and grammar at Padua before 1350 are cited by Nancy Siraisi, *Arts and Sciences at Padua* (Toronto, 1973).

rhetorical lecturing text for the established scholar, though some study of the *De inventione* was probably recommended, and lectures seem often to have taken a much freer form, leading to treatises on rhetoric that cannot be classed as commentaries on the classical treatise. Again, such was the currency of leading interpreters such as "Alanus," Bartolinus, and Guarino that students seem to have acquired copies of their glosses in many cases rather than compiling their own.

Although in the era of printing the study of the *De inventione* seems to have been elevated to the front rank (by the repeated printing of Victorinus), the provision of glosses for both the elementary texts seems to have been left to a less precocious class of scholar not necessarily associated with the front rank of research into the textual history of the classical writings. We may consequently conclude that, in the era of printing, the *De inventione* and the *Ad Herennium,* with their commentaries, made up the basic rhetorical curriculum in the schools and academies. But, meanwhile, close attention was increasingly paid to the other rhetorical works of Cicero, especially his speeches.

II

The mature rhetorical works of Cicero were not glossed or commented on in the Middle Ages and the speeches received only marginal attention, chiefly by way of antique *scholia.*[67] A brief survey, by

67. The ancient scholia to Cicero's speeches which survived in the Middle Ages and are represented by medieval manuscripts are printed/discussed in Orelli (vol. 5); P. Faider, *Répertoire des éditions de scolies et commentaires d'auteurs latins* (Paris, 1931); and in *Ciceronis Orationum Scholiastae,* ed. T. Stangl (Vienna, 1912, rpt. 1964). William of Malmesbury knew perhaps twelve speeches or groups of speeches: see R. M. Thomson, "The Reading of William Malmesbury," *Revue Bénédictine* 85 (1975), 362 ff.; "Addenda et Corrigenda," *Revue Bénédictine* 86 (1976), 327 – 35. The *libri manuales* analyzed by E. M. Sanford, "The use of classical Latin authors in the libri manuales," *Transactions of the American Philological Association* 55 (1924) 190 – 248, esp. pp. 242 – 43, contain fifteen speeches or groups of them, and the *Brutus, De inventione, De oratore, Partit. Or., Topica* (the *Topica* with Boethius's commentary is common enough in medieval manuscripts), and the *Ad Her.* M. Manitius, "Handschriften antike Autoren in mittelalterlichen Bibliothekskatalogen," *Beiheft zum Zentralblatt für Bibliothekswesen* no. 67 (Leipzig, 1935) adds perhaps seven speeches to these. Excerpts from the *De oratore* exist in a s.XII MS at St. Victor, MS Paris Arsenal 711, the *Florilegium Gallicum:* J. J. G. Alexander and M. J. Gibson, eds., *Medieval Learning and Literature: essays presented to Richard William Hunt* (Oxford, 1976), p. 84; and J. Hamacher, *Florilegium Gallicum, prolegomer a und Edition der Excerpte* (Frankfurt, 1975). The text also figures in Hadoard's

contrast, of manuscript evidence for Renaissance scholarly attention to these works marks a change. The material I have assembled (chiefly from Kristeller's *Iter Italicum* 1 and 2 and from Pökel, a kind of random probe) embraces: twelve commentaries (notes and such) on the *Partitiones oratoriae* (including those by Philippus Rinaldus, S. J., Horatius Tursellinus, Paulus Vizanus, S. J., and Poliziano); three on the *Orator* (including 2 manuscripts of the commentary by Mari-Antonio Majoragio); thirteen on the *De oratore* (including three on book 3 only; among the identified works are glosses by Omnibonus Leonicenus, or Ognibene de' Bonissou, by Vicenza, the follower of Vittorino da Feltre and editor of the *De inventione, Ad Herennium,* Quintilian's *Institutes,* and so forth; by Gasparino Barzizza Pergamensis, Poliziano, Petr. Jo. Erpinianus, J. B. Scortia, S. J., Tarquinius Galluzzi, Horatius Tursellinus, G. Bartholdus Pontanus [candidate in philosophy at Prague writing in 1579 in the College of Jesuits], and Achilles Statius). We also have mention of glosses by Pomponio Leto on the *Brutus, Orator,* and *De oratore.*

I have come across thirty-four manuscripts of Antonio Loschi's commentary on eleven of Cicero's speeches and there are doubtless very many more, suggesting that commentaries on the speeches achieved greater manuscript distribution than did commentaries on the *Ad Herennium.* Sabbadini speaks of Loschi's "immensa diffusione," "larghissima diffusione fra gli umanisti." Loschi, the Milanese ducal secretary, wrote this collection in the 1390s; in one of the *reportationes* of Guarino's *Ad Herennium* commentary, Loschi and Veronese him-

---

Cicero collection: P. Schwenke, ed., "Des Presbyter Hadoardus Cicero—excerpte (Cod. Vat. Reg. 1762)," *Philologus* Suppl. -Bd. V Hft. 3 (1889) and that of William of Malmesbury (see Thomson, "The Reading," as already cited).

The *Catilines* and *Philippics* are the most popular speeches, but no speech attains the great popularity of the *De amicitia,* the *De senectute,* or the *De inventione,* or even the *De officiis.* Brunetto Latini studies closely *Marc., Lig., Deiot., Cat.* (my diss. 1.320 – 21) and Adelard of Bath refers to *Marc., Lig, Deiot., Phil.* (diss. 1.309). Oxford Bodleian MS Barlow 40 provides an interesting page illumination of a crowned Cicero illustrating the Catilinarian conspiracy. The Verrines are a common illustration in medieval rhetorical commentaries (see Murphy, *Medieval Eloquence,* p. 51, for example).

An intriguing illustration of the medieval neglect of Cicero's speeches is provided by the evidence of John of Salisbury's *Policraticus.* John's *Metalogicon* is almost entirely without reference to the speeches. Despite the fact that Cicero is commended "for eloquence" in *Policraticus* 3.5, John draws all his information regarding courtroom practice from "medieval" sources: a pithy saying from the *Pro Ligario* is taken from Augustine, details regarding the training of the rhetor and the practice of the orator are taken from Cicero via Macrobius, John's knowledge of the *Pro Roscio* is similarly derived and in 6.19 information regarding oratorical/rhetorical case practice is taken

self are cited as two outstanding scholars on a question of textual authenticity at one point in the *Ad Herennium.* Sicco Polenton's Padua 1413 *argumenta* on the Ciceronian speeches not dealt with by Loschi was also popular (I have noted sixteen manuscripts). Both collections were printed, as were the commentaries by the classical writer Asconius Pedianus.

I have noted twenty further manuscripts containing notes, commentaries, or lecturing material in relation to groups of speeches. Achilles Bocchius has left *argumenta in orationes invectivas Ciceronis* and on some of Cicero's other speeches. Other names include Galuzzi, Andr. Julianus, Gasparino Barzizza, Joannes Schosserus (Isenacensis, 1594 on *Pro. Mil., Rosc., Manil.*); Padre Juan Nuñez on *Red., Sext.*; Rev. P. Ioannis Aquensis (1580, Prague on *Rab., Marc.*). Other manuscripts include notes on particular speeches: *Arch.* by Vinc. Maius; *Cat.* (2), *Lig.* (6, including Trapezuntius [3] and Georgius Merula 1); *Man.* (6, including Achilles Bocchius, dominus Marcilius Professor Eloquentiae, Lazarus Bonamicus *praelectio*); *Marc.*; *Mil.*(5, including Seb. Berettarus, Gregorius Amasaeus, Guarinus, Paulus Manutius); *Phil.* (including Berettarus, Poliziano, Beroaldo,[68] Pomponius Leto [Laetus], Fran. Bencius); *Pis.* (2, including Bencius); *Prov. Cons.* (Petrus Angelius Bargaeus); *Quint.* (3, including Caelius Calcagninus, Julius Camillus Utinensis, Leonardus Florentinus = Bruni?); *Rosc. Am.* (2); *Sext.* (2, including Bencius); Sall.-Cic. *Invectt.* (Jeronimo Zurita, 1469). Some of these works achieved print (e.g., Trapezuntius *Lig.*, Beroaldo *Phil.*); some I have not yet identified in printed editions. Many are doubtless students' notes. A full survey of catalogues of printed manuscripts would vastly extend our impressions. My selection is intended merely to suggest the scope of manuscript survival of this class of material during the Renaissance.[69]

from the *Ad Herennium.*

For Wibald of Corvey and the speeches of Cicero, see L. D. Reynolds and N. G. Wilson, *Scribes and Scholars: a guide to the transmission of Greek and Latin literature,* 2nd ed. (Oxford, 1974), pp. 100 and 232; Ward (diss.), 1.423–34; and on Hadoard of Corbie and Sedulius Scottus and their Cicero excerpts, cf. Reynolds-Wilson, p. 91 and pp. 229–30. The increased interest of the Renaissance in Cicero's speeches is, of course, commonly assumed by modern scholars (cf. Kristeller, *Renaissance Thought,* 1.14, for example).

68. 1435–1505, Bolognese professor who also taught in Milan, Parma, and Paris. R. Pfeiffer, *History of Classical Scholarship from 1300 to 1850* (Oxford, 1976), p. 55; Pökel, p. 22.

69. Titles of speeches are abbreviated according to the style of Lewis and Short's *Latin Dictionary.* On Sicco and Loschi, see Sabbadini, *Storia e Critica di testi latini* (Cata-

The printed material is relatively vast, and though more accessible than the manuscripts, equally without meaningful survey at present. What follows can be taken as a guide only. Although I have looked at many actual editions from the period and worked through the major printed guides, there can be no claim that the basis of my statistics is either exhaustive or even in every case accurate. I have tried to restrict the tendency to inflate the numbers of printed editions by indiscriminate attention to the entries in older, unsystematic reference works (Fabricius, Panzer, Maittaire, Graesse, and so on) but cannot claim total success. What I can claim is that exhaustive figures would reveal more rather than fewer editions than those on which the following remarks are based. I have, for example, excluded from my count all editions recorded in older references without indication of year.[70]

Between 1528 and 1570, every year saw publication of one or more commentaries on a Ciceronian speech or mature rhetorical work; before and after those dates, scarcely a year went by without a similar publication. If we divide the printing of the commentaries into three chronological groupings, we find that in the first period, between 1477 and 1526, attention was divided approximately equally between the speeches and the mature rhetorical works. The only speeches to be glossed individually, apart from the printed collections of Loschi, Polenton, and Asconius Pedianus (the latter saw seven printings at least in this period), were *Phil.* (Beroaldo, Trapezuntius, Franciscus Maturantius Perusinus), *Mil.* (Sylvius, late in the period), *Pro Archia* and *Marc.* (Jakob Locher, who taught classics at Freiburg and Ingolstadt), *Pro Lig.* (Trapezuntius, four editions, and Giorgio Marlani or Merula, 1425–1494, who taught classics at Venice and Milan). A popular early collection printed as a single volume seems to have been Asconius, Trapezuntius in *Lig.*, Luschus and Polenton (Venice 1477 and 1492).

In the same period glosses on the *De oratore* were printed from

---

nia, 1914; 2nd ed. Padua, 1971), pp. 20 ff.; *La Scuola*, pp. 59–60 and pp. 13–144 for Cicero research among the humanists; Galetti, pp. 556–58; G. da Schio, *Sulla vita e sugli scritti di Antonio Loschi* (Padua, 1858); Monfasani, pp. 261, 265, 289–94 on Loschi and Trapezuntius (Monfasani describes Trapezuntius's *Rhetoricorum libri quinque* as "as much a commentary on Cicero's orations as it was a manual of rhetoric, and in writing it . . . George thought not infrequently of Loschi's earlier work").

70. *Marc.* with paraphr. Phil. Mel., Trapez. *Phil.* (three times) Fortunatianus (Milan), Asconius, Mel. in *Orator*, Vict. Pis. *in Orat.*, Boethius *De diff. Top.*, in *Top. Cic.*, Sylvius *in Cat.* (twice), Omnib. Leonic. *in De orat.*, G. Vall. *in Top.*

four authors, including Philip Melanchthon and Leonicenus Omnibonus (who also glossed the *Orator*, as, perhaps, did Merula, although the major *Orator* commentator of the period was Victor Pisanus). The *Topica* was glossed by Giorgio Valla (who also glossed the *partitiones oratoriae*) and by Melanchthon, and the old gloss of Boethius was printed once towards the end of the period. Italians have the edge here, although some German scholars appear. There is only one Frenchman in the group: Franciscus Ambianus Sylvius (du Bois), who taught at Paris and whose commentaries on Cicero's speeches were to dominate the next thirty years. Curiously, no one of these scholars paid any attention (on the evidence of the printed editions) to the *Ad Herennium* or *De inventione*, with the two exceptions of Franciscus Matura(n)tius Perusinus (Francesco Maturanzio, Perugian student of Greek and Latin letters, diplomat, professor of eloquence at Perugia, ca. 1443 – 1518) and Marino Becichemo (Marino da Scutari Becichemo, Marinus Becichemus Scodrensis, an Albanian University classical scholar who lived ca. 1468 – 1526 and taught in Ragusa, Brescia, Venice, and Padua).

I have a record of forty-eight editions of commentaries (notes, *adnotationes, castigationes,* and such) in this period, with no year seeing more than five and no one work being printed more than nine times (including Leonicenus Omnibonus on the *De oratore*, a commentary not printed again after this period). This figure does not include collected editions of Cicero's works, or speeches, with *castigationes,* such as Ciceronis oratt. p. P.B(eroaldum) correcte, 1499, Venice, 1505 (Pökel, p. 22), and for a list of others see Orelli, vol. 6, p. 238 ff. and F. L. A. Schweiger, *Handbuch der classischen Bibliographie: lateinische Schriftsteller* (Leipzig 1830 – 1834; rpt. Amsterdam, 1962, as *Bibliographisches Lexicon der gesamten Literatur der Römer*) 1. 103 ff. In the same period the *Gesamtkatalog der Wiegendrucke* lists twelve editions of the *De oratore*, nine of the *De inventione*, and fourteen of the *Ad Herennium* (including texts with commentary). One edition is listed for the *Orator*, two for the *Partitiones oratoriae*, and two for the *Topica.* Eight of the more popular speeches were printed individually *(In Cat.* reaching six full or part editions, *Pro. Arch.* four), and some fourteen collected or selected editions can be counted from the same source. In the same period Quintilian's *Institutes* was printed eight times, according to the *Indice Generale degli Incunaboli delle Biblioteche d'Italia.*

In the second period, 1527 – 1560, by contrast, I have a record of 566 printed commentaries, glosses, sets of notes (with a further 12 doubtful editions), rising to a maximum of 55 editions in 1539 and tapering away at the beginning and end of the period. This figure does not include 8 editions of all Cicero's works with notes or critical apparatus,[71] 8 collections of glosses on Cicero's speeches,[72] 2 collections of notes on the *De oratore, Orator,* and *Brutus* by Paulus Manutius (Venice 1554, 1559), and one collection of various commentaries on the *Topica* (1559).

Both speeches and mature rhetorical works secured considerable attention, but the emphasis on the speeches in this period increased in comparison with the previous period. In a sample year (1541), twenty-four of forty-six commentaries published were on Cicero's mature rhetorical works. In this period the great French scholars and printers of the day joined forces with the Italians and Germans.

In the last period, 1561 until the end of the sixteenth century, the number of commentaries and such published dwindles to 128, an average of around 3 per year, as against 17 per year for the peak period; never more than 10 commentaries and such were published in any one year in the later period. This figure does not include 9 editions of Cicero's *Opera omnia* with *castigationes, annotationes,* or both,[73] 13 editions of the speeches with commentaries, *castigationes,* or both (or, in the case of Ramus, *praelectiones*),[74] one edition of the *De oratore* and *Orator (de perf. orat. ad M.Brut.)* with *castigationes, annotationes,* and *scholia* (Cologne 1574), and one *Opera rhetorica* by Paolo Manuzio and Pietro Vettori (Petrus Victorius) published in 1585. This period witnesses continued publication of a very thin scattering of old favorites (Asconius, Loschi, Boethius *in Top. Cic.,* Melanchthon) but sees German, Flemish, or Eastern European humanism much more predominant than earlier: Jakob Omphalius, Coelio Secundo

71. Edited by Petrus Victorius (Pietro Vettori), Gothofredus, Camerarius, and Manutius.

72. Sylvius, Melanchthon, Latomus, Basle 1536, Basle 1539, and also such editions in the following years: 1547, 1552, 1553 (Basle), 1554 (Lyons), 1560 (Manuzio and Kämmerer).

73. Including four by Denis Lambin (1565, 1566, 1572, 1573) and three more by the same with Fulvio Orsini (1584, 1585, *bis*), one by Pietro Vettori and Joachim Kämmerer together, one by Manuzio (1577).

74. Including six by Paolo Manuzio (1565, 1578, 1579, 1581, 1582, 1583)· two by Johann Freigius, 1583, 1592; two by Giammichele Bruto, 1579 (Lyons), 1584; one (Lyons, 1567) mentioning Asconius, Vettori, Manuzio, Faerno, Hotmann, and Lambin; one by Sturm (1563); and one by Lambin (1570). Doubtless many more editions of this sort exist that my initial researches have passed over, and primarily for this reason my figures should be taken as an absolute minimum.

Curio, Andreas Patricki, Jacob de Crusque, Johan Fischer (Piscator), Matthaeus Drescher, Johann Freigius, and Friedrich Sylburg. The French and Italian element, however, is still strong, and there may well be an inevitable bias implicit in the available printed handbooks.

If we look at the printing history of Cicero *rhetorica* and speech commentary editions during the period as a whole, the following impressions may be gained. Taking the speech commentaries first, we find that between the invention of printing and the end of the sixteenth century an absolute minimum of 479 printed commentaries, *adnotationes, dispositiones (integrae paraphrases), artificia, argumenta,* and so forth on individual speeches saw the light (with a possible 13 additional commentaries, at least) — almost 4 editions a year on average, between 1477 and 1599. These figures do not include the editions of collected speeches with commentaries, annotations, or critical apparatus already mentioned above, nor do they include information derived solely from Fabricius. The great majority of speeches in the period saw fewer than 5 published commentaries/ glosses each (a little over 150 commentaries in all).

The three most popular commentaries seem to have been Melanchthon's *Pro Archia* (fifteen in the period 1533 – 1592), Latomus's *Pro Milone* (12/1535 – 1571), and the ancient set by Asconius Pedianus (*Corn., Scaur., Pis., Mil., Tog. Cand.,* ed. A. C. Clark, Oxford, 1907) and pseudo-Asconius (a late antique collection, *in Verr., Div. in Caec.,* ed. Orelli [Turin, 1833], vol. 5, pt. 2). I have noted twenty-four printings of part or all of this Asconian ensemble, 1477 – 1553 and 1586. Orelli (vol. 5, pt. 2, pp. vi ff.) notes some eight editions (one of which has the *scholia* of Paolo Manuzio, p. ix); Clark (p. xxxiii) notes ten down to 1563. The popularity of the *Pro Archia* is suggested by a remark of Fabricius (*Bibliotheca Latina Mediae et Infimae Aetatis* [ed. J. D. Mansi, 6 vols. in 3, Florence, 1858 – 1859, hereafter referred to as "Fabricius" or "F"] p. 161): *notis illustravere, certe, voluere plures, ad usus tironum.*

The most popular speeches glossed, excluding the evidence of Asconius, Loschi and Polenton, were those shown in this table. Notable here are the speeches characteristically popular in the Middle Ages (see note 67, above). Curiously, perhaps, the great series of political speeches do not enjoy uniform individual popularity. The *Philippics* are in the most popular group, but the *Catilines* are in the second group, with six to eight commentators and ten to twenty commentaries (with *Man., Agr., Rosc., Red., Rab.*), and the *Verrines* are in the least popular group with fewer than ten commentaries and five or

	Number of Commentators	Number of Commentaries
Marc.	12	36
Lig.	12	34
Arch.	12 (often printed with the *colores* in the margins)	43
Mil.	12 (often published with a *compendium de arte dicendi,* or *de arte dicendi in genere indiciali*)	42
Phil.	10	33
Deiot.	10	23

fewer commentators (this figure almost certainly indicates the limitations of my search), despite the fact that in the medieval *Ad Herennium* and *De inventione* commentaries the Verrine orations are alone almost always cited. Some speeches do not seem to have been commented on individually at all: *Pro Scauro* (Fabricius 1.163 says this is glossed only in Asconius), *Tog.Cand.* (Fabricius 1.159 – only in Asconius), *Pro M. Tullio.* These observations, however, must be set against the popularity of the Asconian collection (dealt with above) and the collections of Loschi and Sicco. I have come across ten printings of the former (1477, 1492, 1536 – 1547, 1586, *Arch., Man., Quint., Clu., Flac., Sull., Planc., Mil., Marc., Lig., Deiot.*) and six of the latter (*Cat., Red., Dom., Arusp.Resp., Sext., Vat., Cael., Prov. Cons., Balb.,* Cic.-Sall. *invectt.;* see Cosenza 4.2874, 5.1448). The apparent lack of emphasis on the Verrines must to some extent be made up for from the contents of the collected editions I have not separately analyzed. Fabricius (1.157), for example, lists Sylvius, Latomus, Hegendorf, Toxita, Camerarius, Nannius, and Eubolus Dynaterus as commentators on the Verrines (all or part) in the Lyons 1553 edition. The Cicero-Sallust invectives attract some interest: six commentators, eight commentaries (i.e., editions), with such leading names as Beroaldo, Valla, Sylvius, Omnibonus Leonicenus, and Josse Badius Ascensius.

The total number of speech glosses, therefore, should probably be fixed at a minimum of twice the number of *De inventione, Ad Herennium* commentaries (not counting the collected editions, which would increase the discrepancy). However, the individual printing of particular commentaries does not seem to equal the printing runs of the most popular *Ad Herennium* commentaries. Overlap between the two sets of glossators seems surprisingly absent. Trapezuntius, Sturm, Giorgio Valla[75] have but the slightest connection with the *De inventione/Ad Herennium* tradition, while Guarino, a staple contributor to the latter, has but a scant foot in the speech gloss world. Badius Ascensius, Maturanzio, and Toxita represent the only real overlap between the two traditions, in some sixty-five names.

The total number of separate commentaries on Cicero's mature rhetorical works is, by my count, and again excluding certain "collections," 255, of which 8 are anonymous. This is considerably fewer than for the speeches and perhaps not appreciably more than for the *De inventione/Ad Herennium* set, although I have more thoroughly investigated collected editions for the latter.[76] However, the mature rhetorical works of Cicero comprise 6 works, which I set out in apparent order of popularity:

Works	Number of Commentaries
Topica ad Trebatium	77
De partitione oratoria, partitiones oratoriae (see Monfasani, p. 269, note 115)	71
De oratore libri tres	56
Orator ad M. Brutum de optimo genere dicendi "*Utrum dificilius . . .*"	28
Brutus de claris oratoribus "*Cum e Cilicia . . .*"	16
De optimo genere oratorum, "*Oratorum genera . . .*"	7

Of these, it should be noted, the *Topica* has the clearest dialectical interest; it also seems to have appealed to lawyers, to judge from the title of Curio's 1553 commentary: *In Top. Cic. explicationes ad iuris civilis rationem quod voluit Cicero accommodata* (Orelli, vol. 6, 433).

Since the *Ad Herennium* alone secured almost 140 editions

75. See above, note 65 and the text between nn. 62 and 63.

76. Since I am, with the late Professor Caplan, responsible for the *CTC* article on these texts.

of notes, commentaries, *castigationes*, and so forth, it may reasonably be concluded that the mature "Renaissance" rhetorical works of Cicero did not replace the "medieval" *dubia* in the period we are considering.

The principal commentators on Cicero's mature rhetorical works are as follows (S=also commented on the speeches, SM=barely figures among the speech commentators; R=also commented the *De inventione* or *Ad Herennium*):

Work by Cicero	Number of Editions	Dates of Editions
	Iacobus Lodoicus Strebaeus Rhemensis (SM)	
Partit. Or.	16	1535 – 1568 (F. 1.150 adds 1564 Basle)
De orat.	7	1540 – 1564
Orat.	5	1536 – 1543 (F. 1.150 adds 1564 Basle)
Brut.	2	1543 – 1546
	Philip Melanchthon (S)	
De orat.	18	1514 – 1564
Top.	10	1523 – 1554
Orat.	6	1534 – 1546 (F 1.150 adds 1564 Basle)
Brut.	2	1543 – 1546
Opt. gen. or.	1	1543
Partit. Or.	1	1560

Denis Lambin (R) also wrote on four of the above texts (*De orat., Top., Brut., Orat.,* 1569) but apparently without much success. Later scholars who wrote on three of the above works are Antonio Riccoboni (R), Pietro Vettori (R), Mari-Antonio Majoragio, Audomarus Talaeus (S), Coelio Secundo Curio (S). Scholars who glossed two works include: Giorgio Valla (R?), Omnibonus Leonicenus (SM), Latomus (S), Hegendorf (S), Io. Rivius Atthendoriensis (Joannes Rivius of Attendorn), Io. Camerarius (S), Estaço Statius (Achilles Statius), Victor Pisanus, Leodegarius a Quercu (S), Ramus (S). Authors of a single gloss (in order of first appearance) are Turnebus, Boethius, Ger. Bucoldianus (S), Io. Visorius Coenomanus, A. Antonius Palmyraenus,

Johannes Sturm (S), Antonio de Gouvea (SM), Guillaume Morel, Sebastiano Corrado, Amerbach (S), Turnebe (S), Erythraeus (S), Petr. Velleus Guevara, Mignault (Minos, S), Ioannes a Reberteria Turonensis, I. Antonius Viperanus, Fabius Paulinus Utinensis, Jean Passerat.

Of a total of thirty-six names, three, perhaps four, glossed the *De inventione/Ad Herennium* and seventeen the speeches as well as the mature rhetorical works. This latter lack of overlap is surprising, but more surprising is the dichotomy between commentators of the *juvenilia/dubia* and those of the mature rhetorical works. Even more striking is the absence of any name attached to all three groups: *De inv./Ad Her.,* speeches, mature rhetorical works.

Part of the explanation of this absence is the differing interests of scholars who paid some attention to the rhetorical works of Cicero. Ramus, Melanchthon, Agricola, Sturm, and Christopher Hegendorf, for example, were all much exercised by logic and dialectic.[77] Sturm's interest in Hermogenes led him to comment upon Cicero's *Partitiones oratoriae,* and a year later he wrote a handbook of logic as a *Partitiones dialecticae.*[78] Riccobono and Pietro Vettori are among the seven Italians who produced a new version of Aristotle's *Rhetoric* to replace the Quattrocento texts of Trebizond and Ermolao Barbaro.[79] This emphasis on logic and Aristotle's *Rhetoric* is, incidentally, yet another illustration of the continuing distinction between the rhetorical south of Europe and the dialectical north.[80]

I think it will follow from the above, and from such research as is undertaken into this subject in the future, that Cicero's less elementary rhetorical treatises were increasingly studied in the Renaissance, but that the intensity of attention devoted to each work was not equal to that devoted to the elementary treatises. Again, it seems clear that those scholars who studied the more sophisticated works were, in general, not the scholars who published aids to the elementary treatises. Scholars like Petrus Ramus, Philip Melanchthon, Georgio Valla,

77. See Monfasani, pp. 321–27; and Cesare Vasoli, *La Dialettica e la Retorica dell' Umanismo: "Invenzione" e "Metodo" nella Cultura del XV e XVI Secolo* (Milano, 1968), pp. 147 ff., 249 ff., 310–601. Valla, Trapezuntius, Latomus, and Gouvea were also caught up with contemporary interest in dialectic and logic (Vasoli, pp. 255 ff, 407, 410–18; Monfasani, pp. 328 ff).

78. Monfasani, p. 326.

79. Ibid., p. 332.

80. See my diss. 1, chap. 3 (c); and Bouwsma, *Venice and the Defense of Republican Liberty* (Berkeley and Los Angeles, 1968), p. 2.

or even Gasparino de Barzizza (whose notes on the *De oratore* seem to have survived in manuscript) represent a class of students whose names are found attached only to the more sophisticated rhetorical works of Cicero. Much the same impression is created by the history of Cicero's speeches in the Renaissance. The overall conclusion, that the speeches were subjected to vastly increased attention in the Renaissance, cannot be contested. As with the mature rhetorical works, however, few commentators linked their study of the speeches with lecturing on the *De inventione,* the *Ad Herennium,* or both. The examples of Alexander Guarinus, who commented on both the *Pro Milone* and the *Ad Herennium,* and of George of Trebizond, who, as we have seen, commented on some of the speeches and wrote a treatise based to a large extent on the *De inventione* and *Ad Herennium,* were not typical. The speeches therefore support the view that commentators tended to specialize, some on the orations, some on the later rhetorical works of Cicero, some on the elementary works, with only a few ranging more widely.

III

All these sources of classical rhetorical theory profited from the researches of Renaissance scholars. We have already spoken of Trapezuntius's researches into Greek rhetoric: Kristeller's *Iter* 1 – 2 lists at least eleven manuscripts of his translation of Aristotle's *Rhetorica* (cf. the editions of Venice 1523, Lyons 1541; and Monfasani, p. 55). Filelfo's translation of the *Rhetorica ad Alexandrum* was common (the *Iter* lists some sixteen manuscripts, two with Trapezuntius's translation of Aristole's *Rhetorica* and cf. printed editions, e.g., 1545). The complete rhetorical art of Hermogenes was published with Greek commentaries by Aldus Manutius in 1508 and incorporated into vast compends like that of Antonius Lullius's seven books of rhetoric, published in 1558.[81] The minor Latin rhetoricians were copied in the Renaissance. Fortunatianus's *Artis rhetoricae libri tres* was printed at

81. A. M. Patterson, *Hermogenes and the Renaissance: Seven Ideas of Style* (Princeton, 1970), p. 18 and chap. 1 generally; on Hermogenes see also Monfasani, index, p. 402; and Kristeller, *Iter Italicum,* 2 vols. (Leiden, 1963 – 1967), 1.335 and 2.90. There is some material on the study of Greek rhetoric in the West in N. Wilson, "The Book Trade in Venice ca. 1400 – 1515," in H. G. Beck et al., *Venezia, centro di mediazione fra oriente e occidente (secoli XV –XVI), aspetti e problemi* (Florence, 1977), pp. 381 ff.

least six times with, for example, his *Dialectica*, Guarino da Verona's *Oratio nuptialis*, Aquila Romanus's *De figuris*, Trapezuntius's translation of Aristotle's *Rhetorica* or his *Rhetoricorum libri quinque*; Sulpitius Victor's *Institutiones oratoriae* were printed at Basle in 1523; also, though not formally classified among the *rhetores latini minores*, Boethius's *De differentiis topicis* was printed in the Renaissance (e.g., 1511, 1534, 1537, 1543). Dionysius Halicarnassus's *De compositione artis rhetoricae* was also printed, for example, in 1546. The influence of these texts, however, was not particularly pronounced in view of the broad range of source material available to Renaissance scholars.[82]

Quintilian's *Institutes of Oratory* aroused great interest after Poggio's discovery of the complete manuscript in 1416. Filippo Beroaldo emended the text in his *Annotationes* (Bologna, 1496); Gasparino Barzizza and Lorenzo Valla devoted much attention to it: Polizian wrote a preface to it and his notes on it are in manuscript. He prepared a course of lectures on Quintilian and there are samples of his use of the ancient rhetorician in his *Miscellaneorum centuria*. The *Institutes* was much excerpted. There are numerous manuscripts of the abridgement by Franciscus Patricius Senensis (Francesco Patrizi Senese, Bishop of Gaeta). Another epitome by "Jona Philologo" was published at Basle, no date, and six more times at Paris, Lyons, and Strassburg to 1568. There are manuscripts of Marinus Becichemus's *quaestiones* on the text of the *Institutes* and Ramus wrote *Rhetoricae distinctiones in Quintilianum* (printed 1549 Paris, 1550 Paris, 1556 Cologne, 1559 Paris, and so forth).[83]

Between 1482 and 1599, upwards of forty editions presented texts of the *Institutes* with annotations, commentaries, and also (or

---

82. On the minor Latin rhetoricians in the Renaissance, see Giuseppe Billanovich, "Il Petrarca e i retori latini minori," *Italia Medioevale e Umanistica* 5 (1962), 103–64; see also Kristeller, *Iter* 2.568, 581 (Fortunatianus); 1.161, 301; 2.319, 423 (Martianus Capella *De nuptiis*, printed 1499 and six times thereafter before 1600); 2.440 (Tacitus, *Dialogus*, printed 1477 and six times thereafter, once, 1539, with the *castigationes* of Beatus Rhenanus); Fredborg in *The Logic of Buridan*, ed. Pinborg, pp. 48–51, dealing with Boethius's *De differentiis topicis* in the later Middle Ages. Certain manuscripts of Guarino da Verona's *Ad Her.* commentary appear with Boethius *De diff. top.* 4, with Julius Severianus *praecepta artis rhetoricae* or with Julius Fortunatianus's *ars rhetorica* (e.g., Milan Ambros. A 36 inf., Vat. lat. 5338), but others show a matching with "modern" works, such as Barzizza's popular *Exempla exordiorum*.

83. On Quintilian in the Renaissance and on the studies of Poggio, Valla, Guarino, and Gasparinus, see Sabbadini, *Storia*, chap. 7; and his *La Scuola* p. 60 (Barzizza's *exordia* and his study of the rhetorical works of Cicero and Quintilian). On Polizian's

instead of) *castigationes* or *argumenta*. Among the editors in this period appear some Cicero speech commentators (e.g., Bucoldianus: cf. Schweiger 2.836). The fourteen earliest commentators are listed below:

Badius Ascensius, who glossed an extract from *Inst.* II.9 in four editions between 1498 and 1500.

Rafaello Regio (Pökel, p.220), a Paduan professor who died in 1520; Regio's commentary on the whole of the *Institutes* saw at least fourteen editions before 1536. He also wrote *Problemata in Quintilianum*.

Lorenzo Valla, whose annotations on *Institutes* I-II (so Graesse; my own inspection of the 1494 Venice edition indicates that his signed notes extend to sig.g vi^v) saw, it seems, but two editions (1493 – 1494).

Pomponius Laetus, the celebrated fifteenth-century classicist (see *CTC* 3.373 – 83), and Joannes Sulpitius (Verulanus, Giovanni Sulpizio? Pökel, p.269) appear only in the 1493 and 1494 editions mentioned above for Lorenzo Valla. Pomponius's annotations cease at the same point in the text of the *Institutes* as Valla's, but neither my own inspection nor that of Graesse can find any trace of work by Sulpitius, despite the presence of his name on the title page.

Peter Schade or Mosellanus, 1493 – 1524 (Pökel, p.181), teacher at Frieburg and Leipzig; his commentary was printed in perhaps fifteen editions between 1528 and 1567; in many of these it is specifically stated to cover only the first seven books of the text.

Quintilian studies, see the index to I. Maïer, *Les manuscrits d'Ange Politien*, Travaux d'Humanisme et Renaissance 70 (Geneva, 1965), esp. pp. 344 – 45. According to Maïer (*La formation d'un Poète Humaniste*, 1469 – 1580, Geneva, 1966, p. 423), Polizian prepared a course of lectures on Quintilian at the studio in Florence, ca. 1480 – 1481, and his *introductio* has been preserved. Kristeller's *Iter Italicum* has numerous citations relating to Quintilian. For example, Polizian's manuscript notes on Q: Kristeller *Iter* 1.176; Valla's *collectanea* on Q: *Iter* 1.397, 2.546; Becichemus's *questiones* on various readings in Q. against Regius: *Iter* 2.268; Andr. Masius's *lectiones Quintiliani: Iter* 2.305; anonymous orations beginning with a lecture on Quintilian: *Iter* 2.215; Aurelius Bienatus commentary on *Inst.* I – IV (1475) *Iter* 1.415, commentary on Q.: *Iter* 2.319. Such examples could be multiplied. See also D. Bassi, "L'Epitome di Quintiliano di Frencesco Patrizi Senese," *Rivista di filologia e d'istruzione classica* 22 (1894), 385 – 470. Quintilian, like *Ad Her.* IV, was often pillaged for *Florilegia* on the *colores* (e.g., Lyons 1525, 1530).

Camerarius, already noted as a commentator on Cicero's speeches, produced a popular gloss to *Institutes* I-II printed in at least sixteen editions between 1532 and 1567, commonly with Schade on I-VII and Pinus (see below) on III.

The *argumenta* (and sometimes *castigationes*) of the Paris professor Pierre Galland (1510 – 1599), who edited the *Institutes* at Paris in 1543 with Polizian's preface, saw some eight printings between 1538 and 1567. It was against him, probably, that Ramus directed his charges in his *Rhet. dist. in Quint.* (1549).

Josse Badius Ascensius, glossator of the *Ad Herennium* and some of Cicero's speeches (but not his mature rhetorical works) had notes on Quintilian's *Institutes* printed three times (1516, 1527, 1528).

Gul(ielmus?) Philander Castilionieus had his *castigationes* printed some eight times between 1536 and 1561.

Antonius Pinus Portodemaeus wrote a gloss on *Institutes* III that was printed six times between 1538 and 1567.

Ioannis Sichardus (Johannes Sichard, 1499 – 1552), a pupil of Ulrich Zazius and professor of law at Tübingen (Pökel, p. 257), edited the *Institutes* for a Cologne printing in 1536 (with Camerarius), but it seems that the 1541, 1543, 1548 *(bis)*, 1555, and 1561 editions also print marginal annotations of the modern, classicizing, textual sort.

Merula, whose name also appears among the Cicero speech commentators, had glosses on the *Institutes* printed in 1516 and 1527.

Jan de Meurs (Meursius, Pökel, p. 175, 1579 – 1639) had a commentary printed in 1587 and 1599.

A number of other scholars seem to have had their notes printed at least once: Melanchthon (1570, a commentator on Cicero's speeches and mature rhetorical works); Morel (1548, also glossed Cicero's *Partit. Or.*); and A. Turnebus (*Breves commentarii* 1586, presumably the Turnèbe who appears among the Cicero speech and mature rhetorical works glossators). There are also at least five anonymous commentaries or sets of notes.

The *Declamationes* (ed. Domitius Calderinus, Rome, 1475) received less attention, being glossed by Schade (four editions?), Badius (1528), Rudolf Agricola (1555; Agricola also glossed Seneca's *Declamationes*), Fernandus Pincianus (once, Pökel, p. 209, Fredenandus Nonius, a Spaniard who worked on Seneca, Pliny, Pomponius Mela and taught at Alcala and Salamanca), P. Aerodius (1563), P. Belingenius Cecus (1567), Pierre Pithou or Pithoeus (Pökel, p. 210), 1580, 1594, 1618, printed with Tacitus *Dialogus*. Anonymous *annotationes* and *argumenta* were printed in 1539 and 1543 (see Sabbadini, *Storia*, pp. 21 and 300 ff.).

In a letter included in the Venice 1494 edition of the *Institutes* (with glosses by Pomponius Laetus, Lorenzo Valla, and Raphael Regius), Joannes Antonius Campanus (1427 – 1477), draws the distinction between Cicero and Quintilian in terms of the former:

> ruling in *conciones* and *subsellia* (courts), the latter *in scholiis et scassibus;* Cicero himself is more effective in practice *(pugnacior),* Quintilian is perhaps a little more devoted to instructing others. Even in regard to the style *(genus dicendi)* there is dissimilitude. Cicero is magnificent and full *(magnificus et plenus),* Quintilian is rather lavishly ornamented *(sumptuosus)* and richly ornate *(locuples).* The one is ample, sublime, overflowing *(amplus/sublimis redundans),* the other is serious, keen, elaborate *(gravis, acer, elaboratus).* The one is naturally more ornate *(natura ornatior),* the other, for his part, just as finished in his studious preparation *(studium).*

Polizian, in his preface to the *Institutes* (printed, for example, in the Paris 1542[84] edition of that text), puts it this way:

> Indeed, we do not, as it were, prefer Quintilian to Cicero, but we judge his *Institutio oratoria* to be fuller and more fecund than the rhetorical books of Cicero. . . . As our philosophers do not put Aristotle, whom they especially follow, before Plato, so we prefer to interpret Quintilian rather than Cicero, not indeed in order to detract from that sacrosanct glory of Cicero but that we might serve your interests as you hasten towards Cicero. . . .

He goes on to stress that Cicero's rhetorical works were intended for beginning orators, or slipped out ill-advisedly, or else do not contain precepts for the orator. "When we take into our hands the books of old authors, we are not searching out unused paths; yet, if such authors enjoy less use and custom among men today, it is not the fault of their quality, but rather the fault of time and fortune. . . ," and there follows a humanist denunciation of the barbarous Middle Ages. In

---

84. I have used Chicago Univ. Regenstein Lib. PA 6649 f.A2, 1542. The preface is listed in Aldus Manutius's 1513 catalogue of books (cf. H. Omont, *Catalogues des livres Grecs et latins imprimés par Alde Manuce à Venise* [1498, 1503, 1513], Paris, 1892).

the early sixteenth century,[85] the works of Quintilian, Cicero, Aristotle, and Trebizond were selected as the key books on classical rhetoric. However, it seems likely that Trebizond's own treatise, with its twenty-one manuscripts from the fifteenth century, and a string of printed editions beginning in 1472,[86] outbid the Roman writer as a popular compend of rhetoric and continued to exercise some influence on the reading of Hermogenes when the appearance of new translations and epitomes of the Greek writer after the middle of the sixteenth century resulted in widespread attention to Greek rhetoric and stylistic.[87] That Aristotle's *Rhetoric* should have been seen as a central text is to be expected. There are over ninety-seven Latin manuscripts of Aristotle's *Rhetorica* in the later Middle Ages, many with *scholia* and *marginalia*. There are up to twenty-two manuscripts of a single commentary on the *Rhetoric*—that of Giles of Rome.[88] As early as 1310–1320 we have the *Summa rethorice* or *opusculum rethorice* of Guido Vernani de Arimino, O.P., lector at the *studium* of Bologna in those years. Lohr classifies this as a commentary on Aristotle's *Rhetoric*,[89] but it presents a broad treatise on rhetoric

85. Monfasani, pp. 318–19.

86. Ibid., pp. 320–21. Trebizond, of course, made great use of Quintilian. Seb. and Antoine Gryphius put out a steady stream of coupled *Ad Her.* and *De inv.* editions, but hardly a Trapezuntius *Rhetoricorum*, from the 1520s through to the end of the sixteenth century. The original compositions by Valla and Melanchthon saw more editions by Gryphius than Trebizond's. See H. L. Baudrier, *Bibliographie Lyonnaise*, 12 vols. (Lyons, 1895–1921), 8.17.

87. Monfasani, pp. 322 ff.; Patterson, pp. 18 ff.

88. Which was printed. See Fredborg, in *The Logic of Buridan*, ed. Pinborg; and Lohr, *Traditio* 23 (1967), 334–35 on Giles of Rome (there are five early editions of his commentary and five manuscripts and four early editions of his *de differentia rhetoricae, politicae et ethicae*). On Aristotle's *Rhetoric* in the universities and mendicant *studia*, see Murphy, *Medieval Eloquence*, pp. 54–56. The 1330 Dominican regulations at Toulouse prescribed Aristotle's *Politics* as the first reading in the second year of *studia moralis philosophiae*, and his *Rhetoric* as second reading; see A. Maierù, "Techniche di insegnamento," *Le scuole degli Ordini Mendicanti secoli XIII–XIV: Atti del XVII Convegni di Studi Todi 1976* (Todi, 1978), p. 323. Kristeller's *Iter* lists at least twelve manuscripts of Aristotle's *Rhetoric* (Latin) excluding Trapezuntius's version (including Abraham de Bodmes and Hermolao Barbaro as translators). Lohr's articles in *Traditio* 23–24, 26–30 (1967–1968, 1970–1974) cover the medieval Aristotle commentaries.

89. Lohr *Traditio* 24 (1968), 191–92; Kristeller, *Iter* 2.239. Vernani makes one of the few references to Augustine *De doctrina Christiana* 4 to be found in medieval rhetorical literature, despite the cardinal importance of that work in the eyes of modern scholars (e.g., Murphy, *Rhetoric in the Middle Ages: A History of Rhetorical Theory from Saint Augustine to the Renaissance*, Berkeley and Los Angeles 1974, esp. pp. 47–64, 286–92; and his *Medieval Eloquence*, p. 27).

and rhetorical persuasion in its own right. The *Rhetoric* is cited and used in many manuscripts of the Latin or Ciceronian tradition, and the attention the Renaissance devoted to the work had firm foundations in the later medieval curriculum.[90]

Despite this increased attention to non-Ciceronian ancient sources of rhetorical doctrine, it would nevertheless seem that the elementary Ciceronian texts and new compositions enjoyed the greater utilization during the Renaissance. Some remarks on these new compositions are now in order.

IV

It would be a mistake to suppose that formal commentaries on any of the classical works of rhetoric formed the exclusive or even the preponderant didactic base for Renaissance rhetoric. Even if we exclude the wealth of epitomes and treatises that pillage the *Ad Herennium* for orientation in the fields of letter-writing, law or prose, and poetic composition (the *colores*),[91] there is still a vast mass of ill-sorted school and didactic writing that derives from or is crudely based upon the *Ad Herennium* and the *De inventione,* and to a lesser extent other rhetorical sources. This material ranges from the most jejune student notes, summaries, abridgements, or compends (some of which were even printed, such as the twelve-page "brief introduction to the *Ad Herennium*" by Iacob Haligraeus, Paris, 1574) to learned, novel, or original works by such scholars as Valla, Trapezuntius, and Barzizza, and includes such curiosities as panegyrical orations on rhetoric exemplifying rhetorical rules and a versified version of *Ad Herennium* I-II.[92] It would be impossible to categorize this material

90. Mixed traditions: 'de arte rhetorica libri tres ex Aristotele, Cicerone et Quintiliano precipue deprompti' by Cyprianus Soarius, S.J. (Baudrier V. 282) is typical of many Renaissance compends. MS 482 of the Chicago University Regenstein Library contains a large ca. 1440 *florilegium* on ethical problems with extracts from Aristotle's *Rhetoric,* Cicero's *De oratore,* the *Ad Herennium,* "Gualfredus in Poetria," Quintilian *Decl.* and so on; topics covered include "on shameful speech," "on replying sweetly," "on avoidance of insult," "on not speaking angrily or with anger," "on wise speech," "on temperance," "concerning those who are powerful," and *de rethorica* f.202ᵛ, *de exordio* f.203ʳ, *de multiloquia* f.206ᵛ.

91. For instance, MSS London BL Add. 15,108 f.228 ff.: *Parvulus Rethorice;* Harley 670; Reg. 12.B.XVII.

92. To give one example: MS London BL Add. 22,862 fols. 50–76 includes a s.XV hexametric *Ad Her.* I–II with glosses, preceded by an *epitome iuris canonici.* The

adequately here, but in volume and range future research may ultimately suggest that it formed an important didactic addition to the
classical text-plus-commentary (though obviously deriving much
material from both) and indicates a need felt by Renaissance students for greater flexibility and adaptability on the part of the rhetorical curriculum of their day.

A few sample illustrations of this material will indicate the extent
to which it provides material beyond the range of an *Ad Herennium*
commentary. MS Basle F. VIII.5 for example is a large fifteenth-century grammar collection of 332 folios, made up of late classical, medieval, and humanist authors. Folios 285 – 328 contain a rhetorical
treatise on the *tria genera causarum*, founded on the *Ad Herennium* but
with an emphasis upon demonstrative oratory. There are elaborate
tables of arguments and sources for that kind of oratory, including a
page obviously devoted to the needs of the preacher. The treatise
then moves on to deliberative and judicial oratory, dealing with *insinuatio, narratio, constitutio* in a manner suggesting reliance upon the
Ad Herennium and, to a discernible extent perhaps, the teaching tradition of the twelfth and thirteenth centuries on that text. There is a
figura divisionis dictaminis, including addresses to *cives* in criminal
cases. Another of the Basle manuscripts, also once owned by
Iohannes Heynlin,[93] contains a *De preceptis rhethorice facultatis*, a treatise on rhetoric in two books, the second of which is on *elocucio*, following the doctrine of the *Ad Herennium*. It contains Heynlin's marginal glosses. There is also a treatise on prose composition and
colores, well illuminated, paragraphed for reference, with sample *exordia* called *arenge*, and material on *dictamen*; the treatise begins:
"whoever desires to acquire the skill of the *dictator*, and the ornaments of *elocutio* in accordance with the *viridarium* of rhetorical
amenity. . . ." The manuscript also contains *Domini Guarini Veronensis
inter rethores haud ab re facundissimi de arte dicendi precepta et a Tullio et
Demostene excerpta ad orationem conponendam* . . . , in four pages.[94] We

---

colores naturally attracted compends and summaries: for example the common prose
tract *Tria sunt circa que* . . . , London BL Harl. 2432 f. 141, Cotton Cleop. B.VI f. 33, Add.
41,490, Reg. 12.B XVII. A properly dissected discussion of this class of manuscript
material has never been attempted. The printed literature is immense. Renouard (*Répertoire des Imprimeurs Parisiens,* Paris, 1965) lists thirty-three editions of Lorenzo Valla's
De Latinae linguae elegantia from one press alone, 1501 – 1544.

93. Basle Öffentl. Bibl. der Univ. F.VIII. 14.

94. I have to thank Dr. Martin Steinmann, assistant keeper of manuscripts at the
OBU, for sending me a Xerox copy of the first page of this treatise.

also come across in the same manuscript Guillaume Tardif (Guilielmus Tardivus), a native of au Puy (1440–ca. 1500) who wrote a *Compendium ex Cicerone, Quintiliano que rhetorice artis oratorieque facultatis* at Paris around 1475. His *ex gravissimis auctoribus exordiorum praxis excerpta* contains extracts from the *De inventione,* together with epigrams, verse, miscellaneous *exempla,* rules for versification, word lists, and aids for literary composition including examples of consolation. The *Epitome in utramque Ciceronis rhetoricam* of the German humanist Conrad Celtis (1459–1508), published at Ingolstadt in 1492 as a guide for his lectures,[95] suggests the need to adapt the rhetorical curriculum to the requirements of the day in a manner not possible in a formal commentary on a classical text: part 1 contains familiar material from the *De inventione* and the *Ad Herennium,* part 2 rules for memorizing, and part 3 is a formal treatise on letter-writing. Vives himself, as I have mentioned, wrote a *Praelectio in quartum Rhetoricorum ad Herennium,* as well as a *De ratione dicendi,* a treatise on deliberative oratory and letter-writing, and six declamations; Antonio Mancinelli's epitomes and schoolbooks on versification, style, and related matters were often printed too. There is, however, an important difference here: Vives wrote no gloss on the *Ad Herennium* or *De inventione*; Mancinelli did. Why did many scholars, whose exposure to the traditional classical *originalia* was considerable, nevertheless not choose to issue glosses?

Some part of the answer may be found in the fact that it was not usually up to the *magister* to issue versions of glosses on the *originalia* but up to his students. An author therefore who wanted to publish something with his own imprint may have naturally thought of a nongloss form. Again, the currency of a famous gloss version may have dissuaded publication of a new gloss. An example might be provided by Friar Lorenzo Guglielmo Traversagni. In his *Nova Rhetorica* of 1478 and its *Epitome,* Traversagni pillaged the *Ad Herennium* and, to a much lesser extent, the *De inventione.* In 1476 and the years following, he lectured on the *Ad Herennium* at Cambridge, yet in 1452 he is found transcribing Guarino's commentary: he did not, it seems, write a commentary of his own.[96] Another curious case is Magister Gas-

95. MS Berlin Deutsche Staatsb. lat. fol. 910 fols. 1 ff. contains what appears to be a Celtis text (ca. 1489) and this presumably is what Orelli, 6.434–35, refers to as *"Epitome in utramque Ciceronis rhetoricam cum arte memorativa nova et modo epistolandi utilissimo,"* s.l. et a.

96. Monfasani, p. 261. The *Epitome* is edited by R.H. Martin, "The *Epitome Margaritae Eloquentiae* of Laurentius Gulielmus de Saona," *Proceedings of the Leeds Phil-*

parino Barzizza of Bergamo,[97] a scholar and classicist of some depth, ducal orator, and letter-writer under Filippo Maria Visconti. He taught Vittorino da Feltre and professed rhetoric at Padua. His rhetorical works, apart from letters and orations, seem to concentrate on providing practical examples of *exordia,* in accordance with the prescriptions of the *Ad Herennium* and with instruction on style, the *colores,* elocution, imitation, and the structure of Latin discourse. Barzizza died in 1431, before Guarino's *Ad Herennium* commentary became available. Did Barzizza write a commentary? Did he lecture on the *Ad Herennium* but feel the *originalia* were adequate without comment? Or did he see that his students used Bartolinus? In any event, his own compositions reflect the peculiar emphases of the humanists; and in this respect, it is clear that the *Ad Herennium* was insufficiently flexible as a text. In the early sixteenth century, the Span-

---

osophical and Literary Society (Literary and Historical Section) 14, pt. 4 (1971), 99 – 187. Martin (p. 107) records only one printed version of Laurentius de Saona's *Epitome margaritae eloquentiae* (= epitome of his larger *Nova Rhetorica,* of which there are two s.XV editions), in the Library of Ripon Cathedral. MS Vat. lat. 11,441 contains both the *epitome* and the *Nova Rhetorica.* Schägl MS 131 contains an *Ad Her.* with, on fol. 57^r, a colophon indicating that it was completed in 1450. December 3 "in castro montis Silicis" by Frater Guilelmus Savonensis de Traversagnis, O.F.M. It is entitled *Perutile et breve compendium artis rhetorice nove Marci Tulii Ciceronis ad Herennium.* The *Epitome* (Martin, p. 119) is based mainly on the *Ad Her.,* with a few passages from the *De inventione.* Traversagni also wrote an *Ars seu modus epistolandi,* included in the same manuscript. See Murphy, "Caxton's Two Choices," *Medievalia et Humanistica* n.s. 3 (1972), 241 ff.

97. The bibliography is extensive: see Sabbadini, *Scuola di Guarino,* p. 60; Monfasani, pp. 265 – 66; and R. P. Sonkowsky, "A fifteenth-century rhetorical *opusculum,*" *Classical, Medieval and Renaissance Studies in honour of B. L. Ullman,* ed. C. Henderson, vol. 2 (Rome, 1964) pp. 259 – 81. There are two works associated with the name of Gasparino which approach the nature of a partial commentary on the *Ad Herennium:* his *Exempla exordiorum super rethoricam novam* (a collection of sample speech openings to illustrate precepts from the *Ad Herennium*) and a "De exornationibus verborum atque sententiarum ex rhetorica ad Herennium" beginning "cum exornationes verborum atque sententiarum." The latter is a kind of treatise on the *colores* adopting the order of *Ad Herennium* IV. 19 – 68 and is found in three manuscripts. Cf. Daniela Mazzuconi, "Per una sistemazione dell' epistolario di Gasparino Barzizza," *Italia Medioevale e Umanistica* 20 (1977), 184. Kristeller (*Iter Italicum* 2.417) seems to ascribe the work to Gasparinus, but in another place (2.264) refers to it as an "anonymous commentary." According to Mazzuconi these *exornationes* are different from Gasparino's compilation entitled "hec sunt exornationes et constructiones." Tau, "Il *contra oblocutores et detractores poetarum* di Francesco da Fiano," *Archivio italiano per la storia della pietà* 4 (1964), 268, ascribes the work, from MS Vatican Ottob. lat. 1438, to "Gasparino pergamense." I owe thanks to Professor G. W. Pigman III of the California Institute of Technology for information about these *exornationes* and Gasparino's rhetorical oeuvre. Professor Pigman is editing Gasparino's life of Cicero.

iard Ferdinandus Herrariensis said as much: "nam liber *Ad Herennium* tam brevis est ut nihil fere contineat quod votis adolescentulorum satisfaciat."[98] He also criticized the *De oratore* and *Orator* for all but advanced students and felt Quintilian to be too prolix. He recommended, in fact, the study of George of Trebizond's *Rhetoricorum libri quinque,* which survives in more manuscripts, for example, than any extant individual *Ad Herennium* commentary.

A little later Vives, in his *De ratione dicendi,* recommends the rhetorical works of Cicero, Quintilian's *Institutes,* Hermogenes *De dictionum formis* (see Kennedy *Roman World* [note 100, below] p. 619 ff.), especially book 5, and Trebizond, "for the most part the expositor of Hermogenes." He also approves the use of Demetrius Phaleron's *Peri Ermeneias,*[99] Aelius Aristides' *Peri tou politikon logoi,*[100] and Dionysius Halicarnassus.[101] The pupil will also "take into his hands" Martianus Capella's *De nuptiis* V, Rutilius Lupus, Julius Rufinianus, Aquila Romanus, and Sulpitius Victor. Martianus V or Melanchthon is recommended as "an easy and short compendium of the art (of rhetoric)" "or the four books of Rhetoric to Herennius" (which Vives thinks were probably taken from the works of Quintilian and put together by Cornificius). Then the pupil should proceed to Quintilian's *Institutes* III, IV, VIII, IX, X, Cicero's *Orator,* Aristotle's *Rhetoric to Theodectes* (i.e., the *Rhetoric*), followed by private study of the rest of Quintilian's *Institutes,* Cicero's *Partitiones oratoriae, De oratore, Brutus,* the *Rhetorica ad Alexandrum,* and "the treatise of George of Trebizond."[102] Whether this curriculum reflects sixteenth-century practice or Vives's idiosyncratic ranking is difficult to say, but it certainly preserves the primary — if elementary — status of the *Ad Herennium,* indicates the parallel currency of the *rhetores latini minores* and new compositions, and relegates Trebizond and, to a lesser extent, Quintilian to the status of "reference" rather than curriculum material.

98. Monfasani, p. 319.

99. George Kennedy, *The Art of Persuasion in Greece* (Princeton, 1963), pp. 284–87.

100. George Kennedy, *The Art of Rhetoric in the Roman World. 300 B.C.–A.D. 300* (Princeton, 1972), pp. 582–85, 629.

101. Ibid., pp. 342–63.

102. See J. F. Cooney, "*De ratione dicendi:* a Treatise on Rhetoric by Juan Luis Vives, Books 1–3" (Ph.D. diss., Ohio State University, 1966); M. J. Thomas, "The Rhetoric of Juan Luis Vives" (Ph.D. diss., Pennsylvania State University, 1967), pp. 121–22; I. G. Gonzalez, "Juan Luis Vives: his Contributions to Rhetoric and Communication in the 16th Century with an English Translation of the *De consultatione*" (Ph.D. diss., Indiana University, 1973), pp. 189 ff.; and Foster Watson, *Vives on Education* (Cambridge, 1913), pp. 182–83.

V

A final consideration of the problems raised in the preceding section must conclude this essay. If we look back over the 1,650-year history of commentaries and glosses on Cicero's *Rhetorica* surveyed in this and a preceding article,[103] a pattern emerges. For the first 1,000 years the *De inventione* and *Ad Herennium* are advanced texts serving particularly intense moments of interest in communication, systems of knowledge, or sources of antique learning (Victorinus, Grillius, Alcuin, Lupus of Ferrières, the period of textual reconstruction towards the end of the 1,000-year period). In the ensuing 500 years these texts become the basis for theoretical study of the ancient art of rhetoric and are equipped with elaborate glosses and commentaries. If we recall the two aspects of ancient rhetoric, the Aristotelian, or scholastic, and the dynamic, linguistic, or "Gorgian,"[104] we will need to note that in this second period of our survey, specialized applications of rhetorical theory appear (*dictamen, poetria,* and so on), but language experimentation, or the "Gorgian" aspect of rhetoric, does not necessarily accompany the scholastic study of the *De inventione* and *Ad Herennium:* Mussato and Lovato at Padua must not be confused with Bartolinus or Giovanni del Virgilio at Bologna.[105] Yet the two classical texts are the most thoroughly studied learned writings from antiquity on rhetoric, especially in twelfth-century France and fourteenth- and fifteenth-century Italy.[106]

The last 150 years of our 1,650-year period see tremendous diversification. The *Ad Herennium* and *De inventione* are frequently printed, with commentaries and glosses or alone, but the glosses are associated with relatively undistinguished scholars and have to compete with a great variety of new sources of eloquence, especially the mature rhetorical works of Cicero, Quintilian, and ancient Greek rhetorical texts. Great names such as Lorenzo Valla and Leonardo Bruni, pioneers in "Gorgian" rhetoric, are not schoolmen, and others, such as Melanchthon, show far more interest in the mature rhe-

103. Murphy, *Medieval Eloquence,* pp. 25 ff.

104. See Jacqueline de Romilly, *Magic and Rhetoric in Ancient Greece* (Cambridge, Mass., 1975).

105. See Guido Billanovich, *"Veterum Vestigia Vatum* nei carmi dei preumanisti padovani: Lovato Lovati, Zambono di Andrea, Albertino Mussato e Lucrezio, Catullo Orazio (*Carmina*), Tibullo, Properzio, Ovidio *(Ibis),* Marziale, Stazio *(Silvae),"* *Italia medioevale e umanistica* 1 (1958), 155–243; and in the same journal [4 (1961), 181–200], Paul Oskar Kristeller, "Un *ars dictaminis* di Giovanni del Virgilio."

106. Murphy, *Medieval Eloquence,* p. 38.

torical works of Cicero, or in dialectic, or Cicero's speeches, than they do in the *Ad Herennium* or *De inventione*. Perhaps the most significant aspect of this last 150 years, however, is the appearance of the new compositions and manuals noted in our previous section, designed to replace the primacy of the *Ad Herennium* and *De inventione*. That they did not entirely do so is indicated by the statistics of printing history, but their appearance and popularity are facts. What did the "new compositions" have to offer that the *De inventione* and *Ad Herennium* did not? What was the principal reason for the loss of primacy on the part of the latter texts? If we look at two randomly selected examples of these new elementary Renaissance rhetorical manuals that are not specifically oriented towards preaching, *poetria* or *dictamen*, we can gain some idea of what qualities were needed that the classical treatises and their commentaries did not provide.

The two works I have chosen are Melanchthon's *Elementorum rhetorices libri* and Traversagni's *Epitome Margaritae eloquentiae*, an abridgement of his *Nova rhetorica* or *Margarita eloquentiae*.[107] Two initial incentives for the composition of new manuals that emerge from these two works are, first, the fact that new treatises simply did away with the need to have both classical text and commentary before the student, and, second, the fact that the classical *originalia* were in some respects unsuited as basic texts — the *De inventione* was plainly incomplete; the *Ad Herennium* lacked adequate prefatory material[108] and did not necessarily reflect the emphases of Renaissance practitioners. Quintilian and the mature rhetorical works of Cicero were too diffuse, the *rhetores latini minores* too thin. A consideration of Traversagni's *Epitome* will amplify these initial impressions.

In his preface Traversagni provides a modernized version of the usual commentary prefatory material.[109] He then follows *Ad Heren-*

---

107. The latter work is oriented towards preaching: see Murphy, "Caxton's Two Choices," p. 243. On the editions of these two texts used, see above, note 96, and M. J. La Fontaine, "A critical translation of Philip Melanchthon's *Elementorum Rhetorices libri duo*" (diss., University of Michigan, 1968).

108. As a consequence medieval commentators developed a standard preface: N. Haring, "Thierry of Chartres and Dominicus Gundissalinus," *Mediaeval Studies* 26 (1964), 281–86.

109. Ed. R. H. Martin, pp. 128 ff. Traversagni provides a broad but formal definition of rhetoric, using that given in Isidore of Seville's *Etymologies* as a basis. The three occasions for formal oratory are modernized (*iudicialis* occurs "in conspectu principum et iudicum" and is now the province of advocates and procurators instead of, as formerly, orators; *deliberativum* occurs "in commotione," that is, where "viri graves" assemble to consult persuasively or dissuasively about things that pertain to the com-

nium I.3.5 ff. but his rewriting offers ample opportunity for thorough modernizing and Christianizing illustrative content.[110] It is worth noting here that Traversagni's rewriting is not necessarily in the interests of brevity: in fact, his section on *exordium* is almost three times as long as that in the *Ad Herennium*,[111] while his section on *narratio* is somewhat shorter.[112] The rest of the *Epitome* expresses most clearly Traversagni's departures from the presentation found in the *Ad Herennium*, which becomes lost, at this point, in the judicial *constitutiones* and rhetorical proof techniques (enthymemes).[113] Traversagni has no use for these, despite their popularity in medieval commentaries. He plunges into a description of the *topoi* of argumentation, very much in the language of the medieval commentators.[114] This rewriting allows a complete modernization of context[115] for Traversagni and a reduction of fifty-four pages in the Marx *editio minor* of the *Ad Herennium* to five in his. Traversagni then

mon good of a king's state or a republic). *Materia* (cf. Thierry of Chartres, above note 108, sections 8 – 12) follows, then *finis* (Thierry, sections 14 – 15). These passages represent a succinct handling of what is treated discursively in the *De inventione* I.5.6 and I.5.7 to I.6.8. The *partes* come next (see Thierry, 16 – 18) but the description is fuller than is found in the summary coverage at *De inv.* I.7.9 and *Ad Her.* I.2.3. This is sometimes achieved by incorporating instruction located elsewhere in the *Ad Her.* (cf. e.g., Martin, pp. 131 ff., notes) and provides an opportunity to comment on current controversy, for example, a sideswipe at those who depict rhetoric simply as a matter of *colores* rather than as excellent reasoning and judgment carefully and wisely researched, prudently arranged and adapted to the task of rendering probable what we wish to persuade of. Traversagni then proceeds through *artifex* (Thierry, 20), *officium artificis*, and *instrumentum oratoris* (Thierry, 19).

110. For example, on *insinuatio*, Martin, pp. 141 –42.

111. This was apparently a sensitive area in which the curriculum could be expanded: Gasparino Barzizza's collection of *exordia* occurs frequently in the manuscripts and we have in MS Stuttgart Württ. Landesbibl. HB VIII.13, fols. 189 – 194ᵛ a collection of sample *exordia:* "in causa dubia ad captandum benivolenciam . . . in re honesta in genere deliberationis ad constituendum propositionem de causa agenda . . . pro retorquendo exordium in partem adversarii ad captandum benivolentiam in re turpi sumptum a Tulio contra Salustium . . ." etc. The collection is entitled "exordia super novam Ciceronis rhetoricam anno domino 1461ᵃ Parisius collecta per egregium virum Ferariensem nacione de ordine minorum religiosum communicata autem in Lipczk. Expliciunt anno domini 1470ᵒ" (colophon, f. 194ᵛ).

112. Largely by omitting *Ad Her.* I.8.13, nonoratorical *narrationes*, which medieval commentators greatly developed.

113. The remainder of *Ad Herennium* I and as far as II.29.46.

114. Who inserted at this point (*omnes res, De inv.* I.24.34) elaborate theoretical discussions of the *topoi (sedes argumentorum)* and the *circumstantiae* that particularized a case.

115. E.g., Martin, pp. 158 –59.

takes over the *Ad Herennium* terminology of *amplificatio* and *commis-seratio* in *conclusiones,* matches it with the descriptive content of the *De inventione's loci indignationis* and *conquestionis,* divorces both from a strict applicability in conclusions and, as a consequence, is better able to handle the subject of the *conclusio,* after he has dealt with the three *genera causae.*[116] He omits entirely *pronuntiatio, memoria,* and *elocutio.*

Traversagni's rewriting of the *Ad Herennium,* then, effects more than simply the provision of a treatise on *inventio.*[117] It allows, first, a more expeditious and less repetitious presentation of the information contained in the classical treatise; second, it allows a moderniza-tion and Christianization of context; third, it enables the deletion of anachronistic material (the *constitutiones*) or material taught else-where or felt to be overrated;[118] fourth, it allows a concentration on speeches of the sort most likely to be provided by Renaissance stu-dents — panegyrics, speeches at church councils, and before major ecclesiastical and secular dignitaries, sermons, and the like.

For Melanchthon, too, the opportunity of writing an indepen-dent treatise allows a full preface in which the nature of rhetoric is discussed and its broad applicability in the reading and judging of important material as well as in the pleading of cases is canvassed. Melanchthon's view of rhetoric is oriented towards its place in help-ing with the comprehension and articulation of argument and in the evaluation of speeches. Hence he includes a discussion of its relation-ship with dialectic,[119] adds a fourth *genus cause (didascalicon)* dealing with dialectic and stresses in general the fundamental significance of dialectical *topoi* for rhetoric seen as the analysis and description of all kinds of concepts. However, the greatest advantage of new composi-tion for Melanchthon is twofold: first, he had the ability to modern-ize the curriculum and adapt it to his own background and context as a professor and university lecturer in Greek, theology and biblical exegesis in Wittenberg. With reference to the first aspect, he is able to point out the irrelevance of instruction in *memoria* and *pronuntiatio,*[120]

116. *Ad her.* II.30.47; *De inv.* I.53.100 – I.56. 109; *Ad Her.* III.2.2 – 9.16; *De inv.* II.52.157 ff.

117. Martin, p. 118; Traversagni has carefully worked the *Ad Herennium* remarks on *dispositio* into his text (Martin, p. 131) and he does deal briefly with *elocutio, memoria* and *pronuntiatio* (pp. 132 – 35) in his prefatory material.

118. *Elocutio,* cf. remark at Martin, p. 130 line 16, paraphrased in note 109, above.

119. And notes that some reject the equation *res* =dialectic, *verba* =rhetoric.

120. "Since memory receives inadequate assistance from art, and *actio* (delivery) is now quite otherwise than it was among the ancients." Melanchthon also excludes treatment of *insinuatio* and the *tertium genus narrationis* from his text.

and, a little later on, to point out that the ancient emphasis on the judicial kind of case was hardly appropriate in his own day, since there was little trace of the ancient art of pleading in the courts of the sixteenth century. Yet, he adds, the *iurisconsulti* who in his day pleaded cases in their own way, yet read rhetorically influenced texts and the precepts of judicial rhetoric, were still taught to facilitate the judging of speeches by others and to instruct young men in the handling of controversies *in epistolis et ad ecclesiastica negocia.*[121] Melanchthon is, in fact, anxious to point out how ecclesiastical disputes can profit from *status* theory and judicial rhetorical precepts, and he devotes much attention to both; in fact, what Traversagni omits altogether Melanchthon sees as the most necessary part of the art (even to the extent of reviving the outmoded "legal stases" of *De inventione* I.13.17 and II.40.116 ff.), especially in comprehending any *controversia* and in interpreting, for example, Paul. So extensive is Melanchthon's treatment of the *status* that it dominates his presentation of more conventional material: the parts of speech, for example, are dealt with inside the conjectural *status.*[122]

The second aspect of the advantage of a new composition for Melanchthon was the opportunity to include references to Quintilian, Cicero's speeches and mature rhetorical works, Greek practitioners such as Demosthenes and Lysias and, above all, to his own specialty: biblical exegesis.[123] Book 2 of his treatise, for example, on *elocutio,* is drawn from the *De oratore* and *Orator,* Quintilian, Cicero's speeches, and a good deal of Greek rhetorical theory (presented in the original). It also includes a section "on the four ways of expounding sacred literature." *Dispositio* is illustrated with the epistles of Paul, and, if we may conclude by returning to the element of modernization and Christianization in Melanchthon's rhetoric, we should note that his handling of the deliberative and demonstrative kinds of cases, and of the *loci communes* (*De inventione* II.15.48), provides an

121. Elsewhere he refers to the role of rhetoric in "teaching ordinary people about religious beliefs or the dignity of laws and magistrates."

122. He deals also with the rhetorical syllogism, omitted by Traversagni, and the *loci communes, De inv.* II.15.48, beloved of medieval commentators.

123. The format of a new composition allowed a good deal of flexibility with regard to Cicero's speeches. Trebizond, for example, was able to include a great amount of comment on the *Pro Ligario* in his *Rhetoricorum libri quinque,* and Melanchthon was able in his treatise to refer often to his favourite Ciceronian speech, the *Pro Archia.* He is able to point out that, although this latter is a judicial speech, it relies heavily on the principles of *demonstratio.*

opportunity of illustrating by reference to German history and to ecclesiastical orations.

In conclusion, then, it would be unwise to try to fit Renaissance rhetorical didacticism into one particular mold — the differences between Melanchthon and Traversagni should demonstrate this. Yet, in important ways, the old classical rhetorical curriculum as presented in the *De inventione* and *Ad Herennium* was too inflexible for accelerated Renaissance interest in speech and pleading situations, in argument and exegesis, and in the classical past. As a consequence new compositions acquired increasing vogue. The element of surprise that confronts the modern inquirer is not this latter circumstance, but the fact that the *Ad Herennium* and *De inventione* with their commentaries and glosses were printed at all in the Renaissance. That they were we may ascribe to the dead weight of (medieval) tradition and to the enhanced Renaissance respect for (classical) *auctoritas*.

The Byzantine Rhetorical
Tradition and the Renaissance

JOHN MONFASANI

Some eighty years ago Karl Krumbacher complained that "the pre-
paratory work for a detailed history of middle Greek production in
rhetoric and epistolography is still completely lacking."[1] In the time
since, thanks especially to the labors of Hugo Rabe and others on
Hermogenes and his commentators as well as to the continued publication of Byzantine correspondence, sermons, and orations, many of
the *Vorarbeiten* demanded by Krumbacher are in place. Much of a
fundamental nature remains to be done, including a census of rhetorical texts and manuscripts, but the fact remains that Byzantine
rhetoric has become a subject ripe for attempts at synthesis, as witness the stimulating essays of George Kustas[2] and the brilliant, detailed survey by Herbert Hunger in the new history of Byzantine
literature replacing Krumbacher's classic.[3]

In contrast, when we come to the history of Byzantine rhetoric in
the Renaissance, we enter an almost virgin land. Annabel Patterson
has written on Hermogenes of Tarsus;[4] I have worked on George of
Trebizond; the late Bernard Weinberg gathered material on two
lesser authorities of the Byzantine tradition, Demetrius Phalereus

1. *Geschichte der byzantinischen Literatur von Justinian bis zum Ende des öströmischen Reiches (527–1453)*, 2 vols. (Munich, 1897), 2.455.
2. Cf. his "Function and Evolution of Byzantine Rhetoric," *Viator* 1 (1970), 55–73; and *Studies in Byzantine Rhetoric* (Thessalonica, 1973).
3. H. Hunger, *Die hochsprachliche profane Literatur der Byzantiner*, 2 vols. (Munich, 1978), 1.65 f. H. G. Beck's eminently useful *Kirche und theologische-Literatur im byzantinischen Reich* (Munich, 1959) should also be mentioned.
4. *Hermogenes and the Renaissance* (Princeton, N.J., 1970).

and pseudo-Longinus;[5] and Walter Ong has made some observations concerning the influence of Hermogenes on Renaissance concepts of method.[6] Consequently, I will not be offering any sort of synthesis but merely attempting to note certain traits of the history of Byzantine rhetoric in the Renaissance that I find interesting and relevant.

In the Latin Middle Ages, the chief sources for the classical art of rhetoric were the two manuals attributed to Cicero, a mutilated Quintilian, some late antique authors now collected in Halm's *Rhetores Latini minores,* and one translated Greek work, Aristotle's *Rhetoric,*[7] which was used more as a text in ethics and psychology than as a handbook in oratory.[8] The early humanists transformed the medieval conception of rhetoric. They made it the core subject in a new program of literary and classical education.[9] They discovered and, for the first time in a thousand years, fully valued Cicero's orations and dialogues concerning oratorical culture. However, they failed to create a similar revolution in the sources of classical rhetoric beyond finding a complete Quintilian and adding some lesser items, such as Cicero's *Partitiones oratoriae.*[10]

The rhetorical tradition of the Greek Middle Ages was dramatically different from that of the Latin West. Except for a gap in the seventh and eighth centuries, when there still must have been some schools, the late antique tradition of rhetoric maintained itself with notable success in the thousand-year history of Byzantium. Unlike their Latin counterparts, medieval Greek scholars read and imitated

5. In vol. 2 of the *Catalogus translationum et commentariorum. Mediaeval and Renaissance Latin Translations and Commentaries,* eds. F. E. Cranz and Paul Oskar Kristeller (Washington, D.C., 1971), 27–41 (Demetrius), 193–98; and "Translations and Commentaries of Demetrius, *On Style* to 1600: A Bibliography," *Philological Quarterly* 30 (1951), 353–80.

6. *Ramus, Method, and the Decay of Dialogue* (Cambridge, Mass., 1958), pp. 232 f.

7. Only three manuscripts of the pseudo-Aristotelian *Rhet. ad Alex.* are listed in *Aristoteles Latinus,* 2 vols., eds. G. Lacombe, A. Birkenmajer, M. Dulong, E. Franceschini, L. Minio-Paluello (Rome, 1939–Cambridge, 1955). For the unique manuscript of Demetrius Phalereus's *De elocutione,* see B. V. Wall, *A Medieval Latin Version of Demetrius' De elocutione* (Washington, D.C., 1937).

8. Cf. James J. Murphy, *Rhetoric in the Middle Ages* (Berkeley and Los Angeles, 1974), pp. 90 f.

9. Cf. Paul Oskar Kristeller, "Humanism and Scholasticism in the Italian Renaissance," *Byzantion* 17 (1944–1945), 346–74; rpt. in his *Studies in Renaissance Thought and Letters* (Rome, 1956), pp. 92–119.

10. Cf. R. Sabbadini, *Le scoperte dei codici latini e greci ne' secoli XIV e XV,* 2 vols. (Florence, 1905–1914), 2, chap. 4, "Riassunto filologico."

the classical models of oratorical and epistolographic eloquence from Demosthenes to Libanius. The Byzantines also studied, paraphrased, commented upon, and excerpted from a set of classical rhetorical manuals different in content from those available to the Latins. Aristotle, Dionysius of Halicarnassus, and other authorities were available, but it was the corpus of writings attributed to the second-century rhetorician Hermogenes of Tarsus that dominated the curriculum and rhetorical culture of Byzantium. Given the profound influence rhetoric exercised in Byzantine culture, touching even theology[11] and mathematics,[12] the Hermogenean corpus must rank as one of the most important formative elements in medieval Greek civilization. The differences between Hermogenes and the traditional Latin authorities are numerous, but two are fundamental. First of all, Hermogenes structured argumentation around what he called the "method of division." This method involved breaking off into a series of dichotomies all possible categories of issues and all possible arguments within issues. *Method* is such a favorite word in the Hermogenean corpus that the last piece in the corpus, an apocryphal work, is even entitled "On the Method of Awesomeness." For stylistics, the other major part of rhetoric, Hermogenes offered a system quite unlike the standard Latin division of style into grand, middle, and plain. Instead, Hermogenes described twenty-one stylistic categories, such as clarity, ethos, beauty, vehemence, grandeur, and truth, which he analyzed into their component parts, namely, diction, notions, figures of thought, figures of speech, cadence, rhythm, syllabic composition, and cola.

Now, it is virtually a truism that in accepting classical Hellenism from Byzantium, the humanists willy-nilly also accepted certain traits characteristic of medieval Hellenism. One cannot understand the choice of Platonic texts used by Marsilio Ficino without knowing something about the Byzantine sage Gemistus Pletho; Erasmus's Greek New Testament was basically the Byzantine recension of the Bible;[13] Byzantine minuscule and, for a long time, Byzantine pronunciation provided the way classical Greek was printed and spo-

11. Cf., for instance, Kustas, *Studies*, pp. 120 f., and Gregory Palamas's *Prosopoeia*, cited below.

12. Cf. J. Mogenet, "L'introduction à *Almagest*," *Académie royale des sciences, des lettres et des beaux-arts de Belgique* (Brussels), Mémoires 8°, ser. 2, vol. 51, fasc. 2, 18–20, comparing rhetorical *prolegomena* to mathematical introductions.

13. Cf. F. G. Kenyon, *The Text of the Greek Bible*, 3rd ed., rev. A. W. Adams (London, 1975), pp. 105, 173.

ken in the Renaissance.[14] Rhetoric can also be seen as a prime example of the way and to what extent Byzantine culture passed to the West in the age of the Renaissance.

In 1397, Manuel Chrysoloras, the first major Byzantine teacher of the Renaissance, took up his chair in Florence.[15] At Florence and later in Lombardy and Constantinople, Chrysoloras did well to teach Greek effectively. However, his pupils almost immediately inaugurated the Renaissance absorption of the Byzantine rhetorical tradition. Leonardo Bruni translated the orations of Demosthenes and Aeschines, as well as writing a celebrated imitation of Aelius Aristides' Panathenaic oration.[16] Cencio de' Rustici turned Aristides' oration *Ad Dionysum* into Latin,[17] and Guarino Veronese rendered four orations of Isocrates.[18] Clearly, classical Greek oratory was the first and remained the favorite interest of humanists in the Byzantine rhetorical tradition. Indeed, before the end of the fifteenth century, Demosthenes' oration *On the Crown* was translated six times,[19] and there were at least fifteen Latin versions of each of the Isocratean orations *Ad Nicoclem* and *Ad Demonicum*.[20] It is striking how many of the humanists who learned Greek tried very early in their careers to translate some piece of Greek oratory. Not only do Bruni, Guarino,

14. Cf. the lively lecture of Ingram Bywaters, *The Erasmian Pronunciation of Greek and its Precursors: Jerome Aleander, Aldus Manutius, Antonio of Lebrixia* (London, 1908); and D. Geanakoplos, *Greek Scholars in Venice* (Cambridge, 1962), pp. 273 f.

15. G. Cammelli, *I dotti bizantini e le origini dell' Umanesimo*, 1: *Manuele Crisolora* (Florence, 1941), chap. 2.

16. Cf. H. Baron, *Leonardo Bruni Aretino. Humanistisch-philosophische Schriften* (Leipzig and Berlin, 1928); and his *The Crisis of the Early Renaissance*, rev. ed. (Princeton, 1966), pp. 192 f.; and L. Bertalot, *Studien zum italienischen und deutschen Humanismus*, 2 vols., ed. Paul Oskar Kristeller (Rome, 1975), 2. 277 f., 295 f.

17. Bertalot, *Studien*, 2. 132.

18. *Econ. Helenae, Nicoles, Ad Demonicum* and *Evagoras*; but not the *Ad Nicoclem*, as once said; cf. R. Sabbadini, *La scuola e gli studi de Guarino Veronese* (Catania, 1896), pp. 125–126; T. Kaeppeli, "Le traduzioni umanistiche di Isocrate e una lettera dedicatoria de Carlo Marsuppini a Galeotto Roberto Malatesta (1430)," *Studi Romagnoli* 2 (1951), 57–65; L. Gualdo Rosa, "Niccolò Loschi e Pietro Perleone e le traduzioni dell'orazione pseudo-Isocratea 'A Demonico,'" *Atti del R. Istituto Veneto di Scienze, Lettere ed Arti* 131 (1972–1973), 825–56, esp. 826.

19. J. Monfasani, *George of Trebizond. A Biography and A Study of his Rhetoric and Logic* (Leiden, 1976), pp. 61–68.

20. Cf. Gualdo Rosa in note 18 and her article "Le traduzioni latine dell' *a Nicole* di Isocrate nel Quattrocento," in *Acta Conventus Neo-Latini Lovaniensis*, eds. J. IJsewijn and E. Kessler (Louvain and Munich, 1973), pp. 275–303. I also made an independent tally based on the leading manuscript and incunabula catalogs, especially Paul Oskar Kristeller, *Iter Italicum*, 2 vols. (Leiden, 1963, 1967).

and Cencio de' Rustici fit this pattern, but so do Lapo da Castiglion-chio the Younger,[21] Francesco Filelfo,[22] Carlo Marsuppini,[23] Bernardo Giustiniani,[24] Benedetto Bursa,[25] Niccolò Perroti,[26] Rudolph Agricola,[27] and, to give only one more example, Erasmus, who translated three declamations of Libanius soon after learning Greek.[28] Even nonoratorical works fed the humanist appetite for Greek oratory, as witness Bruni's version of the speeches in the *Iliad*[29] and Battista Guarini's rendering of Mark Antony's oration in Dio Cassius.[30]

However, while the classical oratory preserved by the Byzantine tradition came naturally to the early humanists, they had to be taught to appreciate the technical rhetoric preserved by the same tradition. In this connection, Byzantine rhetoric served a secondary, material function. For it provided the vehicle by which émigré Greek scholars, who lacked the antecedent reputation of someone like Chrysoloras or the ecclesiastical position of a Cardinal Bessarion, could somehow make their way in early Renaissance Italy. This is true of the two greatest Byzantine teachers in Italy in the decades after Chrysoloras, George of Trebizond and Theodore Gaza.

Trebizond first attracted attention in the 1430s when he published his *magnum opus*, the *Rhetoricorum libri V*.[31] It made his reputation, as events proved it to be a major document of Renaissance cul-

21. Cf. Gualdo Rosa, "Nicolò Loschi," pp. 277, 289 (notes 20 – 23), 296 – 297; and "Le traduzioni latini dell' *A Nicocle*," pp. 826 – 27.

22. A. Calderini, "Ricerche intorno alla biblioteca e alla cultura greca di Francesco Filelfo," *Studi italiani di filologia classica*, 20 (1913), 204 – 424, esp. 342; and cf. Kristeller, *Iter*, 1.25, 260.

23. Cf. the article of Kaeppeli cited in note 18, above.

24. P. Labalme, *Bernardo Giustiniani* (Rome, 1969), pp. 45 f.; and Gualdo Rosa, "Le traduzioni latine dell' *A Nicocle*," p. 296.

25. Monfasani, *George of Trebizond*, p. 23, note 100, but I only recently discovered the identity of the author.

26. G. Mercati, *Per la cronologia della vita e degli scritti di Niccolò Perotti arcivescovo di Siponto*, Studi e Testi, 44 (Rome, 1925), pp. 70 f.

27. L. Spitz, *The Religious Renaissance of the German Humanists* (Cambridge, Mass., 1963), p. 35.

28. Cf. P. S. Allen's introduction to the preface in Erasmus, *Opus epistolarum* (Oxford, 1906), 1.390; and the new Erasmus *Opera omnia* (Amsterdam, 1969), 1.1.175 f.

29. Cf. Bertalot, *Studien*, 2.280 f.

30. Cf. MS. Vienna, Nationalb. lat. 109, ff. 9ᵛ – 17ᵛ (*Tabulae codicum manuscriptorum praeter graecos et orientales in Bibliotheca Palatina Vindobonensi asservatorum*, 1, Vienna, 1864, 15 – 16).

31. Monfasani, *George of Trebizond*, chaps. 9 and 11.

ture. It exposed to the Italians in a large way for the first time the chief authorities of Byzantine rhetoric and showed by extensive examples drawn from Cicero, Vergil, Livy, and other Latin classics how much Byzantine rhetoric could do to reveal the secrets of Latin eloquence. At the same time, George deftly integrated the Byzantine authorities, such as Dionysius of Halicarnassus, Maximus the Philosopher, and especially Hermogenes, in a synthesis with the traditional Latin authorities. In short, George's *Rhetoric* succeeded because he had found the right formula, accommodating Latin rhetoric with Byzantine rhetoric. It was the unique humanist *summa* of classical rhetoric of the Italian fifteenth century. It also was one of the first humanist works to gain a following north of the Alps. As early as 1470, Guillaume Fichet in Paris complained that there was a group of *Georgiani* at the university, whose adulation of George's *Rhetoric* he found a scandal.[32] I recently discovered Fichet's own copy of George's work, whence he lifted parts for his own *Rhetoric*.[33] I also found in the Sorbonne another copy of George's rhetoric that apparently circulated in the later fifteenth century and may have been the copy Robert Gaguin lent Erasmus for his own study.[34] In the early sixteenth century, Trebizond had become such an authority that Philip Melanchthon justified his own short *Rhetoric* as simply a means of sparing students the expense of otherwise having to buy Trebizond's *summa* of Latin and Greek rhetoric.[35] Into the late sixteenth century, George remained an authority to be compared with Cicero, Quintilian, and Aristotle.

Ironically, George's archrival, Theodore Gaza, also capitalized on Byzantine rhetoric to find the road to success in Italy. We can first place Gaza in Italy with surety in 1440 when he appeared at the University of Pavia.[36] By 1442 or 1443, he had come to Mantua to work with Vittorino da Feltre in his school. At Mantua, Gaza published his first work. Pointedly, it was a translation of chapters from Dionysius of Halicarnassus's *Rhetoric* and more specifically of those dealing with nuptial poetry and oratory,[37] a genre popular in Italy since the Middle Ages, but one in which the West lacked classical

32. Ibid., pp. 321 – 22.

33. Paris, B.N. lat. 16233.

34. Paris, Université, cod. 629. Cf. Monfasani, *George of Trebizond*, p. 318.

35. T. W. Baldwin, *William Shakespere's Small Latin and Lesse Greek*, 2 vols. (Urbana, Ill., 1944), 2.9, note 31.

36. R. Sabbadini, *Il carteggio di Giovanni Aurispa* (Rome, 1943), pp, 168 f.

37. Ibid.

manuals.[38] Gaza knew well how to cater to his Italian audience. With Vittorino's death, Gaza transferred to Ferrara, where he took up the chair in Greek and eloquence. We have his inaugural address of October 18, 1446.[39] Until now all we knew is that he made a brilliant success of the opportunity. Soon after he was offered a chair at Florence by Cosimo de' Medici and the Florentine government.[40] In 1448 he was elected rector of the University of Ferrara;[41] and a year after that he received the call to come to the Rome of Pope Nicholas V.[42] Our only hint for this great success after 1446 is the remark, in Lilio Gregorio Giraldi's dialogue *De poetis,* that Gaza had interpreted "non nullas Demosthenis orationes."[43] However, Paul Oskar Kristeller has called my attention to a manuscript in the Folger Shakespeare Library containing some opuscula of Gaza.[44] These texts have proven to be the lectures Gaza gave upon taking up his chair at Ferrara. The first lecture series seems to have been the commentary on Demosthenes' oration *On the Crown* (as we have already seen, a great favorite of the early Renaissance). The rubric to the commentary tells us that it was given in the fifth year of Leonello d'Este's reign, which means a date in 1446, the very year Gaza started to teach in Ferrara. The second commentary is on Plato's brilliant critique of rhetoric, the *Gorgias,* a text already known to Latins from Leonardo Bruni's translation. Gaza explained in the introduction that, since he had already treated the supreme example of civil oratory in Demosthenes, he was now turning to the supreme example of demonstrative style in Plato. It is true, Gaza continued, that the purpose of the dialogue was to dissuade students from the rhetoric of the Sophists; nonetheless, in eloquently arguing his case, Plato proves the great power and worth of rhetoric. Thus it was the translation of a Greek rhetorical work and then these two lectures in the field of rhetoric that first made Gaza famous in Quattrocento Italy.

A decade later, in 1457, the fourth great Byzantine master in

38. Cf. Paul Oskar Kristeller, *Studies,* p. 566, note 36; and especially F. Brandileone, *Saggi sulla storia della celebrazione del matrimonio in Italia* (Milan, 1906), pp. 115 – 210.

39. L. Mohler, *Kardinal Bessarion . . .* , 3 vols. (Paderborn, 1923 – 1942), 3. 253 f.

40. Gaza's reply is edited in A. Gherardi, *Statuti della Università e Studio Fiorentino dall'anno MCCCLXXXVII . . .* (Florence, 1881), p. 455.

41. Cf. Gaza's inaugural address in Mohler, 3.259 f.

42. Cf. Monfasani, *George of Trebizond,* pp. 80 – 82.

43. É. Legrand, *Bibliographie hellénique des XVe et XVIe siècles,* 4 vols. (Paris, 1855 – 1906), l.xxxiii.

44. MS. V a 123. I am preparing a study of these texts.

Renaissance Italy, John Argyropoulos, began to lecture in Florence. His instruction reflects the maturity of humanism beginning about the mid-century. For he taught not simply Greek or rhetoric, but ethics, logic, physics, and metaphysics.[45] It was the development of Italian humanism rather than simply the scientific interests of Argyropoulos that had wrought the change.[46] After all Argyropoulos had taught rhetoric back in Constantinople.[47]

We have support in arguing for a change in humanist attitudes towards their Byzantine teachers sometime about mid-century from the career of George of Trebizond. In the 1440s, George began to translate the Aristotelian *libri naturales,* initially with the encouragement of friends, but after 1447 under the direct orders of Pope Nicholas V, for whom he rendered Aristotle's zoological works and Ptolemy's *Almagest* as well as some patristic texts. To his Aristotelian versions George felt competent to append extensive *scholia,* while in the case of Ptolemy's *Almagest* he wrote a massive commentary. By the same token, when Gaza arrived in Rome, he was put to work turning into Latin Theophrastus's botanical works.[48] Eventually he too translated Aristotle's zoological works; and recently his lengthy *scholia* to Aristotle's zoology, addressed to Giovanni Andrea de' Bussi, have also turned up.[49] Indeed, by the late 1450s, another Greek émigré, Andronicus Callistus, was hired to teach moral philosophy in addition to Greek at the University of Bologna.[50] Clearly, these Byzantines no longer felt bound by the more narrow humanist rhetorical expectations of the early Quattrocento. After mid-century, Italians no longer perceived their Greek masters as simply teachers of language and rhetoric. Thus, to be successful in their new home, Byzantine

45. G. Cammelli, *I dotti bizantini* . . . , 1: *Giovanni Argiropulo* (Florence, 1941); J. Seigel, "The Teaching of Argyropoulos and the Rhetoric of the First Humanists," in *Action and Conviction in Early Modern Europe: Essays in Memory of E. H. Harbison,* eds. T. K. Rabb and J. Seigel (Princeton, N.J., 1960), pp. 237–60; E. Brown, "Giovanni Argiropulo on the Agent Intellect: An Edition of Ms. Magliabecchi V 42 (ff. 224–228ᵛ)," in *Essays in Honour of Anton Charles Pegis,* ed. J. R. O'Donnell (Toronto, 1974), pp. 160–75.

46. Seigel (see note 44), working from too narrow a perspective, attributes the change to Argyropoulos. This question is one I hope to return to in the future.

47. Cf. Cammelli, *Argiropulo,* p. 185; Monfasani, *George of Trebizond,* p. 255.

48. Cf. C. B. Schmitt, "Theophrastus," *Catalogus translationum* (see note 5 above), 265 f.

49. MS. Montecassino 649; cf. Kristeller, *Iter,* 1.395.

50. Cf. A. Perosa, "Inediti di Andronico Callisto," *Rinascimento* 4 (1953), 3–15. It was not unusual for a humanist to hold such a position, but for a Byzantine émigré to teach more than language was unusual until then.

scholars had to cater to broader literary and scientific interests. Certainly, later Byzantine émigrés, such as Constantine Lascaris at Messinia,[51] did teach rhetoric; and certainly rhetoric and oratory continued to play a large role in the culture of the Byzantine émigrés (for instance, late in life Cardinal Bessarion translated Demosthenes' *First Olynthiac* to encourage a crusade against the Turks);[52] but it is instructive to see that Marcus Musurus, who was partly responsible for the epochal Aldine edition of the Greek rhetoricians, had only one manuscript of these rhetoricians and only three manuscripts of the Greek orators in the fifty-five manuscripts that have recently been identified as making up his library.[53]

However, the critical event in the history of Byzantine rhetoric in the Renaissance after Trebizond's *Rhetoricorum libri V* of the 1430s was not so much the expanding perspectives of humanism as rather something that began to take shape at the close of the Quattrocento. Between 1499 and 1513 at Venice, Aldus Manutius with the help of Byzantine scholars published a corpus of Greek epistolographers, a corpus of Greek orators, and a corpus of Greek rhetoricians, including the chief Byzantine commentaries on Hermogenes.[54] With these core texts of the Byzantine rhetorical tradition now easily available, the Renaissance basically had what it wanted from the Byzantine tradition of rhetoric. As far as I am aware, works of specifically medieval Greek rhetoric, not included in the Aldine corpora, were printed only sporadically in the Renaissance. The Latin *ars epistolandi* of Nicholas Secundinus was printed in 1472 and otherwise survives in a *codex unicus*.[55]

In 1523, Doxopatros's introduction to Hermogenean rhetoric was printed in the Latin version of Hilarion of Verona and reprinted thirteen years later.[56] In the middle of the century, Guillaume Morel edited Gregory Palamas's *Prosopoeia*, which was a judicial debate be-

51. Cf. H. Rabe in *Rheinisches Museum* n.s. 62 (1907), 586–90; and 63 (1908), 526 f.

52. Mohler, *Kardinal Bessarion*, 1.417.

53. E. Mioni, "La biblioteca greca di Marco Musuro," *Archivio Veneto* ser. 5, 93 (1971), 5–28; and M. Sicherl, "Musuros-Handschriften," in *Serta Turyniana. Studies . . . in honor of Alexander Turyn*, ed. J. L. Heller (Urbana, Ill., 1974), pp. 564–608.

54. Cf. Legrand, *Bibliographie*, 1.51, 82 for the epistolographers and the rhetoricians.

55. P. A. Mastrodemetris, *Nikolaos Sekoundinos (1402–1464). Bios kai ergon* (in Greek) (Athens, 1970), pp. 194 f.; and F. Babinger, *Johannes Darius (1414–1494) . . .*, in *Bayer. Acad. der Wissenschaften, ph.-hist. Kl. Sitzungsberichte*, Jahrgang, 1961, no. 5 (Munich, 1961), pp. 106 f.

56. See C. Walz, ed., *Rhetores Graeci*, 8 vols. (Stuttgart and Tübingen, 1832–1836), 6.1 f.

tween the mind and the body concerning responsibility for sin.[57] In 1554 at Paris, Henri Etienne published the treatise *On Insoluble Objections* of Maximus the Philosopher, which George of Trebizond had once plagiarized from for his *Rhetoric*.[58] Finally, the reputation of the philosopher Gemistus Pletho is probably responsible for the printing in 1595 of his epitome of rhetoric.[59] No doubt more items can be added to the list, but the basic fact remains: the Latins had only a *selective* interest in Byzantine rhetoric. The Aldine corpus of the *Rhetores Graeci* contained virtually all the texts from the Byzantine tradition that interested the Latins and would be translated in the Renaissance; but substantial parts of the Aldine corpus, namely, the Byzantine commentaries on Hermogenes, never were subsequently translated.[60] Not every text that the Byzantine scholars included in the *Rhetores Graeci* provoked the interest of the humanists.

Indeed, the different Greek rhetorical texts that did receive attention tell us much about how this Byzantine tradition was transmuted in the Renaissance. The mainstay of Byzantine rhetoric, Hermogenes, enjoyed a significant influence in the West but never came near approaching the dominance he had achieved in Byzantium. Antonio Bonfinio translated the whole Hermogenean corpus in the 1480s, but his version had a minimal manuscript diffusion and was printed only in 1538.[61] In the middle of the sixteenth century, two important teachers and translators of rhetoric, Natale de' Conti in Italy and John Sturm in the north made new Latin versions of Hermogenes.[62] Sturm, I may add, was the single most important proponent of Hermogenes in the sixteenth century. He apparently was responsible for the Greek editions of Hermogenes in Paris starting in 1531. In some copies of these editions blank folios are interleaved. This indicates that someone at Paris intended to lecture on the Greek text of Hermogenes. Later at Strasbourg, Sturm produced from his lecture notes voluminous commentaries that were eventually printed. And in works of pedagogical theory he regularly

57. See Krumbacher, 1.486.

58. As part of an anthology entitled *Dionysii Halicarnassei responsio ad Gn. Pompeii epistolam* . . . , H. Stephanus, 1554.

59. Walz, 6.544.

60. I should note that Alexander Sophista's *De schematibus* was translated from the Aldine edition by Natale de' Conti in an edition of 1557. I consulted a copy at Columbia University Library, New York; cf. Walz, 8.416.

61. I could not find any copy listed in the major manuscript catalogs.

62. Cf. Patterson (note 4, above), pp. 219–20, for some indications.

preached the value of Hermogenes.[63] It was under his influence that the tutor of King Edward VI and Queen Elizabeth, Roger Ascham, also recommended Hermogenes.[64] In the statutes of the new St. John's College, Oxford, in 1555, and in the statutes for Cambridge issued by Queen Elizabeth in 1579, Hermogenes is listed as one of the school authorities in rhetoric.[65] At the end of the century, several Italian versions appeared.[66] Anyone who goes through Bernard Weinberg's four-volume anthology of Italian Renaissance critics and rhetoricians will have no trouble finding numerous references to and uses of Hermogenes.[67] In fact, a leading interpretation of Ariosto and Tasso hinged precisely on the application of the Hermogenean stylistic forms.[68] To the north, Julius Caesar Scaliger made extensive use of Hermogenes' forms in his massive *Poetics*.[69] And all the while, George of Trebizond's *Rhetoric*, with its Hermogenean overlay, continued to be printed.

Dionysius of Halicarnassus was also translated in the sixteenth century and available in many editions, as were Demetrius Phalereus and Aphthonius.[70] These authors were significant authorities for the Byzantines, and in accepting them, the West was accepting a Byzantine perspective, a reality of cultural transmission illustrated in a negative way by the case of pseudo-Longinus. Pseudo-Longinus had been virtually ignored by the Byzantines. He was not even included in the Aldine *Rhetores Graeci*. Not surprisingly, he was also ignored by the Latin humanists until the second half of the sixteenth century; and even then he was not much studied. It was not until the late seventeenth century that the West freed itself of the Byzantine valu-

63. C. E. Lass, *Die Paedagogik des Johannes Sturm* (Berlin, 1872), p. 78; C. Schmidt, *La vie et les travaux de Jean Sturm* (Strasbourg, 1855), pp. 260 f.; Baldwin, 1.284 ff.; 2.24.

64. Baldwin, 2.22; L. V. Ryan, *Roger Ascham* (Stanford, Calif., 1963), index.

65. Baldwin, 1.106 – 7.

66. Patterson, pp. 219 – 20.

67. *Tratti di poetica e retorica del '500,* 4 vols. (Bari, 1970 – 1974).

68. Cf. B. Weinberg, *A History of Literary Criticism in the Italian Renaissance,* 2 vols. (Chicago, Ill., 1961), 1.176; Patterson, pp. 180 – 81.

69. *Poetices libri septem* (Lyons, 1561), pp. 174 – 83.

70. For Dionysius this is my impression from consulting the major published catalogs of printed books and other sources. For Demetrius we have a comprehensive list in Weinberg's article cited in note 5. For Aphthonius see the *Index Aureliensis. Catalogus librorum sedecimo saeculo impressorum*, prima pars, tomus 4 (Baden-Baden, 1966), nos. 106.231 – 396 (*sic:* read 106.231 – 296. After edition no. 106.251 the numbering suddenly jumps to 106.352, and the mistaken numeration is continued for the subsequent editions).

ation of pseudo-Longinus and finally recognized the *De sublimitate* for a masterpiece.[71]

Aristotle's *Poetics* experienced a similar *fortuna*. The *Poetics* survived the Greek Middle Ages in no small measure because in the tenth or eleventh century it was made part of a Byzantine rhetorical corpus intended to compete with the Hermogenean rhetorical art.[72] The attempt, of course, failed, but the *Poetics* did remain as a lesser rhetorical text for the Byzantines. The Greek émigrés to Italy hardly referred to it. Its place as a smallish item in the Aldine *Rhetores Graeci* represents a proper Byzantine conception of its value. In the 1490s, its first Renaissance translator, Giorgio Valla, was still clearly working within the Byzantine tradition since he scarcely gave Aristotle's *Poetics* any weight when he came to write his own *Poetics* and *Rhetoric*.[73] Again, it was only the late Renaissance, further removed from the Byzantine provenance of the text, that made the Aristotelian *Poetics* what it had never been in Byzantium: a sovereign authority in all matters literary.

Some Renaissance transformations of Byzantine rhetoric had nothing essentially to do with literature. John Sturm, for instance, seized upon Hermogenes' method of division and universalized it as one of the three methods of learning and investigation. Sturm undoubtedly depended on Plato and Galen for much of his theory, but the influence of Hermogenes is demonstrable.[74] Consequently, Sturm and, behind Sturm, Hermogenes stand at the origin of one stream of the Renaissance obsession with method, an obsession that will eventually lead to Descartes, but in the short term led to Sturm's friend and student Peter Ramus at Paris. Subsumed under Ramism, the Hermogenean method exercised a profound influence on Western education into the seventeenth century.[75]

---

71. See Weinberg's article on pseudo-Longinus in the *Catalogus translationum*, 2.193–98.

72. See W. Schmid in *Rheinisches Museum* 72 (1917–1918), 114–19.

73. Cf. E. N. Tigerstedt, "Observations on the Reception of the Aristotelian *Poetics* in the Latin West," *Studies in the Renaissance* 15 (1968), 7–24; E. Lobel, *The Greek Manuscripts of Aristotle's Poetics*. Supplement to the *Transactions of the Bibliographical Society*, London, no. 9 (Oxford, 1933); A. Wartelle, *Inventaire des manuscrits grecs d'Aristote et de ses commentateurs* (Paris, 1963). It is significant that Wartelle knew only one commentary on the *Poetics* (no. 1673, p. 124) found in a sixteenth-century manuscript.

74. Cf. my *George of Trebizond*, pp. 325 f.; Ong, pp. 232 f.

75. Ong, *passim*. A. Schindling, *Humanistische Hochschule und freie Reichsstadt, Gymnasium und Akademie in Strassburg 1538–1621* (Wiesbaden, 1977), pp. 216–19, down-

Another remarkable transformation rendered Hermogenes into a magician. In the first half of the sixteenth century, Giulio Camillo Delminio became an important authority in literary theory. He also translated Hermogenes into Italian. However, for Delminio, Hermogenes' stylistic forms were embodiments of specific cosmic powers, and the use of these forms in speech would magically create the desired effects. In his wondrous *Theater of the World,* Delminio made sure to integrate Hermogenes into his gnoseo-magical system. A short time later, Fabio Paolini in Venice, who in another work had explained the literary value of Hermogenes, also preached the possibilities of attracting down astral influences into one's speech by inspired use of the Hermogenean forms.

I would like to call attention to one final nonliterary use of Hermogenes. Michelangelo was the dominant artist of the first half of the sixteenth century. To describe his overpowering impact and the greatness of his art, contemporaries seized upon a new category of artistic criticism, *terribilità,* which became a byword in describing Michelangelo's art. In a forthcoming book, David Summers argues persuasively that the *terribilità* of Renaissance artistic criticism derives directly from the rhetorical category of *deinotes,* popularized in the Renaissance by the new Greek sources and especially by Hermogenes, who explained it as virtually synonymous with oratorical perfection.[76] *Terribilità* is, of course, a literal translation of *deinotes.* I myself find this argument all the more persuasive because the same critics, such as Vasari, used the term *gravità* as a synonym for *terribilità.*[77] But these words simply are not synonymous. However, the anomaly makes perfect sense if one grants the Hermogenean origin of *terribilità* and knows that, beginning with George of Trebizond

plays somewhat Sturm's admiration for Hermogenes, but I am not convinced by his arguments that Sturm's commentaries on H. were only posthumous and that on two occasions Sturm criticized H.

76. Professor Summers generously allowed me to read an early draft of chapter 8 of his forthcoming *Michelangelo and the Literature of Art* (Princeton, 1981). Cf. also K. Borinski, *Die Antike in Poetik und Kunsttheorie vom Ausgang des klassischen Altertums bis auf Goethe und Wilhelm von Humboldt* (Leipzig, 1914), 1.181; P. Barocchi, ed., *Giorgio Vasari, La vita di Michelangelo nelle redazioni del 1550 e del 1568,* 5 vols. (Milan and Naples, 1962), 2.472 f.; and J. Bialostocki, "Terribilità," *Stil und Ueberlieferung in der Kunst des Abendlandes. Akten des 21. Internationalen Kongresses für Kunstgeschichte in Bonn 1964* (Berlin, 1967), pp. 222–24. Prof. Summers first provided me with these references.

77. Cf. R. J. Clements, *Michelangelo's Theory of Art* (New York, 1961), pp. 93–94; cf. also Summers, chap. 8 between notes 10 and 11, though he generally stresses the conjoining of *difficoltà* with *terribilità* in the categories used about Michelangelo.

and Antonio Bonfinio, the first two translators of Hermogenes, as well as with Marcus Antonius Antimachus, the first Renaissance translator of Demetrius Phalareus, humanists tended to Latinize *deinotes* by *gravitas* in an attempt to identify the traditional Greek category of supreme oratory with the term most expressive of supreme oratory in the Latin tradition.[78]

This and the other examples I have given are the type of topics that must be investigated if we are ever to have a true and complete picture not only of Byzantine rhetoric in the Renaissance, but also of the much broader process of the Hellenization of the West in the age of the Renaissance.

78. Cf. *Auctor ad Herennium* IV.11; Cicero *De oratore* III.177. I believe it was George of Trebizond who, based on these indications, made the identification of *deinotes* and *gravitas* for the Renaissance. Latin authors did use other terms; cf. the note of H. Caplan to his edition of the *Ad Herennium,* Loeb Classical Library (Cambridge, Mass., 1954), p. 244.

PART THREE

Ethics, Politics, and Theology

Lorenzo Valla: Humanist Rhetoric and the Critique of the Classical Languages of Morality

NANCY STRUEVER

A consideration of rhetoric and ethics in the oeuvre of Lorenzo Valla suggests a much larger project that would study the cluster of rhetorical canons, premises, and strategies as they guide both the ethical inquiry of the Renaissance humanists and the ethics *of* humanist inquiry. Valla's rhetoric, recall, is exemplary of Renaissance rhetoric as ambitious, as an embedding strategy, analogous to Quintilian's tactic of integrating grammar and dialectic, psychological theory and general reading, within a single course of rhetorical training, a training that is more than a pedagogical episode, indeed, represents and invests a life-long engagement. As ambitious, Valla's rhetoric is not simply late embellishment but early procedure, and his rhetorical clarifications make a powerful contribution to his definition of successful inquiry; as inclusive, his rhetoric includes the rhetor's own behavior, affects moral conduct as well as ethical insight.

The project would stipulate two very rich forms of interrelationship: it would focus on the connection between rhetorical and ethical theory, and thus study the humanist appeal to rhetorical assumptions in their revisionist program of critique of classical ethics; it would also assume a connection that is usually expressed as a stricture, that is, that rhetorical and ethical practice are inseparable. In turn, the definition of *praxis* as topic of inquiry could support a further claim about mode of inquiry; the project would stipulate a heuristic relationship between modern rhetorical analytic competence and Renaissance rhetorical performance, and thus require the modern historian to resort to contemporary rhetorical techniques in order to analyze the humanist discursive practice that is the evidence for humanist *behavior,* their conduct of inquiry. The project then would be a history of the discursive practice as well as theory of humanist investigators, with special reference to ethical issues.

Lorenzo Valla (1407 – 1457), astute in theory and aggressive in practice, scholar and polemicist, philologue and pamphleteer, interested as much in religious substance as literary form, is an easy choice for initiating a study of humanist rhetoric and ethics. Valla's *De vero falsoque bono,* as an exercise in ethical theory, is a very strong instance of humanist revisionism that makes constant appeal to rhetorical premises in the development of a new ethical lexicon and syntax. This is an obvious point, and I shall merely suggest as particularly illuminating the passages in the later versions of the *De vero bono,* which Professor Lorch has identified as related to the contemporaneous revisions of his *Dialecticae disputationes* (1444 – 1449).[1] Here we find rhetorical canons of accessibility, flexibility, and responsiveness, and the rhetorical privileging of ordinary, natural usage over arcane, esoteric choice, used to locate a series of faults in the classical ethical lexicon and to suggest remedies for the faults. One must recall that one of the contexts of Valla's reworking of the *Dialecticae disputationes* and the *De vero bono* is his close reading of the more complete Quintilian manuscript.[2] His is a critique of the use of words in propositions, of malfunctioning definitions, and his rhetoric is a Quintilianesque discipline that provides the analytical axioms and techniques for resolving equivocations and confusions; Valla then combines rhetorical with Christian postulates to construct a filter to screen out undesirable classical discursive and hence cognitive practices.

In the *De vero bono,* then, Valla has his protagonists in the dialogue, the "Stoic," "Epicurean," and "Christian" *personae,* exemplify or subvert errors in classical ethical usage: reifications, concealed or self-deceived figurative uses, tautologies, and false attributions of

1. See the preface of Prof. M. Lorch's edition of Valla's *De vero falsoque bono* (Bari, 1970), pp. xlix ff.; hereafter cited as *DVB.* Most other citations from Valla's works are from *Opera Omnia* (Basel, 1540, rpt. Turin, 1962); hereafter cited as *OO.* The *DVB* variants of ms. γ, which Lorch relates to the *Dialecticae disputationes* version, focus on such issues as *quid est bonum? substantiane an actio an qualitas* (*DVB,* 62; *OO,* 654–58); *virtutem non esse medium inter duo extrema* (*DVB,* 98; *OO,* 660, 665–66).

2. See S. Camporeale, *Lorenzo Valla; Umanesimo e teologia* (Florence, 1972), p. 75 f.; he claims that the Parisian manuscript Valla acquired in 1443 was "senza dubbio piu coretto e molto meno lacunoso" than the manuscript he already possessed, p. 76.

transitivity or intransitivity. This series of lexical faults locates for Valla the sources of instability in the foundation of premise and motive of classical ethics. Thus, for example, the lengthy attack on Aristotelian "moderation" as virtue Valla assigns to Antonio da Rho is an attack on the tendency of Aristotelians, for the logical purpose of purifying, or regularizing, the terms of their arguments, to transform relation constructs ("the mean") into entities ("moderation"), and thus to make empty forms into moral imperatives.[3] Similarly, Valla resists the temptation to attribute substance to *bonum*, which is rather, as he has Vegio say, an *actio;* his resistance is rooted in Valla's general tactic of reduction of all predicaments germane to the sphere of human events from the Aristotelian ten to two, *qualitas* and *actio.*[4] The false strategy of reification is behind another dysfunctional classical practice, the unselfconscious use of trope as deviation from normal use; Valla argues, again through da Rho, that virtue is called a good only through metonymy.[5] But da Rho argues not only against the classical dialectical prejudice for hypostatization, but in defense of a rhetorical bias for a *contextualist* attribution of virtue and vice, according to "nature and the lives of men," to "time and place," — *separatim et vices*, to specific context — "melius itaque singulos actus et singulas res iudicamus."[6] Valla employs contextualism, which finds expression in the canons of rhetorical decorum, to confute Aristotelian reifications, then; but further, Valla asks us to distinguish contexts, to look to an inclusive, generic contextualism for the attribution of generic virtue, as opposed to the specificity of contextualist reference for the characterization of particular acts. Here proper definition stems "ex perpetuitate ac frequentiore usu actionum," rather than from deduction of place in a philosophical system of formal relations.[7]

In characterizing Valla's ethical lexicon, while we must note that

3. *DVB*, 95 f.; *00*, 665 – 66.
4. *DVB*, 62; *00*, 654 – 58; Valla uses the third predicament, *substantia*, sparingly.
5. *DVB*, 112; "Quin etiam si recte estimemus, ne bonum quidem virtus dicitur, nisi per metonomiam sive hypallagen ut domus, ager, divitie bona sunt quia bonum parant, que est voluptas."
6. *DVB*, 96 – 97; "Eadem hora subinde temperatus et intemperatus, prope dixerim milies et milies eadem hora recte aut secus facere possum; adeo unicum verbum laudari vel vituperari solet."
7. *DVB*, 100; "Nam liberalis, parcus, avarus, prodigus non ex singulis actibus nominatur, licet ex singulis actibus laudari vituperarive possint, sed ex perpetuitate ac frequentior usu actionum; nec earum parvitate, mediocritate, magnitudine et, ut dixi, mensura sed ratione atque scientia."

his rhetorical canons specify a flexible, ad hoc approach to ethical judgments, they also stipulate economy as perspicacity in the definition of virtues; but classical ethics, Valla complains, errs in that it redounds in tautological virtues, for *fortitudo, iustitia,* and *caritas* have the same structure, the same force.[8] But economy does not preclude commodiousness; in another lexical strategy, in the discussion of the predicaments "action" and "passion" in the *Dialecticae disputationes,* Valla suggests a significant enlargement of the domain of human activity, of transitivity, in his reduction of passion to action: to feel a passion is no different from knowing a danger, he claims.[9] Here I would suggest he anticipates the tactic of Descartes, who characterizes certain passions as "juste et honnête," as part of an ethical competence, in his treatise on *Les passions de l'âme;* in both cases the revised lexical force serves to enlarge the ethically charged domain to include these states of mind.[10] Economy, inclusiveness, but also austerity: the most serious challenge to an ethical lexicographer is to avoid a threadbare optimism. Valla combines rhetorical canons of definition, one of the major argumentative *topoi,* with an austere Christian doctrinal stance to assert that the one truly vital activity, the supremely relevant transitivity, is a possession of God; for example, man's love of God cannot be defined as a product of a human aim, since it has a divine source, and so is an effect of divine ordinance.[11] The proper function of religious or metaphysical hypotheses in Valla's theory is to deny human omnicompetence while asserting, in a precise manner, human responsibility.

Valla also uses rhetorical premises, of course, to revise the structure or syntax of argument as well as the lexicon of terms employed in argument. Both Vasoli and Camporeale have discussed this structural revision of syllogism, of the schemes of consequence; the program expresses, on the one hand, a growing lack of faith on Valla's part in the usefulness of the elaborate technical accomplishments,

8. *DVB,* 99; *00,* 663 f.

9. *00,* 679,686: "Quid enim patior si diligor, aut timeor, aut audior, aut etiam vocor, nisi audio, in audio iam actio est; est igitur ut dicebam, pati actio; quoniam sentire passionem perinde ut actio est; ut intelligere periculum." Valla goes on to discuss how *passio* can be a *qualitas* as well.

10. Descartes's argument assumes the veridical nature, the immediacy and autonomy of the passions pertaining *only* to the soul; see in particular pp. 45–46, 146, 150, 158 in *Les passions de l'âme* (Paris, 1953).

11. *DVB,* 114–15; *00,* 668; see also Valla's *Defensio questionum in philosophia,* ed. G. Zippel, *Italia medioevale e umanistica* 13 (1970), 86. For the variety of arguments drawn from the meaning of a term, *ex nota,* see, for example, Cicero, *Topica* ii. 9 f.

the refinements of the structures of valid inference of late medieval logical formalism, and on the other, a growing interest in the concrete depiction of the conventions and rules of discourse that affect reference in some significant way.[12] The structure of the *Elegantiae,* a grammar for rhetoricians, is illustrative of Valla's antiformalism, for the *Elegantiae* eschews syllogistic rigor for an unsystematic, "topological" approach. Recall that the rhetorical *topoi* are organized in lists, not systems; a *topos* is an armamorium of flexible, responsive debating tactics, a series of argumentative wrestling holds; just so, the *Elegantiae* represents a list of lexical maneuvers, initiatives derived from historical discursive events, a repertoire that the reader as author may draw from at will in response to specific discursive demands. This accessibility helps explain its enormous popularity in the Renaissance, but it also indicates how the form as well as the content of the *Elegantiae* supports the hegemony of invention over judgment, how it asserts the priority of discovery of issue and the cultivation of a taste for a variety of approaches as opposed to an investment in technical virtuosity in the formal criticism of validity, an initiative that remains a characteristic of humanist inquiry through Vico.[13]

It is Valla's stress on the importance of social convention and authorial intention that controls his critique of the logical structures of argument. The firm relegation of dialectical forms to a subordinate role in the construction of discourse, as well as the stipulation of the hegemony of *consuetudo,* custom, are, of course, Quintilianesque motives. But I would suggest that Valla projects, in his concern with the depiction of the force of discursive conventions in controlling meaning, a new encapsulating frame for the relation between inference and reference. Valla, in fact, presses the critique of logic to the point of forming a "rhetorical theory of truth": that is, discursive exchange establishes a proposition as "true," accepted as immune, self-standing.[14] Rhetorical inclusiveness would entail the stipulation

12. See C. Vasoli, *La Dialettica e la retorica dell'Umanesimo; Invenzione e'metodo' nella cultura del XV e XVI secolo* (Milan, 1968), "Filologia, critica, e logica in L.V.," pp. 28–77; and Camporeale, *L.V.; Umanesimo e teologia,* pt. 1, "Dialettica e retorica," pp. 33–87; "Riscoperta di Quintiliano," pp. 89–146.

13. *DVB,* 113: "At quanto satius erat oratorie quam dialetice loqui! Quid enim ineptius philosophorum more ut si uno verbo sit erratum tota causa periclitemur? At orator multis et variis rationibus utitur, affert contraria, exempla repetit, similitudines comparat et cogit etiam latitantem prodire veritatem."

14. For a contemporary discussion of a "rhetorical theory of truth," see L. Apostel, "Further Remarks on the Pragmatics of Natural Languages," in *Pragmatics of Natural Languages,* ed. Y. Bar-Hillel (Dordrecht, 1972), p. 16; as in the Valla passage above,

that a general pragmatic theory (of the relation of word to user) must include, surround a general semantic theory (of the relation of the word to extra-linguistic referent). This is not simply a devaluation of the obligatory force of arcane deductive schemata, but a new, or at least a polemical, valuation of discursive contextual force. To be sure, this is a matter of Valla's practice as well as his theory; certainly in his choice of the dialogue as moralizing genre we are made to see that a frame of speaker's intentions and debating convention encapsulates the argumentative structures of inference; insights are expressed within a matrix of beliefs and allegiances. But his pragmatic bias may claim theoretical refinement; Valla's subtle distinction between specific and general contextual force perhaps anticipates the modern distinction of Saul Kripke between speaker's reference and semantic reference.[15] If we recall Valla's separation of the act of general definition of virtue from the act of specific attribution of virtue, we can appreciate his sensitivity to the different *kinds* of contextual force, of the types of obligation that govern the creation of meaning. But where Kripke's distinction functions to explain ambiguity, Valla's awareness of the contingency of types of reference on types of intention represents a more positive, or naive, attempt to exploit a linguistic capacity, the ability to select context. And the *ethical* value of Valla's distinction lies in its specification of ethical domain as well as semantic scope; thus definition and attribution of virtue are two separate types of responsibility, and the responsible inquirer does not call a specific activity by a general name, ascribe infelicitously, breaking an understanding.

This theory, then, is a theory of practice: it suggests that Valla's most basic innovations are not those in theme or subject matter, but those in the canons of proper practice and relevant rule in serious,

---

"true" is related to "conviction"; "A proposition is called by Hintikka self-sustaining if it is immune to certain types of criticism; (if it can be shown that there are no types of arguments an addressee would accept that would lead from premises he also accepts to the negation of the proposition mentioned)."

15. S. Kripke, "Speaker's Reference and Semantic Reference," *Midwest Studies in Philosophy* 2 (1977), 255–76; Kripke distinguishes between a general and a specific intention on the part of the speaker; where the semantic referent is by a *general* intention of the speaker to refer, "the speaker's referent is given by a *specific* intention, on a given occasion, to refer to a certain object," p. 264; the references may not coincide, but one reference functions in the domain of semantics, the other in the domain of pragmatics, speech acts. Recall Valla's observations on disjunction of reference in notes 6 and 7.

ethically charged, debate; his contributions are more to the theory of well-motivated ethical inquiry than to ethical theory. There is, indeed, an analogous and illuminating Renaissance initiative that appears in the political-historical discourse of Machiavelli and Guicciardini. Machiavelli changed not so much the subject matter as the rules for the discussion of political history: the "content" is not new, the political structures and narrative examples that illustrate them are traditional, but the shift is in the rules that constrain the discussion of political structures and historical events, the conventions that stipulate what is appropriate or inappropriate for debate.

To summarize our brief consideration of Valla's discursive theory: since language is presumed by the humanists to be a mirror of nature, a change in language strategies and values is necessarily a change in truth discovery procedures and values.[16] Further, proper use of language, tactful discursive interventions, can dissolve ethical as well as metaphysical knots. Valla's procedures not only force the rejection of the reifications of the Aristotelian and Stoic moral lexicon as producing "inappropriate," sterile debate, but sponsor a shift to "ordinary" issues as.well as language, that is to say, issues both intractable and highly sensitive, such as the question of the moral uses of pleasure. Thus when we turn to focus on Valla's discursive practice, his conduct of inquiry, we notice a powerful combination of motives: Valla's penchant for intractable issues gives rise to highly motivated quarrels; at the same time, Valla's rejection of many of the elaborations of formal logical structures insures that the conduct of the argument will be less formal, less rule-bound. The result is a discourse that deals with intractable issues in a less restrained manner.

To investigate humanist ethics of inquiry by means of analysis of this discursive conduct, I would suggest, raises immediately the modern issue of genre and of generic organization of discourse in a very interesting way. Genette has claimed that genre was originally, and correctly, a problem of mode or "voice" in classical culture; that is to say, generic definition was primarily a definition based on the consideration of the relation of the discourse to the speaking subject, to the enunciative situation.[17] But further, Stierle has claimed that the

16. For a debate on whether the "unproblematic" classical *impalcatura* dominated all semantic theory through the Renaissance, see P. Rossi, "Linguisti d'oggi e filosofi del Seicento," *Lingua e stile* 3 (1968), 1–20.

17. G. Genette, "Genus, 'types,' modes," *Poétique* 32 (1977), 389–421; see also R. Dupont-Roc, "Mimesis et énonciation," in *Écriture et théorie poétiques* (Paris, 1976), on Greek notions of genre as mode, pp. 6–14.

study of genre should be more concerned with the establishing of the discursive identity of author and reader than with self-closed structures of textual coherence: the student must focus on the discourse's historical place in the context of contemporaneous speech activity, in the process of production and reception of texts, rather than seek to establish the lack of self-contradiction of the content of an isolate text. For, Stierle points out, the reader is never content to simply "perceive" a text, but organizes it into discourse, puts it in its place in a historical spectrum of discursive activity; thus each reader addresses the issue of the institutionalization, of the normative stablization of discursive behavior, and thus judges the text's subversive or conservative bent.[18]

Within the range of humanist discourse, two of the most important and most political genres are the invective and the "academic" letter; as genres, they are modes of control of speech as exchange, modes that define the horizon of expectations of the reader as well as project the values and channel the force of the speaker's argument. Both function, then, as modes of exchange in a variety of issues, to structure humanist inquiry: the invective, with its premise of *malevolence* of receptors, communal disjunctions, and the letter—with, normally, the premise of the *benevolence* of the receptor—which functions as one of the important modes of diffusion of learning before the advent of the learned journal. The object of a generic analysis would be the definition of the roles of locutor and receptor in letter and invective, the relations to previous and successive modes of discourse, and the structure of argument as it shapes role and theme.

I shall focus on invective as genre since it represents a difficult but essential topic in the study of rhetoric and ethics in humanism; their verbal combat may not be elevating, but it is integral. And invective, to be sure, constitutes an extraordinarily thick *rhetorical* experience: invective demands the production of highly stylized, "rhetorical" texts that argue the rhetorical identity, competence, of the protagonists by raising issues about grammatical, lexical, and discursive practices that are considered to be controlled by rhetorical canons, and which in turn produce rhetorical values in speech activity. In Valla's invective there are, of course, the expected Christian themes: the assertion of militant Christian heroism or of equally militant defense against charges of Christian heresy. But the militancy relates to

18. K.-H. Stierle, "Identité du discours et transgression lyrique," *Poétique* 32 (1977), 422–41.

a peculiar domain of Christian discourse; his shift into high gear of invective is related to his shift to a new sphere of investigation of the biblical text. Here Valla abandons the hypothesis of a received text for that of a problematic text, resituated in a social domain of scribal error and scholarly stupidity. "I emend not the Holy Scripture," he states, "but the interpretation of the Holy Scripture"; not Jerome's doctrine, but the competence of the historical communities of scribes and the ascription of direct personal responsibility are at issue.[19]

In both his invective tactics and in his initiatives of textual criticism, Valla embarks on a redefinition of the role of the author/ speaker, and in both cases we find the premise of contextual relevance taken seriously. The primacy of usage in determining reference develops a sensitivity to role, to the responsibility of the user of words; humanist quarrelling is itself a direct effect of the seriousness of the contextualist hypothesis. The humanist lexicon of textual emendation is a lexicon of praise and blame, as Rizzo has pointed out; the vocabulary underlines the obligation of purification, the duty of rejection of corruption.[20] Valla's initiatives in biblical textual criticism are part not only of the history of the development of philological science, but also of a general revaluation of intellectual, or verbal, currency from cheap to dear. His New Testament investigations are a serious statement that an accessibility that is cheaply earned is less valuable than one that is dearly won; he requires an investment in expensive, strenuous strategies. The mental frame that recognizes the merit of the most difficult reading as potentially the most historically sound is entirely different from that which attempts to simplify all passages by recourse to a theological system, to self-gratulatory, circular reasonings.

We see, then, a change in the structures of obligation and constraint, in the rules that emphasize both the responsibility and the vulnerability of the discussants. Thus, Valla may claim that he addresses *vitia*, not *homines*, but the *ad hominem* component, for example, his description of Poggio Bracciolini as an elephant doing more damage to his own side in retreat than to the enemy in advance, is a necessary extension of the generic rule that enunciative situation is relevant context.[21] Whereas in the scholastic *disputatio* the conventions demanded that the speaker address "impersonally" the prob-

19. *Antidoti in Pogium, Lib.* 1, in *OO*, 268 –69.
20. S. Rizzo, *Il lessico filologico degli umanisti* (Rome, 1973).
21. *Antidoti in Pogium, Lib.* 1, in *OO*, 253,268.

lem of constructing a logical/ontological system or of filling in details of a given, approved system, the task for the humanist author of invective assumes personality as parameter, that he must refuse to divorce what is said from how and why it is said.

Of course, Valla's use of the dialogue form in invective also underlines authorial intervention as praiseworthy or blameful, as having ethical implications.[22] But it is unenlightening for Reynolds and Wilson to speak of the "vain and aggressive" nature of Valla as marring his scholarship; "vanity" is less an adequate explanation of personal motive than an effect of social situation, a result of being forced to function in rough discursive games.[23] Also, there is difficulty in the current reading of Renaissance rhetorical initiatives as "opportunistic"; Jardine speaks of Baconian "presentation," divorced from the mission of the discovery of truth and from the rigors of Bacon's discovery procedures as thus freely exploitative, unrestrainedly manipulative, and therefore "opportunistic"; opportunism represents a new, irresponsible consciousness of role.[24] Bacon, to be sure, concentrates on narrowly defined issues of power and tactics of domination and mastery. But the fifteenth-century humanists are less rugged individualists than embattled communitarians. Humanist invective needs a hypothesis not of "possessive individualism" but of "possessive intellectualism"; invective rules treat erudition as a personal acquisition or possession and insure the fragility, vulnerability of the inquirer, subject to constant revaluation: a very different kind of responsibility from the scholastic allegiances to a domain of immutable ideas agreeably expressed. Humanist contextualism represents loss as well as gain; we tend to view the discovery of the philological construct of anachronism, the prime contextualist tool of text criticism, as pure gain, but it is impossible to separate context as gain from relativism as loss when the loss is a loss of ingenuousness, of intellectual innocence, and where the struggle for purity of text is inevitably a struggle for reputation.

22. See C. Nisard, *Les Gladiateurs de la République des Lettres au XVe, XVIe, et XVIIe siècles* (Paris, 1860), 1.207.
23. L. D. Reynolds and N. G. Wilson, *Scribes and Scholars, A Guide to the Transmission of Greek and Latin Literature* (London, 1974), p. 126. See E. Veron, "Linguistique et sociologie," *Communications* 20 (1973), p. 246–96; Veron claims that "motive" is not an internal state but a public method utilized to decide the social existence or nonexistence of the action.
24. L. Jardine, *Francis Bacon: Discovery and the Art of Discourse* (Cambridge, 1974), pp. 15–16.

Within invective, the configuration of the receptor's or audience's role changes as well; whereas the scholastic *disputatio* had presumed and elaborated an ahistorical logical and ontological structure, and hypothesized a homogeneous, well-motivated community of inquirers, the humanist invective presumes a heterogeneous community of well- and ill-motivated inquirers who address historical issues of convention, usage, allegiance, and style. While the use of the dialogue form in an invective would seem to direct the accusation of malevolence to a particular receptor, the invective actually functions so as to involve a general audience as well in the attribution of malevolence. It was a widespread, enduring practice of the humanists to describe with precision and violence a very wide range of intellectual perfidy; consider the roster of antagonists in Boccaccio's defense of poetry in the *Genealogie deorum*, for example.[25] While the invective seems to appeal to the ideal judgment of a universal readership, the existence of an ideal readership is neither described nor confirmed. The invective dialogue, after all, publicizes a private quarrel; the arguments, which concern social usage, inevitably pertain to communities, groups; and the extent to which the audience as community is accomplice in the adversary role is left imprecise, unclear in an unsettling manner.

The issue of receptor role arises in the noninvective genres, such as the *De vero bono*, as well. Valla's description of his role as that of a "David" confronting a "Goliath" is again an assumption of generalized hostility that places in question at the outset a model of easy consensus and deliberately creates a distance between author and audience.[26] Then his repudiation of the Epicurean point of view, in this and in other texts, may simply be a standard Christian defense against charges of unorthodoxy. But what, precisely, did he intend his readers to do with the *personae*, which he insists over and over again are the *fictae personae*, of Stoic and Epicurean? Within and without this dialogue, his reader is the recipient of subtle and not so subtle tactics of subversion: thus the Epicurean *persona*, in particular, seems inadequately undermined, not exploded. His apologetic strategy, pointing out that the Stoic and the Epicurean of the dialogue as "fictions" obviously had nothing to do with the staunch Christians appointed the roles, may actually simplify, make easier, the reader's

25. G. Baccaccio, *Genealogie deorum gentilium libri*, ed. V. Romano (Bari, 1951), 2, chap. 14.
26. *DVB*, 3.

task of coming to terms with the radical doctrine he has the Epicurean espouse. Valla uses disjunction heuristically: note, he claims,
"dum pro Epicureis loquor, Stoicum agere."[27] The counterfactual
personae confront the reader's expectations and by denying normal
positions, by distancing, force fresh consideration of the arguments.
The task of the audience, set by Valla, is the discovery of something
new, divergent from the familiar Neo-Aristotelian notions of virtue
as informed by Stoic prejudices; certainly Valla, in addressing his
contemporaries, is both self-conscious and proud of the novelties of
the *De vero bono.*[28]

Iser has described the innovative force of fictions for an audience in this way in his essay in *Rezeptionsästhetik, The Implied Reader:*

> The reader discovers the meaning of the text, taking negations as
> his starting point; he discovers a new reality through a fiction
> which, at least in part, is different from the world he himself is used
> to, and he discovers the deficiencies inherent in prevalent norms
> and in his own restricted behavior.[29]

The adversary relation, which the invectives utilize, is essential to the
task of innovation. Valla's notion of rhetorical decorum requires a
psychologistically sound mode of expression for the plausible psychological story he has devised in his invective to convey his moral
precepts. Like Quintilian, Valla postulates the necessary violence, the
necessary pleasure of discursive practice; new insight is not achieved
by means of a calm consensus or a mild didacticism.[30] Discourse is
not only the vehicle of insight, but its working is the metaphor for the
workings of the soul; forceful, varied discourse, rather than formal
logic, is the best evidence of the useful activity of mind. His new
moral doctrine is, I would maintain, a psychologistically clever Christian Epicureanism, and the rhetorical canon of decorum underwrites a coherence among natural feeling, discursive practice, and
ethical insight; that is to say, self-discovery proceeds through the
production and reception of discursive strength and sweetness.[31]

In this way the rhetorical analysis of humanist discursive prac-

27. Ibid.
28. Valla, Letter to Tortelli, cited by Lorch, *DVB,* xlviii; see also *OO,* 2.84.
29. W. Iser, *The Implied Reader* (Baltimore, 1978), p. xiii.
30. See Quintilian, *Institutio Oratoria* V. 14 f; VI, pref.; recall that Valla incorporated V. 8 – 14 in the *Dialecticae disputationes.*
31. Apostel (see note 14) distinguishes between the *monologic* and *dialogic* models
of language competence; just so, I would maintain, Valla shifts easily from a dialogic
model of language to a notion of morality as dialogue-constructed. Recall *DVB,* 91:

tice may contribute to the historical definition of humanism as a complex of roles, disciplines, pedagogic institutions, and civic initiatives; contribute, that is to say, to a nonvacuous definition of humanism as "transitional." For within the context of the late Renaissance changes in method, Valla loses credit as a mere precursor. Jardine is correct in stipulating that late Renaissance methodologists, and Bacon in particular, separate out the function *docere* from the rhetorical triad that includes *movere* and *delectare;* Valla's emphasis on the latter two functions argues against Valla as a precursor of early modern methodologists, points rather to Valla as a practitioner of the both flighty and enduring trade of fictional subversion in the manner of Rabelais, or Defoe, or Swift.[32] Subversion as a program, in turn, undermines the characterization of humanists as either *epigoni* or "forerunners"; and humanist discursive practice in general gives evidence of "transitional," separate, identity: the practice is no longer bound by the communicative and role conventions of the medieval university with its formalized disputations, theological institutions of *docere;* but its teaching roles and communicative modes do not yet possess the professional resonances of early modernity; the pedagogic and research institutions described in Ramism, Protestant scholasticism, Jesuit reform, encyclopedism, are not yet in place. Nor is a humanist such as Valla prototypical of a city-centered, "civic" humanism or an "aulic," courtly humanism; rather, he represents a fifteenth-century humanism that is freer, less structured—structured, as a matter of fact, by actions of dispute and exchange; the ties and bonds are those of highly communicable quarrel and friendship: their structures are the structures of genre.

Both the invectives and letters as genres mark the lines of allegiance in disputes and thus provide a map of the social bonds of the humanist community of inquiry. Their social bonds are ties of partisanship in disputes, which are, by and large, disputes over language use, connection to social conventions. The political structure of humanism is not a simple reflex of a Renaissance political-social structure, but an internal structure, a function of their own social needs and technical accomplishments. It is possible to draw a map of the significant bonds of the humanist community based on the ties and

---

"Nunquid hic persuadebit aliis quod non persuaserit sibi? Num audientes ad iram misericordiamque commovebit, nisi prius eisdem se affectibus permoverit?"

32. *DVB,* 3: "magna vis oratoris in delectando est." See Jardine, *Francis Bacon,* chap. 1.

antagonisms of the various issues. The thicker lines, reinforced by many alliances, would represent the dominant structures, the norms and values that invest the community; a list of hypotheses defended would be a list of their major contested social, ethical values. Recall that the sixteenth-century epistolary preface of Carlowitz to Valla's invective against Poggio in the Basel *Opera* provides a defense of verbal combat as a legitimate part of inquiry. Rhetorical education, discursive practice are law-worthy, the preface claims, apt for regulation; they need to be recalled to the severity of discipline that had produced the ingenuity and energy invested in verbal combat in Valla's time, which Carlowitz contrasts with the invidious present and its negligence and inertia.[33] The preface, in short, supports Perelman's hypothesis that epideictic is the central genre of rhetoric and that praise and blame constitute the essential rhetorical exercise of affirmation of values and of creating intensified adhesion to values.[34] In the preface, epideictic function — praise of virtue, blame of vice — underwrites invective as a useful institution, *vere germana exercitatio,* as a *simulacrum* of combat, *pugna,* which prepares for real combat, *justa pugna.*[35]

This part of our project has required, then, a shift in focus from the reassertion of the dictum that eloquence is power to the analysis of the practice of eloquence as the practice of power. The humanists as a community are united not only by ties of alliance but also by relations of domination and submission. The sixteenth-century scholars such as Dolet and Scaliger made their reputations by attacking the powerful, not the weak; only Erasmus could feed Dolet's reputation.[36] Then, granting these motivations, consider the shifts in structure, tone, and point of view in the very broad Renaissance genre of treatises of advice and counsel; shifts in actual power rela-

33. *OO,* 249 f.; Carlowitz's preface was quite popular in the early sixteenth century and appeared in several more editions.

34. Charles Perelman and L. Olbrechts-Tyteca, *La nouvelle rhétorique* (Paris, 1958), 1.62 ff.

35. *OO,* 251; recall W. Ong on ritual combat as a dominant form in academic curricula for a millennium and a half, in *Rhetoric, Romance, and Technology* (Ithaca, N.Y., 1971), p. 17.

36. An interesting project would be the history of the reception of the *Elegantiae* as text, as receptive strategies manifest themselves in the various abridgements, epitomes, editions, and in the literature of erudition in general; one could employ M. Foucault's techniques of revealing discursive structures as power structures; on the wider implications of Foucault's methods see L. Bersani, "The Subject of Power," *Diacritics* (Fall, 1977), 1–21.

tions in the community at large may not necessarily be symmetrical with shifts in verbal tactics of the projection of power in the literature of good counsel. Invective is simply the extreme case that tests rhetoric as ethical, where most genres affirm rhetoric as having its own politics, and stipulate as a necessary attribute of an intellectual elite rhetorical virtuosity.

Let me suggest, in conclusion, three tentative hypotheses for a rhetorical analysis of the relation of rhetoric and ethics in Renaissance humanist inquiry: hypotheses that are tentative but that, I must admit, sound self-evident.

First, gross shifts in the problematic of inference and reference, that is, problems of unrecognized ambiguity or equivocation, of false reifications, of tautologies, of reductive definitions, as well as shifts in the notion of the structure of argument, shifts largely under the influence of rhetorical canons and premises, have implications not only for the critical program, but for the discursive performance of the humanists; that is to say, not only for the issues of inquiry but also for the institutionalization, the social conduct, of inquiry. Thus Valla's program of demonstrating that classical moral language is equivocal, reified, reductive, and tautologous affects humanist pedagogic, research, and publication practices.

Second, we must, therefore, investigate the political *structure* of humanist inquiry; it is not enough to simply specify some vague political goals, to speak of "civic humanist" imperatives; rather, a precise analysis of changes in rules of debate, in the constraints on discourse, is needed. We must also be able to confront the cases wherein the conduct of inquiry undermines or subverts the ostensive goals, or even the cases wherein seemingly subversive behavior actually contributes to success. Then, on the premise that "good politics gives rise to good inquiry," the definition of political structure of inquiry defines the proper domain for the consideration of prescriptive or normative rules of inquiry, for raising ethical issues as issues of social structure, of the discipline of a community of inquirers.

Third, conduct, discursive practice itself, can be a source for the redefinition of goals; invective, for example, forces a very rich and detailed experience of responsibility on the inquirer. Then, the form of conduct reinforces one of the most important perspectives of humanist inquiry, which has strong ethical as well as intellectual implications. For the humanist perspective is both social and historical in an interesting way. On the one hand, humanists recognize a temporal dimension of social bonding, a recognition motivated by both critical program and investigative behavior; both define the community of inquirers as a historical one, both focus on continuities and discontinuities in the investigation of the past. Conduct also generates a grasp of the historical dimension of moral imperatives; a moral dictum is not a mere axiom, but an experience, an inductive conclusion, at least for the party of the "Ancients." On the other hand, the ties of language are not simply ties of individual to individual, of, say, classical author to modern reader, but of one social usage to another, later one; linguistic ties are social ties, bonds that communicate social imperatives and connect two societies, not two individuals. And this is certainly the strong ethical charge carried by Valla's investigation of usage, *consuetudo*, and the ordinary usage of the populace at that, as the most important canon of propriety. The humanist model of reading is not that of isolate reader confronting an isolate text, but of a continuity of acts of interpretation on the part of a later society confronting an earlier one: learning is in structure social, and historical, and ethical.

The Question of Truth
in Renaissance
Rhetoric and Anthropology

CHARLES TRINKAUS

La querelle des rhetores et des philosophes dans la renaissance has become almost as notorious to modern scholars as that between ancients and moderns. Generated by criticisms of scholastic dialectic as lacking eloquence on the part of humanists and by the reciprocal criticism of the contentlessness of mere poetry and mere rhetoric on the part of scholastic apologists,[1] it was a Renaissance of Plato's "ancient quarrel of poets and philosophers."[2] Today it has become a battlefield of modern scholars enacting in some large or small ways their participation in C. P. Snow's conflict between scientific and literary cultures.

Once and for all a truce should be declared in this war, with some mutually agreeable concessions so that we may free the study of the Renaissance from the needless burden of a partisanship within the humanities. The importance of Renaissance scholasticism should be conceded — particularly that of the Aristotelianism of the Italian universities — and the continuation of the far more intensive study of its figures and phases begun in this country by the students of Paul

1. See, above all, Paul Oskar Kristeller's classic essay "Humanism and Scholasticism in the Italian Renaissance," printed in a number of places, perhaps most available in *Renaissance Thought, The Classic, Scholastic and Humanist Strains* (New York, 1961), pp. 92 – 119. For a survey of humanist critique of scholastic dialectic see Cesare Vasoli, *La dialettica e la retorica dell'Umanesimo* (Milan, 1968). For the controversy between Giovanni Pico della Mirandola and Ermolao Barbaro and the adjoinders of Philip Melanchthon, see Quirinus Breen's "Three Renaissance Humanists on the Relation of Philosophy and Rhetoric," chap. 1 of his *Christianity and Humanism, Studies in the History of Ideas* (Grand Rapids, Mich., 1968), pp. 1 – 68.
2. Plato, *Respub.* X (607B).

Oskar Kristeller and John H. Randall, Jr., should be encouraged, on the one hand. On the other, the importance of such Renaissance philologists as were concerned with the precise interpretation of ancient philosophical and scientific and mathematical texts should also be conceded for the contributions they made to the history of philosophy and science. It should be recognized that the Renaissance of Platonism, despite its deep roots in medieval theology and philosophy, began under the auspices of the long humanist nostalgia for Aristotle's greatest rival, known through the pages of Cicero, Macrobius, and Augustine. The revival of Platonism continued through the sixteenth century with many friendly associations of humanists and Platonists. But it should be reaffirmed that the Renaissance Platonists, too, were genuine philosophers, and that however much individual ones may, like some of the humanists, have been at odds with scholastic Aristotelianism, many others sought a synthesis or a reconciliation of Plato and Aristotle, commencing with Giovanni Pico della Mirandola. It may be mentioned that Paolo Beni not only taught natural philosophy at the *Sapienza* in Rome in 1595, but that, on becoming professor of the humanities at Padua in 1598, he declared that Plato and Cicero were the two founders of the *studia humanitatis* and that it was difficult to decide whether Plato's eloquence or his wisdom was the greater. He later prepared a volume of extracts from Plato's writings, which he titled *Rhetorica Platonis*.[3]

Paolo Beni may well be a late and extreme example of a humanist who also possessed credentials as a philosopher and a theologian. There were, however, other humanists, beginning with Petrarch, who encountered and discussed genuine problems of philosophy as a necessary part of their functioning as rhetoricians, particularly those who were concerned with the theoretical foundations of their disci-

3. Although his interpretation is debatable, see on Beni the article of Giancarlo Mazzacurati in *Dizionario biografico degli italiani*, s.v. Beni's comment on Plato and Cicero in his *Oratio . . . quibus omnibus Perfectus Humanitatis Doctor decribitur ac fingitur, Habita Patavii in Publico Gymnasio XVI Kal. Aprilis Anno MDC,* in his *Quinquagintae orationes* (Padua, 1613), p. 17: "Nam Plato, quem elegantiae, urbanitatis, eloquentiae Humanitatis ipsius sive fontem sive Magistrum merito appellaveris, sine quo nostra haec studia in squalore ac situ iacerent, e cuius spatiis (ut multa complectar paucis) extitit noster Cicero, difficile est iudicare an eloquentia magis excellat quam sapientia, disputandi suavitate quam subtilitate, orationis ubertate et copia, quam doctrinae magnitudine et varietate." On the rhetoric of Plato, see his *Oratoriae disputationes, seu Rhetoricae controversiae. Et Platonis Rhetorica subjicitur, ex variis locis excerpta.* Venetiis, Apud Io. Guerilium. 1625. *In Platonis Rhetorica* begins at p. 111.

pline. It is well known that many humanists in their apologetic de-
fenses of their studies claimed to have a more comprehensive (or a
more appropriate, or more usable) command of philosophy than the
university-trained philosophers, but these claims, which were frequently not serious, are not at issue. Rather it is a legitimate claim that
humanists, in the very pursuit of rhetorical goals and methods, could
become philosophical in the questions they handled. There definitely were genuinely "philosophical humanists," although this does
not mean that they should be called, or confused with, philosophers.

I will attempt to show how the critique of dialectic by three Italian humanists derived from and contributed to their own rhetorically determined need to investigate and understand human motivation and behavior, and how in the pursuit of such understanding
they were compelled to take positions on questions concerning truth
that must at least be considered para-philosophical. Committed by
their art to generating intention and action in their audience and
public, Renaissance humanists attempted to become more precise in
determining what kind of language and what kind of reasoning
would produce meaningful persuasion, that is, a state of mind that
would lead to the corresponding appropriate action. Pragmatic and,
perhaps, opportunistic, such considerations also involved the establishment of certain norms concerning human nature that, if they
were not strictly determined by the precedents of ancient philosophy, at least may be called "anthropological."

In our concern with rhetoric as an art and its employment by the
rhetorician, we sometimes forget the recipient of rhetoric, the reader
and the audience. There is a tendency to assume that Renaissance humanists identified only with the deliverers of rhetoric, with their classical models, Isocrates and Demosthenes, Cicero and Quintilian,
Augustine and Jerome. We forget that the humanists were in many
cases readers if not hearers of rhetoric and famous as critics and
interpreters of texts. They viewed the rhetorical relationship certainly as much from the viewpoint of the recipient as of the deliverer,
both in their actuality as living citizens and theoretically as critics and
analyzers of eloquence.

A question of major concern to the humanists that links rhetoric
to philosophy, however much the two traditions might differ in its
discussion, was that of truth. It has bothered and outraged some of
our colleagues to encounter Petrarch's famous quip in the *De suiipsius
et multorum ignorantia:* "It is better to love the good than to know the

truth."[4] This is a clear sign, it is alleged, of his anti-intellectualism, or at best what could be expected of a devotee of the rhetorical tradition who would place an emotional attachment ahead of the knowledge of reality. What is forgotten is that this was an age in which what had for long been held to be philosophical reality was being reduced to the status of mere names by the philosophers of the new dispensation of the *via moderna,* call them "nominalists" or what you will. Petrarch also had a role in these philosophical debates, as is evidenced by his invectives against the physicians and the young Venetian students of natural philosophy who provoked his work.

But it is an earlier work (at least in inception) that best provides his fundamental position, though this is not always recognized. In the prologue to the first book of the *Secretum,* first written in 1347 but much revised in 1349 and 1353, as it is now thought, Petrarch presented the spirit of Truth, who will silently watch and listen while the human figure of "Saint Augustine" endeavors to persuade "Franciscus" of the right path. It is not enough to suggest that there are echoes of Beatrice, Virgil, and Dante in these three of whom Petrarch declares that "Franciscus's" "steps had gone astray" and that he knew "not the gravity of his disease."[5] Petrarch is undoubtedly signalling that his dialogue is concerned with the Truth, with man's capacity to grasp the Truth, with his susceptibility to be transformed by knowledge for the Truth and to live his life in accordance with it. The argument between "Augustinus" and "Franciscus" in this first part of the dialogue develops over whether a man who knows his misery by deep meditation and wishes to remove it can do what he wishes. The recollection of Saint Augustine's agony and conversion under the famous fig tree is to provide example for the wavering and doubting

4. *Francisci Petrarce De sui ipsius et multorum ignorantia liber,* ed. Pier Giorgio Ricci, in *Francesco Petrarca Prose,* eds. G. Martellotti, P. G. Ricci, E. Carrara, E. Bianchi (Milan and Naples, 1955), p. 748, "Satius est autem bonum velle quam verum nosse." Translation by Hans Nachod, in *The Renaissance Philosophy of Man,* eds. E. Cassirer, Paul Oskar Kristeller, J. H. Randall, Jr. (Chicago, 1948), p. 105. Subsequent citations will be to *Prose.*

5. *De secreto conflictu curarum mearum libri tres,* ed. E. Carrara, in *Prose,* pp. 22–215; translation by W. H. Draper, *Petrarch's Secret, or the Soul's Conflict with Passion* (London, 1911), hereafter Draper. See *Prose,* 24–26; Draper, 4–5. Latin passages will not be given in subsequent notes on the *Secretum* because of the accessibility of this edition. Translations will sometimes vary from Draper's. The old dating of 1443 has been all but disposed of by Francisco Rico. See his *Vida u obras de Petrarca, I, Lectura del Secretum* (Padua, 1974), pp. 453–535, and esp. pp. 468–71; and his "Precisazioni di cronologia Petrarchesca; Le 'Familiares' VIII ii–v, e i rifacimenti del 'Secretum,' " *Giornale storico della letteratura italiana* 105 (1978), 481–525.

"Franciscus." The saint's own final conflict of will, which held him back from emotional acceptance of his intellectual conviction of the Truth of catholic Christianity, it is agreed, was resolved, by divine grace.[6] In Petrarch's similar case, not a miracle but an intellectual exercise, intensive meditation on man's last ends, is proposed.

It is at exactly this juncture that the definition of man as an animal but one which is rational and mortal is put forth, and Petrarch turns to an attack on scholastic dialectic. As "Augustinus" puts it: "although a host of little pinpricks play upon the surface of your mind, nothing yet has penetrated the center. The miserable heart is hardened by long habit, and becomes like some indurable stone; impervious to warning however salubrious, you will find few people considering with any seriousness the fact that they will die." "Franciscus" immediately responds: "Then few people are aware of the very definition of man, which nevertheless is so hackneyed in the schools, that it ought not merely to weary the ears of those who hear it, but is now long since scrawled upon the walls and pillars of every room."[7] It is, of course, this existential condition of the *vulgus* (in which he includes himself) that is the true barrier to comprehending the Truth, but Petrarch makes its persistence the special fault of the defective methodology of the scholastic dialectician who plays with mere words with the resulting educational shambles. As "Augustinus" puts it: "This prattling of the Dialecticians will never come to an end; it throws up summaries and definitions like bubbles, matter indeed for endless controversies but for the most part they know nothing of the real truth of the things they talk about *(plerunque autem, quid ipsum vere sit quod loquuntur, ignorant)*. . . . Against this kind of men, so fastidiously negligent and vainly curious, they should be questioned as follows: Why this everlasting labor for nothing, this exercise of wit on silly subtleties? Why in total oblivion of reality do you grow old conversant only with words, and with whitening hair and wrinkled brows do you spend all your time on childish ineptitudes?" *(Quid, obliti rerum, inter verba senescitis . . . ?)*.[8]

It is in the context of this discussion of the epistemological failure of scholasticism that "Augustinus" presents his description of what it is really like to live according to reason and his long exposition of death and dying graphically depicting the powerful physical

6. *Prose,* 40; Draper, 19–20.
7. *Prose,* 50; Draper, 29.
8. *Prose,* 52; Draper, 29–30.

and emotional effects the witnessing of a horrible death-bed scene and meditation upon it can produce. Then, and only then, can a man understand the truth of the standard definition of man as a rational and mortal animal that is bandied about in the schools. "Augustinus" adds: "This then is what I meant by sinking down deeply into the soul — not while, perchance by force of habit you name 'death' or reiterate 'nothing more certain than death, nothing more uncertain than the hour of death' and other sayings of this kind in daily use. For these fly right by and do not sink in."[9] Moreover, meditation is translated into written language and may be seen as a form of rhetoric practiced on the self and upon one's readers.

Dialectical philosophy, as here and in the probably contemporary group of letters in *Le familiari*,[10] and Aristotelian natural philosophy and moral philosophy, as argued in the *De ignorantia*, fail for Petrarch not because he despises the intellect, knowledge, and truth but because they are inadequate roads to the Truth, based as they seem to him on too shallow a conception of human nature. Poetry and rhetoric, which he learned from his own practice and from Cicero, Seneca, Horace, Virgil, and Saint Augustine (the *De doctrina Christiana* and the *Contra academicos*), are better instruments for acquiring the deep knowledge of the truth that reaches and moves the will. Only this and not mere verbalizing is sufficient. Hence Petarch avers, "Satius est autem bonum velle quam verum nosse."[11]

His is a different conception of learning that involves a new integration of the self and a discovery of the road to God. Man, however, is rational (as well as mortal) as the definition held, but man's rationality is only a potential until he has truly learned to direct his life by reason. *Ratio*, moreover, along with *oratio*, is the faculty by which he impersonates himself and guides the reader to the transcendence of fortune and its excessive effects in the *De remediis*.[12]

For Lorenzo Valla truth was only definable subjectively. Valla says in his *Repastinatio:* "The true or the truth is a quality present in the sense of the mind and in speech, as in 'Does he truly feel that?' 'Does he speak truly?' For when we inquire whether there is one world or many, we do not ask thus whether it is true that there is one world but out of the contradiction, either the alternative [position], 'Does he

9. *Prose*, 56; Draper, 33 – 34.   10. *Rer. fam.*, 1.7 – 10.   11. See note 4, above.
12. See Klaus Heitmann's discussion in his *Fortuna und Virtus, Eine Studie zu Petrarcas Lebensweisheit* (Cologne and Graz, 1958), passim. On Petrarch's moral philosophy in general, see my *The Poet as Philosopher: Petrarch and the Formation of Renaissance Consciousness* (New Haven, Conn., 1979), chaps. 3, 4, and 5.

truly believe there are many worlds?' or ours, as when we set up two or more sides among us as we do in deliberating. For there is no investigation of the true before a controversy over the matter arises. Therefore truth is knowledge of a disputed subject, and falsity lack of knowledge concerning the same; that is a species of prudence or imprudence, or of wisdom or folly. Or we may say truth is both the knowledge of the mind concerning some matter and the signification of a speech derived from the knowledge of the mind. For the speech is taken in two ways: one whether anyone speaks true when he speaks thus as he feels; the other whether he speaks forth what he feels or something different through simulation or dissimulation. Therefore there may be a double falsehood in the statement, the one out of ignorance, the other out of malice; the first of imprudence, the other of injustice because in actions, as will appear in the sequel."[13]

The passage above is translated as literally as I am able from Valla's first book of his *Repastinatio dialecticae et philosophiae* in a chapter where he argues that the transcendentals of ancient philosophy — the good, the true, and the one — are qualities derived from human linguistic usage and are not metaphysical entities. As the last two sentences quoted indicate, Valla closely links the question of truth and falsehood with that of virtue and vice. Both are qualities of the soul, one pertaining to the intellect or reason, and the other to the will or love.[14]

Following Saint Augustine's *De Trinitate*, Valla sets up a parallel between the divine Trinity and the human soul. But the relationship and character of Father, Son, and Spirit are differently stated by Valla, who introduces Quintilian's three categories of controversy —

13. Lorenzo Valla, *Repastinatio dialectice et philosophiae,* Biblioteca Apostolica Vaticana, Cod. urb. lat. 1207 (hereafter Urb. lat. 1207), ff. 50^v – 51^r: "Verum sive veritas . . . qualitas est quae sensui mentis inest et orationi, ut 'vere ne ille sentit?' 'vere ne hic loquitur?' Nam quom quaerimus an unus mundus sit an plures, non ita quaerimus an verum sit unum mundum esse, sed ex contradictione aut alterius, ut 'vere ne ille sentit plures mundos esse?' aut nostra quom ipsi apud nos duas pluresve partes sicut in deliberando suscipimus. Nec ante veri inquisitio quam rei controversia nascitur. Itaque veritas est notitia rei controversae, falsitas vero eiusdem inscitia; quae est speties prudentiae aut imprudentiae, seu sapientiae aut insapientiae. Seu dicamus: Veritas est tum notitia animi de aliqua re tum orationis ex notitia animi profecta significatio. Nam orationem duobus modis accipi volo: uno an quis verum loquatur quum ita loquatur ut sentit; altero an quod sentit proloquatur, an diversum per simulationem dissimulationemve. Ideoque duplex erit in oratione mendacium: illud ex ignorantia, hoc ex malitia; illud imprudentie, hoc iniustitie, quia in actis ut in sequentibus apparebit."

14. Urb. lat. 1207, 51^{r-v}.

An sit? Quid sit? and *Quale sit?* — into his exposition. *An sit?* of course is an axiomatic affirmation that God exists. *Quid sit?* raises the question of the divine substance.[15] But Valla has already set forth his own notion that the orator's subject matter—*res*—is the only transcendental, and it is divided threefold into "substance," "quality" and "action."[16] To describe a thing or to speak of God, it is necessary to recognize that there are only two basic substances—matter and spirit—and their possible combinations. But matter and spirit, including God and the human soul (as well as animal souls) in the latter, are too abstracted for usage in relation to any actually existing *res*, such as God, so that Valla proposes the use of the term *consubstantial* as a better and more inclusive term than *substance*.[17]

The divine consubstantial (as all others) should include the threesome of substance, quality, and action. The divine three-in-one then, following Valla's rhetorical or Quintilianic mode of reasoning, consists of the Father, who "is properly the life, power and eternity of God," the Son, who "is the wisdom of God, born from the power itself," and the Holy Spirit, "who is the love of God." All three have one substance but different qualities, as just described, and actions: the Father gives forth power, creates and emanates; the Son shines with wisdom; the Spirit burns with holy love — all on the analogy of the sun.[18]

Made in the image of God, the human soul is also compared to the vibration, light, and heat of the sun: "in the soul or substance of the soul there are three perpetual qualities: memory, which is the life of the soul, intellect, which is the same as reason, and . . . love." As for its actions: "the soul comprehends and retains other things by memory, examines and judges by the intellect whether things are, what they are and how they are *(an sit, quid sit, quale sit?)*, and embraces or rejects them by the affect."[19]

15. See section of book one of his *Repastinatio*, titled "Quid sit Deus?" Urb. lat. 1207, ff. 66ʳ – 69ᵛ, followed by "Quid sit anima hominis et bruti?" Urb. lat. 1207, ff. 69ᵛ – 76ᵛ.

16. See first and second sections of book one of *Repastinatio*: "Omnia tribus elementis sive predicamentis comprehendi" (i.e., substance, quality and action), Urb. lat. 1207, ff. 42ᵛ – 44ʳ; "Nec ens nec aliquid esse transcendens, sed tantum res," Urb. lat. 1207, ff. 44ʳ – 46ʳ.

17. See sections "De distributione substantiae," Urb. lat. 1207, ff. 58ʳ – 59ʳ and "De substantia," Urb. lat. 1207, ff. 65ᵛ – 66ʳ.

18. Urb. lat. 1207, ff. 67ᵛ – 68ᵛ.

19. Urb. lat. 1207, f. 71ʳ: ". . . in anima seu substantia animae tres perpetuae qualitates: memoria quae vita animi est; intellectus eadem est ratio . . . [et] amor . . . ; . . .

In accordance with this conception of the soul, Valla thinks of the moral virtues, in contrast to the prevailing Aristotelian notions, as emanating only from the affects and as reducible to one, strength of soul, manifested in the vigor of love or hate, joy or sorrow (past, present, and future). Again, he follows Augustine's criticism of the Stoic conception of the virtues in book 14 of *The City of God.* Prudence, so favored by Cicero and many of the humanists, is regarded as a purely intellectual virtue, or rather, as Valla would have it, as knowledge of virtue. Cato and Catiline used their knowledge, the one for justice and the other for injustice. "Therefore [prudence's] praise is for justice, not knowledge." Prudence, if called by its right name of knowledge or cognition, should not be praised or blamed, "but action proceeding from cognition and understanding through good will." In fact, for Valla the whole range of intellectual powers or virtues is removed from the realm of rhetoric, which is reserved for stimulating the actions of the will or for the moral virtues and vices. Hence he carefully distinguishes between *right (ius),* which is the knowledge of justice and law, and *justice,* which is "action, right, good and equitable." "That quality [right] is part of prudence. . . . From adhering to right and doing what right orders, this quality [justice] is named. That quality [right] emanates from truth, this [justice] from will."[20]

Moral action follows from knowledge of what is moral, and a man can sin out of ignorance or out of ill will toward an object of his hate. But ignorance is also censurable as a symptom or a consequence of a weakness of soul that prevents the necessary effort and study to discover right reason or truth. Magnanimity and pusillanimity are the paramount virtue and vice, and are manifested in fortitude and charity or their absence. Man is for the most part driven by his passions but also can sometimes exercise free will. "Fortitude," he says, "is a certain resistance against the harsh or the pleasant things which prudence has declared to be evils. Is not such action justice? Yes, except that justice seems to be the result of a freer will and to occur mostly in easier circumstances."[21] There is, then, a realm for

anima res alias memoria comprehendit et retinet, intellectu examinat et iudicat an sit, quid sit, quale sit, affectu amplectitur vel repellit."

20. Urb. lat. 1207, ff. 71ʳ – 72ᵛ: "Laus ergo iustitiae fuit non cognitionis. . . . . . Sed actio ex cognitione et scientia prodiens per bonam voluntatem. . . . Iustitia vero non scientia neque ars, sed actio racta, bona, et aequa. Illud prudentiae est. . . . . . Haec a stando iuri et ab agendo quod iubet ius nominat. Illud a veritate manat; hoc a voluntate."

21. Urb. lat. 1207, f. 72ᵛ: "Est enim fortitudo reluctatio quaedam contra aspera et

instruction and a realm for rhetorical appeal. Since man is motivated by the desire for the experience of loving, which can be reduced to mere pleasure or elevated to holy beatitude, epideictic rhetoric would be the most potent type of appeal for Valla, though there is also room for the judicial and the deliberative.

As sin is from weakness and virtue from strength, he has a vision of man impressing himself on the exterior world rather than being moulded by externals or written upon as on a *tabula rasa*. The mind is not a *tabula rasa* but is more like a flame or the sun: "And to stay with the same comparison, just as a flame seizes and devours and renders into ashes the material by which it can be fed, so the soul is nourished by learning and hides what it perceives within itself and transfigures it in its own heat and light; hence it paints others rather than is painted by others; . . . the soul, advancing into exterior things by its own light, projects and paints upon them a certain image of its memory, intellect and will."[22]

Rhetoric and the study of language and literature are for Valla the key to man's discovery of rightness and wrongness and truth. Hence it is Valla's project to reform dialectic within a Quintilianic context in the remaining two books of this work. But the intellectual virtues, which include faith and hope, are subordinate to charity, or goodness of the will, in their striving for fulfillment in the act of *amatio,* or loving. "As charity is located in the ultimate part of the soul, so faith and hope are in the prior ones where knowledge, wisdom and truth dwell. For to know, or be wise, or understand, is nothing except to believe and feel about things just as they are constituted *(credere ac sentire de rebus ita ut sese habent),* and this is called truth."[23]

Should Valla be called a philosopher? Since he did his best to

---

blanda quae mala esse prudentia dictaverit. An non talis iustitia? nisi quod et liberioris arbitrii videtur et plerunque versari in facilioribus."

22. Urb. lat. 1207, f. 76[r-v]: "Atque ut eadem in similitudine versemur, sicut flamma ignis materiam qua ali potest apprehendit, devorat et in prunas convertit, sic anima alitur discendo et ea quae percipit in se recondit, suoque calore ac sua luce transfigurat ut ipsa potius pingat alia quam pingatur ab aliis. . . . anima fulgore suo in exteriora prodiens memoriae, intellectus, voluntatisve quandam obiicit et depingit imaginem."

23. Urb. lat. 1207, f. 74[v]: " . . . ut caritatem in ultima parte animae ita fidem et spem in prioribus sitas ubi scientia et sapientia et veritas habitant. Nihil est enim scire et sapere et intelligere, nisi credere ac sentire de rebus ita ut sese habent, et haec vocatur veritas." For a discussion of this, as yet, unpublished work of Valla with a somewhat different emphasis, see my *In Our Image and Likeness, Humanity and Divinity in Italian Humanist Thought* (Chicago, 1970), pp. 150–65.

dissociate himself from philosophy, ancient, medieval, and Renaissance, it would probably be wrong so to consider him. But if it is asked whether, by virtue of his consideration of philosophical problems, he was a systematic thinker who constructed an orderly and coherent theory of knowledge derived from the study of rhetoric and linguistic usage and a conception of human nature and motivation based on his conception of man's experience as an image and likeness of the divine, an honest reader, it seems to me, would have to say "Yes."

Gioviano Pontano, another ardent student of ancient rhetoric and ethics, visualized the overall structure of human society as determined by the formation of linguistic character types. Developing the ancient sophistic and Ciceronian vision of rhetoric as calling men together into cities and families from an original wild existence, Pontano in his *De sermone* sees the bonds of social existence as growing out of discourse. "Just as reason," he says, "is the guide and mistress for directing actions, so speech *(oratio)* is the manager of all those things which, conceived in the mind and activated by thinking, are pushed forth into the public world, for, as it is said, we are born social and must live in multitudes. Wherever discourse is greater and more frequent, there is a richer supply of all those things in which life is naturally lacking (since need is present as a companion to all men at their birth). By means of speech life itself is rendered far more adaptable as well as more capable of acquiring virtues and of attaining happiness."[24]

What he has in mind is not formal oratory and rhetoric by which, he says, "men who are especially distinguished in elocution establish the greatest position and the highest authority for themselves in the most populous cities and the largest enterprises." "For," he adds, "we are not at all referring to that part of rhetoric which is called the oratorical power or faculty or art, but only to that common discourse itself by which men, in approaching friends, in carrying on their daily tasks, use language in get-togethers, conversations, family and civic meetings and practices. For this reason those who are engaged in such matters are to be commended according to a quite different criterion than those who are called orators and the eloquent."[25]

Within this wider context of universal discourse, Pontano finds

24. *Ioannis Ioviani Pontani De Sermone Libri Sex*, eds. S. Lupi and A. Riscato (Lugano: 1954), 1.1.3. Latin quotations will not be given because of the availability of this excellent edition. Hereafter *De serm.*

25. *De serm.* 1.3.3-4.

that urbanity and truth are specific qualities that especially contribute to the enhancement of society and the good life for man. The latter quality, truth, is of special interest to us because to Pontano truth becomes a moral virtue — *veracitas.* "Because right reason should preside in handling and managing affairs and truth is its special friend," it is held to be of the highest value by all men. "Through truthfulness human conciliation is established and faith flourishes in the city and a kind of bonding of all our actions and affairs takes place as well as the observance of promises and statements. That this is so Christ, both God and at the same time man, has intimated to us, since He has professed himself to be the Truth."[26]

As was just seen, the virtue corresponding to truth is *veracitas.* Since habitual virtues lead to distinctive character types, on the one hand, there results the *verax* or the truthful man. On the other hand, a considerable number of unpleasant types result from the lying, opposite kind of man, and much of Pontano's disquisition will be about the various forms of *ostentatio, simulatio,* and *dissimulatio.* But truth and veracity also have their cognates. "It follows, therefore, that the study of truth is that virtue which is named *veridicentia* [truthsaying], and those who use it are *veridici;* hence those who prophesy truly are *vates* or soothsayers *(harioli),* truthsayers likewise and truespeakers." Truthful men "engage in investigations of things and natural causes or of right and wrong and either in forensic affairs or in physical and mathematical researches." Speaking well of something *(benedicentia)* also follows from speaking truly *(veridicentia),* for it is the part of an upright man to speak well and to be a truthspeaker and to be himself an especially upright and good man and citizen. And if any crime ought to be disparaged, the veracious man will not spare the truth but he will speak in such a way that he does not seem to do it out of zeal for speaking ill or detracting but in order that honesty (uprightness, *honestas*) may be vigorous in the city itself and at the same time there may be liberty and the common good of all citizens, and in order that crime and wickedness will be driven far away.[27]

In the course of developing his exposition of truthfulness, Pontano projects an ideal of a scholarly man and professor *(studiosus, professor)* who in every action and speech assumes in his own person the role of defending truth. "Moreover," he says, "since all virtue is

26. *De serm.* 1.7.8.   27. *De serm.* 2.2.52-53.

voluntary *(gratuita)* and sought for its own sake, and veracity is laudable among the very first of the virtues and is very helpful for maintaining and expanding human society, no wonder that the truthful men *(veraces)* themselves are scholars *(studiosi)* of the true itself solely for the sake of the truth; and they both cultivate truth for its own sake and, because they understand it to be an especially durable bond of human society, they know that they themselves have been born for cultivating it."[28] Surely this is a fine and, to us, early acknowledgment of the existence and the moral and social necessity of the man of learning and science. Pontano proceeds to enumerate the duties or *officia* of the truthful man: he should speak freely and openly and never deceptively about himself when this is needed, and he should invent nothing concerning himself beyond what he is and has, and not subtract anything remaining modest all the while. He will not twist the truth or distort by words in any way and will not be windy or intemperate or frigid in tone and manner. "He will be straightforward and true to himself and no different in explaining and speaking of the affairs of others. These he will refer to and expound in circles and councils and gatherings in such a way that he will not seem merely to speak graciously and in order to please the ears but in zeal for and for the sake of the truth alone."[29]

Pontano's discussions of modes of speech as types of virtue and character here and elsewhere are full of descriptions of the shadier and less admirable habits and stratagems he knew well and presented with sharp and telling insight. Side by side with the humanist-scholar was the courtier-civil servant-counselor, a role Pontano also successfully fulfilled. One must guess, however, that when he wrote the passages above it was not without some conflict between the two ideals, and especially with that of the companionable, facetious type he also so patently admired. At any rate he asks whether the truthful man can ever be permitted to shade the truth, to simulate, or to invent, for the pressure of the times on the person who acts in their circumstances is very great. "Now," he says, "they invent much, now on the contrary conceal in adverse and dangerous circumstances—those wise men who are administrators of public affairs, commanders of armies. So also do many learned physicians in the most perilous diseases, and not a few priests who are called preachers where they add their own authority to the facts; nor yet are they held

28. *De serm.* 2.2.53-54.   29. *De serm.* 2.2.54-55.

to be liars from this, or less than truthsayers, when their purpose is not to lie or deceive but to help in this manner and to avert danger, which is entirely the practice and duty of prudent men."[30]

Pontano's concerns, like Petrarch's and Valla's, are highly moral but are projected from a quite different social context, more secular, public, and courtly, perhaps. Like the others, Pontano is highly original, though his ancient sources were Aristotelian and Ciceronian in contrast to Petrarch's employment of Cicero, Seneca, and Augustine and Valla's overt promotion of the concepts of Quintilian and his tacit Augustinianism and pretended Epicureanism. But in each of the three cases, the question of truth is expounded in a self-consciously grasped nexus of relationships among God, man, nature, history, and society, which nexus seemed more crucial to these humanists for the discovery and implementation of truth than the institutional isolation and methodological purity of the scholastic philosophers of their day. These broader, more experiential and anthropological modes of conceptualization and motivation can in great part be understood as a consequence of Renaissance humanist study of ancient ethics and rhetoric. The importance of rhetorical humanism in the history of Western thought thus needs to be conceded regardless of whether any humanist is granted a niche in the hall of famous philosophers.

30. *De serm.* 2.2.57–58.

The First German Treatise on Homiletics: Erasmus Sarcer's *Pastorale* and Classical Rhetoric

JOACHIM DYCK

Rhetoric is, as Klaus Dockhorn has said, a *Weltanschauung* in the truest sense of the word: it has its own epistemology, its own moral laws, and, above all, its own anthropology.[1] And even though this statement cannot be strictly applied to every single epoch in the history of rhetoric from Aristotle to the twentieth century, it most certainly *is* valid for Protestant humanism in the sixteenth century, when rhetoric, together with dialectic, was for the reformers the methodological foundation on which they based their conception of the hermeneutics of the new doctrine and how it was best to be propagated.

I

The relationship between the propagation of the new doctrine and its reception was of central importance in the German Reformation; it differed vastly from the medieval conception of how opinions on theological content were to be established. The revolutionary ideas required new vehicles and thus new forms of communication: this was the age when the sermon became the most important instrument in the propagation of the new teaching and in the instruction of the faithful on the basic conceptions of this religious reform

---

1. Klaus Dockhorn, "*Rhetorica movet*: Protestantischer Humanismus und karolingische Renaissance," in *Rhetorik: Beiträge zu ihrer Geschichte in Deutschland vom 16.-20. Jahrhundert,* ed. H. Schanze (Frankfurt, 1974), p. 17.

movement. And this is the reason Luther calls the ministry the highest office in Christendom.[2]

It is obvious why the sermon as a vehicle for propagating the new doctrine resorted both to the structure and to the language of rhetoric, and this explains why Melanchthon is of the opinion that the art of preaching is to a certain extent either a part or a reflection of rhetoric ("rhetorica quoniam ratio concionandi illius artis quedam vel pars vel imago est"),[3] from which he borrowed several paradigms, though with slight modifications of their form. Rhetoric is the study of the principles of persuasion developed out of classical oratory by which the orator is enabled to persuade his listeners to accept views that he, the orator, considers right and important. Rhetoric aims at a psychological effect, and thus Aristotle's definition (that it is the capacity for selecting in each individual case the best possible means of persuasion) was valid until well into the nineteenth century.

II

The psychological target of the reformers was the congregation. Before the Reformation the congregation played a very minor role, but now it becomes central to the church and is given a totally new function. This is clearly reflected in the acceptance of the demand of the peasants that congregations should be permitted to appoint their own ministers.

For the congregation the sermon has, in turn, a particular function; it is no longer just one of the many parts of the liturgy but takes on central significance. Its function is not only to communicate doctrine but also to enable the individual to establish a personal relationship with his God on the basis of the Bible: "*Officium praedicatorum* is actually a form of judgment, *ut semper diligant, ut praedicent,* to help and advise the people and to hold them to faith and love" (Luther, 1538).[4] Burdened with original sin, man is inherently incapable of real perfection. As an idea, however, man has to be conceived as an image of God endowed with perfectability. And the congregation,

2. Ulrich Nembach, *Predigt des Evangeliums: Luther als Prediger, Pädagoge und Rhetor* (Neukirchen-Vluyn, 1972), p. 11.

3. Uwe Schnell, *Die homiletische Theorie Philipp Melanchthons* (Berlin and Hamburg, 1968), p. 65.

4. Nembach, *Predigt des Evangeliums,* pp. 37–38.

together with one of their own number, the preacher, is eager to realize at least some aspects of perfection in each individual (i.e., confession, penance, forgiveness of sins). The function of the sermon changes with Luther's definition — that is, it is supposed to deal with teaching and exhortation *(doctrina et exhortatio)*. It is no longer an instrument in the hands of an elite to impose the supremacy of the doctrine from above to below; its function now is to communicate the teaching that, ideally, should be accessible to each member of the congregation in the vernacular of the Bible.

III

In classical antiquity, rhetoric was exclusively verbal communication, the practice of oratory. Rhetoric becomes an instrument of interpretation only when Christians start to examine critically both Roman civilization and the view that the Bible is a text for discriminating and educating readers written in accordance with the rules of rhetoric. The humanists, according to their concept of the role of eloquence, hold that the postulates of true education are *first* a literal understanding, *second* an understanding of the subject matter, and *third* a clear exposition of the insight thus gained. It is immaterial whether the written or spoken word is used as the means of communication. A prerequisite is the recognition that the writers of classical antiquity always observed the rules of rhetoric in their works. Thus, literary sources can only be properly understood by those who are themselves acquainted with the rules of form in accordance with which such works were originally written. A knowledge of rhetoric is therefore an important element in the understanding of literature. The rules for the interpretation, the hermeneutics of an oration or of any other literary product, must be immediately visible in the exposition of its structure.[5] Since the divine secrets are concealed in words as if in a sanctuary, it is necessary to understand the meanings and the figures of speech contained in the Bible.

For the reformers the appropriate hermeneutics for the Holy Scripture, as for any other literary text, consisted in the unconditional acceptance of the rules of classical rhetoric, and there are nu-

5. Cf. Schnell, *Die homiletische Theorie,* p. 19.

merous testimonies to the fact that it was Melanchthon's expert knowledge and perfect mastery of rhetoric and related dialectics that caused Luther to support Melanchthon's appointment to a professorship in Wittenberg. Again and again Luther stressed how much he was indebted to his younger colleague's knowledge of theological methodology. Through increasingly systematic study Luther became convinced of the necessity for reform, and again and again in his *Table Talks* he drove home his message of "Dialectica docet, rhetorica movet" — the most pertinent and striking summing-up of his unconditional acceptance of rhetoric as the underlying hermeneutics and anthropology of his whole theological system, his perfect synthesis of doctrine and faith.[6]

IV

With this new and radical change in the function of the sermon in Luther's humanism — that is, the central importance of the propagation of the new doctrine — it becomes clear why the reformers laid so much stress on the best possible training for preachers. A proper understanding of the Bible is a prerequisite for interpreting the Holy Scripture to the faithful. But to understand the Bible properly, the preacher needs both a knowledge of language and facts — in short, an academic education. The reformers regarded the liberal arts of the *trivium* as the best foundation for a better understanding of the Holy Scripture and their doctrine of faith, man's station and his justification through faith. The student of theology must therefore concern himself both implicitly and explicitly with rhetoric, for rhetoric, as part of that *trivium*, is a basic subject of study and is, at the same time, the hermeneutic method of text interpretation. As a matter of fact, we know from Melanchthon's visitation reports that the reformers were eager to improve religious ministration in the villages and towns and raise the standard of training for the ministry, so that congregations would no longer have to put up with ministers who had neither the moral nor educational qualifications for such an office. Thus, training in rhetoric became for the very first time in history a basic requirement in the training for the priesthood.

6. Cf. Dockhorn, *"Rhetorica movet,"* p. 21.

From the Middle Ages on, numerous treatises had appeared in Latin on the art of preaching, *rationes concionandi*. Since the church no longer represented the sole source of revelation, but the presence of verbal revelation had itself assumed the center of divine worship, the art of oratory was becoming more and more important, particularly because the sermons were delivered in the vernacular and the congregation was thus enabled to share in the process of interpretation. This change from a representative church to a congregationally centered church, coupled with the translation of the Bible into German, ensured that all theological problems could be dealt with in the vernacular. Thus the vernacular was extended to genres that previously were the exclusive domain of Latin. In addition, the ministry became a public institution in the course of the Reformation and the German educational treatises of the time addressed themselves to the educated middle classes in the towns that supported the Reformation.

V

Erasmus Sarcer was the first reformer to deal with the problems of the ministry in the German language.[7] Note his 1559 title: *Pastorale on the office, nature, and discipline of pastors and servants of the church, and how they should study from their youth up and thereafter most profitably instruct in the course of their whole ministry, setting an unparalleled example both in teaching and conduct, it being their duty to proclaim the true religion where it has not been told and to maintain it where it has already been proclaimed.* This detailed title is in itself a program — the humanism that it proclaims is confirmed rhetoric. Sarcer demands a basic course of academic study for the ministry, what he calls the "good arts," the *bonae literae:*

> and albeit these good arts may not impart the eternal bliss that belongs to the kingdom of Christ, yet are they useful and good

7. *Pastorale Oder Hirtenbuch / vom Ampt / Wesen / und Disciplin der Pastorn / und Kirchendiener / Und wie sie von jugend auff studieren sollen / und hernach auch nützlich leren / in jrem gantzen Kirchenampt / in Lere und Leben sich unverweislich verhalten / desgleichen in schweren / und ungewönlichen fellen erzeigen / welche sich umb / und neben jrem Ampte teglich zutragen. Dienstlich die ware Religion recht anzustellen / da sie nicht ist / und zuerhalten / da sie ist* (Eisleben, 1559).

enough to impart the teachings of the Holy Scripture in proper and fitting manner to those who are simple and evil for their own improvement, for there be many servants of the Church who may as well know the Holy Scripture and can draw from it the necessary doctrine, but who, when it be required of them that they should impart to others what they honestly know and understand of the word of God, are not able to instruct for the use and benefit of others without the help and support of the good arts.[8]

Sarcer never tells us exactly what he means by the "good arts," but this is not necessary: they include rhetoric and dialectic, and from these comprehensive systems, which he himself has presented in Latin manuals, he derives the most important rules for the preacher in the chapter on the training and studies for servants of the church — in full accordance with the pattern set by Luther, who had required that the preacher be

a rhetorician and a dialectician, that is, he must teach and exhort. If he is to teach, he must be able to expose accurately, then to define; thirdly, he must be able to quote relevant passages from the Bible; fourthly, to illustrate with examples from the Bible or elsewhere; fifthly to embellish his words with parables; sixthly, he must be capable of admonishing the evil-hearted, the unruly and the indolent.[9]

Luther does not explicitly distinguish between dialectic and rhetoric in this passage, and the transition from *docere* to *exhortari* is very gradual. Melanchthon, too, maintained that dialectics and rhetoric were

8. Sarcer, *Pastorale,* fol. II[r]: "Und wiewol diese sc. guten Künste von den dingen der Seligkeit/die da zum Reich Christi gehören/nichts leren können/so sein sie doch hierzu nützlich und gut/das man die Leren der Schrifft/ordentlich und geschicklich/ andern einfeltigen und schlechten möge furtragen/und das zur besserung. Denn viel Kirchendiener sein/welche die Schrifft nur sehr recht und wol verstehen/und hieraus auch nötige Leren fassen können/aber wenn sie ander Leute leren sollen/ was sie rechtschaffens wissen und verstehen von Gottes sachen/so vermögen sie solchs doch nützlich und besserlich niemand zu leren/one hülffe und beistand guter Künste."

9. Luther, *Table Talks* 2216. Cf. Birgit Stolt, *Wortkampf: Frühneuhochdeutsche Beispiele zur rhetorischen Praxis* (Frankfurt, 1974), p. 52: "Ein Prediger muss ein Dialektiker und Rhetoriker sein, das heisst, er muss lehren und ermahnen. Wenn er etwas lehren will, muss er es zunächst genau bezeichnen, danach definieren; drittens muss er Bibelstellen dazu anführen, viertens es mit Beispielen aus der Bibel oder anderswoher beleuchten, fünftens diese seine Worte mit Gleichnissen weiter ausschmücken; sechstens die Schlechten, Widerspenstigen und Faulen tadeln."

so closely related that one could hardly draw a distinction between them. Sarcer is therefore in agreement when he refrains from drawing a clear distinction between them in his curriculum.

VI

"For such orderly and improved instruction," says Sarcer, "the method taught by the good arts is the instrument and proper tool."[10] What Sarcer calls the method, *methodus,* is the sum of all the technical considerations deriving from dialectics and rhetoric. The method provides the order required for teaching, it is largely "a certain and proper way of learning in an orderly manner, and of teaching how to teach the world."[11] Sarcer is concerned with a systematizing of hermeneutic problems and how they are to be taught, whereby he lays great stress on the fact that this classification should not be confused with the methodology of philosophical syllogism, "to construct something for purposes of demonstration." Sarcer's concern is a reflection on doctrinal content and its mediation through the *trivium,* presented in the form of an introductory manual for future preachers and all those interested in the current problems of the Reformation.

Sarcer explains his concept of studying and learning in the form of an interpretation of a main concept from the field of dogmatics, in this case the concept of faith, *locus communis,* as the appropriate terminology would express it. Melanchthon puts these *loci* into the context of a system of theological theory in his work of 1521, *Loci communes rerum theologicarum* (Wittenberg, 1521), and sees a *locus* as a basic theological concept. Sarcer retains the Latin terminology but also talks about "main articles of Scripture":

> Whoever will study Holy Scripture, either for his own benefit or that of others, must first take notice of the particular and significant words called *locus communes,* main articles of Scripture, as evident in such words as faith, righteousness, penance, etc.[12]

10. Sarcer, *Pastorale,* fol. II: "Zu solchem ordentlichen und besserlichem leren/ ist nu der Methodus/den gute Künste leren/das Instrument und der recht Werckzeug."

11. Sarcer, *Pastorale,* fol. III: Der Methodus ist "ein gewisse und rechte weise/ ordentlich zu lernen/und zu leren der Schrifft Leren."

12. Sarcer, *Pastorale,* fol. III: "Wil einer für sich selbst in der heiligen Schrifft

The explanation of such a *locus communis* is a *thema simplex*. A *thema compositum* would be the statement "Charity is built upon faith" and it can be presented in two ways — by means of hortation or discouragement, or by means of praise or rebuke.

In the following section Sarcer interprets the *locus communis* of faith, basing his presentation of this theme on the categories of rhetoric, wherein the *genus demonstrativum* employs *laudatio* and *vituperatio,* and the *genus deliberativum* the concepts of persuasion and dissuasion. Practice requires the application of these categories of rhetoric, the *genus demonstrativum* for praise and rebuke, and the *genus deliberativum* for admonition. Sarcer restricts himself to a demonstration of only one concept, that of faith, to give his readers a simple illustration of how this practice of interpretation and communication works.

How should one proceed to interpret the word *faith* for the congregation? This first stage is an investigation of the meaning of the word *faith*. In rhetoric the instrument for investigation and the discovery of arguments is the *inventio*. As demonstrated in the *Auctor ad Herennium,* the function of *inventio* lies in the *excogitatio rerum verarum aut vero similium,* that is, in the discovery of true or probably true arguments.[13] But he who wants to find must roughly know where to look. The task of systematizing this search and of evolving a doctrine that describes where to search falls upon the much-discussed *topic* within the category of the *inventio*. This is the doctrine of the places (*topio, loci*) within which the arguments are to be found and with the help of which the orator has to prove his thesis and make it credible. Sarcer does not specifically mention this technical term, *inventio,* but he describes metaphorically the function of the topic along the same lines:

> The purpose for which the method is useful and good: namely, that it opens the eyes forces one to look around at great length so that one has at all time sufficient material to talk or preach about and thus less need of labour and work as others see little or are completely blind and can take no notice of those around one and must

---

nützlich studieren oder ander Leute fruchtbarlich leren/was er studieret hat/so mus er erstlich der sonderlichen und deutlichen wörter warnemen/die man nennet *Locus communes,* Haubtartickel der Schrifft/als da sein solche und dergleichen wörter/ Glauben/Gerechtigkeit/Busse etc."

13. *Auctor ad Herennium* I.2.3; cf. Quintilian, *Institutio oratoria* III.3.1.

therefore most often have with ignominy to cease to orate and to preach because of a lack of subject matter.[14]

The *loci* listed by Sarcer himself in his Latin treatise on rhetoric (published in 1536) are the following: *quid sit (a definitione), quae partes vel species (a partibus), quae causae (a causis), qui effectus (a effectibus), quae cognata et pugnatia (a pugnantibus)*.[15] And in accordance with these topics, Sarcer interprets the term *faith* without the slightest attempt to explain the rhetorical origin of his deliberations: "It is fitting that you should first investigate the meaning of the word *faith* as it appears in the Bible." From the *topoi ex definitione* and *a partibus*, he then derives the different meanings of the term ("*faith* means constancy, means wholehearted trust and hope"). Sarcer does not limit himself to the definition proper, but gives possibilities of amplification, whereby he uses the metaphor of vision to characterize the search: "in such an investigation to discover the meaning of the word *faith* a wide field of vision is opened up." At the same time the contrary opinion must be "countered" and "refuted," must be "challenged," "considered," and "kept in view."[16]

The *topoi causa, effectus, contrario* follow this presentation of the *topos ex definitione,* and Sarcer continues with a vernacular formulation for the German reader:

> After this description of what faith is, you must continue to investigate what the real sources of faith are, that is, where it has its origin and whence it comes. It will then be discovered that the Holy Ghost is the real source of faith. The Word of God, however, is the outward manifestation of this moving of faith in the Holy Ghost.[17]

14. Sarcer, *Pastorale,* fol. VI[v]: "Es ist auch allhier zu sehen/warzu doch der ordentlich Methodus welchen gute Künste leren und vorschreiben/nütze und gut sey/ neben andern vielen nutzen. Nemlich das er weite Augen mache/das man sich weit-leufftig umbsehe/damit man allzeit Materia zu reden oder predigen gnug hab/und deste weniger mühe und arbeit/da sonst ander Leute wenig sehen/oder schier stock blind sein/keiner umbstende war nemen können/aus mangel der Materien/zum offtermal mit schanden zu reden und zu predigen auffhören müssen..."

15. Erasmus Sarcer, *Rhetorica plena ac referta exemplis, quae succinctarum declamationum loco esse possunt* (Leipzig, 1539), pp. 125 ff. For the *logi argumentorum* in Melanchthon's rhetoric, compare Schnell, *Die homiletische Theorie,* p. 38.

16. Sarcer, *Pastorale,* fol. IIII[r]: "... In solcher erkündigung/was eigentlich der Glaube heisse/thut sich zu gleich ein weites felt auff"; "widerfechten" and "widerlegen," "anfechten," "hinzusetzen" and "weiter sehen."

17. Sarcer, *Pastorale,* fol. V[r]: "Nach der beschreibung des dings/was der Glaube sey/hastu als dan weiter umbzusehen/welchs die wircklichen ursachen des Glaubens sein/das ist/woher er seinen ursprung neme/und woher er kome. Als dan wird sich

(All this was expressed much more easily and concisely in Latin within the technical vocabulary of rhetoric; in his *Rhetorica* Sarcer explores the *thema coniunctum* through all his *topoi:* "An fides charitatis fundamentum sit." And under the *topos causae* we find recorded with consummate precision: "Verbum et spiritus sanctus: subjectum mens est." This is followed by the description of the *topos partitio*— "whether faith has many parts or consists of one thing only"— though Sarcer cannot apply this *topos* here, as "faith is in itself indivisible," for as he says in Latin under the *topos partes:* "Fides in partes secari non potest. Est enim unus quidam motus animi, intuens in promissiones dei.")[18]

We can sum this up by saying that Sarcer makes the topics of dialectic and rhetoric available to the German preacher and shows how to use them in preparing sermons. These topics are thus multifunctional for Sarcer: they function both in the form of a hermeneutic principle for an explanation of the term under examination and also as a means of amplifying a subject, a sentence, or a theme. In addition, Sarcer recommends that the preacher make his own collection of *loci,* which will greatly increase his own fund of knowledge; moreover, academic studies, education, and material knowledge must be ordered and classified, and it is certainly not a coincidence that word order becomes a *leitmotif* in Sarcer's concept of education. For the humanists the ordering of material according to *loci* was an integral part of their educational and literary activities, for "the enormous increase in material discovered as a result of a more intensive study of classical antiquity and the Bible urgently needs both classification and organization."[19] The student is expected to make notes while reading and to collect fitting maxims, sentences, appropriate examples, or useful rules of conduct under particular headings, which are called *loci communes;* Rudolf Agricola says that they are called *communes* because "they include everything that can be said about a particular subject as well as all the relevant arguments."[20] The humanist depended on the fruits of his own reading, which he collected in special notebooks of *loci communes,* for he needed the support of authorities on a subject to prove a thesis, to underline a

finden/das der heilige Geist die wirckliche ursache des Glaubens sey. Gottes wort aber ist das eusserliche mittel/dadurch der heilige Geist/den Glauben wircket."

18. Sarcer, *Rhetorica,* p. 130.

19. Edgar Mertner, "Topos und Commonplace," in *Strena Anglica: Festschrift für Otto Ritter,* eds. G. Dietrich and F. W. Schulze (Halle, 1956), p. 194.

20. Mertner, "Topos und Commonplace," p. 195.

statement of opinion, or even to employ as embellishment. And this is exactly what Sarcer recommends:

> There are other ways of learning method [*methodus*], as, for instance, to enter *loci communes* out of the Scripture in a certain book and to classify them according to this method and thus to strengthen argument with quotations from the Scripture, as an example of faith.[21]

But this was not to be all. After the Bible had been classified according to *locis communes,* the same should be done with the writings of the Church Fathers, the reports of the councils and even the writings of contemporary Protestant authors, whose "many edifying sayings will adorn and strengthen" the collection.[22]

Sarcer stresses the genuine rhetorical intention of the *loci,* that is, not to miss any aspect that could be relevant in the search for suitable arguments. Aids for the memory — this is how Cicero too defined the function of the *topoi.*[23] It would be easy to produce further evidence that Erasmus Sarcer produces a pattern for a sermon in the first chapter of his *Pastorale* without explicitly bringing a specific text. This is the illustration of a *locus communis* according to the rules of rhetoric and as part of Protestant teaching. But I will not enlarge on this here: all that needs to be emphasized is that this is the first treatise on homiletics in German, presenting the principles and structure of a rhetoric and hermeneutics derived, in somewhat laborious German, entirely from the principles of classical rhetoric. This, again, is a contribution to the development of a national language, whereby Sarcer, at the beginning of the Renaissance, points to both the "reacquisition" of language and its connection with true doctrine:

> So that we Germans once more acquire and achieve the correct application of all good arts, the right understanding of the pure teaching of the divine word, the true path to righteousness and bliss and the proper use of God's holy sacraments and the liturgy. I will not mention here the wisdom, cleverness, caution, eloquence,

21. Sarcer, *Pastorale,* V II[r]: "Uber das so sein auch weiter andere mittel/dienstlich den Methodum zu lernen/als das jm einer Locos communes in ein gewis Buch versamle/aus der Schrifft/und einen jeden von diesen/nach des Methodi teile abteile/ und diese mit Sprüchen der Schrifft befestige/als Exempels weise vom Glauben."

22. For this method of using rhetorical *topoi,* see Joachim Dyck, *Ticht-Kunst: Deutsche Barockpoetik und rhetorische Tradition* (Bad Homburg, 1969), pp. 59–65.

23. Cicero, *De oratore* II.30.130.

skill, and other great virtues that have to our amazement within so
few years increased so mightily in Germany.[24]

In the *aemulatio* of the nations, the Germans are here characterized
by virtues amongst which eloquence has a recognized place.

VII

But I do not want to create a false impression with this modest
attempt to characterize Sarcer's work: The *Pastorale* is not just a German treatise on homiletics in the technical sense of the term. His
following chapters lay a great deal of stress on questions of church
organization and dogma, and apart from *inventio* and *amplificatio*
other aspects of eloquence such as disposition and style are not elaborated. There is no room here for the characteristic function of rhetoric, namely, adornment and persuasion, as Luther has defined it
(*rhetorica ornat et suadet*).[25] Sarcer merely advises the preacher to resort to the great writers and their Latin works, here mentioning
Agricola, Reuchlin, Melanchthon, Hepinus, and Artopeus, and gives
exact sources. He explains this reference by saying that, because so
much had already been recorded, it was not necessary to give so
many precepts and examples, for otherwise his manual would have
become too voluminous a compendium. He also has enough self-
esteem to refer the reader to his own Latin *Dialectica* and *Rhetorica*.
Sarcer is not purposely avoiding drawing up exactly technical instructions for the writing of a sermon; he simply safely assumes that,
as far as the details are concerned, he can refer his reader to the
Latin tractates that have already appeared. For him, and this is an
important manifestation in Protestant humanism that reappears in
the early years of the Age of Enlightenment, it is not so much a ques-

---

24. Sarcer, *Pastorale*, II[r]: "... also das wir Deutschen nu den rechten gebrauch
aller guten Künste/den rechten verstand der reinen lere göttlichs worts/den waren
weg zur gerechtigkeit/und seligkeit/und den rechtschaffenen gebrauch der hoch-
würdigen sacramente/und den wahrhafftigen Gottesdienst/wider erlanget/und zu
wegen gebracht haben. Ich wil hier nicht sagen von Weisheit/Klugheit/Vorsich-
tigkeit/wolberedenheit/Geschicklichkeit/und andern tewern und hohen Gaben/
hieran Deutschland/in kurtzen jaren/nur uber alle mass/auch mit verwunderung
zugenommen hat."
25. Cf. Stolt, *Wortkampf*, p. 53.

tion of the importance of the *praecepta* as of the *exercitium*. He is more concerned with the practice than the theory:

> In the arts that teach the method [*methodus*] it is more a question of practice than of precepts, just as method [*methodus*] itself is learnt more from practice than from rules.[26]

Classical rhetoric involved three possibilities of realization in practice: *scribendo, legendo, dicendo.*[27] Sarcer has read his Quintilian and therefore advises his readers:

> I think it advisable that every preacher write out in full [*scribendo*] the sermon that he intends to preach and that he arrange it in orderly manner according to the method [*methodus*] and according to the precepts of the rhetoricians.[28]

The *lectio* is the reception of the written work of art in the mind of the reader. It can be repeated again and again. The repeated reading is recorded in the memory and in the end leads to imitation.[29] Sarcer recommends moderation in reading:

> One should read little and only what is good and should diligently apply oneself to this, for whoever is to be found everywhere is at home nowhere and much reading will distract hearts and minds so that when required they will not know which of the many things before them they must seize and will therefore out of this multiplicity now seize upon the worst thing as the best.[30]

This is good advice indeed in times of upheaval: strength is to be derived from the great masters. One should rely only on what is absolutely certain; in this sea of opinions, "multum est legendum, verum non multa."

26. Sarcer, *Pastorale,* fol. VII^r: "Denn es ist umb die Künste/so den Methodum lernen/also gelegen/das Sie mehr durch ubunge/als durch Precepta wollen gefasset sein/wie dan auch der Methodus an sich selbst/mehr aus ubung/als aus Regeln wil gelernet sein."

27. Quintilian, *Institutio oratoria* X.1.1.

28. Sarcer, *Pastorale,* fol. VII^v: "So düncket mich auch gut sein/das ein jeder Prediger/seine Predigten/die er zu thun gedencket/vollig schreibe/und dieselbige nach dem Methodo/und wie sonst die Precepta der Rhetoren mit sich bringen/disponire ordentlich und anstelle."

29. Quintilian, *Institutio oratoria* X.1.19.

30. Sarcer, *Pastorale,* fol. VII^v: "Denn er allerwegen ist/der ist nirgend daheim/ und werden durch viel lesen/die Hertzen und Gemüther distrahiret und verrucket/ das sie zur zeit der not nicht wissen/welchs sie fur vielen dingen ergreiffen sollen/ und ergreiffen mannichmals in solcher vielheit/als balde das ergste als das beste."

VIII

Up to this point I have emphasized only that the German homiletics of the Protestant ministers is based upon rhetoric and that the propagation of the word must conform to the principles of persuasion, for the sermon has two functions: to preach penitence and the forgiveness of sins.

> But to preach penitence means nothing else than to proclaim by the preaching of the law, to Christ's flock their sin and evil-doings, which they have committed against God's will and command. To preach forgiveness of sin, on the other hand, means to comfort and to strengthen the frightened and the meek by preaching the Gospel. The congregation must become aware of God's wrath and punishment of their sins, but not lose heart though they continue to sin.[31]

The congregation must be convinced that "God will pardon and forgive their sins and that He will withdraw his anger and punishment."[32] But how can they be convinced of faith? This opens up an extremely important field of rhetoric, namely, the emotive field, which has not been mentioned so far. For classical rhetoric and especially Quintilian, who was one of Luther's and Melanchthon's favorite authors, rhetoric was clearly the art of persuasion, and the secret of its capacity to produce an emotional response lay in an ability to be moved by emotion oneself (*ut moveamur ipsi*).[33] Sarcer accepts this too. For him it is clear that "he who moves others with his teaching and persuades them to accept and believe what he teaches must have been moved in his heart likewise."[34] The reference to this central thesis in Quintilian's definition of the emotions is obvious, and Sarcer

31. Sarcer, *Pastorale,* fol. XXXIIII^v: "Busse aber Predigen heisset nichts anders/ dan das Christi Scheflein/durch die Predigte des Gesetzes jre Sünde und Missethat verkündigen/wider Gottes willen und befelch begangen. Vergebung der Sünden aber predigen/heisset das eigentlich/widerumb durch die Predigte des Evangely/ die erschreckten und beengstigten Gewissen/aus der Predigte des Gesetzes/und von wegen der erkenntnis jrer sünden/Göttlichs zorns und straffe hierüber/trösten und auffrichten/damit sie in jren Sünden nicht verzagen und unter dem zorn und straffen Gottes verzweiffeln."

32. Sarcer, *Pastorale,* fol. XXXIIII^v.

33. Quintilian, *Institutio oratoria* VI.2.26.

34. Sarcer, *Pastorale,* fol. XLV^r: "Und wil nu hier heissen/wer ander Leute durch leren und Predigen bewegen/und sie der Lere und Predigte bereden/das sie diese ding annemen und gleuben/zum nutze und besserung/der muz zuvorn in seinem hertzen beweget sein."

emphasizes it once more with the Latin commonplace: "Oportet docentem prium affectum esse & prius persuasum, qui vult alios adficere, & aliis de re aliqua persuadere."[35] He who is not moved by the word will not be able to move others. He will remain cold, *frigidus.* The orator must believe wholeheartedly in what he teaches and must establish an emotional rapport with his listeners.

But we can go one step further and incorporate the concept of faith, as formulated by Sarcer, in the rhetorical theory of the emotions. In the first edition of the *Loci communes,* Melanchthon launched a sharp attack on the scholastic concept of faith and had supplemented the intellectual with the emotional understanding. Klaus Dockhorn has documented that both Melanchthon and Luther derived their concept of faith from Quintilian's rhetorical theory of emotions, insofar as faith for them means the capacity to visualize that which is absent and to conjure it up emotionally, that is, the capacity of the orator to actualize and make present by means of persuasive speech, his capacity to produce the impression of direct participation and immediate involvement.[36] This is, after all, to Sarcer the function of the Holy Ghost: "Rhetoricatur Spiritus sanctus iam ut exhortatio fiat illustrior."[37] With this he takes up the thought with which Quintilian concludes his deliberations on "visualizing and making present." Thus *illustrior* is the adjective that expresses that gift of participation which is a function of the eye but which the eloquent orator can impart to his listeners.[38]

Sarcer defines faith exactly in this context, for "the place of faith is in the heart or the soul," and faith is indivisible because, as Sarcer says in his *Rhetorica:* "Fides in partes secari non potest. Est enim unum quidam motus animi"[39]; or in the German version from his *Pastorale:* "Faith means a simple and unsophisticated state of emotion, by means of which one believes in and accepts God's word."[40]

Against this background of the fundamental rhetorical origin of the Protestant concept of faith, it is only of peripheral importance

35. Sarcer, *Pastorale,* fol. XLV[r].

36. Cf. Dockhorn, *"Rhetorica movet,"* pp. 26 ff. Dockhorn, "Luthers Glaubensbegriff und die Rhetorik. Zu Gerhard Ebelings Buch Einführung in die theologische Sprachlehre," *Linguistica Biblica* 21/22 (February, 1973).

37. Luther, WA XL/3, 59 f. and cf. Dockhorn, "Luthers Glaubensbegriff," p. 30.

38. Quintilian, *Institutio oratoria* VI.2.32 – 36.

39. Sarcer, *Rhetorica,* p. 130.

40. Sarcer, *Pastorale,* fol. V[v]: "Denn [der Glaube] allein einen schlechten und einfeltigen Affect der bewegnis bedeutet/dadurch man Gottes verheissung gewis gleubet und vertrawet."

that Sarcer attributes the role of systematic structuring of the sermon to dialectic, and that he sees rhetoric as having the function of embellishing or polishing. It is the traditional belief that the function of rhetoric is to adorn. But the *ornatus*, the body of rules covering the use of tropes and figures of speech, is also part of the emotional effect to be achieved by words; it is not an adornment to delight the intellect but a means of producing and reducing emotion. How could one otherwise explain such figures of speech as *motus* in classical antiquity, as mentioned by Quintilian?[41] Sarcer, in his description of the task at hand, continues by conjuring up the emotional effect of style while he says:

> Part of this function of extending and polishing is borne by a simple, ornamental, and eloquent form of speech that helps elaborate the theme and bring it to the attention of the hearts and souls of those listening.[42]

The concept behind the German terms is not clear in Sarcer's references to the generally ornamental and eloquent form of speech. Cicero allowed the orator three modes of persuasion: he should either convince with proofs *(probare, docere)*, or awaken a feeling of goodwill and favorable predisposition in the listener *(delectare, ethos)*, or move him to enthusiastic and passionate approval *(movere, pathos)*. If the orator wants to convince his listeners with the help of clear facts, he does so with the *genus humile*, which imitates the vernacular *(consuetudo)*, or as Sarcer puts it, "the ordinary way of speech." If he is aiming at powerful and passionate emotion, that is, *pathos*, then he will use an elevated style *(genus grande)*, which is then given every conceivable form of adornment.[43] Quintilian invokes Cicero when he defines figures of speech as such expressions: "quae essent clarissima et ad movendum auditorem valerent plurimum."[44] *Ornamental* is the word Sarcer applies to the style of *pathos* as opposed to the simple style. But if the speaker intends to win the goodwill of his listener, then he must choose the style that lies between these two extremes: he must speak "eloquently," as Sarcer puts it.

Sarcer was thus the first to invoke in German Cicero's demand

41. Quintilian, *Institutio oratoria* VIII.5.35.
42. Sarcer, *Pastorale*, fol. VIᵣ: "Und gehöret zu diesem ausbawen und polieren fur das erste/eine gemeine/zierliche/und flüssige art zu reden/die den gantzen handel hilfft fortsetzen/und in der Zuhörer hertzen und gemüter bringen."
43. Cicero, *Orator* LXIX; *De oratore* II.53.212.
44. Quintilian, *Institutio oratoria* IX.1.25.

for the adaptation of style to the effect intended, which practice has become so significant in the European esthetic movement, and he did so long before the poetics of the seventeenth century. His "comprehensive manual of practical and pastoral theology" not only provides detailed information about the vocation of a Protestant minister in the second generation of the Reformation from a minister's point of view, but also gives much useful information about the social standing and training of those who had taken up this vocation.[45] As a humanist and therefore a rhetorician too, he postulates qualifications for the Protestant preacher that are identical with those postulated by Cicero and Quintilian for the orator. "For the Renaissance, oratory became a pedagogical ideal, in fact, one of the objectives of any form of higher education."[46] Rhetoric, whose province is the emotional communication of content, thus becomes the vehicle to express the new values of Protestant thought.

45. Catalogue Antiquariat M. Edelmann Reformationsdrucke, bearbeitet von Walther Gose (Nürnberg, 1972), p. 179.

46. K. Hartfelder, *Philipp Melanchthon als Praeceptor Germaniae* (Berlin, 1889), p. 328; cf. Schnell, *Die homiletische Theorie,* p. 16.

Content and Rhetorical
Forms in Sixteenth-Century
Treatises on Preaching

JOHN W. O'MALLEY

I recently published a book on the sacred oratory of the papal court from about 1450 until the death of Pope Leo X in 1521.[1] The book shows, I believe, that the revival of the *genus demonstrativum* of classical oratory explains the transformation in structure, purpose, and content in the sermons at the court during this period. Besides indicating that the negative judgments historians have commonly made about "Renaissance preaching" need revision,[2] the book provides grounds for suspecting that an examination of how authors of works on preaching deal with the three classical *genera* — judicial, deliberative, demonstrative — is a good entrance into the total network of assumptions that govern their understanding of preaching and its relationship to rhetoric, as well as its relationship to general culture. That is the approach I should presently like to follow for a highly

1. *Praise and Blame in Renaissance Rome: Rhetoric, Doctrine, and Reform in the Sacred Orators of the Papal Court, c. 1450 – 1521,* Duke Monographs in Medieval and Renaissance Studies, no. 3 (Durham, N.C., 1979).

2. With ill-concealed disdain, for instance, Johann Baptist Schneyer dismisses the whole phenomenon of Renaissance preaching in Italy and Spain with four pages in his *Geschichte der katholischen Predigt* (Freiburg, 1969). This tradition, related though it is to Luther's antipathy for things Italian, derives more directly from Erasmus's caricature of a sermon at the papal court that he describes in his *Ciceronianus.* See my *Praise and Blame,* pp. 29 – 31. Though it must be used with caution, there is still some useful discussion of the relationship between form and content in P. W. von Keppler, "Beiträge zur Entwicklungsgeschichte der Predigtanlage," *Theologische Quartalschrift* 74 (1892), 52 – 120, 179 – 212, esp. 82 – 103. See also Joseph M. Connors, "Homiletic Theory in the Late Sixteenth Century," *The American Ecclesiastical Review* 138 (1958), 316 – 32, esp. for a study of rhetorical form in Agostino Valerio and Luis de Granada.

selective sampling of sixteenth-century treatises on preaching. First, however, some background will be helpful.

In Italy by the late fourteenth century, there were sacred orations that broke with medieval traditions of preaching and that show the unmistakable impact of the Renaissance revival of classical rhetoric. The first fully classicizing orations of which I am aware are the panegyrics honoring Saint Jerome composed by Pier Paolo Vergerio in Padua and elsewhere between about 1392 and 1408. Vergerio was a member of the circle led by Giovanni di Conversino da Ravenna that included other notable humanists like Guarino da Verona and Vittorino da Feltre. Vergerio's orations abandon all the features of the medieval *laudes sanctorum*—theme, division, authorities, structure, dialectical style of argumentation—and adopt the principles and *topoi* of the classical *genus demonstrativum*.[3]

By 1410 there is evidence that the adaptation of that *genus* to Christian saints was a standard exercise at Padua, and there is also evidence that at about the same time the *genus* was put to the same use elsewhere in Italy, especially wherever the orations were delivered in Latin.[4] Simultaneously, there was an adaptation of the *genus* to Christian funeral oratory. Poggio Bracciolini's eulogy of Cardinal Zabarella at the Council of Constance, September 27, 1417, is an early and important example of the new approach, which would be widely imitated in the major cities of Italy during the course of the century.[5]

An even more interesting, slightly later, development was the adaptation of this *genus*, of this "art of praise and blame," to doctrinal sermons or sermons dealing with events from the life of Christ. Gasperino Barzizza was among the first to inaugurate this change, which was known in a mature form at the papal court by the middle of the century in several sermons there by Pietro del Monte, the noted canonist and humanist, disciple of Guarino. During the rest of the century, this new form contended at the court with its medieval, thematic rival, and by the death of Leo X it had won a considerable, though by no means total, victory over it.[6] The new form was em-

3. See my *Praise and Blame*, pp. 85 – 86. See also David Robey, "P. P. Vergerio the Elder: Republican and Civic Values in the Work of an Early Humanist," *Past and Present* no. 58 (February, 1973), pp. 3 – 37, esp. 27 – 31.

4. See *Praise and Blame*, pp. 86 – 87.

5. See ibid., pp. 80n, 89 – 90, as well as John M. McManamon, "The Ideal Renaissance Pope: Funeral Oratory from the Papal Court," *Archivum Historiae Pontificiae* 14 (1976), 9 – 70.

6. See *Praise and Blame*, pp. 81 – 119.

ployed outside the court and outside Italy, as Rudolf Agricola's sacred oration at Heidelberg on Christmas Day 1485 clearly proves, but its use seems generally to have been restricted to refined audiences and formal settings.[7]

Though limited in the audiences it reached, this adaptation of classical rhetorical form wrought a change in preaching that was striking. The least important feature of the change was the substitution of classical vocabulary, syntax, and figures of thought and diction for their medieval equivalents. Much more important was the change in the materials with which the sermons dealt — the *res*. These became focused more clearly on God's deeds and actions — his *beneficia* — and less on the abstract doctrines that were the standard materials for the thematic, that is, the scholastic, sermon of the Middle Ages. "History," if you will, replaced "philosophy." Moreover, the very purpose of the sermon was transformed from an exercise in proof and dialectical argumentation to an exercise in praise. Admiration, gratitude, and desire for imitation were the sentiments the sermons were now meant to inspire and for which they now had the appropriate rhetorical techniques. Whereas the thematic sermon emphasized *docere* at the expense of *movere* and *delectare,* the demonstrative oration more effectively coordinated teaching with persuasional aims. Perhaps most important of all, the new style of sermon, through its employment of praise, conveyed a religious vision that was uncommonly positive in its appreciation of God, man, and the world. It was a "rhetoric of congratulation" applied to God and his works, especially man. The emergence of the peculiarly Renaissance theme of the "dignity of man" is due in considerable measure to the employment of the principles of the *genus demonstrativum.*

As far as I have been able to ascertain, this extraordinary development was not heralded by any treatises advocating it or describing how to accomplish it. In 1478, however, Lorenzo Guglielmo Traversagni wrote his *Margarita eloquentiae* in Cambridge. Traversagni's book securely locates all sacred oratory, including even thematic and popular sermons, in the *genus demonstrativum.* This long and still inadequately studied work betrays an awareness of the new type of oratory I described, but the book's influence has yet to be determined and its "modernity" must not be exaggerated.[8]

7. See ibid., pp. 120–22.
8. See ibid., pp. 43n, 46–47, 49n. Traversagni's *Epitome* of his longer work also locates sermons in the *genus demonstrativum;* see Ronald H. Martin, "The 'Epitome Margaritae Eloquentiae' of Laurentius Gulielmus de Soana," *Proceedings of the Leeds*

Aurelio "Lippo" Brandolini's treatise on letter-writing, completed at the papal court sometime before 1485, is an important and neglected work. Generally speaking, it was the most elaborate of its kind in the Quattrocento, anticipating by several decades Erasmus's similar treatise. Its significance for sacred oratory lies in a few digressions that indicate that sacred oratory pertains to the *genus* of ceremonial oratory, to the oratory of praise and blame. Brandolini criticizes preachers at the court who do not know the difference between a lecture, suitable for the classroom, and an oration, proper to a church. He thus rejects the thematic sermon.[9] Brandolini's few pages document a revolution taking place in certain circles in the Quattrocento due to the revival of classical rhetoric. Nonetheless, during that century it was the medieval *artes praedicandi* that continued to be written and published in Italy and elsewhere.

North of the Alps a modest break comes with Reuchlin's *Liber congestorum de arte praedicandi* of 1504.[10] The *Liber* is brief, sketchy, and noteworthy more for indicating a transition from the medieval tradition than for providing anything coherent to replace it. Without developing the idea, the *Liber* allows the preacher use of all three of the classical *genera*.

Reuchlin pales in importance alongside Melanchthon, his grandnephew, who from his first book on rhetoric in 1519 all through his subsequent career repeatedly addressed the problem of preaching.[11] He had almost immediate impact on other Lutheran theorists like Veit Dietrich and Johannes Äpinus (Hoeck), with whose works on preaching two short treatises of his own were published in Basel in 1540.[12]

Philosophical and Literary Society (Literary and Historical Section) vol. 14, pt. 4 (1971), 99–187, esp. 177–78. See also James J. Murphy, "Caxton's Two Choices: 'Modern' and 'Medieval' Rhetoric in Traversagni's *Nova Rhetorica* and the Anonymous *Court of Sapience*," *Medievalia et Humanistica* n.s. 3 (1972), 241–55.

9. *De ratione scribendi libri tres* (Cologne, 1573), first published in Basel in 1549. See esp. pp. 94–101.

10. (Pforzheim, 1504), esp. fol. [5v] on the *genera*.

11. The most complete study of Melanchthon's theory on preaching is Uwe Schnell's *Die homiletische Theorie Philipp Melanchthons*, Arbeiten zur Geschichte und Theologie des Luthertums, no. 20 (Berlin, 1968). Also useful is Wilhelm Maurer's *Der junge Melanchthon zwischen Humanismus und Reformation*, 2 vols. (Göttingen, 1967–1969), esp. 1.171–214.

12. *De arte concionandi formulae ut breves, ita doctae et piae, Ioanne Reuchlino Phorcensi, anonymo quodam Rhapsodo [Dietrich], Philippo Melanchthone, D. Ioanne Hepino autoribus. Eiusdem Melanchthonis discendae theologiae rationem ad calcem adiecimus* (Basel, 1540).

Melanchthon at one point was so apprehensive about the *genus demonstrativum* for sacred oratory that he rejected it. Like most sixteenth-century theorists, he also minimized or eliminated the use of the *genus iudiciale* in the pulpit.[13] His most distinctive achievement was the introduction of a new, fourth *genus,* the so-called *genus didascalicum.*[14] This new *genus* had teaching as its purpose. Melanchthon asserted that he in fact transferred the *genus* to sacred rhetoric from dialectics, which he described as the *ars recte docendi.*[15]

Melanchthon wrote his *De officiis concionatoris* in 1529. Though not altogether expressive of his mature thought on preaching, it was, after the revised treatise on rhetoric, his most influential statement on it. In the *De officiis* Melanchthon defines his theory of preaching by employing three *genera:* the *didascalicum,* which teaches true doctrine; the *epitrepticum,* which exhorts to faith; the *paraeneticum,* which exhorts to good morals.[16] The *epitrepticum* and *paraeneticum* are considered exhortations, adaptations of the classical *genus deliberativum.* For such an understanding of the *genus deliberativum,* Melanchthon was influenced by the authority of Erasmus's *Opus de conscribendis epistolis.*[17] In Melanchthon's view, the *didascalicum* and *epitrepticum* are far more important than the *paraeneticum* because they deal with faith, while the *paraeneticum* deals with action.

There are several aspects of Melanchthon's achievement that deserve mention. First, his treatises are more directly and obviously influenced by classical rhetoric than were the medieval *artes.* Second, he nonetheless finds it necessary to add the *genus didascalicum* to the traditional three, to redistribute the *genus deliberativum* into two species of *epitrepticum* and *paraeneticum,* and practically to reject both the judicial and demonstrative except insofar as the latter was an "ornamented" version of the *didascalicum.* Third, Melanchthon specifies the *res* that the sacred orator teaches as the Lutheran doctrines of law, sin, and grace; Scripture is characteristically understood as a

---

Besides Melanchthon's "Ratio" on how to learn theology, his other work published in this volume was the *De officiis concionatoris.*

13. See his *De officiis concionatoris* in *Supplementa Melanchthoniana,* eds. Paul Drews and Ferdinand Cohrs, vol. 5, pt. 2 (Leipzig, 1929), pp. 5 – 7. See also, however, his *Elementa rhetorices,* in *Corpus Reformatorum,* ed. Carolus Gottlieb Bretschneider (1846, rpt. New York, 1963), 13.421 – 23, 429, 448 – 49.

14. See *Elementa rhetorices,* cols. 421 – 28; *De officiis concionatoris,* pp. 5 – 10.

15. See *Elementa rhetorices,* col. 424.

16. *De officiis concionatoris,* pp. 5 – 7.

17. See *Elementa rhetorices,* col. 422.

book of threats and promises; thus Melanchthon's treatises and those of his followers are never doctrinally neutral — res and verba are inextricably intertwined. Finally, his theory of sacred oratory is considerably more complex than I have here suggested and is intimately related to his teaching on the use of "commonplaces" or topoi in theology, on the relationship he postulates between rhetoric and dialectics, and on other major issues like biblical hermeneutics.[18]

It was the genus didascalicum that caught the attention of Melanchthon's contemporaries and of succeeding generations. In that genus he continues an attention to doctrine propositionally and dialectically articulated that was, surely unintentionally, reminiscent of the thematic sermons of the scholastics. At the same time, he explicitly rejected the emphasis on the deeds of Christ and on the praise of Christ that he quite correctly says characterized Italian "declamations."[19]

Along with Melanchthon, Erasmus is the second figure of towering significance for the theory of sacred oratory in the first half of the sixteenth century. The Ecclesiastes of 1535, his last major work, was eagerly awaited for years before it was finished.[20] Though it failed to satisfy Erasmus's contemporaries and his critics through the ages, it was the single most important treatise on the theory of sacred oratory since Augustine's De Doctrina Christiana, a work by which the Ecclesiastes was profoundly influenced.[21]

In all his writings Erasmus saw Christ as, essentially, a great teacher, and he viewed Scripture as the book containing the "philosophy" that Christ taught. Erasmus thus tends to transform all the books of the Bible into a species of "wisdom literature." We should

18. See, e.g., his Quomodo concionator novitius concionem suam informare debeat, De modo et arte concionandi, and De ratione concionandi, in the Supplementa, pp. 17 – 79. See also Schnell, Homiletische Theorie, pp. 46 – 53, 115 – 21; Maurer, Der junge Melanchthon, 1.171 – 214; 2.139 – 51, 230 – 63; and Quirinus Breen, "The terms 'Loci Communes' and 'Loci' in Melanchthon," in his Christianity and Humanism: Studies in the History of Ideas, ed. Nelson Peter Ross (Grand Rapids, Mich., 1968), pp. 93 – 105.

19. See De officiis concionatoris, p. 6.

20. Ecclesiastes, sive Concionator evangelicus, in Opera omnia, ed. J. Clericus, 10 vols. (Leiden, 1703 – 1706), 5.769 – 1100.

21. See James Michael Weiss, "Ecclesiastes and Erasmus: The Mirror and the Image," Archive for Reformation History 65 (1974), 83 – 108; Charles Béné, Érasme et saint Augustin, ou Influence de Saint Augustin sur l'Humanisme d'Érasme, Travaux d'Humanisme et Renaissance, no. 103 (Geneva, 1969), esp. pp. 372 –425; André Godin, "Érasme et le modèle origénien de la prédication," in Colloquia Erasmiana Turonensia, ed. Jean-Claude Margolin, 2 vols. (Toronto, 1972), 2.807 – 20.

not be surprised, then, that preaching is defined in the *Ecclesiastes* principally as an act of teaching. Though Erasmus located preaching in the charism of "prophecy," he defines the prophet's task not as predicting the future or thundering against sin and misbelief, but as explaining and teaching the mysteries of Scripture, "the philosophy of Christ."[22]

For Erasmus, truly Christian teaching is never dialectical or argumentative, never frigidly abstract, for it must always be persuasive of a godly life. Erasmus constructs five *genera* appropriate to the sacred orator, but at least four of them can be reduced to the *genus suasorium,* that is, an equivalent of the *genus deliberativum* of classical oratory. The fifth, the *genus laudatorium,* represents the demonstrative; Erasmus practically restricts it to panegyrics of the saints and heavily imbues it with elements from the *genus suasorium.*[23]

Erasmus's treatise seems to have been responsible for a widespread tendency among Catholics in the sixteenth century to establish the *genus deliberativum* as the *genus* most appropriate for the pulpit. In 1595 Ludovico Carbone, for instance, stated in his *Divinus orator* that the deliberative was the *genus* proper to the preacher, for the preacher always has some persuasion in mind.[24] Even for Lutherans, under the influence of Melanchthon, the *genus deliberativum* ranked a close second behind the *genus didascalicum* as the *genus* proper to the pulpit.[25]

Erasmus does not explain why he lifts a literary form intended for a deliberative assembly and transfers it to a church setting. His location of preaching in the deliberative genre, as well as his definition of it as teaching, tended to give preaching a more moralistic and professedly didactic quality than was evidenced in the demonstrative sermons at the papal court. Due partly to Erasmus's influence, demonstrative oratory in the sixteenth century becomes, at least in many important treatises, ever more restricted to panegyrics of the saints and to funeral eulogies; it loses its earlier prerogative, apparently taken for granted in Italy in the Quattrocento, as the *locus* for all sacred oratory.

22. See *Ecclesiastes,* cols. 798, 824–26.   23. See ibid., cols. 877–92.

24. *Divinus orator, vel De rhetorica divina libri septem* (Venice, 1595), esp. p. 125. This Ludovico Carbone (d. 1597) is not to be confused with the fifteenth-century humanist of the same name.

25. See Schnell, *Homiletische Theorie,* pp. 172–76; and John S. Chamberlin, *Increase and Multiply: Arts-of-Discourse Procedure in the Preaching of Donne* (Chapel Hill, N.C., 1976), pp. 67–91.

The paths through which the influence of Melanchthon and Erasmus was diffused have yet to be explored by modern scholars. At present I will offer a single example of that diffusion, the *De sacris concionibus recte formandis* published in Rome in early 1543 by the Spanish cleric Alfonso Zorrilla.[26] In Zorrilla's dedicatory letter to Juan Alvárez de Toledo, one of the Roman Inquisitors appointed by Pope Paul III in the previous year, he rejects Erasmus's *Ecclesiastes* as too "diffuse, prolix, and confused" to be practical. Somewhat in desperation, then, Zorrilla tells the Inquisitor, he composed the present work "almost as a compendium" of what some others had written on the subject.

Zorrilla's book was influential in Catholic circles. We should not be surprised at this. It seems to have been the first treatise on preaching printed in Italy that broke with the medieval *artes*. It was published, moreover, almost under the auspices of the Inquisition and was singled out for special commendation by Saint Robert Bellarmine about fifty years later. What neither the Inquisitor nor Bellarmine nor anybody else suspected until I recently established it is that Zorrilla's book is constructed out of wholesale borrowings from Lutheran sources — Melanchthon, Dietrich, and Äpinus. Zorrilla made extensive use of the Basel volume of 1540 as well as of Melanchthon's *Elementa rhetorices*. The Lutheran origins of the substance of the book stand as dramatic testimony to the fervid search in the first half of the century for substitutes for the medieval styles of preaching.

Important public documents in the century tend to ignore questions of structure, genre, and rhetoric, and deal largely with content; considerable attention is also given to issues like jurisdiction and the prerequisites of knowledge and virtue in the preacher. Among such documents are the decrees of the Fifth Lateran Council, 1516,[27] of the First Council of Cologne, 1536,[28] of the Second Council of Trier, 1549,[29] of the Council of Trent, 1546 and 1563,[30] of the First Provincial Synod of Milan, under Saint Charles Borromeo, 1563, and the

26. See my "Lutheranism in Rome, 1542 – 43: The Treatise by Alfonso Zorrilla," *Thought* 54 (1979), 262 – 73.

27. See *Conciliorum Oecumenicorum Decreta*, ed. Giuseppe Alberigo et al., 2nd ed. (Basel, 1962), pp. 610 – 14.

28. See *Sacrorum conciliorum nova et amplissima collectio*, ed. Giovanni Domenico Mansi (Paris, 1901), 32.1248 – 55.

29. See ibid., cols. 1441 – 43.

30. See *Conciliorum Oecumenicorum Decreta*, pp. 645 – 46, 739. See also Johann Ev.

saint's influential *Instructiones praedicationis verbi Dei* issued some years later.[31]

Cardinal Gasparo Contarini, the most exciting figure associated with the Roman Curia from about 1536 until his death in 1542, also ignores form in favor of content in his brief "Modus concionandi" of 1540.[32] Like some other theorists in the long history of Christian preaching, Contarini seems to suggest that the study of rhetoric is unnecessary, even dangerous, for the preacher; he requires in him only humility, charity, and a right understanding of the law, sin, faith, and forgiveness. Although Contarini explicitly rejects the "Lutheran pestilence," his teaching on the key doctrines in the "modus concionandi" is only subtly different from Lutheran teaching.

By the time Zorrilla compiled his book in 1542, however, questions of form *(verba)* had become as crucial as questions of content *(res)*. Zorrilla follows Melanchthon (by way of Äpinus) and lists three *genera* for the preacher: *didacticum, demonstrativum,* and *deliberativum.*[33] He accordingly gives special attention to the *genus didacticum* or *didascalicum* and seems to be the first to introduce it, under the unwitting but magnificently orthodox sponsorship of Alvárez de Toledo and Bellarmine, into the Catholic tradition.

Zorrilla makes allowance almost as an afterthought for a fourth *genus,* which he does not name but which is the equivalent of the homily, in the sense of an informal and familiar discourse that follows the text of a biblical pericope — verse-by-verse sometimes, or even phrase-by-phrase.[34] By virtue of this structure (i.e., nonstructure) and by virtue of the patristic models available for imitation, the homily favored allegorical senses of Scripture. There is no doubt that the patristic revival in the Renaissance contributed to renewed interest in this "ancient form."

The homily, known and practiced in the Middle Ages, enjoyed,

Reiner, "Entstehungsgeschichte des Trienter Predigtreformdekrets," *Zeitschrift für katholische Theologie* 39 (1915), 256–317, 465–523; and A. Larios, "La reforma de la predicación en Trento (Historia y contenido de un decreto)," *Communio* 6 (1973), 223–83, which also contains a brief review of preaching theory and practice before and after Trent.

31. See *Constitutiones et decreta condita in provinciali synodo Mediolanensi* (Venice, 1566), pp. 7–14; and the *Instructiones* in *Acta Ecclesiae Mediolanensis,* ed. Achille Ratti (Milan, 1890), 2.1205–48. See also Joseph M. Connors, "Saint Charles Borromeo in Homiletic Tradition," *The American Ecclesiastical Review* 138 (1958), 9–23.

32. Printed in *Regesten und Briefe des Kardinals Gasparo Contarini,* ed. Franz Dittrich (Braunsberg, 1881), pp. 305–9.

33. Zorrilla, *De sacris concionibus,* fols. 25r–26v, 59v–76r. 34. Ibid., fol. 74.

therefore, new attention in the sixteenth century. Erasmus, for instance, admired its use by his friend, Jacques Vitrier.[35] Despite Erasmus's advocacy of the classical *genera* in the *Ecclesiastes,* he elsewhere seems to favor the homily over them. This great classicist seemed uncertain about just how appropriate for the pulpit were the classical forms of oratory.

The homily, often commended as a "Christian" form in contrast with the "pagan" forms of classical rhetoric, was to a large extent adopted by the Fathers from the classroom style of the "grammarians," the teachers of the pagan classics. Its origins therefore are hardly more Christian than those of its oratorical counterparts. However, once the Bible is perceived as a "wisdom" or a "philosophy" of Christ, the loose and lecture-like structure of the homily is a suitable way to expound it.[36]

Many years after Erasmus, Robert Bellarmine, overtly hostile towards sermons constructed according to principles of classical oratory, particularly commended the homily, as well as sermons from theological *topoi.* According to Bellarmine, use of these forms by the Fathers established their authority. As Bellarmine's preacher expounded Scripture, he would interpret it in the light of the patristic commentaries. But, in the spirit of the Counter Reformation, he would use Saint Thomas and the *Catechism of the Council of Trent* for his exposition of doctrine. Interestingly enough, though Bellarmine approved of Aquinas's doctrine, he was cool towards the thematic (scholastic) sermon.[37]

35. See André Godin, *L'homélaire de Jean Vitrier: Texte, étude thématique et sémantique,* Travaux d'Humanisme et Renaissance, no. 116 (Geneva, 1971), esp. pp. 14 – 18; *Opus Epistolarum Des. Erasmi Roterodami,* 11 vols. (Oxford, 1906 – 1947), 4.509. See also Godin, "De Vitrier à Origène: Recherches sur la patristique érasmienne," in *Colloquium Erasmianum* (Mons, 1968), 47 – 57.

36. See the introduction by Pierre Nautin to Origen's *Homélies sur Jérémie,* eds. Pierre Husson and Pierre Nautin, Sources chrétiennes, no. 232 (Paris, 1976), esp. pp. 112 – 57; and see also my "Grammar and Rhetoric in the Theology of Erasmus," to appear in *Paideia,* Special Renaissance Issue (forthcoming). For the development of the homily as part of an informal worship service, see James J. Murphy, *Rhetoric in the Middle Ages: A History of Rhetorical Theory from Saint Augustine to the Renaissance* (Berkeley and Los Angeles, 1974), pp. 55 – 56; 298 – 300; for the traditional opinion that the homily was a direct outgrowth of the synagogue service and apostolic preaching, see August Brandt, "Abriss der Geschichte und Theorie der Homilie," in Fritz Tillmann's *Die sonntäglichen Evangelien im Dienste der Predigt* (1917; rev. ed. by Paul Goedeke, Düsseldorf, 1965), 19 – 58.

37. "De ratione formandae concionis," in *Auctarium Bellarminianum: Supplément aux oeuvres du cardinal Bellarmin,* ed. Xavier-Marie le Bachelet (Paris, 1913), pp. 655 – 57.

One of the most insistent advocates in the second half of the century for a return to patristic forms, homiletic and topical, was Diego de Estella, the renowned Franciscan mystic and stylist. His *Modus concionandi,* first published at Salamanca in 1576 and many times reprinted, urges his "sermo evangelicus," a kind of homily, almost to the exclusion of all other forms. Estella is familiar, however, with the thematic sermon and with the principles of classical rhetoric.[38] Even so, he is reluctant to allow panegyrics even of the saints.[39] Sacred oratory should be based on the text of Scripture, not on the lives of men.

Consonant with the Franciscan tradition and characteristic of Estella is his turning the "teaching" of the sermon to a moral purpose.[40] His preacher will draw copiously on the "moral sense" of Scripture that underlies the literal sense.[41] Estella seems to assume that the audience facing the preacher is invariably living in sin and

---

For a description of the scholastic and nonhumanistic style of Bellarmine's theology, see Robert W. Richgels, "Scholasticism Meets Humanism in the Counter Reformation, The Clash of Cultures in Robert Bellarmine's Use of Calvin in *Controversies," The Sixteenth Century Journal* vol. 6, no. 1 (1975), 53 – 66.

38. *Modo de predicar y Modus concionandi: Estudio doctrinal y edición crítica,* ed. Pio Sagüés Azcona, 2 vols. (Madrid, 1951). On Estella, see E. Allison Peers, *Studies of the Spanish Mystics,* 3 vols. (London, 1951 – 1960), 2.171 – 94; and Donat de Monleras, "Estella (Diego de San Cristóbal)," in *Dictionnaire de spiritualité,* 4.1366 – 70. Besides the account by Pio Sagüés Azcona in his edition of the *Modo de predicar* (1.226 – 73), the history of treatises on preaching in Spain in the sixteenth century is reviewed by Félix G. Olmedo in the "prólogo" of his edition of *Don Francisco Terrones del Caño: Instrucción de predicadores,* Clásicos castellanos, no. 126 (Madrid, 1946), pp. lii – clvi; and by Antonio M. Martí, "La Retórica Sacra en el Siglo de Oro," *Hispanic Review* 38 (1970), 264 – 98. Two more general studies are Martí's *La preceptiva retórica española en el Siglo de Oro,* Biblioteca románica hispánica, 1: Tradados y monografías, no. 12 (Madrid, 1972); and José Rico Verdu, *La retórica española de los siglos XVI y XVII* (Madrid, 1973). I am indebted to Professor Donald Abbott of the University of California, Davis, for many of these references. Now see also Hilary Dansey Smith, *Preaching in the Spanish Golden Age: A Study of Some Preachers of the Reign of Philip III* (Oxford, 1978); and Antonio Cañizares Llovera, "La predicación española en el siglo XVI," in *Repertoria de Historia de las Ciencias Eclesiásticas en España, Siglos I – XVI,* 6 (Salamanca, 1977), pp. 189 – 266.

39. See *Modo de predicar,* 2.370 – 75.

40. Saint Francis himself, in his Rule for the friars, set the Franciscan tradition that sermons were to deal with "vices and virtues, punishment and reward." See *Seraphicae Legislationis Textus Originales* (Quaracchi: Collegium S. Bonaventurae, 1897), p. 44. This passage is quoted by Estella, *Modo de predicar,* 2.210. See also the chapter on preaching (esp. no. 118) of "The Capuchin Constitutions of 1536," in *The Catholic Reformation: Savonarola to Ignatius Loyola,* ed. John C. Olin (New York, 1969), pp. 172 – 76.

41. See *Modo de predicar,* e.g., 2.214, 223, 225.

must be moved to virtue and to good works.[42] The preacher will insist on the reality of death, judgment, and hell.[43]

This attitude contrasts with the "rhetoric of congratulation" and the emphasis on the "dignity of man" operative in the Italian demonstrative sermons described earlier. Estella's emphasis on good works is demanded by his moralism, but is also advanced by him as an antidote to the Lutheran heresy. The Venice, 1584, edition of his treatise was dedicated to Charles Borromeo, archbishop of Milan and great saint of the Counter Reformation. Borromeo is known to have been influenced by it and quoted from it, without acknowledgment, in his own important instructions on pastoral care.[44]

Estella's Dominican contemporary and fellow mystic, Luis de Granada, shared some of his pessimism about the low spiritual state of the preacher's congregation and also shared the viewpoint that the preacher's task was principally moral. Following the tradition initiated by Erasmus, he locates preaching in the deliberative genre; it is through use of this genre that men are persuaded to justice and piety and are dissuaded from vice. Granada then reserves the demonstrative solely for panegyrics of the saints, and, seemingly with some reluctance, admits the possibility of the *genus didascalicum* as well as the homily. Consciously dependent though he was upon the classical tradition, he was apprehensive about it and yearned for the day when somebody would create a "fully Christian rhetoric."[45]

That ideal was also espoused and even attempted by the great Lutheran theorist from Marburg, Andreas Hyperius, whose *De formandis concionibus sacris* of 1553 was translated into English by John Ludham a few years later.[46] For Hyperius, Scripture alone is the source from which to draw the forms for preaching. He rejects the attempt to make preaching conform to the three classical *genera*, "as though she [Divinitie] had not furniture and implements sufficient, especially for th'ecclesiasticall function, in hir owne proper house and home."[47] He discovers his five scriptural forms in Paul's Second

42. See ibid., 203 – 5, 210 – 12, 314 – 18.   43. See ibid., 316.   44. See ibid., 1.259.

45. *Ecclesiasticae rhetoricae, sive De ratione concionandi libri sex* (Lisbon, 1576), esp. pp. [viii – ix], 12 – 14, 34 – 35, 69 – 77, 150 – 51, 165, 171, 178 – 87. On Luis de Granada, see Peers, *Spanish Mystics,* 2nd rev. ed. (1951), 1.25 – 61; and Alvaro Huerga, "Louis de Grenade," in *Dictionnaire de spiritualité,* 9.1043 – 54, with excellent bibliography.

46. *The Practis of Preaching, otherwise called, The Pathway to ye Pulpet* (London, 1577). On this treatise, see Chamberlin, *Increase and Multiply,* pp. 67 – 91.

47. *Practis of Preaching,* fol. 18ʳ.

Epistle to Timothy (3.16), but the first and most important of them in fact corresponds to Melanchthon's "doctrinal or didascalicsk" *genus.*[48] Hyperius, profoundly influenced as he was by the classical tradition, eventually admits that there is correspondence between some of his forms and even the traditional *genera.*[49]

Alfonso García Matamoros, on the other hand, unequivocally reconciles classical rhetoric with the pulpit. His *De methodo concionandi* was first published in 1570.[50] Since the Inquisition in Spain forbade owning and reading Erasmus's *Ecclesiastes,* Matamoros felt an obligation to try to meet the needs of his fellow countrymen that this prohibition created.[51] In fact, while proposing "the life of our Lord and teacher" as material for preaching, he also proposes the typically Erasmian "philosophy of Christ."[52] However, though he respected Erasmus and had studied the *Ecclesiastes,* he judged that in some precepts Erasmus (as well as others) departed from the teaching on eloquence of Cicero and Quintilian. That he could not approve.[53]

Matamoros reproached anybody who would tamper with the three classical *genera* and he rejected as unnecessary all the other *genera,* like the *didascalicum,* that recent authors had invented. According to García Matamoros, a proper understanding of classical rhetoric would show that the three traditional *genera* were sufficient for the sacred orator and that all others could be reduced to them.[54]

More important than García Matamoros's affirmation of the classical *genera* is the theological justification he offers for it. We do not lose our human nature, he asserts, by being Christians, so we should not think it necessary to introduce into the pulpit some new rhetoric fallen directly from heaven. If we accept Aristotle's dialectics and philosophy for use in theology, why not on the same grounds accept classical rhetoric for Christian use? Moreover, Christ by his exaltation on the cross has drawn all things, including rhetoric, to himself and rendered them holy.[55] In this rationalization of García Matamoros, we see a clear instance of an attempt to correlate a vast theologi-

48. See ibid., fols. 18ʳ – 19ʳ.
49. See ibid., fols. 19ᵛ – 20ʳ.
50. In *Opera omnia* (Madrid, 1769), pp. 523 – 700.
51. See his *De tribus dicendi generibus,* pp. 436 – 37.
52. See *De methodo concionandi,* pp. 591, 593 – 94, 693. See also, however, p. 622.
53. See ibid., pp. 524, 529. See also pp. 645 – 47 on Erasmus.
54. See ibid., pp. 529 – 33. But see also p. 609 on the *genus didascalicum.*
55. See ibid., pp. 529 – 33, 545 – 46, 551 – 52.

cal position with the relatively pedestrian question of how to use, adapt, or reject classical forms.

Agostino Valerio (Valier), bishop of Verona and later cardinal, is the last author I will mention. His immensely popular *De rhetorica ecclesiastica* was first published in 1574, shortly after Matamoros's treatise. It is more serenely, but no less uncompromisingly, classical than Matamoros's; except for a brief and unobtrusive paragraph on the homily,[56] he never entertains even the suggestion that there might be alternatives to classical oratory.

Just as classical as the preaching theory that Valerio adopts is the *humanitas* that seems to me to animate the treatise. Besides embodying the classical virtues of clarity, order, and simplicity, the treatise emphasizes the human or humane values in Christianity. Valerio, for instance, rejects Stoic apathy and urges the preacher to awaken or instill good affections in his listeners. The preacher should especially arouse the emotion of love—love for God, of course, but also love of parents for their children, of children for their parents, of citizens for their native land, of friends for their friends. He should even try to make the good among his audience love themselves.[57]

Limitations of space now force me to move to the proposal of an agenda for future scholarship. The first task is the completion of the Caplan-King lists of sixteenth-century treatises, especially by taking note of works existing only in manuscript.[58] Second, the sermons preached by the authors of the treatises must be studied to see how practice corresponded to theory.[59] (Ironically, the two most important theorists—Melanchthon and Erasmus—left us no sermons!)[60]

56. See *Libri tres de rhetorica ecclesiastica* (Paris, 1575), fol. 103^r.

57. See ibid., fols. 38^v–42^v.

58. Harry Caplan and Henry H. King, "Latin Tractates on Preaching: A Book-List," *The Harvard Theological Review* 42 (1949), 185–206, esp. 187–95; "Italian Treatises on Preaching," *Speech Monographs* 16 (1949), 243–52, esp. 244; "Spanish Treatises on Preaching: A Book-List," *Speech Monographs* 17 (1950), 161–62; "Scandinavian Treatises on Preaching: A Book-List," *Speech Monographs* 21 (1954), 1–9; "Dutch Treatises on Preaching: A List of Books and Articles," ibid., pp. 235–47; "French Tractates on Preaching: A Book-List," *Quarterly Journal of Speech* 36 (1950), 296–325.

59. Frederick McGinness has completed such a study for preaching at the papal court in the late sixteenth and early seventeenth centuries, "Rhetoric and Counter-Reformation Rome: A Study in the Preaching at the Papal Court, 1563–1621" (Ph.D. diss. University of California, Berkeley, 1982). I am grateful to Mr. McGinness for reading an earlier version of this article and making some useful suggestions.

60. See my "Grammar and Rhetoric."

This would be an enormous undertaking, and judicious samplings will perhaps suffice to disclose dominant patterns. Then comparisons must be made between northern and southern humanism, between Erasmians and anti-Erasmians, between pre-Reformation and post-Reformation, between Catholic and Protestant. Never before had there been such variety in theories of sacred oratory as in the sixteenth century. The very names of the authors of works on preaching—Melanchthon, Erasmus, Contarini, Borromeo, Bellarmine, to name a few—indicate we are dealing with a crucial issue. It is a curious commentary on our scholarship that this phenomenon has never been studied in any systematic or comprehensive way.

It is my persuasion that studies like those I am advocating will uncover not only important information about the history of rhetoric and its adaptation to the Christian pulpit, but will also throw light on larger religious and cultural issues. García Matamoros explicitly relates his stance vis-à-vis classical rhetoric to a theological position. Other authors may be less explicit, but their rhetorical decisions are surely conditioned by their religious anthropology and their doctrinal convictions. In the controversy over rhetorical forms, deeper problems lurked beneath the surface.

Similarly, the authors' understanding of the nature of Scripture—as a book of the "philosophy of Christ," as a book of historical deeds, as a book of threats and promises, as a book of moral precepts—determines their choice of the *genus* that is most appropriate for propounding that book from the pulpit. Their choice of the *genus*, in turn, influences the hermeneutics with which they approach the sacred text, so that rhetoric has implications, here too, for literary interpretation. We can ask, further, what the purpose of a sermon is—to lead to understanding, to faith, to conversion of morals, or to inspiration by the vision of a beautiful deed. This question is implicitly answered by the *genus* in which the author places the sermon. An understanding of the use of the *genera* in preaching is an entrance into the deepest values that sixteenth-century cultures cherished and that its religions reflected and helped create.

Rhetoric, Politics, and Society:
From Italian Ciceronianism
to French Classicism

MARC FUMAROLI

We are in the first stages of a new discipline, the history of rhetoric. This discipline, as James J. Murphy has in a timely way reminded us, has not yet even catalogued its sources. *A fortiori*, it hasn't yet explored its possibilities nor defined its place in the academic *arbor scientiarum*, itself in the very midst of mutation, as witnessed by the growth of new disciplines such as our own. It may, then, seem premature, given the present state of our knowledge and intellectual landscape, to throw up a bridge between the history of rhetoric and political and social history. In actual fact, this step is not new. It even has ancient letters patent of nobility. One could trace it back to Plato, in whose works reflection on laws, the city, civism, is inseparable from the examination of the art of speech; to Aristotle, who ties rhetoric, that art of the probable, to politics, the art of the possible; to Tacitus, who, in the *Dialogue of the Orators*, links the evolution of Roman eloquence to the passage from republican to imperial institutions. Without going back so far in time, one can justifiably maintain that what we call Renaissance was, among other fundamental characteristics, the affirmation in itself, within Christian Europe, of a civil society, distinct in its very finality from religious and military society: in opposition to religious salvation and the glory of bearing arms, in opposition to the modes of language, the dogma, and the violence that permit their attainment, rhetoric appears as the connective tissue peculiar to civil society and to its proper finalities, happiness and

Translated from the French by Ruth B. York.

political peace *hic et nunc*. In the course of the sixteenth century, the ideal of chivalry was metamorphosed into the ideal of the *cortegiano*, nourished by the *De oratore* of Cicero, and the monastic ideal gave way to that of the priest-orator, of which the Jesuit is the example in the Catholic milieu. This fact underlines the force of the conquering expansion of civil society, which imposes on religious and warrior societies its own common denominator, the *vir bonus dicendi peritus*, whose authority rests on wisdom endowed with eloquence. Even before the history of rhetoric was constituted as an independent discipline, the historians of Italian humanism perceived the complementarity of rhetorical reflection and political thought in the culture of the Quattrocento and the Cinquecento. As early as 1937, in a pioneer article published by the *Journal of Warburg and Courtauld Institute,* Delio Cantimori had stressed the relationships between rhetoric and politics in Italian humanism (1.83–102). In his fundamental works—from the 1938 article in the *Bulletin of the John Rylands Library* (22. 32–97) to the collection published in Chicago in 1968 (while he was still at the Newberry Library), *From Petrarch to Leonardo Bruni, Studies in Humanities and Political Literature*—Hans Baron distinguished between a Florentine civic humanism and the aulic humanism of the Italian courts, the one linked to a republican political ideal, the other to a monarchic ideal. In the first case, eloquence and the orator, taking as paradigm the senatorial eloquence of the Roman republic, take on a heroic dimension; the spoken word, fed by wisdom and sustained by virtue, makes itself the responsible guide of the city. In the second case, the only hero is the prince, and public speech has no other function than the celebration of the prince; it is the festive link between him and the people; politics retires into the secret of the court and into the deliberation between the prince and his counsellors. Naturally, it would be abusive to force the antithesis: in both cases this same humanist ideal of *eloquentia cum sapientia conjungenda,* the same innervation of the *vita civile* by rhetoric, is at work. But depending on whether this *vita civile* is joined to "republican" or monarchic and autocratic types of institutions, the form and spirit of the alliance between wisdom and eloquence change. It is even possible, as we shall see in the case of France, that in a monarchy that nonetheless enjoys a unanimous *consensus*, certain institutions may adopt, within the regime, a more or less mythical ideal inspired by the Roman republican senate to counterbalance the autocratic tendency of the prince and his court. "Civic" humanism in the Europe of sixteenth- and seventeenth-century monarchies is perhaps more on the order of representations than on the order of institutional realities. There nevertheless remains, thanks to the mythical prestige of the Roman republic and the ideal of the orator set forth by Cicero in his dialogues on eloquence, an active force that will be spread more vigorously in the eighteenth century and that will be actualized dramatically in the assemblies of the French Revolution.

One finds a remarkable amplification of all the humanist *loci communes* I have just summarized in *L'Avant Discours de Rhétorique ou traitté de l'Eloquence,* which the young Davy Du Perron composed for Henry the Third, probably in the 1580s, in the Académie du Palais. Du Perron begins by establishing that eloquence was born in the states of republican constitution and that it is in a way consubstantial to such constitution:

> ... The places where eloquence has always reigned and triumphed more have been in Republics and popular governments, for the reason that in those States, where deliberations depend on the multitude, the first particular that must be sought is that the people, who are, as they say, a many-headed animal, agree on a self-same intention; otherwise, as long as the people are divided amongst several opinions, there will be no progress toward the execution of what is useful and necessary. And that is a thing that cannot be obtained by particular schemes, by going to solicit them one after another, because the time of the execution passes in the doing of all this; consequently it is necessary to have recourse to a public and popular instrument which can move infinite persons at the same time and make them consent to a common resolution. A thing which must be attributed to eloquence, either alone or above anything else: for it is eloquence which manages whole assemblies of men by the spoken word, makes itself mistress of their affections, shapes their wills as it suits these affections, and withdraws them from whatever it does not please to see them inclined to. It is through it that Peoples most fierce and jealous of their liberty voluntarily take on the yoke and servitude of laws for the establishment and the conservation of Republics: even though the institutions of civil life are beautiful and favorable in themselves, nevertheless they are more efficacious in governing simple and popular souls when the splendor and majesty of the oration illustrate the beauty, the excellence, and the dignity of things.[1]

---

1. Jacques Davy du Perron, "Avant-Discours de Rhetorique ou Traitté de l'Eloquence," *Les diverses oeuvres de l'illustrissime Cardinal Du Perron, Archevêque de Sees, Primat des Gaules et de Germanie, et Grand Aumônier de France* (Paris, 1622), in fol., p. 759.

In this speech pronounced before a king, and addressed to him personally, the humanist Du Perron cannot keep himself from linking his enthusiasm for eloquence ("the splendor and majesty of the oration") to a republican form of "civil life": it's that the power of eloquence can never be manifested so openly and obviously as in the direct exercise of the spoken word seizing hold of the minds of a crowd. By a logic supposing a certain nonrecognition of the effects of printing, in other respects celebrated with enthusiasm, the wager the humanists had placed on *eloquentia cum sapientia conjungenda* disposed it to cherish preeminently an archaic, or, if one prefers, utopic form of government, one that gave the orator the opportunity to manifest immediately, by his hold on a crowd, the power of eloquence. The example of the two great ancient orators, Cicero and Demosthenes, which only the republican regime of Rome and Athens had made possible, reinforced this inclination. Thus it is not without a fleeting touch of regret that Du Perron, abandoning his dream of a republican golden age of eloquence, comes back to reality, to the king before him and the monarchic form of the kingdom of France:

> Thus, as for Kingdoms and Monarchies, because deliberations in them depend on the will of a single man, who is ordinarily better acquainted with and prepared for the state of things than a gross and ignorant multitude could possibly be, and therefore does not allow himself to be so easily charmed by spoken words but wants to see to the heart of matters, it [eloquence] does not have so much power.[2]

It reserves to itself, even here nevertheless, according to the orator, "a good and great part." He enumerates them: embassies, propositions to the council of state, accounts, harangues. But, wresting the monarchy from its purity of principle, only a crisis, such as "civil wars led by popular pretexts, such as for religion" can give full flight to public deliberative eloquence before a "people wishing to be with full knowledge of the facts and itself rendered equal to the state of affairs." This is obviously the case in 1580. Far from complaining, Du Perron observes that in this quasi-republican situation, the opportunity is offered to eloquence, as in the time of the ancient forums, either to precipitate the people "into disorders, acts of insolence, and confusions" or to "recall and divert it from them."

2. Ibid., p. 760.

At about the same time, Montaigne, starting from premises similar to Du Perron's, comes to contrary conclusions. He writes, in fact, in the essay *De la vanité des paroles:*

> It [rhetoric] is a tool invented to manipulate a mob and disorderly commoners, and is a tool used only in sick states, like medicine, in those where the vulgar, the ignorant, where all were in power, as in Athens, Rhodes and Rome, and where things were in perpetual tempest, there orators thronged. . . . Eloquence flourished best in Rome when affairs were in their worst state and when the storm of civil wars agitated them: as a free and indomitable field bears the most vigorous weeds. From that it seems that the policies that depend on a monarchy need it less than the others: for the stupidity and facility that is found in the common people and which make them subject to be led and twisted by the sweet sound of that harmony without coming to weigh and know the truth of things by force of reason, this facility, I say, is not so easily found in a single man, and it is easier to keep him safe, by good education and advice, from the effect of this poison.[3]

The experience of the civil wars rallies Montaigne to the point of view suggested by Tacitus in the *Dialogue of the Orators* through the voice of Maternus: public deliberative eloquence, which believes it can maintain the crowd on the road to wisdom, is but a pernicious illusion. Montaigne draws from that a defense of the monarchy. A prudent defense, nonetheless: the monarch is preferable only on the condition that he be protected against himself by "good education" (it's the whole problem of the education of princes) and by "good advice" (it's the whole problem of the good advisor to the prince).

Again at the same time, in 1580 but in Rome this time, in the inaugural lesson of his course at the *Sapienza* concerning the *Annales* of Tacitus, Marc Antoine Muret meditated on the same theme, burningly topical. After reminding us that Cosimo de' Medici, founder of the Grand Dukedom of Florence, and Paul III Farnese, restorer of the pontifical monarchy after the sack of Rome and the victories of the heresy, were both assiduous readers of Tacitus, he then adds:

> One must observe that today, republics are no longer very numerous: there are hardly any more peoples who are not dependent on the orders and the will of a single man, who don't obey a single man, who are not governed by a single man.[4]

3. Montaigne, *Essais* (Paris, 1958), pp. 342 – 43.
4. Marc Antoine Muret, *Opera omnia* (Leipzig, 1848), p. 384.

And in 1582, in another inaugural lesson, this time of a course devoted to Cicero, Muret draws the consequences of this universality of monarchic regimes in the Europe of his time:

> Eloquence, as if the privilege of age had won for it a sort of retirement, must content itself with our dusty scholastic disputes, with the holy sermon, the only one that has a popular audience, and, from time to time, with acknowledgments to Princes, and with their funeral orations.[5]

The secret mourning for the great eloquence celebrated and practiced by Cicero is here, as it was with Du Perron, very keen. Muret, who knows Italian history well, implicitly opposes the Florence of the Medici, as he knows it, to the Florence of the fifteenth-century republic, where the eloquence of the humanist chancellors, studied by Hans Baron, the Salutati, the Bruni, had thought to reawaken the civism of Cicero. The Golden Age has withdrawn into the past. Must one despair of eloquence? If the public deliberative genre, of which Montaigne wished to see only the risks, is incompatible with the government of a single individual, orators still have, even under this regime, means of expressing themselves and exerting their influence. Muret observes then:

> Of the three genres defined by Aristotle, only the epideictic, which was formerly little esteemed, remains in use. It remains, however, so that they who are in a position to write letters well, that is to say eloquently, with prudence, and taking into account things, persons, and circumstances may easily reach the intimacy of Princes, be entrusted with the most important affairs, and grow from honor to honor. It is by this path that, among so many others, Jacques Sadolet and Pierre Bembo have raised themselves to a high position close to the papal tiara.[6]

Like Montaigne, Muret sees no other orator possible in a monarchy than the counselor to the prince. And to exercise the authoritative power of *eloquentia cum sapientia conjungenda,* he has recourse to the deliberative only through the epideictic. In other words he can counsel the prince, act for the best on his mind, only by taking the detour of praise. Epistolary art and its oral counterpart, the art of conversation, sum up the eloquence at court. Both suppose an art of pleasing whose essential values are clarity, elegance, urbanity (in French, *hon-*

5. Ibid., p. 404.   6. Ibid.

nêteté), polite and ingratiating pleasantness, wit (*ingenium*). The model of this eloquence can be found not in the *Orationes* but in the *Epistolae* of Cicero. So that for Muret, and contrary to what Morris Croll believed,[7] the political analysis of eloquence leads him to remain faithful, essentially, to the Ciceronianism of Bembo, which was in fact a courtly art. Even if Muret (and on this point Morris Croll was right) takes into consideration the lessons of Erasmus and the directives of the Council of Trent in order to refuse to make of *elocutio* an order in itself and submits it to learned *inventio,* nourished by Seneca and the Fathers, he does not, for all that, sacrifice *inventio* to *elocutio*: the values required by Cicero for the latter, *latinitas, urbanitas, elegantia,* the art of flattering the ear by the harmonious music of the style, are, for him, not incompatible with the Christian and philosophic erudition of the wise man. On the contrary, it is through this Ciceronian music that the wise man at court will succeed in having his wisdom listened to and in having it enter into the exercise of power. In this, Muret is opposed to Lipse, whom Morris Croll thought he could place in the same "anti-Ciceronian" movement as Muret. An academic far from the courts, the melancholy, erudite Lipse uses a jerky style imitated from Seneca, embellished with his allusive obscurity, the emblem of his touchy moral and intellectual independence in a world fallen from virtue. Between Muret and Lipse, the debate is rather analogous to the one Molière will establish in *Le Misanthrope* between Alceste and Philinte. And it is a debate in which morality, politics, and rhetoric are intimately tied: what is at stake in this debate is the possibility for *docta eloquentia* to live at court without denying itself, yet all the while yielding to the rule of the game that passes through the sacrifice of deliberative "candor" to the benefit of epideictic "flattery."

In this light, the Ciceronian quarrel, which goes well beyond the *Ciceronianus* of Erasmus, is revealed as a political debate as well. It is not by chance that Erasmus, founding father of the *respublica litterarum,* is the spiritual master of Lipse, typical citizen of the republic of letters. The anti-Ciceronianism of Erasmus and Lipse assumes that the intellectual has a margin of considerable independence in relation to monarchic power. This independence of the *sçavant* is symbolized by the divergence of his style from the Ciceronian norm.

7. Morris W. Croll, *Style, Rhetoric and Rhythm,* eds. J. Max Patrick and Robert O. Evans (Princeton, N.J., 1968), pp. 167–202, passim.

Montaigne belongs to the same tradition and he was considered a spiritual brother by Lipse. On the contrary, for anyone who, like Muret, thinks (i.e., frequents with the prince and not at a haughty distance, in the interior of the court and not in some learned retreat) that the intellectual must make wisdom heard and triumph, Ciceronianism, which Bembo had made the symbol of eloquence fitting for the courts, must be the rule. It offers, in fact, through *claritas* and *delectio verborum,* a rule of the game suited to allowing a dialogue within a ruling elite. It is up to the wise man to use this rule of the game to impose, by the detour of elegance and urbanity, his own views. This politico-rhetorical debate, we shall see, will find fertile ground in France in the seventeenth century.

The premises of this debate are posited as early as the sixteenth century under the reign of Henry III. They can be summed up in the antithesis between the rhetorical positions of Jacques Amyot and Guillaume Du Vair. In both cases we must take into account the slight inflexibility supposed by transposition of a conflict that appeared in Neo-Latin prose, on the register of the vernacular language. But the basic political and moral principles remain identical. Preceptor of King Henry III and an eminent member of the palace academy, Jacques Amyot is at the same time a scholar and a man of the court. Translator of Plutarch, he is also the translator of the Greek novels of Longus and Heliodorus, which are at the origins of the pastoral literature dear to the court of France, from d'Urfé to Fénelon. Like Du Perron, and probably in the same context of the palace academy, Amyot drafted for Henry III a *Projet d'éloquence royale,* which remained in manuscript form until 1806. One finds in it already all the features of what has come to be known as French classic style, which will triumph under Louis XIV. The sources of the *Projet* are Italian: the Bembo of the *Prose della volgar lingua,* the Vettori commentator in 1562 of the *De elocutione* of Demetrius of Phaleron, two masters of Ciceronian Atticism. As a man of the court addressing himself to the king, Amyot is less interested in invention, learned, erudite, or inspired by the speech, than in its elocution and the eloquence of that elocution. He takes as reference for elegant prose not a civic eloquence unseemly in a monarchic regime, or else reserved for the prince on great occasions (the States General, for example), but rather the art of conversation of the king and his entourage, governed by a just equilibrium between *spezzatura, neglegentia,* and the *decorum* inseparable from the royal *persona.* For him the essential value of the best style is "pleasantness":

In choosing [the words], we will take those that are the most fit to mean the thing we wish to speak of, those that seem to us the most pleasant, which sound best to the ear, which are most customarily in the mouths of those who speak well who are Frenchmen and not foreigners.[8]

These four criteria of the *delectio verborum (Proprietas, euphonia, elegantia, latinitas)* are those of the *De oratore* and of Bembo. And Amyot adds:

The words having been chosen, it is fitting to join and tie them together so that there be no harsh encounter of letters or syllables. And when the ear, on which one must rely, causes us to judge that the suit is too flat or too harsh, by changing the order of the words and arranging them in another way, we find at the end that it will become more firm and more pleasant. . . . Among other things one must study the clauses together, and, in so far as is possible, diversify and change the conjunctions that link them in order that nothing be loose or interrupted so that all may flow smoothly and all the parts be assembled as the members of the same body.[9]

This art of the harmoniously proportioned period, rhythmic and pleasant to the ear, is a transposition into French of Bembo's *ciceroniana norma.* It takes into account technical analyses extracted by Pietro Vettori from Demetrius of Phaleron's *De elocutione,* a manual of Atticism colored by Isocratism. That this French Atticism, whose recommendation of *latinitas* and *urbanitas* is the usage of the *sanior pars* of the court, aspired from then on to impose itself as the royal norm of style in France is what Du Perron, under Henry IV, reveals to us in a passage from the *Perroniana:*

Dialects [and he means by that the idiolects proper to the diverse social and provincial milieux] are in use in popular and aristocratic States and one must accommodate oneself to them; but in monarchic States, one must strive to speak only the language of the Court, where one finds all that is politeness in the Kingdom, which is not true in Republics and Democracies.[10]

What eloquence loses in political power in a monarchic regime it regains somehow in the realm of elegance and esthetic refinement,

---

8. Jacques Amyot, *Projet d'éloquence royale composé pour Henri III, Roi de France, d'après un manuscrit autographe de l'auteur* (Versailles, 1805), p. 44.

9. Ibid., p. 46.

10. *Perroniana, sive excerpta ex ore cardinalis Perronii, J. et P. du Puy,* ed. by I. Vosio (Geneva, 1667), p. 310.

in the realm, then, of the epideictic. If, under Henry III and in a time of civil wars, Du Perron had been able to manifest a lively interest in deliberative eloquence and in its capacity to surmount the division of minds, under Henry IV when the monarchy is solidly reestablished, he sees the urgency elsewhere: "dialects" have invaded the court — these are the gasconisms come from Béarn — damaging its power of example of "good usage." To fight against a "bad taste" that diminishes the splendor of the court, Du Perron announces a doctrine of best style very close to Amyot's; this doctrine is also a Ciceronian Atticism transposed into the French language. From the *imitatio ciceroniana* it takes its normative, examplary, centripetal character, and like that ideal of style of the Roman High Renaissance, it is, by its epideictic and not deliberative essence, attuned to the law of the spoken word in the regime of the monarchic court, which law is to make everything pass through the filter of attractiveness, praise, and flattering beauty.

Such as Du Perron poses it, the problem of the "best French style" in the seventeenth century is thus intimately tied to the purely political problem of the French monarchy's progress toward its own principle and the progress of the Court of France as theater and instrument of this power. One of the obstacles on this road was obviously the feudal aristocracy, and, indeed, until the defeat of the Fronde, small courts grouped around greats such as the Duke of Montmorency or the Prince of Condé will secrete their own "dialects," their own literary style, rivals of those of the royal entourage. But another obstacle, less apparent because it emanates from the milieu that traditionally furnishes the French monarchy its theoreticians, its apologists, and its financial and judicial officers, is the rhetorical tradition proper to the aristocracy of the Robe. And this aristocracy is *sçavante* par excellence: as Eugene Rice has shown, this is the aristocracy that, from Guillaume Budé to Jacques-Auguste de Thou, from Henri de Mesmes to Guillaume Du Vair, has sponsored the high French humanist erudition. Linked by its responsibilities to the Court of France, to the royal government, and to the parliaments, this learned aristocracy has at first parliamentary roots. And the Parliament of Paris, and after it the ensemble of French parliamentary bodies, willingly considers itself a republican senate *à la romaine* whose highest task is less judiciary than deliberative and political: that of maintaining, beyond the succession of reigns, respect for the "fundamental laws of the kingdom" and therefore the task of limiting, by its *arrests* and *remonstrances,* the arbitrary inherent in the monarchy. The parliamentary milieu considers itself, then, all the more faithfully monarchist as it watches jealously over the kingdom's traditions and restrains that which, in the policy of the court, might seem to clash with or overthrow those traditions.

The parliament, mother-institution of the aristocracy of the Robe, defines itself, then, willingly *through opposition* to the court, to its Machiavellianism, to the liberty of morals, the spirit of flattery that reigns there, foreign imports hostile to French "candor" and Christian morality. The high magistrates gladly affect a severe and austere mask *à la Caton*. Their ancient models are willingly the heroes of the Athens and the republican Rome of Plutarch, the Phocions, the Catos, or the Stoic senators according to Tacitus, the Senecas, the Thrasea Paetus. On several occasions after the violent death of Henry III, then of Henry IV, the Parliament of Paris truly played the role of a deliberating assembly, deciding the succession to the throne or the form to be given to the regency. This magistrature of censors sustained by an immense juridical and historical culture is not without a certain conception of eloquence. This humanist conception perpetuates, while refining it, a medieval tradition codified by, among other things, Guillaume du Breuil's *Stilus curie parlementi,* which condemned the advocates to a severe utilitarian style devoid of *ornatus* other than juridic or scriptural quotations. This tradition, keyed to the "republican" spirit of the high magistrature and to the myth of the hard and pure Rome of Cato the Elder, is enriched in the sixteenth century by the views expressed by Erasmus in the *De copia* and the *Ciceronianus.*[11] The parliamentary milieu, as we have said, is the one from which is recruited and the one which sponsors the French republic of letters. The *forma mentis* fashioned by the style of judiciary eloquence practiced in the parliaments of France and by the style of deliberative eloquence of their Remonstrances to the Crown, was determinant in the generalized adoption of rhetorical Erasmism within the bosom of French humanism. The epideictic elegance, the aulic urbanity of the *stylus ciceronianus,* could not serve as interpretors for the learned and severe magistrates. What is more,

11. See the work of Terence Cave, *The Cornucopian text, problems of writing in the French Renaissance* (Oxford, 1979), which penetratingly analyzes Erasmus's *De copia* as the rhetorical matrix of French learned humanism. On the influence of the *Ciceronianus* in France and on what I call, in a sense, close to the "cornucopian text" of Terence Cave, see my "rhétorique des citations," *L'Age de l'éloquence, rhétorique et res literaria en France de la Renaissance au seuil de l'époque classique* (Geneva, 1980).

the *stylus ciceronianus* was irremediably compromised in their eyes by having been the official style of the Court of Rome and by having served as model for the Italian style of Castiglione's *Cortegiano,* of Della Casa's *Galateo,* treatises according to which the courtiers of the Valois patterned themselves.

The principal difference between the Ciceronian style, Latin, vulgar, or both, and the style descended from the *De copia* and the *Ciceronianus* resided in an inverse relationship that the two styles attributed to *inventio* and to *elocutio.* The Ciceronian style gives predominance, or at least an equal importance, to elocution: its elegance supposes, then, that the "sources" of the speech are not to be apparent and are not to break its smooth and shining surface. On the contrary, the scholarly style issued from the *De copia* gives primacy to invention: the sources of the speech, the *semina dicendi* of which it is the efflorescence, must remain apparent, and, among others, the quotations, sentences, apothegms in their original language. To the antithesis pleasantness/rough strength must be added, then, the antitheses science/ignorance, sincerity/dissimulation. The way of pleasantness, ignorance, and dissimulation is obviously the courtly art of flattery; the way of rough strength, encyclopedic knowledge, and sincerity is the learned eloquence of the wearers of the Robe. The polemic of Adrien Turnèbe against Pierre Paschal,[12] his *Commentarii* on Quintilian's *Institutio oratoria,* the polemics of Henri Estienne against the "pseudo-Ciceronians" and the "Italianized French language" uphold the cause of a scholarly style whose harmonics are evident with the style of parliament. And Montaigne's polemic against Cicero, but also against Bembo, in the *Essays* sums up for the use of a vaster public the theses of the anti-Ciceronianism of the learned men of the Robe. Friend of La Boétie (who had written the *Contr'un*), the former Counselor to the Parliament of Bordeaux remained profoundly faithful to the spirit of his original milieu. He even makes himself its

---

12. On this quarrel, in which Turnèbe attacks in Paschal the "Ciceronian" at court, see P. Bonnefon, *Pierre Paschal, historiographe du roi* (Paris, 1883). The rhetorical doctrine of Turnèbe, enemy of Ramus, is formulated in his *Commentarii* on the *Institutio oratoria* of Quintilian. He abundantly quotes Erasmus. He prefers Cato's example to that of Cicero. He places the moral *auctoritas* of the orator and his scholarly, juridic, and philosophic *inventio* far above his elegance in the handling of the *ornatus* of the style. Of this rhetoric, whose very form, a series of glosses, announces the doctrine, the addressees seem to have been essentially the magistrates and advocates of the parliament. It is the antithesis of a rhetoric for the use of a courtier, such as the *Cortegiano,* or later, *L'Honneste homme* of Nicolas Faret. On the anti-aulicism in the sixteenth century, see Pauline M. Smith, The *Anti-Courtier Trend . . .* (Geneva, 1966).

vulgarizer. Moreover, his monarchic loyalism finds its limit, quasi-republican, in a philosophy of the spiritual autonomy of the individual vis-à-vis the state.

In spite of this dominant current, Ciceronianism found advocates in the scholarly milieu in France of the sixteenth century. The case of Christophe de Longueil, of whom Bembo and Sadolet had made a *civis romanus,*[13] was an argument in the polemic of French humanism against the pretensions of Italian humanism. Even an anti-Ciceronian like Henri Estienne publishes in 1581 — urged, it's true, by Henry III — a volume of *Epistolae ciceroniano stylo scriptae:*[14] its preface avers that he who is capable of the greatest thing is capable of the least thing and that the *ciceronianus stylus* of Longueil and Bunel, two Frenchmen, is as good as that of the Italians Manuce and Bembo. But in his view it's a matter of a tournament of virtuosity: the scholarly style of true erudites could not conform to this sterile discipline. Contrary to Longueil, an "Italianized" Frenchman, Jules Cesar Scaliger was an Italian who had become French and was installed at Agen. His work as a grammarian and *poéticien*[15] is the most profound attempt to ground in theory the fundamental myth that sustains Ciceronianism: there was a Golden Age of language and Latin poetry, the age of Virgil and Augustus. Before, everything was "primitive," including Greek letters; then everything enters into decadence. Imitation of the authors of this Golden Age is the only track that can lead it back to modern Europe. This is the way the "Ciceronian" humanists of the Courts of Julius II and Leon X reasoned already.

And it is this historic myth, fusing with the French national ambition to reincarnate the Rome of the Golden Age, that will uphold classicism under Louis XIV. This thesis had political implications: it's under an enlightened monarchic regime, wished for, moreover, by Cicero at a certain moment of his political career, that Latin litera-

13. On Longueil, see Philip-August Becker, *Christophe de Longueil* (Bonn and Leipzig, 1924); and Théophile Simar, *C. de Longueil humaniste (1488–1522)* (Louvain, 1911).

14. On Henri Estienne, see Louis Clément, *Henri Estienne et son oeuvre française . . .* (Paris, 1898); and Jean Jehasse, *Renaissance de la critique* (Saint-Etienne, 1976), pp. 234–35 and p. 329.

15. On the work of Scaliger, grammarian and poetician, see Rose Mary Ferraro, *Giudizi critici e criteri estetici nei Poetices libri septem* (Chapel Hill, N.C., 1971). But Scaliger is also the author of *Epistolae,* which justifiably was considered a masterpiece of the *stylus ciceronianus.* This proved, as his son, Joseph Juste, occupied himself showing, that one could be, contrary to the theses of Erasmus's *Ciceronianus,* a giant of erudition and an accomplished Ciceronian.

ture had known its full bloom. This theory, then, ran contrary to the cult of Cato the Elder professed by the erudite French magistrature. It supposed that the full flowering of the arts is tied to the luxury of the epideictic and poetry over the utilitarianism of the judiciary and deliberative. And the epideictic genre, which makes prose contiguous to poetry, is more at home in a monarchic court than in the forums of republics. Whereas, as we have seen, humanists at court, such as Amyot or Du Perron under Henry III, work to create an *art* of French prose, the whole effort of the scholarly humanism of the sixteenth and the beginning of the seventeenth century tends to preserve the utilitarian character of prose and reserve art for poetry alone. Here again there are exceptions and resistances. The itinerary of Etienne Dolet, from his pamphlets against Erasmus's *Ciceronianus,* his editions of Cicero, to his treatise on translation[16] becomes clear in this light: it is a tenacious and continuous quest to endow Neo-Latin, then French prose, with *ornatus* that alone will make it worthy of the masterpieces of eloquence of antiquity. More prudent because it depends on the philhellenic prejudice of learned Frenchmen, the work of Louis Le Roy goes in the same direction: his translations from the Greek aspire to be for French prose the counterpart of the work of the Pléiade in poetry. Thus it is that Du Bellay, who gave hardly any place to prose in his *Deffence et Illustration,* salutes Le Roy's work in a poem that figures at the beginning of Le Roy's translation of the *Banquet* (1558):

> Til now we have taken the flower for the fruit
> The bark for the wood, the color for the live,
> Using our minds only in poetic labor.

> But instructed and impressed we will be this time
> Since Louis Le Roy, our French Plato
> Teaches us eloquence and the Attic doctrine.[17]

More daring, the work of Blaise de Vigenère, the translator, will break the interdict that scholarly prejudice causes to weigh on the development of an art of French prose. At the same time an erudite and courtier, at once Latinist, Hellenist, Hebraist and acquainted with Italian language and literature, Vigenère was well placed to play

16. On the polemic of Etienne Dolet against Erasmus, see *L'Erasmianus sive Ciceronianus XX d'Etienne Dolet (1535)* (Geneva, 1974). His treatise on translation.

17. In Louis Le Roy, trans., *Le Banquet de Platon* (Paris, 1558). On Le Roy, see W. L. Gundersheimer, *The Life and Works of Louis Le Roy* (Geneva, 1966).

a mediatory role between learned and aulic humanism. In the preface to his celebrated translation of the *Images et Tableaux de Philostrate,* he denounces the prejudice that weighs against *ornatus* in prose:

> If our forebears had put themselves at the duty of trying all that the good minds of our time, likewise the Poets, have undertaken and perfected with good results and if prose had had the courage and the boldness to second them following the example of the Greeks and the Latins, for the lights of free oration have always taken their first step and growth in poetry, we would be, at this hour, ready to gather and collect the sweet fruits in order to be able to enjoy them at our ease and contentment. But having wished to cling fearfully to a too severe and religious routinism, thinking to commit a greater sacrilege and heinous crime by changing the least syllable of Antiquity already replete and chosen, I don't believe anyone wants to debate the fact that the old stocks of the French language have good need of being layered, and the trees renewed by some good nursery; for being all covered with moss, they no longer produce anything any longer but a few coarse and arid leaves.[18]

The "layering" of French prose can come only from a grafting onto the prose of Latin and Greek art, and above all onto the style of Cicero:

> We must endeavor to pattern our style on the one amongst them all which with the voice and consent of learned men is considered the best, as Cicero shows his contemporaries the true Attic, clear, clean and moderated, not poor nor run down, as he himself practiced it over all the others.[19]

For Vigenère as for Dolet, Cicero is the symbol and rallying point for those among the French humanists who want the *ornatus* of the prose of antique art to penetrate French prose and purify it from Gothic barbarism. The resistance to Cicero comes from those among the French humanists who dread the idea that this art of prose may seal the authority of the court in matters of language and may diminish the learned prestige of the high magistrates, "Catos" who watch severely over the lapses of the court. What is at stake in the debate is therefore political: it is no less a matter than determining the place of the parliaments in the wheels of decision in the kingdom.

18. Preface to *Images et Tableaux de platte peinture de Philostrate* (Paris, 1578).
19. Ibid.

A Robert Estienne in his *Grammaire françoise* thought the king's court and the supreme courts of justice and finance equally qualified to act as referees on "good usage" in the French language:

> I rely on those who during their entire lifetimes have frequented the courts of France, that of the king as well as of his Parliament in Paris and also his Chancellery and Chamber of Accounts in which places the language is written and pronounced in greater purity than in all others.[20]

But an Estienne Pasquier goes further, and reserves for the scholarly men of the Robe the privilege of fixing the norm for good French prose:

> Whoever would like to acquire judgment and intelligence in this language and take any degree, I would counsel him to frequent practicing law people, for besides having exquisite speech, proper and familiar, making themselves accessible to the common populace (which is principal among them), the courtly or the most delightful speech of the King and the Court is well-known to them, sent back and forth by Letters or by Edicts of the ones or the others.[21]

It is evident that for Estienne Pasquier the words *courtly* and *delightful* are somewhat pejorative and designate the excess of art, *ornatus*, the luxurious and flattering character of the language of the court. In his opinion, French prose must have above all a character of usefulness in the service of competent *sçavants*. The fact remains that this refusal by scholarly men of the Robe to let prose escape from the limits of the *utilitas* nourished by erudite quotations was somewhat contradictory to the desire to confer on parliament and its magistrates a function both moral and political as tutors and censors of royal power. This contradiction becomes apparent in the course of the civil wars when, as Du Perron pointed out, the monarchy was colored by the republic and had to take into account factions supported by the people. The Calvinist orators, or orator-members of the Ligue, did wonders to fanaticize the populace, and the Parliament of Paris felt then the weakness of its own eloquence, too schol-

20. As quoted by Louis Clément in *Henri Estienne et son oeuvre française*, p. 450. See, quoted by the same author, this other affirmation: "Bad language is as rare in the Parlement as it is frequent at the Louvre," p. 451.

21. As quoted in D. Thickett, *Choix de Lettres d'Estienne Pasquier* (Geneva, 1956), p. 88. See also Ferdinand Brunot, *Histoire de la langue française*, 3. pt. 1, republished in 1966, pp. 21–23.

arly and stiff. Drawing lessons from this cruel experience, Guillaume Du Vair in 1594 published his treatise *De l'Eloquence françoise et pourquoy elle est demeurée si basse*,[22] which proposed a reform of the traditional attitude of the French humanists vis-à-vis the art of prose. Counselor to the Paris Parliament, a future First President, Du Vair does not rally to the doctrine of Amyot, nor less still to Vigenère's. He does not envisage the blooming in France of an epideictic art of prose that would give the advantage to the court. Instead, he wishes the appearance in parliament of an art of deliberative eloquence that raises the judicial style above "chicanery" and confers on it the majesty and efficacy of the "orations" of Demosthenes and Cicero. Thence he places the accent of the discourse on *la force*, which remains in his eyes the antithesis of the sophisticated *douceur* of the courtier-Machiavellians. In the final analysis, this strength reposes on the encyclopedic erudition of the orator, on the resources of his *inventio:* but instead of showing itself as it is, with its "bones and muscles" (let us understand sentences and ancient quotations in their original language), it must cover itself with a "skin" and a "complexion" breathing health: the abraded skeleton of scholarly prose must give way to the vigorous "body" of persuasive eloquence. For "skin" and "complexion" one must understand an art of the well-rhythmed period, and one that Latin and Greek quotations no longer interrupt: these last, "meditated" and translated into French, must content themselves with invisibly nourishing the uninterrupted and powerful flux of the discourse.

Du Vair's treatise, which remained faithful to the severe tradition of the erudite magistrates' rhetoric, nevertheless opened a breach in the interdict that tradition caused to weigh on the quest for *elocutio* in the French language. But this breach was opened in the name of an ideal too utopian to find a practical application. Except for periods of grave crisis, the court cannot accept that the Parliament of Paris transform itself into a deliberating assembly trampling on the power of the king and his direct counselors to decide without appeal. Under Henry IV, and even more, beginning in 1630 under Richelieu, the parliament is brought back to purely judiciary role and Richelieu in its high ranks sets apart functionaries and intendants destined to carry out the royal policy. By a remarkable paradox, the Gallican humanist jurists, who through hostility towards the temporal power

22. Guillaume Du Vair, *De l'Eloquence françoise. . .* , ed. René Radouant (Paris, 1907, rpt. Geneva, 1970).

269

of the Holy See had forged the juridic and historical arguments for royal absolutism, are caught in their own trap. Absolutism ceases to be for external use; it surges back onto the very organization of powers in France; it constructs a state apparatus fit to carry out rapidly and without useless discussion the decisions of the king and his ministers. It becomes evident, under Richelieu, that the deliberative eloquence Du Vair dreamed of has no place in such a system. It will reappear during the Fronde, but caught in a vice between monarchic loyalism and the refusal of absolutism inside the kingdom, it will offer only a spectacle of confusion and failure. It will disappear then, or almost, until the Revolution, which, in order more freely to begin to speak, will do away with the Ancient Regime parliaments.

As early as the years from 1620 to 1630, this impossibility of deliberative eloquence in a monarchic regime became obvious to the best minds of the French republic of letters. The consequence was ineluctable: for lack of being able to prevent the triumph of the court as warrantor of "good usage" in language and the triumph of the aulic art of praise as the specifically monarchic mode of eloquence, the French erudites decide, not without hesitation or remorse, to tyrannize over what they cannot prevent. To this logic of facts is added the prestige of Joseph Juste Scaliger, faithful to the intellectual legacy of his father, who takes it upon himself to spread abroad in the French and Dutch republic of letters the theses of Jules Cesar Scaliger concerning the classic Golden Age of Latinity. As may be seen in the *Scaligerana*,[23] he combats Erasmus's rhetorical heritage and maintains that the *ciceronianus stylus*, by its clarity, its elegant precision, and the universal norm of language it authorizes, is the surest instrument of critical intelligence, the most efficacious agent of scholarly research. So he topples the major argument that, since the *Ciceronianus*, had made Ciceronian Atticism suspect within the bosom of the republic of letters. There is a learned elegance and it is capable of judging and tasting with *acribia* the other forms of elegance. Scaliger's *Poétique* and the erudite tradition consecrated to Aristotle's *Poetics* and *Rhetorics* offer to the learned sure principles of appreciation and authoritative power over the prose and poetry of the court. The circle of the Dupuys, which under Louis XIII is the intellectual general staff of French humanism, gradually rallies to these views at the same

23. *Scaligerana, sive excerpta ex ore Josephi Scaligeri, par F.F.P.P.* (Fratres Puteanos) (Geneva, 1666, 8ᵛᵒ); and *Scaligerana, Thuana, Perroniana. . . ,* 2 vols. (Amsterdam, 1740, 8ᵛᵒ).

time that it grants its aid, not without remorse and inner hesitations, to Richelieu's policies.

In 1638 a member of the Dupuy circle, Nicolas Perrot d'Ablancourt, publishes in collaboration with Olivier Patru a translation of *Eight Orations* of Cicero in a prose that aspires to be itself a model of French Ciceronianism.[24] The editor of this translation, Jean Camusat, is close to the Académie Française, founded by Richelieu, and there is every reason to think that the work is in some way sponsored by the Académie. Thus there was in operation, under the authority of Richelieu, the synthesis of the aulic Ciceronian tradition (which in France went back to Amyot and Du Perron) and the scholarly Ciceronian tradition (which in France went back to Etienne Dolet and Jules Cesar Scaliger). This synthesis presents two sides: one turned toward an alliance of utility and elegance in the service of the sciences and the affairs of state, the other toward an alliance of attractiveness and a regulated elegance in the service of the amusements of the court. Such a compromise, correcting each by the other, prudently blends the *force* of the scholarly style and the *douceur* of the aulic style; this compromise rests on the idea Richelieu forms of the Court of France, the theatre of royal power, whose actors are the nobles of the sword, reduced to the role of ornaments, and whose stagehands are competent and scholarly men of the Robe. The function of classic Atticism is to permit dialogue between the two aristocracies and to favor their coexistence at court. It supposes that in the last analysis, the court is the criterion of French "good usage." It makes the traditional authoritative power of the Parliament of Paris precarious, in this domain as in the political one, and throws back into "pedantry" or "the bourgeois look" the language of men of the Robe not employed at court. Inversely, the royal, moral, and rhetorical *decorum* to which it is subjected by the learned members of the Academy rules out the temptations of "baroque" excess that characterized the art of the small feudal courts under Henry IV and the young Louis XIII and that is still threatening in the "irresponsible" milieu of the young courtiers. This masterpiece of diplomacy and rhetorical politics is, then, a powerful instrument of royal prestige and the consent it demands of its subjects and servants. One understands why the revolt against absolutism during the Fronde might be accompanied not only by the reawakening of parliamentary eloquence but also by the development of centrifugal styles such as the burlesque and the pre-

24. Patru, D'Ablancourt, et al., *Huit oraisons de Cicéron* (Paris, 1638).

cious. Mazarin's victory and above all the taking of power by Louis XIV will assure, this time on wider and stabler bases than in Richelieu's time, the triumph of classic Atticism in France.

It is not surprising, then, that this triumph is accompanied by an extraordinary reviviscence of the Ciceronianist myth par excellence: the Augustan Golden Age. As soon as the king personally takes power, he is hailed as a new Augustus whose reign is to make France the new classic Rome of modern Europe. But this new classic Rome is also Christian, which makes her superior to her pagan model. So that in the classic French synthesis even the heritage of the *Ciceronianus* has its place and safeguards the "century of Louis XIV" from the objections of which the "century of Julius II" had been the victim. This is to say to what point the elegant and measured simplicity of classic French Atticism conceals, under its smooth and vigorous form, an extraordinary richness of motifs in which all the debates of the Renaissance and Catholic Reformation in their most contradictory tendencies are summed up. The republican, scholarly, and Christian severity that remains very much alive in it acts as counterweight to the courtly, brilliant, libertine lightness in it; the irony of Erasmus that Molière's comedy preserves, is in it a counterweight to the Borromean gravity of Bossuet. As absolutist as it has become, the French monarchy remains the unifying principle of a diversity, and not a sterilizing totalitarianism. A Ciceronian and Christian monarchy, it bases its reign not on a systematic ideology but on a rhetoric both firm and liberal, whose *topique* is the complex and diverse heritage of Christian humanism and whose style is itself a compromise, wavering between two exclusive extremes, that results from the humanist debate about the best *elocutio.* Rather than adherence of doctrine, Louis XIV's monarchy awaits an adherence of taste; it has enough confidence in itself to seduce rather than convince or do violence to. In this sense, and on the whole, it was the least political evil slowly elaborated by the humanism of the French Robe, neither republican utopia nor tyranny.

This monarchy that makes seduction a means of government, that organizes its own seduction by mobilizing in its service the most brilliant talents in the kingdom, carried out in its own way the humanist program of *eloquentia cum sapientia conjungenda* and it accomplished it in the epideictic mode of praise, in the classic style of Attic beauty. In an essay on political philosophy written in Rome under Richelieu, the "erudite libertine" Naudé had seen clearly that only eloquence can make the political order acceptable and lasting:

For me, I deem discourse so powerful that I have found nothing to this point exempt from its empire; it persuades and makes the most fabulous religions believed, it incites the most iniquitous wars, gives cloak and color to the blackest deeds, calms and appeases the most violent seditions, excites rage and fury in the most peaceful souls. In short, it is discourse which plants and cuts down heresies, which makes England revolt and Japan be converted. . . . And if a Prince had twelve men of such a stamp devoted to him, I would esteem him more strongly and would believe he'd be better obeyed in his Kingdom than if he had two powerful armies. But more especially as one can use eloquence two ways, to speak and to write, it still must be noted that this second part is not of less consequence than the first, and I dare say it surpasses it to some extent; for a man who speaks can be heard in only one place and by three or four thousand persons . . . , whereas he who writes can declare his conceptions everywhere and to everyone. I add that many good reasons often escape the ear through the haste of the tongue, reasons which cannot so easily deceive the eyes when they pass several times over the same thing. . . .[25]

This variation, after so many others, on the theme of eulogy such as the *De oratore* has fixed it, admirably sums up my remarks. One of the newest contributions the history of rhetoric can bring to political and social history is to give it back this sense, appropriately humanistic, of the powers of the spoken word, not only as a political instrument but as a political stake as decisive in the final analysis as the resources of armaments and raw materials. The history of speech, and—in relation to it—of societies, of institutions and of social groups, is a capital chapter in the history of *homo loquens*. To a certain extent, Greco-Latin rhetoric remains the instrument of analysis that not only allows us to understand how this history was made, but also why, on more than one occasion, this history could be mastered, could to a slight extent escape violence, and could give way to the *bonheur d'expression*.

25. Gabriel Naudé, *Considérations politiques sur les coups d'état* (n.p., 1667), pp. 266–68.

Lawyers and Rhetoric
in Sixteenth-Century England

RICHARD J. SCHOECK

If, with Aristotle, we take rhetoric to signify "the faculty of observing in any given case the available means of persuasion," and if we note with him that this faculty is not a function of any other art, then we recognize that we are concerned with an art that uniquely leads to action in others and to action (as Ong has observed) "in the sense of something other than contemplation."[1] Rhetoric, thus, is essentially and ineluctably involved in the world of action; it is (to use a term of Hoyt H. Hudson) a strategy, and always a strategy for action. It is not surprising therefore to find that the profession of law, which is always primarily concerned either with the defense of a client or with the administering of justice, should be deeply involved with rhetoric, philosophically speaking, and that its involvement has always been part of the history of rhetoric, and, until our own century, of law.

From the *Rhetoric* of Aristotle and the dialogues of Cicero through the medieval schools for the *ars dictaminis* in tenth- and eleventh-century Bologna out of which came the university, this relationship between law and rhetoric has always been characteristic. Indeed, only with Irnerius in the early twelfth century did law cease to be a subdivision of rhetoric: then the study of law became a subject in its own right, and we witness the rise of the law schools at Bologna and elsewhere as part of the universities.[2] The history of European

1. Aristotle, *Rhet.* 1.2.1355b. See further W. J. Ong, "The Province of Rhetoric and Poetic," *Modern Schoolman* 19 (1942), 24–27.

2. The history of that relationship has not been written in full or with sufficient sense of its continuity over many centuries. For the development from schools for the *ars dictaminis* into faculties within the universities, see Charles H. Haskins, *The Renais-*

thought for the next five centuries at least — and I am thinking of the history of education and the history of ideas as well as the history of legal and political thought — can only be written when we have a full account of the contribution of the law schools of Italy, Spain, France, Germany, and England and Scotland. To repeat a quotation I used in my report of 1967 on the history of law in the Renaissance, given to the Renaissance Society of America, "among all the things that actually happened in the Middle Ages [add Renaissance], not the least important was the fact that thousands of influential men spent the formative years of their youth studying Roman and canon law."[3] Like rhetoric, law was an essential part of the fabric of the Renaissance; and on both the Reformation had a significant impact: the cutting of canon law ties with Rome in the 1530s produced immense, if still not fully studied, changes in England (comparable to the changes in Protestant countries on the Continent), and the anti-Aristotelianism so generally associated with the Reformation in philosophy spilled over into rhetoric, contributing to the popularity of the Ramistic logic and rhetoric.

The division into deliberative, forensic, and epideictic that was conventional in the classical period of rhetoric was carried forward into the Renaissance in both the Ciceronian and Aristotelian traditions; but it must not be thought of as an absolute division that excluded other categories or taxonomies.[4] Besides, sixteenth-century lawyers learned some rhetoric at the universities (which increasing numbers of them attended before beginning their legal studies at an Inn of Chancery or Inn of Court), and some seem likely to have begun some kind of study of rhetoric first in an Inn of Chancery and then in an Inn of Court; others, we know, deepened their command of rhetoric by private study. Therefore we cannot assume that the same texts, methods, or concepts were uniform everywhere among sixteenth-century English lawyers.

sance of the Twelfth Century (1927, rpt. 1957), esp. chaps. 7, "The Revival of Jurisprudence," and 12, "The Beginnings of the Universities"; and H. Rashdall, The Universities of Europe in the Middle Ages, rev. ed. (Oxford, 1936), 1.208 ff. For an introduction to the sixteenth-century chapters of this story, see R. J. Schoeck, "Rhetoric and Law in Sixteenth-Century England," Studies in Philology 50 (1953), 110 – 27 —with the reply of D. S. Bland, "Rhetoric and the Law Student in Sixteenth-Century England," Studies in Philology 54 (1957), 498 – 508.

3. Quoting Brian Tierney: cf. Renaissance Quarterly vol. 20, no. 2 (1967), 279 – 91, "Report on Scholarship: Recent Scholarship in the History of Law."

4. For my rationale, see "On Rhetoric in Fourteenth-Century Oxford," Mediaeval Studies 30 (1968), 214 – 25.

To be sure, lawyers were primarily concerned with what we traditionally look for in forensic rhetoric, the persuasion towards judgment of past action, although they were involved in the other two areas of rhetoric as well: deliberative (to determine future courses of action, for lawyers dominated Parliament and other assemblies), and epideictic (the praise or blame of the past in terms of the existing, for lawyers were well represented in councils and as public orators). There are several kinds of questions: what was their training in rhetoric and which rhetorical texts were used, what were their educational forms and how did these relate to conventional forms, and what kind of role did the lawyers play in the development of rhetoric in Renaissance England? We shall first want to begin with what is known of the education in institutions of the lawyers, the Inns of Chancery and of Court. I shall then turn to examine, or at least to point to, the contribution to rhetoric of a small number of highly influential lawyers: Thomas More and his less well-known but distinguished and immensely influential adversary Christopher St. German, Sir Thomas Elyot, Sir Thomas Smith, and George Puttenham. Bacon and Coke, not to speak of Plowden, Caesar, Lambarde, and Egerton — all these would belong in a complete history of lawyers and rhetoric in Renaissance England, and we would want to continue the story to such scholars as that most learned man of his age, John Selden. But I must be selective, and I shall end my account with Puttenham in the 1570s.[5]

5. There are the two discrete disciplines of the history of Renaissance rhetoric and of the history of law in sixteenth-century England: until the Newberry Conference on Rhetoric in the Renaissance, the first had been very much neglected, and the second still is. A study of the relation of the two is very much *terra incognita.*

At the legal history conference at Aberystwyth (July 1972), J. H. Baker could still speak of "The Dark Age of English Legal History"—see his essay in *Legal History Studies 1972,* ed. Dafydd Jenkins (Cardiff, 1975), pp. 1–27 for a splendid survey of the state of the art. One may add the following: Wilfrid R. Prest, *The Inns of Court under Elizabeth I and the Early Stuarts, 1590–1640* (London, 1972); and Louis A. Knafla, *Law and Politics in Jacobean England: The Tracts of Lord Chancellor Ellesmere* (Cambridge, 1977), chap. 1 of which ("The Making of a Legal Mind") incorporates a good deal of his earlier *Huntington Library Quarterly* essay, "The Law Studies of an Elizabethan Student," *Huntington Library Quarterly* 32 (1969), 221–40. Elsewhere I have cited the vital work of Samuel E. Thorne on the readings in the Inns of Court (Selden Society, 1954). But the essential fact remains that we know very little as yet about the place of rhetoric or the kinds of rhetoric in the curriculum of the Inns and about the role of rhetoric in sixteenth-century English common law.

As for rhetoric in the universities and among humanists, I am happy to refer to the survey by Paul Oskar Kristeller on philosophy and rhetoric in his most recent

As I have written recently in *The State of Scholarship in Sixteenth-Century Literature* (1978), "the vital question of the relation of rhetoric and law — vital for traditional reasons and more specifically because of the role of lawyers in the writing and shaping of rhetoric in sixteenth-century England — remains pretty much where I left it in ...1953."[6]

Let us first consider some aspects of England's differences from the larger European movements. The uniqueness of the English common law and those still more extraordinary institutions, the Inns of Court, made for special developments in England. On the Continent the law schools were part of the universities; they were not so in England. On the Continent the civilians and canonists all shared with theologians and philosophers a common education in the liberal arts; this was not the case in the latter Middle Ages in England, and only in the sixteenth century did the custom begin to grow of attending Oxford or Cambridge first before attending the Inns — as Thomas Elyot and Coke recommended, and as Thomas More and so many other leading lawyers had done.[7] Besides, in England the language of lawyers' education and technical writing was law French, not the universal Latin.[8]

Renaissance Thought and Its Sources (New York, 1979), pp. 242–59, with bibliographical notes on pp. 323–27.

6. "English Literature," in *The State of Scholarship in Sixteenth-Century Literature,* ed. William M. Jones (Columbia, Mo., 1978), p. 122.

7. See Prest, *Inns of Court;* and B. Vickers, *Francis Bacon and Renaissance Prose* (Cambridge, 1968), p. 272.

In this study I am primarily, but not exclusively, interested in common lawyers. Given that many individual common lawyers were also at some stage of their careers also students of the civil law, and given that in a number of courts in Renaissance England there was an overlap of common lawyers and civilians, one could not assume that there were closed compartments here (or elsewhere) in the study and practice of law. Knafla, to cite but one example, has indicated that Egerton not only cited precedents from Justinian but "later he would use such works to make occasional analogies between the rules of common and civil law" (*Law and Politics,* p. 40). For the Continent there is the excellent work of Donald R. Kelley in *Foundations of Historical Scholarship* (New York, 1970). At the end of the century in England, a legal scholar and humanist like Gabriel Harvey was a close student of civil law, common law, and rhetoric (as Virginia Stern has recently demonstrated in *Gabriel Harvey: A Study of His Life, Marginalia, and Library* [Oxford, 1979]). We must guard against facile compartmentalizations with lawyers of the caliber of Thomas More, Christopher St. German, Francis Bacon, Edward Coke, and many others as well.

8. For a convenient summary of the history of law French, see my article in *The New Catholic Encyclopedia* (New York, 1967).

The reception of the Roman law on the Continent had a wider influence than meets the eye, for reception influenced not only the lawyers and judges, but also—as Gilmore and others have shown—the political thinkers, and it continued to influence theologians, as it had done from the earliest years of the Church; and because reception brought with it a well-established mode of thinking and its own rhetorical traditions, it influenced style greatly.[9] Thus Rabelais must be seen as reacting against the style and habits of thought as well as simply the catalogues of books of the canonists and civilians; yet thousands of others who had been, like Rabelais, trained in the two laws, did not question Bartolus and the glossators. The revolt against the Italian mode, the *mos italicus*, began early in the sixteenth century with Budé, Alciati, and others; but even with humanist-masters like Bodin, the *mos gallicus* never completely displaced the older *mos italicus*, even in France.[10]

In a full history of lawyers and rhetoric in the Renaissance, there are, or will be, many other confluences and collocations to comment upon. Lawyers were among the earliest builders of libraries in the Renaissance, as I have noted in *Manuscripta* (1962), and the great libraries like that of Coke, for which we have the catalogue, clearly demonstrate the breadth of learning—if we needed such external verification. It is well known that earlier in the century, such lawyers as St. German in England or Busleiden and Budé on the Continent built great libraries. Sir Edward Coke had in his library Aristotle's and Quintilian's rhetorics, several grammars and books of logic, a "Fiore della Retorica" (1560), some Cicero, and a book of elocution—*Catalogue of the Library of Sir Edward Coke*, ed. W. O. Hassall, with preface by S. E. Thorne (New Haven, Conn., 1950), pp. 61ff. As Professor Thorne remarks, the catalogue proves Coke a more widely read man than has been suspected ("Rhetoric and Law in Sixteenth-Century England," p. 127). The question of what editions of and therefore what commentaries on Cicero, Quintilian and others they studied

9. Myron P. Gilmore, *Argument from Roman Law in the Political Thought 1200 – 1600* (Cambridge, Mass., 1941, rpt. 1967).

The question of the so-called reception of the Roman law into English common law of the Renaissance, argued so brilliantly by Maitland, has recently been challenged by S. E. Thorne—but that is a question outside the province of this essay.

10. See first of all Linton C. Stevens, "The Contribution of French Jurists to the Humanist of the Renaissance," *Studies in the Renaissance* 1 (1954), 92 – 105. For a history of the *mos gallicus* in a larger framework, see Donald R. Kelley, *Foundations*, cited above, note 7. For Rabelais (a critical figure) see Enzo Nardi, *Rabelais e il Diritto Romano* (Milan, 1962), which deals also with the correspondence with Budé.

and themselves annotated has yet to be investigated. We know that, although Quintilian was not often specified in school curricula, he was widely read, and Puttenham records (as Vickers has noted) the following anecdote:

> I have come to the Lord Keeper *Sir Nicholas Bacon,* & found him sitting in his gallery alone with the works of Quintilian before him, in deede he was a most eloquent man, and of rare learning and wisedome, as ever I knew England to breed....[11]

Lawyers in England studied their classical rhetoric long before the time of Thomas More, and in fact the relation between law and rhetoric may already have had a firm tradition before Chaucer (who studied both) and John Gower. But clearly Sir John Fortescue (1394? – 1476?) wrote his *De laudibus legum Angliae* and his last work, *The Governaunce of England,* with a rich sense of the tradition of which I have been speaking. Whether he learned his rhetoric mainly in early fifteenth-century Oxford (where he is supposed to have been educated in Exeter College) or in a more technical way in early fifteenth-century Lincoln's Inn, Fortescue was a master of the English language as well as Latin — and of course law French — and his style merits study for its mastery of traditional rhetoric. The *OED* and *MED* credit Fortescue with the earliest instances for such words as *abating, incorporation, tributory, feasable, depopulation, miscounselling, importunity,* and he has usages earlier than the first recording in the *OED* of *body politic, borrowing, deserved, proportioned,* and *impoverish.*[12] All of this manifests a remarkable creativity in the language, yet without going to the extremes of aureate diction that was so much the vogue in fifteenth-century England, with its Lydgates and Hoccleves, or in fifteenth-century Latin in England, with its *verborum florida venustas* of the clerks (of which E. F. Jacob has written so well).[13] Stylistically, Fortescue is very much a pioneer in English in his use of balance and parallelism, repetition, and what has been called syntactical

11. *The Arte of English Poesie,* eds. G. D. Willcock and A. Walker (Cambridge, 1936), p. 140.

12. I am here indebted to the section on language in Winifred G. Keaney's *The Governance of England* (Ph.D. diss., University of Maryland, 1975) and to D. S. Bland, "Sir John Fortescue's Vocabulary," *Notes and Queries* 196 (1951), 529 – 30.

13. See H. S. Bennett, *Chaucer and the Fifteenth Century* (Oxford, 1947), chap. 6; and E. F. Jacob, "Verborum Florida Venustas," in *Essays in the Conciliar Epoch,* rev. ed. (Manchester, 1953), with its stress on clerks and letter books. "In every age convention has dictated the tone and phrasing of letters and speeches, but in few epochs has it been so much king in learned, that is Latin, composition" (p. 185).

correlation — which is not Vickers's "syntactical symmetry," but rather an appropriateness of syntax to meaning, or style to purpose. Fortescue's explication of a system of universal order — to cite but one example — merits being placed in the company of Elyot's description in book 1 of *The Governour*, and of Hooker's in book I of *On the Laws of Ecclesiastical Polity*; and indeed Tillyard, in his well-known *Elizabethan World Picture*, quotes extensively from Fortescue's account in his *De natura legis naturae*, a neglected work on natural law theory. Fortescue masters a convincing argument in prose: we can ask no more of rhetoric and its students.

What is known about education in the early Tudor Inns of Court is frustratingly little: we have no curricula, no book prescriptions, few documents to indicate how the teaching was done. There is in fact no documentary evidence to indicate that rhetoric was taught within the four Inns of Court themselves.

But we do know several immensely important things about education in the Inns: first, that all practicing lawyers took part in that education during their own years of practicing law — that the learning-teaching relationship came to an end only with the promotion to serjeant, at which time the lawyer withdrew from his Inn and became a member of Serjeants' Inn. Second, we know a fair amount about the teaching method of the Inns: there was a great stress on argument and upon the special forms of moots and bolts (of which I shall say more); and this stress leads, almost unmistakably, to the conclusion that there must have been rhetorical training somewhere along the line: at the universities, if the student went there first, or in one of the subsidiary Inns of Chancery, where he certainly would have gone had he not attended university and probably would have attended even with one or more years of university education — or perhaps in the Inns of Court proper, though it seems more likely that there would be some trace in the records if that had been the case.

Much of the student's time (as I have outlined elsewhere) was taken up in learning statutes and cases: lawyers since time immemorial have always stressed *memoria* (witness Chaucer's Man of Law):

> In termes hadde he caas and doomes alle
> That from the tyme of Kyng William were yfalle.
> Therto, he coulde endite and make a thing,
> Ther coulde no wight pinche at his writyng;
> And every statut coude he pleyn by rote. (GP. 325 – 29)

In his most useful book *Francis Bacon and Renaissance Prose,* Brian Vickers has made an important contribution in his analysis of division: of the distinction between *partitio* and *divisio,* and then of the centrality of partition among lawyers, and therefore of the importance of law in rhetoric. Jardine goes so far as to say that "Cicero and Quintilian are concerned first and foremost with the study of law and techniques of legal argument." On the question of *partitio,* Vickers writes:

> But in addition to these channels [the schools, and so forth] there was another source of influence open to Bacon, and one which (considering the amount of time and energy which he devoted to it) has been too much neglected by his critics, that of the Law. Although some of the stages of transmission have yet to be studied in detail it seems clear that the use of *partitio* in legal rhetoric continues (despite intermediary breaks) from Cicero and Quintilian to Bacon and Coke in substantially the same form. The whole question of rhetoric's influence on legal oratory does not seem to have excited the interest of legal historians. . . .[14]

The major exercise for the student came — after attendance at Westminster Hall and after much work with actual cases — in the moots and bolts, which was essentially an elaborate case argument; and with utter-barristers sitting as judges and students acting as opposing counsel, there was apparently all of the atmosphere of a mock trial. The importance can be seen in the proliferation of kinds of moots: petty and grand, chapel, hall, library, and such — but the general principle of function seems to have been much the same. Cases were formulated by the barristers, and the arguments by the students then proceeded. Sir Thomas Elyot discusses moots as "a shadowe or figure of the auncient rhetoricke" in *The Governour* (Croft ed., 1.148–49), thereby emphasizing in yet another way the traditional relation of law and rhetoric.

The readings in the Inns have been called the most ceremonious and sophisticated exercises, and here I would turn to Sir William Dugdale's seventeenth-century account:

> After much pomp and ceremony, the Reader's assistant begins:
> the Sub-Lecturer doth first, with an audible voice, read over the statute or at least that branch of it, that he hath chosen to read on. This ended, the *Reader* begins with a grave speech, excusing his own

14. Brian Vickers, *Sir Francis Bacon and Renaissance Prose* (Cambridge, 1968), p. 39.

weakness, with desire of their favourable censures; and concluding with the Reasons, wherefore he made choice of that Statute: Then he delivers unto them his divisions made upon the Statute, which are more or fewer, as he pleaseth; and then puts ten or twelve Cases upon his first division; of the which, the puisne Cupboardman, before spoken of, makes choice of one to argue, being followed in turn by the senior members of the Society, the Reader having the last word to "maintain his own conclusion." The exercise would be repeated after dinner, and the Reader would proceed through his various divisions during the Reading, which usually lasted two weeks, on alternate days. . . . [15]

Regulations required participation by the student-lawyers in the learning exercises — dialectical, formalistic, highly traditional — that were peculiar to the Inns, and that were analogous to the scholastic disputations. (Indeed, comparisons between serjeants and doctors, between readings and disputations, occur in more than one treatise.) These exercises obviously developed great skill in developing arguments *pro* and refuting those *contra,* and at the heart of the matter was the great use of division. I take this skill to be the force of Sir Thomas Smith's mid-century exclamation over the skill of the young common lawyers:

> In an inaugural lecture at Cambridge Sir Thomas Smith, Professor of Roman Civil Law (who was a contemporary with Plowden as Master of the Bench at the Middle Temple), exclaimed upon the skill in disputation shown by the students of English law at the Inns of Court. Their skill extended to matters of philosophy and theology: "Etiam cum quid e philosophia, theologiave depromptum in quaestione ponatur, Deus bone! quam apte, quamque explicate singula resumunt, quanta cum facilitate et copia, quantaque cum gratia et venustate, vel confirmant sua, vel refellunt aliena! Certe nec dialecticae vim multum in eis desideres, nec eloquentiae splendorem."[16]

Though what I have sketched is only a part of a still more complex whole — a whole that included revels, as a constituent element in which drama had a key role (in ways that we do not yet fully understand) — it was, all in all, a highly technical, formalistic education that was tradition, *mutatis mutandis,* from the time of Fortescue in the fifteenth century to that of Selden in the seventeenth. The descrip-

15. Ibid., p. 40.
16. As quoted in Richard O'Sullivan, *The Inheritance of the Common Law* (London, 1950), p. 45.

tions of the Inns and the education within them that we find in Fortescue are remarkably like those in Dugdale.[17]

Let me now turn to some lawyers of the sixteenth century, and first to Christopher St. German. Little known outside the history of common law, Christopher St. German exercised an enormous influence upon the development of the law in England. Born mid-fifteenth century and living until 1540, St. German was a barrister of the Inner Temple who was well read in the common law and also some aspects of canon law; and he was deeply interested, as the recent edition by J. B. Trapp of Thomas More's reply to him in *The Apology* indicates, in the religious controversies of his time and in such theologians and religious writers as Jean Gerson and St. Gertrude. Much influenced by Gerson, he studied the development of equity from Aristotle through certain medieval thinkers, and he tried to apply it to correct and supplement rules of English law. St. German embodied his ideas in two dialogues between a doctor of divinity, expressing the canon law, and a student of the common law, a serjeant. Although originally published in Latin under another title, it is generally known by the English title of *Doctor and Student,* and from 1530 until the twentieth century there were several editions, and it was cited by every writer on equity down to the time of Blackstone in the eighteenth century. We can sum up three reasons for its importance: First, "the English version of the first dialogue put into a popular and intelligible form the canonist learning as to the reason for the existence of a system of equity," and the answer was found in conscience, "the executive agent in the work of applying equity to the individual hard cases which were brought before the Chancellor" (thus Holdsworth).[18] It was thus the basis and starting-point of the English system of equity. Second, the timing was opportune, for it came at the end of the period of ecclesiastical chancellors and the beginning of the development of equity by the common lawyers; and *Doctor and Student* figures significantly in promoting continuity in the development of equity. Third, the canonist principles of equity were expressed clearly in a popular form — which is to say that the rhetoric of St. German was most successful, although it remains unstudied.

17. See the work of Knafla, Prest, and others, cited above.

18. Sir William Holdsworth, *History of English Law,* 2nd ed. (London, 1937), 5.266–67; Paul Vinogradoff, "Reason and Conscience in Sixteenth-century Jurisprudence," *LQR,* 24 (1908) 374.

The controversy between More and St. German is one of the two or three great controversies of the sixteenth century, and More clearly regarded St. German (who wrote anonymously) as a major threat to orthodoxy and the establishment; each of the controversialists employed a wide range of polemical techniques, and there is much that yet needs study. But I cannot pass on without calling attention to two or three areas in More himself that have not received sufficient study. A good deal of further analysis and investigation is called for with More's letters.[19] More's masterful rhetoric in his letter to Oxford is well known, but it is worthy of observation that More had had only two years at Oxford: may we not inquire whether a good deal of the rhetoric employed so magnificently in this letter may not have been learned *after* leaving Oxford? (Possibly in private studies with Erasmus and others, and possibly, too, in his studies in the Inns of Court—Lincoln's Inn.) Another rhetorical matter to which I merely call attention is that of the kind of, or reason for, More's citation of rhetorical authorities. When Cicero is cited by More in the *Utopia*, for example, it is on the question of laws (Yale ed., 164/20 – 1): More was richly aware of the extent to which Cicero was concerned with the study of law, as well as with legal argument (I am adverting to Jardine's observation cited earlier). We are, to summarize, still lacking a thorough study of either the rhetoric or law of Thomas More, one of the century's consummate rhetoricians and lawyers.

Sir Thomas Elyot's *The Boke of the Governour* is celebrated as "the first book on the subject of education written and published in the English language" (thus Foster Watson, in the introduction to his 1907 Everyman edition, p. xi). But let us emphasize also that it is a book that is centrally concerned with law and justice, and that it is written for lawyers and governors. I have commented on the importance of Elyot's work in my earlier essay, "Rhetoric and Law in Sixteenth-Century England" (*Studies in Philology*, 50 [1953]), and I will simply repeat that a whole chapter in book 1 (chap. 14) is devoted to the study of the law, and that book 3 is concerned initially, and I think primarily, with justice.

Perhaps the most significant synthesis of law and rhetoric in the sixteenth century is to be found in the work of Thomas Wilson — a civilian and an advocate of the arches, as well as ambassador, privy councillor, secretary of state, and lay dean of Durham—whose ex-

19. See Richard J. Schoeck, *The Achievement of Thomas More* (Victoria, B.C.: University of Victoria, 1976).

tremely influential *Arte of Rhetorique* of 1553 was reprinted seven times before the end of the century and has been termed "the only English rhetoric of the sixteenth century which goes beyond translation or close paraphrase." A doctor of civil law of the University of Ferrara and master of requests, Wilson was as a civilian outside the common law tradition, yet in his *Arte of Rhetorique* he has the highest regard for that tradition.[20]

At the beginning of the *Arte of Rhetorique*, Wilson states that the orator "must be able to speake fully of al those questions, which by lawe & mans ordinance are enacted," and the marginal gloss emphasizes: "Rhetorique occupied about all lawes, concerning man." In a somewhat conventional fashion law and justice are worked into the discussion of an oration demonstrative (17 ff.), and an Oration deliberative (29 ff.): thus the law is honest, godly, profitable, and necessary. Therefore Wilson advises one "to studie the lawes of England":

> Againe, when we see our frend enclined to any kind of learning, we must counsaile him to take that way still, and by reason perswade him, that it were the meetest way for him to doe his Countrie most good. As if he giue his minde to the lawes of the Realme, and finde an aptnesse thereunto, we may aduise him, to continue in his good entent, and by reason perswade him, that it were most meete for him so to do. And first we might shewe him that the studie is honest and godly, considering it onely foloweth Iustice, and is grounded wholy vpon naturall reason (p. 31).

For Wilson declares that the law maintains and safeguards the commonweal:

> Take away the Law, and take away our liues, for nothing maintaineth our wealth, our health, and the saueguard of our bodies, but the Law of a Realme, whereby the wicked are condemned, and the Godly are defended (pp. 38–39).

The discussion of an oration judicial (86 ff.) is traditional; in analyzing the point in question or debate between contending parties, and considering the division of states, Wilson employs the rhetorical *state* rather than the legal *issue* or *case*. His sections on interpretation of a law (94 ff.) do not use the legal jargon of law French, as the common lawyer would, and his explanation of "chalenging or refusing" seems rather from the point of view of a civilian. Yet he is not as biased or

20. See Schoeck, "Rhetoric and Law," p. 118.

prejudiced as many of his fellow civilians were — for this was, it must be remembered, a period of conflict between the common law and the civil law, a conflict which began under Wolsey, was mollified by More, and smouldered during the century — and his account of "chalenging or refusing" (that is, appeal from common pleas to Chancery, p. 97) is objective enough. Wilson seems to write with a desire to appeal not only to the civilian but also to the common lawyer; there is nothing of the partisan feeling of Starkey's earlier *Dialogue,* or even his own *Discourse upon Usury.*[21]

Here again we find that crossing of lines between the common and civil law of which I have spoken earlier.

One must of course point out that the emphasis on law that we find in the *Rhetorique* was to some extent ready at hand for Wilson in Quintilian, in Cicero's rhetorical writings, and in the *Rhetorica ad Herennium,* but it is Wilson's desire to make traditional rhetoric available and applicable to the needs of his own times that gives this emphasis on law its place in his writings when we do not find it, so conspicuously, in the earlier rhetoricians of the Renaissance. And this desire to fit traditional rhetoric to the needs of his times is also apparent, of course, in Wilson's linking of rhetoric and preaching. Crane has declared that "it was principally for young noblemen who did not have time and patience to master rhetoric from the Latin textbooks that Thomas Wilson compiled his *Arte of Rhetorique,* 1553." I would suggest that for a large part of his intended audience Wilson had in mind the young noblemen and gentlemen who were students at the Inns of Court; this is supported by the legal content and the frequent resorting to legal experience for illustration, and by the dedication. Though Wilson, again, is writing to make rhetoric serve contemporary needs and is addressing those professions which especially spoke, and wrote: preachers and statesmen-diplomats — one should remember, however, that a large part of the diplomatic and political ranks were filled from the Inns of Court.

We may find it surprising that a humanist like Wilson should be so much the lawyer in a rhetorical treatise, and perhaps even more surprising that Wilson, a civilian, should make so much use of the common law and think so highly of it. But he was of Elyot's metal, and bore the same stamp of the older humanism of men like More: in the words of Mair, "he was one of a band of grave and dignified scholars,

21. Ibid., pp. 119–20.

men preoccupied with morality and citizenship as well as with the lighter problems of learning and style," and in Tawney's view, "Wilson for all his scholarship, belonged to the older tradition, the tradition which held that 'this is the true ordering of the state of a well-fashioned commonwealth, that every part do obey one head, one governor, one law, as all parts of the body obey the head, agree among themselves, and one not to eat up another through greediness, and that we see that order, moderation, and reason bridle the affections'" — a tradition of men whose social philosophy (and theories of communication) was based ultimately on religion, therefore on an order of law and justice:

> For by an order we are borne, by an order we liue, and by an order
> we make our ende. By an order [one ruleth] as head, and other obey
> as members. By an order Realmes stande, and Lawes take force . . .
> (pp. 156 – 57).[22]

Sir Thomas Smith (1513 – 1577) did not leave us an important book of rhetoric, although he did write a vitally important book in the sphere of politics. Smith's *De republica Anglorum* (STC 22857) was first published in 1583 and enlarged in 1589, and it was frequently reprinted. In 1610 there was a new continental edition in Latin — "nunc primum J. buddeni fide in Latinum conversi" (STC 22868) — which provides some evidence both to the continuing importance of Latin and to new motives for now presenting the work in Latin. Outside Smith's career as diplomat and councillor to Queen Elizabeth, he is significant in the history of scholarship primarily for his endeavor to reform Greek pronunciation at Cambridge. But there is an importance to his testimony concerning rhetoric that we must note here. Smith had been a scholar and fellow of Queen's College, Cambridge, and received the M.A. in 1533, then was made public orator at Cambridge in 1538; he studied at Paris and Padua, from which university he received the D.C.L. In his inaugural lecture as Henry VIII's first Regius Professor of Civil Law at Cambridge (1544), Smith exclaimed at the eloquence and skill in disputation shown by the students of the Inns — and Smith was not a common lawyer himself. *Deus bone!* he exclaimed: praising their skill — as I have already quoted in discussing legal education. Evidence of this kind, although it cannot be used to prove a case, is immensely valuable in supporting and color-

---

22. Ibid., pp. 120 – 21. One should note Wilson's long commendation of justice.

ing what we know from other kinds of evidence, and again it enables us to conclude that many things besides law were taught — including rhetoric.

With George Puttenham we come to one who was born in a legal family — he was related to the Elyot family (the nephew of Sir Thomas Elyot), to Sir James Dyer the judge and legal writer, and to the Throckmortons — and he was himself a lawyer. He was, as Willcock and Walker observe in their introduction to the 1936 edition of *The Arte of English Poesie,* "at the Middle Temple in the late fifties when the Inns of Court were the chief centre of literary activity" (p. xxii). In Puttenham's *Arte,* there are many anecdotes relating to the law courts and lawyers, as well as frequent references to Cicero and Quintilian. His references to legal practice and oratory are worth our observation.

It quickly becomes evident — and especially from his many illustrations drawn from the law — that Puttenham's sense of *poesie* is more nearly that of a Sidney than, let us say, of a Francis Meres. The legal anecdotes, perhaps a dozen in number, in general illustrate the effects of rhetoric, and there are several that have to do with oratory more specifically. I shall draw upon two developed anecdotes for comment. The first occurs in the third book, "Ornament" (Willcock and Walker ed., p. 233), where Puttenham refers to *expeditio,* or the speedy dispatcher:

> This is done [that is, achieving a quick and swift argument] by manner of speech, both figurative and argumentative, when we do briefly set downe all our best reasons serving the purpose, and reject all of them saving one, which we accept to satisfie the cause: as he that in a litigious case for land would proove it not the adversaries, but his clients.

> No man can say its his by heritage,
> Nor by Legacie, or Testatours device:
> Nor that it came by purchase or engage,
> Nor from his Prince for any good seruice.
> The needs must it be his by very wrong,
> Which he hath offred this poore plaintife so long.

A second illustration Puttenham develops in discussing, in chapter 2 of the same book, "How our writing and speeches publike ought to be figurative, and if they be not doe greatly disgrace the cause and purpose of the speaker and writer" (p. 138). Puttenham, in a long quotation which merits reading in its entirety, turns to the law for effect:

> And though grave and wise councillors in their consultations doe not use much superfluous eloquence, and also in their judiciall hearings do much mislike all scholasticall rhetoricks: yet in such a case as it may be (and as this Parliament was) if the Lord Chancelour of England or Archbishop of Canterbury himself were to speake, he ought to doe it cunningly and eloquently, which can not be without the use of figures: and neverthelesse none impeachment or blemish to the gravitie of their persons or of the cause: wherein I report me to them that knew Sir *Nicholas Bacon* Lord keeper of the great Seale, or the now Lord Treasorer of England [Pawlet?], and have bene conversant with their speeches made in the Parliament house & Starrechamber. From whose lippes I have seene to proceede more grave and natural eloquence, then from all the Oratours of Oxford or Cambridge, but all is as it is handled, and maketh no matter whether the same eloquence be naturall to them or artificiall (though I thinke rather naturall) yet were they knowen to be learned and not unskilfull of th'arte, when they were yonger men: and as learning and arte teacheth a schollar to speake, so doth it also teach a counsellour, and aswell an old man as a yong, and a man in authoritie, aswell as a private person, and a pleader [lawyer] aswell as a preacher, every man after his sort and calling as best becometh: and that speach which becommeth one, doth not become another, for maners of speaches, some serve to work in excesse, some in mediocritie, some to grave purposes, some to light, some to be short and brief, some to be long, some to stirre up affections, some to pacifie and appease them, and these common despisers of good utterance, which resteth altogether in figurative speaches, being well used whether it comes by nature or by arte or by exercise, they be but certaine grosse ignorants of whom it is truly spoken *scientia non habet inimicum nisi ignorantem.*   (pp. 139–40)

And then, as we have already seen, after these two long sentences Puttenham describes his coming upon Sir Nicholas Bacon with the works of Quintilian.

The humanistic qualities of *The Arte of English Poesie* indeed link it with Elyot's *Governour,* Wilson's *Arte of Rhetorique,* and Ascham's *Scholemaster,* that is to say, with humanistic forms like the dialogue and humanistic essay rather than with scholastic and quasi-scholastic forms like the manual (to bring to bear the most useful division of Alain Michel). And although *The Arte of English Poesie* is one of the least utilitarian of humanistic treatises, it nonetheless offers a sense of the varying roles of rhetoric among the lawyers — in the courts, with clients, and in council chambers — that is unique in English Renaissance literature.

Much more needs to be said about a number of mutual concerns of law and rhetoric. Even the study of *topoi* will throw light on what Vickers has called "the continuing mutual influence between rhetoric and law."[23] Thus, as Vickers further notes, the "modesty formula" (or humility *topos*) was originally derived, as in Quintilian IV.i.8, from judicial oratory; and there is need to inquire into the continuing role of that *topos* among lawyers, as well as characteristic employments of other *topoi*. There is the quite complex question of *status*, where there is a difference of more than emphasis between the usages of lawyers and of rhetoricians. There is the question of axioms and maxims, and while historians of the civil law enjoy Peter Stein's lovely study of Roman maxims, we have little comparable for common lawyers; the fondness of many common lawyers and judges, as reported especially in the Yearbooks, for proverbs and tales is closely related but of course distinguishable. There is the question of interpretation, and in the sixteenth century we find commentators like Edmund Plowden reaching into the techniques for scriptural exegesis to discover tools for explicating and interpreting statutes; I know of nothing that compares interpretation of common and civil law in the sixteenth century. And finally there is the vast area of equity, for the continuing development of which common lawyers who followed St. German went back to Aquinas, and to Cicero,[24] and to Aristotle; and the more scholarly lawyers explored the commentaries on this question (as I shall note in my commentary on Thomas More's controversies with St. German, specifically in the *Debellation*). These are questions that I merely name yet wish to identify as needing further study both for their own importance and as contributions to our fuller understanding of the complex relations between rhetoric and the law in Renaissance England.

The Tudor lawyers, we may conclude, needed and valued their rhetoric. We twentieth-century scholars who wish to understand more fully the manifold role of rhetoric in Tudor society, government, thought, and letters must give fuller account of those lawyers and their part in the continuing development of rhetoric in the Ren-

23. Vickers, p. 272.
24. The role of Cicero in bridging the territories of rhetoricians and lawyers needs fuller study, and the revival of Stoicism later in the sixteenth century produces further currents of thought.

aissance. I have named only a few of these lawyers and have not discussed any of them with fullness; and while it is clear that Fortescue, More, St. German, Elyot, Smith, Wilson, Puttenham, Bacon, and Coke deserve much greater study and merit full scope in any history of Renaissance rhetoric, there are many others who, for diverse reasons, must at least be named in a closing summary to a jury of readers: Abraham Fraunce (that most romantic of Ramists), William Fulbeck, William Lambarde (whose charges to juries merit editing), John Hoskins, Gabriel Harvey, and others. Above all we must bear in mind that rhetoric must have been useful to lawyers in many ways: to discover the means of persuasion available, to organize (and as Knafla has shown for Egerton, there is a kind of rhetoric of study), to persuade, to fix in the memory, and lastly to ornament speech and writing.

In his foreword to *Lee's Lieutenants,* written at the end of many years of reading army reports and countless letters and journals, Douglas Southall Freeman writes that "At first, one had the feeling that these Confederates had ridden so far toward oblivion that one could not discern the figures or hope to overtake them before they had passed over the horizon of time." So too with these often obscure lawyers, from whose books, readings, commonplace books, and other writings and records one may begin to develop names into personalities, and whose *litera scripta* begin to take on the sound of a voice. "In the end," to quote again from Freeman, "there was a sensation of reaching their camp, of watching the firelight on their faces, and of hearing their brave and genial conversation." So too with the Tudor lawyers: we move towards a glimpse of them in the great halls of the Inns in a moot or reading and we begin to understand them at work in the candlelight, with a Quintilian or Cicero open on the table before them. They were men of learning and wisdom, and they knew when and how to be eloquent.

Pascal's Arts of Persuasion

HUGH M. DAVIDSON

The second edition of the Port Royal *Logique ou art de penser* appeared in 1664, two years after the death of Pascal. At the bottom of page 341, printed as a note, one finds an interesting sentence that begins: "Feu Mr Pascal, qui savait autant de véritable rhétorique que personne en ait jamais su. . . ." In a way my remarks are no more than a comment on that tribute: I have come to the conclusion that Pascal's own analyses and practice make it useful for us to distinguish between two and perhaps even three approaches to rhetoric, each leading to works different in structure and texture.

The *opuscule* entitled *De l'esprit géométrique* is a good place to begin. It is made up of one short and two long fragments, totaling about thirty pages. The history of these texts is complicated and unclear. There is a case to be made for believing that Pascal composed them as he was drafting the preface for a work that he later abandoned, *Essai d'éléments de géométrie*. Unfinished and uneven as they are, certain pages of these fragmentary texts give us, nonetheless, some invaluable starting points.

The first thing to note is that Pascal is invariably concerned with the truth. His art or arts of persuasion cannot be understood unless we take fully into account his conviction that art and its efficacy are interesting only insofar as they serve truth. He writes at the start of the first fragment:

> On peut avoir trois principaux objets dans l'étude de la vérité:
> l'un de la découvrir quand on la cherche; l'autre de la démontrer

quand on la possède; le dernier, de la discerner d'avec le faux quand on l'examine.

Je ne parle point du premier: je traite particulièrement du second, et il enferme le troisième.[1]

To tell us what it means to demonstrate the truth and by implication to separate it from error, Pascal turns at once to geometry, for it alone among human sciences observes the true method and produces unerring demonstrations that compel assent. Then later, as he takes up the art of persuasion, he assimilates *persuader* to *démontrer,* a radical tactic signalling that rhetoric apart from truth and quasi-geometrical inference is a waste of time.

Especially interesting for us is the analysis of the process of assent. He introduces the subject by establishing a fundamental distinction: "L'art de persuader a un rapport nécessaire à la manière dont les hommes consentent à ce qu'on leur propose, et aux conditions des choses qu'on veut faire croire" (p. 355). My acquaintance with the works of Pascal leads me to think that the mechanism of assent is never far from his mind. What are the factors and stages involved in it?

There are two entrances whereby opinions come into the soul: understanding and will. The more natural way is via the understanding, and then assent is to demonstrated truths; but the commoner way, though contrary to nature, is via the will, which is motivated to assent or consent not by proof but by pleasure. These two powers, *entendement* and *volonté,* have characteristic principles and prime movers of their operations. Each power, in fact, starts with principles of two kinds, universal and particular. Thus, in the case of the mind, starting points are found either in truths accepted by every one, such as that contained in the statement "the whole is greater than any of its parts" or in what Pascal calls *axiomes particuliers;* and these are received by some but not by all, though once admitted they are just as powerful in causing belief as the universal principles. Similarly, in the will, starting points are found either in certain natural desires that all men have — such as the desire to be happy — or in what Pascal calls *objets particuliers* that we pursue as the means to happiness; and once assumed, these limited objectives work on the will with just as much force as does the end of true happiness. It is worth remarking here that the second category in each instance — the particular axioms or

1. Pascal, *Oeuvres complètes,* ed. L. Lafuma (Paris, 1963), p. 348. All page references are to this edition ("l'Intégrale").

aims — have negative values: Pascal says that they are as powerful as the natural (and universal) truths or desires, in spite of being false or pernicious.

After his discussion of men and their powers of consent, Pascal turns to the second major piece in his argument, having to do with the conditions or qualities of things. The reasoning is perfectly symmetrical: opinions or truths can be imposed infallibly provided they can be established as consequences flowing from the natural and universal principles in the mind of the person to be persuaded. And objects or aims can be imposed certainly and necessarily if they are shown to be means to the happiness that we all desire above everything else.

There is one last and very important case to consider. Let us suppose that the things proposed for acceptance are based on truths known to us but are contrary to our favorite desires. Then the soul becomes the theater of a conflict between truth and pleasure, *vérité* and *volupté*. In such an instance, which happens to be very common, the outcome is uncertain. In order to know what he should do, the would-be persuader would have to know everything taking place in his listener, and not even the listener is likely to have that kind of insight. In a sense, all has been going smoothly to this point. The difficulty leads Pascal to qualify his argument: "De sorte que l'art de persuader consiste autant en l'art d'agréer qu'en celui de convaincre, tant les hommes se gouvernent plus par caprice que par raison!" (p. 356). He goes on to describe briefly an art of persuasion that would be nothing but an *art d'agréer*. It would know how to attach itself to any human wish or wishes, and not simply to those shared by all men. It would adapt itself perfectly to individuals and their caprices, and it would be extraordinarily effective. Pascal does not develop this line of thought. He says that he believes such an art exists at least in theory, but it is beyond his powers and he wonders if anyone is capable of getting it down in a treatise. In any case the art he has decided to sketch in the fragments is the one that builds on constant and universally shared ideas or values.

According to Pascal's conception of assent, everything depends on finding and assembling truths and means that have a demonstrable *rapport* with principles located in the audience. And so this art of persuasion will be sharply conscious of connections and relations among all elements that enter into its discourse. It will require a logical model that proposes rules for insuring precision in its statements, validity in its reasonings, and correct sequence in its elaborations. A generalized version of geometry will meet all these requirements. Pascal lays down three rules for definition, two for axioms, and three for demonstrations. Definitions must be explicit and univocal, axioms self-evident. In demonstrations one should move through all steps necessary to see the dependence of the propositions on the axioms and definitions. Pascal mentions a further step that is essential, though he never develops his idea: "Je passe maintenant à celle [la règle] de l'ordre dans lequel on doit disposer les propositions pour être dans une suite excellente et géométrique" (p. 357).

Such are the main points, it seems to me, in Pascal's theory of assent and the art of persuasion built on it. He passes over the unstable psychological and moral causes in the situation that escape control; he focuses his attention on the ones he can manipulate; he prepares to adapt his message to people and their circumstances; and he chooses a quasi-mathematical mode of discourse.

It is now time to look at Pascal's practice. The *Lettres provinciales* and the *Pensées*, both of which are full of methodological signals, return often to the distinctions we have been discussing; and the mechanism of assent holds for both works. And yet, Pascal introduces such basic changes of emphasis and procedure that I am inclined to say that we shall understand these two masterpieces better and see more interesting things in them if we study them as tending to embody specifically distinct arts of persuasion.

The letters are addressed by the anonymous author as follows: numbers 1– 10 to a "provincial de ses amis," a vaguely evoked friend who lives away from Paris and who wants to know what the disputes in the Sorbonne are about. For him and people of good sense like him, Pascal has enlightenment and reasssurance to offer. Numbers 11– 16 are addressed to the Jesuit fathers taken as a group, and numbers 17– 18 to the R. P. Annat, Louis XIV's confessor and a leader of the Jesuit group. For all these Pascal has charges of doctrinal error, moral laxism, and political intrigue.

We saw earlier that there are three things one can do with truth: discover it, demonstrate it, or separate it from error. The three aims are closely related, of course. But in the *Lettres provinciales* it seems fair to say that the problem is not to discover the truth — it is already known and articulated — but to discriminate it from falsehood. The rhetorical situation fits so well into the framework proposed in the fragments on the *Esprit géométrique* that one would expect Pascal to see the chance of using the concepts and the method advocated there. In my opinion there is much evidence to show that he did just that.

For one thing he seems to conceive of Christian doctrine as constituting itself in a linear fashion. It has taken on over the centuries the character of an axiomatic system having divinely supported starting points in the Bible, fundamental assumptions in the creeds, supplemental developments of theorems — that is, of propositions and positions justifying them — achieved by the Church Fathers and the great theologians, and further elaboration in the decisions of councils and popes. This great sequential synthesis of Scripture and tradition gives Pascal all the criteria he needs for judging the thought and actions of the Jesuits. At any point along the line, he may indicate conflicts with the new doctrines of the Jesuits: now the Gospels, now Saint Paul, now the Fathers are pitted against the casuists, and so on.

The quasi-geometrical way of posing and solving problems extends to even more detailed aspects of letters. In six of them (numbers 1, 2, 3, 4, 17, 18) the main subject is grace, and the problem or confusion is due to conflicting definitions: there is *grâce efficace, grâce suffisante, grâce actuelle* — and the related notion of *pouvoir prochain.* Pascal exposes without mercy the ambiguities and contradictions into which all parties to the dispute are drawn because of the failure to define these terms precisely and univocally. He evens turns up evidence to show that some Jesuits and New Thomists have agreed to use the phrase *pouvoir prochain* without assigning any sense to it.

In letters 5–10 Pascal turns to the *morale des jésuites.* Here the principles and decisions of the casuists are reported as *maximes,* in other words, as propositions. A new aspect of his logical model comes into view. What counts when one advances propositions is, of course, the proof or justification that lies behind them. Pascal has a field day with the Jesuit doctrine of *opinions probables,* which are justified by the reasoning and authority of those who write them. To him the issue is ultimately that of man's reasons versus God's reasons. Moreover, on any point opposed *opinions probables* tend to occur, which makes the principles of morality contradictory and leaves the sinner to choose the least burdensome opinion as his guide.

The *Lettres provinciales* show, then, how Pascal's first art of persuasion works. In them we follow an evolving rhetorical situation, along with the adjustments that ensue as the addressees change; we establish without difficulty the principal logical aim, which is separation of truth from falsehood; we see many signs of the model of reasoning Pascal had in the back of his mind — that of geometry; and as the letters succeed one another, we discern under the surface a compendent set of terms, statements, and positions to which additions have been and may be made, providing they respect the status of what is already in place and observe the strict etiquette of a generally deductive process.

Pascal addresses the first *Lettres provinciales* to those who share his convictions, inviting them to examine with him the views and behavior of the Jesuits. In the later *Provinciales,* without forgetting the readers who sympathize with him, he addresses his opponents directly and engages in a kind of duel with them, intending to expose their errors as before, but also to reduce them to confusion and silence. The situation changes fundamentally in the *Pensées.* The essence of the matter is indicated by the image of the *chercheur.* Men fall into three groups: (1) those who are not seekers; (2) those who are; and (3) those who have found. Clearly, Pascal will focus his efforts on the first group and attempt to turn them into seekers. They are indifferent or hostile to the Christian religion because they find it contrary to reason, unhelpful, unattractive. His art of persuasion has in this case the very specific task of reversing this negative attitude.

The logical aim here is not to discern the truth from falsity, though attention is given locally to the claims of philosophers and of rival religions; nor is it to discover truth, though in a sense the reader comes to see for himself what the apologist has seen before him. Pascal's objective is rather to *demonstrate* or, better, to *prove* the truth. I say that because if one studies his usage in the *Pensées,* one sees that he prefers by far to speak of *preuves* rather than of *démonstrations.* The means of persuasion that he proposes to his addressee are clusters of convergent proofs that are fitted to a mental and moral itinerary. It leads from uncertainty to a state of readiness for faith. This is the logic of the heart, the *ordre du coeur,* as used by Christ, Saint Paul, and Saint Augustine. Pascal defines it thus: "Cet ordre consiste à faire des digressions sur chaque point, qui a rapport à la fin, pour la montrer toujours."

Instead of using or building as before an axiomatic system, Pascal embarks on a dialectic of paradoxes and resolutions. The argument unfolds in two perspectives, depending on whether we are speaking of *l'homme sans Dieu* or *l'homme avec Dieu.* The meaning of every important word is fixed according to the contrary term to which it is bound and according to its point of emergence in one or the other perspective.

Here is an example. In the negative phase of the argument, man is the subject of contradictory tendencies, toward *misère* and toward *grandeur.* But in the positive phase the conflicting tendencies are transformed and reoriented: *misère* becomes *pénitence,* and *orgueil* becomes *humilité;* then these positive counterparts of the original terms are turned toward God as the unifying end. The fragment on the wager offers another example of this kind of conflict and resolution. Pascal's aim is to *ôter les obstacles.* The obstacles come from two sources, *l'esprit* and *le coeur.* The mind is brought, by the terms of the wager, to a provisional state of submission. It recognizes that betting on the existence of God is not contrary to reason. Similarly, the contrasting principle of the heart is brought by repeated acts and force of habit to a new moral disposition. By a kind of double *as if*—the mind thinking as if and the heart acting (or causing us to act) as if God exists—we reach a posture receptive to faith. Once more the antithetical tendencies of concupiscence and intellectual pride have been transformed and redirected toward the same end.

Of course Pascal knows that he cannot give faith: he can only prepare for it. With faith we enter the zone of God's initiative. In an important fragment Pascal tells us that there are three means of belief, *trois moyens de croire:* reason, habit, and inspiration. His *art de persuader* in the *Pensées* bears directly on the first two, and if they come to be rightly qualified, the apologist has accomplished his task. One thinks of Plato, whose rhetoric is transformed into dialectic so that one may reach an intuition of the Good; Pascal's rhetoric, likewise under the sway of dialectical procedures, is designed to make clear the *viam Domini,* to prepare his seeker for grace.

The contrast with what we have seen in the *Lettres provinciales* is so complete that I think we are justified in speaking of a second art of persuasion here. All the aspects of Pascal's method — initial situation, aim, typical form of argument, elaborations of particular points — have undergone essential changes. Perhaps the best way to sum up what has happened is this: in the *Lettres provinciales* we begin with certainty, with *évidences* like those of geometry that lend their compelling force to the consequences derived from them; whereas in the *Pensées* we begin with uncertainty, with contradictions that are resolved by stages into a synoptic view that is finally guaranteed by faith: for the certainty attained at the end works retroactively over all that has preceded.

The fate of rhetoric in the hands of Pascal illustrates events or choices that have occurred more than once in the history of the discipline. It is not easy to state the point briefly or unambiguously, but let me put it this way. He works changes both in the fundamental *subject matter* of rhetoric and in its *method*. As for subject matter: in schools, in the program of the French Academy, in the works of critics, poets, moralists, historians, even in some philosophers, a large place is made for rhetoric in the period from roughly 1635 to 1685. It is not hard to verify that statement in *belles-lettres,* but it holds for social intercourse as well. The subject matter of that literary rhetoric and of its extension into the moral code of *honnêteté* tends to be *words* and *actions,* which are judged according to the criterion of appropriateness or decorum. But words and actions are less real to Pascal than *things* or *beings*—in this he follows the scientific and theological preferences of the period in which he lived. Bodies are, minds are, hearts moved by charity are; and after things comes correct thought about things. Thus it is the mission of rhetoric to show—for discernment or for conversion—the path by which finite beings may be eventually united with an infinite Being.

As for method: here one may observe changes on two levels, one having to do with the status of rhetoric and the other with its constitutive principles. During the period in question the rhetoric of words and actions tends to become the discipline of disciplines, the fundamental attitude and technique from which other arts are derived and to which they are subordinated. Pascal reacts strongly against this trend; he knows that the *véritable rhétorique* is not universal in scope, nor is it independent in status: it follows from and extends some more basic discipline. Then the question becomes: On what will it be made to depend? Here Pascal joins Descartes, the Port Royalists, and other anti-Ciceronians in promoting geometry, and more precisely, its method to the place of honor. The old rhetoric of invention, arrangement, and elocution, of *agrément* and *bienséance,* must give way to the new and authentic rhetoric of definition, composition, and demonstrative sequences. There, it seems to me, is the intuition that guided Pascal in much of what we see in the *Lettres provinciales.* But that is not all. When Pascal moves from the polemic of the *Provinciales* to the apology of the *Pensées,* he is obliged to recognize that the *esprit de géométrie* will not work: it is too technical, too intellectual, too far from the reasons of the heart. Rhetoric remains, as before, in a subordinate place, but he shifts his allegiance from geometry and discourse in the Euclidean mode to theology and discourse after the manner of Saint Augustine. Persuasion turns on proofs rather than demonstrations, and the former art of precise definitions and linear reasoning must yield to a new rhetoric of analogical terms, of conflicts and resolutions: and there you have, it seems to me, the essential formula of much that we see in the *Pensées*.

Of course my contrast is too starkly drawn; it calls for qualification; it does not do justice to some significant points of contact and interpenetration. And I have set aside in the preceding analyses important aspects such as Pascal's dramatic imagery, his changing pathos, and other traits that join to give to the letters and fragments their extraordinary power. I have concentrated instead on the intellectual armature that underlies the qualities we find so impressive in Pascal's work.

I hope it is now clear that to analyze Pascal's arts of persuasion is also to become aware of certain typical revolutions in which rhetoric may be involved: changes in its subject matter; changes in its relative status among the intellectual disciplines; and changes in the models set for it when it is no longer the discipline of disciplines. Shifts such as those we have seen here in the works of one man are in fact *péripéties* that have recurred in the history of rhetoric and will no doubt continue to do so.

PART FOUR

Rhetoric
and Other
Literary Arts

Grammar and Rhetoric
in the Renaissance

W. KEITH PERCIVAL

Nonne satius est mutum esse quam quod nemo intellegat dicere?
Cicero, *Phil.* III.22, quoted by Valla, *Opera* (Basle, 1543, p.634)

By Renaissance grammar we mean the discipline *grammatica* as it was practiced by Renaissance humanists.[1] Grammar, in brief, was the branch of the *trivium* responsible for teaching students to speak and write Latin correctly.[2] Thus, a definition often cited in the Quattrocento reads: "Grammatica est scientia recte loquendi recteque scri-

1. The term *humanist* was, of course, not in general use in the Quattrocento. The vernacular *umanista* seems first to have referred to teachers of classical literature, later also to students. See A. Campana, "The Origin of the Word Humanist," *Journal of the Warburg and Courtauld Institutes* 9 (1946), 60 – 73; and R. Avesani, "La professione del-l'umanista nel Cinquecento," *Italia medioevale e umanistica* 13 (1970), 205 – 32. Terms such as *humanism, Humanismus, umanesimo,* and the like are, conversely, of very recent coinage.
2. That the concepts of "grammar" and "Latin" were closely related in the Renaissance is shown by the fact that the word *Latin* did not regularly appear in the titles of Latin grammars until late. The first grammarian who used the word in the title of a textbook seems to have been Antonio de Nebrija, but the practice did not become general until well into the sixteenth century. The humanists discovered, and quite early, that it is hardly possible to acquire a profound acquaintance with Roman antiquities without a thorough knowledge of Greek, and many of them studied the language assiduously and gained proficiency in it. But throughout the Renaissance and beyond, Latin remained the principal language in which humanistic studies were carried on. On the study of Greek and the vernacular languages during the Renaissance, see my article "The Grammatical Tradition and the Rise of the Vernaculars," in *Current Trends in Linguistics,* ed. Thomas A. Sebeok, *Historiography of Linguistics,* vol. 13 (The Hague, 1975), pp. 231 – 75; A. Pertusi, Ἐρωτήματα: per la storia e le fonti delle prime

bendi, origo et fundamentum omnium liberalium artium."[3] The subject was divided into four parts, each one dealing with one of the four basic grammatical units: orthography, with letters; prosody, with syllables; etymology, with words; and syntax, with sentences. Characteristically, the Latin grammar of Guarino Veronese begins with the following statement: "Partes grammaticae sunt quattuor, videlicet littera, syllaba, dictio, et oratio; littera, ut *u*, syllaba, ut *vi*, dictio, ut *Victor*, oratio, ut *Victor amat Andream*."[4] These four topics constituted grammar in the narrow sense of the term.

It should be noted, however, that grammar textbooks did not necessarily cover all four divisions of the discipline. It was a common practice for teachers of grammar to use more than one manual for teaching their subject. There were texts specially designed for the beginning student, there were others for the more advanced, and the coverage of topics varied considerably. Two widely disseminated primers were the *Ars minor* of Donatus (fourth century A.D.) and the *Ianua,* a medieval compilation based largely on Priscian's *Institutiones.*[5] For the intermediate level, the *Doctrinale* of Alexandre de Villedieu and the *Graecismus* of Evrard de Béthune, both of them medieval products, were often used.

Many texts were relatively short and covered only one of the four parts of grammar; some were even more restricted in scope. It was a common practice, for instance, to compose separate treatises on such topics as irregular preterites and supines, syntactic figures, nominal genders, and the like. For elementary manuals, the question-and-answer format was popular. This is the style in which Donatus wrote his *Ars minor,* and it was the style used by textbook writers in other disciplines in antiquity.[6] In the Renaissance, some of the new

grammatiche greche a stampa," *Italia medioevale e umanistica* 5 (1962), 321–51; and Roberto Weiss, *Medieval and Humanist Greek: Collected Essays,* Medioevo e umanesimo 8 (Padua, 1977).

3. See, for example, Florence, Biblioteca Riccardiana, Cod. 678, f. 1ʳ.

4. Oxford, Bodleian Library, MS. Lat. misc. e. 123, f. 1ʳ.

5. The *Ianua* begins with a set of elegiac couplets, the first line of which reads "Ianua sum rudibus primam cupientibus artem." The grammar itself begins "*Poeta quae pars est?*" See Charles Thurot, *Extraits de divers manuscrits latins pour servir à l'histoire des doctrines grammaticales au moyen âge* (Paris, 1869), p. 47; and Wolfgang O. Schmitt, "Die Ianua (Donatus): ein Beitrag zur lateinischen Schulgrammatik des Mittelalters und der Renaissance," *Beiträge zur Inkunabelkunde* (Dritte Folge) 4 (1969), 43–80.

6. See, for example, Jutta Kollesch, *Untersuchungen zu den pseudo-galenischen Definitionen medicae,* Akademie der Wissenschaften der Deutschen Demokratischen

grammar texts were cast in this format: Niccolò Perotti's *Rudimenta grammatices,* for example. Regardless of whether the manual used was in the catechetical style or not, students were usually required to learn their grammatical rules and the associated examples by heart.[7]

Besides the catechetical style, many grammars utilized mnemonic verses. This was a tradition inherited from the Middle Ages: the *Doctrinale* and the *Graecismus* are entirely in verse. The advantage of metrical rules was that they could be more easily memorized. But the drawback was that they were at times difficult to understand. Significantly, when the medieval verse grammars came under fire from the humanists, it was their pedagogical ineffectiveness that was focused upon, rather than the errors they contained. But the practice of composing rules in metrical form continued unabated throughout the Renaissance and well into the modern period.

In contrast, another popular medieval mode of presentation disappeared: the humanists did not write commentaries on standard grammatical texts. However, it is interesting that two successful Renaissance grammatical textbooks, namely, Antonio de Nebrija's *Introductiones* (1495) and Manuel Alvares's *De institutione grammatica* (1572), were provided with commentaries by their respective authors. But this activity must be regarded as a different genre from the medieval commentary. What Nebrija and Alvares aimed at was to elucidate, illustrate, and in some instances justify the rules they had presented. Theoretical issues are occasionally raised but without the sustained care and rigor of which the scholastics had been capable.

An essential feature of grammar during the Renaissance was that it was not merely a linguistic but also a literary discipline. Grammar rules were learned as a preparation for the study of literature.

Republik, Zentralinstitut für alte Geschichte und Archäologie, Schriften zur Geschichte und Kultur der Antike 7 (Berlin, 1973), pp. 39–46, esp. p. 39.

7. This is particularly emphasized by Battista Guarini in his treatise *De modo et ordine docendi ac discendi:* "Sed illud a magistro observari volumus, ut quas proponit pueris earum regularum declamationes, eas tum scribant, tum absque scriptura componant. Si enim rescripserint tantum, evenit plerumque ut rogati nihil ex tempore sciant respondere, utpote soliti in omnibus partibus multum diuque meditari. Contra vero si memoriter solum respondere didicerint saepe numero quibus inter se litteris syllabae connectuntur ignorant: quod si ad utrumque ut diximus assuefacti simul fuerint, expeditam consequentur et in scribendo et in loquendo promptitudinem, quam illud quoque vehementer augebit si Latine loqui continue assuefiant." Heidelberg: Henricus Knoblochtzer, December 18, 1489; Hain *8131, Proctor 3139, Guarnaschelli 4521, Goff G-530, BMC III, p. 671, sig. A4r.

As one sixteenth-century grammarian expressed it, "Grammatica est iter nobis ad studium litterarum et omnium liberalium artium."[8] Grammarians, therefore, pursued many problems that lay outside the limits of grammar proper, specifically the study of poetic meters (metrics), the study of the types and categories of poetic composition (poetics), and composition itself, both prose and verse. They also compiled dictionaries and glossaries, and studied word origins (etymology, in the more usual, present-day sense of the term). In pre-Renaissance Italy, the grammarians had taught the *ars dictandi,* which was part of rhetoric. They remained the teachers of composition throughout the Renaissance and beyond.

This dual function of the grammarian, as teacher of grammar in the narrow sense and as teacher of composition and literature, was a legacy from antiquity. It is clear, for instance, from Quintilian's *Institutio oratoria* (first century A.D.) that it was customary at that time for grammarians to train their students in a proper understanding and appreciation of literature.[9] It was their function, in fact, to explain and interpret archaisms, poetic conceits, geographical and mythological names, in short any words encountered in literary texts that did not lend themselves to straightforward literal interpretation. To underline the dual responsibility of the grammarian, Quintilian divided grammar into two parts: one dealing with the technical part of the subject and the other with the interpretation of the poets: "Haec igitur professio," he says, "cum brevissime in duas partes dividatur, recte loquendi scientiam et poetarum enarrationem, plus habet in recessu quam fronte promittit."[10] In another passage, he gives these two parts names, calling the first *methodice* and the second *historice.*[11] After the complete text of Quintilian's *Institutio* became available in the early fifteenth century, many humanists adopted this terminology, perhaps because it reflected so well the functions of the grammarian in their own day.

That grammar from its beginnings had been more than its name connoted was a fact of great historical significance. For of all the basic

8. Naples, Biblioteca Nazionale, Cod. V C 5, f. 2ᵛ, as quoted by Paul Oskar Kristeller, *Iter Italicum,* 1 (Leiden, 1963), p. 400a.

9. Diomedes puts the matter thus: "Tota autem grammatica consistit praecipue intellectu poetarum et scriptorum et historiarum prompta expositione et in recte loquendi scribendique ratione." Heinrich Keil, *Grammatici Latini,* 1 (Leipzig, 1857), p. 426. Literary criticism was clearly also part of the Greek *technē grammatikē,* see Karl Barwick, *Remmius Palaemon und die römische ars grammatica* (Leipzig, 1922), pp. 215 f.

10. Quintilian, *Institutio oratoria* I.4.2.   11. Ibid., I.9.1.

school subjects taught in antiquity, grammar was the only one to survive the barbarian invasions intact. This was so because the institutions, both lay and ecclesiastical, that arose on the ruins of the western Roman Empire were united in one important respect: they all utilized Latin as their medium of communication. In practical terms, this meant that any student who had the slightest ambition to become a man of substance, either in civil administration or in one of the learned professions, had to be able to handle the language competently. Therefore, when educational institutions expanded their intellectual scope in the High Middle Ages, the demand for effective grammatical instruction grew: lectures in the newly established universities were conducted in Latin, and the technical literature of the two lay professions, medicine and law, was likewise in Latin.[12] In these circumstances, the ability to express oneself fluently in that language was a prime necessity. In pre-Renaissance Italy, where the universities were dominated by the faculty of law, the study of Latin grammar and composition was an indispensable prerequisite both for the lowly notary and the advanced student of the Roman civil code and its medieval glossators. For law, even more than medicine, was a discipline that relied on sophisticated hermeneutical skills, and the technical literature the student of law had to master was of quite extraordinary complexity.[13] Grammar was, therefore, not merely the gateway to the other liberal arts; it was the foundation of the whole educational edifice. It is important to emphasize that the dominant position of Latin instruction in the curriculum persisted throughout the Renaissance and was, if anything, further reinforced by the prestige of the *studia humanitatis.*

12. See, for instance, Augusto Gaudenzi's significant comment: "Ma ciò che non si è ancora abbastanza osservato è che la scuola di rettorica seguitò a procedere parallela a quella di diritto, anche per il motivo, che l'insegnamento della grammatica, che non fu mai troppo bene separata dalla rettorica, diventò una preparazione a quello del diritto, *il quale . . . si impartiva in latino*" [italics mine]. "Sulla cronologia delle opere dei dettatori bolognesi da Buoncompagno a Bene di Lucca," *Bulletino dell'Istituto storico italiano* 14 (1895), 85.

13. As Paul Koschacker expressed the matter: "Die Schwierigkeit des Corpus iuris erfordete ... spezifisch gelehrte Forschung, die ihren Platz im 12. und 13. Jahrhundert an den in Italien und den westeuropäishen Ländern entstehenden Universitäten fand. Auf der anderen Seite waren diese *studia generalia,* die Studenter aller, d.h. der europäischen Länder offenstanden, die geeignetsten Repräsentanten dieser europäischen Kulturgemeinschaft, die äusserlich getragen wurde durch die lateinische Sprache sowohl im Schrifttum wie im Unterricht." *Europa und das römische Recht,* Berlin, 1947, p. 82.

It may come as something of a surprise, therefore, to discover that throughout the Renaissance the general attitude to grammar was strangely ambivalent. On the one hand, it was lauded as the foundation of the liberal arts, but on the other hand it was, after all, an irksome school subject and could, therefore, be thought of as a puerile pursuit unsuitable for an adult, and especially unsuitable for a member of one of the money-making professions. It may have been in part to defend themselves against detractors that grammarians were fond of emphasizing the notion that a knowledge of grammar would serve a student well throughout his whole subsequent career.

This argument is well illustrated in Battista Guarini's inaugural "Oratio de septem artibus liberalibus" (1453), which introduces the subject of grammar in the following way: "Sequitur deinde sermocinalis seu logica, tres in partes distributa, primoque in grammaticam, quam scio plerosque imperitos tamquam tenuem et ieiunam cavillari (Quintilian, *Institutio* I.4.5); qui si eius fructus intellegant, non video certe quo pacto eam parvi pendere valeant, multo plus utilitatis in recessu habentem quam fronte promittere videatur (I.4.2). Per eam ad rhetoricam, ad ius civile, ad medicorum libros, ad omnes denique disciplinas transitus datur. Nam si fundamenta iacta non fuerint, quidquid supra construas corruat necesse est."[14] Studying grammar is, therefore, not just a rite of passage imposed on the young, but a solid foundation on which competence in the two mundane professions, law and medicine, is built.

Alternatively, a less straightforward argument could be used: one could concede that grammar was a low-ranking discipline compared with the others but insist that it is, for that very reason, beneath the dignity of a mature scholar to make trivial mistakes in such an area. Thus, Pierpaolo Vergerio, in his influential pedagogical treatise *De ingenuis moribus* (1404), admonishes his readers as follows: "Ante omnia igitur, si quid proficere de doctrinis volumus, congrui sermonis habenda est ratio, et curandum ne, dum *maiora* prosequimur, turpiter in *minoribus* labi videamur."[15]

A more positive argument in favor of grammar was based on the notion that, in addition to understanding the meanings of terms, the

14. Karl Müllner, "Acht Inauguralreden des Veronesers Guarino und seines Sohnes Battista: ein Beitrag zur Geschichte der Pädagogik des Humanismus," *Wiener Studien* 18 (1896), 283–306; 19 (1897), 139.

15. *De ingenuis moribus et liberalibus studiis,* ed. Attilio Gnesotto, Atti e memorie della R. Accademia di scienze, lettere ed arte in Padova, 34.2 (Padua, 1918), p. 123.

competent grammarian must necessarily know what they refer to and be familiar with the disciplines to which they belong. Coluccio Salutati expresses this point of view as follows: "Et eadem ipsa grammatica sine notitia rerum et quibus modis rerum essentia variatur et omnium scientiarum concursu praeter necessitatem notitiae terminorum maxima ex parte sciri non potest."[16] Salutati then goes on to assert that in general a knowledge of one discipline is an essential component of a knowledge of all the others: "Conexa sunt humanitatis studia; conexa sunt et studia divinitatis, ut unius rei sine alia vera completaque scientia non possit haberi."[17]

However, not all humanists advocated blurring the boundary between grammar and the other disciplines. In one of his dialogues, the Westphalian humanist Alexander Hegius, more traditional in this regard than Salutati, has his two characters exchange the following remarks:

> A. An anima pertinet ad considerationem grammatici?
> B. Non.
> A. Quare?
> B. Quia grammatica nomina rerum tractat, non res ipsas, nisi quatenus significantur nominibus. Itaque grammaticus neque substantiam animae, neque vires eius, neque operationes, neque organa tractat, sed de nomine animae pronuntiat, unde derivetur, et quae significata habeat.[18]

But a more practical objection could be leveled at Salutati's grand perspective. How could pupils still at the elementary stage of learning the rudiments of grammar be expected to grasp concepts they would not encounter until they studied the higher disciplines? In this vein, Antonio de Nebrija deplored the use of definitions that presupposed knowledge on the part of pupils which they did not have. It had been customary in the Middle Ages, for instance, to define the active verb as one that governs a direct object denoting a "rational animal," that is, a human being. Accordingly, *amo* "love" qualified as an active verb, while *aro* "plough" did not. But, says Ne-

---

16. *Epistolario, di Coluccio Salutati,* ed. Francesco Novati, Fonti per la storia d'Italia pubb. dell'Istituto storico italiano, no. 18, vol. 4 (Rome, 1905), letter 24, p. 216.

17. Ibid.

18. *Dialogi* (Deventer, 1503), sig. B1ᵛ. This occurs in a dialogue entitled "Dialogus *peri tes psyches,* id est de anima, et primo de anima in genere, et eius definitionibus et aliis multis" (sigs. B1ʳ – C5ʳ).

brija, how can we require a mere beginner to be concerned about the distinction between a rational and a nonrational animal?[19]

In practice, therefore, the humble status of grammar in the curriculum deprived it of much of its potential cognitive significance, and the humanists strengthened this tendency by emphasizing the practical function of grammar as a preparation for the study of literature. Accordingly, they made a point of getting their students past the technical part of grammar as quickly as possible and into the more interesting activity of reading authors and composing their own Latin. This attitude to elementary preceptive grammar is reflected in the following remarks from Erasmus's *De ratione studii:* "Verum ut huiusmodi praecepta fateor necessaria, ita velim esse quantum fieri possit quam paucissima, modo sint optima. Nec umquam probavi litteratorum vulgus, qui pueros in his inculcandis complures annos remorantur."[20]

The result of this was that the humanist grammarians trimmed the grammatical curriculum rather drastically. Indeed, not only was the course of study skimpier as regards coverage, but the intellectual content of the discipline was also watered down. The grandiose attempt of the scholastic grammarians to transform grammar into a demonstrative science, an attempt that had culminated around 1300 in the treatises on the modes of meaning, was abandoned. There is a characteristic reference to the modes of meaning in Lorenzo Valla's encomium on Thomas Aquinas, in which Valla castigates the theologians for their exaggerated reverence for "what they call metaphysics and the modes of meaning and other things of that kind." These notions, he says, are being regarded with almost as much respect as a newly discovered sphere or the planetary epicycles! But he hastens to add that it really makes no difference to him whether one knows about them or not. However, he says finally, it is perhaps better after all to remain ignorant of them since they are obstacles in the way of better things: "Ista autem quae vocant metaphysica et modos significandi et alia id genus, quae recentes theologi tamquam novam

19. "Ego hoc loco non possum satis mirari quae dementia grammaticos ceperit, partim iuniores, partim etiam quosdam ex antiquioribus, ut verbum activum definiant 'quod potest construi cum accusativo nominum significantium animal rationale.' Neque enim aliam ob causam illos hoc scripsisse arbitror, nisi ut difficultatem augere iis in rebus in quibus nulla erat difficultas. Nam quid per Deum immortalem obsecro te ad grammaticum rei litterariae praesertim adhuc rudem scire attinet quid sit transire in animal rationale, quid in animal (ir)rationale?" *Introductiones Latinae,* Salamanca, 30 September 1495; Reichling 641, GW 2231, Palau y Dulcet 188901, Goff A-905, sig. n6ʳ.

20. *Opera omnia* 1, ed. Joannes Clericus (Leiden, 1703), col. 521C.

sphaeram nuper inventam aut planetarum epicyclos admirantur, nequaquam ego tantopere admiror, nec ita multum interesse arbitror scias an nescias, et quae forte satius nescire tamquam meliorum impedimenta."[21]

Later in the fifteenth century, in the 1480s, Alexander Hegius devoted a whole treatise to an attack on the modistic grammarians, his *Invectiva in modos significandi*,[22] but the arguments he advances are by and large nontheoretical. The modistic writers are, he claims, corrupters of Latinity; the Church Fathers wrote excellent Latin without knowing anything about the modes of meaning; the *modistae* are impostors and obtain money from their pupils on false pretenses; and so forth. Significantly, however, Hegius does not debate with the modistic grammarians on their own ground, and the same must be said of subsequent humanist critics of modistic grammar, such as Erasmus and Juan Luis Vives. The humanists had, it must be admitted, a completely untheoretical approach to grammar, if by theory we mean an explicitly formulated system of general principles independent of the specific facts to be accounted for.

Another basic trait of humanist grammarians was their notion of what validates a grammatical rule. They reinstated the principle that a rule is valid if it accords with the usage of classical authors. Ancient usage was, thus, the final court of appeal, not the prescriptions of grammarians, either ancient or modern. It cannot be said, however, that this principle had ever been explicitly denied, but in practice the grammarians of the Middle Ages had described the Latin used in their own day, that is, the Latin of the learned professions.

Reasserting the primacy of *ancient* usage had far-reaching consequences. We should recall that by the end of the fifteenth century the bulk of the Latin literature to which we have access today had already been made generally available — this was one of the achievements of the humanist movement. This literature included a number of grammars that had been unknown (or virtually so) for most of the Middle Ages. This meant that the humanists had access, for the first

21. Joannes Vahlen, "Lorenzo Valla über Thomas von Aquino," *Vierteljahrsschrift für Kultur und Literatur der Renaissance* 1 (1886), 394. On modistic grammar, see Jan Pinborg, *Die Entwicklung der Sprachtheorie im Mittelalter*, Beiträge zur Geschichte der Philosophie und Theologie des Mittelalters, 42.2 (Münster and Copenhagen, 1967); and the same author's *Logik und Semantik im Mittelalter: ein Überblick*, Problemata, 10 (Stuttgart-Bad Cannstatt, 1972).

22. *Dialogi* (Deventer, 1503), sigs. 02^r – 04^v. For a modern edition, see J. IJsewijn, "Alexander Hegius (d. 1498): *Invectiva in modos significandi*," *Forum for Modern Language Studies* 7 (1971), 299 – 318.

time, to the entire range of Roman grammatical literature. Authors such as Varro, Probus, Diomedes, and Asper were now usable both as sources of information about Latin and as representatives of hitherto unknown theoretical positions.

What the humanists discovered as these works came to light was that there was disagreement among the grammatical authorities of antiquity on many important issues, and also that some statements of the revered Donatus and Priscian, whose works had formed the basis of grammatical instruction hitherto, were clearly erroneous. The realization that ancient authorities were discordant and in some instances even fallible forced grammarians to set about constructing the grammar of Latin for themselves, or at least adjusting it wherever necessary to fit the facts of usage. Indeed, the process of renovating the readjusting Latin grammar went on steadily throughout the Renaissance and continued in the following centuries. This activity explains a rather puzzling feature of Lorenzo Valla's famous *Elegantiae linguae Latinae,* namely, that Valla bandies relatively few words with his immediate medieval predecessors, but devotes one whole book out of six to a point-by-point criticism of *ancient* grammarians and lexicographers, such as Macrobius, Aulus Gellius, Festus Pompeius, and the authors of the Roman civil code. Indeed, the humanists were so confident of their command of Latin that they could on occasion accuse the Romans themselves of not knowing their own language, as when Valla says of Boethius: "I shall show this Roman that he does not know how to speak Roman."[23]

Another consequence of the emphasis on imitating ancient usage was that the ultimate goal of grammatical instruction was now not merely to train students to produce correct Latin, that is, sentences in which the nouns are in their proper cases, the verbs and subject nominatives agree in number and person, and so forth, but to write Latin indistinguishable from that which had been written by the ancients themselves. Needless to say, this was a remarkably ambitious project, and to approach the goal a student needed to acquire a complete grasp of phraseology, word order, style and diction, all of which went far beyond the traditional province of the grammarian as it had previously been defined in the textbooks. One might say, therefore, that grammar in the Renaissance gained in breadth whatever it may have lost in depth.

23. "Sed huic homini Romano ostendam Romane loqui nescire," *Opera* (Basle, 1543), sig. 04ʳ.

At this point a brief chronological survey of Renaissance grammar is in order. If we regard humanism of the Renaissance variety as first emerging in the activities of the Paduan circle represented by Lovato Lovati (1246–1309) and his pupil Albertino Mussato (1261–1329), it is surely a significant fact that these early humanists were, to all appearances at least, content with the current grammatical literature. Lovato and his colleagues devoted themselves to the actual composition of literary works, their favorite genres being history and drama. But it is also noteworthy that Lovato himself wrote a short treatise on the meters of Seneca, describing such hitherto unknown forms as the iambic senarius.[24] The significance of this event lies in the fact that the only classical meters commonly cultivated previously were the hexameter and the pentameter.[25] In our broader sense of the term *grammar,* this kind of activity may legitimately be considered part and parcel of the discipline. Lovato's treatise was, therefore, the first piece of Renaissance grammatical literature.

Like the Paduan humanists, Petrarch seems also to have been satisfied with grammar as it was practiced in his day. Two interesting facts may be adduced in this connection. First, he included two medieval lexica, the anonymous *Papias* (from the mid-eleventh century) and the *Catholicon* of John of Genoa (1286) in a list of his favorite books, in company with the ancients Priscian and Donatus.[26] A second glimpse at Petrarch's attitudes to grammar is provided by one of the *Epistolae seniles* in which he has occasion to compare medicine unfavorably, in terms of its effectiveness as a discipline, with both grammar and rhetoric.[27] It is perhaps significant, however, that the only grammatical authority he mentions explicitly in this passage is Priscian. We cannot be sure, therefore, to what extent his favorable opinion of grammar extended to contemporary practitioners of the discipline.

With Petrarch's protégé Coluccio Salutati (1331–1406), we observe an unequivocal assertion of the new linguistic standards. In some ways, Salutati sets the tone of much of the subsequent critique

24. *De Senecae tragoediarum lectione vulgata,* ed. R. Peiper (Breslau, 1893), pp. 32–35. (Festschrift zur Jubelfeier des Gymnasiums zu St. Maria Magdalena.)

25. See Charles Thurot, *Extraits de divers manuscrits latins,* p. 440.

26. See Berthold L. Ullman, "Petrarch's favorite books," *Studies in the Italian Renaissance,* Storia e letteratura, 51 (Rome, 1955), pp. 117–37.

27. *Epistolae seniles,* 12.2; see Francisci Petrarchae, *Operum tomus II* (Basle, 1554), sigs. 2A2^v–2A3^r.

of medieval Latinity. It is in essence a *negation* of the usage of the present and immediate past. Interestingly, the area in which this attack is first concentrated is orthography, a topic for which rhetoricians (in their role of teachers of *dictamen*) had a particular fondness. The force of Salutati's censure can be gauged from the following sentence in his famous letter to Fra Giovanni Dominici: "I would like all churchmen to have been and to be proficient enough in grammar so that we would hear them using *no* barbarous words, *no* syntactic errors, *no* words coined at variance with analogy, *no* words in inappropriate meanings, *no* words placed where they do not belong."[28] On the positive side, we must register Salutati's passion for orthographical questions, an interest that was to be shared by many of the prominent humanists of the Quattrocento, beginning with Gasparino Barzizza (in his *Orthographia* of 1418) and culminating in the great Salamanca humanist Antonio de Nebrija at the end of the century.[29] Notice also that this sentence from Salutati's letter to Dominici reveals in embryo a complete program of grammatical renovation: the avoidance of barbarisms (nonclassical words), solecisms (syntactic mistakes), unjustifiable lexical coinages, and words with impermissible meanings and in impermissible collocations.

The first grammatical manual composed by a humanist was the *Regulae grammaticales* of the great educator Guarino Veronese (1374–1460).[30] The earliest known reference to it occurs in a letter of Guarino's written in early 1418, a decade before he was invited to Ferrara by Niccolò d'Este. The salient feature of this remarkable work is its extreme brevity. This brevity occurs in part because the *Regulae* was not intended for complete beginners and thus does not treat such topics as inflectional paradigms and definitions of the parts of speech. We have evidence, in fact, that Guarino used his *Reg-*

28. *Epistolario,* vol. 4, p. 217.

29. Barzizza's *Orthographia* (note the opening sentence: "Quoniam recta scriptura, quam Graeca appellatione orthographiam dicimus, *proxime videtur ad oratoris officium accedere*") is contained in Venice, Biblioteca Marciana, MS. Lat. XIII.89 (=4478). On orthography in the Quattrocento, see Sabbadini, *La scuola e gli studi di Guarino* (for full reference, see next footnote), pp. 47–52.

30. On the *Regulae grammaticales,* see Remigio Sabbadini, *La scuola e gli studi di Guarino Guarini Veronese* (Catania, 1896, rpt. in *Guariniana,* ed. Mario Sancipriano, Turin, 1964), pp. 38–47; see also Sabbadini's two articles, "Dei metodi nell'insegnamento della sintassi latina," *Rivista di filologia* 30 (1902), 304–14, and "Elementi nazionali nella teoria grammaticale dei Romani," *Studi italiani di filologia classica* 14 (1906), 113–25; and my article, "Textual Problems in the Latin Grammar of Guarino Veronese," *Res Publica Litterarum* 1 (1978), 241–54.

ulae in conjunction with other manuals, in particular the *Ianua* and the *Doctrinale*.[31]

Moreover, as Sabbadini clearly showed over seventy-five years ago, Guarino's grammar is almost entirely unoriginal: the ingredients can be found in the manuals written in the late Trecento, and in few instances does Guarino have anything new to add. Nevertheless, the *Regulae* differs noticeably from the grammars current in the pre-humanistic period in that it completely lacks the logical and meta-physical underpinnings characteristic of the grammatical products of scholasticism. Paradoxically, therefore, Guarino's grammar is humanistic in what it excludes, not in what it contains. Thus, it is note-worthy that Guarino did not indulge in that typical humanistic prac-tice of using quotations from classical authors to back up the rules of grammar. His examples are, in fact, the same concoctions that one encounters in a typical medieval grammar.[32]

Another remarkable feature of the *Regulae* is the coverage of topics. Like the Latin grammars of the Trecento, a large part of it is devoted to verbal syntax. Guarino provides an elaborate classifica-tion of verbs on the basis of the nominal cases they govern. All the verbs that govern a particular combination of cases, say, an accusative and a genitive, are placed in the same class. This syntactic property is first described in a formulaic statement; a sentential example fol-lows, to which is appended a more or less extensive list of member verbs in their principal parts with vernacular glosses. Finally, a mne-monic verse is given. For instance, the class containing verbs that take two accusatives is described as follows:

"Nota quod sunt quaedam verba activa quae volunt ante se nominativum personae agentis et post se accusativum personae pa-tientis et ultra accusativum alium accusativum, ut *ego doceo te gram-maticam.*

Doceo	es	per amaestrare
Instruo	is	
Vestio	is	per vestire
Oro	as	per pregare
Rogo	as	

31. On the use of the *Ianua* and the *Doctrinale* by Guarino, see Sabbadini, *La scuola e gli studi di Guarino,* pp. 42–43.

32. Typical examples are the following: "Animal homo currit," from the section on figures, and "Antonius est Venetus cuias est Andreas," from the section on relatives.

Peto	is	
Posco	is	per domandare
Flagito	as	

Flagito posco peto rogo calceo celo,
Vestio cubcingo cingo monet instruit oro,
Postulat exorat duplices adiungito quartos."[33]

This section is followed by one devoted to active verbs that take an accusative and genitive (model sentence *ego emo equum decem ducatorum*), a section on verbs that govern an accusative and dative (model sentence *ego do tibi panem*), a section on verbs that take an accusative and an ablative without preposition (model sentence *ego spolio te cappa*), and finally active verbs that take an accusative and ablative with preposition (model sentence *ego audio lectionem a magistro*). Neuter verbs are similarly subdivided into classes, which are given names. Thus, those that take a dative (model sentence *ego servio tibi*) are termed "acquisitive" and are so referred to in the introductory formula: "Nota quod verbum neutrum acquisitivum est illud quod vult ante nominativum personae agentis et post se dativum personae patientis."[34] This system had taken shape in the previous century, and it continued to be used, with variations, by Italian grammarians of Latin throughout the Renaissance.

After this central section on verbal syntax, the *Regulae* then consists of a series of brief chapters on a wide variety of topics ranging from patronymics and relative pronouns to heteroclite nouns and derivative verbs.[35] This is another feature inherited from the Latin grammars of the Trecento. One of the more important of these later chapters is devoted to the so-called syntactic figures. In the terminol-

33. This transcription is based on the following manuscripts: Milan, Biblioteca Trivulziana, Cod. 631; Venice, Biblioteca Marciana, MS. Lat. XIII. 113 (=4042); Oxford, Bodleian Library, MS. Lat. misc. e. 123; Bologna, Biblioteca Universitaria, Cod. 818; New York, Columbia University Library, Plimpton 145.

34. I have discussed this feature of the *Regulae* in my article "Textual Problems in the Latin Grammar of Guarino Veronese." See note 30 for a full reference.

35. The topics covered in the *Regulae* are orthography, enumeration of parts of speech, accidents of the noun, accidents of the verb, basic rules of concord, the impersonal verb, syntax of personal verbs (the central section to which I refer above), adverbs of place, the participle, comparative adjectives, superlative adjectives, syntactic figures, patronymic nouns, inchoative, meditative, frequentative, desiderative, and diminutive verbs, relative pronouns, heteroclite nouns, the syntax of *quis* and *uter*, and the syntax of *solvo, nubo,* and *lateo.*

ogy current at that time, a construction was called a figure if it appeared to violate a basic syntactic rule. In other words, a figure was a justifiable syntactic error, and the *Regulae* so defines it: "Figura est vitium cum ratione factum." To take a simple example, a construction such as *milites et tribunus currunt*, "the soldiers and the tribune are running," is a figure because *tribunus*, a singular noun, is immediately conjoined with *currunt*, a plural verb. A classification of such permissible deviations from strict syntactic rules had been worked out by the medieval grammarians, and Guarino's grammar contains all the customary types with the stock examples.[36]

Guarino also wrote three other short grammatical works, namely, the *De orthographia* and the *Carmina differentialia*, both in verse, and the *De diphthongis*, in prose.[37] Manuscripts and early printed editions of the *Regulae* usually include one or more of these shorter pieces.

Guarino's grammatical output, therefore, was predominantly in orthography, syntax, and lexicography, all three areas of great importance for students oriented towards Latin composition. Moreover, as we have seen, the *Regulae* itself contained lexical lists in the central section on verbal syntax. Clearly, this way of presenting grammatical facts was motivated by considerations of pedagogical expediency. As regards the exclusion of so many topics that had occupied a place in medieval grammars, Guarino offered no justification. He evidently felt, as his son Battista put it, that the *Regulae* contained everything that was necessary to enable the student to compose sentences correctly: "sicut nihil est superflui, ita omnia facile reperiuntur quae ad orationem recte struendam conducere videantur."[38]

36. Guarino's list of syntactic figures follows: prolepsis *(aquilae volant una sursum altera deorsum)*, syllepsis *(rex et regina albi)*, zeugma *(ego et tu scribo)*, synthesis *(pars in frusta secant)*, antiptosis *(de aqua non est)*, evocatio *(ego Vergilius cano)*, appositio *(miratur molem Aeneas magalia quondam)*, and synecdoche *(Aethiops albus dentes)*. The tropes are not referred to by Guarino, but receive treatment from later grammarians, e.g., Perotti, who reproduces Donatus's list in its entirety.

37. The *De orthographia* begins "*A* separans *m* vel *u*, *abs c q t*, cetera vult *ab*." The *Carmina differentialia* begins "Dicitur esse *nepos* de *nepa* luxuriosus." See Sabbadini, *La scuola e gli studi di Guarino*, pp. 52–58. The treatise on diphthongs begins "Non sine causa factum esse certo scio." On Guarino's version of the *Erōtēmata* of Manuel Chrysoloras, see Sabbadini, *Epistolario di Guarino Veronese*, 3, Miscellanea di storia veneta, 3rd ser., vol. 14 (1919), pp. 76–77. Guarino also wrote a treatise on composition, beginning "Corpus ut in membra, rursum membra ipsa licebit"; see Sabbadini, *La scuola e gli studi di Guarino*, pp. 73, 228–30.

38. Battista Guarini, *De modo et ordine docendi ac discendi*, sig. A4ʳ.

After Guarino's *Regulae,* the next landmark is undoubtedly the massive *Elegantiae linguae Latinae* of Lorenzo Valla (1407 – 1457), which was published in the mid-1440s. However, it cannot be categorized as a grammar in the narrow sense defined above, for it is by and large concerned with the proper choice and use of individual words and it is not organized like a typical grammatical work. Instead, what we find is a series of chapters, each devoted to a particular word or group of semantically or syntactically related words.

Two conspicuous features of the *Elegantiae* are the extensive, but by no means exclusive, use of direct quotations from ancient authors to back up the rules, and an all-pervasive critical attitude. As regards the first, recall that Valla did not advocate imitating any and every turn of phrase to be found in some ancient writer or other. In his view, the usage of the ancients must be followed with discrimination.[39] It is also interesting that he did not hesitate to criticize the grammarians of antiquity, a practice that appears to have displeased his contemporaries. In his apologia to Eugenius IV, for instance, he felt it necessary to mention that he had been accused of comparing Priscian with the sun, a heavenly body that on occasion suffers eclipse: "...Priscianum quidem solem grammaticae, sed aliquando passum esse eclipsim."[40]

Valla, moreover, drew the ultimate consequence from his stringent linguistic principles by applying them in a variety of areas. Thus, it was largely on linguistic grounds that he challenged the authenticity of the donation of Constantine, and his New Testament criticism (his *In Novum Testamentum adnotationes,* which, however, did not appear until long after his death) was imbued with the same principles. That he was conscious of the philosophical implications of his new approach is clearly shown in the *Dialecticae disputationes,* where he demonstrates that it is impossible to philosophize without a clear realization of the nature of language.[41] Philology could, therefore, be harnessed for higher purposes, a fact to be demonstrated repeatedly in subsequent decades and centuries.

39. See my article "The Grammatical Tradition and the Rise of the Vernaculars," p. 254.

40. *Opera* (Basle, 1543), sig. 2R$_x$9^r. Cf. Max von Wolff, *Lorenzo Valla: sein Leben und seine Werke* (Leipzig, 1893), p. 69.

41. See Cesare Vasoli, "Le *Dialecticae disputationes* del Valla e la critica umanistica della logica aristotelica," *Rivista critica di storia della filosofia* 12 (1957), 412 – 34; 13 (1958), 27 – 46, esp. p. 45.

A few years after the *Elegantiae,* in mid-century, Giovanni Tortelli's encyclopedic *Orthographia* appeared, based on all the ancient sources (especially Greek ones) available at that time, and in 1468 — another milestone — Niccolò Perotti's *Rudimenta grammatices.* The latter was the first humanistic grammar to include elementary morphology, that is, noun and verb paradigms, definitions of the parts of speech, and so forth. The central section of Perotti's grammar is devoted to verbal syntax; it is, in fact, an amplified version of the corresponding part of Guarino's *Regulae.* However, Perotti broke new ground by including in his grammar a manual of epistolary style, headed "De epistolis componendis." The *Rudimenta* could, therefore, be used as the basis for a complete course of study in Latin, and it was perhaps for this reason that it was so popular, appearing in many printed editions both in Italy and north of the Alps. (An adaptation of it was written by Bernard Perger of Vienna University with the impressive title *Grammatica nova,* the first edition of which came out around 1479.) It is interesting that Perotti's sentential examples have a more classical ring to them than Guarino's. Thus, *ego amo Petrum* makes way for *Pyrrhus amat Penelopen,* and *ego spolio te cappa* for *pasce te liberalibus studiis.* Notice, however, that Perotti continues the traditional practice of placing the verb in the middle of the sentence, between the subject and the complement.

Significantly, printed editions of the *Rudimenta* often include Perotti's two metrical treatises, the *Artis metrices opusculum* and the *De ratione carminum quibus Horatius et Severinus Boethius usi sunt,* both composed in 1453. Finally, Perotti left behind his monumental *Cornucopiae,* a massive commentary on Martial and a treasure house of Latinity, which was published posthumously (1489).

Another influential grammarian of the second half of the fifteenth century was Giulio Sulpizio Verulano, who taught for a while in Rome as a member of Pomponio Leto's circle. Unlike Perotti, Sulpizio did not compose a complete manual of Latin grammar, but a series of separate pieces, which were often transcribed together in manuscripts and usually appear together in printed editions. We have a *rudimenta,* a work on nominal declensions, a treatise on nominal genders, one on preterits and supines, a manual of epistolary style *(De componendis et ornandis epistolis),* and a treatise on scansion and syllabic quantity. Sulpizio was something of an innovator: he paid more attention than his predecessors to the syntax of the noun and adjective, and he streamlined the presentation of syntactic facts by omitting some of the less important information, such as the vernacular glosses.[42] However, Sulpizio's grammatical compendium was not as popular as Perotti's *Rudimenta,* judging by the number of printed editions the two works went through.

A grammar even more comprehensive than Perotti's was written by the Spanish humanist Antonio de Nebrija (ca. 1441 – 1522). The first printed edition of his *Introductiones Latinae explicitae* appeared in Salamanca in 1481, and the work assumed final shape in 1495 and was reprinted many times both in Spain and elsewhere for over three hundred years. In Spain it achieved the status of a pedagogical classic, and not even the *Minerva* of Francisco Sánchez (1587) was capable of supplanting it. Like Perotti's *Rudimenta,* it is lucidly written and well organized. Its coverage includes orthography, prosody, etymology, syntax, and metrics; some editions end with a compact Latin-Spanish word list. All editions from 1495 on are provided with a copious commentary in which Nebrija carefully explains and justifies his intentions. Perhaps his most startling innovation was to add the gerund and the supine to the customary eight parts of speech.

Nebrija also compiled a Latin-Spanish and a Spanish-Latin dictionary, wrote a grammar of the vernacular (1492) and a treatise on the correct pronunciation of Latin and Greek (*De vi ac potestate litterarum deque illarum falsa prolatione,* first edition Salamanca, 1503), and produced a lexicon of the civil law (*Lexicon iuris civilis,* first edition Salamanca, 1506). In his work on pronunciation, Nebrija claimed that the Romans pronounced *c* and *g* as stops in all positions and *ae* and *oe* as true diphthongs; he recommended that these letters and letter combinations should be pronounced now as they were pronounced in ancient times. He was, therefore, the originator of the so-called Erasmian pronunciation of Latin. (Whether Erasmus knew

42. In the preface to his treatise on syntax, Sulpizio refers to his endeavors as follows: "Ad quod opus aggrediendum impulit me etiam caritas quaedam et pietas erga adolescentes, qui fraudati sunt simplicitate doctrinae. Nam cum multi licet doctissimi hac aetate viri de constructione scripserint, id tamen quod erat non negligendum praeterierunt, nominum videlicet constructionem. Illorumque alii nimis impliciti et parci fuerunt, alii sicci incautique in tenuissimos inciderunt errores, alii nimis profusa sed non plena tradiderunt praecepta. Ego autem conatus sum ita breviter rem colligere, ut brevitas ipsa non pariat obscuritatem, et ita accurate, ut nihil praeteream necessarium, nec aliorum sequar errores, neque tam vulgariter scribere volui, ut nihil laboris in pectore docentis relinquerem. Nam verborum significata non posui, neque secundas personas, et praeterita et supina, ut alii posuere. Est enim huius libelli titulus solummodo de constructione." *Grammatica Sulpitii Verulani,* Modena, Biblioteca Estense, MS. Campori 43 =γ: D.6.5, ff. 81^v – 82^r.

of Nebrija's work before writing his famous dialogue on the pronunciation of Latin and Greek, in 1528, is an interesting question.)

Another innovative grammar appeared in printed form in 1484 in Venice, written by the famous Roman humanist Giulio Pomponio Leto (1428–1498). What distinguishes Pomponio is that he was steeped in the terminology and theories of what we might call the noncanonical Roman grammarians, that is, authors such as Diomedes, Probus, and above all Varro, whose *De lingua Latina* exemplified an approach to grammar quite different from that of the familiar Donatus and Priscian. It is clear that Pomponio was rather exhilarated by his exposure to this literature, and not surprisingly, his own grammar departed from tradition more radically than any other that had hitherto appeared in the new humanistic style. But perhaps for this very reason it was not a commercial success. Only one edition other than the first has been reported, namely, a Paris imprint from around 1505.[43] However, at least two of Pomponio's innovations were influential. He was the first grammarian to arrange paradigms in tabular arrays, a practice adopted by Nebrija. (Our earliest manuscript copy of Pomponio's grammar, namely MS. Lat. XIV. 109 [=4623] at the Biblioteca Marciana in Venice, is dated 1466: we may, therefore, safely attribute the innovation to him, rather than to Nebrija.)[44] Pomponio was also the first grammarian to call *amavero* a future perfect indicative, instead of a future subjunctive, an analysis he found in Varro.[45]

In northern Europe, several new humanistically inspired textbooks were written in the early years of the sixteenth century: in Germany the manuals of Heinrichmann and Brassicanus, in France the works of Jean Pellisson and Josse Bade, in England those of John Stanbridge and Robert Whittington. The most successful of these new contributions was the vast grammatical *opus* of the Flemish humanist Johannes Despauterius (Jan Despauter), which spans the period from about 1510 to 1520 and includes a compact *Rudimenta*

43. See *British Museum General Catalogue of Printed Books,* vol. 192 (London, 1963), col. 672.

44. Concerning Pomponio's Latin grammatical works, see José Ruysschaert, "Les manuels de grammaire latine composés par Pomponio Leto," *Scriptorium* 8 (1954), 98–107; and the same author's "A propos des trois premières grammaires latines de Pomponio Leto," *Scriptorium* 15 (1961), 68–75.

45. See Aldo Scaglione, *Ars grammatica,* Janua Linguarum, Series Minor, 77 (The Hague, 1970), pp. 90–94; and my comments in reviewing this interesting monograph, *Language* 51 (1975), 440–56, esp. 444–47.

(1514) and treatises on accidence (1512), syntax (1513), versification (1510), accents (1511), poetic genres (1511), epistolary composition, and orthography, covering thus the entire spectrum of topics thought to constitute the grammarian's province in the Renaissance. It is interesting that the longest of these works is the *Ars versificatoria*, which in the magnificent collected edition of Despauter's grammatical output, printed in Paris by Robert Estienne in 1537/38, runs to over two hundred pages, or between a quarter and a third of the whole volume.[46] Despauter's works continued to enjoy favor until the mid-eighteenth century.

Another highly successful grammar that came out later in the sixteenth century may be mentioned, namely, the *De institutione grammatica libri tres* (Lisbon, 1572) by the Portuguese Jesuit Manuel Alvares (1526 – 1582). After it was adopted by the Society of Jesus as its official grammar, Alvares's work continued in constant use until the nineteenth century. The coverage of topics is broad: after accidence (book 1) and syntax (book 2), there are a number of separate chapters on prosody, figures, metrics, and patronymic nouns (book 3). Like Nebrija's grammar, it contains a commentary by the author himself. The rules in some sections are in verse; most of them, however, are in prose.

Throughout the Renaissance, medieval grammatical works continued to be used, especially, of course, in northern Europe. Two medieval lexica, the *Papias* and the *Catholicon,* appeared in a number of printed editions before 1500. The most notable case, however, is the *Doctrinale* of Alexandre de Villedieu, a verse grammar that had been a staple of the curriculum since the early thirteenth century. Reichling, the modern editor of the *Doctrinale,* counted 163 incunabular editions and over 100 sixteenth-century imprints.[47] We also have the testimony of Battista Guarini, who speaks with approval of the *Doctrinale* in his *De modo et ordine docendi ac discendi* (1459).[48] In the course of time, however, the humanists discovered errors in Villedieu's work

46. Iohannis Despauterii Ninivitae *Commentarii grammatici* (Paris, Robertus Stephanus, 1537, colophon dated March 19, 1538), pp. 356 – 576.

47. Dietrich Reichling, *Das Doctrinale des Alexander de Villa-Dei: kritisch-exegetische Ausgabe mit Einleitung, Verzeichniss der Handschriften und Drucke nebst Registern,* Monumenta Germaniae paedagogica 12 (Berlin, 1893).

48. Speaking of prosody and metrics, Battista says, "Ad eam sententiam non inutilis erit is liber qui sub Alexandri nomine versibus habetur, ex quo etiam praeteritorum verbi et generum nominis et declinationum formulas percipient. Nam praeterquam quod omnia sumit a Prisciano, facilius etiam quae carminibus scripta sunt memoriae commendantur conserventurque" (sig. A5^{r-v}).

(Valla pointed out a certain number in a short piece entitled *Emendationes quorundam locorum ex Alexandro*), and serious questions were raised about its pedagogical effectiveness. It was, accordingly, condemned by Sulpizio Verulano in a rather detailed critique.[49] The *Ianua,* erroneously attributed to Donatus, continued to be used throughout the Renaissance. It is noteworthy that Pomponio Leto published an edition of the *Ianua* in which he arranged the paradigms in the same tabular form he had used in his own grammar.[50]

In the sixteenth century, several attempts were made to reform grammar in a more fundamental fashion than hitherto. An outstanding example of the revolutionary advocate is Julius Caesar Scaliger (1484–1558), who wrote a devastating critique of traditional grammatical definitions and terminology in his *De causis linguae Latinae,* first published in Lyons in 1540. Scaliger's point of departure was avowedly philosophical; he maintained that grammar was an integral part of philosophy and that the distinction between lower- and higher-ranking disciplines was a product of human stupidity.[51] One might say, therefore, that the wheel had come full circle. From a total rejection of philosophical approaches to grammar, humanism had returned to a fresh examination of the rational bases of language. Scaliger's project was continued, albeit in a somewhat diluted form, by the Spanish humanist Francisco Sánchez de las Brozas (Franciscus Sanctius Brocensis), whose *Minerva sive de causis linguae Latinae,* first appearing in Salamanca in 1587, achieved considerable popularity outside Spain from the mid-seventeenth century on for over 150 years. Sánchez's ideas influenced, for instance, the authors of the famous Port Royal grammar, the *Grammaire générale et raisonnée* (Paris, 1660), a seminal work in the philosophical grammar tradition of the Enlightenment. To conclude this brief chronological survey, therefore, we may say that the Renaissance humanists created a solid cur-

49. See my article "Renaissance Grammar: Rebellion or Evolution?" in *Interrogativi dell'umanesimo II: Atti del X Convegno internazionale del Centro di studi umanistici "Angelo Poliziano,"* ed. Giovannangiola Tarugi (Florence, 1976), pp. 73–90, esp. pp. 87–89.

50. The editors of the *Gesamtkatalog* describe this edition as follows: "Die Rezension ... sucht durch Rotdruck, Klammern und eine spaltenweise Anordnung der Paradigmen bei der Flexion den Text übersichtlicher zu gestalten" (*Gesamtkatalog der Wiegendrucke,* 2nd ed., Stuttgart and New York, 1968), 7. col. 675.

51. "Cuius (*scil.* Aristotelis) profecto iudicio grammaticam non solum esse philosophiae partem, id quod nemo sanus negat, sed ne ab eius quidem cognitione dissolvi posse intellegeremus.... Neque enim scientiae minores a superioribus suapte natura disiungi possunt, sed ingeniorum tantum imbecillitate dissociari solent." *De causis linguae Latinae* (Lyons, 1540), sig. 2bl$^{\rm v}$.

ricular foundation on which grammar continued to be based until the advent of comparative philology in the nineteenth century.

It is clear from the preceding discussion that grammar and rhetoric started out in antiquity as part of a single educational program, grammarians being in charge of the beginners and rhetoricians of the more advanced students. Within grammar, the study of correctness (*recte loquendi scientia,* as Quintilian called it) preceded the study of texts *(poetarum enarratio).* The precise boundary between grammar and rhetoric, however, was unclear. In practice, the study of the poets tended to be reserved for the lower grammatical level and the study of prose writers, especially orators, for the higher rhetorical level. But there were inevitable jurisdictional disputes. Quintilian remarks at the beginning of book 2 of his *Institutio oratoria,* for example, that in his day grammarians had begun to intrude so far on the accustomed domain of rhetoric that they had in effect appropriated most of the higher-ranking branches of knowledge *(prope omnium maximarum artium scientia).*[52] Specifically, he accuses them of teaching certain varieties of declamation (the so-called *suasoriae,* for example) that had originally fallen within the sphere of the rhetoricians. Clearly, after the demise of ancient forensic rhetoric this kind of encroachment necessarily ceased.

Another factor that blurred the boundaries between grammar and the other two branches of the *trivium* was the narrow conception many grammarians had of the scope of grammar. By and large, the center of gravity lay on the lower side of syntax, in the areas of orthography and word inflection. A great deal of grammatical instruction was concerned with the problem of avoiding errors *(vitia),* and the grammarians of antiquity even evolved an elaborate typology of grammatical mistakes (Donatus, for example, lists no fewer than twelve types of *vitium*). In general, a sentence was grammatically correct if it contained no errors. As Quintilian expresses it, "prima barbarismi ac soloecismi foeditas absit."[53] Conversely, grammarians had little to say of a positive nature about how sentences should be put together. Even Priscian, who alone among the Latin grammarians of antiquity paid attention to syntax, had nothing substantive to prescribe about phenomena such as word order, the sequence of tenses, and relations of subordination and predication. When these problems eventually forced themselves on the attention of scholars in the Middle Ages, it was typically the logician and rhetorician who han-

52. *Institutio* II.1.1–6.   53. Ibid., I.5.5.

dled them, not the grammarian. Word order was treated in rhetoric, while basic intrasentential relations (subject and predicate, dependency relations between adjectives and nouns, and so forth) were referred to the logician. The result of this distribution was to break up the study of Latin among all three branches of the *trivium*.

To complicate matters further, the final centuries of the Middle Ages were marked by the hegemony of logic, and no discipline escaped the influence of the syllogistic method. As one writer put it, "logica est regula syllogizandi in omni scientia."[54] Thus, in grammar, we witness not only the rise of the *modistae*, but constant reference, even by writers of teaching grammars, to concepts of logical origin. An illuminating example appears in the discussion of the relative pronoun in the *Doctrinale*, which includes the following lines:

> Occurritque tibi quandoque relatio simplex:
> *Femina quae clausit vitae portam, reseravit.*[55]

To paraphrase, the relative pronoun may sometimes refer to a different instance of a class from the one referred to by its antecedent. Thus, in the sentence quoted ("Woman, who closed the gate of life, opened it"), the relative pronoun *quae* refers to Eve, while its antecedent, *femina*, refers to the Virgin Mary. The writer of the *Glosa notabilis*, a popular fifteenth-century commentary on the *Doctrinale*, adds the example *Petrus laborat eo morbo quem Iacobus habet*, "Peter is suffering from the same disease that Jacob has," pointing out that Peter and Jacob are in reality suffering from different diseases *numerically:* "... quia est alius morbus numeraliter distinctus ab illo qui est in Petro et qui est in Iacobo."[56] As oversubtle as this may seem, it is nevertheless a valid observation about the way language is normally used; a modern example might be the sentence *John drives the same car*

54. Robertus de Basevorn, *Forma praedicandi*, see Th.-M. Charland, *Artes praedicandi: contribution à l'histoire de la rhétorique au moyen âge*, Publications de l'Institut d'études médiévales d'Ottowa 7 (Paris, 1936), p. 233. It should nevertheless be emphasized that the spheres of logic and grammar were clearly distinguished in the scholastic period, see Thurot, *Extraits*, pp. 128–30.

55. Reichling, *Das Doctrinale des Alexander de Villa-Dei*, p. 92, lines 1449–50. In the *Catholicon* of John of Genoa, composed in 1286, this rule is formulated thus: "Simplex vero relatio dicitur quando relativum et antecedens supponunt pro eodem in specie, sed non in numero, ut *mulier damnavit quae salvavit*, alia fuit mulier quae damnavit numero, quia Eva, et Alia que salvavit, quia Maria." Venice, September 24, 1483; Hain 2257, GW 3188, Proctor 4785, sig. b8[rb].

56. *Glosa notabilis secunde partis Alexandri* (Deventer, September 18, 1490; Copinger 339, GW 1092), sig. s2[r].

as Peter. However, it was an observation suggested by the study of logic and was linked to the theory of supposition.[57] Indeed, the fifteenth-century reader was warned of the logical provenance of the notion of *relatio simplex* by the marginal heading "Impedimentum contra regulam *logicalem*."

An analogous situation existed in relation to rhetoric. When grammarians cited sentences, for example, they customarily placed the words in the order subject-verb-complement. Thus, in the popular *Regule* of Francesco da Buti (1324 – 1406), we find examples such as *ego egeo denariorum et tu abundas scientie.*[58] This practice was continued by the humanist grammarians: Guarino cites sentences exemplified by *virtus debet placere hominibus;* Perotti has *Pyrrhus amat Penelopen, ego doceo te artem grammaticam,* and the like; and at the end of the fifteenth century we have Nebrija discussing such sentences as *ego video lapidem.*

It was up to the rhetorician to point out that the verb is normally placed at the end of the sentence in Latin, and the rhetoricians of the Quattrocento gave prominence to this fact. For instance, at the beginning of the century, Gasparino Barzizza states in his *De compositione:* "Laudatur igitur oratio illa quae in verbum saepius quam in aliam partem orationis finitur, ut in hoc exemplo *sola virtus est quae hominem beatam facit.*"[59] But from the way Barzizza expresses himself it is clear that he regards this as a stylistic precept, not a statement about how Latin sentences are customarily constructed. Thus, he immediately goes on to make another such stylistic recommendation, namely, that one should start sentences with the object rather than the subject:

---

57. See C. H. Kneepkens, "The Relatio Simplex in the Grammatical Tracts of the Late Twelfth and Early Thirteenth Century," *Vivarium* 15 (1977), 1 – 30. Supposition, briefly, was the referential function of a term in a specific proposition. Thus *homo* has a different referential function in the sentence *homo ambulat* from the one it has in *homo est species.* See Alan R. Perreiah, "Approaches to Supposition Theory," *The New Scholasticism* 45 (1971), 381 – 408; I. M. Bocheński, *A History of Formal Logic,* 2nd ed. (New York, 1970), pp. 162 – 73; and William and Martha Kneale, *The Development of Logic* (Oxford, 1962), pp. 246 – 74. The grammatical term *relatio simplex* suggested the corresponding logical term *suppositio simplex,* which was defined as the use of a term to refer to a mental concept (e.g., *homo* in *homo est species,* or *animal* in *animal est genus*); see *Ockham's Theory of Terms: Part I of the Summa Logicae,* translated and introduced by Michael J. Loux (Notre Dame, Ind., 1974), p. 198.

58. Pisa, Biblioteca Cateriniana del Seminario, Cod. 182, f. 8ʳ.

59. Joseph Alexander Furiettus, ed., *Gasparini Barzizii Bergomatis et Guiniforti Filii Opera* (Rome, 1723), p. 4.

"Commendatur praeterea oratio illa quam obliquam dicimus, id est quae a posterioribus dictionibus incipiat, ut *neminem fere comperies qui satis sibi in rebus adversis constet.* Ab apposito quidem, non a supposito verbi incipit oratio."[60]

To relegate questions of word order entirely to the rhetorician had the disadvantage that students started out learning sentences in one order while they were studying grammar, and had to switch to another order when they went on to the study of rhetoric. To obviate this disparity, Battista Guarini recommended in his *De modo et ordine docendi ac discendi* that elementary students should recite their basic syntactic rules with the verb at the end of the sentence, not in the middle: "Erit autem illud perquam utile ut in his regularum declamationibus consuescant ornate componere, ut, exempli causa, oratio plerumque verbo claudatur, et quicquid ab illo pendet anteponatur quam id a quo dependet. Facilius enim postea ad stili elegantiam perducuntur."[61]

But it is not clear whether Guarini's suggestion had any influence on pedagogical practice, for we observe other rhetoricians still contrasting the word order taught by the grammarians with the word order appropriate for the orator. For instance, Agostino Dati, in his influential *Elegantiolae,* makes the distinction very explicit: "Scis plenam orationem tribus constare partibus, quas suppositum (ut ipsorum vocabulis utar), verbum, et appositum vocant. Dicunt igitur grammatici *Scipio Africanus delevit Carthaginem.* Ornatioris vero eloquii homines converso potius utuntur ordine: *Carthaginem Scipio Africanus delevit.*"[62] The contrast is further systematized by Josse Bade in his commentary on Dati's manual, in which we find two long sets of numbered rules for handling word order, one for the grammarian and the other for the rhetorician.[63]

We observe a similar opposition between grammar and logic. A good example appears in the treatment of intrasentential relations.

60. Ibid.   61. Sig. A4ᵛ.

62. *Artis dicendi et scribendi preceptorium utilissimum* (Leipzig, 1497; Hain 6022, GW 8132), sigs. 2A2ᵛ – 2A3ʳ.

63. To take one example, the grammarian is said to begin the sentence with a noun in the vocative case, while the rhetorician places that constituent in third or fourth position, or even farther still from the beginning of the sentence: "Vocativus igitur, tametsi apud grammaticum primum locum efflagitat, nunc tertio, nunc quarto loco, nunc etiam remotiore a principio pones, ut Cicero: 'Quamquam te, Marce fili, annum iam audientem Cratippum, idque Athenis, abundare oportet praeceptis insti-

Although these were studied mainly by the logicians, and the grammarians, therefore, derived their notions on the subject from logic, the two disciplines developed separate terminologies to deal with what were, in essence, the very same phenomena. For instance, the terms *subiectum* and *praedicatum* were used exclusively by logicians, the grammarians preferring their own *suppositum* and *appositum*. Conversely, the term *copula* referred in grammatical analysis to the sentence connectives (*and, or,* and so forth), while the logicians used the same term to refer to the sign of predication. It is also significant that logicians felt free to use, if necessary, ungrammatical sentences in the course of analyzing propositions. Thus, Paul of Venice (d. 1429), in his monumental *Logica magna*, resolves the sentence *utinam non legerem,* "Oh that I might not read," into the ungrammatical *opto quod non legerem,* "I wish that I might not read," adding the interesting comment: "If this analysis is objected to by an appeal to grammarians' rules, it should be pointed out that the logician has a different way of speaking from the grammarian, as is obvious from many cases."[64] In practice, therefore, the student learned a different version of logical syntax from the grammarian from the one taught by the logician.

To sum up, we observe both overlap and opposition in the relation among the various branches of the *trivium.* In the case of grammar and rhetoric, the overlap was already noticeable in antiquity, as is revealed by the remarks of Quintilian I have quoted above. Later, in the Middle Ages, a different kind of overlap developed, when the teaching of *dictamen* was in the hands of grammarians and when, as we have seen, the presentation of grammatical facts in the textbooks was influenced by the needs of the prospective *dictator.* Another permanent factor that contributed to this overlap was that grammar, in the wider sense of the term, had traditionally always included such topics as poetics, metrics, and even the tropes and *colores rhetorici.*[65] Finally, we should not forget that grammatical correctness was regarded as one of the indispensable constituents of *elegantia,* which was, in turn, one of the basic requirements emphasized by both the

---

tutisque philosophiae.'" *Augustini Dati Elegantiocule cum duplici commentario* (Nuremberg, September 16, 1504), sig. D4ᵛ.

64. "Et si contra hoc instatur adducendo regulas grammaticorum, dicatur quod logicus habet alium modum loquendi quam grammaticus, sicut patet in multis." *Logica magna Pauli Veneti* (Venice, October 24, 1499, Hain *12505), f. 101ᵛᵃ.

65. A complete list of the *colores rhetorici* may be found, for instance, in the *Catholi-*

medieval and the ancient rhetorician.[66] In a real sense, then, grammar was an integral part of rhetoric.

During the Renaissance, rhetoric dramatically enhanced its standing vis-à-vis the other two branches of the *trivium*. Formal logic of the kind practiced by the scholastics made way for a rhetoricized *ars disserendi*. The previous ties between grammatical and logical analysis loosened, while the long-standing association between grammar and rhetoric was strengthened. One might plausibly suggest, for instance, that Erasmus conveyed the closeness of this latter association by his choice of the title for his manual *De duplici copia verborum ac rerum*, indicating, as it does, that the two facets of *copia*, form and matter, though separable in practice, are in essence indissoluble.[67]

At the same time, we must not overlook the other side of the coin: the two disciplines retained their separate identities and in many ways developed along different lines. This is especially noticeable in the matter of new textbooks. Guarino, for example, wrote several grammatical works in spite of the fact that he was not interested in grammar for its own sake, while in the realm of rhetoric he was content to use an ancient manual, the *Rhetorica ad Herennium*. Similarly, when Nebrija was once asked why he had never written a rhetoric textbook comparable to his *Introductiones Latinae* on grammar, he replied that he had had many new things to say about gram-

---

con of John of Genoa. See also the *Doctrinale* and the *Graecismus* for coverage of these areas that lie outside grammar in the narrow sense of the term.

66. Thus, we read in the *Rhetorica ad Herennium:* "Elegantia est quae facit ut locus unus quisque pure et aperte dici videatur. Haec tribuitur in Latinitatem et explanationem. Latinitas est quae sermonem puram conservat ab omni vitio remotum. Vitia in sermone, quo minus is Latinus sit, duo possunt esse: soloecismus et barbarismus" (4.12.17). This passage is echoed in the opening paragraph of the *Regulae rhetoricae* of Francesco da Buti (1324 – 1406): "Ex quo primo sciendum est quod tria in omni exquisito dictamine requiruntur, scilicet elegantia, compositio, et ornatus, quorum primum est adeo necessarium, quod sine ipso nullum potest dictaminis aedificium permanere. ... Nam primum, elegantia est quae reddit orationem Latinitate puram et explanationem perspicuam. Latinitas est quae servat orationem puram ab omni artis grammaticae vitio Latinitati contrario. Vitia enim Latinitati contraria sunt soloecismus et decem vitia annexa, de quibus traditur documentum a Donato in *Barbarismo*." Rome, Biblioteca Angelica, Cod. 1375, f. 91ᵛ.

67. Erasmus makes the point himself: "Hae [*sc.* copia rerum et copia verborum] quamquam alicubi sic coniunctae videri possunt, ut haud facile dignoscas, ita alteri inservit altera, ut praeceptis potius quam re atque usu discretae videantur; nos tamen docendi gratia ita separabimus, ut neque superstitionis in secando, neque rursum negligentiae merito damnari possimus." *De duplici copia*, 1.7; *Opera omnia*, ed. Clericus, 1.col.6A.

mar, whereas in rhetoric everything had already been said and was familiar to everybody.[68]

We have seen that grammar and rhetoric were the most important linguistic disciplines practiced by Renaissance humanists. Grammar was the more elementary of the two, in the curricular sense, and perhaps for that reason it was the area in which the humanists were in a position to contribute a great deal of their own. In rhetoric, by contrast, the legacy of antiquity was much more substantial and hence not so easy to emulate — one thinks of such literary masterpieces as Cicero's *De oratore* and Quintilian's *Institutiones*. The relation between the two disciplines was close, but in this regard the humanists were in debt to their immediate medieval predecessors, who had also oriented much of their grammatical instruction towards the distant goal of stylistic fluency. The most significant change we observe between medieval and Renaissance grammar was a consequence of the new attitude to formal logic, which ceased to provide the basic conceptual framework for all the other disciplines. Further research will undoubtedly reveal what wider repercussions the shift from medieval to Renaissance rhetoric had on the overall complexion of European intellectual life.

68. The statement occurs in the prologue to a compilation made by Nebrija of various rhetorical works by Aristotle, Cicero, and Quintilian, which appeared at Alcalá in 1515. He reports there that Cardinal Cisneros put the following question to him: "¿Por qué no haceis unas Introducciones Retóricas como las que para tanta gloria vuestra y de nuestra nación hicisteis a la Gramática?" To this Nebrija replied as follows: "Porque allí tenía muchos como yo a quienes imitar y aquí pocos, y que no pueden facilmente ser imitados. Allí tenía yo muchas cosas nuevas que decir, aquí no, porque todo está dicho ya y anda en boca de todos." This may be found in Antonio Palau y Dulcet, *Manual del librero hispanoamericano*, 2nd ed., vol. 10 (Barcelona, 1957), p. 488b.

Erasmus on the
Art of Letter-Writing

JUDITH RICE HENDERSON

Erasmus's *Opus de conscribendis epistolis* (Basel: Johann Froben, 1522) has been described by Aloïs Gerlo as "a vigorous attack on the medieval *formulae* for letter-writing," "a manifesto against the outdated manuals and old-fashioned methods of the day."[1] This judgment seems to me more applicable to the early drafts of the treatise written during Erasmus's years in Paris (1495 – 1499) and later published in unauthorized editions: *Brevissima maximeque compendiaria conficiendarum epistolarum formula* (Erfurt: Mattheus Maler, 1520) and *Libellus de conscribendis epistolis* (Cambridge: John Siberch, 1521). In these drafts Erasmus, like his humanist contemporaries in Germany, drew upon fifteenth-century Italian handbooks on letter-writing and classical models to promote a new epistolography in opposition to the medieval *ars dictaminis* still alive in the schools of northern Europe. By 1522, when Erasmus completely revised and greatly enlarged his treatise, he had already begun to react to those extremes of classicism in sixteenth-century Italy that he would attack six years later in the *Ciceronianus* (Basel: *in officina Frobeniana*, 1528). Without approving

---

1. "The *Opus de conscribendis epistolis* of Erasmus and the Tradition of the *Ars epistolica*," in *Classical Influences on European Culture* A.D. *500 – 1500*, ed. R. R. Bolgar (Cambridge, 1971), pp. 107, 109. Similar views have been expressed by Wesley Trimpi, *Ben Jonson's Poems: A Study of the Plain Style* (Stanford, Calif., 1962), pp. 69 – 70; Cecil H. Clough, "The Cult of Antiquity: Letters and Letter Collections," in *Cultural Aspects of the Italian Renaissance: Essays in Honour of Paul Oskar Kristeller*, ed. Cecil H. Clough (Manchester, 1976), pp. 47 – 48; and Marc Fumaroli, "Genèse de l'épistolographie classique: rhétorique humaniste de la lettre, de Pétrarque à Juste Lipse," *Revue d'histoire littéraire de la France* 78 (1978), 886 – 905.

the legalism of the medieval tradition, in the *Opus de conscribendis epistolis* Erasmus opposed those Ciceronian purists who would confine the genre within the limits of the familiar letter and purge humanist epistolography of all vestiges of the *ars dictaminis*. If the letter was to remain the important tool of intellectual and religious reform that it had become in the hands of Erasmus and his contemporaries, it must be flexible in subject matter and style, unencumbered by the new prescriptions of the Ciceronians.[2]

The humanists were, as Paul Oskar Kristeller has demonstrated, "the professional successors of the medieval Italian *dictatores*," inheriting their offices "either as teachers of the humanities in secondary schools or universities, or as secretaries to princes or cities."[3] Founded in the 1080s by Alberic of Monte Cassino, the *ars dictaminis* came of age at Bologna in the first half of the twelfth century and by the end of that century had spread to France, Germany, and England.[4] Essen-

2. Gerlo has remarked, "The *Opus de Conscribendis Epistolis* contains the germs of the *Ciceronianus*" (p. 112), but by this he apparently means only that Erasmus showed his opposition to the exclusive imitation of Cicero by recommending Pliny and Poliziano as additional epistolary models. Fumaroli has also seen a relationship between the *Opus de conscribendis epistolis* and the *Ciceronianus*. He has argued that the Ciceronians continued the impersonal, official epistolography of the *dictatores* (pp. 887–88). Opposed to this professional epistolography was the personal, private epistolography of Petrarca, Erasmus, and Lipsius, to whom the letter collection was "une autobiographie morale fragmentée" and the letter "déjà un 'essai' au sens de Montaigne, abordant tous les sujets à partir d'un *moi* méditant et central" (p. 888). Thus Erasmus's opposition to "l'Ancien Testament légaliste des *Artes dictaminis médiévaux*" in the *Opus de conscribendis epistolis* anticipated his attack on "un légalisme rhétorique paganisant" in the *Ciceronianus* (p. 891). While I agree that Erasmus opposed legalism, whether medieval or Ciceronian, I see the *Opus de conscribendis epistolis*, like the *Ciceronianus*, as primarily an attack on Ciceronian legalism. Furthermore, while admiring much about Professor Fumaroli's perceptive analysis of Erasmus's treatise on letter-writing, I would describe the opposition between an official and a private epistolography in the Renaissance rather differently. I believe that the neoclassic tradition of the private (or familiar) letter initiated by Petrarca resulted in Ciceronianism and, ultimately, in the *Epistolica institutio* of Justus Lipsius. Although Erasmus gave the familiar letter an important place in both his theory and his practice, I would argue that the *Opus de conscribendis epistolis* promoted the official, professional epistolography inherited from the *ars dictaminis* as a tool of humanist reform. The present essay is part of a work in progress: "The Art of Letter-Writing in the Renaissance."

3. *Renaissance Thought: The Classic, Scholastic, and Humanist Strains* (New York, 1961), pp. 11–12.

4. James J. Murphy, *Rhetoric in the Middle Ages* (Berkeley and Los Angeles, 1974), pp. 194–268, is my principal source for the following description of the *ars dictaminis*, but I have also consulted, besides editions and studies of individual *artes dictandi*, which are too numerous to mention here, the following general studies: Natalis Valois, *De arte*

tially, the *ars dictaminis* applied classical rhetoric to letter-writing, which, with the demise of the classical institutions that had bred the orator, had become the political skill most in demand in the Middle Ages. In imitation of the structure of the classical oration, the *ars dictaminis* divided the letter into parts, usually five: *salutatio, exordium* or *captatio benevolentiae, narratio, petitio,* and *conclusio.* The *salutatio* received the most attention in the medieval handbooks that provided formulas for courteously addressing all ranks in the hierarchy of feudal society. In fact, its division into parts or sometimes its *salutatio* alone were considered the defining features of the letter, distinguishing it from other kinds of *dictamen.*[5] The letter also had its

scribendi epistolas apud Gallicos Medii Aevi scriptores rhetoresve (Paris, 1880); Louis John Paetow, *The Arts Course at Medieval Universities,* in University of Illinois Studies, vol. 3, no. 7 (January 1910), 67–91; Reginald L. Poole, *Lectures on the History of the Papal Chancery* (Cambridge, 1915), pp. 76–97; Charles Sears Baldwin, *Medieval Rhetoric and Poetic* (New York, 1928), pp. 206–27; Charles Homer Haskins, *Studies in Mediaeval Culture* (New York, 1929), pp. 1–35, 124–47, 170–92; N. Denholm-Young, *Collected Papers on Mediaeval Subjects* (Oxford, 1946), pp.26–55; J. de Ghellinck, *L'Essor de la littérature latine au XIIe siècle,* 2nd. ed., in *Museum Lessianum, Section Historique,* nos. 4–5 (Brussels, 1955), pp. 278–92; Franz-Josef Schmale, "Die bologneser Schule der Ars dictandi," *Deutsches Archiv für Erforschung des Mittelalters,* 13 (1957), 16–34; Giuseppe Vecchi, *Il magistero delle "Artes" latine a Bologna nel medioevo,* in *Pubblicazioni della Facoltà di Magistero Università di Bologna,* no. 2 (Bologna, 1958); Harris Fletcher, "Latin Prose Rhythm in the Late Middle Ages and Renaissance," in *Classical Studies Presented to Ben Edwin Perry,* Illinois Studies in Language and Literature 58 (Urbana Ill., 1969), pp. 248–91; Helene Wieruszowski, *Politics and Culture in Medieval Spain and Italy,* Storia e Letteratura 121 (Rome, 1971), pp. 331–77, 387–474, 515–61, 589–627, 641–46; Charles Faulhaber, *Latin Rhetorical Theory in Thirteenth and Fourteenth Century Castile,* University of California Publications in Modern Philology 103 (Berkeley and Los Angeles, 1972), passim; James R. Banker, "The *Ars dictaminis* and Rhetorical Textbooks at the Bolognese University in the Fourteenth Century," *Medievalia et Humanistica* n.s. 5 (1974), 153–68. I have not yet been able to obtain Marian Plezia, "L'Origine de la théorie du *Cursus* rhythmique au XIIe siècle," *Archivum Latinitatis Medii Aevi* 39 [1974], 5–22; Tore Janson, *Prose Rhythm in Medieval Latin from the 9th to the 13th Century,* Acta Universitatis Stockholmiensis, Studia Latina Stockholmiensia, 20 (Stockholm [1975]); or Carol D. Lanham, *Salutatio Formulas in Latin Letters to 1200: Syntax, Style, and Theory,* Münchener Beiträge zur Mediävistik und Renaissancen Forschung (Munich, 1975). They are cited by Faulhaber, "The *Summa dictaminis* of Guido Faba," in *Medieval Eloquence: Studies in the Theory and Practice of Medieval Rhetoric,* ed. James J. Murphy (Berkeley and Los Angeles, 1978), pp. 85–111.

5. An example of the first type of definition can be found in an anonymous *Summa dictaminis* (ca. 1200–1210), ed. Ludwig Rockinger, *Briefsteller und Formelbücher des eilften bis vierzehnten Jahrhunderts,* in Quellen zur bayerischen und deutschen Geschichte 9 (Munich, 1863–1864), p. 103: *Epistola sic diffinitur, epistola est oracio congrua suis e partibus conuenienter conposita affectum mentis plene significans. . . . suis e partibus dixi,*

own style, the *cursus*, a rhythmical prose developed in the Papal Curia and incorporated into the handbooks on letter-writing beginning about 1180.

The formal letter of the *dictator* was entirely different from the familiar letter of classical tradition. Classical theory had distinguished the *sermo* or ordinary language of the letter from the *contentio* or formal speech of the oration. Therefore letter-writing had not been treated in the rhetorical works of Cicero and Quintilian, although Demetrius did discuss it in his section on the plain style in *De elocutione*.[6] There he warned against "making an oratorical display" (p. 441) in a letter: "It is absurd to build up periods, as if you were writing not a letter but a speech for the law courts" (p. 443). The letter, he thought, should be brief and, like the dialogue to which it was closely related, "should abound in glimpses of character. It may be said that everybody reveals his own soul in his letters" (p. 441). The subject matter should be as simple as the style: "If anybody should write of logical subtleties or questions of natural history in a letter, he writes indeed, but not a letter. A letter is designed to be the heart's good wishes in brief; it is the exposition of a simple subject in simple terms" (p. 443).

The discovery of the letters of Cicero by Francesco Petrarca and Coluccio Salutati led to a vogue of classical imitation that was to culminate in the Ciceronianism of the early sixteenth century.[7] How-

---

quia quinque sunt partes dictaminis: salutacio, exordium, narracio, peticio, et conclusio. An example of the second type of definition can be found in *Die Ars dictandi des Thomas von Capua.*, ed. Emmy Heller, in *Sitzungsberichte der Heidelberger Akademie der Wissenschaften, Philosophisch-historische Klasse* (1928 – 1929), 4.15; *Est ergo epistola litteralis legatio diversarum personarum capax, sumens principium cum effectu salutis.* Typically the definition of the letter ended a series of definitions, first *dictamen*, then its three or four parts — *metricum, rhythmicum, prosaicum,* and sometimes *prosimetricum* or *mixtum* — and finally *epistola*, a division of *prosaicum*.

6. *On Style*, trans. W. Rhys Roberts, rev. ed., The Loeb Classical Library (London, 1932), pp. 438 – 45.

7. Cicero's letters were copied from time to time during the Middle Ages. See L. D. Reynolds and N. G. Wilson, *Scribes and Scholars: A Guide to the Transmission of Greek and Latin Literature* (London, 1968), pp. 86, 92, 96, 105. However, Petrarca first called attention to them in his letters to dead authors after his discovery of a manuscript of the *Letters to Atticus, Quintus, and Brutus* in the Chapter Library at Verona in 1345. Salutati found the *Ad Familiares* in 1389 in the Cathedral Library at Vercelli. He became the first humanist to own copies of both collections of Cicero's letters. For accounts of these "discoveries" and their influence on humanist letter-writing, see John Edwin Sandys, *A History of Classical Scholarship*, vol. 2 (Cambridge, 1908), pp. 7, 18, 31; Reynolds and Wilson, *Scribes and Scholars*, pp. 109, 112; and Rudolph Pfeiffer, *History of Classical Scholarship from 1300 to 1850* (Oxford, 1976), pp. 9 – 11, 26.

ever, for most humanists Cicero was not the only epistolary model. Angelo Poliziano summarized the situation in the late fifteenth century when he defended the eclecticism of his own letter collection in the dedication to Piero de' Medici:

> I acknowledge the style of my letters is very unequal; for which I expect not to escape reprehension. But let it be remembered that the writer was not always in the same humour; and that one mode of writing is by no means suited to every person, and every subject. . . . However, among so many discordant opinions of those who write, or who give rules for writing letters, I do not despair of finding an apology. One will say, for instance, "these letters are very unlike Cicero's." I shall answer, not without good authority, that Cicero is not to be regarded as a proper model in epistolary composition. Another will pronounce me the mere echo of Cicero. To him I shall reply, — that I feel myself highly gratified in being deemed able to express even a faint resemblance of such an original. A third could wish I had adopted the manner of Pliny the orator, whose taste and judgment are so highly spoken of. — My answer will be, I entertain a thorough contempt for all the writers of Pliny's age. Does my style, in the opinion of a fourth, savour strongly of that very author? I shelter myself under the authority of Sidonius Apollinaris, an authority by no means to be contemned, who assigns to Pliny the palm in letter-writing. Is it discovered that I resemble Symmachus? I blush not to imitate one whose brevity and frankness are admired. Am I thought unlike him? It is because I object to his dryness.

He might defend himself against his critics by citing other classical authorities — he named more than fifteen others — but he concluded, "to their censures I am comparatively indifferent."[8]

On the Ciceronians and their controversy with Erasmus, see Remigio Sabbadini, *Storia del Ciceronianismo* (Turin, 1885), pp. 1–74; John Edwin Sandys, *Harvard Lectures on the Revival of Learning* (Cambridge, 1905), pp. 145–73; Izora Scott, *Controversies over the Imitation of Cicero,* in Contributions to Education, no. 35 (New York, 1910); Walter Rüegg, *Cicero und der Humanismus: Formale Untersuchungen über Petrarca und Erasmus* (Zürich, 1946), esp. pp. 117–25; Giuseppe Toffanin, *Il Cinquecento,* 6th ed. rev. and enl. (Milan, 1960), passim; Giulio Vallese, *Studi di letteratura umanistica da Dante ad Erasmo,* 2nd ed. (Naples, 1964), pp. 101–26; Desiderio Erasmo da Rotterdam, *Il Ciceroniano o della stile migliore,* ed. Angiolo Gambaro (Brescia, 1965), pp. xxi–cxii; Emile V. Telle, ed., *L'Erasmianus sive Ciceronianus d'Etienne Dolet (1535),* Travaux d'Humanisme et Renaissance 138 (Geneva, 1974), pp. 9–95.

8. The Rev. W. Parr Greswell, trans., *Memoirs of Angelus Politianus, et al.,* 2nd ed. augmented (Manchester and London, 1805), pp. 124–27. For the original, see *Omnia Opera Angeli Politiani* (Venice, 1498; rpt. in facsimile, Rome, n.d.), a3$^{\mathrm{r-v}}$.

In spite of this frenzy of classical imitation, the *ars dictaminis* only gradually gave way to the new epistolography. Gudrun Lindholm has demonstrated, for example, that the *cursus* was used regularly in the fourteenth century by Cola di Rienzo and Coluccio Salutati. The fifteenth-century humanists Leonardo Bruni, Gasparino Barzizza, and Poggio Bracciolini abandoned the medieval rhythms in their secular letters, but the *cursus* continued to appear in papal correspondence until it was rejected in the early sixteenth century by Pietro Bembo and Jacopo Sadoleto, those ardent Ciceronians who served as secretaries to Pope Leo X.[9]

Ronald G. Witt's *Coluccio Salutati and his Public Letters* is a valuable study of epistolography in this transitional period from the Middle Ages to the Renaissance.[10] Witt sees Salutati "more as the last of the great medieval chancellors rather than as the progenitor of a line of humanist ones" (p. 3). Not only did Salutati continue to use the *cursus* in his public correspondence, but he even reinstated "a style of aulic rhetoric, the *stilus rhetoricus,* which had been employed a century before in the chancery and which in the meantime had been replaced by humbler or at least less dynamic forms of composition" (p. 33). In August and September 1375, a few months after his election to the Florentine chancery, Salutati experimented with substituting the singular *tu* for the plural *vos* in addressing individuals but abandoned this attempt at humanist reform, "perhaps as a result of complaints from the addressees" (p. 26). He elaborated rather than simplified the flattering salutations medieval courtesy demanded in letters to great powers (pp. 27 – 28). Witt concludes that "apart from the abortive effort to substitute *tu* for *vos* in some cases where the latter was customarily used in addressing individuals, it would be difficult to define any specific stylistic details in the missives which owe their inspiration unambiguously to humanism" (p. 28). Salutati's humanism is revealed, rather, by his skillful rhetoric: his closely reasoned arguments, his use of historical *exempla,* and his flexibility in adapting to the dramatic situation of each letter (pp. 38 – 40).

Fifteenth-century Italian handbooks on letter-writing defined the letter, following classical authorities, as a conversation between absent friends on their own affairs.[11] Yet in their enthusiasm for the

9. *Studien zum mittellateinischen Prosarhythmus: seine Entwicklung und sein Abklingen in der Briefliteratur Italiens,* in Acta Universitatis Stockholmiensis, Studia Latina Stockholmiensia 10 (Stockholm, 1963), pp. 198 – 201.

10. Travaux d'Humanismé et Renaissance 151 (Geneva, 1976).

11. For example, the section *De componendis epistolis* of Niccolò Perotti's *Rudimenta*

newly discovered rhetorical works of Cicero and Quintilian, they not only continued but even enlarged the debt of letter-writing to the art of oratory.[12] The *Novum epistolarium* of Giammario Filelfo opened with *Praecepta artis rhetorices*, a description of the divisions of the oration, the *colores rhetorici* or figures of speech, the *genera dicendi* or styles of the orator, and *pronuntiatio* or oral delivery, which, as even Filelfo admitted, is irrelevant to letter-writing.[13] The *De componendis et ornandis epistolis* of Giovanni Sulpizio of Veroli described the divisions of the oration, the *genera dicendi*, the *virtutes dicendi* or virtues of style, the *colores rhetorici*, the *causae orationis* or kinds of orations (*demonstrativa, deliberativa, judiciale*), *pronuntiatio*, and *memoria*, which, like *pronuntiatio*, was one of the five parts of rhetoric important to the orator but useless to the writer.[14]

Erasmus's attitude toward this rhetorical content in the letter-writing handbooks of his Italian predecessors is unclear. In a letter to

grammatices (London, 1512; orig. pub. 1473) began, *Quare invente sunt epistole? Ut eos cum quibus sive propter absentiam sive propter ruborem (seu ob aliam quamvis causam loqui non licet) certiores facere possumus si quid sit quos eos scribere oporteat, sive nostra, sive illorum, sive aliorum causa* (L4^r). Francesco Negro's *Opusculum scribendi epistolas* (Venice, 1492; orig. pub. Venice, 1488) defined the letter as *oratio pedestris: quae absentes amicos praesentes facit tam ad voluptatem: quam ad utilitatem tum publicam tum privatam: divinitus excogitata* (A3^r). Negro had previously cited a similar definition by the Latin comedian Sextus Turpilius (A2^v). In quoting Renaissance editions I have expanded abbreviations and modernized the use of *i, j, s, u, v,* and *w.*

12. A complete copy of Quintilian's *Institutio oratoria*, known to Petrarca only in a mutilated version, was discovered by Poggio Bracciolini in 1416. Cicero's *De inventione* and the pseudo-Ciceronian *Rhetorica ad Herennium* (popularly called the *Rhetorica vetus* and *Rhetorica nova*, respectively) were used throughout the Middle Ages, but Cicero's *Brutus* and the complete texts of his *Orator* and *De oratore* were discovered in 1421. See Sandys, *A History of Classical Scholarship*, 2.26–27, 31–32; Pfeiffer, pp. 32–33.

In *Praise and Blame in Renaissance Rome: Rhetoric, Doctrine, and Reform in the Sacred Orators of the Papal Court, c. 1450–1521*, Duke Monographs in Medieval and Renaissance Studies, no. 3 (Durham, N.C., 1979), John W. O'Malley has observed that in his letter-writing treatise, *De ratione scribendi libri tres* (composed before 1485), the Florentine humanist Aurelio "Lippo" Brandolini "communicates at least as much about his understanding of oratory as he does about how to write letters" (p. 45). Erasmus does not mention this treatise, which as far as I can determine was not published during his lifetime. Cf. O'Malley, p. 45, note 17. In the edition published at Basel by Joannes Oporinus in 1549, which I have seen in the Newberry Library, the letter-writing treatises of Juan Luis Vives, Conrad Celtis, Christoph Hegendorf, Erasmus's *Brevissima formula*, and a portion of *De verborum electione & collocatione* by Jacobus Lodovicus Strebaeus are appended.

13. Milan, 1487; orig. pub. Milan, 1484.

14. Rome, 1491; orig. pub. Venice, 1489.

William Blount, Lord Mountjoy, of November 1499, accompanying an early draft of his own treatise on letter-writing, Erasmus asked concerning the *Novum epistolarium* of Filelfo, "what was the use of repeating, at the very beginning of the book, the rules of rhetoric which are so often given extensively elsewhere? Was it to make children abandon the books of Cicero and Quintilian in order to read this man's rubbish?"[15] In the same letter he approved the comments on letter-writing of Sulpizio and Niccolò Perotti—whom he elsewhere described as the two best Latin grammarians of the age—because they appeared in "books of grammar, not of rhetoric."[16] Erasmus must have read Sulpizio's *De componendis et ornandis epistolis* in an edition of the same author's *Grammatica,* to which it was sometimes appended, but one wonders how he could have overlooked Sulpizio's dependence on classical rhetoric.[17]

Perhaps, like his Italian predecessors, Erasmus found rhetoric a natural guide to letter-writing. One suspects that he disliked Filelfo's "rules of rhetoric" because they were not based squarely on Cicero and Quintilian, as Sulpizio's were, and because they were applied too mechanically. Filelfo divided each of his eighty kinds of letters into three modes—familiar, very familiar, and serious—and assigned one of the *genera dicendi* to each: the middle style to the familiar letter, the plain style to the very familiar letter, and the grand style to the serious letter. This scheme, in addition to ignoring the classical definition of the letter as *sermo,* bred such strange mutations as the *epistola jocosa gravis,* the "serious jovial letter." Erasmus complained, "we might have endured his irritating insistence on imposing a different style on each kind of letter had he not done so incompetently" (*CWE,* ep. 117). To the *Opusculum scribendi epistolas* of Francesco Negro, Erasmus likewise objected that the rules were "pedantically petty and not even based, as they should have been, upon the fundamental texts in the authorities on rhetoric" (*CWE,* ep. 117). In the *Libellus de conscribendis epistolis,* a manuscript of which probably ac-

15. R. A. B. Mynors and D. F. S. Thomson, trans., in *Collected Works of Erasmus* (Toronto; 1974–), 1, ed. Wallace K. Ferguson, ep. 117. For the original see *Opus Epistolarum Des. Erasmi Roterodami,* ed. P. S. Allen et al. (Oxford, 1906–1958), ep. 117. Hereafter these editions will be cited as *CWE* and Allen, respectively.

16. See *CWE,* 1 ep. 101; and *De ratione studii,* ed. Jean-Claude Margolin, in *Opera omnia,* 1.2 (Amsterdam, 1971), 148. Hereafter the Amsterdam edition will be cited as *ASD.*

17. For example, the edition entitled *Regulae Sulpitii* (n.p., n.d., but the Newberry Library, where I saw a copy, suggests Venice, ca. 1495), g2^v–h6^r.

companied epistle 117, as I shall argue below, Erasmus criticized Negro for demanding that every letter contain an *exordium* (B3^r). Each of the sample letters in Negro's treatise was divided into three to five parts, continuing the tradition of the *ars dictaminis*. In epistle 117 Erasmus also criticized Filelfo's synonyms and Negro's sample letters. Sulpizio's handbook was less medieval than those of Filelfo and Negro. Although he treated the composition of both orations and letters, Sulpizio insisted upon simplicity of epistolary style and explained clearly the classical forms of *salutatio, valedictio,* dating, and *subscriptio.*

The humanist enthusiasm for classical rhetoric was not the only factor that worked against a wholesale adoption of the classical tradition of the familiar letter. Like the *dictator,* the humanist established his professional reputation largely on the basis of his skill in letter-writing. With the example of classical letter collections before him, he naturally began to collect and publish his own letters, and inevitably he used these letters not only to prove his skill as a writer but also to spread the doctrines of humanism. As Cecil H. Clough has remarked, the letter became "the prime means by which scholars, and particularly those devoted to the cult of Antiquity, disseminated their ideas and made their case in scholarly controversy."[18] Erasmus's correspondence is typical in this respect. Wallace K. Ferguson has noted that, particularly after his return to the Continent from England in 1514, Erasmus's letters "to a far greater degree than hitherto contain illuminating comments, sometimes developed into full-scale essays on classical, biblical, and patristic scholarship, on contemporary literary criticism, on the reform of education and theology through a combination of *bonae litterae* and the *philosophia Christi,* on the horrors of war, and on all the problems raised by the Lutheran Reformation. At a time when there were no learned journals in which scholars could have their articles published, letters, whether intended to be printed or merely to be circulated in manuscript, served much the same purpose" (*CWE,* 1.xii). Certainly the humanists, encouraged by classical example, wrote familiar letters, but these formed only part of their correspondence. In practice if not in the-

18. "The Cult of Antiquity," p. 33. Cf. Pierre Mesnard, "Le Commerce épistolaire, comme expression sociale de l'individualisme humaniste," in *Individu et société à la Renaissance,* in Université libre de Bruxelles: Travaux de l'Institut pour l'étude de la Renaissance et de l'Humanisme 3 (Brussels and Paris, 1967), pp. 15–31.

ory, the letter continued to be defined not by its subject matter and style but only by its *salutatio*.[19]

Nevertheless, to Erasmus's contemporaries in Germany at the beginning of the sixteenth century, when Italian humanism had just begun to cross the Alps, the differences between medieval and humanist epistolography were clear. In his *Commentaria epistolarum conficiendarum*, Heinrich Bebel, professor of rhetoric and poetry at Tübingen from 1497 to 1518, attacked the authors of the "barbaric" handbooks then circulating in German schools: Paulus Lescher, Joannes Borida of Aquilegia, Pontius, Carolus Virulus, and Samuel de Monte Rutilo.[20] Bebel appealed to classical authority to prove that a letter is a conversation between absent friends on their own affairs and should therefore be written not in an oratorical style but in pure

19. Juan Luis Vives was, as far as I can discover, the first humanist to consider the implications of defining the letter by its *salutatio*. In the *De conscribendis epistolis*, first published at Antwerp by Michael Hillen in 1533, Vives observed that by this definition Cicero's *Tusculan Disputations, De finibus, De senectute, De amicitia*, and *De officiis* would be letters because they were addressed either to Brutus or to Atticus or to Cicero's son Marcus. Vives, whose epistolography was more consistently classical than his predecessors', argued that the letter could be distinguished from the treatise by its simple style. See *Opera omnia* (Valencia, 1782, rpt. in facsimile, London, 1964), 2.264–65, 298. As I shall argue below, to Erasmus, flexibility, not simplicity, of style was the distinguishing characteristic of the letter.

20. (Pforzheim, 1509; orig. pub. Tübingen, 1500), A4^v–5^r. The *Rhetorica pro conficiendis epistolis accommodata* of Paulus Lescher was printed at least six times between 1487 and 1493. See L. Hain, *Repertorium Bibliographicum* (Stuttgart, 1826–1838), no. 10033–38. Hain records only one edition (no. 13255) of the *Rhetorica* of Poncius or Pontius (n.p., 1486). The *Epistolarum formulae* (Louvain, 1476) of Carolus Virulus, regent of the Lily at Louvain from 1437 to 1493, was frequently reprinted in the last quarter of the fifteenth century but came to be held in contempt by the new humanist generation of the early sixteenth century. Erasmus's comments on it are typical. See *Opus de conscribendis epistolis*, in *ASD*, 1.2.230–31,265–66, 284, and *Dilutio eorum quae Iodocus Clithoveus scripsit adversus declamationem Des. Erasmi Roterodami suasoriam matrimonii*, ed. Émile V. Telle, in *De Pétrarque à Descartes*, ed. Pierre Mesnard, 15 (Paris, 1968), p. 71. I have not been able to identify the handbooks of Joannes Borida of Aquilegia and Samuel de Monte Rutilo; however, Eduard Böcking, ed., *Ulrichi Hutteni Equitis Operum Supplementum* (Leipzig, 1864–1869), 2.463–64, offers some speculations about the latter. With Pontius and Carolus Virulus, Samuel de Monte Rutilo is among those satirized in the *Epistolae obscurorum virorum*. According to Bebel, the treatise by Joannes Borida de Aquilegia was entitled *Practica seu usus dictaminis*. As this essay was going to press, Professor Emil J. Polak of Queensborough Community College, Bayside, New York, pointed out to me that Rockinger in *Briefsteller und Formelbücher* published a treatise entitled *Practica sive usus dictaminis* by Johannes Bondi of Aquilegia. However, most manuscripts attribute the work (ca. 1300?) to Lawrence of Aquilegia, perhaps his teacher. See Murphy, *Rhetoric in the Middle Ages*, pp. 258–63.

Latin *sermo.* He added, citing Symmachus, that a letter should be brief without being dry and jejune, faults Bebel found in the letters of Seneca. The five parts "our Germans" require in a letter and for which they provide formulas are, he asserted, inappropriate or unnecessary. The *exordium* has been usurped from the oration, while not every letter requires *narratio* or *petitio.* Our purpose may be rather to persuade or dissuade, to declare our friendship, to exhort to virtue or deter from vice. As Quintilian said, good writing cannot be reduced to a few precepts (A5^{r-v}). In place of the handbooks he mentioned, Bebel would have the student read the models he had named in an earlier treatise, *Qui auctores legendi sint ad comparationem eloquentiae* (A5^v). There he recommended Cicero, Pliny, and Filelfo in letter-writing but had reservations about allowing the young student to imitate Sidonius Apollinaris and Symmachus.[21]

After treating vices and virtues of composition (A5^v-6^v), Bebel attacked the formulas for *salutatio* found in contemporary handbooks. As he described them, the differences between the medieval and humanist *salutatio* were these:

1. If the letter was addressed to a superior, the medieval *dictator* placed the name of the addressee before his own; the humanist, following classical practice, placed his own name first, even if he was a man of humble station writing to the pope or emperor: *H. Bebelius iustingensis poeta. Maximiliano Romanorum imperatori semper augusto* (A6^v).

2. The recipient of the letter was to be addressed in the singular, not in the plural. Bebel found especially distasteful the medieval custom of addressing the correspondent by the "polite" plural *vos* rather than by the singular *tu* (A6^v-7^r).

3. The greeting was to be expressed as *salutem dicit* or *salutem plurimam dicit* (A7^{r-v}). In *Contra epistolas Caroli,* which was appended to the *Commentaria* in 1503, Bebel laughed at the old-fashioned flourishes of Carolus Virulus: *Immensas perenni favore salutes; Salutes foelicium votorum datrices; Amiciciam supra quam dici*

---

21. *Opusculum . . . de institutione puerorum . . .* (Strasbourg, 1513). This treatise had appeared at least as early as 1504 with Bebel's *Oratio ad regem Maximilianum de laudibus atque amplitudine Germaniae,* published by Thomas Anshelm. For a bibliography of Bebel's works, see G. W. Zapf, *Heinrich Bebel nach seinem Leben und Schriften* (Augsburg, 1802). Bebel is probably recommending Francesco (rather than Giammario) Filelfo as a model.

potest pro salute; Salutes ad astra usque ferentes.[22] They were not only too ornate but also ungrammatical, for *salus* has no plural form (e2ʳ⁻ᵛ).

4. Simple titles might be added to the names of the correspondents in the *salutatio,* such as *poeta* and *Romanorum imperatori semper augusto* in the example above, but not the obsequious epithets used by "barbaric" letter writers: *purpureis literarum flosculis gemmisque decorato; nitido scientiae cingulo insignito; septem artium lampade refulgenti* (A7ᵛ). Bebel concluded the *Commentaria* with four pages of more appropriate epithets to be used in addressing correspondents of different ranks and occupations (A7ᵛ-b1ʳ).

Bebel similarly criticized the ornate *valedictiones* of Carolus Virulus: *Tu foelix vale et quidem valentius quam qui valentissimus; Tu laetius vale quam apis in thymo quam piscis in undis* (e4ᵛ). He would write simply *Vale,* or *Vale, et me commendatum habeas,* or *Vale, et me ut soles ama,* or *Vale et me apud principem tuum commenda* (e5ᵛ).

That Bebel's views on letter-writing were typical of the new humanists of Germany is proved by the *Epistolae obscurorum virorum,* in which a few years later they closed ranks against the scholastic theologians over the Reuchlin controversy. The "obscure men" struggled in their medieval Latin to produce letters according to the precepts of the *ars dictaminis.* Albert Strunck apologized to Magister Ortwin Gratius that the hot Roman weather had left him no energy to write letters:

> And well you know what heavy labour it is to frame theses [*facere dictaminas*], for you told me at *Cologne* that you could scarce put together a seemly exercise [*unum bonum dictamen*] in a sennight. You cited Horace to me — how that poet hath laid it down that we ought to spend nine years in the inditing a fair treatise [*unum bonum dictamen*]. And that, I trow, is the manner fit. For it behoves us to be wary, and to take heed that there are no false concords. Sometimes congruity sufficeth not, for embellishments are needed — according to the twenty precepts of the *Elegantiae,* and the Art of Letter-writing of *Pontius* or of *Paulus Schneevogel,* who was Magister of *Leipsic.* Those Poets too, now-a-days, are vengeance captious, and when one

---

22. I have not seen the edition of the *Commentaria epistolarum conficiendarum* published at Tübingen in 1500, but in Zapf the *Contra epistolas Caroli,* as well as *Contra epistolandi modos Pontii et aliorum* and *Commentaria de abusione linguae latinae apud Germanos,* is first mentioned in the title of the 1503 edition published by Johann Grüninger at Strasbourg.

writes anything they straightway cry, "See, in this place and that, there is sorry latinity!" and they come here with their newfangled whim-whams, and subvert the good old grammar.[23]

M. Petrus Hofenmusius told M. Ortwin Gratius of a teacher who scolded him for wishing to read Sallust in order to learn good composition, saying, "You must needs be well drilled in *Alexander's* 'Parts,' and the Epistles of *Carolus,* which are taught in the Grammar School. I never read *Sallust,* and yet I can write theses in verse and prose [*dictamina facere metrice et prosaice*]" (ep. 1.7, pp. 22, 303). The result of studying the handbooks of Pontius and Carolus Virulus instead of classical models was such salutations as *tot salutes dicit quot aucae comedunt gramina,* "greetings as many as are the blades of grass in a goose's supper" (ep. 1.37, p. 361), or the following, which violates Bebel's first, third, and fourth rules:

> *Profundissimo necnon illuminatissimo magistro Ortvino Gratio theologo, poetae, et oratori in Colonia, domino ac praeceptori suo observandissimo Ioannes Schnarholtzius mox licentiandus salutes exuberantissimas dicit, cum sui humilima commendatione ad mandata.* [Johann Schnarrholtz, licentiate, *in posse,* sendeth exuberant greetings, together with his humblest duty, to the most erudite and enlightened Magister Ortwin Gratius, Theologian, Poet, and Orator, of Cologne, his most venerated master and preceptor.]
>
> (ep. 1.30, pp. 78, 347)

Like the handbooks they studied, the "obscure men" worried endlessly over the proper titles to use in addressing men of various ranks. Should "a candidate eligible for the degree Doctor in Divinity" be addressed as *magister nostrandus* or *noster magistrandus,* they wondered (ep. 1.1, p. 292). They were scandalized that one of these new poets, though "a mere student should 'thou' [*deberet tibisare*] the Rector of a University and a Doctor of Divinity" (ep. 1.14, pp. 42, 317). And their valedictions were as "barbaric" as their salutations:

> *Valete superaeternaliter. Et salutate dominum Ioannem Pfefferkorn cum sua uxore: dicatis quod ego opto sibi plures bonas noctes, quam Astronomi*

---

23. Francis Griffin Stokes, trans. (London, 1909), ep. 2.31, pp. 201–2, 458–59. Böcking, *Operum Supplementum,* 2.361, suggests that "the twenty precepts of the *Elegantiae*" may be the *Opusculum scribendi epistolas* of Francesco Negro. Paulus Schneevogel (Niavis) published three collections of model letters, dividing them by length: *Epistole breves, Epistole mediocres,* and *Epistole longiores.* The copies I have seen in the British Museum are dated ca. 1490–1495. Unlike the humanists, Niavis obviously did not consider brevity an important virtue in letter-writing.

habent minutas. [Fare ye well, more than eternally. Greet for me Herr *Johann Pfefferkorn* and his wife: tell them that I wish them more good nights than the minutes that the astonomers reckon.]

(ep. 1.41, pp. 104, 369)

Augustin Renaudet has shown that, in spite of an essentially medieval education in the schools of the Brothers of the Common Life at Deventer and Bois-le-Duc, Erasmus enjoyed more contact with Italian humanism during his formative years in the Low Countries than he was to have in Paris after his arrival there in September 1495. In the monastery at Steyn and as secretary to Henry of Bergen, bishop of Cambray, Erasmus absorbed the classics and the works of such Quattrocento humanists as Agostino Dati, Gasparino da Barzizza, Lorenzo Valla, Poggio Bracciolini, and Francesco Filelfo and found like-minded friends in William Hermans, Cornelius Gerard, and James Batt.[24] The early drafts of the *Opus de conscribendis epistolis,* which Erasmus wrote with other pedagogical works for his students Christian and Henry Northoff, Thomas Grey, Robert Fisher, and William Blount, Lord Mountjoy, in Paris between 1495 and 1499, show an enthusiastic, although critical, acceptance of the new humanist epistolography.[25]

Although it is difficult to date precisely the composition of these early drafts, Erasmus's letters and the treatises themselves provide a few clues. The *Brevissima formula* may have been published from the draft Erasmus sent to Fisher with a prefatory letter about March 1498 (*CWE*, 1. ep. 71). James D. Tracy has speculated that the *Brevissima formula* represents an earlier draft than the *Libellus,* since it alone contains no sample letters by Erasmus himself, only two by Pliny the Younger.[26] Besides the problem of dating, there is some doubt that the treatise as published is entirely Erasmus's work. Erasmus refused to acknowledge the *Brevissima formula* in 1521 (Allen, ep. 1193). He did not authorize its publication until 1536, when it appeared with the *De conscribendis epistolis* of Juan Luis Vives (Basel: T. Platter and B. Lasius). In the preface to that edition and in another letter written concurrently (Allen, eps. 3099, 3100), Erasmus claimed

24. *Erasme et l'Italie,* Travaux d'Humanisme et Renaissance 15 (Geneva, 1954), pp. 11–23. Cf. Raymond Marcel, "Les dettes d'Erasme envers l'Italie," in *Actes du Congrès Erasme* (Amsterdam, 1971), pp. 159–73.

25. The history of the composition of Erasmus's letter-writing treatise has been traced by Jean-Claude Margolin in *ASD*, 1.2.157–73.

26. "On the Composition Dates of Seven of Erasmus' Writings," *Bibliothèque d'Humanisme et Renaissance* 31 (1969), 359.

that he had produced the work in two days some forty years earlier for an English student (*nimirum rudem rudi, crasso crassum*), who had added his own material, including the prefatory letter to a fictitious Petrus Paludanus, to that which he had culled from Erasmus's treatise. The English student was apparently Robert Fisher, of whom Erasmus had spoken harshly in the dedication of the *Opus de conscribendis epistolis* as *cuidam amico parum syncero* (*ASD*, 1.2.205). In the section of the *Opus* on *Exercitatio et imitatio*, Fisher was likewise described as *ingratam discipulum et perfidum amicum* who, having wasted his youth in greedy self-seeking, demanded a *compendiaria* (the word recalls the title of the *Brevissima maximeque compendiaria conficiendarum epistolarum formula*) to teach him the difficult art of writing painlessly in a few simple precepts (*ASD*, 1.2.227-228).

In fact, however, the *Brevissima formula* is general advice about letter-writing rather than a *compendiaria* of formulas, and in spite of Erasmus's claim that Fisher had mixed his own material with that of his teacher, the advice seems typically Erasmian. The treatise begins with Libanius's definition of the letter as *absentis ad absentem colloquium*. Erasmus defines *colloquium* as daily speech, *sermo*. A letter should seem unlabored and spontaneous; those who anxiously seek obsolete or uncommon words or coin neologisms and sometimes write an entire letter for the sake of one brave new word reveal themselves to be barbaric. Purity and propriety of style are achieved by diligent exercise in writing accompanied by careful revision and the study in depth of many diverse writers. (If indeed Fisher was a lazy student, Erasmus's advice should have spurred him to greater effort.) The best models should be imitated, in letters Cicero, Pliny, and Poliziano, who would remain Erasmus's favorite contemporary model; Seneca is suitable for mature but not for beginning students. Because letters are not all alike, the student should study not only diverse authors but diverse works of the same author; those who read only the epistles or *De officiis* of Cicero should not call themselves Cicero's disciples. Although Erasmus asserts that those who imitate Cicero will never have reason to repent, he adds that they are deceived who think imitation alone is sufficient: as the ancients said, no one can equal the model he follows. The individual genius of the best authors cannot be imitated. Some (clearly he means some humanists) claim that there is no "art" of letter-writing and laugh at such diligent study and practice, but if building, weaving, and forging a vessel from clay require art, then surely speech, the glory of man's reason, cannot do without it. It is true, however, that one who writes a letter to a friend should not take refuge in rhetoric. The division of the letter into *salutatio, exordium, narratio,* and *conclusio* is not always or even frequently suitable. Conversely, one should not babble without labor, method, or discipline. Erasmus concludes with a classification of three kinds of letters borrowed from rhetoric: demonstrative, deliberative, and judicial. This classification will reappear in both the *Libellus* and the *Opus.*

Erasmus's definition of the letter as *sermo* places the *Brevissima formula* firmly in the humanist tradition, as does his emphasis upon diligent practice, especially through imitation of the best models. However, Erasmus is not a Ciceronian purist: he recommends diverse models, including the eclectic Poliziano, insists that a student read widely, and encourages him to develop his individual genius. Nature and practice are thus important to good composition, but what of art? Here Erasmus, like his Italian predecessors, is ambivalent about the role of rhetoric, the only art of writing then available. He easily discards the medieval divisions of the letter, but in classifying letters into demonstrative, deliberative, and judicial, he assigns to each a rhetorical purpose: to praise or blame, to persuade or dissuade, to accuse or defend. Like his predecessors, Erasmus seems not yet to have distinguished clearly the familiar letter of classical tradition (in which, as he admits, rhetoric is inappropriate) from the official letter of medieval tradition, with its many political purposes. He first makes this distinction in the *Opus de conscribendis epistolis.*

The *Libellus de conscribendis epistolis* appears to have been published from the "copy of the enlarged and improved *De conscribendis epistolis,*" which Erasmus sent from Oxford to Lord Mountjoy in November 1499 (*CWE,* 1. ep. 117). As Tracy has observed, "Siberch's volume and Erasmus' letter to Mountjoy . . . both contain the same criticisms of Francesco Niger [Negro]" (p. 359). In the *Libellus,* too, we find a distinction between mixed and simple letters, which Erasmus might have borrowed from Negro, and a description of the humanist *salutatio,* the sources of which appear to be the handbooks of Sulpizio and Perotti.[27] I would suggest that Erasmus first read in 1498–1499 the handbooks he evaluated in his letter to Lord Mountjoy and that this reading spurred him to rewrite his own treatise. His ignorance of

27. Negro classified letters into twenty kinds: *commendatitium, petitorium, munificum, demonstrativum, eucharisticum, amatorium, lamentatorium, consolatorium, expositivum, gratulatorium, exhortatorium, dissuasorium, invectivum, expurgativum, domesticum, commune, jocosum, commissivum, regium,* and *mixtum* (A3^r). His "mixed" letter, like Erasmus's, is that which has more than one purpose.

important contemporary literature when he wrote the *Brevissima formula* may also help explain his reluctance to acknowledge it when it was first published in 1520. The *Libellus* could have been composed as late as 1501 or early 1502. Three letters Erasmus wrote to Jacob Batt between May 2, 1499, and December 11, 1500, show that he was still revising the treatise with the intention of dedicating it to Batt's student, Adolph of Burgundy, heer van Veere (*CWE*, 1. eps. 95, 130, 138). To Adolph's mother, Anna van Borssele, vrouwe van Veere, Erasmus promised on January 27, 1501, "a work 'On Letters' and also another 'On Variation of Style' [*De copia*] . . . to assist the studies of your son" but added, "If these should happen to appear later than could have been wished, please do not blame this on my remissness but on my misfortune, or, if you prefer, on the difficulty of the task; for, while it is sheer madness to publish bad books, it is extremely difficult to publish good ones" (*CWE*, 2. ep. 145). Erasmus mentioned working on the treatise again in a letter to Roger Wentford written about November 1511 (*CWE*, 2. ep. 241), but Tracy has argued that "Siberch's text cannot be a reproduction of the 1511 version, since it mentions as among the living James Batt (d. 1502), Henry of Bergen, the bishop of Cambrai (d. 1502) and Prince Phillip the Fair of Burgundy (d. 1506)" (p. 359).

The *Libellus* opens with an assertion that theatrical grandiloquence is indecorous in a familiar letter. Erasmus compares the style of a letter not to shouting in a theatre but to whispering in a corner with some friend. The letter writer should strive, within the limits of *sermo* and below the *contentio* of the oration, for acumen, appropriate diction, wit, humor, charm, and brevity. The worst violation of brevity is an ostentatious salutation that flatters the correspondent by comparing him to the sun, morning star, shining lamp, mirror, flower, gem, sunshine, paradise, and so forth. The *salutatio* should simply name the correspondents, with the name of the writer placed first— *Robertus N. Erasmo suo S. D.* — following the usage of Cicero, Pliny the Younger, and other ancient models. To the names simple titles indicating an office or profession may be added: *M. Cicero Proconsul, C. Caesari Imperatori S. D.; Henricus Antistes Cameracensis, Philippo Burgundiorum duci S. P. D.; Jacobus Battus publicus scriba asecretis Erasmo theologo S. D.* Epithets, which Erasmus lists by rank, should be reserved for the body of the letter. A close friend may be addressed as *mi Cicero, mea Tulliola, mi frater, mea Katharina.* Where the names of the correspondents have not been given in a *salutatio*, a *subscriptio* is appropriate. Erasmus asserts that an *exordium* is not always necessary, criticizing

Francesco Negro, but he then distinguishes simple letters from mixed letters, perhaps recalling Negro's classification. If the mixed letter aspires to any formal structure, it should follow chronological order or else a logical order suggested by the subject matter, not the divisions prescribed by the *ars dictaminis*. The simple letter Erasmus divides into the same three categories he used in the *Brevissima formula:* judicial, deliberative, and demonstrative. The remainder of the treatise describes and gives examples of the kinds of letters in each category.

The *Libellus* does indeed seem "a vigorous attack on the medieval *formulae* for letter-writing," "a manifesto against the outdated manuals and old-fashioned methods of the day." After reading the *Libellus,* especially Erasmus's description of the *salutatio,* one is hardly prepared for the attack on Ciceronian letter-writers that some thirty years later Erasmus would deliver through his character Bulephorus in the *Ciceronianus:*

> Cicero does not date his letters by the year, only by the day of the month. Then a person will not be a Ciceronian, will he, if he dates the year from the birth of Christ, which is often necessary and always useful? These same persons do not permit one, as a courtesy, to put the name of the one to whom he writes before his own; for example, *Carolo Caesari Codrus Urceus salutem.* And they consider it as great a fault if one adds to a proper name any word of dignity or honor, as "Velius greets Ferdinand the Great, King of Pannonia and Bohemia." They cannot pardon Pliny the Younger because he uses the word *suum* in addressing a letter to a friend, simply because no example of this kind is extant in Cicero. They refuse the title to one who follows the model which some scholars have borrowed from *The Duties of Princes* and have recently begun to adopt; viz, to place at the beginning the main point of the letter which they are preparing to answer, because this has never been done by Cicero. I have known some to be criticised as guilty of a solecism because instead of S. D. in the salutation they placed S. P. D., that is, *salutem plurimam dicit,* which was said not to be in Cicero. And some think that even this little thing is Ciceronian, to put the salutation on the back of the letter instead of the front because the carrier is thus told without omitting the courtesy of salutation which letter he is to deliver to each person. Such a little thing causes us to lose the palm of glory? Indeed far from a Ciceronian is he who uses in the salutation this formula, *Hilarius Bertulphus, Levino Panagatho totius hominis salutem, aut salutem perpetuam;* and farther the one who begins his letter

Gratia, pax, et misericordia a Deo Patre, et Domino Jesu Christo or instead of *cura ut recte valeas,* closes it with *Sospitet te Dominus Jesus* or *Incolumen te servet Dominus totius salutis auctor.* What peals of laughter, what jeers would the Ciceronians raise at this![28]

In some cases Erasmus does not contradict his earlier precepts here: the title "King of Pannonia and Bohemia," which he adds to the name Ferdinand the Great in his example of a *salutatio,* is no more flattering or ornate than the titles he had approved in the *Libellus.* In other cases, as when he complains that the name of the writer is always put before that of the recipient of the letter by the Ciceronians, he is criticizing his own directions in the *Libellus.* Even if we allow for satiric exaggeration, Erasmus often seems in this passage to be siding with the *magister noster* against the poet. In truth, he is faithful to the ideal of simplicity in letter-writing, which he had expressed in the first drafts of his *Opus de conscribendis epistolis.* The humanists had once complained against turning letter-writing into an "art" and had laughed while the "obscure men" sweated in the heat to produce a simple greeting according to the precepts of the *ars dictaminis.* Now they were laboring so diligently to imitate Cicero that, like Nosoponus, they must lock themselves in an inner room, sealed from all disturbances, on nights proclaimed auspicious by astrology, eat only ten small currants and three coriander seeds coated with sugar to avoid distracting the brain, shun marriage and family and turn down public office, all to produce a letter of six periods asking a friend to return a book.[29]

Contemporaries believed that in Nosoponus Erasmus had caricatured Christophe de Longueil, whose orations and letters had been collected by Reginald Pole after Longueil's early death on September 11, 1522.[30] Erasmus's letters suggest that he conceived the idea of the *Ciceronianus* after Thomas Lupset had complained to him of the Ciceronians in a letter dated from Padua August 23, 1525 (Allen, ep. 1595) and had sent him the slim volume of Longueil's works. In the *Ciceronianus* Erasmus lamented that Longueil, although a talented young man, had wasted his ability on trivia. His

28. Izora Scott, trans., *Controversies over the Imitation of Cicero,* pt. 2, pp. 49–50; Cf. *ASD,* 1.2.627–28.

29. See Scott, pt. 2, pp. 28–32; *ASD,* 1.2.612–14.

30. *Christophori Longolii orationes duae. . . .* (Florence, 1524, rpt. in facsimile, Farnborough, Hants, England, 1967).

letters impressed Erasmus as affected because, although Longueil had been sequestered in the contemplative life, he had attempted to imitate the letters of Cicero, who had been active in affairs of state. Erasmus found Longueil's orations anachronistic because they described contemporary life in terms borrowed from the institutions of ancient Rome and trivial because they concerned Longueil's trial for *lèse majesté*. Longueil could have done much for the Christian religion, for scholarship, or for the state if he had applied himself to serious studies, Erasmus concluded.[31]

Although attacks on the "apes of Cicero" do not begin to appear in Erasmus's letters and *Colloquies* until 1526, he must have been aware of the "disease" of Ciceronian imitation when he revised the *Opus de conscribendis epistolis* in 1521–1522. The controversy over the imitation of Cicero, which had begun in Italy in the mid-fifteenth century, had already found written expression in the exchanges of Lorenzo Valla with Poggio Bracciolini, of Angelo Poliziano with Bartolomeo Scala and Paolo Cortesi, and of Gianfrancesco Pico with Pietro Bembo.[32] Erasmus discussed the Poliziano-Scala-Cortesi debate in the *Ciceronianus*.[33] He denied that before he wrote his satire he had read the Pico-Bembo polemic, written at Rome in 1512–1513, but Mario Pomilio has argued that he must have known these letters published at Basel by Froben, Erasmus's own publisher, in 1518. Pomilio finds a number of parallels between the arguments of Pico and those of Erasmus. However, Erasmus could not risk alienating Bembo and Sadoleto, together with Pope Clement VII and the Roman Curia, in a time of religious turmoil by seeming to accuse Bembo of paganism. His denial of any knowledge of the Pico-Bembo debate would seem to have been a political necessity.[34]

Erasmus's wide correspondence with humanists throughout Europe would have kept him in touch with the intellectual currents of sixteenth-century Italy, but he had also had some personal experience with the Ciceronians. While living in Italy (1506–1509) he had heard at Rome the sermon addressed to the pope on Good Friday

31. See Scott, pt. 2, pp. 110–15; *ASD*, 1.2.692–96.

32. Scott, pt. 1, pp. 10–23, summarizes these debates and in pt. 2, pp. 1–18, translates the letters of Pico and Bembo. Cf. *Le epistole "De imitatione" di Giovanfrancesco Pico della Mirandola e di Pietro Bembo*, ed. Giorgio Santangelo, in *Nuova collezione di testi umanistici inediti o rari*, 11 (Florence, 1954).

33. Scott, pt. 2, pp. 125–26; *ASD*, 1.2.706–7.

34. "Una fonte italiana del *Ciceronianus* di Erasmo," *Giornale italiano di filologia* 8 (1955), 193–207.

which he later satirized in the *Ciceronianus*.[35] On February 15, 1517, Erasmus wrote a letter to Guillaume Budé from Antwerp in which he described Giovanni Pontano as a Ciceronian (*CWE*, 4. ep. 531). In October 1519 Froben published at Basel among a *Farrago nova epistolarum* of Erasmus a letter written by Christophe de Longueil on January 29 of that year to Jacques Lucas, Dean of Orleans, in which Longueil compared Erasmus unfavorably with Budé, describing Erasmus as charming, fluent, and popular but Budé as more serious and profound (Allen, ep. 914). A temperate reply to Longueil, dated from Louvain April 1, 1519, appeared in Erasmus's *Epistolae ad diversos* (Basel: Froben, August 31, 1521). Erasmus's reply was filled with compliments to both Budé and Longueil, but he nevertheless defended himself against the charges of carelessness and superficiality (Allen, ep. 935). On October 15 – 16, 1519, Longueil, having fled from his trial for *lèse majesté* at Rome, visited Erasmus at Louvain. Erasmus was irritated at the interruption of his work but claimed in a letter to Andrew Alciati, written about May 6, 1526, four years after Longueil's death, that he had tried to be a good host to the young scholar. How had Longueil conceived that resentment against Erasmus that his letters, published in 1524, revealed? Perhaps, Erasmus conjectured, he had seemed inattentive or unsympathetic when Longueil complained of mistakes in Froben's publication of his letter to Erasmus and when Longueil bewailed the misfortune of his trial (Allen, ep. 1706). To Erasmus, Longueil's trial was a ludicrous display of Italian chauvinism and slavish Ciceronianism.[36] The *Opus de conscribendis epistolis* appeared a month before Longueil's death. The time was not yet ripe for Erasmus to engage his pungent wit against the Ciceronians, but in a treatise on letter-writing he could hardly avoid criticizing their excesses in that genre.

The *Opus de conscribendis epistolis* begins with eight chapters that describe the nature and style of the letter (*ASD*, 1.2.209 – 27). The first sentence of the treatise summarizes Erasmus's argument: "Those who either require or prescribe one certain style in letters,

---

35. Scott, pt.2, pp. 62 – 65; *ASD*, 1.2.637 – 39. In the same passage Erasmus mentions Tommaso Fedra Inghirami and Giulio Camillo Delminio; elsewhere he reports that he had roomed with them (Allen, ep. 3032). Renaudet, *Érasme et l'Italie*, p. 205, believes that Inghirami was the orator of the Good Friday sermon. Camillo would later (ca. 1530) write a reply to Erasmus's *Ciceronianus*, published in *Due trattati* (Venice, 1544). The treatise *Della imitazione* has been edited by Bernard Weinberg, *Trattati di poetica e retorica del Cinquecento*, Scrittori d'Italia, no. 247 (Bari, 1970), pp. 159 – 85, 599 – 601.

36. See *Ciceronianus*, in Scott, pt. 2, pp. 112 – 14; *ASD*, 1.2.694 – 95.

which I see has been done even by some erudite men, seem to me to treat that undoubtedly great multiplicity of subject matters, almost infinite in variety, too narrowly and briefly."[37] As he soon makes clear, Erasmus is criticizing not the *magistri nostri* but the neoclassicists: "They deny that a letter should be tolerated unless it is one which restricts itself to the humble style, unless it flows spontaneously and freely and lacks all the sinews of *contentio,* unless it is constructed with words borrowed from the crowd, unless, finally, by its very brevity it merits the name of letter rather than of volume" (*ASD,* 1.2.209 – 10). These are the men, Erasmus says, who now reign in the classroom. Erasmus does not deny that the familiar letter, "the heart's good wishes in brief," should be, as Demetrius had said, "the exposition of a simple subject in simple terms"; in fact, he devotes the seventh chapter *(Peculiaris epistolae character)* of this introductory section of the treatise to the familiar letter. But he contends that the letter serves many other purposes and treats many subjects; therefore, for the sake of decorum its style must be flexible. One by one he discusses the qualities the neoclassicists demand in the familiar letter, although in a different order from that in which he lists them in the passage above: (1) brevity (the remainder of *Quis epistolae character*); (2) the humble style *(De illaborata epistola, De gravitate epistolae)*; (3) "words borrowed from the crowd" *(De perspicuitate epistolae)*; (4) a loose sentence structure *(De compositione).* Finally, he summarizes his own principles of style in the chapters *De habitu epistolae* and *Elegantia.*[38]

The neoclassicists demand that a letter be brief. Erasmus describes his imaginary opponent as ruling that a letter be limited to twelve sentences. But suppose that the subject matter requires amplification? Quintilian said that it would be absurd to dress a baby in the mask and tragic shoe of Hercules; how much more absurd to try to dress Hercules in the swaddling clothes and booties of the baby. A letter of twelve sentences may be more prolix than the *Iliad,* while

37. *ASD,* 1.2.209. This and other translations of the treatise are my own.

38. A manuscript in the Royal Library at Copenhagen (Thottske Saml. 73 Fol.) contains the first chapter of the *Opus de conscribendis epistolis (Quis epistolae character)* and the title of the second chapter *(De illaborata epistola)* written in Erasmus's own hand. If C. Reedijk is correct in dating these leaves (ff. 321ʳ – 323ᵛ) to 1511 on the basis of Allen, ep. 241, and the evidence ("by no means conclusive," as he says) of the watermarks, Erasmus may have conceived the opening chapters of the treatise, his answer to neoclassic letter writers, during or shortly after his sojourn in Italy. See "Three Erasmus Autographs in the Royal Library at Copenhagen," in *Studia Bibliographica in Honorem Herman de la Fontaine Verwey,* ed. S. van der Woude (Amsterdam, 1967), pp. 343 – 44.

perhaps in a letter containing thousands of sentences not one will be redundant. Brevity should be measured by the subject matter and by the leisure of the correspondents, not by the amount of paper used.

The neoclassicists criticize letters written in a grave or ornate rather than a humble style. Erasmus answers that the style must be suited to the person addressed; some men are offended to receive an artless letter, as if it showed contempt for them. Grave matters must be treated in a grave style, as Cicero himself showed by the example of the letter he wrote to Octavius.

The neoclassicists insist that the letter use only colloquial diction, avoiding all erudite words in the name of perspicuity. But why should erudite men not enjoy playing scholarly games in letters, as when, Erasmus recalls, he wrote to Thomas Linacre in trochaic tetrameter? Perhaps those who complain of obscurity in learned letters are merely ignorant themselves, but should the nightingale exchange its song for the cuckoo's to please an ignorant judge?

As for the neoclassic requirement that the periodic speech of the oration be excluded from letters, Erasmus would leave the matter to the judgment of the mature writer. He would prefer that the beginning student practice writing periods so that he will be able to do so in future when the subject matter calls for them.

Erasmus says that the ancients argued the relative merits of the Attic, Rhodian, and Asiatic styles, but Quintilian rightly said that the best style was that most suitable to the subject, time, place, and audience. In a passage reminiscent of Poliziano's defense of his own letters, quoted above, Erasmus argues that any style in letter-writing can be defended on the ground of decorum. If the style is loquacious, it can be justified as having been written to an avid reader or to one with leisure; if erudite, to an erudite man; if artless, to an ignorant reader or one pleased by simplicity; if ornamented, to an antiquarian of ancient words; if soothing, to a friend; if frank, to a familiar; if harsh, to an inferior; if flattering, to an ambitious man.

The second section of the *Opus de conscribendis epistolis* (*ASD*, 1.2.227–66) is addressed to the teacher. Although Erasmus attacks the handbooks of Carolus Virulus and his contemporaries, he instructs the teacher to show his students how to find good arguments, how to write an appropriate *exordium* and *divisio*, and in other ways how to apply rhetoric to letter-writing. The pedagogical section of the treatise nevertheless reveals little about Erasmus's position in the contest between the medieval and classical traditions of letter-writing in the Renaissance, for as Marc Fumaroli has suggested, Erasmus consistently distinguishes between the exercises of the student and the epistolography of the mature writer.[39]

Erasmus next turns to a consideration of the *salutatio* and *valedictio* (*ASD,* 1.2.266 – 300). The correspondent should be addressed in the singular, not in the plural, which some still consider the "polite" form. The name of the writer should be placed before that of the recipient of the letter in the *salutatio.* Erasmus admires the ancient simplicity of addressing the correspondent by his name alone, but he allows the use of a title designating an office or profession. Any flattery, however, is indecorous in a *salutatio:* he ridicules specifically the formulas of Carolus Virulus. Erasmus recognizes that the correspondent was not addressed as *suo* or *suae* until the age of Pliny the Younger and that such formulas as *salve multum, salve etiam atque etiam, salve pro tuis meritis,* and *multam optat salutem* are more recent substitutes for the classical *salutem dicit,* but he does not object strongly to these un-Ciceronian expressions. Flattering epithets may be used in the body of the letter when they are appropriate. For example, a letter thanking a prince for a gift might describe him as *munificentissimus* or *benignissimus.* Erasmus lists titles he considers appropriate to churchmen, princes, magistrates, and kinsmen. He attacks as "superstition" the medieval custom of indicating differences in rank by minute distinctions in epithets, calling cardinals, for example, *reverendissimas dominationes;* archbishops, *reverendissimos;* bishops and abbots, *reverendos;* priors, *venerabiles;* deans, *spectabiles.* Erasmus provides a number of formulas for the *valedictio: vale; vale recte; bene vale; cura ut quam rectissime valeas; vale, nosque, quod soles, ama;* and others. He finds such Christian formulas as *incolumen te nobis diu servet Optimus Maximus Jesus* acceptable, but not affectations such as *vale in eo qui vastum cingit fluctibus orbem.* Finally, Erasmus explains the proper dating of the letter. His many examples include dating the year from the birth of Christ. In short, Erasmus here takes a middle position between his description of the humanist *salutatio* and *valedictio* in the *Libellus de conscribendis epistolis* and his attack on the Ciceronian formulas in the *Ciceronianus.* He describes the classical formulas for the student and warns him against medieval barbarisms, but he is not a strict Ciceronian nor is he willing to condemn all formulas invented since the classical period. In particular, he recognizes the place of Christian expressions in contemporary letter-writing.

In his chapter *De ordine epistolari* (*ASD,* 1.2.301 – 2) Erasmus con-

39. "Genèse de l'épistolographie classique," pp. 890 – 91.

demns the superstitious division of the letter into parts. He distinguishes between mixed and simple arguments, as he had done in the *Libellus*. In simple arguments the purpose should suggest an appropriate order. In mixed arguments either the writer will say whatever comes first to mind or he will devise an order based on time, place, person, or subject matter. In both kinds of arguments, the writer should provide transitions to promote coherence. After giving *Mixtae epistolae exemplum* (*ASD*, 1.2.303 – 9), in the next two chapters, *Epistolarum genera* and *Tres omnium generum fontes* (*ASD*, 1.2.309 – 15), Erasmus classifies simple arguments. Here he repeats his earlier division of letters into deliberative, demonstrative, and judicial, but, significantly, he adds a fourth classification, *familiare*. The remainder of the treatise (*ASD*, 1.2.315 – 579) describes and gives models of the many subdivisions of letters in this fourfold classification.

Earlier treatises on letter-writing, including the first drafts of Erasmus's *Opus de conscribendis epistolis*, had struggled to confine the professional epistolography inherited from the *dictatores*, with its manifold political and scholarly uses, within the narrow classical definition of the letter as a conversation between absent friends. In the final draft of his treatise, Erasmus separated the familiar letter from the letter written to serve a rhetorical purpose but included both under a new definition of the genre. Although books are written in a style designed to please the most learned of their many readers, Erasmus argued, the letter need please only the correspondent. It can therefore be distinguished from other genres by its flexibility of style (*ASD*, 1.2.213,223). This redefinition of the letter allowed Erasmus to synthesize the medieval and classical traditions of epistolography while rejecting the legalism of both the *magistri nostri* and the "apes of Cicero." The *Opus de conscribendis epistolis* described letter-writing as it was practiced by most Renaissance humanists, not as it was narrowly defined by a few Ciceronian purists whose prescriptions threatened to deprive the letter of its efficacy as an instrument of educational and religious reform. Benoît Beaulieu has demonstrated that the ideal of utility, not pure beauty, is the informing principle of all Erasmus's works.[40] That observation is as true of the *Opus de conscribendis epistolis* as of the *Ciceronianus*.

40. "Utilité des lettres, selon Erasme," *Études littéraires* 4 (1971), 163 – 74.

The Place and Function of
Style in Renaissance Poetics

HEINRICH F. PLETT

I

Towards the end of his *Apology for Poetry,* Sir Philip Sidney bursts out
in the ironical complaint:

> But what? methinks I deserve to be pounded for straying from
> Poetry to Oratory: both have such an affinity in this wordish consid-
> eration, that I think this digression will make my meaning receive
> the fuller understanding — which is not to take upon me to teach
> poets how they should do, but only, finding myself sick among the
> rest, to show some one or two spots of the common infection grown
> among the most part of writers; that, acknowledging ourselves
> somewhat awry, we may bend to the right use both of matter and
> manner: whereto our language giveth us great occasion, being in-
> deed capable of any excellent exercising of it.[1]

The digression for which the author virtually apologizes here is devoted to stylistic criticism. The theory of style forms the link between
rhetoric and poetics. In the tradition of the rhetorical model, it constitutes the third phase in the production of a text; it is preceded by two
other phases, the *inventio,* or the search for arguments, and the *dispositio,* the structuring of these arguments. The rhetorical theory of style
regularly comprises the stylistic principles *(virtutes elocutionis),* manners *(genera dicendi),* and, above all, figures *(figurae).* By incorporating
stylistic elements into his poetics, Sidney is availing himself of an already existing convention. It originates in the *Poetics* of Aristotle, chap-

1. Sir Philip Sidney, *An Apology for Poetry or The Defence of Poesy* (London, 1965), pp.
139 – 40.

ters 19 to 22, which deal with questions of grammar, metaphor, and rare words. Ever since Aristotle's treatise, which expressly refers the reader to the same author's *Rhetoric* for a full treatment of these topics, doctrines of poetry have repeatedly been influenced by the neighboring discipline of rhetoric. Some of them display so extensive an influence that they might justifiably be referred to as rhetorical poetics. Sidney's *Apology*, then, far from being an isolated case in the history of rhetoric reception, is but one of many instances within a development, culminating in the Renaissance.

That Sidney and other theorists of poetry regard stylistics as part of their discipline gives rise to the question of what the status of language and style was in the Renaissance. The answer has long been known: in the light of present knowledge, it seems scarcely an exaggeration to say that the Renaissance was as much a renaissance of style as of anything else.[2] The beginnings of this revival can be traced back to Petrarch's rediscovery of Cicero; its end is in sight when in 1667 Thomas Sprat calls for an exact equivalence of words and things: *quot res tot verba*.[3] Between these historical milestones the idea of style enjoyed a great prestige — in spite of the controversies it was subjected to (e.g., inkhorn terms vs. pure English, Ciceronianism vs. Senecanism) — because language was thought of as a social indicator both of man's individual character and his way of communicating with his fellow beings. Wherever the question of style was debated, the larger issues of anthropology, sociology, and politics were sure to be involved. Thus a history of Renaissance stylistics possesses a seismographic quality in that it constantly points to the general history of man's attitudes towards himself and others.

Irrespective of the kind of treatise in which the theory of style is

2. Cf. K. O. Apel, *Die Idee der Sprache in der Tradition des Humanismus von Dante bis Vico,* Archiv für Begriffsgeschichte, 8 (Bonn, 1963 and 1975); C. S. Baldwin, *Renaissance Literary Theory and Practice* (New York, 1939, rpt. 1959); D. L. Clark, *Rhetoric and Poetry in the Renaissance* (New York, 1922, rpt. 1963); M. W. Croll, *Style, Rhetoric, and Rhythm,* eds. J. M. Patrick, R. O. Evans, with J. M. Wallace and R. J. Schoeck (Princeton, 1966); R. Adolph, *The Rise of Modern Prose Style* (Cambridge, Mass., 1968); H.-J. Lange, *Aemulatio Veterum sive de optimo genere dicendi: Die Entstehung des Barockstils im XVI. Jahrhundert durch eine Geschmacksverschiebung in Richtung der Stile des manieristischen Typs* (Bern and Frankfurt, 1974); G. A. Padley, *Grammatical Theory in Western Europe 1500–1700: The Latin Tradition* (Cambridge, 1976).

3. Thomas Sprat, "The History of the Royal Society" (1667), in *Critical Essays of the Seventeenth Century,* ed. J. E. Spingarn, 3 vols. (Bloomington, Ind., 1957), 2.118: ". . .to return back to the primitive purity and shortness, when men deliver'd so many *things* almost in an equal number of *words*."

articulated in the Renaissance, whether it be a Ciceronian, an epistolary, a Ramistic or a stylistic rhetoric,[4] its exponents would appear to
have the following aims in common:

1. Some kind of systematic representation, generally based on
linguistic levels and various forms of deviation from the linguistic norm,

2. A functional explanation of the stylistic devices in terms of
the emotions they are likely to engender,

3. An evaluation of the stylistic devices characterizing them as
either acceptable or unacceptable in specific communicative situations.

All three of these aspects — systematic, functional, and evaluative —
form what can be considered the stylistic norm. It changes according
to the verbal and cultural contexts of which it is a part.

There are two basic types of Renaissance poetics containing two
different types of stylistic theory, humanistic and courtly. Each arose
from different motives and serves a different social purpose. Thus
they also differ in their organization. Julius Caesar Scaliger's *Poetices
libri septem* (1561) and George Puttenham's *The Arte of English Poesie*
(1589) will serve, in the main, as representative specimens of each type.

II

Scaliger's *Poetics,* a Neo-Latin treatise, is the work of a humanistic
scholar who in his great erudition aspired to the ideal of the "uomo
universale."[5] The practicing physician of later years had not only
studied botany and medicine but had also distinguished himself with
his extensive knowledge of philosophy, theology, art and, of course,
philology. His classical erudition is exceptional even for a humanist,
as is illustrated not only by the large-scale comparison of Virgil with
Homer and other authors in the fifth book, but above all by the sixth
book of the treatise, in which Scaliger traces the history of literature
in the Latin language back to its origins. This example shows further-

4. For a typology of Renaissance rhetorics, see W. S. Howell, *Logic and Rhetoric in
England, 1500 – 1700* (Princeton, 1956, rpt. New York, 1961).
5. Scaliger's vita is analyzed by V. Hall, Jr., "Life of Julius Caesar Scaliger (1484 –
1558)," *Transactions of the American Philosophical Society* n.s. 40/2 (1950), 87 – 170. On the
genesis of his poetics consult the article by L. Corvaglia, "La 'Poetica' di Giulio Cesare
Scaligero nella sua genesi e nel suo sviluppo," *Giornale critico della filosofia italiana* 38
(1959), 214 – 39.

more that he was not particularly interested in contemporary vernacular literature. He was concerned rather to restore Latin poetry to the heights of classical achievement, an ambition that in view of the development of Neo-Latin since Petrarch he was confident of being able to fulfill. With this purpose in mind, Scaliger aimed at making his poetics as complete a compendium as possible of all available contemporary knowledge of literature. Not only was it to afford information about the intricacies of technical rules but also to expound their philosophical foundations. Not only did it aim to open up historical perspectives but also to set up critical standards for the evaluation of literature. The result of this complex synthesis of literary theory, history and criticism is a bulky volume containing seven books on poetics published in Lyon three years after the author's death. Its readership consisted of an elite, not one of fixed social class such as the aristocracy, but one that shared the necessary standards of humanistic education. These necessary standards included a profound knowledge not only of classical literature but also of the most important sources for Scaliger's poetics: the *Poetics* of Aristotle, the *Epistola ad Pisones* of Horace, and Marco Girolamo Vida's treatise *De arte poetica libri III* (1527).[6]

It is an indication of how important a role Scaliger accorded to language and style in the framework of his poetic theory that he devoted a great deal of the third ("Idea") and fourth ("Parasceue") books to discussing them. Even more telling is perhaps the fact that the first chapter of his treatise opens with a discourse on the theme "Orationis necessitas, ortus, vsus, finis, cultus" (1.1.). He makes it quite clear that for him human speech is no less than a source of culture. It is speech that makes possible such important cultural achievements as philosophy, rhetoric, historiography, and poetry. As Scaliger emphatically asserts,

> Est sanè portitor animi quasi quidam sermo noster, cuius communicationi ciuiles conuentus indicuntur, artes coluntur, sapientiae necessitudines homini cum hominibus intercedunt.[7]

6. Cf. E. Brinkschulte, *Julius Caesar Scaligers kunsttheoretische Anschauungen und deren Hauptquellen,* Renaissance und Philosophie, 10 (Bonn, 1914), pp. 43 – 98. Scaliger's deviations from Aristotle are discussed by Bernard Weinberg, "Scaliger versus Aristotle on Poetics," *Modern Philology* 39 (1942), 337 – 60. His relations with baroque aesthetics are dealt with by M. Costanzo, *Dallo Scaligero al Quadrio* (Milano, 1961), pp. 9 – 66; his influence on French neo-classicism is taken account of by R. Bray, *La formation de la doctrine classique en France* (Paris, 1963).

7. IVLII CAESARIS/*SCALIGERI, VIRI*/CLARISSIMI,/Poetices libri septem:

By virtue of its esthetic quality, poetry occupies a special place among the *artes* mentioned. But Scaliger stresses that it would be wrong to look on pleasure alone as its ultimate objective; its proper aim is rather the Horatian unity of instruction and delight: "Poeta etiam docet, non solùm delectat."[8] Moreover, it shares with the other arts the rhetorical element of the *persuasio;* however, it is distinguished from these by its use of verse and its imitation of fictitious objects.

According to Weinberg, Scaliger's conception of poetry as language results in its entering into a double relationship: (a) with the objects signified by the words used, and (b) with the public for whom the meanings of the words are intended.[9] In the further argument the aspect of the public is discussed mainly in terms of the functions of ethical persuasion poetry exercises; according to this conception poetry has the task "vt scilicet humana vita compositior fiat" or "vt bonos amplectamur atque imitemur ad agendū: malos aspernemur ob abstinendum."[10] Viewed in this light, poetry appears as part of a practical social ethics. Conversely, there is the aspect of representation that concerns the relationship of *verba* and *res.* To Scaliger's mind words are not independent of things; they are the images of things *(imagines rerum).* At the beginning of the third book their relationship is described more precisely. Things are said here to have primacy over words: "Res autem ipsae finis sunt orationis, quarum verba notae sunt."[11] The further discussion abides by this principle. It plays an important part in the definition of style and levels of style, for example. The concept of style underlying the passage at the beginning of the fourth book "Est autē Character, dictio similis eius rei, cuius nota est, substātia, quātitate, qualitate"[12] is a "material" one (i.e., one that bears on the object of representation) or an "ontological" one.

The rhetorical figures are treated by Scaliger at two different points of his treatise: in the third book beginning at chapter 29, the semantic figures or tropes, in the fourth book beginning at chapter

---

/ ... / APVD ANTONIVM VINCENTIVM. / *M.D.LXI.*, p. 1.

8. Ibid.

9. Bernard Weinberg, *A History of Literary Criticism in the Italian Renaissance,* 2 vols. (Chicago, 1961), 2.744.

10. Scaliger, *Poetices libri septem,* pp. 80, 348.   11. Ibid., p. 80.

12. Ibid., p. 174; cf. p. 183. For the notion of a "material" concept of style see F. Quadlbauer, *Die antike Theorie der genera dicendi im lateinischen Mittelalter* (Vienna, 1962).

26, the remaining figures. Corresponding to this division there is more than one definition of the term *figure*. The third book presents an ontological as well as an epistemological characterization of the figure.

> Cvm re & verbo omnis constet oratio, & figura in vtroque repe-
> riatur ...

> Figura est notionum quae in mente sunt, tolerabilis delineatio, alia
> ab vsu communi. Notiones voco rerū species externarum, quae per
> sensus delatae, in animo repraesentantur.[13]

The fourth book, by contrast, stresses the decorative aspect of the rhetorical figure, its deviation from everyday language:

> Figura loquutionis, quam superiore libro Tropon agnoscebamus,
> est decora facies orationis à vulgari diversa.[14]

This distinction is certainly not to be explained merely by reference to a certain disunity Scaliger's argumentation occasionally exhibits. The different definitions derive from different conceptions of the inventory of stylistic categories. The tropes are accorded an unmistakable priority since these stylistic devices are most amenable to the author's "ontological" conception of language. Scaliger sets up six classes according to the image of reality presented. The first (*significatio* or *aequalis tractatio*) reflects reality precisely, the second *(hyperbole)* signifies more, the third *(eclipsis)* less, the fourth *(allegoria)* something different, the fifth *(ironia)* the opposite; the sixth class comprises all tropes that do not fit into any of the categories mentioned. As each class is subdivided further, the result is an abundance of semantic categories of textual change.

The classification of the remaining figures is performed in a similarly scholastic manner. It is not, however, the *res-verba* relationship that plays the main role, but the principle of grammatical deviation, although cases of overlap with the tropes do occur. Classification according to this principle yields figures of abbreviation (e.g., *ellipsis*), word repetition (e.g., *anadiplosis*), amplification (e.g., *periphrasis*), opposition (e.g., *antithesis*), position (e.g., *hyperbaton*), quantity (e.g., *parison*), and quality (e.g., *homoeoptoton*). The rather formalistic character of these stylistic forms is the more obvious as Scaliger follows up his remarks on the figures with his theory of metrics. At the beginning

13. Scaliger, *Poetices libri septem,* p. 120.   14. Ibid., p. 198.

of the same book the traditional three-style doctrine is expounded in terms of *affectus;* these *affectus,* however, which are divided into general and particular, remain peculiarly abstract, so that it is scarcely appropriate to speak of the concrete elaboration of a dimension of stylistic effect.[15]

What Scaliger considers relevant to his conception of style is evidenced particularly by the "quat[t]uor virtutes poetae" outlined in the third book (chapter 25). These are *prudentia* (chapter 26), *efficacia* (chapter 27), *varietas* (chapter 28), and *suavitas,* which as the product of the other qualities does not receive special attention. These *virtutes* are obviously meant to supplant the four classical principles of style: *puritas, perspicuitas, ornatus,* and *aptum.* Scaliger departs from the assumption that all poetry seeks to teach and delight and goes on to say:

> Quorum vtrunque consecuturi sunt ii, qui & res vero propiores, ac sibiipsis semper conuenientes exequuti fuerint, & operam dederint vt omnia varietate condiantur. Nihil enim infelicius, quàm saturare auditorem antè, quàm expleatur. Quae enim epulae quibus fastidium pro voluptate pariatur? Tertia res ea est, quam ego Efficaciam, Graeci quo designent nomine suo loco dictum est. Eam paucis in Poetis reperies. Est autem vis quaedam tum rerum, tum verborum, quae etiam nollentem propellit ad audiendum. Quarta est suauitas, quae efficaciae illius vim vegetam deducit ex asperitate, cui saepenumero est affinis, ad certam temperationem. Haec igitur esto summa sic: Poetae prudentia, varietas, efficacia, suauitas.[16]

Prudentia demands of the poet a rich and well-ordered invention, *efficacia* vivid and effective depiction, *varietas* a varied arrangement

15. Ibid., pp. 184 – 193. For the development of the theory of the passions in Renaissance rhetorics and poetics see H. F. Plett, *Rhetorik der Affekte: Englische Wirkungsästhetik im Zeitalter der Renaissance,* Studien zur englischen Philologie n.s. 18 (Tübingen, 1975).

16. Scaliger, *Poetices libri septem,* p. 113. F. M. Padelford makes available the following translation of this passage: "Now to realize these ends one's work must conform to certain principles. In the first place his poem must be deeply conceived, and be unvaryingly self-consistent. Then he must take pains to temper all with variety *(varietas),* for there is no worse mistake than to glut your hearer before you are done with him. What then are the dishes which would create distaste rather than pleasure? The third poetic quality is found in but few writers, and is what I would term vividness *(efficacia);* there is also a Greek name for it which will be given in the proper place. By vividness I mean a certain potency and force in thought and language which compels one to be a willing listener. The fourth is winsomeness *(suavitas),* which tempers the ardency of this last quality, of itself inclined to be harsh. Insight and foresight *(prudentia),* variety, vividness, and winsomeness, these, then, are the supreme poetic qualities." *Select Translations from Scaliger's Poetics,* Yale Studies in English 26 (New York, 1905), p. 53.

of ideas and words, *suavitas* a pleasant and winning tone. If we take *efficacia* as a representative example of all the *virtutes*, we recognize that here again the ontological perspective dominates: "Nam tametsi in verbis esse videtur [efficacia]: tamen in rebus ipsis est primò." Later on this definition is extended to include the intellect as well: "Efficacia est, aut in facto, aut in dicto, aut in animo."[17] The conclusion to be drawn from these considerations is that stylistics has no claim to independence in Scaliger's work; it is embedded in a general ontology of the work of art. It is obviously inadmissible here to reduce poetry to poetic language. The *Poetices libri septem* presents a poetics of representation, not a rhetorical poetics, even though the adoption of various rhetorical concepts suggests the latter. Weinberg, however, exaggerates the ontological standpoint when he concludes, "There can be thus no independent science of poetics; poetry can be considered only in relationship to the scheme of things entire."[18] Scaliger's treatise does not disavow esthetics.

Scaliger's theory of style and his poetics as a whole are not topical but retrospective in character. The authorities cited in the treatise are from classical antiquity, just as are the vast majority of the examples used to illustrate stylistic concepts and rules. Contemporary literary production plays a role only insofar as it attempts — in Latin — to emulate the classics. Classical theorists (Aristotle, Horace) and poets (Virgil) provide the foundations of a poetics claiming normative validity. This claim is evidenced not only by the recommendation of certain stylistic concepts but also by the prohibition of such *vitiosae formae* as the *genus siccum* and the *genus pingue* (4.24). Socially, however, despite its precision in laying down certain norms and standards, Scaliger's poetics is peculiarly abstract in character. Apart from various references to contemporary science and the traditional *Ständeklausel* (i.e., the adaptation of stylistic level to social rank), the author refrains from comment on the social circumstances and the forms of political power that shape his own life and those of his contemporaries. This fact might be seen as typifying the seclusion of scholarly life; in its broader implications it reflects the socio-political abstinence espoused by those humanists who preferred knowledge to concrete action.[19]

17. Scaliger, *Poetices libri septem*, p. 116. For ἐνέργεια, the Greek equivalent of *efficacia*, see note 44.

18. Weinberg, *A History of Literary Criticism in the Italian Renaissance*, 2.750.

19. This remark seems to be contradicted by Scaliger's report on action: "Aristoteles ita censuit: Quum poema comparatū sit ad eam ciuium institutionem, quae nos

III

The *Arte of English Poesie* appeared anonymously in 1589, almost thirty years after the first appearance of Scaliger's poetics. Its place of appearance is not the French country town Lyon, but London, the capital of Queen Elizabeth, who had just delivered Philip's armada a devastating blow. The author of this poetics, who has been identified by literary scholarship as George Puttenham,[20] tells us that he has spent time at the courts of France, Spain, Italy, and the Empire. Thus it is no wonder that he does not address himself primarily to scholars and schoolmasters but to the lords and ladies of the court, "idle Courtiers" who wish to perfect their command of their mother-tongue and perhaps now and again to write a poem for their "priuate recreation."[21] As well as this, Puttenham's treatise pursues a further aim: to instruct an uneducated man how to become a court poet, in the somewhat drastic words of the author:

> pulling him first from the carte to the schoole, and from thence to the Court, and preferred him to your Majesties seruice, in that place of great honour and magnificence to geue enterteinment to Princes, Ladies of honour, Gentlewomen and Gentlemen.[22]

At the same time he makes it clear that it is not sufficient for the poet who has become a courtier to command the technical equipment of

---

ducit ad beatitudinē: beatitudo verò nihil aliud quàm perfecta sit actio: neutiquam ad mores cōsequendos deducet poema, sed ad facta ipsa. Rectè sané, neque verò aliter sentimus nos" (*Poetices libri septem*, p. 348). This *actio* is not, however, specified in concrete socio-political terms.

20. Cf. G. D. Willcock and A. Walker's introduction to their edition of *The Arte of English Poesie* (Cambridge, 1936, rpt. 1970), pp. xi–xliv. Until recently only very few articles and book chapters were dedicated to other topics of the *Arte*, e.g., by La Rue van Hook, "Greek Terminology in Puttenham's *The Arte of English Poesie*," *Transactions of the American Philological Association* 45 (1916), 111–28; J. W. H. Atkins, *English Literary Criticism: The Renascence* (London, 1947, rpt. 1968), pp. 156–78; Philip Traci, "The Literary Qualities of Puttenham's *Arte of English Poesie*," *Renaissance Papers* (1957), 87–93; D. M. Knauf, "George Puttenham's Theory of Natural and Artificial Discourse," *Speech Monographs* 34 (1967), 35–42; D. Javitch, "Poetry and Court Conduct: Puttenham's *Arte of English Poesie* in the Light of Castiglione's *Cortegiano*," *Modern Language Notes* 87 (1972), 865–82. The best study hitherto written on Puttenham's treatise is D. Javitch's monograph *Poetry and Courtliness in Renaissance England* (Princeton, N.J., 1978).

21. Puttenham, *The Arte of English Poesie*, eds. G. D. Willcock and A. Walker, p. 158.

22. Ibid., pp. 298–99. Perhaps in this context the fact is not insignificant that a copy of the *Arte* was owned by Ben Jonson.

the verse-smith but that he must also satisfy the requirements of courtly etiquette. In the context of the court, poetry means the artistically sublimated expression of a way of life. Conversely, the representative of this social class must allow the esthetic standards of this construct to be applied to himself. The highest authority supervising the observance of this "socio-esthetic" system of standards is the monarch herself. This is evidenced by the fact that the treatise — according to the printer Richard Field — was written "to our Soueraigne Lady the Queene, and for her recreation and seruice."[23] Furthermore, the reverse side of the title page is embellished by a copperplate portrait of Elizabeth I; and the closing pages of the book contain a declaration of homage combined with the entreaty to "conceiue of myne abilitie to any better or greater seruice" — an indication that the author's dedication was designed to further quite concrete political or social ambitions.[24]

The instruction of the courtly poet in the *Arte* is performed in three steps, to each of which the author dedicates one book: 1. "Of Poets and Poesie," 2. "Of Proportion," and 3. "Of Ornament." Besides a general discussion about poet and poetry, the first book contains a theory of literary genres, while the remaining two are devoted to prosody and the doctrine of style, respectively. Thus the structure corresponds broadly to the rhetorical scheme of *inventio, dispositio,* and *elocutio,* with the reservation that *inventio* and *dispositio* are subjected to a poetological reinterpretation.[25] In books 1 and 2 elements of the courtly code are incorporated into the poetological argument, for instance, the panegyric attitude that informs the epideictic genre classification, or the conservative concept of order underlying the derivation of the prosodic *dispositio* from the musical harmony of the spheres.[26] The third book displays particularly clearly the interpre-

23. Ibid., p. 2.

24. Ibid., p. 308. As D. Javitch points out in "Poetry and Preferment at Elizabeth's Court," George Gascoigne similarly published his early poetry, according to his own words, "To the ende that thereby the vertuous might bee incouraged to employ my penne in some exercise which might tende both to my preferment, and to the profite of my Countrey" (in *Europäische Hofkultur im 16. und 17. Jahrhundert,* ed. August Buck et al., 3 vols. [Hamburg, 1981], 2.163–69).

25. In this respect Puttenham follows a well-established practice of humanistic poetics, which is, for instance, illustrated by M. G. Vida's *De Arte Poetica,* "with Book I devoted to the training and indoctrination of the poet and to the defence of poetry, Book II to invention and disposition, Book III to elocution." Weinberg, *A History of Literary Criticism in the Italian Renaissance,* 2.715.

26. On these topics see H. F. Plett, "Typen der Textklassifikation in der engli-

tative dependence of esthetic categories from the norms of courtly conduct. In the broad view, this influence is unmistakably visible in the constant use of courtly *adagia* or *analoga* to explain or justify esthetic rules. The language of court, or rather of the monarch, provides the ideal for the language of poetry. To cite some concrete examples, this dependence can be clearly observed in the following concepts: (1) in the norm of *decorum*, (2) in the ornamental concept of style, (3) in the *sprezzatura* concept, (4) in the esthetic sensualism of language. Each of these concepts is a constituent of style, which Puttenham, in accordance with an old topos, calls "the image of man"; he might have called it more aptly "the image of the courtier."[27]

Decorum has always comprised both a socio-ethical and a socio-esthetical component.[28] This is clearly reflected in the fact that Puttenham's chapter on stylistic decorum (23) is immediately followed by another on social decorum: "Of decencie in behauiour which also belongs to the consideration of the Poet or maker" (24). The author is quite well aware that it is unusual thus to incorporate a short courtesy book into a poetics. For in his introductory remarks he explicitly points this out and furthermore draws the reader's attention to another book he has written under the title *De decoro,* which contains additional material; about this book nothing more is known. In the chapter in question he restricts himself to an abundance of examples supposed to illustrate the normative restraints to which all social behavior (e.g., the wearing of clothes) is subject. Anyone who infringes them is not only violating a prevailing social convention but is ultimately calling the entire social and political system into question. The ruling monarch is the guarantor of its stability; the hierarchy of norms borne by him reflects feudal habits of thought. Style, by transference, is adapted to the social norms in accordance with the various components of the

schen Renaissance," *Sprachkunst* 12 (1981), 212–27; and Catherine Ing, *Elizabethan Lyrics: A Study in the Development of English Metres and Their Relation to Poetic Effect* (London, 1951, rpt. 1971), pp. 42–55, 89–96.

27. Puttenham, *The Arte of English Poesie,* p. 148. For the history of the topos, see W. G. Müller, "Der Topos 'Le style est l'homme même,'" *Neophilologus* 61 (1977), 481–94.

28. A (necessarily incomplete) history of the critical term up to the English Renaissance is to be found in D.A. Richardson's "Decorum and Diction in the English Renaissance" (Ph.D. diss., University of North Carolina, Chapel Hill, 1972), pp. 1–100. The social aspect of *decorum* is emphasized by L. Fischer, *Gebundene Rede: Dichtung und Rhetorik in der literarischen Theorie des Barock in Deutschland* (Tübingen, 1968). Its formal structures are briefly discussed in chapter 9 ("The Criterion of Decorum") of R. Tuve's *Elizabethan and Metaphysical Imagery* (Chicago, 1947, rpt. 1961), pp. 192–247.

communication model (in terms of rhetoric, the "circumstances": speaker, hearer, object of reference, time, place, and so forth). Puttenham stresses that an emperor, for example, is not referred to in the same way as a "meane souldier or captaine."[29] Each of the three estates is accorded a style appropriate to it, be it in depiction, address, or self-expression; "the nature of the subiect" has ordained it thus.[30] "Nature" in this case has the character of a topos used to sanction the existing hierarchy of values and society. To meet the required stylistic standard is, according to Puttenham, to display not only the correct kind of social morality but artistic distinction as well: "good grace." An adequate stylizing of the poetic *inventio* results in esthetic gracefulness, as is expressed by such translations of πρέπον or *decorum* as *seemelynesse* ("for his good shape and vtter appearance"), *comelynesse* ("for the delight it bringeth comming towardes vs"), and *pleasant approche*.[31] At the bottom of this line of argument is the ideological thesis: beauty is affirmation. Anything that fails to fulfill this postulate is ugly, unseemly, unpleasant. It is significant that when the reader is cautioned about an indecorum these warnings do not have the form of negative literary examples but are couched in political anecdotes in which a subject behaves in a linguistically inappropriate manner towards his sovereign. In every case the offender is punished by being banned from court and hence from social and political activity. An undesirable stylistic *vitium* can be avoided by learning the rules governing each stylistic level. Puttenham impresses them on the reader's mind with vivid examples. He advises strongly against too great a flexibility in applying them and even more against departing from them altogether, as he foresees undesirable consequences. Thus the decorum concept obstructs social as well as esthetic development, albeit the latter to a lesser extent. It does not permit a change of values, much less a revolution.

How Puttenham would like his stylistic concept to be understood is explained concisely in the title of the third book ("Of Ornament") and in detail in a comparison elsewhere:

> And as we see in these great Madames of honour, be they for personage or otherwise neuer so comely and bewtifull, yet if they want their courtly habillements or at leastwise such other apparell as cus-

---

29. Puttenham, *The Arte of English Poesie*, p. 273.

30. Ibid., p. 151. On the gradual dissolution of the *Ständeklausel* and the ideological and social developments accompanying it, see P. Szondi, *Die Theorie des bürgerlichen Trauerspiels im 18. Jahrhundert* (Frankfurt, 1973).

31. Puttenham, *The Arte of English Poesie*, p. 262.

tome and ciuilitie haue ordained to couer their naked bodies, would be halfe ashamed or greatly out of countenaunce to be seen in that sort, and perchance do then thinke themselues more amiable in euery mans eye, when they be in their richest attire, suppose of silkes or tyssewes & costly embroderies, then when they go in cloth or in any other plaine and simple apparell. Euen so cannot our vulgar Poesie shew it selfe either gallant or gorgious, if any lymme be left naked and bare and not clad in his kindly clothes and coulours, such as may conuey them somwhat out of sight, that is from the common course of ordinary speach and capacitie of the vulgar iudgement, and yet being artificially handled must needes yeld it much more bewtie and commendation.[32]

The comparison takes up the traditional personification of rhetoric as a female figure, commonly known ever since Martianus Capella's *De nuptiis Philologiae et Mercurii*.[33] As Puttenham expresses it, the decorum of courtly dress etiquette demanded in the courtesy books and elsewhere is used to provide the basic justification for a theory of style that might be referred to as artificial, decorative, and hedonistic. The courtly style of poetry is artificial because its deviant linguistic structures alienate everyday language, but not to the excess of violating decorum.[34] This style can be said to be decorative because it embellishes the depicted object by means of the figures. Despite the metaphorical terms of description chosen by the author (colors, flowers, precious stones, gold, fine fabrics), it would be wrong to dismiss this decorative rhetoric as a mere esthetic accessory, for it is an essential constituent of courtly literature just as much as magnificent clothing is an integral part of the courtier's existence. The informing principle is

32. Ibid., pp. 137–38.

33. For the iconographical history of Rhetorica, see Plett, *Rhetorik der Affekte*, pp. 144–54.

34. Puttenham, *The Arte of English Poesie*, p. 159: "Figuratiue speech is a noueltie of language euidently (and yet not absurdly) estranged from the ordinarie habite and manner of our dayly talke and writing and figure it selfe is a certaine liuely or good grace set vpon wordes, speaches and sentences to some purpose . . . ." Puttenham's concept of style evidently belongs to the tradition of the *genus mediocre:* see G. L. Hendrickson, "The Origin and Meaning of the Ancient Characters of Style," *American Journal of Philology* 26 (1905), 249–90; F. Quadlbauer, "Die genera dicendi bis Plinius d. J.," *Wiener Studien* 71 (1958), 55–111; and *Die antike Theorie* . . . (cf. note 12); H. Friedrich, *Epochen der italienischen Lyrik* (Frankfurt, 1964), pp. 49–83, 88 ff., 458 ff.; I. Sowton, "Hidden Persuaders as a Means of Literary Grace: Sixteenth-Century Poetics and Rhetoric in England," *University of Toronto Quarterly* 32 (1962), 55–69; M. E. Hazard, "An Essay to Amplify 'Ornament': Some Renaissance Theory and Practice," *Studies in English Literature 1500–1900* 16 (1976), 15–32.

the Neoplatonic idea that outer appearance is an image of inner being and that physical beauty reflects the beauty of the soul. In accordance with the same principle, high social rank calls for adequate representation and noble poetry for an abundance of figurative adornment. This symmetry ("proportion") creates a harmony that gives esthetic pleasure. The courtly poet is called upon to afford his listeners "mirth" and "sollace" by his treatment of "pleasant & louely causes."[35] Elsewhere Puttenham writes: "Poesie is a pleasant maner of vtteraunce varying from the ordinarie of purpose to refresh the mynde by the eares delight."[36] Hence "vnworthy" objects and themes are excluded from this poetry. (In selecting illustrations of his theory, Puttenham shows a preference for the poetry of the early "courtly makers.") Just as style reflects the matter depicted, poetry must reflect the court. Should a discrepancy arise, the claim to beauty is forfeited. On these premises a "l'art pour l'art" conception that presupposes an autonomy of style is neither permissible nor possible.

The *sprezzatura* concept, which Castiglione — in accordance with classical authorities on the *celare artem* (e.g., *Ad Her.*, Cicero, Quintilian) — applied to the courtly code of conduct, means in brief the alleged artlessness of art or the pretended effortlessness with which the artificiality of the courtly code is practiced in social life.[37] The courtier fashions his existence into a work of art, but he does so in such a way that it has the appearance of supreme naturalness, an *altera natura*. The illusion that thus arises presupposes the ability to disguise oneself. The courtier is an actor playing roles; he takes pleasure in fictionalizing his existence, that is to say, in practicing detached self-control. The consequence of this process is an attitude of dissimulating irony. Puttenham now transfers these constituents of the courtly code to poetry. Both share the aim of pleasing illusion: "*beau* semblant, the chiefe professiō aswell of Courting as of poesie."[38] Dissimulation, the ability to conceal art, is called for in both cases. According to Puttenham poetic dissimulation is linguistically

---

35. Puttenham, *The Arte of English Poesie*, pp. 154–55.
36. Ibid., p. 23.
37. On the classical sources of the *celare artem* concept, see H. Caplan's note in his edition of the *Rhetorica ad Herennium* (London and Cambridge, Mass., 1954), pp. 250–51 (4.7.10). Very illuminating is J. A. Mazzeo's chapter "Castiglione's *Courtier:* The Self as a Work of Art" in his book *Renaissance and Revolution* (New York, 1965), pp. 131–60. On Sidney consult K. Myrick, *Sir Philip Sidney as a Literary Craftsman* (Cambridge, Mass., 1935; 2nd ed., Lincoln, Neb., 1965), pp. 298–315 ("Sprezzatura").
38. Puttenham, *The Arte of English Poesie*, p. 158.

realized in tropes. The author selects allegory as the basic trope and renames it *sub nomine agentis* as "Courtier or figure of faire semblant."[39] This principle has two corollaries: (1) allegory and a number of other tropes are a prerequisite of esthetic illusion, and (2) they imitate courtly role playing. The latter remark can be corroborated by two further observations. First, Puttenham describes various rhetorical figures by reference to the category of dissimulation (e.g., *enigma, ironia, periphrasis*); second — and this is exceptional in Elizabethan stylistic rhetoric — many figures in the *Arte* are assigned an English translation identifying them — in analogy to the equation of allegory and courtier — with a social role: e.g., *meiosis* = "the Disabler," *tapinosis* = "the Abbaser," *antitheton* = "the Quarreller," *aporia* = "the Doubtfull," *sententia* = "the Sage sayer," *hyperbole* = "the Ouerreacher," and so on.[40] In these examples stylistic forms indicate social roles, which implies the converse truth, that social roles are manifested in certain stylistic categories. However, Puttenham warns against the unthinking equation of artistic and social norms. While role playing in the social sphere can lead to moral depravity by turning the courtier into a hypocrite — the stereotype of satirical criticism of court[41] — it is restricted in the esthetic sector to the type of artistic practice: "we doe allow our Courtly Poet to be a dissembler only in the subtilities of his arte."[42]

The decorative esthetics of courtly conduct inclines to sensuous exhibition. It is with good reason that Puttenham chooses to elucidate his stylistic ideal by using the image of the magnificently attired ladies of the court. This was indeed in accordance with the courtly code. To choose an example from Castiglione, speaking of the "jestes or merrie conceites" of gallant conversation he refers to

> some men that with so good an utterance and grace and so pleasantly declare and expresse a matter that happened unto them or

39. Ibid., p. 299; cf. p. 186 ff. On the "socio-esthetic" context of this trope, see H. F. Plett, "Konzepte des Allegorischen in der englischen Renaissance," in *Formen und Funktionen der Allegorie,* ed. W. Haug (Stuttgart, 1979), pp. 310 – 35, esp. pp. 324 ff.

40. Puttenham, *The Arte of English Poesie,* pp. 185 (219), 185 (259), 191, 210, 226, 236.

41. Cf. C. Uhlig, *Hofkritik im England des Mittelalters und der Renaissance: Studien zu einem Gemeinplatz der europäischen Moralistik* (Berlin and New York, 1973); and M. C. Miller, "Courtliness in the English Renaissance" (Ph.D. diss., The Johns Hopkins University, Baltimore, 1978).

42. Puttenham, *The Arte of English Poesie,* p. 302. The moral ambiguity of *dissimulatio* is again made clear by Puttenham's rendering of *allegoria* as the "Figure of false semblant" (p. 186).

that they have seene and heard, that with their gesture and wordes they set it before a mans eyes, and (in manner) make him feele it with hand, and this peradventure for want of an other terme we may call Festivitie or els Civilitie.[43]

The principle underlying this thought is the rhetorical category of ἐνάργεια (Latin evidentia), occasionally identified with ἐνέργεια, that is, vividness, efficacy.[44] The principle of *sprezzatura*, however, remains a necessary restraint on its practical realization. An excess of art *(mala affectatio)* is just as harmful as a lack of it *(barbarolexis)*.[45] To characterize affectation, Sidney reverses Puttenham's image; the courtly Lady Rhetoric turns into a painted whore: "that honey-flowing matron eloquence apparelled, or rather disguised, in a courtesan-like painted affectation."[46] This does not, however, prevent him from demanding of the lyric *energia*, that is, sensuous and emotional diction. Both rhetorical categories of effect, *enargeia* and *energeia*, occur in Puttenham's work, assuming the criterial function in the setting up of classes of figures. This process is unique in that it departs from rhetorical tradition by classifying according to receptive rather than formal criteria. Figures of style are divided up according to whether they appeal to the ear, the intellect, or both. Correspondingly, the following classes are distinguished:

1. *auricular figures* = enargetic figures
("seruing to giue glosse onely to a language"),

2. *sensable figures* = energetic figures
("to giue it efficacie by sence"),

3. *sententious figures*
("for bewtifying them with a currant & pleasant numerositie, but also giuing them efficacie, and enlarging the whole matter with copious amplifications").[47]

Expressions such as "pleasant and agreable to the eare" or "pleasant sweetenesse"[48] characterizing the "auricular figures" indicate that

43. B. Castiglione, *The Book of the Courtier*, trans. Sir Thomas Hoby (London and New York, 1928, rpt. 1959), p. 134.
44. Cf. Plett, *Rhetorik der Affekte*, passim.
45. Cf. Puttenham, *The Arte of English Poesie*, pp. 249–61. Cf. also Scaliger, *Poetices libri septem*, p. 116.
46. Sidney, *An Apology for Poetry*, p. 138.
47. Puttenham, *The Arte of English Poesie*, pp. 143, 160.
48. Ibid., p. 160; cf. pp. 162, 163. These expressions are, moreover, indicative of

the language of poetry is regarded as a source of esthetic sensualism. The same phonesthetic quality is manifest in the description of prosody in the second book. In the detailed discussion of *carmina figurata* and emblems, it is joined by the graphesthetic component that appeals to the eye. The most courtly and at the same time most sensuous of all Renaissance art forms, the *Gesamtkunstwerk* of the masque, is omitted from Puttenham's treatise. In the masque, stagecraft, music, and language unite in a single appeal to the eye, ear, and intellect. The controversy between Ben Jonson and Inigo Jones over the superiority of poetry or stagecraft is a striking illustration of how seriously the different modes of perception in this panaesthesia were taken.[49]

Taking critical stock of the foregoing discussion, we arrive at the following results. *The Arte of English Poesie* was written at a time when a courtly, as distinct from a humanist, poetics was being called for. The demand arose from the court's need for sublimated self-articulation and the esthetic affirmation of its own claim to power. The adoption of Italian theories of courtly conduct (Della Casa, Castiglione, Guazzo) had provided a general response to this need. What now required special attention was the application of this general response to poetry. The conversation theory of the courtesy books and their conception of "wit" served as models for literature, but more lasting in their effect were the concepts discussed above: *decorum*, the ornamental, *celare artem*, and the sensual. These provide the point of departure for the estheticization of the courtly ethos; but at the same time they have the function of committing art in turn to a social class with an esthetic consciousness of self. This interdependence of the two codes indicates a remarkably self-contained ideology, but it also betrays a want of realism that precludes their realization. With regard to this initial situation, the difference between courtier and poet was such that it seemed infinitely easier for the latter, living as he did in the realm of fantasy, to endow the "beau

the oral (conversational) nature of courtly culture. A detailed study of this aspect of the English Renaissance has yet to be written. W. J. Ong in his contribution "Oral Residue in Tudor Prose Style" to his *Rhetoric, Romance, and Technology* (Ithaca, N.Y., 1971), pp. 23–47 only touches upon the humanistic strain, whereas D. A. Berger devotes himself to the seventeenth and eighteenth centuries' development: *Die Konversationskunst in England 1660–1740* (Munich, 1978).

49. Cf. D. J. Gordon, "Poet and Architect: The Intellectual Setting of the Quarrel between Ben Jonson and Inigo Jones," *Journal of the Warburg and Courtauld Institutes* 12 (1949), 152–78; Stephen Orgel, "To Make Boards to Speak: Inigo Jones's Stage and the Jonsonian Masque," *Renaissance Drama* n.s. 1 (1968), 121–52.

semblant" with existence, or in the words of Shakespeare, to give "to airy nothing/A local habitation and a name" (*MND*, 1.I. 16 – 17).

IV

In Renaissance poetics the structure and function of style vary with the kind of treatise of which they form a part. Two basic types can be distinguished, a humanistic one and a courtly one. The first type, which is illustrated by Scaliger's *Poetices libri septem*, represents a scholarly approach to the subject. Its main features are the use of Latin, a retrospective interest in classical literature, a learned display of the *ars*, and a primarily ontological interpretation of style that manisfests itself in the heavy emphasis laid on the tropes. The courtly idea of style can be exemplified by the third book of Puttenham's *Arte of English Poesie*. It is different from the humanistic one in that both its language and its literary examples are English, its intention not a demonstration of art but rather its concealment and its conception of the figures more pragmatic than semantic. Whereas Scaliger's affective aim is to teach and delight (in a modified Horatian way), Puttenham primarily seeks to please. A synopsis of the basic differences between the two approaches may lead to the dichotomies shown in Table 1. This classification, which certainly admits of still further subcategorizations, presupposes two sets of social rules. Of these only fragmentary details could be specified here. Suffice it to say that the humanistic style concept is primarily addressed to the learned *respublica literaria* and that it implies a pedagogical ethos that ascribes to the language of poetry a civilizing power of immense effect. Such is the ideology of what historical scholarship has come to term "civic humanism."[50] Still, the aims of the courtly poet are of a much more modest nature. His principal objective is not social reform but to "retaine the credit of his place, and profession of a very Courtier, which is in plaine terms, cunningly to be

---

50. See H. Baron's classical work, *The Crisis of the Early Italian Renaissance*, rev. ed. (Princeton, N.J., 1966). The role eloquence played for humanism is concisely dealt with by Hannah H. Gray, "Renaissance Humanism: The Pursuit of Eloquence," *Journal of the History of Ideas* 24 (1963), 497 – 514. For the English development see, among others, F. Caspari's *Humanism and the Social Order in Tudor England* (Chicago, 1954, rpt. New York, 1968). This study needs, however, to be complemented and partly corrected by more recent research (e.g., L. Borinski, K. Charlton, J. Simon). The humanists' dilemma and eventual failure are excellently described by O. B. Hardison, "The Orator and the Poet: The Dilemma of Humanist Literature," *The Journal of Medieval and Renaissance Studies* 1 (1971), 33 – 44.

TABLE 1
Renaissance Theories of Style

Stylistic Principles	Humanistic: Scaliger	Courtly: Puttenham
Type of poet	scholar	courtier
Aim	teach-delight (*utile/dulce*)	delight (recreation) (*dulce*)
Attitude towards art	*demonstrare artem* (scholastic)	*celare artem* (sprezzatura)
Classification of figures	1. according to semantic categories: tropes (3.29)	according to sensorial/mental perception
	(a) *aequalis tractatio* (b) *hyperbole* (c) *eclipsis* (d) *allegoria* (e) *ironia* (f) remaining tropes	(a) auricular (= enargetic) figures (ear) (b) sensible (= energetic) figures (conceit) (c) sententious (= enargetic/energetic) figures (ear + conceit)
	2. according to formal operations: figures (4.26)	
	(a) abbreviation (b) word repetition etc.	
Description of figures	primarily semantic (ontological)	primarily pragmatic: (a) dissimulation (b) social roles
Illustrative texts	mainly classical (Latin, Greek) — retrospectivity —	mainly contemporary (English) — topicality —

able to dissemble."[51] In the hands of a poet who has turned a "cunning Princepleaser," literary style becomes the instrument of panegyric affirmation.[52] During the Renaissance persons with both scholarly and courtly ambitions had to be acquainted with the humanistic as well as the courtly code as is, for instance, shown by the life and works of Ben Jonson.

Scaliger's and Puttenham's poetics do not remain isolated phenomena in the literary landscape of the sixteenth century, for each has its antecedents and successors. Scaliger's treatise looks back on Vida's poetics as its immediate predecessor and in its turn exerts great influence on the rise of French, English, and German classicism. Conversely, Puttenham's poetics is rivaled by the literary theory of his famous contemporary, Sir Philip Sidney. Sidney's *Apology* shares the *Arte's* anti-scholastic attitude towards style, which is clearly marked by its opposition of "smally learned courtiers" and "professors of learning" (i.e., humanists) in the following passage:

> Undoubtedly (at least to my opinion undoubtedly) I have found in divers smally learned courtiers a more sound style than in some professors of learning; of which I can guess no other cause, but that the courtier, following that which by practice he findeth fittest to nature, therein (though he know it not) doth according to art, though not by art: where the other, using art to show art, and not to hide art (as in these cases he should do), flieth from nature, and indeed abuseth art.[53]

This antithesis, however, proves artificial in that men like Sidney and Puttenham had acquired enough scholarship to be able to compete with the best humanists of their day. Thus the contrast between "humanistic" and "courtly" stylistics is not primarily one of *ars* but of its adaptation to heterogeneous social circumstances. It only reaffirms Puttenham's dictum of 1589 that style is the "image of man" and what Buffon declared more than 150 years later in his famous aphorism: "le style est l'homme même."

51. Puttenham, *The Arte of English Poesie,* p. 299.

52. On the contrast between humanism and courtliness, see G. K. Hunter, *John Lyly: The Humanist as Courtier* (London, 1962), esp. chap. 1 (pp. 1–35, 350–54.). The panegyric attitude is discussed by M. F. Muth, "Elizabethan Praise of the Queen: Dramatic Interaction in Royal Panegyric" (Ph.D. diss., Ohio State University, 1977). Cf. also F. A. Yates, *Astraea: The Imperial Theme in the Sixteenth Century* (London, 1975); and R. Strong, *The Cult of Elizabeth: Elizabethan Portraiture and Pageantry* (London, 1977).

53. Sidney, *An Apology for Poetry,* p. 139.

The Ascendancy of Rhetoric
and the Struggle for Poetic
in Sixteenth-Century France

ALEX L. GORDON

What is poetry? Is it merely a branch of rhetoric, *la seconde rhétorique* as it is called in the manuals of the early sixteenth century, or does it have its own unique essence? This question, raised especially by the poets of the Pléiade and by others close to them, is of critical importance for Renaissance literature. The answers, as we shall see, map out for poetry its own domain. Poetry will retain its links with rhetoric of course, but the Renaissance view of it will include new criteria. To be a poet of humanist stripe is no longer to arrange words in a special order; it is also to look beyond the words to their divine source and civilizing power.

   The ascendancy of rhetoric in the early sixteenth century is clearly seen in Pierre Fabri's *Le Grant et vray art de plaine rhétorique* of 1521 (ed. A. Héron, 3 vols. [Rouen, 1889 – 1890]). For Fabri the orator and the poet approach the art of writing in a similar spirit. Composition for both proceeds through the traditional operations of invention, disposition, and elocution. The poet differs only in that his text is also governed by metrical and prosodic restrictions. The poet in short is a versifier. Practically, this means that he will emphasize his unique role by sophisticated refinement of the verse form. In *Le Grant et vray art de plaine rhétorique* the various possibilities of acoustic affinity are pushed to their extreme end. The results are vertiginous. Fabri quotes a text (3. 47) that by virtue of ingenious rhyme may be read horizontally from top to bottom or the reverse. It may also be read vertically in sequential columns from left to right or from right to left, and from top to bottom or from bottom to top. "Take care of the sense, and the sounds will take care of themselves," says Lewis Carroll. Fabri has reversed this position to the extent of eclipsing sense almost entirely. The signifier in Fabri's quotation has so upstaged the signified that the text seems primarily a demonstration of its own possibilities as a verse form. The author appears far removed from the letter writer or public speaker who is the object of concern elsewhere. Fabri persists, however, in calling him an "orateur." "Grands orateurs" is the title given in the prologue to the rhétoriqueur poets Chastellain and Molinet. In spite of his additional metrical skills, the poet still remains then a worker in words like the orator. He may even become the supreme linguistic craftsman. Fabri writes that Alain Chartier, the great poet of the fifteenth century, "a passé en beau langage élégant et substancieux tous ses prédécesseurs" (2. 11).

Poetry's identification with rhetoric continues in many ways throughout the sixteenth century. The principal exponents of the poetic art,[1] Sebillet (1548), Du Bellay (1549), Peletier du Mans (1555), Ronsard (1565, 1572), and Laudun d'Aigaliers (1597) all describe poetic composition in terms of the rhetorical triad: invention, disposition, elocution. The continued use of these terms by theoreticians who are themselves practicing poets indicates a belief that writing poetry involves the same disciplines as the composition of a speech. In particular rhetorical analysis of style, as embodied for instance in the teaching on figures and tropes, is a rich field of inspiration for the poet. In *La Deffence et illustration de la langue françoyse*, Du Bellay refers him directly to the rhetorical manuals on this subject. In the manuals the poet learns also of the levels of style, of the laws of decorum, and of the techniques of persuading and praising. The latter, discussed in rhetoric under the heading of the demonstrative genre, are of special interest to him since his task consists largely in the celebration of great men and noble achievement. The mid-century poet thus schooled in the compositional laws of rhetoric still does not differ too much from the orator. As with Fabri, his claim to distinction continues to lie, at least in part, in his additional skills as versifier. Pierre de Deimier will write as late as 1610 in his *Académie de l'art*

1. Thomas Sebillet, *Art poétique françoys*, ed. Félix Gaiffe (Paris, 1910); Joachim du Bellay, *La Deffence et illustration de la langue françoyse*, ed. Henri Chamard (Paris, 1948); Jacques Peletier du Mans, *L'Art poétique*, ed. André Boulanger (Paris, 1930); Pierre de Ronsard, *Abbregé de l'art poëtique françois* (1565) and *Préface sur la Franciade* (1572), in *Oeuvres complètes*, 18 vols. ed. Paul Laumonier, vols. 14 and 16, respectively (Paris, 1914 – 1967); Pierre de Laudun d'Aigaliers, *L'Art poëtique français*, ed. Joseph Dedieu (Toulouse, 1909).

poétique that "le propre de la Poësie [c'est] d'estre discourue en vers" (Paris, 1610, p. 9). Du Bellay, spokesman for the Pléiade in its early years and advocate of a type of poetry concerned with more than verse alone will still write of the orator and poet that "les vertuz de l'un sont pour la plus grand'part communes à l'autre" (*Deffence*, p. 85). Thomas Sebillet, in many ways too an apologist of a new poetic, will so confound the orator and poet as to ask with Macrobius who was the greatest rhetorician, Virgil or Cicero. Such a question is only possible if Rome's greatest poet and greatest prose writer are considered exclusively from the point of view of the linguistic medium in which they work. The question neglects all concern for content or for the motivation that lies behind the writing act in the first place.

Rhetoric's importance for poetic in sixteenth-century France cannot then be denied. Its essential role in the corresponding poetry of England was early recognized, as for instance in the practical criticism of Rosemond Tuve's *Elizabethan and Metaphysical Imagery* (Chicago, 1947). Among students of French literature such recognition has been more slowly granted. Recently, however, it has brought rewarding results in theoretical studies such as Grahame Castor's *Pléiade Poetics* (Cambridge, 1964) and in critical readings such as those of Robert Griffin (*The Coronation of the Poet, Joachim Du Bellay's Debt to the Trivium* [Berkeley and Los Angeles, 1969]) and of Louis Terreaux (*Ronsard correcteur de ses oeuvres. Les variantes des Odes et des deux premiers livres des Amours* [Geneva, 1968]). It is particularly important that rhetoric's role be recognized in this way, since acknowledgment of this kind can act as a corrective to certain romantic views of poetry as passionate expression. In this respect we may recall the model of linguistic communication offered by modern theorists. According to this model an addressor sends a message to an addressee. The message, bearing on a referent, is couched in terms borrowed from the linguistic code. Traditional rhetoric tends to emphasize the code or linguistic means and the addressee or the audience whom the orator must move and persuade. Readers of what we shall call a romantic sensibility emphasize the addressor and the referent. They are interested in the person of the poet and in the world he interprets. Such a preference may lead to an inadequate reading of Renaissance poetry with its strong rhetorical bent. It forgets that a rhetorical poetry is concerned as much with audience as with poet. The rhetorical poet like the orator seeks to manipulate the passions of his listeners; their feelings, and the possibility of directing them, may be of more interest to him than his own. Hence a treatise like that of Daniel d'Auge, *Deux dialogues de l'invention poétique* (Paris, 1560), will contain a long if rather dry list of passions to be moved by various techniques. The rhetorical poet is moved perhaps, but above all he wishes to move others. Du Bellay recalls the pure rhetorical tradition when he describes the emotional effect the good poet should exert on him:

> Saiches, Lecteur, que celuy sera veritablement le poëte que je cherche en nostre Langue, qui me fera indigner, apayser, ejouyr, douloir, aymer, hayr, admirer, etonner, bref, qui tiendra la bride de mes affections, me tournant ça & la à son plaisir. (*Deffence,* p. 179)

If the recognition of rhetoric's place in poetic has obvious advantages, an undue emphasis on rhetoric in the writing of poetry is not without drawbacks. Originally conceived as an art of speech-making in order to win an audience, rhetoric does not always fit easily onto the art of poetry. Poetic compositions may contain speeches, especially in the epic and drama, but they are not primarily speeches, nor is their performance, private reading for example, the same as that of a speech declaimed aloud before an audience of some size. Certainly the spinoff from rhetorical reflexion, especially as we have seen in the area of style, is applicable to poetic too, but are poetic genres such as elegy or sonnet best understood in the light of a rhetorical genre such as the demonstrative? Points of contact exist, but they are often on matters of detail; the broad aims of poetry may be different from those of rhetoric, and not just on the simple level of versification as with Fabri. In sixteenth-century France this sense of poetry's unique quality led theoreticians of literature to reflect more deeply on those components of the art of communication that rhetoric may seem to downplay: the addressor and the referent. The poet, in other words, acquired an interesting personality in his own right, and it was believed that what he had to say was important not only for its form but also for the light it might shed on the world of men and things.

Rhetoric, to be sure, speaks to us of the orator, especially in the important texts of Quintilian and Cicero. Quintilian's orator is a good man, since good speech and good morals are inseparable. Cicero's orator is a man of wide experience and learning, since wisdom is a necessary attribute of the speaker who would win an audience. In sixteenth-century France such culture is emphasized in the rhetorical texts of Germain Forget, Cardinal du Perron, and Guillaume du

Vair.[2] The orator of these works remains, however, a rather shadowy, abstract figure. By contrast the poet of mid-century poetic is vividly incarnate. In the *Deffence et illustration*, Du Bellay describes his natural talent, his training in the art of poetry, his knowledge of public life, and his vast culture acquired through study both day and night. We also read of the calm the poet must enjoy to write his greatest work, of inspiration sought indoors and outdoors according to the season, and of work habits that involve self-criticism as well as that of friends. Du Bellay's poet is ambitious and elitist. Scorned by the masses of his own time, he writes for posterity and achieves immortality both for himself and for those of whom he sings. Such a poet has found a new type of salvation, a religion of art by which he ascends to the heavens. Du Bellay's portrait has its precedents of course, particularly in Horace; but the precedents were always there. What is important is that they are suddenly invoked again and developed; and by others as well as Du Bellay — by Sebillet, by Ronsard, by Laudun d'Aigaliers, and most arrogantly perhaps by Peletier du Mans. For him as for Shakespeare all the world's a stage, and the poet on this stage plays the most conspicuous role. "C'et qu'il se presante pour la plus spectable personne du Teatre: e ce Teatre et l'Univers" (*L'Art poëtique*, p. 223).

The apotheosis of the poet is most evident of course in the renewed Renaissance claim to divine inspiration. Mentioned briefly by Sebillet and Du Bellay, the platonic view of the inspired poet is most developed by Pontus de Tyard in his *Solitaire Premier ou Prose des Muses et de la fureur poetique, plus quelques vers lyriques*, 1552, and by Ronsard in the celebrated "Ode à Michel de l'Hôpital." For Fabri the poet was an orator who possessed additional technical skills in verse. Ronsard rejects this role of artisan-versifier. His poet is inspired through the muses by Jupiter and his poetry is an inspiration to mankind. The poet is an essential link in a magnetic chain that binds the soul of everyman to its divine source. Such a charge involves severe moral constraints. To receive the gift of inspiration, the soul must

2. Germain Forget, *Rhétorique françoise faicte particulièrement pour le Roy Henri troiziesme* (Bibliothèque de Carpentras: ms. no. 1789, fol. 148 – 157-fonds Peiresc). An edition of this work based on a manuscript of the R. Biblioteca Estense of Modena was published by Giulio Camus under the title *Precetti di rettorica scritti per Enrico III, re di Francia*, Memorie della Regia Accademia di Scienze, Lettere ed Arti in Modena, series 2, vol. 5 (1887); Cardinal Jacques Davy Du Perron, *Avant-Discours de Rhétorique ou Traité d'Eloquence* in *Les Diverses Oeuvres de l'illustrissime Cardinal du Perron . . . .* (Paris, 1622); Guillaume du Vair, *De l'éloquence française* (1590), ed. René Radouant (Paris, 1908).

remain pure and virtuous. The poet is a secular priest concerned as much with his availability to God as with his skill in the poetic forms through which the divine message is passed. Significantly, Ronsard's *Abbregé de l'art poëtique françois* (1565) begins with lengthy admonitions on the poet's cult of the muses. They must be revered, for ultimately all poetry derives through them from the highest source: the grace of God.

The difference between the subject matter of poetry and of rhetoric is analyzed in various ways by the Renaissance theoreticians. Generally, poetry's subject matter is both more abstract and more elevating. In his comparison of orator and poet, Peletier du Mans sees the orator as constrained by the immediate demands of particular circumstances. He must speak of a well-specified matter before a well-defined audience in order to achieve a precise practical end. The poet feels none of these responsibilities. He may choose his subject matter freely, enrich it as he pleases, and leave aside the details of immediate existence that are the orator's first concern. The orator is time-bound. The poet speaks for eternity and speaks not of the accident but of the core of truth, "le neu, le segret et le fons d'un argumant" (*L'Art poëtique*, p. 84).

Such idealism is supported in the second half of the century by the rediscovery of Aristotle's *Poetics*. As we know, the great lesson of this work was to define poetry not by its metrical form but by its content seen as imitation of ideal rather than empirical truth. Ronsard invokes the principle of imitation both in his *Abbregé de l'art poëtique françois* and in his 1572 preface to the *Franciade*. The orator, he claims, seeks to persuade; the poet, unconcerned with addressee, seeks only to represent the "vraisemblable." In the *Franciade* preface Ronsard distinguishes the historian who relates the facts from the poet who describes what is possible although never perhaps realized. Poetry is thus freed from any constraining principle of realism. Aristotle's *Poetics* renders great service to poetic theory in France insofar as it makes room for the fictional content of literature, self-evident of course to most readers, but inexplicable if poetry is viewed only in the practical terms of the rhetorical tradition.

Although poetry, unlike oratory, serves no immediate practical purpose, it is not, however, disinterested. Its goal is the moral edification of the reader. This didactic aim had been recognized throughout the Middle Ages and continued to be acknowledged in the sixteenth century. Fabri mentions it at some length in the prologue to his rhetoric. Citing the authority of Boccaccio's *Genealogiae deorum*, he

defends poetry as an art that presents the truth in the form of allegory; he adds that all Scripture is full of allegory and that Christ
himself was a poet-allegorist in his parables. The later humanists
continue to favor the allegorical interpretation of literature. Dorat,
teacher of the Pléiade, interprets the classical epics allegorically, and
Ronsard himself describes the earliest poetry of man as a "theologie
allegoricque" (*Abbregé*, p. 4). The allegorical view, like the Aristotelian,
recognizes the "fables plaisantes & colorées" (ibid.) of literature, but
discovers in these fictions a moralizing intention. Literature is not
concerned with the practical truth of rhetoric, but with the timeless
truths of a divine order.

It will be clear now that the referent of poetry and the conception of the poet defined in the Renaissance are connected. A divinely
inspired poet transmits a divine message. Practically, this meant that
poetic could no longer define the poetic genres exclusively in terms
of formal structure as in the early manuals of the century such as that
of Fabri. Their content also becomes important. With Sebillet specific
content is prescribed for the sonnet, rondeau, chant royal, and com-
plainte. With the Pléiade grave content is encouraged as a general
norm. The *Deffence et illustration de la langue françoyse* marks a clear
preference for serious literature over a mere literature of entertain-
ment. Peletier du Mans, the most eloquent theoretician in the Pléiade
circle, distinguishes four subjects for poetry: war, love, *pastoralité*, and
agriculture. French literature, he believes, has given adequate treatment only to love. War, which includes all varieties of human behavior and experience, is the most challenging subject for the poet and
the most worthy of serious attention. Hence Peletier's passion for the
epic, which he expounds through a long analysis of the *Aeneid*. This
study has been condemned as derivative (based largely on Macrobius by way of Vida), but it is closely based on Virgil's text and hardly
seems a travesty of Rome's epic. Peletier's reading is that of an earnest
student who expects to be improved by his books. Such a student
looks for moral insights rather than esthetic pleasure. He may be
more concerned with truth than with beauty and not too interested
in their possible identity.

If we view sixteenth-century poetry in its entirety, it is clear that
the evolving definitions of poetry correspond to the evolving practice of the poets. Fabri's rhetoric anatomizes the different features of
the linguistic system, and the poetry of the *rhétoriqueurs* from which
Fabri draws his examples is highly logocentric. In Molinet's "La Res-
source du petit peuple" (1481), we find for example a type of "poésie

pure." Highly self-conscious, Molinet's poetry is a maximized manipulation of the signifier. It foregrounds all the formal elements that make it possible: sound, metre, parts of speech, syntax. With the poets of the Pléiade, the linguistic medium of poetry declines in relative importance, although of course the Pléiade style bears its own distinctive mark. This style, however, is neither phonocentric nor grammocentric. Its distinction lies in the way it imitates the style of classical and Italian literature. This imitation bears on signified as much as on signifier. It brings to literature a new content, the heroic vision for instance of the classical epic or the perception of love embodied in the Petrarchan style. Du Bellay insists in *La Deffence et illustration de la langue françoyse* that the study of classical languages is useful mainly for increasing the poet's store of ideas. The Pléiade poet has a more than formal message to communicate. Inspired and inspiring, he is the teacher of the nation. Ronsard, the prince of poets, became the poet of princes and an eloquent voice in the royal policy of the Valois. His alliance with the king recalled the classical precedent of Virgil and Augustus so often cited in the Renaissance. Like Virgil, Ronsard enshrined the values of a nation in his writing, and these values were paramount in the creative act. Rhetorical techniques were treated no longer as an end as they had been in the early years of the century, but as a means. Although the generous vision of rhetoric no doubt admits the same priority, this priority is often lost as, at times, with Fabri in the narcissistic contemplation of style, or again at the end of the sixteenth century and at the dawn of French classical literature. The orphic poet of the Pléiade has no place for instance in Pierre de Deimier's *Académie de l'art poétique* of 1610. Deimier pays lip service to poetic content in his definition of poetry as "vn don de Nature perfectionné de l'Art: par lequel auec la plus grande bonté du langage on chante les affections & les loüanges des Dieux & des hommes" (p. 1), but his treatise deals primarily not with the poetic subject matter of feelings and great deeds, but with the means that express them. These means are all subject to severe rational and social constraint. Poetry has so many rules, writes Deimier, that if one is ignorant of them, "on peut faire en vn Poëme plus de fautes que de vers" (p. 13). In language the final arbiter is popular usage, and Deimier condemns Du Bartas for using doublets such as "floflotant" that have no currency in the language of the people. Such strictures recall the normative tendencies of classical rhetoric. The latter with its emphasis on effective audience contact attaches great importance to the judgment of listeners on questions of linguistic use. The orator must find a level of style acceptable to the reasonable man. In this way rhetoric tends to become a conservative instrument of culture since the reasonable listener is not usually prepared for radical change in linguistic habit. But rhetoric is not always restrictive. The social responsibility shown by Deimier in the area of language is less strongly felt in the rhetoric of Fabri. The verbal mechanisms Fabri uncovers in the language, especially in that of poetry, are developed to their extreme end. They absorb the attention of the writer to a point where he forgets the normal usage of his audience. Hence the great difference between the rhetorical poetry of the early sixteenth century and that of the early years of the seventeenth. Molinet's verse is a flamboyant, self-regarding demonstration of verbal art. That of Malherbe, who best incarnates the teaching of Deimier, is a sober exposition in rhyme of the wisdom held in common by society and poet. With Malherbe we are far removed from the Pléiade ideal of the poet divinely inspired and teacher of men. According to his pupil Racan, he saw in the poet only an excellent arranger of syllables who was of no more use to the state than a good skittles player. The code and the addressee of rhetoric have triumphed once again, and the humanist concern for addressor and referent, which had allowed poetic to define its own ground, is again relegated to obscurity.

Today rhetoric enjoys a new vogue. Avant-garde sympathies may well lie more with Fabri and Deimier than with the "personal" poet of the Pléiade who believes that his words are the way to things and finally to meaning. In our time the very notion of the person is questioned. At our most despairing moments we may feel that we no longer choose our words. They come to us in a fully functioning system through which we are constituted. We do not write them; they write us. To many the humanist's struggle for poetry's own truth may seem little more than a proud illusion.

Rhetoric and Fiction
in Elizabethan England

ARTHUR F. KINNEY

In a striking portrait that fills the verso of the title page in the Bod-leian Library's unique copy of the *Sphaera Civitatis* by John Case of St. John's College, Oxford (1602), a reasonably good likeness of Eliza-beth I embraces a globe of concentric circles, the taxonomy of which discloses Case's own vision of the state: the circles are labeled stellata (and Heroes), Maiestas, Prudentia, Fortitvdo, Religio, Clementia, Fecvndia, and (nearest the center, or Iustitia Immobilis), Vbertas Re-rvm — Eloquence.[1] This medular positioning of the art of rhetoric signifies not only Case's leanings but the queen's; earlier her tutor Roger Ascham has told us that when he was permitted to visit the Princess Elizabeth during Mary Tudor's reign they read Latin and Greek together, their favorite being that disputatious chestnut, the opposing orations of Demosthenes and Aeschines concerning the latter's embassy to Philip of Macedon.[2] Yet the apt pupil merely fol-lowed her mentor; lesser known, perhaps, but just as revealing, is Ascham's own remark to a friend of Archbishop Lee of York in 1544 that he would take a copy of Lee's *Rhetores Graeci* in lieu of half a year's pension then owed him;[3] least known, but likewise indicative, is a remark of one C. W. of St. John's College, Cambridge, who justifies his translation of the first book of Polybius and appends an abstract

---

1. Bodleian Library A. 14.18 Linc.; sig. 1ᵛ.
2. Lawrence V. Ryan, "Introduction" to *The Schoolmaster (1570) by Roger Ascham* (Charlottesville, Va., 1967), p. xxi.
3. *The Whole Works of Roger Ascham*, coll. and ed. the Rev. Dr. Giles (London, 1865), I.i.58–60.

of Henry V's biography because, he admits, he was moved by an oration in Halle's chronicles. These various indices to an age in which the study of eloquence ripened as the foundation of a humanist curriculum show the pervasive force of the humanists; even Richard Sherry adds an Erasmian declamation to his 1550 book of schemes and tropes: "That chyldren euen strapt frō their infancie should be well and gently broughte vp in learnynge."[4] Thus the cultural hero advanced by the humanists is not the military Achilles but the rhetorical Odysseus as received through Golding's Ovid: "The Lords were moued with his woordes, & then appeered playne/The force that is in eloquence. The lerned man did gayne/The armour of the valeant" (13.463–65).[5]

"You cannot read Renaissance literature for long," Richard A. Lanham sums, "without noticing everywhere a delight in words, an infatuation with rhetoric, a stylistic explosion."[6] Even so, rhetoric was hedged about with a wary skepticism educators and writers alike knew — rhetoric discovered probabilities rather than taught truth. Thus for Leonard Cox rhetoric is "right pleasaunt" as a "persuadible art,"[7] his understanding echoing the Tudor commonplace sources in Aristotle and Cicero, while Sir Thomas Wilson writes in his *Arte of Rhetorique* of 1553 that "The findyng out of apte mater, called otherwise Inuencion, is a searchyng out of thynges true, or thynges likely, the whiche maie reasonably sette furth a matter, and make it appere probable" (a3ᵛ). "We hold many doctrines as probable which we can easily act upon but can scarcely advance as certain," Cicero notes in the *Lucullus*;[8] and the writers of the Renaissance show repeatedly their awareness that persuasion may rest not with the truth of statements but equally with the right impressions of the speaker's character or the emotions of the judges, ideas fundamental to Aristotelian rhetoric. In this sense, as in the search after topics and commonplaces on which to arrange and build arguments and reports, the cogency and success of rhetoric depended on resources and on resourcefulness. The models so devoutly imitated in Richard

4. *A treatise of Schemes & Tropes very profytable for the better understanding of good authors, gathered out of the best Grammarians & Oratours* (1550), title page.

5. *The .xv. Bookes of P. Ouidius Naso, entytuled Metamorphosis, translated oute of Latin in English meeter, by Arthur Golding Gentleman* (1567), sig. Y3ᵛ.

6. *The Motives of Eloquence: Literary Rhetoric in the Renaissance* (New Haven, Conn., 1976), p. 33.

7. *The Art of crafte of Rhetoryke* (1532 ed.), sig. A2ᵛ.

8. *Lucullus*, II.iii.7–8.

Rainolde's redaction of Aphthonius, for instance, or the rules formu-
lating a chria, an encomium, or a fable, emphasize Tudor caution —
necessary because, in such a verbal culture, Thomas Newton noted in
1577, *"there is nothinge so incredible, but by artificiall handelynge maye bee
made probable: nothinge so rugged and rustye, but by Eloquence maye bee
poolyshed (and as it were glitteringly burnished . . .)"* (M5).

Newton's comment comes in the preface to his translation of Cicero's *jeu d'esprit,* the *Paradoxia,* and his isomorphic marginal note is
revealing: "What learning and Eloquēce is able to doe." This conscious acceptance of the lubricious possibilities inherent in language
in a culture persistently trained in antilogy, or the ability to argue
either side of a question with equal skill, leads Wilson to issue a long
catalogue of warnings. "Not onely it is necessarie to knowe, what
maner of cause wee haue taken in hande, when wee firste enter vpon
any matter," he admonishes his readers, his pupils,

> but also it is wisedome to consider the tyme, the place, the man for
> whom we speake, the man against whom we speake, the matter
> whereof we speake, and the iudges before whom we speake, the rea-
> sons that best serue to further our cause, and those reasons also,
> that maie seme somewhat to hynder our cause, and in no wise to vse
> any suche at all, or else warely to mitigate by protestation, the euill
> that is in theim (sig. bl).

Eloquence for many Tudor writers was not — could not have been, in
any realistic sense — the golden language of the good and wise man
as Quintilian has seemed to premise, but the manipulation of words
in a country where eristics was respected and daily practiced. Elizabethan authors were, if anything, suspect of those characteristics
Plato (and later Sextus and others) found in argumentation — *euché-
reia* (dexterity) and *agchinoia* (sharp-wittedness), those practices that
seemed to align *sophia,* or "wysedome," to sophistry, "a craftye and
deceytefull sentence, an Oracyon or inuention, whiche seemeth to be
trewe, when it is false," as Elyot defines them in his dictionary.

Yet as the Tudors continued to develop their own high age of
rhetoric, they drew more and more on what we should call imaginative or creative techniques to attract their listeners and persuade
their audiences. As ambassadors, they needed oratory: as orators,
they became, in Lucian's word, actors.[9] And as writers they became
poets. "Poetes firste inuented fables, the whiche Oratours also doe
vse in their perswasions, and not without greate cause, both Poetes

9. *Of Pantomime* 65.

and Oratours doe applie theim to their vse," Richard Rainolde comments.[10] A rooted need for verisimilitude joins both arts. Both gravitate, naturally, toward narrative form, a form taught too in Rainolde's rhetorical handbook. This indiscriminate practice of what we today would distinguish as rhetoric and poetic is also seen in Erasmus's *De copia* where his *exempla* as frequently employ simile and metaphor as they do analogy and syllogism, or in the common practice, begun in the Tudor grammar schools, of delivering orations and disputations by what Sherry calls "effiguration" or *prosopographia* or *prosopopoeia*, the description of a feigned person or the act of feigning.[11] By supplying much practice in form, persona, and illustration, rhetoricians so merged rhetoric and poetic in what they felt a condign use of language to approximate truth and to persuade men to believe the credible to be the probable, that there seemed precious little room left for writers of pure fiction to make their own works of the imagination clearly fables. As consequence, they did not: they borrowed the forms of the oration and the disputation and the techniques of a rhetoric of figures for their own purposes, writing a fiction that invented tales for their audience to judge as if they too were in attendance at a formal rhetorical occasion. Thus the act of methaxis — the complicit participation by an audience in actively judging a fiction — became the common means not only of ambassadors, orators, and actors, but of fiction writers too at the dawn of the English novel.

Nowhere is this more astonishingly plain than in the brilliant display of ironic wit that comes very early in the development of Elizabethan fiction, in John Lyly's *Euphues* (1578) and *Euphues and His England* (1580). In retrospect this could not have surprised his contemporaries, for as the grandson of Henry VIII's official grammarian and the author of a Latin grammar authorized by four successive Tudor monarchies, Lyly was the most visible heir of the humanist movement that had introduced rhetoric alongside grammar as the basis of Tudor education and culture. Even the obvious *propositio* of *Euphues*, given by the older man Eubulus, echoes the Christian humanism urged by men like Erasmus, Sturm, and Ascham at the outset of their writings. "Descend into thine owne conscience," Eubulus tells Euphues,

> and consider with thy selfe, the great difference betweene staring and starke blynde, witte and wisedome, loue and lust: be merry, but

10. *A booke called the Foundacion of Rhetorike* (1563), sig. A3.
11. Sherry, *treatise*, sigs. E1ᵛ – E2.

with modestie: be sober, but not too sullen: be valyaunt, but not too venterous. Let thy attyre bee comely, but not costly: thy dyet wholesome, but not excessiue: vse pastime as the word importeth to passe the time in honest recreation. Mistrust no man without cause, nether be thou credulus without proofe: be not lyght to follow euery mans opinion, nor obstinate to stande in thine owne conceipt. Serue GOD, loue God, feare God, and god will so blesse thee, as eyther heart canne wish or thy friends desire.[12]

This excessive monishment deals rhetorically — even copiously — with issues of probability, not fact: fictionally, Lyly makes it one side of a *controversia:* the stability of Eubulus's prophylactic position balances the regnant hypocrisy of his city of Naples, just as his argument for restraint counteracts the atmosphere of freedom he feels will threaten Euphues, the urgency for self-discipline and his humanist particularizations for illustration (appealing eventually to the Trojans, Lacedaemonians, Persians, and Parthians) in deliberate counterpoise with the more general, almost fatuous precepts that have permitted some critics, seeing things rather too simply, to compare Eubulus with Polonius. Further, the subsequent debates or *controversiae* that compose the bulk of *Euphues* — formalized disputations on nature and nurture, conscience and concupiscence, friendship and lust — are precisely those topics John Lyly disputed publicly in his examinations in the Church of St. Mary the Virgin in Oxford, much of *Euphues* seemingly extrapolated from earlier college notes. This is, I think, no coincidence, no otiose act in the anatomy of wit, but rather an openly connected and concentrated testing of the efficacy of rhetoric and a rhetorical education Lyly here means to analyze.

Lucilla sums this for us in *Euphues*: "If Nature canne no waye resist the furye of affection," she inquires pointedly, "how shoulde it be stayed by wisedome?" (sig. 13/I.231). The question for her is an urgent one since it is learning itself — humanist wisdom at its most accessible and applicable — that creates her difficulty as she struggles to reason her way to an appropriate behavior. She defines the object of her natural, unruly affection for Euphues with *exempla* from her storehouse of humanist learning and secures it in the amber of a traditionally accepted humanist rhetoric. See how familiar this sounds on the surface of it:

12. *Euphues* (1579 ed.), sig. B4ᵛ; *The Complete Works of John Lyly*, ed. R. Warwick Bond (Oxford, 1902, rpt. 1973), I.189–90.

> I knowe so noble a minde could take no Originall but from a noble
> man, for as no bird can looke again the Sunne but those that bee
> bredde of the Eagle, neyther any Hawke soare so hie as the broode
> of the Hobby, so no wight can haue suche excellent qualyties except
> hee descends of a noble race, neyther be of so highe capacitie,
> vnlesse hee issue of a high progeny (sig. I2^V/I.231).

And yet to love Euphues is to break her pledge to Philautus, and this
reminds her, with equal force, of still other historical examples—of
Myrhha, Biblis, Phaedra—who were victimized by natural passions
that, similar to hers, they could not control. Her education in books
of the past as patterns for the present is so comprehensive, then, that
rather than holding no answers for her, they sanction all possibilities:
her humanist learning and rhetorical inquiries result in a stalemate
of idea and action fixed in a revealingly symmetrical prose.

Lucilla's father, Fernardo, seizing Lucilla's inability to determine
her own best course of behavior by such rhetorical investigations
through the commonplaces, interrupts her the better to defend Philautus, before whom Lucilla is also confessing.

> *Lucilla,* as I am not presently to graunt my good wil, so meane I not
> to reprehend thy choyce, yet wisdome willeth me to pawse, vntill I
> haue called what may happen to my remembraunce, and warneth
> thee to be circumspect, least thy rash conceipt bring a sharpe re-
> pentaũce (sig. I2^V– 13/I.231).

This reply provides Lucilla with another wide-ranging accumulation
of possibilities equal to those that disturbed her in the first place. I do
not like this, Fernardo tells his daughter, then adds, I will not rebuke
(censure) your choice in men; and, I will delay responding until all of
this blows over; and also, I will wait until I can determine the cause of
your defection and then I will act; and finally, do whatever you wish, if
you must, but do be discreet about it. The father who would be school-
master here correlates to the earlier Eubulus; and both teachers say
and know too much. Their learning exposes their *in*sufficiency, just as
their humanist rhetoric, traditionally employed, tries desperately to
conceal their uncertainties, the disturbing multivalences of their own
thoughts. What Lucilla senses in her father's response—apparently
fulsome, actually vapid—Euphues sees and tells Eubulus openly: "If
Nature be of strength or force," he argues with a strong logic, "what
auaileth discipline or nurture? [And] if of none, what helpeth nature?" (sig. C2/I.192). The *isocolon, parison,* and *paramoion* of Lyly's elaborate style, traced back variously to classical rhetoricians, medieval

preachers, and the Oxford lectures of John Rainoldes, are not simply decorative: they are here — with Lyly now — probative, strategic, and vital — intellectual consequences of an agile, inventive, and confused mind caught in a bewildering array of rhetorically familiar self-examinations. *"The whole worlde is become an Hodge-podge,"* Lyly will lament (sig. A2ᵛ) in *The Woman in the Moone* (1597), while he compares his play *Sapho and Phao* to a *"Labyrinth"* (sig. G2). Equivocations in language so useful to a rhetoric dealing with the probable as credible or true both conceal and expose equivalencies in thought. The rhetorical riches of humanism could be suicidal.

It is just such possibilities as these — words put to wrong purpose and facilitating wrong ends — that cause Tudor writers of fiction to protest, too frequently and stridently, perhaps, the useful ends of fable and story; and it is no coincidence, either, that just as Lyly was composing his fictions, Sidney was establishing his witty, synthetic *Defense of Poesie*. Sidney's apology rests, as his understanding of a successful and worthwhile poetics does, on its rhetorical ability to move men to particular virtuous actions. Yet his work is not a simple formulary, for he refuses to argue (as others of the period do) that truth rests only, or even finally, on the foreconceit of the poet. Rather, Sidney contends, meaning rests in the complicit judgment of the reader. Sidney makes his point openly when he admires the irony of Erasmus (and Agrippa) and when he scorns readers who are content to believe everything literally — readers content *not* to judge. By the virtue he awards icastic art (divinely revealed or humanly counterfeited) juxtaposed with the fantastic shows of wantonness (unreal because evil in God's and the poet's created universes) Sidney reawakens, without admitting it, the caution of Plato, the cynicism of Sextus. Even when such evil is not present, the inherent conflict between icastic and fantastic representation demands a third response in the reconciliation by the reader in his well knowing: an act of triangulation through which the reader gives the final significance on the inherent disputation of any text using images — on any act of poetic fiction.

Sidney's poetics is realized as well as anywhere in his own triumphant fiction, the *Arcadia* (1590; 1593). So marvelously rich and complex a work as this one cannot be analyzed sufficiently in a few sentences, but the disputation between Pamela and Cecropia in Book III, generally acknowledged to be a chief climax in the work, will illustrate Sidney's own strategies in simultaneously advancing different arguments so as to force upon the reader an act of triangulation.

Praising the embroidery of the captured Pamela, Cecropia argues for the superiority of marvelous art — "It is the right nature (said *Cecropia*) of Beauty, to worke vnwitting effects of wonder" — while Pamela counters with her sense of the realistic properties of the purse she is working — "I valued it, but euen as a verie purse."[13] This open-and-shut debate is complicated still further by Sidney's own rhetorical presentation of the scene; he notes that "the flowers [Pamela] had wrought, caried such life in thē, that the cūningest painter might haue learned of her needle," but he continues without pause or transition,

> which with so prety a maner made his careers to & fro through the cloth, as if the needle it self wold haue ben loth to haue gone frō-ward such a mistres, but that it hoped to return thitherward very quickly againe: the cloth loking with many eies vpon her, & louingly embracing the wounds she gaue it (sig. Z4ᵛ/483),

the very hyperbole rendering the scene delightfully absurd, impairing its high seriousness by being too highly serious. This complication is not an isolated one in the *Arcadia*. The discussion of art, which urges the naturalness of the colors against the exaggeration of the ornamentation, is subsumed by a more important disputation on the proper use of beauty. Pamela defends beauty as her own representation of God's harmony and order in the universe, while Cecropia sees beauty as a transitory possession the wise will put to good use; she argues, that is, for woman's misappropriation of beauty in a speech that is analogously sophistic, an anatomy of what Sidney (following Lyly) calls her "mischieuous witte" (sig. Z5ᵛ/487). Pamela appears to get the best of this disputation, for within the fiction she has the last, long declamation, arguing for "a Nature of wisdome, goodnes, & prouidence" (sig. Z6ᵛ/490) in which "each thinge being directed to an ende, and an ende or preseruation" (sig. Z6ᵛ/491) argues in turn God's existence, perfection, and generosity. So excerpted, we have no difficulty in choosing Pamela as the victor in this verbal match; but placed in the context of Sidney's fiction we realize that life in Arcadia is governed not by a single and intelligible Creator (or poet) but by chance and by the accidents of Fortune as well. Pamela's devotion to a transcendent faith is, in the plot, mocked by the tested efficacy of Basilius's oracle sounding more pagan mysteries. Moreover, Pamela's

---

13. (1593 ed.), sig. Z4ᵛ; *Arcadia*, ed. Maurice Evans, The Penguin English Library (Harmondsworth, 1977), p. 484.

faith in the power of her own language ignores the potentialities of Cercropia's eristics just as her willingness to see all language as an honest revelation of character is undercut by Sidney himself in the sophistic pretenses of Pyrocles and Musidorus and in the disguises that force their rhetoric to be as counterfeit — that is, as beautiful and as artificial — as the roses on Pamela's hand-stitched purse. Whether we are to judge the ends of their speeches (which are determined by their various senses of the good) or the means (which are often at odds with their chief purposes) grounds the *Arcadia* in a dialectic that even Euarchus, commanding all his wisdom and faith in an un-eroded justice, cannot resolve. For the final disposition of events in *Arcadia* comes neither from the faith of Pamela nor the reason of Euarchus, but the mistakes of all the main characters in thinking a drugged Basilius to be dead and in Basilius's own foolishness in at-tempting to seduce his wife by his own self-indulgent rhetoric. Nor does *Arcadia* — new or old — ever come to a conclusion: Sidney, in promising more to come, suggests that a plot grounded either in fortune or in providence — it is up to us to judge which and to defend our choice — is not all there is to tell. Sidney's conclusion is inconclu-sive, enigmatic because it brings us back to the beginning of *Arcadia* and to a sense of promise rather than of completion. If *Arcadia* has closure, then, it is we who supply it.

This imaginative poetics utilized by Lyly and Sidney whereby the form of rhetorical oration and the employment of rhetorical dis-putation become a chief means of fabling, persuading to the credible as rhetoricians argued the probable, marks the main body of Elizabe-than fiction while guaranteeing that, in its reliance on a triangulation with the reader (or listener) it could outstretch its place, its age. The fiction is, as a consequence, wonderfully alive, wonderfully witty; it turns its own skepticism to the advantage of satire and even self-mockery (as in the cases of Lucilla and Cecropia). Seen rightly, Eliza-bethan fiction is wonderfully lambent, rich in shifting perspectives and tonalities, various in its implications, forceful in its purposive employment of audience. Even Francis Bacon could recognize the value of this, much as he dismissed Ciceronian rhetoric for paying more attention to words than matter: "Reade not to contradict, nor to belieue," he tells us in the 1597 *Essays*, "but to waigh and consider" (sig. A4ᵛ). This sense of the dynamic process of reading, as well as listening, shows how the Tudor fiction writers, inheriting classical rhetoric, forged a poetics suitable too to the new age of science just then being born.

Reading Milton Rhetorically

THOMAS O. SLOANE

About *inventio* in classical and humanist theories of composition, one observation is inescapable: It was the chief art of rhetoric. Finding what to say — or, more precisely, choosing the appropriate ideas — is always and everywhere the primary task facing anyone composing discourse, a truism not even eccentric theories could abuse. In some traditional rhetorics *inventio* is discrete, in others it pervades the remaining four arts, and in all it is central. Even the Ramists only underscored the importance of *inventio* when they assigned it to their more dignified discipline "logic." Assuming the barest correlation between theory and practice, one would expect that the principles of rhetorical invention suffused all composition in the English Renaissance. And since poetry in that period was usually considered a major rhetorical accomplishment, we can further assume that poets as well as orators made use of *inventio*. Our assumptions can be readily confirmed by scholarship and sealed by such categorical statements as Dryden's: "The first happiness of the poet's imagination is properly invention, or finding the thought."[1]

But we also know that rhetoric was designed to help *audiences* as well as speakers, readers as well as writers. That is, *inventio* not only systematized part of the speaker's creative process but in some way assisted the audience's interpretive process. If poets created by means of rhetorical invention, their audiences surely read by the very same means. However, that historical axiom has yet to reach our

1. Letter to Sir Robert Howard, *The Works of John Dryden*, ed. Sir Walter Scott (Edinburgh, 1821), 9.98.

394

level of practical criticism. How is it possible to read rhetorically? Or to rephrase the question by specifying its terms: if *inventio* means finding the thought, how could it assist the reader's understanding? In light of our increasingly refined historical information concerning the role rhetoric played in the work of every major poet from Wyatt to Dryden and in light, too, of the documented prominence of rhetoric in the literary education of their readers, the question seems worth pondering. Doing so may be heuristic, adding yet another dimension to our views of rhetoric, poetry, and criticism. Let us begin with the observation, suggested earlier, that the implications of *inventio* are seldom considered in practical criticism and concentrate in particular on that criticism which most looks like rhetorical reading.

Consider two ostensibly rhetorical approaches to interpreting Milton. Those critics for whom rhetorical analysis means an examination of style seldom give much attention to style as a strategy on the reader. It is not that they sever body and mind, as Crassus puts it, divorcing style from thought,[2] but that they sever the poet's *elocutio* from the reader's *inventio*. They separate considerations of style from the process whereby a reader finds the thought. Many of these rhetorical critics demonstrate well the means whereby style performs its functions of adorning, clothing, or ornamenting what they assume was the poet's thought; their analyses are frequently packed with figures and tropes, the names of many of which have not appeared in print for centuries. Certainly these analyses have extended considerably our knowledge of *elocutio*. But insofar as they omit the reader's interaction with a text they stop short of rhetorical reading. Should not a rhetorical reading show how the reader's mind is led toward the discovery of thought that has been, one should assume, strategically adorned, clothed, or ornamented? Second, the opposite extreme, which amounts to emphasizing the reader's invention exclusively, in isolation not simply from the poet's style but from *all* rhetorical considerations (particularly those that are the major components of meaning and intention), may seem radical but in our time it is not rare. Indeed, one of our most successful Milton critics virtually proposes allowing the reader to invent the poem with very little help from the poet's craft. And it is demonstrably the case with Milton that that craft centered (to borrow a comparison from Milton, who noted, in speaking of an ideal scheme of education, that poetry was both "subsequent" and "precedent" to rhetoric) in the arts of rhetoric. In

2. *De oratore* III.vi.24.

fact, from Wyatt to Dryden poets created and their readers read primarily by means of *inventio*—and *inventio* is a rhetorical art, connected with and conveying rhetoric's deep view of discursive meaning as a compound of speaker, speech, and audience, and of intention as a construct of convention and expectation.

I do not propose to offer full rhetorical readings in this short essay. I propose to do no more than suggest the ways in which such readings might proceed. I wish above all to propose that what passes for rhetorical reading—whether an examination of style or a positing of a hypothetical reader's momentary responses—must be grounded in assumptions concerning the poet's own rhetorical knowledge. So far as Milton is concerned, both of the approaches I have so briefly reviewed are misapplications of the rich rhetorical traditions in which he himself placed his own work. Antithetical as they are, I should like to use these two—a noninventive analysis of style and a free-wheeling inventiveness in reading—as my *divisio*. I shall argue that each is flawed by a certain shortsightedness: each has ignored the precise function of *inventio* in analysis because each lacks a wholly rhetorical approach, one that would examine style and consider the reader's interpretive process while never straying from the concept of the poem as in part at least a rhetorical act. In developing my argument, I shall try to explain what I mean by the poem as a rhetorical act, and I shall try to justify my critique of these two approaches by suggesting that restoring *inventio* to a central position in a genuinely rhetorical reading is important, for doing so may provide us with yet another basis for assessing Milton's achievement.

The first intensive study of rhetoric in Milton's poetry, offered twenty years ago, is a prime example of noninventive stylistic analysis.[3] J. B. Broadbent's "pioneering demonstration" has been found to be partial at best. Brian Vickers faulted it for failing to take into account the "organic literary function" of stylistic devices.[4] I should argue that Broadbent failed to pursue the function of style because he divorced his analysis from a total rhetorical attitude toward what a poem is and how it means. The analysis of style, rhetorically conceived, should lead one ineluctably toward the discovery of thought by leading one consciously closer to the very strategies whereby that thought is presented and controlled. Rhetorically conceived, style is no more and no less than an embodiment of strategies whereby the poet exerts control

3. J. B. Broadbent, "Milton's Rhetoric," *Modern Philology* 56 (1959), 224–42.
4. Brian Vickers, *Classical Rhetoric in English Poetry* (London, 1970), p. 153.

over the range of associations he might reasonably expect his reader to bring to the task of understanding. Not necessarily any reader, but particularly the reader the poet could have imagined. At the very least, therefore, a rhetorical reading must impute an audience's response to style, and in spite of an impressive knowledge of rhetorical theory, Broadbent stops short of that imputation.

In sum, I take invention in rhetorical reading to mean exactly what it means in rhetorical composition, finding the thought already present in the materials. It is a process of including some ideas and excluding others, a process in which the poet's style is a means of control over an implied reader's invention. Insofar as rhetorical composition is linear, proceeding from invention to style, rhetorical reading merely reverses the process, in order to—as Milton might put it—distinguish first the kinds of style and then the various ideas with which each kind is associated.[5] Indeed, the Hermogenean ideas of style, to which Milton was adverting in that reference, provide a body of conventions that may prove useful in our reading of his poetry, not simply because they were well known to the poet (though, obviously, this poet knew many rhetorical conventions) but also because they signify the profound linkage of *inventio* with *elocutio* in rhetorical reading.[6] It is that linkage which is crucial to my argument. But let us begin by acknowledging the vastness of the problem and the presumption of too easily identifying conventions, associations, and influences.

5. In *Apology for Smectymnuus,* Milton takes to task those clergymen so ignorant that they do not "know how to write, or speak in a pure stile, much lesse to distinguish the *ideas,* and various kinds of stile," *Works* (New York, 1931), 3.347.

6. See Annabel M. Patterson, *Hermogenes and the Renaissance: Seven Ideas of Style* (Princeton, N.J., 1970). The book contains much useful information concerning Johannes Sturm's edition of Hermogenes and Minturno's use of the Hermogenean ideas. George L. Kustas discusses Hermogenes and his early medieval commentators in *Studies in Byzantine Rhetoric* (Salonika, 1973). The work of Trapezuntius, the most important commentator on Hermogenes for the Renaissance, is thoroughly discussed by John Monfasani, *George of Trebizond: A Biography and a Study of his Rhetoric and Logic* (Leiden, 1976). At the very least, the Hermogenean conventions, however vast and complex, would be more appropriate in a rhetorical reading of Milton than those provided by Ramism, the dominant rhetorical theory of his formative years, toward which he took a curiously avuncular stance; see for example, P. Albert Duhamel, "Milton's Alleged Ramism," *PMLA* 67 (1952), 1035–53; and Christopher Grose, "Milton on Ramist Similitude," in *Seventeenth Century Imagery,* ed. Earl Miner (Berkeley and Los Angeles, 1971), pp. 103–16. I detect an "avuncular" tone in Milton's intention in his recension of the *Dialectique,* to dispel the shortcomings of Ramist theory by helpfully explaining it. For suggesting the possible relationship of Hermogenean rhetoric and Milton's poem, I am grateful to Mr. Scott Selby.

It is not too much to assume, I think, that any text will provoke certain associations in a reader's mind — for example, the reader might associate Petrarchan conventions with a certain tone or stance, Orpheus with vitalism, rosebuds with the *carpe diem* theme. So far as Hermogenes is concerned, another critic with a more thorough understanding of the *Peri ideon* than I have might demonstrate its function in Milton's rhetoric as a body of conventions offering associations Milton sought to control in his audience. However, my concern here is not with establishing the identity of these conventions. It is, rather, with demonstrating a method of rhetorically reading the elements of style, and this method, as I have indicated, always presumes that within a text we shall discover signs of the poet's control over a reader's invention, over a reader's use of associations to arrive at the poet's meaning and intention. For my task, only the possibility that the associations I shall imagine — or ones like them — are operative need be admitted. After all, in imagining Milton's own ideal (or implied) reader, we could posit an intellect whose range of associations and knowledge of conventions is vast. For the poet, you will recall, saw himself as an individual talent operating within a great confluence of rhetoric and poetry extending at least from the Old Testament prophets through Spenser. But this acknowledgement, rather than vitiating our efforts to grasp context, should only make them err on the side of modesty and tentativeness.

On the question of influences, let me reassert my thesis. It is not the demonstration of rhetorical influences (the presence, say, of Hermogenes' theory in Milton's practice) that makes a reading rhetorical. It is, rather, the centering through the text on the poet-reader relationship. To put the matter stylistically, rhetorical reading presupposes a certain attitude toward language: language reflects a speaker's designs as he confronts an audience, who he assumes are not possessed of *tabulae rasae* but of minds filled with associations, conventions, expectations, which he must direct, control, or take advantage of. This is the attitude that distinguishes rhetorical reading from other types of close analysis. Good rhetorical reading preserves the greatest potential complexity of reader's response and poet's control; in the case of Milton's poetry, considering the vast intellectual range of response and control, a rhetorical reading can do no more than suggest this complexity. Nonetheless, it is this complexity that is, in the rhetorician's eyes, sufficient warrant for details pertaining to such matters in textual criticism as the omission of a comma or in textual explication as an apparently abrupt biblical allusion — as we shall see in the following example:

On Time

Fly envious *Time*, till thou run out thy race,
Call on the lazy leaden-stepping hours,
Whose speed is but the heavy plummets pace;
And glut thy self with what thy womb devours,
Which is no more then what is false and vain.
And meerly mortal dross;
So little is our loss
So little is thy gain.
For when as each thing bad thou has entomb'd
And last of all thy greedy self consum'd.
Then long Eternity shall greet our bliss
With an individual kiss;
And Joy shall overtake us as a flood,
When every thing that is sincerely good
And perfectly divine,
With Truth, and Peace, and Love shall ever shine
About the Supreme Throne
Of him, t'whose happy-making sight alone,
When once our heav'nly-guided soul shall clime,
Then all this Earthy grosness quit,
Attir'd with Stars, we shall for ever sit,
    Triumphing over Death, and Chance, and thee O Time.[7]

The presentation of the poem — including its intended appearance on a clock case — produces at least a moment's confusion in which other notions of time may be brought to bear upon one's reading. Consider a possible context. To fly time was the exhortation of the contemporary Cavalier poet, who played variations on the themes of the earlier Elizabethans. Seize the moment, use your time, fear the passing of youth, the Cavalier argued. The Elizabethan lyricist, conversely, had argued that we should find in art monuments that outlast time, building in sonnets pretty rooms.[8] Correlative to

---

7. *Works* (New York, 1931), 1.25 – 26.

8. "Milton's intention is not to capture time or to seize the day, but to let it run to its own dissolution. In fact one of the major themes of Milton's most serious poetry is quite simply resistance to the temptations posed by those arguments of time that had so clearly emerged in the earlier Renaissance," Ricardo J. Quinones, *The Renaissance Discovery of Time* (Harvard, 1972), p. 451.

these was a rhetorical commonplace tradition (which Patterson associates with the Hermogenean idea of speed)[9] that considered flying any sort of danger, such as the ravages of time, an act of bravery. The idea in all these conventions is courage born of fear, a theme that one of Milton's contemporaries was later to exploit in advising his coy mistress to devour time through erotic pleasures.

Among unquestionably many others, these associations (which, admittedly, for all but Milton's ideal audience, his "fit but few," might be arcane) are stimulated initially by the grammatical ambiguity in the opening lines of the poem. The imperative does not make immediately clear who is being ordered to "fly." Is Time being told to fly or are we? (Let "we" in this discussion mean implied readers, that audience with a grasp of those conventions that seem to be at work in this poem. "Milton," or "poet," is also hypothetical though implied.) If we imagine, however uncertainly, that we are being addressed, then our initial identification with the qualities of Time would cause us to see ourselves as gluttons, feeding on the false and vain, fattening on the material inconsequence of this world. Gradually the ambiguity lessens, to be totally dissolved by the "our-thy" distinction in lines 7 and 8. By then, our initial confusion, if not actual identification with Time, could only sharpen the contrast when we are invited to concentrate on that feature of our being that is not temporal. In other words, the ambiguity is rhetorically functional, and it thereby justifies the practice of those select, careful editors who since 1645 have printed the poem without a comma following the first word,[10] however strange the punctuation might seem to modern eyes.

Functional, too, is a certain lexical ambiguity in the opening three words. Time is often taken as a reference to "Chronos" and "envious" glossed as an epithet, signifying Chronos's jealousy of his own children, whom he devoured. Though the association of Chronos with a kind of grisly gluttony is explored in the comparisons of the following lines, the association of Chronos with flight is less conventional and may consequently heighten the initial impression that it is the reader who is being told to flee a jealous monster. Moreover, the lexical construction might recall for the reader not Chronos but Petrarch's *Trionfi*, in which winged Time moves inexo-

9. Patterson, chap. 6.

10. The medieval heritage of using punctuation rhetorically, to ensure that one's readers perceive the text in a certain way, is suggested in M. B. Parkes, "Punctuation, or Pause and Effect," in *Medieval Eloquence,* ed. James J. Murphy (Berkeley and Los Angeles, 1978), pp. 127–42.

rably through space, who in his envy claims for himself and destroys all the monuments and trophies of Fame. In the century before Milton, Petrarch's *Trionfi* had become assimilated to the Elizabethan love of pomp and display, particularly those processions supposedly patterned after Roman ideals and called "triumphs." In tapestries and allegorical paintings, envious Time's winged chariot moved in a stately procession, awesomely triumphing over Fame and the world.[11] A further importance of this possible association becomes apparent at the conclusion of the poem.

All these associations create expectations whose fulfillment or thwarting reveals the poet's control in engaging the reader. Though winged, Milton's Time moves slowly, at the pace of heavy plummets. Envious and gluttonous, it ironically feeds on itself. Like Spenser's Error, the children whom the mother had swallowed destroy themselves by devouring the mother. In these paradoxes, one set of associations gives way to another. More conventionally, Time becomes the serpent with its tail in its mouth: "'Time swallows all that's past and more,' wrote a forgotten poet of the seventeenth century, 'yet time is swallowed in eternity.'"[12] Speed becomes only a mortal perception of Time's vast slowness: *tempus edax rerum*, Ovid has Protagoras say, "Time devours all things/With envious Age, together. The slow gnawing/Consumes all things, and very, very slowly."[13] The meaning as well as the tonal defiance of Milton's opening lines gradually become explicit, and the reader's search for thought, his *inventio*, has encouraged him to examine the craftsmanship of the poem — has brought him, that is, into the fully rhetorical resonances of the poet's *elocutio*.

Then, in a striking imitation of the very concept it articulates, just when the poem, like Time, seems to end, the poem rises — and I think successfully carries the reader with it — to a higher form of defiance. Time is defied in praise of Eternity. Using *anaphoras* Milton creates a repetitive "when . . . then" syntactical pattern arranged climactically. Line 12 completes the bare argument of the poem, with the triumph of Eternity. The following line names the emotion that is the theme of the remaining 10 lines and serves as a conjunction between the

11. See E. E. Carnicelli, ed., *Lord Morley's Tryumphs of Fraunces Petrarche* (Cambridge, Mass., 1971).

12. Marjorie Hope Nicholson, *The Breaking of the Circle,* rev. ed. (New York, 1960), p. 48.

13. Ovid, *Metamorphoses* 15.234. The translation is from Rolfe Humphries (Bloomington, Ind., 1964), p. 372.

two "when . . . then" constructions. In this second half of the poem, we are again encouraged to recall Petrarch, whose *Trionfi* sequence ends with the triumph of Eternity over Time. In both poems, the emotion of joy is central. But in his poem Milton gives special controlled meaning to the "triumph." It is not a stately, moving procession. In fact, it involves no movement at all, no "triumphing" in a secular sense, but an elevation to a supreme stasis. The reader is led toward this stasis through the majestic style we have come to call Miltonic, though there may be more specifically rhetorical names for it, such as grandeur or magnitude, one of the seven Hermogenean ideas, whose positive force was meant for purposes of praise and whose praising effects were conveyed through such stylistic elements as structural antithesis, circumlocution, and impressive syntactic control.[14] Marked by paradox, the poem seems to shift from the style of speed — in this case, ironically plodding movement — to the style of grandeur, which absorbs the first style as part of its own antithetical structure. The "And" of line 13 seems additive, but just as we are anticipating the completion of a compound construction, the poet leads us into an amplified version of the "when . . . then" pattern. Sensing the poet's control over the syntax, we are led to a particular appreciation of his own individual contribution to the style of grandeur, the alexandrine of the final line.

One final association reverberates through the last line, the voice of the Old Testament preacher who was haunted by Time and who grieved for all men under the sun, for "time and chance happeneth to them all." Death is implicit in the first part of the poem. But the listing of "chance" is warranted by its commonplace association with Time in Ecclesiastes. That is, the association is commonplace for the audience, who most likely would not find the listing of "chance" either abrupt or justified merely by the poet's desire for prosodical ingenuity.

I mention this final matter to restore emphasis on the unique features of rhetorical reading. It may be that Milton patterned his work after Hermogenes or what he could see of him through Trapesuntius or Sturm or other commentators, or after Petrarch, or even after Minturno's description of Hermogenean grandeur as illustrated by Petrarch's "triumph of Eternity." But establishing influence is not the point; the point is to show evidence of Milton's influence in the poem, his control over the reader, and over what he could have

14. Patterson, p. 74.

assumed about his reader's expectations and potential interpretation of topics and manner. O. B. Hardison has examined the many
possible interpretations of the word "individual" in line 12 and ultimately associated it with some extremely complex scholastic controversies.[15] I have tried to examine stylistic controls over a host of possible associations in the poem, without, admittedly, going into any one
of them to Hardison's depth. Hardison suggests a critical rather than
a readerly response, though we may both be urging the same point,
that Milton must be read, insofar as possible, in his context, in his
setting, which for him included his contemporary events, the ancient
and ongoing tradition of humane letters, and the inescapable relevance of an everliving Bible.[16] This may be the oldest view of Milton,
one that has sorely tried his attractiveness for students in the modern
literary curriculum. But I have attempted to give this view a distinctly
rhetorical bearing in order to place our discussions of Milton's poetic
intentions on a firm basis and perhaps give us yet another means of
assessing his achievement, this time as a master of rhetoric.

Several years ago in an analysis of *Lycidas*, Northrop Frye attempted to show how context got into the text of that poem and
became its informing principle. Frye, of course, always has an eye on
literary archetypes, and the conclusion he reaches about *Lycidas* is a
general one: "It is literature as an order of words, therefore, which
forms the primary context of any given work of literary art."[17] But for
the rhetorical critic, I have tried to argue, context is a much broader
principle, just as language, style, and form are more strategic than in
Frye's philosophy. Because, rhetorically conceived, language reflects
the transactions between a speaker and an audience, context is provided not simply by literature but also by the range of associations
the poet might assume his text will provoke in a reader. But limita-
tion is oftentimes seen as an advantage of Frye's approach, for he
preserves the boundary between rhetoric and poetry, which he con-
ceives of as something distinctly nonrhetorical; and for many critics

15. O. B. Hardison, Jr., "Milton's 'On Time' and its Scholastic Background," *Texas
Studies in Literature and Language* 3 (1961), 107–22.

16. As Mary Ann Radzinowicz has suggested, even this short poem is "suffused
with images drawn from the Book of Psalms," *Toward Samson Agonistes: The Growth of
Milton's Mind* (Princeton, N.J., 1978), p. 196. But the source of artistic control over that
suffusion lies elsewhere, as I have attempted to show. Thus we make different uses of
what Radzinowicz calls the "contextualist approach."

17. Northrop Frye, "Literature as Context: Milton's *Lycidas*," *North Carolina Studies in Comparative Literature* 23 (1959), 53. The essay has been reprinted in Frye's *Fables
of Identity* (New York, 1963), pp. 119–29.

that boundary is worth preserving. On one side a poem is viewed as discrete, esthetic, iconographic. On the other, the rhetorical side, a poem is heard as discursive, suasory, existential.

One of the most illuminating readers of Milton in our day has boldly advanced on that boundary in the name of "affective stylistics." For Stanley Fish the poem is in the reader, and what is to be known of the poet's intention and meaning is to be found by examining a knowledgeable reader's process of interpretation.[18] In one of his recent articles, Fish makes plain, again, that the *bête noir* of his critical forays is the formalist, whose search for organic literary function is staunchly anti-audience and who insists that the poem's text alone — not the reader's experience — contains all we can know about the poem. Thus, the formalist's quest for objective meaning disallows the reader's experience. By contrast, Fish states, "it is the structure of the reader's experience rather than any structure available on the page that should be the object of description."[19] Which reader? Fish allows the possible identification of his theoretical reader as the poet's intended reader, "whose education, opinions, concerns, linguistic competences, etc. make him capable of having the experience the author wished to provide."[20] But Fish's primary concern, he insists, is with critical method, a consideration that somehow avoids the responsibility of specifying the readers whose experiences are the very subject of this method. Moreover, it would seem that the "opinions, concerns, and linguistic competences" Fish expects of the reader are actually those like his own, which have been carefully honed against an abrasive antagonism with formalist criticism. It is curious and unfortunate that the "education" Fish expects of the reader apparently does not include knowledge of rhetoric. Curious when one considers that Fish's method itself is similar to what I have called rhetorical reading, but actually not so curious when one considers Fish's dislike of formalism. Viewed in isolation, *elocutio* itself is ostensibly formalistic, as Fish early recognized. In his first book-length study, he disparages rhetoric as offering no more than antiquated names for the poet's textual tools.[21] This characterization, besides being incorrect, may have motivated his efforts in another direction to restore the

18. Fish's best statement of this idea is in his appendix to *Self-Consuming Artifacts* (Berkeley and Los Angeles, 1972), "Literature in the Reader: Affective Stylistics," pp. 383–428.

19. "Interpreting the Variorium," *Critical Inquiry* (Spring, 1976), p. 468.

20. Ibid., p. 475.

21. Stanley Eugene Fish, *John Skelton's Poetry* (New Haven, Conn., 1965). In an

audience to the interpretive process in disregard of deeper rhetorical doctrine. Thus, the approach encourages, as I noted earlier, a certain freewheeling invention; in this case, the reader's *inventio* is severed from the poet's *elocutio* as well as from rhetorical concepts of meaning and intention.

Fish's reading of Sonnet 18 is typical of his foreshortened view:

> Avenge O Lord thy slaughtered saints, whose bones
>   Lie scattered on the Alpine mountains cold,
>   Even them who kept thy truth so pure of old
>   When all our fathers worshipped stocks and stones,
> Forget not: in thy book record their groans
>   Who were thy sheep and in their ancient fold
>   Slain by the bloody Piemontese that rolled
>   Mother with infant down the rocks. Their moans
> The vales redoubled to the hills, and they
>   To heaven. Their martyred blood and ashes sow
>   O'er all the Italian fields where still doth sway
> The triple Tyrant: that from these may grow
>   A hundredfold, who having learnt thy way
>   Early may fly the Babylonian woe.[22]

The uniqueness of Fish's reading of this sonnet centers on his imagined reader's experience of the final 2 lines. This reader takes line 13 momentarily as a sense unit and imagines that it refers to God's seemingly callous abandonment of the Waldensians. That impression, however fleeting, undercuts the possibility of experiencing anything like moral affirmation by enforcing, perhaps even reenforcing a concomitant impression that the Waldensians themselves had already met the speaker's prayed-for condition, that they had in fact learned God's "way," Protestantism, only to suffer God's "way" in another, grimmer meaning, indiscriminate punishment. So interpreted, the line seems to continue the "note of outrage with which the poem began." And the reader will go on to imagine that the poet may be advising him actually to "fly" God's service. But the final three words of the poem provide the necessary correction, and then the

article that preceded the book, Fish warns of using rhetorical analysis on any "poem which in no way depends on rhetoric for its effects," *Studia Neophilologica* 34 (1962), 235.

22. The edition of the poem and Fish's interpretation appear in *Critical Inquiry* (Spring, 1976), pp. 469 – 70. There are no punctuational differences between this edition and the one in *Works* (New York, 1931), 1.66. The latter, however, besides using old spelling capitalizes "Saints," "Fathers," "Stocks," "Stones," "Sheep," "Fold," "Infant," "Rocks," "Vales," "Hills," "Heav'n," and italicizes *Piemontese, Italian,* and *Babylonian* — effects that may be preferable for they guide the reader's voice.

reader understands that he is meant to learn God's way at an early age in order to escape the divinely promised destruction of Babylon itself. Nonetheless, in spite of the ultimate correction, for Fish's reader there remain two "pulls" in the poem: trust in God on the one hand, and troubles with understanding God's justice on the other.

Because Fish insists that the poem *is* the reader's experience of it, his imagined reader must begin with a priori, absolutely nonformalist assumptions that what is to be known of the poet's intention will be found not so much in the text itself as in his, the reader's, experience of reading the text. But in a rhetorical reading, the reader's a priori assumption is that the poet through the text has certain designs on the reader's attention and emotions. In Fish's interpretation of Sonnet 18, the reader merely overhears the poet at prayer. In a rhetorical reading, this overhearing relationship is itself a strategy for involving the reader in a certain way. We do not merely catch the poet, in Sonnet 18, in a moment of intimate utterance in which he reflects the unresolved turmoils and doubts in his mind, as Fish's reader does. Rather, we experience the intimate discourse of a fictive speaker, invested though he may be with the poet's own character, uttering words in a certain strategic manner. It is interesting and probably significant that a rhetorical reading of this sonnet weights the interpretive process toward the meaning and intention that Fish notes are "generally agreed" upon, if somewhat unlike those he finds in his own reading. But perhaps it is even more significant, so far as heuristic value is concerned, that a rhetorical reading while remaining closer to the former ultimately diverges from both.

Generally, the poem is read as offering a series of attitudes, from outrage to acceptance, or from vehement cry to calm petition. If the poem begins in anger, it ends in submission to God's will. This reading is reasserted in the most intensive recent analysis of the poem, by Nicholas R. Jones.[23] In all fairness to Fish, it must be noted that Jones's analysis is more extensive than his, that it examines details far beyond the point Fish intends to examine them for the purposes of his own essay. Nonetheless, the chief distinction remains: Jones sees the poem, as Fish does not, as a rhetorical act. The poem "presents a nameless, fictitious character involved in the universal process of religious self-education," states Jones (p. 168). Bringing to bear on his reading what he can learn about the "rhetoric of prayer" from

23. Nicholas R. Jones, "The Education of the Faithful in Milton's Piedmontese Sonnet," *Milton Studies* 10, ed. James D. Simmonds (Pittsburgh, Penn., 1977), 167–76.

Milton's *Christian Doctrine*, Jones argues that through prayer the speaker in this poem searches for God's will in a way that skillfully, empathically carries the overhearing reader with him. "In the final sentence of the sonnet the speaking voice returns to a modified form of his initial demand. Now, however, instead of an uncompromising demand for vengeance, there are three gentle and ambiguous petitions" (pp. 174–75). The ambiguity, however, is not a tonal one. The ambiguity arises, again (as in "On Time"), through allusions that are ultimately carefully controlled; for example: "The final requests might still include the military vengeance which the sonnet's beginning implies (the possible allusion to the myth of Cadmus makes one think that 'Italian fields' could mean the battlefields of an English invasion of Savoy), but the two major, unmistakable allusions of this passage are more indicative of faith than of revenge. As many have pointed out, these primary references are to the parable of the sower (Matthew 13, 3–9) and to the apothegm of Tertullian, 'the blood of martyrs is the seed of the Church'" (p. 175).

Jones's reading, which is well set within an historical context, could be carried one step farther. Unlike Fish, Jones does not place the poem in the reader. He places it, rather, in a fictive surrogate for the poet—in the experience of a persona so constructed as to encourage the reader's empathic participation. However, the emphasis might also fall more in the area where Fish puts it, on the reader's experience, but this time as a more direct or conscious object of the speaker's strategy. Although this emphasis weakens the poet-speaker distinction crucial to Jones's reading, it serves the rhetorician's view of the poem as a nexus of speaker-text-reader transaction.

Moreover, interposing a persona—particularly an overtly masked speaker such as Jones finds in the poem—between poet and reader is not typical of Milton's mature rhetoric. Milton's characteristic voice in his later poems is vatic, and his mask, if any, is transparent; the persona is frequently a "prophet" speaking to caution, educate, or inspire his audience. To interpose another kind of persona in a dramatically devotional scene somewhere in the middle distance between poet and reader is to alter the lines of Milton's strategy from directness to indirectness — or as Raymond Waddington puts the distinction, to replace the "accommodative" rhetoric of prophecy with the "insinuative" rhetoric of meditation.[24] The meditative persona

24. Raymond B. Waddington, "Milton Among the Carolines," in *The Age of Milton*, eds. C. A. Patrides and R. B. Waddington (Manchester, 1980), p. 342.

seeks his own spiritual illumination and indirectly the self-illumination of his overhearing audience, whereas the prophetic persona brings his truth, again to quote Waddington, "down to the level at which it can be comprehended by his audience, or at least those members of his audience capable of responding."

The latter view when applied to this poem makes the speaker's use of prayer utterly strategic. The mode of address, the prayer, becomes the standard rhetorical apostrophe, the strategy being to place the reader in an ostensibly overhearing relationship. As in the rhetoric of meditation, the strategy allows the speaker to use the conventions of prayer to reach his actual audience. But first let us consider these conventions of prayer as a transparent, more direct rhetorical construction; later we shall note their possible dramatic significance in designating the speaker's preferred battleground in the war for men's minds. The speaker himself may, of course, be an audience of sorts, but he can hardly be the most compelling object of the strategy. Surely, it is Milton's contemporary English readers who are, potentially at least, the primary and most immediate audience. True, the actual audience may be larger and beyond the immediate; it may include succeeding generations and other men throughout Europe, an effect that in this case the apostrophic stance may underscore. What is important to recognize, however, is that it is on the minds of this actual audience — whether immediate or eventual — that the speaker imprints bloody events while ostensibly beseeching God. In so doing, he achieves an intention beyond prayer, meditation, or self-education. He brings the truth he has found in these events down to the level at which it can be comprehended by his audience and on which he may exhort them to action — but action of a certain sort, for the range of meaning is controlled in part by the address to God, who has prior claim on all vengeance.

The speaker is emphatic in calling the occasion of his utterance a "slaughter" and the massacre a martyrdom of "saints." The two concepts control the layered meanings of the various allusions. The fear instilled by the speaker's vehemence is directed ultimately toward any possibility of misperceiving Rome's woeful confusion of military might with moral suasion — in particular, moral suasion of the sort the poem itself represents and enacts. Rome's overwhelming use of military might, against a populace here depicted as meek and passive, argues the failure of its own moral suasion. That is, if there is bravery in courage born of fear — in this case, fleeing the destruction

God will surely visit upon Babylon — there is also bravery in shunning another kind of Babylonian woe, resorting to material advantage. The doomed "triple Tyrant" is attached to imperialistic Rome, Babylon in the Augustinian sense, the earthly city.[25]

These careful distinctions, contrasts, and compounds have their counterpart in (and are made even sharper by) a certain structural move: it is significant that the speaker makes the horror of the slaughter most vivid after the contrast between the early righteousness of the Waldensians and the religious belatedness of the English, in line 4. In the final line, if the word "Early" echoes this contrast, its irony only underscores the urgency in the speaker's voice. For the Waldensians have shown us in stark clarity the precise terms in which the warfare for men's souls will be waged. The speaker's voice — and I hear neither gentleness nor calmness at the conclusion — continually cries for vengeance, never more so and never less so than when he calls for the abandonment of Babylon, which these events reveal in its pristine error and bestiality. But the speaker chooses the battleground of conscience, in contrast to the battleground chosen by the "bloody Piedmontese," and it is there that whatever reproof is applied to Rome becomes ultimately a challenge to wavering hearts in his audience. Thus, the apostrophe, the apparent petition to God for vengeance and memory, is strategic in clarifying the speaker's own choice of action and the poem as, itself, a rhetorical act. Further, the punctuation alone, whether the poem is read silently or aloud, makes "Avenge" and "Forget not" equivalents. But when the poem is read aloud, the intention I have described may be made audible, for then the syntax — perhaps as a result of that impressive control which is the stylistic sign of grandeur, here used not for praise but for reproof — may seem to resolve itself into a single sentence: "Avenge . . . Forget not . . . that from these may grow. . . ." In either event, it is the actual not the putative audience that may accomplish vengeance by never forgetting.

My interpretation only extends Jones's contextual and allusive approach. The issue I would raise concerns not Jones's approach but Fish's. To contrast Jones's reading with Fish's, one need only note that the latter ignores the doctrine that elements of style even when mirroring a speaker's emotion are at once strategies in the poet's contest for the reader's emotions. To sharpen the contrast between my ap-

25. For the implied contrast between Augustine's two cities, see A. J. Weitzman, *Milton Newsletter* 3, 1969, 55 – 57.

proach and Fish's, I would note primarily that the reader Fish posits as the poet's intended reader is cut off from the rich rhetorical and cultural legacy as well as the interpretive habits of the reader Milton himself might have imagined.

Forty years ago Tillyard virtually anticipated the rebuttal of my critique of Fish. He showed that it is possible to carry too far the view I propose. Tillyard's skillful reading of *L'Allegro* imagines an audience of Cambridge undergraduates in the 1620s. Thereby he illuminates certain important structural features of the poem, structural in the sense in which I and, I think, Fish use the term, though with sharp differences in application: formal features that place controls on the reader's response.[26] But Tillyard's ultimate interest is not Milton's poetic skill or artistry but his biography. The poems are mainly historical artifacts. Quite the opposite of Fish, who tries to place Milton's poems in the modern reader's consciousness, Tillyard never lets us forget that these poems are hoary with age and remoteness, and thereby he takes an incipiently rhetorical view to a clearly nonrhetorical end. His final judgment is that "in the last resort Milton's importance is simply that of his own personality."[27]

But surely a modern rhetorician would ask, Which personality? The historical Milton? Or the personality Milton fashioned for the sake of communicating his poems? These are, of course, questions central to that feature in rhetorical criticism known as *ethos,* the character of a speaker, whether poet or persona, which is always implied in style; the *ethos* of the poet in particular is implied in the stylistic controls he places on his implied reader's response. Reading of the sort I have suggested in these remarks, which preserves the primacy of rhetorical *inventio* in the reader's craft as well as in the poet's, shows us that the poem is neither in the implied reader, nor in the implied poet (or his surrogate persona), nor (as Fish makes his enemy the formalist insist) in the text, but in a certain relationship between the three. Fully used, rhetorical reading may show us some of the conscious craft whereby the historical poet turned that relationship into an art.

26. E. M. W. Tillyard, *The Miltonic Setting* (London, 1938), chap. 1.
27. E. M. W. Tillyard, *Milton* (London, 1930, rpt. New York, 1967), p. 312.

"The Power of Persuasion":
Images of the Orator,
Elyot to Shakespeare

BRIAN VICKERS

The handbooks to rhetoric in the English sixteenth century are not, perhaps, among the most impressive literary productions of that period. Even their students and exponents occasionally adopt a defensive or apologetic tone. E. E. Hale, surveying ideas on rhetoric in the Tudor period, concluded that "The greater number of the rhetorics of the sixteenth century are without any ideas at all, certainly upon the present subject."[1] Warren Taylor, in his pioneer attempt to classify and systematize Tudor rhetoric, produced the classic sentence, "Renaissance rhetoric is, at best, mixed"[2] — by which he presumably meant eclectic, although the other sense would also apply. Certainly, there is very little that is original in English, or indeed any other vernacular rhetoric of this period, and the sources are familiar to all: Aristotle, Cicero, Quintilian, Erasmus, Susenbrotus, Aphthonius, Despauterius, and more, the later authorities themselves being compilations from earlier ones. But of course originality is not what one looks for in the maker of a rhetoric book, who ought rather to offer clarity, thoroughness, the sensible illustration of the figures, and a sense of the importance of rhetoric in relation to literature and the other arts. On this count Wilson, Peacham, Hoskins, Puttenham, and Sidney rank with the best vernacular rhetorics of the Renais-

This essay is dedicated to Madeleine Doran.

---

1. E. E. Hale, "Ideas on Rhetoric in the Sixteenth Century," *PMLA* 18 (1903), 439.
2. Warren Taylor, *Tudor Figures of Rhetoric* (1937; Whitewater, Wis., 1972), p. 14.

sance and have a keener awareness of the relevance of their teaching to literary language than do a number of their continental rivals.

The English rhetorics belong firmly to the classical and continental traditions, not least in their fusion of rhetoric and poetics,[3] granting the poet and the orator equal status, similar methods, identical goals—to move, to teach, to please—and distinguishing between them sometimes through the traditional dichotomy of media, prose against verse, sometimes through the presence or absence of fiction. Both the orator and the poet had been attacked by Plato, but from that common inheritance the poet in the Renaissance had received much more criticism for his link with feigning, during that fruitless confusion between fiction and lies, and for his connection with the theatre. Poets and poetry were under attack, and much Renaissance literary criticism, we have known since the pioneer work of Joel Spingarn, takes the form of an apology for poetry.[4] The orator, by contrast, got off lightly, and attacks on rhetoric in English during this period were few, and often mere paradoxes or *jeux d'esprit*, such as that by H. C. Agrippa or John Jewel's *Oratio contra rhetoricam*.[5] Indeed, my feeling is that in England, as in Italy, during the Renaissance, rhetoric had a surprisingly good press, perhaps an unhealthily favorable one. The programmatic statements by the English humanists and rhetoricians give speech and its arts an altogether too benevolent, one-sided presentation. Language is good, therefore its study is good. There is a striking inability, or unwillingness, to conceive that language could be applied to evil ends, or used to deceive or corrupt.

A brief survey of the main texts on rhetoric and eloquence shows the widespread acceptance of the idea—whose classical origins are sufficiently obvious for me not to need to document them—that lan-

3. On the equation of rhetoric and poetry see, e.g., Cicero, *De oratore* I.70; John Rainolde, *Oratio in Laudem Artis Poeticae* (ca. 1572), eds. W. Ringler and W. Allen (Princeton, N.J., 1940), pp. 19–20, 66; I. Sowton, "Hidden Persuaders as a Means of Literary Grace: Sixteenth Century Poetics and Rhetoric in England," *University of Toronto Quarterly* 32 (1962), 55–69; George Puttenham, *The Arte of English Poesie* (1589), ed. A. Walker and G. Willcock (Cambridge, 1936, rpt. 1970), passim.

4. J. E. Spingarn, *A History of Literary Criticism in the Renaissance* (New York, 1899, rpt. 1930).

5. Henry Cornelius Agrippa, *Of the Vanitie and Uncertaintie of Artes and Sciences* (1530), Sandford translation (1569), ed. C. M. Dunn (Northridge, Calif., 1974): see chap. 6, "Of Rhetorike," pp. 42–47; and E. Korkowski, "Agrippa as Ironist," *Neophilologus* 60 (1976), 594–607, who is unaware that he has been partially anticipated by Barbara C. Bowen, "Cornelius Agrippa's *De Vanitate:* Polemic or Paradox?" *Bibliothèque d'Humanisme et Renaissance* 34 (1972), 249–56; and H. H. Hudson, "Jewel's Oration against Rhetoric: a Translation," *Quarterly Journal of Speech* 14 (1928), 374–92.

guage is the gift of God to man. The first comprehensive and coherent rhetoric in English, *The Arte of Rhetorique* by Thomas Wilson, *for the use of all such as are studious of Eloquence* (1553), has a preface with the title "Eloquence first given by God, and after lost by man, and last repayred by God againe."[6] At "the first being," Wilson writes, man was made "an everliving creature, unto the likenesse of God, endued with reason, and appointed Lorde over all other thinges living." But as a result of the fall, sin and corruption overwhelmed "mans reason and entendement," and without God's grace "all thinges waxed savage, the earth untilled, societie neglected," human beings living "like brute beastes." After a while — Wilson is notably vague about the time-scale involved — God,

> still tendering his owne workmanshippe, stirring up his faithfull and elect to perswade with reason all men to societie. And gave his appointed Ministers knowledge both to see the natures of men, and also graunted them the gift of utteraunce, that they might with ease win folke at their will, and frame them by reason to all good order. And therefore, whereas men lived brutishly in open feeldes, having neither house to shroude them in, nor attire to clothe their backes, not yet any regard to seeke their best availe: these appointed of GOD called them together by utteraunce of speech, and perswaded with them what was good, what was bad, & what was gainful for mankind.

The ministers of God found the "rude" people scarcely able to learn, yet they persevered, and effected their reeducation or reclamation:

> after a certaine space they became through Nurture and good advisement, of wilde, sober: of cruell, gentle: of fooles, wise: and of beastes, men: such force hath the tongue, and such is the power of Eloquence and reason, that most men are forced, even to yeeld in that which most standeth against their will.

Indeed, for Wilson rhetoric and persuasion are the *sine qua non* of an ordered society:

> Neither can I see that men could have been brought by any other meanes, to live together in fellowship of life, to maintaine Cities, to deale truely, and willingly obeye one an other, if men at the first had not by art and eloquence, perswaded that which they full oft found out by reason.

6. Quotations from the edition by G. H. Mair (Oxford, 1909), Preface, sig. A6^v – A7^v.

Wilson's account of the civilizing force of rhetoric is imaginative, not historical, is more in the nature of a myth. It has obvious parallels in the claims that poetry brought men from savagery to civilization: such as Thomas Lodge's pronouncement that "Poetes were the first raysors of cities, prescribers of good lawes, mayntayners of religion, disturbors of the wicked, advancers of the wel disposed, inventors of laws, and lastly the very fot-paths to knowledge and understanding."[7] Many of these mythical histories derive ultimately from Plato's *Protagoras* (321d – 322c), Cicero's *De oratore,* and Horace's *Ars Poetica* (verses 39 ff.), often through intermediaries, such as Scaliger.[8] They belong to a wider view of the history of mankind as a movement from chaos to order, that version of primitivism Boas and Lovejoy have labeled "hard," where life is seen not as constantly declining from an initial Golden Age, but as progressing towards greater civilization.[9] Learning from the past is man's unique function, according to Sir Thomas Elyot in *The Governor* (1531):

> And therefore who advisedly beholdeth the astate of mannes life, shall well perceive that all that ever was spoken or written, was to be by experience executed: and to that intent was speche specially gyven to man, wherein he is moste discrepant from brute beastis, in declaring what is good, what viciouse, what is profitable, what improfitable, by them whiche by clerenesse of witte do excelle in knowlege, to these that be of a more inferior capacitie.[10]

In Caxton's *Mirrour of the World* (1480), a translation from the French, the transmission of language and knowledge is credited to the seven liberal arts and to the "clergye," without whom

7. Lodge, *Defence of Poetry, Music, and Stage Plays* (1579), in *Elizabethan Critical Essays,* ed. G. G. Smith, 2 vols. (Oxford, 1904), 1.75.

8. See Sidney, *An Apology for Poetry,* ed. Geoffrey Shepherd (London, 1965, rpt. Manchester and New York, 1973), pp. 147 – 48; William Webbe, *A Discourse of English Poetrie* (1586), in G. G. Smith, 1.231, 234.

9. A. O. Lovejoy and G. Boas, *Primitivism and Related Ideas in Antiquity* (Baltimore, Md., 1935), p. 10; see also A. B. Ferguson, "'By little and little': The early Tudor humanists on the development of man," in *Florilegium Historiale. Essays presented to Wallace K. Ferguson,* eds. J. G. Rowe and W. H. Stockdale (Toronto, 1971), pp. 126 – 50.

10. Elyot, *The Governor,* ed. H. H. S. Croft, 2 vols. (London, 1880), 1.264. See also Wilson's *Arte,* preface, *ad.fin.* ("whereas men are in many thinges weake by Nature, and subject to much infirmitie: I thinke in this one point they passe all other creatures living, that have the gift of speech and reason"); also Puttenham, book 2, chap. 5 and book 3, chap. 4; Sidney, *Apology,* p. 121: "for if *oratio,* speech next to reason, be the greatest gift bestowed upon mortality . . . ," and Geoffrey Shepherd's note on the passage (pp. 195 f.).

we had knowen nothing ne who had be God, ne men shold never have knowen what thing had ben best to doo: and so shold alle the world have ben dampned. Thenne had we ben born in an evyll houre, ffor the men had knowen nomore than do dombe beestis.[11]

This image of rhetoric as the instrument of civilization is adopted by all the English apologists for rhetoric, with the additional claim that it (like poetry) was the origin of human learning.[12] Since rhetoric became linked to society by this quasi-historical account of its origins, the practice of rhetoric was thought to be conducive to the maintenance of order and degree. In Stephen Hawes's didactic poem with the optimistic title *The Pastime of Pleasure* (1517), rhetorical order, or *dispositio,* is seen as not only symbolic of social order but as in some manner creating it:

> Without dysposycyon/none ordre gan be
> For the dysposycyon/ordreth every matter
> And gyveth the place/after the degre[.]
> Without ordre/without reason we clatter
> Where is no reason/it vayleth not to chatter. . . .
> (862 ff.)

The "fatall problems/of olde antyquyte," according to Hawes, were "Ordered with reason" by learned men, and thus were laws created:

> Before the lawe/in a tumblyng barge
> The people sayled/without parfytenes
> Throughe the worlde/all about at large
> They hadde none ordre/nor no stedfastnes
> Tyll rethorycyans/founde Iustyce doubtles
> Ordenynge kynges/of ryghte hye dygnyte
> Of all comyns/to have the soverainte
>
> The barge to stere/with lawe and Iustyce
> Over the wawes of this lyfe transytorye. . . .
> (876 ff.)

11. *Caxton's Mirrour of the World,* ed. O. L. Prior, EETS e.s., 90 (London, 1913), p. 28; cf. also Henry Peacham, *The Garden of Eloquence* (1593), facsimile ed. W. G. Crane (Gainesville, Fla., 1954), on wisdom and eloquence as gifts of God (sig. ABii[v], ABiii[r]); and R. Rainolde, *The Foundacion of Rhetorike* (1563), ed. F. R. Johnson (New York, 1945), fol. i, where rhetoric and logic are said to be "giftes of nature."

12. Cf. Elyot, *Governor,* 1.117, 121; Peacham, *Garden,* sig. ABiii[v]; Sidney, *Apology,* pp. 96, 145 f.; Puttenham, *Poesie,* book 1, chap. 3; book 3, chap. 19; Stephen Hawes, *The Pastime of Pleasure* (1517), ed. W. E. Mead (London, 1928), p. 36, lines 785–91; Caxton, *Mirrour,* p. 36, where rhetoric is seen as inventing and upholding "the droytes and

The connection between speech, reason, and order, which we have already seen in Thomas Wilson's pioneer work, is basic to English sixteenth-century thinking about language and obviously expresses the Renaissance's setting of order against chaos, harmony against discord. Henry Peacham writes that through the working of "apt speech given by nature, and guided by Art wisedome appeareth in her beautie, sheweth her maiestie, and exerciseth her power, working in the minde of the hearer, partly by a pleasant proportion, & as it were by a sweet & musicall harmonie, and partly by the secret and mightie power of perswasion . . ." (sig. ABiii^r). The man "well furnished" with knowledge and speech "hath bene judged able, and esteemed fit to rule the world with counsell, provinces with lawes, cities with pollicy, & multitudes with persuasion" (sig. ABiii^v). That rhetoric is essential to the government of society is a point on which all these sixteenth-century writers would agree;[13] indeed, their own treatises are mostly dedicated to leading public figures,[14] often with a preface including an anecdote from some classical source on the feat of some orator in winning over a city by words alone. That first sketch for a University of London, *Queene Elizabethes Achademy*, by Sir Humphrey Gilbert, includes provision for a teacher of logic and rhetoric who will exercise his scholars by "Orations made in English, both politique and militare, taking occasions owt of Discowrses of histories," the vernacular being especially useful "in preaching, in parliament, in Cownsell, in Commyssion, and other offices of Common Weale." "This kind of educacion is fittest for" the young men attending court, Gilbert writes, "becawse they are wardes to the prince, by reason of knights service."[15] We hear in his simple and utilitarian English that union of rhetoric with the *vita activa* that permeated the whole European Renaissance. Richard Mulcaster, Spencer's teacher, proclaimed that "The qualitie of our *monarchie* wil admit trew speaking, wil allow trew

lawes by whiche the jugements be made, and that by rayson and after right ben kept and mayntened in the court of kynges, of princes and of barons. . . ."

13. Cf. Elyot, 1.73, 76, 117; Rainolde, *Epistle* and fol.i^r – fol.ii^r; A. Munday (or L. Pyott), preface to *The Orator* by Alexander van den Busche (1596), sig. Aiv^r.

14. Elyot's *The Governor* is dedicated to King Henry VIII; Rainolde's treatise is dedicated to Lord Robert Dudley, Master of the House of Privy Councillor; Wilson's to Lord Dudley, "Lord Lisle, Earle of Warwicke, and Master of the Horse"; Peacham's to Sir John Puckering, Lordkeeper of the great seal of England; Puttenham's (by intention) to Queen Elizabeth.

15. *Queen Elizabethes Achademy*, with *A Booke of Precedence* and other courtesy books, ed. F. J. Furnivall, EETS (London, 1869), pp. 2 f.

writing, in both with the bravest, so that it do please, and be worthie praise, so that it preach peace, and preserve the state."[16]

From the civic function of rhetoric we turn to its psychological function. On what we might term the productive or creative side of communication, the generation of language, Renaissance theorists held that rhetoric's primary purpose was to express thought or reveal the mind. The title page of Peacham's work describes itself as *The Garden of Eloquence, conteining the most excellent Ornaments, Exornations, Lightes, flowers, and formes of speech, commonly called the Figures of Rhetorike. By which the singular partes of mans mind are most aptly expressed, and the sundrie affections of his hearte most effectuallie uttered.* In his *Epistle Dedicatorie* Peacham describes how "almightie God ... hath opened the mouth of man, as the mouth of a plentifull fountaine, both to powre forth the inward passions of his heart, and also as a heavenly planet to shew foorth, (by the shining beames of speech) the privie thoughts and secret conceites of his mind" (sig. ABiii[r]). The conception of rhetoric as a means to body forth thought is again virtually unanimous in the sixteenth century, often as a simple dichotomy between the inward and the outward man.[17] John Hoskins, probably echoing Pierre de la Primaudaye, works on just such an inner/outer model:

> The conceits of the mind are pictures of things and the tongue is interpreter of those pictures. The order of God's creatures in themselves is not only admirable and glorious, but eloquent; then he that could apprehend the consequences of things, in their truth, and utter his apprehensions as truly were a right orator.[18]

Rhetoric not only produces or organizes speech as expression, but above all things it controls speech for persuasion. In his translation of the French encyclopedia *Miroir du Monde* of 1480, Caxton defined rhetoric as the art "whyche conteyneth in substance rightwisnes, Rayson and ordynaunce of wordes." When the work was reissued in 1527, in an expanded version made by Lawrence Andrewe, rhetoric was defined as

16. Mulcaster, *Elementarie* (1582), ed. E. T. Campagnac (Oxford, 1925), p. 273.

17. Hawes, *Pastime*, lines 691–93; 753–56; Richard Sherry, *A Treatise of Schemes and Tropes* (1550), facsimile ed. H. W. Hildebrandt (Gainesville, Fla., 1961), pp. 7, 13, 19; Sidney, *Apology*, p. 140 ("the uttering sweetly and properly the conceits of the mind, which is the end of speech"); Wilson, *Arte*, p. 2; Puttenham, *Poesie*, book 3, chaps. 5, 19.

18. Hoskins, *Directions for Speech and Style* (ca. 1599), ed. H. Hudson (Princeton, N.J., 1935), pp. 2, 54–56.

a scyence to cause another man by speche or wrytyng to beleve or to do that thynge whyche thou woldest have hym for to do.[19]

Would that it were true, the professor of rhetoric might say—but there in all its nakedness we encounter the idea almost universal throughout the Renaissance, that rhetoric cannot be resisted. We recall the description of Athens in *Paradise Regained:*

> Thence to the famous orators repair,
> Those ancient, whose resistless eloquence
> Wielded at will that fierce democracy . . .[20]

Milton's reference to Demosthenes and Pericles could be duplicated many times over. Elyot defines eloquence as the expression in words and sententiae of matters so forceful "that they by a vertue inexplicable do drawe unto them the mindes and consent of the herers."[21] Thomas Wilson refers to the myth of Hercules linking all men "together by the eares in a chaine, to drawe them and leade them even as he lusted. For his witte was so great, his tongue so eloquent, and his experience such, that no man was able to withstande his reason, but every one was rather driven to do that which he would, and to will that which he did."[22] Puttenham also uses this image and describes poetry as a form of super-rhetoric, able to carry man's opinion "this way and that, whither soever the heart by impression of the eare shalbe most affectionatly bent and directed."[23] Eloquence "is of great force," Puttenham says, and addresses itself to man's mind,

> For to say truely, what els is man but his minde? which, whosoever have skil to compasse, and make yeelding and flexible, what may not he commaund the body to perfourme? He therefore that hath vanquished the minde of man, hath made the greatest and most glorious conquest.　　　　　　　　　　　　　　　　(p. 197)

That elevation of the act of persuasion to the highest point of human power is astonishing to a modern reader, perhaps, but it is one that the Renaissance rhetorician meant seriously. Henry Peacham even gives practitioners of his craft divine status:

19. Caxton, *Mirrour,* p. 35; Andrewe, as cited by L. Cox, *The Arte or Crafte of Rethoryke* (1524), ed. F. I. Carpenter (Chicago, 1899), p. 26.

20. *Paradise Regained,* book 4, lines 267 ff.

21. Elyot, *Governor,* I. 116 f., 119; also Sidney, passim.

22. Wilson, *Arte,* preface.

23. Puttenham, *Poesie,* book 1, chaps. 3, 4; book 3, chaps. 2, 7, 10, 19.

so mighty is the power of this happie union, (I meane of wisdom & eloquence) that by the one the Orator forceth, and by the other he allureth, and by both so worketh, that what he commendeth is beloved, what he dispraiseth is abhorred, what he perswadeth is obeied, & what he disswadeth is avoided: so that he is in a maner the emperour of mens minds & affections, and next to the omnipotent God in the power of perswasion, by grace, & divine assistance.[24]

Peacham's closing qualification, that man's power in speech is owing to God, brings us to the final stage in the Tudor and Elizabethan humanists' conception of rhetoric, its relation to religion and ethics. Thomas Becon urged that the liberal arts should be applied to "advance the true religion of God. For eloquence without godliness is as a ring in a swine's snout."[25] That forcible expression would find many echoes in English and continental rhetoric books, and we have only to think of the vast traditions of Christian rhetoric from Saint Augustine's *De Doctrina Christiana* to Erasmus's *Ecclesiastae sive de ratione concionandi libri quatuor* (an important and understudied text) and beyond, or to recall the familiar arguments that the Bible cannot be understood without a knowledge of rhetoric, or that the souls of the congregation cannot be thoroughly moved without the use of rhetoric, to see that the concept of Christian eloquence was firmly rooted throughout Renaissance Europe. Richard Sherry ends the epistle to his little *Treatise of Schemes and Tropes* with a prayer:

The lyvynge God from whome all good giftes do procede, gyve us grace so to ordre all our words and speache, that it may be to his honour and glory for ever and ever. Amen.[26]

The same linking of rhetoric with all good things is found on the secular side, where eloquence and ethics are held to be indissoluble. Vives tells his readers that your tongue is "the one instrument Nature gave to you for doing good. . . . Our speech is at the service of reason"; and Puttenham tells his that speech and language are "given by nature to man for perswasion of others, and aide of themselves. . . ."[27] The first stage of rhetoric's application to ethics is the discrimination of good and evil. As Caxton's English has it,

24. Peacham, *Garden*, sig. ABiii[v].
25. *The Catechism of Thomas Becon*, ed. J. Ayre (Cambridge, 1844), pp. 382 f., 386; as cited by Joan Simon, *Education and Society in Tudor England* (Cambridge, 1966), p. 188.
26. Sherry, *Treatise*, p. 16.
27. Vives, *De ratione dicendi*, tr. J. F. Cooney (Ph.D. diss., Ohio State University, 1966), p. 271; Puttenham, *Poesie*, p. 8.

> Who wel knewe the scyence of Rethoryque, he shold know the right
> and the wronge; ffor to doo wronge to another, who so doth it is
> loste and dampned, and for to doo right and reson to every man, he
> is saved and geteth the love of God his creatour.[28]

The poets, Puttenham writes, were "from the beginning the best
perswaders and their eloquence the first Rethoricke of the world," and
because they endeavoured to "reduce the life of man to a certaine
method of good maners, and made the first differences betweene vertue and vice," they were also "the first Philosophers Ethick."[29] The orator, like the poet, is seen as a teacher who praises virtue and attacks
vice: the vigour and prestige of epideictic rhetoric in the Renaissance
derived from its identification with ethics.[30] Stephen Hawes, writing in
1517, looks back to Petrarch and forward to Matthew Arnold in his
linking of poetry with the question of how to live:

> Thus the poetes / conclude full closely
> Theyr fruytfull problems / for reformacyon
> To make us lerne / to lyve dyrectly
> Theyr good entent / and trewe construccyon
> Shewyng to us / the hole affeccyon
> Of the waye of vertue / welthe and stablenes
> And to shyt the gate of myschevous entres.
>
> (1114 ff.)

Rhetoric, like poetry, has a reformative or reclamatory function: for
Hawes it is addressed to

> The erryng people / that are retractyf
> As to the ryght waye / to brynge them againe.
>
> (1123 f.)

The assumption is that men will fall into vice without the good
offices of the orator or poet: to Sidney the poet "doth intend the
winning of the mind from wickedness to virtue."[31] Since, as Richard

28. Caxton, *Mirrour*, p. 36.

29. Puttenham, *Poesie*, book 1, chap. 4, pp. 8–9.

30. Cf. Puttenham, *Poesie*, book 1, chaps. 10, 12–16, pp. 24, 27–36; and Brian
Vickers, "Epideictic and Epic in the Renaissance," forthcoming in *New Literary History*.

31. Sidney, *Apology*, p. 113. Compare his later remarks on the function of comedy:
"Now, as in geometry the oblique must be known as well as the right, and in arithmetic
the odd as well as the even, so in the actions of our life who seeth not the filthiness of
evil wanteth a great foil to perceive the beauty of virtue. This doth the Comedy handle
..." (p. 117).

Rainolde declares, "the ende of all artes and sciences, and of all noble actes and enterprises is vertue," then "the vertue of eloquence" is to persuade "Princes and rulers . . . in good causes and enterprises, to animate and incense them to godlie affaires and business."[32] The Ciceronian union of wisdom and eloquence is celebrated also by Sir Thomas Elyot and Henry Peacham, the latter defining wisdom as "the knowledge of human and divine thinges," and virtue as "the loving & provident mother of mankind," which is shown in its true "beautie" and "majestie" by the power of eloquence. With the use of the figures of rhetoric, those "martiall instruments both of defence & invasion," Peacham claims, we may "defend ourselves, invade our enemies, revenge our wrongs, ayd the weake, deliver the simple from dangers, conserve true religion, & confute idolatry."[33]

Even in this highly compressed and selective survey of sixteenth-century English praises of rhetoric, the reader may already be tired of the universal power and goodness ascribed to it. If we now ask what was their conception of its relation to, or propensity to be used by, evil, we find a virtual blank. Sidney once refers to Xenophon's description of Cyrus's use of stratagems — a passage Machiavelli had singled out in the *Discorsi* for approving comment in his account of fraud — and justifies it as a mode of serving your prince by "such an honest dissimulation"; in another place he concedes that if poetry is abused, "by the reason of his sweet charming force, it can do more hurt than any other army of words," yet he denied that "the abuse should give reproach to the abused."[34] Otherwise he skirts the problem of evil, not willing, as a defender of poetry, to concede too much to its opponents. Anthony Munday, introducing his translation of *The Orator* by Alexander van den Busche, says that from these declamations "thou maiest learne Rhethoricke to inforce a good cause, and art to impugne an ill": it never seems to occur to him or to anyone else that the terms could be reversed and that rhetoric could enforce an evil cause, and impugne a good one.[35] The case of Thomas Wilson is instructive. Drawing on *Ad Herennium* he defines four sorts of oratorical matter, "honest, filthie, doubtful and trifling": as Ian Sowton has noted, "there is no discussion whatever of filthy topics or

32. Rainolde, *Oratio,* preface and sig. Ai[v].
33. Elyot, *Governor,* 1. 75 f., 264; Peacham, *Garden,* sig. ABii[v] – iv[r].
34. Sidney, *Apology,* p. 111 (cf. Machiavelli, *Discorsi,* 2.13), p. 125.
35. Sig. Aiv[r].

tactics."[36] Russell Wagner, in a posthumously published study of the *Arte of Rhetorique,* noted that in it *ethos* is not mentioned: "the concept of ethical proof as proof from the character of the speaker is wholly lacking, and the idea that unlearned or evil men cannot hope to be persuasive, is almost never expressed." Indeed, "the next to last sentence of the *Arte of Rhetorique* . . . seems to be Wilson's only comment on the speaking of wicked men."[37] Here Wilson simply ends by wishing that his work will be successful, but adds: "And yet what needes wishing, seeing the good will not speake evill: and the wicked can not speake wel" (p. 222).

"The wicked can not speake wel": that amazing optimism about the innate goodness of speech and rhetoric is typical of much European Renaissance theorizing, too. Only such an exceptional figure as Coluccio Salutati could publicly concede that language could be abused.[38] But anyone who approaches the panegyrics to rhetoric with an open mind about its ultimate function might conclude that if it has such power over man then it could be a very dangerous art indeed! Imagine an Iago, say, sitting down to read Peacham's *The Garden of Eloquence,* with its promise that by a knowledge of it he would become "the emperour of mens minds and affections," that through it "what he perswadeth is obeied, and what he disswadeth is avoided." He would have read on with great interest. Or imagine his reactions when reading those naive passages which claim that speech automatically shews forth "the privie thoughts and secret conceites" of a man's mind: he would have laughed with contempt, but also with pleasure, since he would realize that by controlling his speech he would be able to suggest "privie thoughtes and secret conceites," while reserving his real feelings to some deeper level of language and dissimulation.

In referring to Iago, I wish to set Shakespeare over against the Tudor theorists, partly to show the limits of their theorizing—no

36. Wilson, *Arte,* pp. 7 f.; Sowton, p. 58.

37. "Thomas Wilson's *Arte of Rhetorique,*" *Speech Monographs* 27 (1969), 19 and note.

38. On continental rhetoric and its glorification of the orator, see E. Garin, *Italian Humanism. Philosophy and Civic Life in the Renaissance,* tr. P. Munz (Oxford, 1965); Hannah H. Gray, "Renaissance Humanism: The Pursuit of Eloquence," *Journal of the History of Ideas* 24 (1963), rpt. in *Renaissance Essays,* eds. Paul Oskar Kristeller and P. P. Wiener (New York, 1968), pp. 199–216. On Salutati's criticism of the misuse of speech, see Nancy S. Struever, *The Language of History in the Renaissance. Rhetoric and Historical Consciousness in Florentine Humanism* (Princeton, N.J., 1970), pp. 55 ff.; and on Poggio Bracciolini's, *ibid.,* pp. 166 ff.

very difficult task, perhaps — and also to provoke thought about the nature of persuasion in Shakespeare. There have been several studies of Shakespeare's knowledge of rhetoric and classical oratory, and demonstrations of the presence of specific rhetorical devices in his poetry and prose.[39] But I do not recall many studies of the nature of persuasion in his plays, that is, the attempt of one person to change the way another person thinks or acts. Certainly, Shakespeare agrees that speech is powerful and that persuasion succeeds. But it is striking that the process is often ambivalent or downright evil. Where the theorists stress the power of rhetoric to reclaim men from evil to good, I can think of only one substantial scene in Shakespeare where a conversion or reclamation takes place, and that is Hamlet's attempt to make Gertrude realize the disgusting nature of her marriage with Claudius[40] — and even that scene is notably difficult to interpret, Hamlet's nausea with their sexuality having been seen by many critics as being "in excess of the facts." One character who refuses to be seduced by evil persuasion is Hal in resisting Falstaff; when he becomes King Henry V he is almost the only full-scale admirable persuader in Shakespeare, incarnating the dual ideal (however improbable the combination) of Christian prince and successful wooer. Otherwise the good people in Shakespeare do not need to be persuaded: they are good already. Cordelia and Imogen do not need to be told or urged to behave rightly; it is in their natures and shows itself in their action. Conversely, the evil people do not need to be persuaded to evil; nor can they be reclaimed from it. Despite all the theorists' blankness on this topic, persuasion in Shakespeare is more often used by the evil people, to corrupt and destroy the good, than by the good to reclaim the evil. Persuasion in his plays is either evil, or has unexpectedly bad results, or is futile. It is seldom glorious, or admirable, or Christian.

To start with an instance of futility: *Troilus and Cressida* is among the most language-conscious of Shakespeare's plays, densely rhetorical, stuffed with strange words — many of them nonce creations, invented for this one use only — and revealing an attempt to imitate what he thought to be Homeric style, having only Chapman's transla-

---

39. See Milton B. Kennedy, *The Classical Oration in Shakespeare* (Chapel Hill, N.C., 1942); Sister Miriam Joseph, *Shakespeare's Use of the Arts of Language* (New York, 1947); Brian Vickers, *The Artistry of Shakespeare's Prose* (London, 1968, rpt. 1979); and his "Shakespeare's Use of Rhetoric," in *A New Companion to Shakespeare Studies,* eds. K. Muir and S. Schoenbaum (Cambridge, 1972), pp. 83 – 98.

40. *Hamlet,* 3.4.

tion to go on. Supposedly about love and war, much of the play turns out to be about speech and persuasion, as in the long and elaborate council scenes, first of the Greeks (1.3.) then of the Trojans (2.2.). Yet speech achieves nothing in this play. The Trojan council, debating whether to return Helen and so end the war, is moved by a speech by Hector, urging her return. Yet, having argued so well, he suddenly collapses his own case:

> Hector's opinion
> Is this in way of truth: yet ne'ertheless,
> My spritely brethren, I propend to you
> In resolution to keep Helen still.... (2.2.188 ff.)

On the Greek side, the cumbrous and swollen oratory of Agamemnon and Nestor is imitated, perhaps even parodied, by Ulysses, one of the most loquacious characters in all of Shakespeare. The purpose of Ulysses' words and deeds is to get Achilles to swallow his hurt pride and return to the battlefield, and to do so Ulysses expends a vast amount of eloquence, both in direct persuasion of Achilles (3.3.), and in attempts to work Ajax up as a rival (4.5.). Yet in the end, when Achilles does enter the battle again, it is not through the power of speech but because his lover, Patroclus, has been killed. As the scabrous commentator Thersites is made to say,

> ...the policy of those crafty swearing rascals—that stale old mouse-eaten dry cheese, Nestor, and that same dog-fox, Ulysses—is not proved worth a blackberry. (5.4.8 ff.)

For an instance of speech not having the intended effect, consider *Measure for Measure.* Here Angelo has sent Claudio to prison for having made his betrothed, Juliet, pregnant. Claudio's sister, Isabella, a novice about to enter an order, comes to plead with this cold-blooded, censorious deputy to forgive Claudio. Lucio had urged her to use "the power you have," the appeal of a maiden who can "weep and kneel" (1.4.76 ff.). When she comes to plead the provost wishes her success: "Heaven give thee moving graces" (2.2.36), a rhetorical injunction repeated in other forms (43 ff., 70, 124 f.). Her persuasion does move Angelo, a man whose blood was "very snow-broth" (1.4.57 f.), but not to forgive Claudio: instead, he falls in love with the pleader. As he says in the soliloquy at the end of the scene,

> Never could the strumpet
> With all her double vigor, art and nature,

424

> Once stir my temper; but this virtuous maid
> Subdues me quite. Ever till now,
> When men were fond, I smiled and wondered how. (2.2.183 ff.)

Speech and virtue do finally triumph over concealment and vice, but only through the resource of the Duke, a *deus ex machina*. Isabella would rather have held her tongue: "O perilous mouths," she exclaims,

> That bear in them one and the selfsame tongue,
> Either of condemnation or aproof,
> Bidding the law make curtsy to their will,
> Hooking both right and wrong to th'appetite,
> To follow as it draws.   (2.4.172 ff.)

As Isabella discovers, speech is the servant of the will. Her victory over Angelo's mind results in the birth of his desire and a whole train of corruption and deception.

Persuasion for evil ends is common in the history plays and tragedies. The hiring and persuading of murderers, for instance, is a process that Shakespeare seems to deliberately pause over, as with Richard III's working of Tyrrel to kill the princes in the tower (*Richard III*, 4.2.65 ff.) or King John's persuasion of Hubert to kill Prince Arthur (*King John*, 3.2.17 ff.) — a process that proves to have the wrong effect, again; for although Hubert is deterred from murder by the young prince's innate virtue (4.1), yet when subsequently the King relents (4.2) the boy kills himself accidentally (4.3). Once he is dead John bitterly attacks the tool he won to the task (5.1.42 ff.). The murderers hired by Macbeth to kill Banquo and Fleance are persuaded at great length, on two consecutive days (*Macbeth*, 3.1.73 ff.); the single man hired by Edmund to kill King Lear and Cordelia, being already desperate, needs less persuasion (*King Lear*, 5.3.26 ff.). Equally ready for murder is Laertes, who takes the persuasion of Claudius even further than that evil man conceived of (*Hamlet*, 4.7). At a far higher social and intellectual level is Cassius's persuasion of Brutus, yet that idealistic defender of liberty is also moved by speech to become a murderer. We see how Cassius's first long persuasion (*Julius Caesar*, 1.2.32 – 181) falls on receptive ears: as Brutus says to him.

> What you would work me to I have some aim.   (163)

Brutus invites Cassius to speak with him again (299 ff.), and at the end of the scene Cassius is left alone onstage, that position which

Shakespeare gives to so many of his evil speakers to reveal themselves and their manipulations to us:

> Well, Brutus, thou art noble; yet I see
> Thy honourable mettle may be wrought
> From that it is disposed. Therefore it is meet
> That noble minds keep ever with their likes;
> For who so firm that cannot be seduced? (305 ff.)

Cassius gives a graphic demonstration of the truth of Wilson's claim that "such is the power of Eloquence . . . that most men are forced, even to yeeld in that which most standeth against their will. The words used for the process — to "work," to "be wrought" — show the speaker as an artificer, or manipulator, the victim as a passive object who will find the process disturbing. As Brutus says in his great soliloquy,

> Since Cassius first did whet me against Caesar,
> I have not slept.
> Between the acting of a dreadful thing
> and the first motion, all the interim is
> Like a phantasma or a hideous dream.   (2.1.61 ff.)

The "insurrection" Brutus suffers is proleptic of that experienced by the state of Rome once Cassius's successful persuasion achieves its goal. The final result of their assassination, though, is their own deaths. Evil eloquence comes to no good end.

In *Coriolanus* Rome and insurrection become coterminous, and in the ensuing political struggle eloquence plays a central role. The newly elected representatives of the people, the tribunes Sicinius and Brutus, foment the people's hatred of Coriolanus, while simultaneously making him angry by their insults. Having played both parties off against each other, they win their own goals but pervert the concepts of democracy and justice.[41] Shakespeare always sets his manipulators and dissemblers directly before us, so that we can see exactly how they operate, usually by aside or soliloquy, but here by their joint conferences, which usually end a scene (2.1.194 –259; 2.2.153 –58; 2.3.250 –58). Who holds the stage last sums up the events just past and controls the actions that follow. In addition, we see the tribunes manip-

---

41. I have developed a fuller analysis of this process in my study of the play in the "Studies in English Literature Series," published by Edward Arnold, *Shakespeare, "Coriolanus"* (London and Boston, 1976), and in "On teaching *Coriolanus*: the importance of perspective," in *Teaching Shakespeare,* ed. W. Edens et al. (Princeton, N.J., 1977), pp. 228 – 70.

ulating their tools, the plebeians, in how to provoke Coriolanus to anger and eject him from his office (2.3.169 – 250). In a later scene, just before the crucial confrontation, they even instruct them in how to shout, giving a practical demonstration of crowd manipulation:

> Assemble presently the people hither;
> And when they hear me say, 'It shall be so
> I'th'right and strength o'th'commons', be it either
> For death, for fine, or banishment, let them,
> If I say fine, cry 'Fine!' — if death, cry 'Death!' . . . (3.3.12 ff.)

Yet despicable though the tribunes are for perverting political speech, at the other end of society the same processes apply. The patrician party loathes the plebeians, yet Coriolanus's mother, Volumnia, gives her son a lesson in how to speak to the people, which is a lesson in hypocrisy. Go to them, she says, take your hat in your hand,

> And thus far having stretched it, — here be with them —
> Thy knee bussing the stones, — for in such business
> Action is eloquence, and the eyes of th'ignorant
> More learned than the ears. . . . (3.2.73 ff.)

Whatever classical source Shakespeare remembers, the point is that he is describing not eloquence, merely, but evil eloquence. Her advice that her son should use that sinister Machiavellian concept "policy," just as much in peace as in war, utterly destroys the distinction between good and evil from which the orator was supposed to start (41 ff.). The ability to "take in a town with gentle words," rightly lauded by Wilson and other rhetoricians as a useful accomplishment in war, can be a very corrupt one in peace. Volumnia's urging that he should speak

> such words that are but roted in
> Your tongue, though but bastards and syllables
> Of no allowance to your bosom's truth . . . (54 ff.)

would corrupt his very nature, as Coriolanus sees. His outburst against evil eloquence links it with hypocrites, harlots, knaves, beggars, mountebanks, and all those who "Cog their hearts from" men (111 – 34). Yet despite his revulsion he resolves to win the election, "Or never trust to what my tongue can do/I'th'way of flattery further" (135 f.). But the patricians have learned the importance of political rhetoric too late: the superior organization of the "voices" of the people defeats Coriolanus and causes his expulsion from Rome.

When he returns, hot for revenge, he is confronted by his mother, leading his wife, Virgilia, his son, Marcius, and a Roman lady, Valeria. All are dressed in mourning, the rhetorical significance of their costume being indicated by Volumnia:

> Should we be silent and not speak, our raiment
> And state of bodies would betray what life
> We have led since thy exile.   (5.3.94 ff.)

Their costume speaks, appeals for pity; so do their gestures. Volumnia bows to him, seated in his official chair, and to the dutiful son Coriolanus this is "As if Olympus to a molehill should/In supplication nod" (30 f.). Yet Volumnia has more expressive gestures in reserve. When Coriolanus kneels to her in filial obedience, she insists that he rise while she kneels, to show that by his actions he has "mistaken" the duty that should run from child to parent. He is, properly, appalled:

> What's this?
> Your knees to me? to your corrected son?
> Then let . . . the mutinous winds
> Strike the proud cedars 'gainst the fiery sun,
> Murd'ring impossibility . . .   (56 ff.)

Coriolanus can see the inversion of relationships represented by her kneeling, but he is too young and inexperienced to see that she is making this inversion to persuade or manipulate him.

The psychological dominance of the mother having thus been asserted, there is something feeble in the son's plea that she should "not bid" him dismiss his soldiers: "Tell me not/Wherein I seem unnatural; desire not" to cool my rage (81 ff.) — in other words, do not control my speech and feelings. Undeterred, Volumnia proceeds to use all possible appeals to the emotions, starting from his family's horror at seeing him in his new role as revenger, triply unnatural:

> Making the mother, wife, and child, to see
> The son, the husband, and the father, tearing
> His country's bowels out.   (100 ff.)

Having used the metaphor of the body politic in its most emotive form, Volumnia proceeds to equate herself with it, should her rhetoric fail:

> if I can not persuade thee
> Rather to show a noble grace . . .
> thou shalt no sooner
> March to assault thy country than to tread —

> Trust to't, thou shalt not—on thy mother's womb,
> That brought thee to this world. (120 ff.)

As his wife and son add their pressure, Coriolanus attempts to rise, the signal in classical ritual that the audience is over and that the suitors have failed in their supplication.[42] But Volumnia returns to the attack in a fifty-line speech, for which Shakespeare blends arguments from patriotism, expediency, and, above all, duty:

> There's no man in the world
> More bound to's mother, yet here he lets me prate
> Like one i'th'stocks. (158 ff.)

The gods will plague him, she threatens, for denying her "the duty which/To a mother's part belongs" (160 f.). Volumnia nakedly exploits the principle of reciprocity within family ties to enforce gratitude and obedience, glossing over altogether the ingratitude shown to Coriolanus by his city, which expelled him. Once again she uses gesture as pressure:

> Down, ladies; let us shame him with our knees.

Her final blow is to withdraw her love, which she has done before, but now in the extreme form of denying his legitimacy:

> Come, let us go:
> This fellow had a Volscian to his mother;
> His wife is in Corioli, and his child
> Like him by chance. (178 ff.)

At this point we have perhaps the most expressive use of gesture in Shakespeare, as Coriolanus, moved by his mother's combination of appeal and threat, tears running down his cheeks (lines 196 f.), stands, as Shakespeare's stage direction puts it, and *Holds her by the hand, silent.* At this moment his resistance breaks; his silence shows that her speech has defeated his argument for revenge: emotional persuasion has triumphed over reason and justice. Knowing that his granting of her suit means that he must betray his new allies, Aufidius and the Volscians, Coriolanus predicts the death that awaits him, while acknowledging the power of her eloquence:

> O my mother, mother! O!
> You have won a happy victory to Rome;

42. See Brian Vickers, *Towards Greek Tragedy* (London and New York, 1973), chap. 8, pp. 438–94; and J. P. Gould, "Hiketeia," *Journal of Hellenic Studies* 93 (1973), 74–103.

> But, for your son — believe it, O, believe it —
> Most dangerously you have with him prevailed
> If not most mortal to him.   (186 ff.)

Yet she does not care: her goal has been achieved, and she will be hailed as "our patroness, the life of Rome!" (5.1.1). Coriolanus's last words to her are another statement of the power of eloquence:

> Ladies, you deserve
> To have a temple built you. All the swords
> In Italy, and her confederate arms
> Could not have made this peace.   (5.3.206 ff.)

Just such an instance of persuasion's power would figure in the preface to a Tudor rhetoric book.

III

The examples of Cassius and Volumnia point up the significance of Shakespeare's presentation of evil rhetoric: it is the use of persuasion to manipulate, to control the others' wills, drive them to do, as Caxton said, what you want them to do. The masters at this art include Richard III, Lady Macbeth, Iago, and Edmund, and an idea of the importance Shakespeare attached to the demonstration of evil speech may be gleaned from the fact that the three longest speaking parts in his plays are those of Hamlet (1,422 lines), Richard III (1,124), and Iago (1,097).[43] Another factor that those three characters have in common — although (obviously) in every other way Hamlet differs from Richard III and Iago — is that they are given an exceptional number of soliloquies, exceptional in frequency, length, and importance. For the evil speakers the soliloquy is used by Shakespeare not merely for definitional purposes but to set up two levels of discourse. The villain speaks directly to the audience, revealing his real nature; since this is arranged by Shakespeare to coincide with the first presentation of the characters, we are enabled, or privileged, to see his subsequent false speech, or "seeming," both from his point of view and from that of his dupes. Our awareness of these two levels of discourse allows us to perceive many forms of irony hidden to the dupes, but it also allows us — in a rather unpleasant way, at times — to

43. See the *Complete Works* (Pelican text), ed. A. Harbage, one-volume ed. (Baltimore, Md., 1969), p. 31.

share their plans to manipulate and control the others. We see the whole "deceptive speech" program from the outset, and are informed of each stage of its development.

So in the last part of the *Henry VI* trilogy, Shakespeare, with an eye to the next play in sequence, which he was already planning to write, makes Richard step forward and declare his abilities in speaking and lying:

> Why, I can smile, and murder whiles I smile, . . .
> And wet my cheeks with artificial tears,
> And frame my face to all occasions. . . .
> I'll play the orator as well as Nestor,
> Deceive more slily than Ulysses could,
> And, like a Sinon, take another Troy.
> I can add colours to the chameleon,
> Change shapes with Proteus for advantages,
> And set the murderous Machiavel to school.   (3.1.182 ff.)

When, in the play that bears his name, Richard III addresses us in the opening scene, he tells us how he has laid plots to entrap his brother Clarence (1.1.30–41, 145–51) and that he plans to marry Lady Anne, even though he killed her husband and her father (153–62). This is the rhetorical process of *propositio,* announcing what you intend to say. But for Richard the intention embraces not only words but action. Having overcome her in a brilliant and forceful scene (1.2.1–227), he exults in his persuasive powers:

> Was ever woman in this humour woo'd?
> Was ever woman in this humour won?
> I'll have her; but I will not keep her long.   (228–30)

Whereas other characters in Shakespeare use the future tense in hope but often without fulfillment, when Shakespeare's evil persuaders use it they go on to effect what they intend. So Richard goes through his career of evil, predicting every step of his machinations until he reaches the crown. Once his ambition is realized, though, the purpose and energy of his speech fail him; the goal is attained, the language loses its function. And once his pretence is exposed, so is his illegitimacy as a ruler. In the optimistic world of Renaissance orthodoxy, since he has no right to rule he is unable to do so. Good deeds and good words will supplant him.

The dialectic of good and evil speech, false and true appearance, runs through *Macbeth* as a symbolic opposition between darkness and daylight. Both Macbeth and Lady Macbeth are consummate hypocrites,[44] and Shakespeare introduces both to us with asides and soliloquies to clarify their evil intent and establish the false level of discourse:

> Stars hide your fires;
> Let not light see my black and deep desires.   (1.3.50 f.)

Macbeth, as the initial agent, trusted by Duncan, is in that privileged position where he can deceive and dissemble. Yet apparently dominant here, from the very outset he is unaware of other forces manipulating him, which are seen by us: the witches — whose ultimate goals are left inscrutable by Shakespeare — and his wife. Lady Macbeth's great soliloquies predict her own power to control him, and cause her nature to dominate his:

> Hie thee hither,
> That I may pour my spirits in thine ear;
> And chastise with the valour of my tongue
> All that impedes thee from the golden round.... (1.5.26 ff.)

To assist her powers of persuasion, she invokes the aid of supernatural "spirits," the unseen "murdering ministers" latent in nature and awaiting use (41 ff.). The two combined make her a truly "resistless" orator, who is able to drive, goad, and shame Macbeth to the deed when his innate moral sense would deflect him from it. Macbeth's reluctant praise of her—"Bring forth men-children only" (1.7.72)— may remind us of the further degree of unnaturalness in Lady Macbeth, for in the Renaissance as in classical times rhetorical instruction was not given to women, who were not expected to take part in public life. Like Volumnia, Lady Macbeth has mastered a male tool, an ominous achievement.

In *Macbeth*, as in *Richard III*, good finally prevails, honest speech and trust are reestablished once evil has gained its ends and revealed its true nature. In the later play, so much more complex in every way, the restoration of trust is articulated as a separate and crucial issue in the scene between Malcolm and Macduff, where language and ethics are tested (4.3). The tragedy is more profound than the history play, also, in its sense of the public effects of evil speech. Richard III devastates England, but the effects on the body of the realm are hardly

44. See Brian Vickers, "Shakespeare's Hypocrites," *Daedalus*, Summer 1979, pp. 45–83.

noticed. In *Macbeth* the evil cloaked behind hypocrisy and false speech results in *res publica* becoming disordered, on the human level (4.3.1–8) as on the animal. Scotland now "cannot/Be call'd our mother, but our grave," where screams of agony and passing bells are not noticed,

> and good men's lives
> Expire before the flowers in their caps,
> Dying or ere they sicken.   (4.3.164–73)

In contrast to Hawes's automatic connection of *dispositio* with civic order—yet in a deeper sense in validation of it—by creating tempests in the cosmos, Shakespeare is declaring to what extent order has been disturbed (2.3.59–68), where unnatural darkness coincides with an owl killing a falcon and horses eating each other (2.4.1–19). These manifestations of chaos show the consequences of the Macbeths' evil: whereas the theorists of rhetoric guaranteed that the art had brought and would bring man from savagery to civilization, in *Macbeth* as in *King Lear* Shakespeare shows men and women using language to realize their own ambitions, in some profound way reversing the whole course of nature and history. In these plays man, the speaking animal, reverts to the level of beast: chaos is come again, but this time through persuasion.

The truth of this connection between language and chaos is so obvious for the play of *King Lear* as to need no further illustration.[45] Where Wilson, Hawes, and Peacham insist on the inevitable link between speech, reason, and good order, in his tragedies Shakespeare shows speech as the means of producing and furthering unreason, discord, and savagery. King Lear's absurd reduction of his daughters' love to an epideictic exercise towards himself, casting them as his own panegyrists, suits Goneril and Regan, who launch into flattery and lies as to their second (or real) nature. The integrity of Cordelia, like that of Coriolanus, cannot stoop to conquer, and she, like him, is disowned, expelled, her very relationship denied. In a sense Lear deserves what happens to him, since he has encouraged the perversion of speech. But in a more important sense Goneril and Regan show that those who corrupt language are capable of any evil, for having gained by their "persuasion" (this is a unique situation, in that Lear had persuaded himself), they go on to violate all bonds of filial affec-

---

45. See A. C. Bradley, *Shakespearean Tragedy* (London, 1904).

tion and indeed common humanity. They become "monsters," not daughters (3.7.102). In the subplot corrupt speech also wins a child great material advantage. Edmund, bastard son of Gloucester, introduced like Richard III and Lady Macbeth by a soliloquy, proclaims his intention to oust the legitimate son Edgar (1.2.15 ff.): within a short while he has done so. Then, resembling Richard in his use of *propositio,* he announces that he will denounce his own father to gain all (3.3.20–25), and does so, coolly and efficiently (3.5.1–20). But the great invention of the double plots in *King Lear* is that Shakespeare joins them, brings together the three children who have gained power through evil speaking, and involves them in a triangular love plot. Here a contest of persuasion is played out between Goneril and Regan for the hand—or rather, body—of Edmund, a competition that oddly echoes their contest before King Lear. When it looks as if Edmund will choose the widow rather than the married woman, the defeated persuader turns to poison—an extension of what she has done to language and truth. In the persons of Edgar, Kent, and Albany, finally, good speech and virtue reassert faith in the transparency of language. When Henry Peacham praised speech for its power in showing forth the privy thoughts and secret conceits of man's mind, he had not read *King Lear.*

Yet that comment is not entirely just. Edmund does reveal his privy thoughts, but only to the audience; Goneril and Regan also do so to us only, in their private conversations. What the theorists utterly failed to consider—and showed themselves to be bad rhetoricians and bad psychologists—is the nature of human dissimulation, an activity that is especially suited to representation in drama, and above all, in tragedy. Shakespeare's greatest rhetorician and greatest dissimulator is Iago. *Othello* was written immediately after *Hamlet,* and there are important carry-overs between the two characters who dominate those plays. Both Hamlet and Iago are given long roles with many soliloquies; both are thereby brought into close relationship with the audience, one sympathetic, the other loathsome. Both are gifted linguistically, or rhetorically: they can imitate other men's styles, can improvise and extemporize rhymes and witticisms. Unlike other leading characters in the tragedies, both Hamlet and Iago move easily between verse and prose, speakers, great actors, great pretenders. Iago's self-revelations announce his hatred for Cassio, Roderigo, Othello, and Desdemona, from which basis he plans to destroy them, which plans are predicted and fulfilled, one by one. Iago, like Richard III and Edmund, is given the orator's method of announcing his intentions before the event (*propositio*), and — in this even more in control than the other two — of summing them up afterwards. Iago's manipulation of two levels of discourse has the further ability to make his dupes see the world in the way he presents it. What they see is a vision made out of words, words that are designed to echo their own hopes or fears. These are purely verbal constructs, as the audience knows. When Othello, driven to madness by Iago's insinuations that Desdemona has betrayed him, exclaims as if in self-excuse,

> It is not words that shakes me thus (4.1.42),

we know that it is only words — marshalled brilliantly by Iago, to the most destructive intent — that have destroyed him. As Iago stands exultantly over the body of Othello, writhing on the floor, the hero having been reduced first from verse to prose, the medium of mad-men on the Elizabethan stage, and finally from language to gabble and silence; his reason gone, Iago presents it as a triumph of science:

> Work on,
> My medicine, work! (4.1.44 f.)

One might recall Plato's attack on rhetoric, that it was but an art like cooking (*Gorgias,* 462d ff.); Iago has elevated it to the level of a science for the control of human reason. I am irresistibly reminded of Puttenham's paean to the "great force" of eloquence when addressed to the mind of man:

> For to say truely, what els is man but his mind? which, whosoever have skil to compasse, and make yeelding and flexible, what may he not commaund the body to perfourme? He therefore that hath vanquished the minde of man, hath made the greatest and most glorious conquest.[46]

I conclude that Shakespeare knew more about the power of persuasion than did its theorists.

46. *Poesie,* book 3, chap. 19, p. 197.

Select Bibliography

The following citations were contributed by speakers
in the twenty-sixth annual Newberry Renaissance Conference,
which was the basis for this book. Each speaker was asked to submit
ten titles, and a double asterisk marks titles that speakers named
three or more times. This bibliography is alphabetized by author,
regardless of whether the item is a book, monograph, or journal article.
It is not comprehensive, but indicates basic modern secondary
sources useful for anyone pursuing further study
of rhetoric during the European Renaissance.

Apel, Karl Otto. *Die Idee der Sprache in der Tradition des Humanismus von Dante bis Vico.* Bonn: 1963, 2., durchgesehen Aufl. 1975. (Archiv für Begriffsgeschichte. Bd. 8.)

Baldwin, Charles S. *Renaissance Literary Theory and Practice.* New York: 1939, rpt. 1959.

Banker, J. R. "The *ars dictaminis* and rhetorical textbooks at the Bolognese University in the fourteenth century." *Medievalia et Humanistica* n.s. 5 (1974), 153–68.

Barner, Wilfried, *Barockrhetorik. Untersuchungen zu ihren geschichtlichen Grundlagen.* Tübingen: 1970.

Baron, H. *The Crisis of the Early Italian Renaissance: Civic Humanism and Republican Liberty in an Age of Classicism and Tyranny.* 2 vols. Princeton: 1955. (Revised to one volume, 1966)
With a focus on the historiographic approach to humanistic literature, Baron brings to light the crucial role played by rhetoric in the socio-political developments of the period. Also of help are the sequels to this study.

Beck, Hans-Georg. "Antike Beredsamkeit und byzantinische Kallilogia." *Antike und Abendland* 15 (1969), 91 – 101.

———. *Kirche und Theologische Literatur im byzantinischen Reich.* Handbuch der Altertumswissenschaft, zwölfte Abteilung, zweiter Teil, erster Band. Munich: 1959.
Especially useful for homiletics.

Béné, Charles. *Erasme et Saint Augustin.* Geneva: 1969.
Esp. pp. 372 – 426 on the *De Doctrina Christiana* and Ecclesiastes.

Bertalot, L. *Studien zum italienischen und deutschen Humanismus.* 2 vols. Rome: 1975

Billanovich, G. "Il Petrarca e i retori latini minori." *Italia medioevale e umanistica* 5 (1962), 103 – 64.

———. "L'insegnamento della grammatica e della retorica nelle università italiane tra Petrarca e Guarino." *The Universities in the Late Middle Ages.* Eds. J. IJsewijn and J. Paquet. Leuven: 1978, pp. 365 – 80.

Bleznick, D. W. "Las *Institutiones Rhetoricae* de Fadrique Furió." *Nueva revista de filologia hispanica* 13 (1959), 334 – 39.

Böhlig, Georg. "Untersuchungen zum rhetorischen Sprachgebrauch der Byzantiner mit besonderer Berücksichtigung der Schriften des Michael Psellos." Diss., Munich: 1956.

Bolgar, R. R., ed. *Classical Influences on European Culture, A.D. 1500 – 1700.* Cambridge: 1976.

Borinski, Karl. *Die Antike in Poetik und Kunsttheorie.* 2 vols. Leipzig: 1914.

Boyle, Marjorie O'Rourke. *Erasmus on Language and Method in Theology.* Toronto: 1977.
An important analysis of the rhetorical basis of Erasmus's theology of the *logos.*

Breen, Quirinus. *Christianity and Humanism, Studies in the History of Ideas.* Grand Rapids: 1968.
Contains the Barbaro-Pico-Melanchthon debate and Calvin and rhetoric article. See also his Nizolius articles and edition.

———. "Three Renaissance Humanists on the Relation of Philosophy and Rhetoric." *Christianity and Humanism.* Grand Rapids: 1968, pp. 1 – 68.

Burger, Heinz Otto. *Renaissance, Humanismus, Reformation: Deutsche Literatur im europäischen Kontext.* Bad Homburg: 1969.

Buisson, Ferd. *Le Répertoire des Ouvrages Pédagogiques du XVIᵉ Siècle.* Paris: fasc. 3, 1886.

Camporeale, Salvatore. "Lorenzo Valla tra Medioevo e Rinascimento: Encomion s. Thomae (1457)." *Memorie Domenicane* n.s. 7 (1976), 11 – 94.
Esp. pp. 28 – 62. The most detailed study of Valla's panegyric from rhetorical viewpoint.

———. *Lorenzo Valla, Umanesimo e teologia.* Florence: 1972.

Caplan, Harry, and Henry H. King. "Latin Tractates on Preaching: A Book-

List (1500 ff.)." *The Harvard Theological Review* 42 (1949), 185 – 206.
Most complete list of 16th-century treatises.

Castelli, Enrico, ed. *Retorica e barocco: atti del III Congresso internazionale di studi umanistici,* Venezia, 15 – 18 giugno 1954. Rome: 1955.

Castor, Grahame. *Pléiade Poetics.* Cambridge: 1964.

Chamberlin, John S. *Increase and Multiply: Arts-of-Discourse Procedure in the Preaching of Donne.* Chapel Hill: 1976.
Impact of Augustine, Erasmus, and classical revival on preaching.

Clark, Donald L. *John Milton at St. Paul's School: A Study of Ancient Rhetoric in English Renaissance Education.* New York: 1948.

————. *Rhetoric and Poetry in the Renaissance.* New York: 1922, rpt. 1963.

Constable, Giles. *Letters and Letter-Collections.* Turnhout: 1976.

Cosenza, Mario Emilio. *Biographical and Bibliographical Dictionary of the Italian Humanists and of the World of Classical Scholarship in Italy, 1300 – 1800.* 2nd rev. ed. 6 vols. Boston: 1962 – 1967.

Crane, William G. "English Rhetorics of the Sixteenth Century." In *The Province of Rhetoric.* Eds. J. Schwartz and J. A. Rycenga. New York: 1965.

————. *Wit and Rhetoric in the Renaissance.* New York: 1937.

Crescini, Angelo. *Le origini del metodo analitico, Il cinquecento.* Udine: 1965.

Croll, Morris W. *Style, Rhetoric, and Rhythm.* Eds. J. Max Patrick, R.O. Evans, with J. M. Wallace and R. J. Schoeck. Princeton: 1966.

Curtius, Ernst Robert. *Europäische Literatur und lateinisches Mittelalter.* Bern: 1948. Translated as *European Literature and the Latin Middle Ages,* by Willard R. Trask (New York: 1953).

Davidson, Hugh M. *Audience, Words, and Art: Studies in Seventeenth-Century French Rhetoric.* Columbus: 1965.

Dockhorn, Klaus. *Macht und Wirkung der Rhetorik.* Bad Homburg: 1968.

Dyck, Joachim. *Athen und Jerusalem. Bibel und Poesie in der Tradition ihrer argumentativen Verknüpfung.* Munich: 1977.

————. *Ticht-Kunst. Deutsche Barockrhetorik und rhetorische Tradition.* Bad Homburg: 1969.

Eisenstein, Elizabeth L. *The Printing Press as an Agent of Change: Communications and Cultural Transformations in Early-Modern Europe.* 2 vols. New York: 1979. Reprinted, in one vol., Cambridge: 1980.

Fischer, Ludwig. *Gebundene Rede, Dichtung und Rhetorik in der literarischen Theorie des Barock in Deutschland.* Tübingen: 1968.

Flynn, Lawrence, S. J. "The *De Arte Rhetorica* of Cyprian Soarez, S. J." *Quarterly Journal of Speech* 42 (1956), 367 – 74.

————. "Sources and Influence of Soarez' *De Arte Rhetorica.*" *Quarterly Journal of Speech* 43 (1957), 256 – 65.

Fontanini, G. *Biblioteca dell' Eloquenza Italiana.* Vols. 1–2. Venice: 1753.
  With notes by Apostolo Zeno, this early effort at a critical analysis of Italian elo-
  quence presents a beginning reference point for works in grammar, rhetoric,
  poetry, and drama among others.
France, Peter. *Rhetoric and Truth in France, Descartes to Diderot.* Oxford: 1972.
  Esp. bibliographical essay, pp. 265–77.
Fumaroli, Marc. "Genèse de l'épistolographie classique: rhétorique humaniste
  de la lettre, de Péttrarque à Juste Lipse." *Revue d'Histoire Littéraire de la
  France* 78 (1978), 886–905.
———— . *L'Age de l'éloquence: rhétorique et 'res literaria' de la Renaissance au seuil
  de l'époque classique.* Geneva, 1980.

Gallardo, Bartoleme Jose. *Ensayo de una biblioteca española de libros raros y curio-
  sos.* 4 vols. Madrid: 1863–1889.
**Galletti, A. *L'Eloquenza (Dalle Origini al XVI Secolo).* Milan: 1938.
  A pioneer effort offering a view of practical and theoretical works on sacred and
  profane eloquence in Italy from ca. 100–1600.
Garin, E. *Italian Humanism.* Trans. Peter Munz. New York: 1965.
———— , P. Rossi, and C. Vasoli. *Testi Umanistici sulla Retorica.* Rome: 1953.
  A concentrated effort to provide some critical appraisal of certain published and
  unpublished works of selected Renaissance rhetoricians.
Gerl, H. B. *Rhetorik als Philosophie: Lorenzo Valla.* Munich: 1974.
Gilbert, Neal. *Renaissance Concepts of Method.* New York: 1960.
  On role of rhetoric in methodology debates of sixteenth century.
Gordon, Alex L. *Ronsard et la Rhétorique.* Travaux d'Humanisme et Renais-
  sance 111. Geneva: 1970.
Grassi, Ernesto. *Rhetoric as Philosophy: The Humanist Tradition.* University
  Park: 1980.
Gray, Hannah H. "Renaissance Humanism: the Pursuit of Eloquence." In
  Renaissance Essays from the Journal of the History of Ideas. Eds. Paul Oskar
  Kristeller and P. P. Wiener. New York: 1968, pp. 199–216.
Green, Otis H. "On the Attitude toward the Vulgo in the Spanish *Siglo de
  Oro.*" *Studies in the Renaissance* 4 (1957), 190–200.
———— . "Se acicalaron los auditores: An Aspect of the Spanish Literary Ba-
  roque." *Hispanic Review* 42 (1959), 413–22.
———— . *Spain and the Western Tradition.* 4 vols. Madison: 1963–1966.
Griffin, Robert, *Coronation of the Poet, Joachim Du Bellay's Debt to the Trivium.*
  Berkeley: 1969.

**Hardison, O. B. *The Enduring Monument.* Chapel Hill: 1962.
Hathaway, Baxter. *The Age of Criticism: The Late Renaissance in Italy.* Ithaca:
  1962, rpt. Westport, Conn.: 1972.
———— . *Marvels and Commonplaces: Renaissance Literary Criticism.* New York:
  1968.
Heath, Terrence. "Logical Grammar, Grammatical Logic, and Humanism in

Three German Universities." *Studies in the Renaissance* 18 (1971), 9 – 64.

**Howell, Wilbur S. *Logic and Rhetoric in England, 1500 – 1700.* New York: 1960.

Jaffe, Samuel O. *Nic. Dybinus.* Wiesbaden: 1974.

Jardine, Lisa. *Francis Bacon: Discovery and the Art of Discourse.* Cambridge: 1974

**Joseph, Sister Miriam. *Shakespeare's Use of the Arts of Language.* New York: 1947.

Kennedy, George. *The Art of Persuasion in Greece.* Princeton: 1963.

————— . *The Art of Persuasion in the Roman World (300 B.C. – A.D. 300).* Princeton: 1972.

** ————— . *Classical Rhetoric and Its Christian and Secular Tradition from Ancient to Modern Times.* Chapel Hill: 1980.

Kennedy, William J. *Rhetorical Norms in Renaissance Literature.* New Haven: 1978.

Kibédi Varga, A. *Rhétorique et Littérature.* Paris: 1970.

Knowlson, James. *Universal Language Schemes in England and France, 1600 – 1800.* Toronto: 1975.

Kristeller, Paul Oskar. "An Unknown Humanist Sermon on St. Stephen by Guillaume Fichet." In *Mélanges Eugène Tisserant,* 6, Studi e Testi, no. 236. Vatican City: 1964, pp. 459 – 97.
Edition with indication of figures of thought and diction.

————— . *Renaissance Thought.* New York: 1961 and 1965.

————— . *Studies in Renaissance Thought and Letters.* Rome: 1956, rpt. 1967.

————— . *Iter Italicum.* 2 vols. Leiden: 1963 – 1967.
A prodigious effort that offers a list of uncatalogued medieval and Renaissance manuscripts in Italian and other libraries. Volume 1, *Italy: Agrigento to Novara;* volume 2, *Italy: Orvieto to Volterra; Vatican City.*

————— . "Un *Ars dictaminis* di Giovanni del Virgilio." *Italia medioevale e umanistica* 4 (1961), 181 – 200.

Krumbacher, Karl. *Geschichte der byzantinischen Literatur* (Handbuch der Altertumswissenschaft, neunte Abteilung). 2nd ed. 2 vols. Munich: 1897.
Old but still indispensable.

Kustas, George. "Function and Evolution of Byzantine Rhetoric." *Viator* 1 (1970), 55 – 73.

————— . *Studies in Byzantine Rhetoric.* Salonika: 1973.

Lange, Hans-Joachim. *Aemulatio veterum sive de optimo genere dicendi. Die Entstehung des Barockstils im 16. Jahrhundert durch eine Geschmacksverschiebung in Richtung der Stile des manieristischen Typs.* Bern and Frankfurt: 1974.

LaRusso, Dominic. "Rhetorical Education: Italy 1300 – 1450." *Western Speech* 4 (1960), 213 – 19.

Lausberg, H. *Handbuch der literarischen Rhetorik.* 2 vols. Munich: 1960.

Lechner, Joan Marie. *Renaissance Concepts of the Commonplaces.* New York: 1962.

Leeman, A. D. *Orationis ratio, the stylistic theories and practice of the Roman orators, historians and philosophers.* Amsterdam: 1963.

Lida De Malkiel, Maria Rosa. *La tradición clásica de España: Esplugues de Llobregat.* Barcelona: 1975.

Lyons, Bridget Gellert. *Voices of Melancholy: Studies in Literary Treatments of Melancholy in Renaissance England.* New York: 1971.

Marti, Antonio. *La preceptiva retórica española en el Siglo de Oro.* Biblioteca remánica hispánica. 1: Tradados y monografías, 12. Madrid: 1972.

McKeon, Richard. "Creativity and the Commonplace." *Philosophy and Rhetoric* 6 (1973), 199 – 210.

––––––– . "The Methods of Rhetoric and Philosophy: Invention and Judgment." In *The Classical Tradition: Literary and Historical Studies in Honor of Harry Caplan.* Ed. Luitpold Wallach. Ithaca: 1966, pp. 365 – 373.

––––––– . "The Transformations of the Liberal Arts in the Renaissance." In *Developments in the Early Renaissance.* Ed. Bernard Levi. Albany: 1972, pp. 158 – 223 (incl. 16 pp. bibliography).

––––––– . "The Uses of Rhetoric in a Technological Age: Architectonic Productive Arts." In *The Prospect of Rhetoric.* Eds. Lloyd F. Bitzer and Edwin Black. Report of the National Development Project sponsored by the Speech Communication Association. Englewood Cliffs, N.J.: 1971, pp. 44 – 63. Report of the Discussion Group "Wingspread — The Final Session," pp. 182 – 85.

McManamon, John M. "The Ideal Renaissance Pope: Funeral Oratory from the Papal Court [1447 – 1521]." *Archivum Historiae Pontificiae* 14 (1976), 9 – 70.
Comparison of thematic and classical eulogies.

––––––– . "Renaissance Preaching: Theory and Practice: A Holy Thursday Sermon of Aurelio Brandolini." *Viator* 10 (1979), 355 – 373.
Critical edition plus study of figures of thought and diction.

McNally, J. R. *"Rector et Dux Populi:* Italian Humanists and the Relationship between Rhetoric and Logic." *Modern Philology* 67 (1969), 168 – 76.

Menéndez y Pelayo, Marcelino. *Historia de las ideas estéticas en España.* 2 vols. Madrid: 1974.

Michel, Alain. *Rhétorique et philosophie chez Cicéron, essai sur les fondements philosophiques de l'art de persuader.* Paris: 1960.

**Monfasani, John. *George of Trebizond: A Biography and a Study of His Rhetoric and Logic.* Leiden: 1976.

Müller, Wolfgang G. *Die politische Rede bei Shakespeare.* Tübingen: 1979.

Murphy, James J. "Caxton's Two Choices: 'Modern' and 'Medieval' Rhetoric in Traversagni's *Nova rhetorica* and the Anonymous *Court of Sapience.*" *Medievalia et Humanistica* n.s.3 (1972), 241 – 55.

_____ . *Renaissance Rhetoric: A Short-Title Catalogue of W
ory from the Beginning of Printing to A.D. 1700, with
Holdings of the Bodleian Library, Oxford. With a Sele
Secondary Works on Renaissance Rhetoric.* New York:
_____ . *Rhetoric in the Middle Ages: A History of Rhetorica
tine to the Renaissance.* Berkeley and Los Angeles: 1

Newton-de Molina, David. "Reflections on Literary Cr
    Durham University Journal 65 (n.s. 34) 1972, 1 – 40.
Norden, Eduard. *Die antike Kunstprosa vom VI. Jahrhund
    Zeit der Renaissance.* 2 vols. Leipzig: 1898.

O'Malley, John W. *Praise and Blame in Renaissance Rome.
    Reform in the Sacred Oratory of the Papal Court, c.
    N.C.:* 1979.
    Study of revival of *genus demonstrativum* and its impac
    tant study of epideictic rhetoric in Renaissance curial prea
_____ . "Preaching for the Popes." In *The Pursuit
    Trinkaus and H. Oberman. Leyden: 1974.
Ong, Walter J. "Ramistic Rhetoric." In *The Province of Rl
    and J. A. Rycenga. New York: 1965, pp. 56 – 65.
_____ . *Ramus, Method and the Decay of Dialogue.* Cambr
_____ . "Tudor Writings on Rhetoric, Poetic, and Liter
    ric, Romance, and Technology.* Ithaca: 1971, pp. 48 – 1

Padley, G. A. *Grammatical Theory in Western Europe 1500
    tion.* Cambridge: 1976.
    More than 30 of the authors discussed also wrote works
**Patterson, Annabel M. *Hermogenes and the Renaissai
    Princeton: 1970.
Plett, Heinrich F. *Rhetorik der Affekte: Englische Wirkung
    Renaissance.* Studien zur englischen Philologie, n.s
_____ . *Textwissenschaft und Textanalyse: Semiotik, Ling
    berg: 1975; 2nd ed. 1979.
    Rhetorical analyses of texts by Spenser, Shakespea
    others.

Rico Verdu, José. *La retórica española de los siglos XVI y)

Sabbadini, R. *Le scoperte dei codici latini e greci ne' secoli
    ence: 1967.
_____ . *Storia e critica di testi latini.* 2nd ed. Padua: 197
Santini, Emilio. *Firenze e i suoi Oratori nel Quattrocento.*
_____ . "La protestatio de iustitia." *Rinascimento* 10 (1

lione, Aldo. *The Classical Theory of Composition from its origin to the present, an historical survey.* Chapel Hill: 1972.

hanze, Helmut. *Rhetorik: Beiträge zu ihrer Geschichte in Deutschland vom 16. – 20. Jahrhundert.* Frankfurt: 1974.

nell, Uwe. *Die homiletische Theorie Philipp Melanchthons.* Arbeiten zur Geschichte und Theologie des Luthertums. Bd. 20., 1968.

beck, R. J. "On Rhetoric in 14th Century Oxford." *Mediaeval Studies* 30 (1968), 214 – 25.

Important for understanding the full story of the teaching of rhetoric in Oxford in the 14th (and 15th and 16th) centuries.

___ . "Rhetoric and Law in 16th Century England." *Studies in Philology* 50 (1953), 110 – 27.

Important for the relationship between rhetoric and law.

igel, Jerrold E. *Rhetoric and Philosophy in Renaissance Humanism.* Princeton: 1968.

___ . "The Teaching of Argyropulos and the rhetoric of the first Humanists." In *Action and Conviction in Early Modern Europe.* Ed. T. K. Rabb. Princeton: 1969, p. 237 – 260.

ty and History in the Renaissance. Report on the Renaissance Conference at the Folger Shakespeare Library, April 23 – 24, 1960. Washington: 1960.

Essays by Syme, Mattingly, Gilmore, and others are bolstered by commentary from Bennett, Wiley, Nelson, Haller, Martz to name a few. New fields and new looks at old fields, persons and concepts.

na, Marcial. *Historia de la filosofía española.* 3 vols. Madrid: 1941.

nino, Lee Ann. *A Handbook to Sixteenth Century Rhetoric.* London: 1968.

dman, John M. *The Lamb and the Elephant: Ideal Imitation and the Context of Renaissance Allegory.* San Marino, Calif.: 1974.

t, Birgit. *Studien zu Luthers Freiheitstraktat mit besonderer Rücksicht auf das Verhältnis der lateinischen und deutschen Fassung zueinander und die Stilmittel der Rhetorik.* Stockholm: 1969.

___ . *Wortkampf.* Frühneuhochdeutsche Beispiele zur rhetorischen Praxis. Frankfurt: 1974.

ruever, Nancy S. *The Language of History in the Renaissance: Rhetoric and Historical Consciousness in Florentine Humanism.* Princeton: 1970.

___ . Review of J. E. Seigel's *Rhetoric and Philosophy in Renaissance Humanism.* In *History and Theory* 11 (1972), 64 – 74.

or, J. "The Epitome Margaritae Eloquentiae of Laurentius Gulielmus de Saona." *Proceedings of the Leeds Philosophical and Literary Society (Literary and Historical Section)* 14, pt. 4 (1971), 99 – 187.

npi, Wesley. "The Quality of Fiction: The Rhetorical Transmission of Literary Theory." *Traditio* 30 (1974).

On the impact of the rhetorical tradition on the development of literary theory.

Trinkaus, Charles. "A Humanist's Image of Humanism; the Inaugural Orations of Bartolommeo della Fonte." *Studies in the Renaissance* 7 (1960).
Study of academic orations.

———. *"In Our Image and Likeness": Humanity and Divinity in Italian Humanist Thought.* 2 vols. Chicago: 1970.

Tuve, Rosemond. *Elizabethan and Metaphysical Imagery.* Chicago: 1947.

———. "A Critical Survey of Scholarship in the Field of English Literature of the Renaissance." *Studies in Philology* 40 (1943), 204–55.
Albeit concerned with the "state of the art" in English Literature, Tuve includes a marvelous critical appraisal of most major (and seminal) studies on Renaissance social, political, educational, and rhetorical developments. This is a must for anyone interested in the Renaissance regardless of any special focus.

Unger, Hans-Heinrich. *Die Beziehungen zwischen Musik und Rhetorik im 16. – 18. Jahrhundert.* Würzburg: 1941, rpt. Hildesheim: 1969.

Ullman, B. L. *Studies in the Italian Renaissance.* 2nd ed. Rome: 1973.

**Vasoli, Cesare. *La dialettica e la retorica dell' Umanesimo: "Invenzione" e "Metodo" nella cultura del XV e XVI secolo.* Milan: 1968.

**Vickers, Brian. *Classical Rhetoric in English Poetry.* London: 1970.

Vilanova, Antonio. "Preceptistas de los siglos XVI y XVII." *Historia general de las literaturas hispanicas.* Ed. D. Guillermo Diaz-Plaja. Barcelona: 1953.

Walker, D. P. *Spiritual and Demonic Magic from Ficino to Campanella.* Studies of the Warburg Institute 22. London: 1958.
Pages 140–41 for Hermogenes as a source of astral magic.

Wallace, Karl R. "Aspects of Modern Rhetoric in Francis Bacon." *Quarterly Journal of Speech* 42 (1956), 398–406.

———. *Francis Bacon on Communication and Rhetoric, or: The Art of Applying Reason to Imagination for the Better Moving of the Will.* Chapel Hill: 1943.

Ward, John O. "Glosses and Commentaries on Cicero's *Rhetorica.*" In *Medieval Eloquence—Studies in the Theory and Practice of Medieval Rhetoric.* Ed. James J. Murphy. Berkeley and Los Angeles: 1978, p. 67.

**Weinberg, Bernard. *A History of Literary Criticism in the Italian Renaissance.* 2 vols. Chicago: 1961.

———. *Trattati di Poetica e Retorica del Cinquecento.* 4 vols. Bari: 1970–1974.
A diverse collection of treatises on philosophical and linguistic themes thought to bear on the development of various positions concerning the literature of eloquence.

Weiss, James Michael. "Ecclesiastes and Erasmus: The Mirror and the Image." *Archive for Reformation History* 65 (1974), 83–108.

Wesseler, Matthias. *Die Einheit von Wort und Sache: der Entwurf einer rhetorischen Philosophie bei Marius Nizolius.* Humanistiche Bibliothek. Reihe 1: Abhandlungen. 15. Munich: 1974.

Wickert, Maria. "Antikes Gedankengut in Shakespeares Julius Caesar." *Shakespeare-Jahrbuch*, 82–83 (1949), 11–33.

Wieruszowski, H. *Politics and Culture in Medieval Spain and Italy*. Rome: 1971.

Weiss, R. *Medieval and Humanist Greek*. Padua: 1977.

Wirth, Peter. *Untersuchungen zur byzantinischen Rhetorik des zwölften Jahrhunderts mit besonderer Berücksichtigung der Schriften des Erzbischofs Eustathios von Thessalonika*. Diss., Munich: 1960.

Yates, Frances A. *The Art of Memory*. London: 1966.

Notes on Contributors
Don Abbott

Don Abbott
University of California,
Davis

Hugh M. Davidson
University of Virginia

Joachim Dyck
Universität Oldenburg

Marc Fumaroli
Université de Paris-Sorbonne

Alex L. Gordon
University of Manitoba

Judith Rice Henderson
University of Saskatchewan

A. Kibédi Varga
Vrije Universiteit Amsterdam

Arthur F. Kinney
University of Massachusetts

Paul Oskar Kristeller
Professor Emeritus
Columbia University

Dominic A. LaRusso
University of Oregon

Gerald P. Mohrmann
University of California, Davis

John Monfasani
State University of New York,
Albany

James J. Murphy
University of California, Davis

John W. O'Malley
Weston School of Theology

W. Keith Percival
University of Kansas

Heinrich F. Plett
Universität Essen

Helmut Schanze
Rheinisch-Westfälische
Technische Hochschule Aachen

Richard J. Schoeck
University of Colorado

Thomas O. Sloane
University of California,
Berkeley

Nancy Struever
Johns Hopkins University

Charles Trinkaus
University of Michigan

Brian Vickers
Eidgenosse
Technische Hochschule Zürich

John O. Ward
University of Sydney, Australia

Index